DATE DUE

DEMCO 38-296

CONTEMPORARY MUSICIANS

ISSN 1044-2197

CONTEMPORARY MUSICIANS

PROFILES OF THE PEOPLE IN MUSIC

LUANN BRENNAN, Editor

VOLUME 25
Includes Cumulative Indexes

GALE GROUP

Detroit
San Francisco
London
Boston
Woodbridge, CT

STAFF

Luann Brennan, *Editor*
Leigh Ann DeRemer, *Assistant Editor*

Mary Alice Adams, Carol Brennan, Gerald E. Brennan, Gloria Cooksey, Tige Cosmos, Kelly M. Cross, Robert Dupuis, Evelyn Hauser, Shaun Frentner, Karen Gordon, K. Michelle Moran, Christine Morrison, Jim Powers, Brenna Sanchez, Ann M. Schawlboski, Sonya Shelton, Shari Swearingen Garrett, B. Kim Taylor, Gretchen Van Monette, *Sketchwriters*

Bridget Travers, *Managing Editor*

Maria Franklin, *Permissions Manager*
Margaret Chamberlain, *Permissions Specialist*
Shalice Shah-Caldwell *Permissions Associate*

Mary Beth Trimper, *Production Director*
Dorothy Maki, *Manufacturing Manager*
Cindy Range, *Buyer*
Barbara J. Yarrow, *Graphic Services Supervisor*
Robert Duncan, Michael Logusz, *Imaging Specialists*
Randy Bassett, *Image Database Supervisor*
Pamela A. Reed, *Imaging Coordinator*
Gary Leach, *Graphic Artist*
Cover illustration by John Kleber

ISBN 0-7876-3250-3
ISSN 1044-2197

Contents

Introduction ix

Cumulative Subject Index 255

Cumulative Musicians Index 281

Introduction

Fills the Information Gap on Today's Musicians

Contemporary Musicians profiles the colorful personalities in the music industry who create or influence the music we hear today. Prior to *Contemporary Musicians,* no quality reference series provided comprehensive information on such a wide range of artists despite keen and ongoing public interest. To find biographical and critical coverage, an information seeker had little choice but to wade through the offerings of the popular press, scan television "infotainment" programs, and search for the occasional published biography or exposé. *Contemporary Musicians* is designed to serve that information seeker, providing in one ongoing source in-depth coverage of the important names on the modern music scene in a format that is both informative and entertaining. Students, researchers, and casual browsers alike can use *Contemporary Musicians* to meet their needs for personal information about music figures; find a selected discography of a musician's recordings; and uncover an insightful essay offering biographical and critical information.

Provides Broad Coverage

Single-volume biographical sources on musicians are limited in scope, often focusing on a handful of performers from a specific musical genre or era. In contrast, *Contemporary Musicians* offers researchers and music devotees a comprehensive, informative, and entertaining alternative. *Contemporary Musicians* is published three times per year, with each volume providing information on over 80 musical artists and record-industry luminaries from all the genres that form the broad spectrum of contemporary music—pop, rock, jazz, blues, country, New Age, folk, rhythm and blues, gospel, bluegrass, rap, and reggae, to name a few—as well as selected classical artists who have achieved "crossover" success with the general public. *Contemporary Musicians* will also occasionally include profiles of influential nonperforming members of the music community, including producers, promoters, and record company executives. Additionally, beginning with *Contemporary Musicians 11,* each volume features new profiles of a selection of previous *Contemporary Musicians* listees who remain of interest to today's readers and who have been active enough to require completely revised entries.

Includes Popular Features

In *Contemporary Musicians* you'll find popular features that users value:

- **Easy-to-locate data sections:** Vital personal statistics, chronological career summaries, listings of major awards, and mailing addresses, when available, are prominently displayed in a clearly marked box on the second page of each entry.

- **Biographical/critical essays:** Colorful and informative essays trace each subject's personal and professional life, offer representative examples of critical response to the artist's work, and provide entertaining personal sidelights.

- **Selected discographies:** Each entry provides a comprehensive listing of the artist's major recorded works.

- **Photographs:** Most entries include portraits of the subject profiled.

- **Sources for additional information:** This invaluable feature directs the user to selected books, magazines, newspapers, and online sources where more information can be obtained.

Helpful Indexes Make It Easy to Find the Information You Need

Each volume of *Contemporary Musicians* features a cumulative Musicians Index, listing names of individual performers and musical groups, and a cumulative Subject Index, which provides the user with a breakdown by primary musical instruments played and by musical genre.

Available in Electronic Formats

Diskette/Magnetic Tape. *Contemporary Musicians* is available for licensing on magnetic tape or diskette in a fielded format. The database is available for internal data processing and nonpublishing purposes only. For more information, call (800) 877-GALE.

Online. *Contemporary Musicians* is available online as part of the Gale Biographies (GALBIO) database accessible through LEXIS-NEXIS, P.O. Box 933, Daton, OH 454012-0933; phone: (513)865-6800, toll-free:800-543-6862.

We Welcome Your Suggestions

The editors welcome your comments and suggestions for enhancing and improving *Contemporary Musicians*. If you would like to suggest subjects for inclusion, please submit these names to the editors. Mail comments or suggestions to:

The Editor
Contemporary Musicians
The Gale Group
27500 Drake Rd.
Farmington Hills, MI 48334-3535

Or call toll free: (800) 347-GALE

John Abercrombie

Jazz guitar

Prolific jazz fusion guitarist John Abercrombie is widely regarded as one of the most versatile and talented guitarists in the post-war jazz era. He was in demand as a sideman from countless bandleaders, including Gil Evans and Gato Barbieri, in the 1970s, and then formed his own jazz fusion group, Timeless, in the early 1970s. By 1975 he had formed his Gateway Trio with Dave Holland and Jack DeJohnette. He collaborated extensively with DeJohnette in the 1980s, performed and recorded voluminous amounts of material, and completed critically-acclaimed duet work with Ralph Towner. He led a quartet featuring Michael Becker, and was involved in an all-star big-bad that recorded Charles Mingus' *Epitaph*.

Beginning around 1974, he preferred a subdued, "chamber" style jazz sound. Abercrombie is a jazz innovator who makes creative use of distorting devices, and utilizes elements of bop, rock, and free-style jazz in his distinctive sound. His thoughtful control of tone-color is especially apparent in his duo performances with acoustic guitarist Ralph Towner. *Down Beat*'s Larry Birnbaum wrote, "John Abercrombie keeps post-fusion guitar relevant in the neo-bop era. He straddles the boundaries between freedom and structure, his dark, slippery lines ringing with mystery and melancholy in contexts ranging from trios to big bands. Although he's known for his spaced-out meditations, his music is firmly grounded in mainstream jazz."

Born John L. Abercrombie on December 16, 1944, in Portchester, NY. Abercrombie began taking guitar lessons at the age of 14 from a local teacher, although he mostly taught himself. He attended the Berklee School of Music in Boston from 1962 to 1966, where he studied guitar with Jack Petersen. He played in rock bands in the 1960s, but also toured with organist Johnny "Hammond" Smith in 1967 and 1968. Touring with an established band such as Smith's, Abercrombie gleaned the sort of practical experience that offset his academic studies perfectly and prepared him for his own success. His musical influences were Jim Hall, Bill Evans, Sonny Rollins, John McLaughlin, Larry Young, Jack McDuff, George Benson, Pat Martino, and John Coltrane.

Abercrombie moved to New York City in 1969. Due to his unusual technical command of his instrument, he had little trouble finding opportunities to play with established musicians Between 1969 and 1974 he played with Randy and Michael Brecker in the group Dreams, and toured with the Chico Hamilton Band. While touring with Hamilton, he traveled to Europe for the first time and appeared at the Montreux Jazz Festival. After playing with Hamilton, he joined Billy Cobham's jazz-rock fusion group Spectrum, where he first gained widespread attention from fans and other musicians alike. Cobham's hard-driving, rock-influenced band was the ideal venue for Abercrombie's prodigious imagination and masterful technique at this early stage in his career, and he was able to expand his musical horizons, develop his technique, and fuse his experience with both jazz and rock guitar. He also played with Jeremy Steig, Gil Evans, and Gato Barbieri, while recording with Dave Liebman.

Abercrombie formed his own trio, Timeless, in 1974 and recorded the album *Timeless*. At this time, it was clear he had grown fond of a more subdued, experimental "chamber" style of jazz while performing with his own small groups or as a popular sideman. He performed as a sideman for Jack DeJohnette's combos, and made jazz inroads by using distorting devices such as the phase shifter and volume pedal with the electric guitar—and occasionally with the electric mandolin. By the mid-1970s, he was discovering his unique and innovative musical "voice," approaching fusion with a softer, more delicate style. He replaced the Timeless trio with the Gateway trio in 1975, which included Dave Holland and Jack DeJohnette. In 1978, the trio was replaced by a quartet, which lasted until 1981. After the trio disbanded, Abercrombie continued to collaborate and record with DeJohnette throughout the 1980s and 1990s. He made important contributions to ensembles led by DeJohnette and took part in numerous recording sessions with him as well. In an interview with *Down Beat*,

Abercombie told Frank-John Hadley, "I always think meeting Jack was one of the turning points because it put me back on a track that I wanted to get back on, which was playing more jazz-influenced music, or multi-dimensional music ... play standard songs, write our own material, improvise and delve into more abstracted, very free rock-type fields."

Abercrombie is cited by many as helping to create the "ECM sound," a patchwork of acoustic and electric sounds created by eclectic musicians who combine jazz with European and Asian/Indian elements and influences. Abercrombiehas recorded with Ralph Towner, Jan Hammer, Dave Holland, Mike Brecker, Richie Beirach, George Mraz, Peter Donald, Marc Johnson, Adam Nussbaum, Peter Erskine, Vince Mendoza, and Jon Christensen, among others.

Abercrombie is mildly irked by the fact that he was pigeonholed as a modernist who can't play swing standards or more traditional fare. He told Hadley, "So many people today hear (my) ECM records, especially the earlier ones, where some of the music gets very spacey and non-harmonic and floaty, and they don't realize I grew up playing "Green Dolphin Street" with an organ trio. I think that's one of the reasons I keep coming back to the traditional format with the organ." Abercrombie takes occasional breaks from his organ trio; he reassembled his historical Gateway trio with DeJohnette and Dave Holland in 1995 to record and tour Europe. When describing to Hadley what it was like to play with DeJohnette and Holland again, he said, "It's like somebody throwing you into a room with all these great foods and saying, 'Go ahead, you can do whatever you want in here'." Abercrombie also works with drummer Peter Erskine and bass player Marc Johnson, a long-standing relationship that flourished anew during a 1995 tour of Europe. Hadley described Abercrombie as a "world-class guitarist," which was as apt a description as any that have been written.

Selected discography

Timeless, ECM, 1974.
Gateway, ECM, 1975.
Cloud Dance, ECM, 1976.
Pilgrim & The Stars, ECM, 1976.
Gateway 2, ECM, 1977.
Characters, ECM, 1977.
Pictures, ECM, 1977.
Arcade, ECM, 1978.
Straight Flight, Jam, 1979.
Abercrombie Quartet, ECM, 1979.
M, ECM, 1980.
Drum Strum, Arch, 1982.
Solar, Palo Alto, 1982.
Night, ECM, 1984.
Current Events, ECM, 1985.
Witchcraft, Justin Time, 1986.
Getting There, ECM, 1988.
Works, ECM, 1988.
John Abercrombie, Marc Johnson & Peter Erskine, ECM, 1988.
Animato, ECM, 1989.
While We"re Young, ECM, 1992.
November, ECM, 1992.
Speak of the Devil, ECM, 1993.
Gateway: Homecoming, ECM, 1994.

(with Ralph Towner) *Sargasso Sea,* ECM, 1976.
(with Ralph Towner) *Five Years Later,* ECM, 1981.

As A sideman

B. Cobham: Crosswinds, Atlantic, 1974.
J. DeJohnette: Sorcery, Prst, 1974.
Untitled, ECM, 1976.
New Directions, ECM, 1978.

Sources

Periodicals

Down Beat, March 1997; November 1994.
Guitar Player, February 1995.

Online

http://www.ecmrecords.com/ecm/artists/96.html

—*B. Kimberly Taylor*

All Saints

Pop quartet

Archive Photos, Inc. Reproduced by permission.

This stylishly-garbed, photogenic female quartet from England would yield inevitable comparisons to other phenomenally successful "girl-power" bands, but even quite early in their career All Saints consciously strove to make such analogies moot. The members formed the group on their own—before they had a contract—wrote their own material, and said whatever they pleased to the press. And unlike the Spice Girls, their music captured a fan base whose spectrum expanded well beyond teenage girls. All Saints sold millions of records with their 1997 debut album, *All Saints*, issuing forth a raft of hit singles. *Vox* magazine called the foursome "Britpop incarnate."

All Saints began with the friendship between Shaznay Lewis, who grew up in London, and Melanie Blatt. The two met as session singers in a west London studio on All Saints Road. Blatt had actually made tea and sat on the couch of the studio for months before getting her first shot at the microphone. She had attended the Sylvia Young Theatre School, which also graduated Spice Girl Emma Bunton and several other British entertainment figures.

In London Lewis and Blatt formed All Saints 1.9.7.5. "the year of their birth" with Simone Rainford in 1994. Their first public performance came at the Notting Hill Carnival that same year and they signed with prominent pop label, ZTT. They released a single that sold poorly, and grew increasingly at odds with their management. ZTT dropped them, and Rainford departed. Blatt became reacquainted by chance with a pair of sisters she had known from the Sylvia Young Theatre School, Nicole (Nicky) and Natalie Appleton. Nicky auditioned for Blatt in the bathroom of a London cafe.

The Appletons were technically Canadian citizens, but had been living off and on in both North America and England for much of their lives. "Our parents had emigrated to Canada before we were born," Natalie Appleton told Madeleine Kingsley in *Hello!* magazine, "but then divorced and my father, who had retail stores, came back to England. I was about seven and from then on it was a back and forth situation going from parent to parent." The sisters loved to harmonize with each other and Natalie Appleton sang semi-professionally for a time at a resort in New York's Catskills'"just like the one in *Dirty Dancing*," she told *Hello!* "I just loved being on stage."

Together the quartet began rehearsing and writing songs that reflected their love of American hip-hop music. They also discovered that their voices sounded great in harmony. "We're not the best singers in the world," Lewis would later tell *Touch* magazine. "We're

For the Record . . .

Members include **Natalie Appleton** (born May 14, 1973), vocals; **Nicole Appleton** (born December 7, 1974), vocals; **Melanie Blatt** (born March 25, 1975), vocals; **Shaznay T. Lewis** (born October 14, 1975), vocals; **Simone Rainford** (1994-95), vocals.

Group formed with Lewis and Blatt as All Saints 1.9.7.5., 1994; first public performance at Notting Hill Carnival, signed with ZTT, 1994; joined by Appleton sisters in 1995; left ZTT, signed to London as All Saints, November, 1996; released single "I Know Where It's At," 1997, released debut album *All Saints,* London, 1998.

Addresses: *Record company*—London Records, 825 Eighth Ave., New York NY 10019.

not Mariah Careys or Whitney Houstons, but I think we all have unique voices. I think there are styles and different sounds in our voices. I think that's why our voices work well together." Artist and Repretoire (A&R) people from other labels thought so too, and by this point were eager to find snappy young girl bands after the runaway success of the Spice Girls. But All Saints rejected several offers from labels that wanted to alter their image and fashion them into Spice Girl knock-offs.

The Sound of London 1997

Signing with London Records, the band recorded their first single, "I Know Where It's At," and released it in the United Kingdom in the summer of 1997. It reached number four by August of 1997, and they were soon appearing in the music press and tabloid newspapers almost as much for their kittenish looks and sassy opinions as for their records. Still, "I Know Where It's At" drew praise for a clear attempt to create their own sound. "You can hear the American rap and swingbeat in the background," declared *Vox* magazine of the song, "but in front of you there's this super-cool wonderland, full of loads of amazing stuff that seems not so much like the street fashion of today as the neoteric style of next month."

Their next single, "Never Ever," would catapult All Saints into the record books and onto the front page of nearly every British tabloid. The song made chart history in England for selling more copies than any other

single not at the number one spot, but the teen-sweet breakup lament would eventually hit that mark in January of 1998. Almost overnight they became a huge success throughout most of Europe and Australia, especially after the European release of their debut album, *All Saints,* in November of 1997. It debuted four months later in the United States, and included the first two singles as well as some unusual covers that would chart well in the England: the Red Hot Chili Peppers' "Under the Bridge", and the disco classic "Lady Marmalade" from LaBelle. They flew to North America early that year to promote the record and, emblematic of their wide appeal, won a musical guest appearance on *Saturday Night Live.*

American critics, wary of Spice Girl-mania, nonetheless gave the All Saints' debut overall positive marks. Reviewing it for *Rolling Stone,* Chuck Eddy described the single "Never Ever" as "an affecting spoken plea about post-breakup guilt and isolation," and found in "War of Nerves" "an aptly unnerving prettiness." A slightly more enthusiastic *Rolling Stone* writer, Kevin Raub, declared that *All Saints* "oozes with sweet, sexual mystique and raw, home-grown talent." Amy Linden, reviewing *All Saints* in *People,* called the groups music "sassy, catchy and disposable, the way pop music should be."

By the summer of 1998, All Saints were massive pop stars in the England. Their first live performance, however, came at the "Party in the Park," a concert in London's Hyde Park, in July of 1998. Several thousand fans attended the show, including Prince Charles, British Prime Minister Tony Blair, and United States President Bill Clinton.

Soggy Night, Sordid Stories

Unfortunately that bit of good PR did not translate to a successful promotional tour when All Saints returned to America. Though "Never Ever" had reached the top tem, their debut at Central Park's Wollman Rink was a lamentable occasion. The weather was humid and rainy, and few people bothered to show, despite the lure of free tickets offered by their label. In California, their management forgot to apply for a permit for a live gig on Venice Beach, which had to be canceled. Reviewing the Central Park show for the *New York Times,* Ann Powers called All Saints' bad luck that night "particularly unfortunate because All Saints did try to push the envelope of teenybop music."

By this point, All Saints were considered superstar divas in England, with their public appearances chronicled in the tabloids. They came under intense media scrutiny, were criticized for almost everything they did, and stalked constantly by paparazzi photographers. As Nicole Appleton told *New Musical Express*" Victoria Segal, "It's frightening, I have people following me everywhere with cameras, asking the same questions. It scares me. I think, 'What are they going to do to get me to answer them'."

Over the course of 1998, the British papers excitedly tracked the various romantic affairs of the band, who were all still in their early 20s. Nicky Appleton would date, become engaged, break up, and reunite with one of Britain's biggest pop stars and heartthrobs, Robbie Williams, formerly of the boy group Take That. Her sister Natalie was dating a well-known television personality, and was cruelly exposed by a former friend in the press as having a six-year-old daughter and a teen marriage that ended in divorce. Blatt was roundly criticized as setting a bad example for the legions of preteen girls who worshipped the singers when she became pregnant by her boyfriend, Stuart Zender of the band Jamiroquai.

Blatt gave birth in November of 1998 and was vastly looking forward to taking some time off. "You get a strong sense—from Natalie and Shaznay in particular—that life is a series of petty frustrations, all controlled by a nebulous 'they' outside of the four corners of the band who insist on interfering," Segal theorized in *New Musical Express*. The following month, the same paper charted a series of rumors and press releases hinting, then denying, that Nicky Appleton had quit the band, and had long been at odds with both their manager and Lewis.

Existing under the glare of huge record sales, "Never Ever"—had sold three million copies—and exhaustive media attention, coupled with a feeling that their label wanted to extract the maximum amount of profit from them before they imploded, would perhaps discourage even the most ambitious of performing artists. "When I saw how this business worked, I vowed to myself I'd never want to do it again, not at this extreme level," Blatt told Segal. "It's demoralizing. I've had to compromise myself a lot." Lewis agreed: "Sometimes we think it's only us that goes through this," she told Segal. "But it's not, it's every artist. When you see people on telly, you never imagine there's any bad with it, and that's what the let-down is."

Selected discography

Singles

"I Know Where It's At," London, 1997.
"Never Ever," London, 1997.
"Under the Bridge," London, 1998.
"Bootie Call," London, 1998.

Albums

All Saints, London (U.K.), 1997; London/Island (U.S), 1998.

Sources

Billboard, February 7, 1998, pp. 16-17; June 27, 1998, pp. 15, 20.
Daily Star, July 10, 1998.
Mirror (London), January 13, 1998.
New Musical Express, August 22, 1998.
New York Times, August 28, 1998, p. E25.
News of the World, December 13, 1998.
People, March 16, 1998, p. 29.
Rolling Stone, March 5, 1998; March 26, 1998.
Sky, October 1998.
The Sun (London), December 12, 1998.
Top of the Pops Supplement (London), December 1997.
Touch, December 1997.
Vox, March 1998.

—*Carol Brennan*

Laurie Anderson

Performance artist

Although best known as a multimedia, performance and recording artist, Laurie Anderson has experimented with every kind of art imaginable during her career. She is a composer, dancer, film director, music producer, photographer, poet, sculptor, ventriloquist, violinist, vocalist, writer, and high tech-freak. Unlike many other performance artists who never break out of their niche groups of art-worshippers and freaks, Laurie Anderson achieved an amazing popularity with her multimedia performance art in the United States and around the world. Contributing to that popularity are her long-term contract since 1981 with the major label Warner Bros., her constant re-invention of herself as an artist, as well as her effort to be understood wherever she performs by presenting her shows in several languages. Anderson's hallmarks are solos with self-designed musical instruments which embrace state-of-the-art electronics technology and the use of Vocoders to transform her voice. Rather than songs, her live performances are typified by spoken stories accompanied by musical arrangements which combine sounds, conventional and electronic instruments, as well as light show, costumes, and film or photographic images.

Many critics have tried to describe Laurie Anderson's work since she began performing in the early 1970s. Ken Johnson writing in the *New York Times* called "mystery, melodrama and humor ... central qualities of Anderson's art." "The accumulation of words and images is intoxicating," wrote Sarah Kenton in *Time Out* of an Anderson exhibition, "you absorb the message without realizing that it is full of profundities disguised as humorous asides." Germano Celant maintained in *Interview* that Anderson's longtime artistic goal was "dissolving barriers between people." Anderson herself noted in *Interview* that all her work involves some kind of escapism, "imagining a body to be somewhere else. Music reminds you about your body, but it also takes you out of it. All art is a form of escape, but music is in particular."

If there is anything constant in her career—from performing "Duets on Ice" on street corners of New York City in 1974 to re-inventing Herman Melville's "Moby Dick" as an electronic musical 25 years later—it is the presentation of "works in progress." In *Interview*, Laurie Anderson described this approach: "I always light performances so I can see people really well in the audience. That's how I learn what to cut out, what to change." She uses big notebooks to write down ideas, events, and thoughts, from which she later draws her lyrics which might be re-used from time to time. While political and social criticism expressed through stories of everyday life has always been part of her work, later pieces focused more on her personal life experience.

Soho's Underground

Laurie Anderson grew up with four brothers and three sisters in a Chicago suburb. She studied violin and played in the Chicago Youth Symphony but abandoned the idea of becoming a violinist. She also loved books and started pursuing a degree in Library Science. But her interest in art finally drew her to major in Art History. After her graduation in 1969, Anderson moved to New York City, studied sculpture at Columbia University until 1972, and made her living as art history instructor at various colleges and as a freelance critic for small art magazines in New York City afterwards.

In the early 1970s, she started creating and presenting her first performance pieces such as *Automotive*, a "concert" of car horns in an open space in 1972, and *O-Range*, in which megaphones were used by ten performers to shout stories across a large empty sports stadium in 1973. In the *Duets on Ice* performed on the streets of New York City in 1973, she played her violin while a tape of herself was playing at the same time, hidden inside the instrument. Standing on skates covered with blocks of ice, she performed until the ice melted. *AS:IF*, her first solo show that dealt with her religious upbringing, was presented at Artists Space in New York City in 1974. Selections of Anderson's works

Born June 5, 1947, Wayne, IL; daughter of Arthur T. and Mary Louise (Rowland) Anderson; *Education:* Barnard College, B. A. in Art History, 1969; Columbia University, M.F.A. in Sculpture, 1972.

Art history instructor at City College of New York, 1973-75; freelance critic for *Art Forum, Art News* and *Art in America;* created multimedia installations and performances such as *Automotive* in 1972, *O-Range* in 1973, *Duets on Ice* in 1973, and *AS:IF* in 1974; designed the Tape Bow Violin with Bob Bielecki in 1976; major performance pieces included *Like a Stream* and *Americans on the Move; United States II* premiered in New York's Orpheum Theater in 1980; recorded several songs for two Dial-A-Poem series in 1980-81; "O Superman" (110 Records release) reached number two on British pop charts; signed contract with Warner Bros. in 1981, released *Big Science,* 1982; toured with the eight-hour-performance *United States I-IV* through the United States and Europe, 1983; released *Mister Heartbreak,* 1984; concert film *Home of the Brave,* 1985; released album of same name, 1986; hosted Ernie Kovacs special on PBS in 1987; released *Strange Angels,* 1989; premiered with performance *Empty Places* at Spoleto Festival in Charleston, SC in 1989; performed *Voices from the Beyond* at the Museum of Modern Art and around the United States in 1991; *Stories from the Nerve Bible,* a performance-retrospective of Anderson's work, premiered at Expo '92 in Seville; published a book with same title in 1994; released *Bright Red,* 1994, released *The Ugly one With the Jewels,* a live recording from the *Nerve Bible* in 1995; released the interactive CD-ROM *Puppet Motel* on Voyager; performed *The Speed of Darkness* in the United States and Europe 1996-98; solo show *Whirlwind* at Artists Space in New York; formed "etc" (Electronic Theater Company) in partnership with Interval Research Corporation.

Awards: Villager Award, 1981; Guggenheim Fellowship, 1982; Distinguished Alumna Award from the Columbia School of the Arts, 1994; "Marlene" award for the Performing Arts from Munich, Germany, 1996.

Addresses: *Home*—New York, NY. *Record Company*—Warner Bros.,3300 Warner Blvd., Burbank, CA 91505-4694. *Management*—Keith Naisbitt, William Morris Agency, 151 El Camino Dr., Beverley Hills, CA 90212.

appeared on two anthologies in 1977: *Airwaves* published by One Ten Records, and *New Music for Electronic Material* published by 1750 Arch Street Records. Between 1977 and 1979, she performed in many avant-garde music festivals in Europe and the United States.

The Big 1980s Shows

Anderson's *United States II* performance, the first one she did in a "real theater", premiered in New York's Orpheum Theater in 1980. Described by Will Annett in *Jones Telecommunications and Multimedia Encyclopedia* as "a dark, near apocalyptic vision that stirred audiences and left them deeply unsettled," it was publicized widely in the media. With her tape bow violin she "produced bizarre and haunting sounds by passing a bow laced with audio tape across a violin 'strung' with playback heads," as Annett noted. One of Anderson's songs from that performance-"O Superman"-was released by 110 Records and reached number two on the British pop charts.

That success led to a Warner Bros. contract in 1981. This step "brought her odd sounds and unusual lyrics to an enormous audience and Anderson became performance art's first rock star and Warner Bros. first conceptualist," as Barbara Stratyner put it in *Contemporary Musicians.* Her first album *Big Science* was released on Warner Bros. In 1982. Her financial success made it possible for her to create her own conceptual multimedia opera. With her seven-hour-performance *United States I-IV* she toured extensively through the United States and Europe in 1983. The opus consisted of the four segments "Transportation", "Politics", "Money", and "Love," and was performed over two consecutive nights. A five-album-set, *United States Live,* was released by Warner Bros. in 1984; the same year saw the release of *Mister Heartbreak,* a collection of material not included on the live album, together with pieces co-produced with Peter Gabriel, Bill Laswell, and Roma Baron. Anderson toured the United States, Canada and Japan with a crew of 35. When she returned to New York City, she put together a film documentary of the tour, which was released in 1986 as *Home of the Brave,* with an album of the same name.

Reception of these works by the media and her audience was mixed and they were not financially successful. Anderson hit the road again with a greatest hits tour *Natural History* in 1986, and her audiences and record sales started rising again. Her commercial success, however, alienated her from New York's art community. After her fame peaked in the second half of the 1980s, "Anderson felt the need of a change," John Howert wrote in *Laurie Anderson*. "I was tired of being Laurie Anderson," Anderson told him, and "I wanted to start over. So I threw everything out of my loft. My next performance was going to be really simple, just one person—me—and a microphone."

Back to Her Roots

Anderson started taking voice lessons. The album *Strange Angels* released in 1989 was the first one where Anderson actually sang, with a melodious soprano voice. Her next performance *Empty Places*—parts of which she presented in twelve different languages—was also a solo show with Anderson telling stories and singing songs, using some slides and movies. *Voices from Beyond* from 1991 was a polemic monologue with a few scattered songs on censorship and the intolerance that drives it.

In 1994, Anderson published *Stories from the Nerve Bible*, a retrospective of her works from the previous twenty years, including fables, pictures, and diagrams. In the liner notes to *The Ugly one With the Jewels*, a 1995 live recording with spoken and sung pieces excerpted from a reading of the "Nerve Bible," Anderson described her feelings about seeing her work in the book: "A lot of the material was made to be spoken, so it was really strange to see it in print. I believe that language is alive and that when you hear something it has an entirely different meaning than when you see it on a page." She went on a book tour through the United States and Europe in 1994 and 1995, calling it "the most low-tech show" she had ever done: "I sat on the stage with keyboards, digital effects machines, a violin and a twenty-four input mixing console and mixed the sound myself," she wrote on *The Ugly one With the Jewels*, "Without all the effects of a multimedia show, it became a kind of mental movie. I really felt like I was in the places I was describing."

In 1993 Anderson performed the *Nerve Bible* show which combined elements from her book, CD, CD-ROM, and earlier works. *Bright Red* co-produced with Brian Eno and released in 1994 was Anderson's first album in five years. In its personal, mostly gloomy pieces influenced by an near-death experience on a trip in the Tibetan Himalayas in 1993, Anderson used the same spare sound underlining spoken words that characterized her early works. It included "Night in Bagdad," a piece on the Gulf War, "Love Among the Sailors" on the toll of AIDS, "The Puppet Motel" describing a world taken over by computers, and "In Our Sleep," a duet with rock singer Lou Reed. In 1995 the software firm Voyager released Anderson's interactive CD-ROM *Puppet Motel*, offering six hours of music and talk. Her 1996-1998 solo show, *The Speed of Darkness*, presented a collection of stories and songs that focused on the themes control and the future of art and technology. Using a theater, a mental hospital, and a control room as sets for her stories, Anderson presented herself in a more personal and emotional manner than ever before.

In November of 1998, to celebrate the 25th anniversary of Anderson's first solo show at the New York Artists Space gallery, objects made for the gallery or used in performances were presented in the solo show *Whirlwind*. Ken Johnson described Anderson's *Small Handphone Table* (1978) in the *New York Times*:"you sit with your elbows on a table and hands over your ears; low, ethereal music runs from the table, through your arms and into your ears."

Whirlwind, a room-size installation from 1996, was described by Martha Schwendener for *Time out New York* as an "installation of 48 speakers grouped together and suspended from the ceiling to emit one large mass of sound. As you walk around under the piece or stand in one place and move your head, you get different perspectives on a wide range of sounds, from dance-track-like beats to the whistling of the wind recorded at the Great Wall of China."

Depressed by Optimism

Anderson's latest project is a performance based on Melville's *Moby Dick,* a theme that had already appeared in earlier works. Promotional material provided by Anderson's office described the show: "Using Melville's text as a point of departure, ... *Moby Dick* takes us into an electronic world of glistening images, unusual vocal styles and daring staging," accompanied by music from various genres including the initial incantation in Latin and Polynesian grooves of Queequeg. "The colorful characters on the doomed Pequod, from the Captain to the crazy Cook, are represented by a cast that doubles as Noah, Jonah, Job and Melville himself." *Moby Dick: Songs and Poems* was scheduled to be presented in Ann Arbor, Michigan, New York City, Los Angeles, and San Francisco in the fall of 1999. It marks the first time Laurie Anderson has directed actors. It was also the introduction of "talking sticks", new musical instruments she designed which translate gestures into sound.

In a conversation with Ingrid Sischy on *Moby Dick* Anderson said: "I'm depressed by optimism. The kind of optimism that's around now. I mean, I'm a dark person and this idea that technology and communication are going to save us is incredibly depressing to me. So *Moby Dick* will be very gritty looking with these techno things sort of hidden." In a *New York Times Magazine* article Anderson wrote: "The electronic age makes us all players in a performance-art piece. Our role: To shout at hardware and to volunteer to colonize the moon." In an interview with Adrienne Redd Anderson described her own vision: "My idea of utopia is that everyone can be an artist."

Selected Performances

United States (I-IV), 1983.
Empty Places, 1990.
Nerve Bible, 1995.
Speed of the Darkness, 1996.
Moby Dick: Songs and Poems, 1999.

Selected discography

Big Science, Warner Bros., 1982, reissued, WEA/Warner Bros., 1987.
Mister Heartbreak, Warner Bros., 1984, reissued, WEA/ Warner Bros., 1987.
United States Live (five-album set), Warner Bros., 1984, reissued as *United States of America* (four-CD box set) WEA/Warner Bros., 1991.
Home of the Brave, (motion picture soundtrack), Warner Bros., 1986.
Strange Angels, Warner Bros., 1989.
Bright Red, Warner Bros., 1994.
The Ugly one With the Jewels, Warner Bros., 1995.

Selected films and videos

O Superman, Warner Bros., 1982.
Sharkey's Day, Warner Bros., 1984.
Home of the Brave, 1986.
Language is a Virus, Warner Bros., 1986.
Beautiful Red Dress, Warner Bros., 1990.
The Collected Videos, Warner-Reprise Home Video, 1991.

Selected Scores

Something wild, (underscoring), 1985.
Swimming to Cambodia, 1987.

Wings of Desire, (several songs called "Angel Fragments"), 1988.
Bridge of Dreams,(score for a dance piece by Molissa Fenley, commissioned by Deutsche Oper Berlin), 1994.

Selected writings

United States, Harper & Row, 1984.
Empty Places, HarperPerennial, 1991.
Stories from the Nerve Bible: 1972-1992 A Retrospective, HarperPerennial, 1994.

CD-ROM

Puppet Motel, Voyager Co., 1995, reissued (Mac/Windows ed.) 1998.

Sources

Books

Howell, John, *Laurie Anderson*, Thunder's Mouth Press, 1992.

Periodicals

Interview, August 1998.
New Yorker, April 10, 1995.
New York Times, February 5, 1995; September 27, 1998; October 9, 1998.
New York Times Magazine, September 28, 1997.
Rolling Stone, December 15, 1994.
Time Out New York, June25-July 2, 1997; October 29-November 5, 1998.

Online

http://www.amazon.com
http://www.cc.gatech.edu/~jimmyd/laurie-anderson
http://www.digitalcentury.com/encyclo/update/anderson.html
http://www.hear.com/hollow/feature/anderson.html
http://www.maths.lth.se/matematiklu/personal/apas/laurie

Additional information for this profile was provided by Laurie Anderson's office.

—Evelyn Hauser

Gene Autry

Singer, guitar, actor

AP/Wide World Photo. Reproduced by permission.

The original singing cowboy, Gene Autry lived by a cowboy creed to fight fair, tell the truth, keep your word, and always help those in trouble. He lived by this creed both in life and on screen. Hall of Fame singer, broadcaster, film star, broadcast tycoon, and founder of the California Angels baseball team, Autry is the only entertainer with five stars on the Hollywood Walk of Fame—for radio, records, movies, television and live performance. His endeavors, like his life, spanned the twentieth century as his career moved from radio to recording to movies to television, paralleling the discovery of each.

Autry generated more than 90 films and 90 television episodes, made 635 recordings, and sold more than 100 million records before his death in 1998. Among his most notable professional accomplishments were the creation of the popular "Melody Ranch" radio program, with its celebrated theme song, "Back in the Saddle Again" and his best-selling recording of "Rudolph the Red-Nosed Reindeer." Sales of more than 50 million copies of the 1949 Christmas single propelled the song to the rank of biggest-selling single in history until Elton John toppled it in 1997 with "Candle in the Wind," his tribute to Princess Diana. Autry's happy-go-lucky nature was as much a trademark as his horse Champion and his white cowboy hat. But under the agreeable personality was an intense ambition, intelligence, and self-confidence that took him to a level of fame and fortune beyond his dreams.

Orvon Gene Autry was born on September 29, 1907, near Tioga, Texas, to Delbert and Elnora Autry. The family moved to Ravia, Oklahoma, where his father, a livestock dealer, exposed him to the traditions of the West and the life of a cowboy. He developed a love for music at age 5 when he sang in his grandfather's Baptist church choir and his mother taught him to play the guitar. By the age of 12 Autry purchased a mail-order guitar from Sears Roebuck's catalog. Three years later he was singing at local cafes where he earned 50 cents a night.

Advice from a Legend

Autry's first love may have been music, but he also developed a passion for baseball. He left school to pursue a career in the telegram business while playing as an American Legion shortstop. He was once offered a minor-league contract with the St. Louis Cardinals, but he couldn't afford to take a 50 percent pay cut from his $100-a-month job as a telegraph operator on a St. Louis & San Francisco railroad line. So he remained in Chelsea, Oklahoma, sending telegrams and spending his spare time singing and plucking his guitar.

According to legend, Will Rogers heard a 17-year-old Autry singing at the telegraph office and encouraged the young man to pursue a career in radio. That tip would change Autry's life forever, leading him to the top of the recording industry and onto the silver screen. He started out singing ballads in blackface make-up for 15 dollars a week with the Fields Brothers' Marvelous Medicine show, but soon traveled to New York where he was advised by Victor recording officials to get some local experience and learn how to sing yodel songs. Autry went home and quickly won his own series on a Tulsa radio station as the "Oklahoma Yodeling Cowboy," emulating the sounds of his musical hero Jimmie Rodgers. Autry returned to New York in 1928 and recorded with such labels as Grey Gull, Gennett, and Velvet Tone.

Autry had a knack for predicting how the public wanted to be entertained. He is considered the creator of the Singing Cowboy genre, beginning with "That Silver-Haired Daddy of Mine," a record that went gold for selling a half-millioncopies. He made 635 records, with more than a dozen receiving Gold and Platinum status. His children's hits included "Rudolph the Red-Nosed Reindeer," "Here Comes Santa Claus," "Frosty the Snowman," and "Peter Cottontail."

When the Singing Cowboy started making motion pictures in 1934, he spent eight consecutive years as Hollywood's top box-office Western star. His first starring role was in the 1935 film, Tumblin' Tumbleweeds. He spent nearly three decades starring in more than 90 movies glorifying cowboy action, comedy and the wide-open spaces of the American West. But the focus of his films was on the music. Autry's appeal didn't subside until he left Hollywood in 1942 to join World War II as a member of the Army Air Corps. He was given the rank of Technical Sergeant and was promptly given his own radio show after being assigned to Special Services as an entertainer. However, Autry insisted on being taught to fly and was appointed Flight Officer and transferred to Air Transport Command.

A New Frontier

Autry was the first motion picture star to exploit the potential of television, the new entertainment frontier. Autry would later admit that his clean-cut image cost him a more varied career in movies, which might explain why he was so willing to help pioneer a new medium such as TV. He formed his own production company to make half-hour Western-themed series for television and began work on his own television series that lasted from 1950 to 1956.

Autry attempted to emulate his on-screen persona, but the man was truer to real life that his movie roles. Nevertheless, he ventured to honor "Gene Autry's Cowboy Code." Under the code, a cowboy never shot first, struck a smaller man or took unfair advantage. He always honored his word and never told a lie. He was a good worker, considerate to children and old folks, and respectful of women, parents, and the law. The "Angle of horseback" image stuck. However, his real-life persona was far from perfect. Autry admitted to a battle with alcohol. "Without knowing it, I had grown dependent on liquor to relax," he admitted in his autobiography *Back In The Saddle Again.* "Drinking was a way to celebrate. I was always on the go, fighting another deadline, racing to a studio or a business meeting. The more tired one gets, the easier it is to look for energy in a bottle."

A Cowboy Broadened His Horizons

Autry's career was far from over when he stopped performing in 1956. By 1995, he had built a corporate empire valued at nearly $320 million and was frequently named one of the 400 richest Americans. By the late 1980s, his holdings included four radio stations, the Gene Autry Hotel in Palm Springs, Western Music Publishing Inc., Golden West Melodies Inc., Ridgeway Music Publishing Inc., Melody Ranch Music, and Gene Autry Records Inc. In the early 1950s, Autry's sharp sense for entertainment trends led him into the business of broadcasting. He operated such award-winning stations as KMPC radio and KTLA television in Los Angeles under the banner of Golden West Broadcasters.

As a station owner in search of radio programming, Autry went to the baseball owners' meetings in St. Louis in 1960. He had recently lost the broadcast rights to the Dodgers and was looking to sign up one of the American League's new expansion teams. He returned home the owner of the Los Angeles Angels, which became the first American League franchise on the West Coast. Autry paid $2.4 million for the team that was reportedly worth $125 million in 1996, when Disney became a managing partner with 25 percent ownership.

Autry and his second wife Jackie opened the Autry Museum of Western Heritage in 1988. An achievement that he cherished deeply, the museum has been praised as one of the finest on Western history. Built with a $54 million donation from the Autry Foundation, it traces the development of the West, from its prehistoric roots to its Gold Rush days, with a nod to the romantic images created by Hollywood cowboys such as Autry and his comic sidekicks. An impressive collection of art and artifacts, it draws thousands of visitors every year.

Loss of a Legend

Autry died at home on October 2, 1998, just three days after his 91st birthday, after a lengthy battle with lymphoma. He had endured a great deal of pain in the year before his death, but he still managed to attend his final Angels game on September 23, when the Angels lost to the Texas Rangers. He had requested that no funeral be held and was buried immediately at Forest Hills Memorial Park in Burbank, California.

Autry is recognized in the entertainment industry for his talent, but more so for the way he transcended expectations along the way, from a Tioga, Texas country music singer to star of films and television, and later as producer of his own films and television programs. He is remembered as a kind, generous man whose greatest charm was that he remained a down-to-earth cowboy despite his success.

Selected discography

Greatest Hits (contains "You Are My Sunshine," "Lonely River," and "Blues Stay Away from Me"), Columbia, 1961.
Golden Hits, RCA Victor, 1962.
Great Hits, Harmony, 1965.
The Essential Gene Autry (contains "The Yellow Rose of Texas" and "Back in the Saddle Again"), Columbia, 1992.

Sources

Dallas Morning News, October 3, 1998
Fort Worth Star-Telegram, October 3, 1998
Gannett News Service, October 2, 1998
Independent-London, October 5, 1996

—Kelly M. Cross

LaVern Baker

Singer

LaVern Baker was one of the most successful female R&B vocalists of the 1950s. In the tradition of Ma Rainey and Bessie Smith, Baker's blues-driven, gospel-tinged vocals paved the way for future female rock and rollers. However, unlike the more liberal 1990s, Baker rose to stardom in a decade where songs recorded by black artists were termed "race records" and thus received little airplay on radio stations. "Whitewashing" was a common practice in which white vocalists would re-record a black artist's single note for note and popularize them beyond the original version's success. Despite these barriers, particularly the incessant competition from white cover artist Georgia Gibbs, Baker succeeded. With novelty rock hits "Tweedlee Dee," "I Cried a Tear," "Bop-Ting-a-Ling" and "Jim Dandy," Baker secured her place in pop culture's collective repertoire and her role as pioneer female recording artist.

Like many of the most influential R&B vocalists of the 1950s, Baker's roots were in gospel music. Born Delores Williams in 1929 in Chicago, music was in her blood. Blues singer and guitarist Memphis Minnie was her aunt, and as early as Baker could speak she was singing on street corners with her friends from the neighborhood. In 1941, only 12 years old, she joined her Baptist Church choir in Chicago. By the time Baker turned 17 she had graduated to the local clubs, working as a professional singer at Chicago's Club De Lisa under the name "Little Miss Sharecropper." She also recorded several fruitless blues singles for RCA in 1949 under this alias.

Although blues music was her forte, her club material was primarily pop music. At one of her regular gigs at Detroit's Flame Show Bar, Baker met Al Green, who became her manager and was responsible for her first recordings at Columbia Records in 1951, this time under the name "Bea Baker." A series of virtually unnoticed recordings followed, including an unaccredited release with Maurice King in 1951 on Okeh Records, a recording for National Records, also in 1951, under the familiar nickname "Little Miss Sharecropper" and an unaccredited duet with Todd Rhodes on King Records the same year. Although she later toured Europe with Rhodes as the band's lead vocalist, success would not reach Baker until her Atlantic Records debut.

When Baker recorded her 1953 debut hit for Atlantic, "Soul on Fire," she was already a seasoned performer. She changed her name again, finally settling on LaVern Baker. Her second single, "Tweedlee Dee," was even more impressive, achieving Atlantic's first Top 20 pop hit and making her one of the first Atlantic artists to succeed on both the R&B and pop charts. But with Baker's first hint of success came the reality of current race relations, made painfully obvious by pop singer Georgia Gibbs' copycat version of "Tweedlee Dee" for Mercury Records, which reached number two on the pop charts. Baker filed suit, enraged by the injustice, but lost. Still, she persevered, and her winning streak continued with playful novelty songs "Bop Ting-a-Ling," "Fee Fi Fo Fum," and "Play it Fair," which reached number 2 on the R&B charts.

Baker had not only become a novelty rock icon, but she was making a comfortable living performing, too. In January of 1957, before leaving on an Australian tour, Baker sent her rival Gibbs a letter. "When I went to Australia with Bill Haley, Big Joe Turner, the Platters, and Freddy Bell and the Bellboys, I left her [Gibbs] my [flight] insurance policy," Baker was quoted in a *USA Today* article upon her death in 1997. "I sent it to her with a letter, 'Since I'll be away and you won't have anything new to copy, you might as well take this.'"

Baker's looks and charm made her a perfect candidate for crossover into television and movies in 1955. She was spotlighted on the R&B segment of Ed Sullivan's TV show and she performed in Alan Freed's *Rock, Rock, Rock* and *Mr. Rock & Roll*. In 1956, producer and founder of Atlantic Records, Ahmet Ertegun, found stronger material for Baker to record, resulting in the popular "Jim Dandy," topped the R&B charts in 1957 and reached number 17 on the pop charts. Baker has

For the Record . . .

Born Delores Williams, November 11, 1929, in Chicago, IL, (died March 10, 1997, Manhattan, NY).

Began singing gospel music in her Baptist Church choir in Chicago, 1941; recorded debut single as "Little Miss Sharecropper" for RCA Victor with Eddie "Sugarman" Penigar's band, 1949; recorded as "Bea Baker" for Columbia Records, recorded unaccredited with Maurice King for Okeh Records, recorded as "Little Miss Sharecropper" for National Records, 1951; joined Todd Rhodes' band as lead vocalist, changed name to LaVern Baker, 1952; signed with Atlantic Records as solo artist, 1953; achieved success on R&B charts with single "Tweedlee Dee" and became Atlantic's first Pop Top-20 hit, appeared in Alan Freed's movies Rock, Rock, Rock and Mr. Rock & Roll, 1955; reached number one on R&B charts with "Jim Dandy;" released biggest pop hit "I Cried a Tear," 1958; left Atlantic Records for Brunswick Records, 1964; became Entertainment Director at the Subic Bay Military Base, 1969; returned to the U.S. to perform at Atlantic Records' 40th anniversary party at Madison Square Garden, 1988; recorded "Slow Rolling Mama" for Dick Tracy movie soundtrack, replaced Ruth Brown for nine months in Broadway musical Black and Blue, 1990; died on March 3 in New York City, 1997.

Awards: Received Rhythm & Blues Foundation's Career Achievement Award, 1990; inducted into Rock and Roll Hall of Fame, 1991.

reap chart success in the early part of the 1960's with the singles "Saved," written by the famed songwriting team Leiber and Stoller, "See See Rider," "Bumble Bee," and "Shake a Hand." Before leaving Atlantic for Brunswick Records in 1965, Baker released a Bessie Smith tribute album, which became one of her most popular recordings. At Brunswick, her most notable recording was a duet with Jackie Wilson, "Think Twice," but by that time, her career was in decline.

Toward the end of the 1960s Baker went overseas to entertain U.S. servicemen in Vietnam, but in 1969 she developed pneumonia and moved to the Philippines to seek treatment. Her intended short stay became two decades, during which time she raised several children and worked as a performer for the Marines and then as Entertainment Director of a nightclub at the Subic Bay Military Base. In 1989 Baker returned to the U.S. to perform at Atlantic Records' 40th anniversary celebration. Her career was revitalized when she took over for fellow ex-Atlantic singer Ruth Brown in the Broadway play Black and Blue and recorded the song "Slow Rolling Mama" for the Dick Tracy movie soundtrack. She was honored in 1990 with the Rhythm & Blues Foundation's Career Achievement Award and inducted into the Rock and Roll Hall of Fame the same year.

Baker had struggled with diabetes for many years, but as the disease progressed, she was forced to have both her legs amputated. After two years of healing both physically and emotionally, she began to play the club circuit again, singing from her wheelchair. Her determination had been the principal factor in her initial success, but it was now clearer than ever. After enjoying renewed success for the greater portion of the 1990s, Baker died on March 10, 1997 in New York City

impacted contemporary artists like Bonnie Raitt, who consider her career vital in the crossover between R&B and rock and roll. Raitt told Steve Jones of USA Today that, "'Jim Dandy' was one of the greatest records I heard as a kid. Even when I was a kid in Southern California, I knew the real deal when I heard it."

Follow ups to "Jim Dandy," "Jim Dandy Got Married" and "Humpty Dumpty Heart," were also successful, but Baker's 1959 ballad "I Cried a Tear," featuring King Curtis on saxophone, became her biggest pop hit, reaching number six on the pop charts and number two on the R&B charts. During the next two years Baker recorded several duets, with BenE. King of the Drifters on "Help-Each-Other-Romance," and Jimmy Ricks of the Ravens on "You're the Boss." Baker continued to

Selected discography

Lavern Baker, Atlantic, 1953.
Her Greatest Hits, Atlantic, 1953.
Lavern, Atlantic, 1956.
Sings Bessie Smith, Atlantic, 1958.
Blues Ballads, Atlantic, 1959.
Precious Memories, Atlantic, 1959.
Saved, Atlantic, 1959.
See See Rider, Atlantic, 1963.
The Best of Lavern Baker, JCI, 1963.
Let Me Belong to You, Brunswick, 1970.
Real Gone Gal, Charly, 1984.
La Vern Baker Live in Hollywood '91, Rhino, 1991.
Soul on Fire: The Best of Lavern Baker, Rhino, 1991.
Woke Up This Mornin', DRG, 1992.
Blues Side of Rock 'n' Roll, Star Club, 1993.

Lavern/Lavern Baker, Collectables, 1998.
See See Rider/Blues Ballads, Collectables, 1998.

Sources

Books

Gaar, Gillian G., *She's a Rebel,* Seal Press, 1990.
Romanowski, Patricia, editor, *The New Rolling Stone Encyclopedia of Rock & Roll,* Rolling Stone Press, 1995.
Warner, Jay, *Billboard's American Rock 'n' Roll in Review,* Schirmer Books, 1997.

Online

"LaVern Baker," *All-Music Guide* www.allmusic.com (January 29, 1999).
"LaVern Baker," *The Rock and Roll Hall of Fame,* www.rockhall.com (January 29, 1999).
"Remembering LaVern Baker, a strong-willed R&B original," USA Today, www.usatoday.com (March 12, 1997).

—*Karen Gordon*

Beastie Boys

Rap group

They started out as a young trio who wanted to fight for their right to party, but the Beastie Boys have grown into socially-conscious rappers in more than 15 years of producing their own rap/punk blend. As their lyrics became more mature, they maintained their loud, aggressive, rebellious sound. The group's success allowed expansion into other business ventures, including owning their own record company, publishing a magazine, and creating a line of clothing.

Michael "Mike D" Diamond, Adam "King Ad-Rock" Horovitz, and Adam "MCA" Yauch met as teenagers hanging out in New York clubs. They all grew up in New York in families that were no strangers to creativity. Adam Horovitz was the son of playwright Israel Horovitz. His parents divorced when he was just three years old, and he was raised by his mother Doris, who was a painter and managed a thrift store. Adam Yauch grew up with a father who was a painter and an architect and a mother who was a social worker. Diamond's father worked as an art dealer, but died when Michael was just 16 . His mother was and interior decorator.

AP/Wide World Photos. Reproduced with permission.

The Beastie Boys started out playing in a hardcore band called the Young and the Useless. While still in high school they released their first punk album on Ratcage Records, called *Polly Wog Stew*, and the following year released a single called "Cooky Puss." Without the band's permission, British Airways used a portion of the single in a commercial. The group won the subsequent lawsuit and were paid $40,000. The money helped them focus on their music full-time, and a contract with Def Jam Records' head Rick Rubin led to greater exposure. The single "She's On It" was released on the soundtrack for *Krush Groove* in 1985.

Fought for Their Right to Party

In 1986, the Beastie Boys released their debut on Def Jam Records titled *Licensed to Ill*. The album included the hit singles "Fight for Your Right (to Party)" and "No Sleep Till Brooklyn," and earned multiplatinum sales. It later became the first rap album to reach number one on the *Billboard* album charts. As a result, the Beastie Boys had earned great success with a less-than-respectable image. But soon, the members began to fall prey to their own "party boy" media hype. "It wasn't until "Fight for Your Right (to Party)" came out that we started acting like drunken fools," Yauch told Akiba Lerner and Mark

LeVine in *Tikkun*. "At that point, our image shifted in a different direction, maybe turning off the kids that were strictly into hip-hop. It started off as a goof on that college mentality, but then we ended up personifying it." Their bad-boy image was fueled by reports that they made a music journalist cry during an interview, and that they had been banned from the executive offices of CBS Records for allegedly stealing a camera. The group didn't win much respect on the music front either. David Handelman wrote in *Rolling Stone*, "When the Boys weren't being called Monkees for not playing instruments, they were being called Blues Brothers for plundering a black music form and making more louie off it."

The Beastie Boys vigorously performed a lengthy tour in support of the album, and *Licensed to Ill* became the first rap album to surpass the four million copies sold mark in 1987. "We started getting sick of each other and of being on the road, even sick of the band and what it represented, like we were ashamed to be a part of it," Yauch told Light in *Spin*. "We decided to take some time apart from each other." Yauch spent his time away from the group on a side project called Brooklyn that performed in clubs around New York.

Branched Out in Style and Business

During this same time, the members of the Beastie Boys got into a dispute with Rick Rubin and Def Jam Records over royalty payments. The argument ended in a split with the record label. "Leaving Def Jam was kind of a blessing in disguise," Michael Diamond told Alan Light in *Rolling Stone*, "because we can make whatever record we want." To further change the pace of their lives and music, the trio moved from New York to Los Angeles and signed a new record contract with Capitol Records.

In 1989, the group released their next album, *Paul's Boutique*, named after the Brooklyn store that appears on the cover. The Beastie Boys also recorded the store's radio advertisement on the album. On *Paul's Boutique*, the group moved in a slightly more mature direction. David Hiltbrand wrote in *People*, "With their second album, the New York trio has created a prodigiously inventive, genre-bleeding, free-for-all style." This unfamiliar musical mix was not well received by fans and the group's popularity waned. The album barely sold 500,000 copies—a significant drop from the multiplatinum sales of *Licensed to Ill*.

The maturation of the Beastie Boys' music also revealed itself in its members' lives. The 'bad boy' party image they had maintained began to slow down to a more low-key pace. "Just as we were finishing *Paul's Boutique*, we got our own places, and I was going to clubs a lot less," Yauch told Joe Levy in *Rolling Stone*. "I got a bit more introverted and spent a lot more time on my own, reading. I would just go down to the esoteric bookstore and wander around." After the release of *Paul's Boutique*, the trio took some more time off and entered into some outside business ventures. They started their own record label and began publishing their own magazine, both under the name Grand Royal. They signed artists they wanted to support to their label, and broadcast news about the band, their lifestyle, and their world view in the magazine. They also went on to produce their own line of streetwear clothing to match their stage image called X-Large.

Played Own Instruments

In 1992, the Beastie Boys decided to return to the studio to record *Check Your Head*. This time, in addition to their rap vocals, each member of the band played his own instrument instead of relying on technological wizardry and sampling to provide the music. Adam Horovitz played guitar, Adam Yauch picked up the bass, and Michael Diamond pounded the drums. The singles "Pass the Mic" and "Whatcha Want" helped boost the sales of *Check Your Head* beyond platinum.

The critics had a mixed response to the album. Hiltbrand wrote in *People*, "The sound is murky and messy, the music sloppy and uninvolving. The lyrics certainly contain none of the smartass cleverness that marked the trio's earlier work. Light had a different outlook in *Rolling Stone*, "They won the fight for their right to party, and then, while no one was looking, the Beastie Boys turned into one of today's most consistently creative bands."

Maintaining an easy-going recording pace, the Beastie Boys waited until 1994 to release their next effort, *Ill Communication*, which included "Get It Together" and "Sabotage." They reclaimed their popularity and high sales when the album debuted at number one on *Billboard*'s album charts. David Browne wrote in *Entertainment Weekly*, "Call it novelty, slacker rap, or sheer white urban noise—whatever the tag, it's the most tantalizing ear candy in years, the incessantly inventive sound of brats dismantling pop and trying to reassemble it in their own ingeniously klutzy ways." During that summer, the Beastie Boys co-headlined the popular Lollapalooza tour with alternative rock band Smashing Pumpkins. The trio also released a compilation of the group's earliest recordings, including their lucky charm "Cooky Puss," titled *Same Old Bullshit*.

Fought for the Rights of Others

In the early 1990s, Adam Yauch began exploring Buddhism, and eventually exclusively studied Tibetan Buddhism. He co-founded the Milarepa Fund to raise the awareness of China's oppression of the Tibetan people. The Beastie Boys donated all the publishing proceeds from "Shambala" and "Bodhisattva Vow" on *Ill Communication* to the Milarepa Fund. Following the tour for the album, Yauch organized several Tibetan Freedom concerts and a film documentary to increase awareness of Tibet's struggle.

The Beastie Boys took nearly four years off before they returned to the studio again. All three members moved back to New York, and each spent their time pursuing their own interests. Yauch worked on the Milarepa Fund, Diamond managed Grand Royal Records and the magazine, and Horovitz sought out talent to sign to the label and produced and recorded with other artists. "It's been four years between records, but it wasn't like we were sitting at home," Horovitz told Light in *Spin*. "We basically saw each other almost every day."

In 1998, the trio returned with the release of *Hello Nasty* and the single "Intergalactic." Within the first week of its release, the album soared to number one on *Billboard*'s album chart and sold a whopping 681,500 copies. "*Hello Nasty* jumps from rap to easy listening to Latin to noise to soul to opera to rock without pausing for a breath," wrote Neil Strauss in the *New York Times*.
The members' individual personalities also made their distinct mark on the album as Ann Powers noted in the *New York Times*, "Attentive listeners will notice an unresolved split between the group's attempts at egoless expression and the consummately ego-driven boasts essential to its raps."

Michael Diamond explained how their personal divisions worked into their own cohesive style to Levy in *Rolling Stone*. "On this record, we went back to the three of us just getting together and sharing ideas, then piecing something together and spreading it out," he said. "So it's much more of a collective where we're all saying each other's lyrics, like on *Paul's Boutique*." After nearly two decades of making music together, the Beastie Boys continue to push the limits of rap and hip-hop music into new directions. They took their musical influences and blended them into their own style, eventually ignoring the praise and the criticism and pursuing their own creative path. "It would be nice to look at ourselves as innovators," Horovitz told Chris Mundy in *Rolling Stone*. "I think we are creative, but in terms of being masterminds, no. We're just making music that we like."

Selected discography

Licensed to Ill, Def Jam , 1986.
Paul's Boutique, Capitol, 1989.
Check Your Head, Capitol, 1992.
Ill Communication, Grand Regal/Capitol, 1994.
Same Old Bullshit, Grand Regal/Capitol, 1994.
Hello Nasty, Grand Royal/Capitol, 1998.

Sources

Billboard, November 14, 1987; April 18, 1992; April 23, 1994; August 1, 1998.
Entertainment Weekly, March 18, 1994; June 3, 1994; July 22, 1994; July 17, 1998; July 31, 1998.
Interview, August 1994.
Newsweek, August 3, 1998.
People, August 28, 1989; June 1, 1992; July 20, 1998.
Playboy, April 1987, June 1987, July 1987.
New York Times, July 14, 1998; July 19, 1998.
Rolling Stone, February 12, 1987; December 17, 1987; August 10, 1989; May 28, 1992; June 2, 1994; August 11, 1994; October 30, 1997; May 28, 1998; August 6, 1998.
Spin, September 1998.
Tikkun, November-December 1996.
Time, May 18, 1992; July 4, 1994; August 10, 1998.

—*Sonya Shelton*

Dock Boggs

Banjo, singer

Dock Boggs played a weird hybrid of hillbilly music and blues. He played "old time" music, the original folk music that so many other musicians in the Cumberland Mountains in the late 1920s and early 1930s played, but his was something different. It was "put together out of junk," wrote Greil Marcus in his liner notes to *Dock Boggs: Country Blues, Complete Early Recordings, 1927-1929*, "hand-me-down melodies, folk-lyric fragments, pieces of Child ballads, mail-order instruments, and the new women's blues records they were making in the northern cities in the early years of the twenties." What's more, Boggs adapted the techniques of black blues guitarists to the banjo—a step most other white players never dreamed of taking. Doing so, he created a style of playing completely unlike the strumming "clawhammer" style used by his white contemporaries. Unfortunately Dock's music never really caught on with the public. He quit performing through most of the thirties, forties and fifties. Only the interest of record collectors and the persistence of folklorists in tracking him down kept Boggs's music alive for future generations.

Moran Lee "Dock" Boggs was born on February 7, 1898 in West Norton, Virginia in the middle of Appalachian coal country. He was the youngest of ten children, his father was a farmer who sold off his land piece by piece to the coal companies and ended his life as a blacksmith and gunsmith in Norton. Dock attended school three months a year—Norton couldn't afford to pay a teacher any more than that—and went into the coal mines at the age of twelve, working ten hour days at seven cents an hour. When his formal education ended, Dock became his own teacher, a Bible, a dictionary, and a speller were his textbooks.

Dock, like his brothers and sisters, took an interest in music at an early age. He learned to play clawhammer banjo, the mountain style in which a player simply frailed, that is strummed, the strings. Listening to the string bands that played in the black community of Dorchester, Dock first heard a banjo played finger-style. "I heard this fellow play the banjo," he relates in *Nothing But The Blues*, "and I said to myself ... I want to learn how to play the banjo kinda like that fellow does. I don't want to play like my sister and brother. I am going to learn to pick with my fingers."

He started following a black guitarist named Go Lightning, who often played the ballad "John Henry" at Dock's request. A black banjo player named Jim White gave him the idea that he could play banjo like a blues guitarist would, picking out melodies while he sang. He was learning songs constantly: ballads from his sisters, gospel songs from his brother-in-law, some blues here and there, from folks passing through Norton, and the radio. He particularly liked the female blues singers that he heard in his brother-in-law's record collection, and adapted their songs to his new banjo style.

In early 1927, Dock was working a coal-cutting machine in Pardee, Virginia, when he heard that the Brunswick Record Company was coming to Norton to hold try-outs for record contracts. Dock wasn't sure it was worth the trouble—the mountains, he reasoned, were full of musicians, professional musicians, who stood a much better chance than he at the contract. A friend convinced him to give it a shot, however, and Dock went to the Norton Hotel's ballroom for the audition, fortified with moonshine, and carrying a borrowed banjo under his arm. When he saw the crowd there he nearly turned around and left. Boggs was one of the last to audition. He played "Country Blues" and "Down South Blues"—songs he later recorded—but only the first couple bars of each song as the agents were in a hurry. By the time the day had ended, 75 musicians had auditioned. Boggs was one of the three who got contracts. Among the musicians who were rejected rejected was A.P. Carter of the Carter Family.

In March of 1927, Boggs bought a new suit and got on the train bound for New York City and his first Brunswick recording session. It was the first time he had ever

For the Record . . .

Born Moran Lee Boggs, February 7, 1898 (died February 7, 1971), West Norton, VA; married: wife Sara.

Learned banjo as a boy, developed his unique "blues-style" banjo listening to local black musicians, records and the radio; awarded recording contract by for Brunswick Record Company, 1927; "Country Blues" and "Sugar Baby" included in Harry Smith's Smith's *Anthology of American Folk Music*; found living in Norton VA in 1963 by Mike Seeger; first public appearance after rediscovery American Folk Festival in Asheville, NC; recorded three albums for Folkway Records.

ventured out of the Virginia mountains. He recorded eight songs, including "Sugar Baby," "Country Blues," and "New Prisoner's Song" Dock took "Down South Blues" from a 1923 record by Rosa Henderson. "Boggs turned the regular, rather predictable rhythm of a mediocre city blues singer into a complex redaction of raw urgent force, mountain blues at its best," wrote Charles Wolfe in "A Lighter Shade of Blue," included in *Nothing But The Blues*. Brunswick wanted Boggs to cut more tunes but he refused, perhaps afraid of being taken advantage of by Yankee businessmen.

His first records changed the way Boggs saw his music. It became more than just a hobby to entertain himself, family and friends, it was suddenly a possible source of livelihood. "I thought ... that I might ... happen to put out a record that would make a hit," Dock is quoted by Greil Marcus, "to where I have an opportunity, that I might ... maybe never have to work in the mines no more." He formed a band called the Cumberland Mountain Entertainers—with whom he never recorded—and hired booking agent. Unfortunately, things didn't turn out the way Boggs hoped. He froze up and could not perform at an OKeh Records audition held live on Atlanta radio. Another time he set up a session in Louisville with the Victor record company but couldn't raise the cash to make the trip. He recorded only more before his rediscovery in the 1960s, with a West Virginia label, Lonesome Ace, in 1929. Lonesome Ace was a vanity label, owned and operated by W.E. Myer, who signed his favorite musicians to contracts to set his own poems to music and record them. Boggs cut four pieces of Myers poems.

Myer went broke early in the Great Depression; Dock's first musical career ended at the same time. His wife Sara, a deeply religious woman, wanted him to give up music too, seeing it as the devil's work. Mrs. Boggs finally refused to sleep with Dock, Marcus relates, unless he gave up the banjo. In the end, Dock gave in and returned to the mines where he worked until the mid-1950s. For a while he played now and then for family and friends, for neighborhood socials and dances but eventually gave that up too and pawned his banjo.

Sara Boggs was wrong if she thought abandoning music would save her husband from the snares of the devil. Boggs became deeply involved in running moonshine in the mountains, a business every bit as violent and deadly as the drug trade of the 1990s. In 1942, he underwent a religious conversion, joined his wife's church, and devoted his life to it completely, helping the poor and needy in his mountain community. When mechanization came to the coal mines in 1954, Dock found himself without work and five years short of qualifying for his miner's pension. Destitute, Dock and Sara were forced to survive on the produce of her vegetable garden.

In 1952, Folkways released Harry Smith's *Anthology of American Folk Music*, a set that included two of Dock's 1927 recordings. The *Anthology* became the audio bible of the 1950s folk revival and reawakened interest in the music of a number of obscure artists who had recorded in the 1920s and 1930s, including Dock's. In the mid-1950s young folkies set out to find any of the old artists who might still be alive. Mike Seeger, a musician and folklorist, tracked Dock Boggs down in Norton Virginia in 1963, at the height of the folk revival. A few weeks later he made his first public appearance in more than thirty years at the American Folk Festival in Asheville, North Carolina. For the next eight years Dock Boggs had his second career as a musician. He performed regularly at folk festivals across the United States and recorded three albums for Folkways. Dock Boggs died in 1971 on February 7, on his seventy-third birthday.

Selected discography

Anthology of American Folk Music, Folkways, 1952
Dock Boggs, Folkways, 1963 *Dock Boggs, Volume 2*, Folkways, 1965
Dock Boggs: His Twelve Original Recordings (1927 & 1929), Folkways, 1983
Dock Boggs: Country Blues, Complete Early Recordings, 1927-1929, Revenant, 1998

Sources

The Encyclopedia of Country Music, Paul Kingsbury, ed.,
    Oxford University Press: New York, 1998

—*Gerald Brennan*

Garth Brooks

Guitar, singer, songwriter

Landing a record deal was the goal when Garth Brooks moved to Nashville in 1987. Becoming the largest-selling musical act of all time was the goal by 1998, when only the Beatles stood in his way. This dynamic country megastar— known for such hits as "If Tomorrow Never Comes," "Friends in Low Places," "The Dance," and "Rodeo"— is the highest-certified solo artist in U.S. music history, according the Recording Industry Association of America (RIAA). With more than 95 million album sales certified since 1989, he is also the fastest-selling album artist in RIAA history. Beloved by fans, Brooks played 350 shows in 100 cities during his 1996-98 concert tour, selling more than 5.3 million tickets.

Brooks had more than 20 number one hits, awards too numerous to count and his share of controversies, but in 1998, it was his sales numbers that drew the most attention. To surpass the Beatles, he would have to sell more than 100 million records, a milestone it took the Fab Four 34 years to reach. After ten short years, he was closing in on that record. "Being mentioned in the same breath with the Beatles is staggering for me," Brooks told Brian McCollum of the *Detroit Free Press.* "Because no matter how many records we sell, we'll never be on the same planet as the Beatles." Capitol Nashville president Pat Quigley told Bryan Mansfield of *USA Today,* "If you were a betting man, a hundred million by the millennium is a good bet on Garth Brooks." "I don't want to be remembered as a scorekeeper," Brooks told McCollum. "I just want to focus on the music. Then the number thing will take care of itself."

Troyal Garth Brooks was born in Tulsa, Oklahoma, and raised in the small town of Yukon with country music in his blood. His mother performed on Capitol Records in the 1950s and his father taught him to play his first guitar chords. His sister, Betsy, who later became his bassist, was considered the musician among the six Brooks' children. Garth was the athlete of the family, excelling at track, baseball, football and basketball in high school. His musical tastes ran more toward the rock of the day, such as KISS and Journey. He attended Oklahoma State University on a partial track scholarship for javelin, graduating with a degree in advertising in 1984.

Left for Nashville

Playing clubs while in college, Brooks first talked of Nashville before he completed his degree. His mother told Karen Schoemer of *Newsweek,* "I begged Garth not to go. I cried. I said, 'I want you to get a real job. That's why we sent you to college'." Heeding his mother's plea, Brooks stayed in school, working as a bouncer in

For the Record . . .

Born Troyal Garth Brooks Feb. 7, 1962, in Tulsa, OK; son of Troyal and Colleen Carroll (a Capitol Records recording artist in the 1950s) Brooks; married Sandy Mahl, 1986; children: Taylor Mayne Pearl, August Anna, Allie Colleen. *Education:* Graduated from Oklahoma State University in 1984.

Played in bands in high school and college, also worked as a bouncer during college; signed with Capitol Records, in 1988; released *Garth Brooks,* 1989, with first number one hit "If Tomorrow Never Comes"; released *No Fences,* 1990; released *Ropin' the Wind,* 1991; released *Beyond the Season,* 1992; released *The Chase,* 1992; released *In Pieces,* 1993; released *The Garth Brooks Collection,* 1994; released *The Hits,* 1994; released *Fresh Horses,* 1995; released *Sevens,* 1997; released *The Limited Series,* 1998; released *Garth Double Live,* 1998; subject of six NBC television specials; *Garth Live from Central Park* was highest-rated original program on HBO in 1997, and drew largest concert audience ever in Central Park.

Awards: Country Music Association music video of the year, 1990-91; Country Music Association Horizon Award, 1990; Academy of Country Music video of the year, 1990 and 1993-94; Academy of Country Music top male vocalist, 1990-91; Academy of Country Music song of the year, 1990; Academy of Country Music single of the year, 1990; Academy of Country Music entertainer of the year, 1990-93 and 1997; TNN/Music City News video of the year, 1991; Grammy, best male country vocal performance, 1991; Country Music Association single of the year, 1991; Country Music Association entertainer of the year, 1991-92, 1997-98; Country Music Association album of the year, 1991, 1992; American Music Awards favorite single, 1991-92; TNN/Music City News entertainer of the year, 1992; American Music Awards favorite male artist, 1992-97; American Music Awards favorite album, 1992 and 1996; Country Music Association vocal event of the year, 1993; ASCAP songwriter of the year, 1993-94; Academy of Country Music Jim Reeves Memorial Award, 1994; Academy of Country Music special achievement award, 1997; Grammy, best country vocal collaboration, 1998.

Addresses: *Record company*—Capitol Records, 3322 W. End Ave., Nashville, TN 37203.

addition to playing with a band. He met his future wife, Sandy Mahl, when he was called upon to remove the fist she had pitched at a romantic rival from a bathroom wall. When he graduated from college, Brooks handed his mother his tassel and asked for her blessing to go to Nashville. She refused, and offered her prayers instead. He went to Nashville in 1985 but headed home less than 24 hours later. He married Mahl in 1986 and set out for Nashville once more in 1987, determined to make a go of it. He sang demos and worked in a boot shop until he signed with Capitol Records in 1988. In 1989, Brooks' self-titled debut was released and a superstar was born.

Alanna Nash summed up Brooks' early work in *Entertainment Weekly;* "From his first album ... [Garth Brooks] has recognized that younger country fans demand more than three-chord celebrations of drinking and cheating, so he has deftly wed classic country vocal and instrumental elements with 1970s confessional folk-pop. With *No Fences* in 1990, he began to address such ... subjects as wife beating, the topic of his controversial video for 'The Thunder Rolls.' *The Chase* is Brooks' most mature and ambitious album. If he can alter country's traditionally redneck attitudes toward blacks, homosexuals, and women, Brooks' feat as a record-seller will pale by comparison."

While his controversial message songs gained him praise, some of Brooks' other choices drew criticism. He had his share of trouble adjusting to stardom, noted Schoemer in *Newsweek.* Brooks admitted infidelity in 1991, outed his sister as a lesbian in 1993 without first consulting her, and even refused an American Music Award for favorite artist of the year in 1996. Through it all, his fans remained loyal, and Brooks never forgot that they were responsible for his rise to fame and fortune. He insisted that concert tickets be held to a $20 average. At every arena he played, he moved through each section, checking the view and the sound. Producer Allen Reynolds said, "I've never known an artist who loves what he does any more than Garth Brooks. Nor an artist who loved his audience more."

Gave Fans His All

Brooks told Ray Waddell of *Amusement Business* magazine, "Everybody talks about paying dues. I don't remember that part. It's always been a blast, whether it was 20 people in a club or 20,000 in an arena. The audience keeps me fresh. But there's another factor. When I step out on stage each night, there's a thought running around in my head. What if something happened to me? What if this was the last show I ever played? Is it the one I'd want to be remembered for?"

Brooks gave his all for the fans, even if it meant losing lucrative endorsements. He told Waddell, "Our promoters don't have any front-row seats to give out. We've never done an endorsement because of one phrase in every contract: 'We need 20 of your best tickets every night.' When you've got 20 people that would be somewhere else if they didn't have free tickets, that sucks. We want everyone to be there because they want to be there. We've turned down $10 million, $15 million and $20 million endorsements because of that clause. We will not do it."

Kate Meyers summarized the fan relationship in *Entertainment Weekly;* "He's got Springsteen-like energy, but never screams; a Madonna-style mouthpiece, but he never grabs his crotch; fist pumps a la Arsenio, but he never barks. To me, a great performer is someone who, when it's over, you'd walk through hell with them. You feel like, 'Yeah, I believe!' And sure enough, at the end of his shows he uncaps bottles of Evian and baptizes the adoring crowd, true believers all."

Adored by millions of true believers, it seemed Brooks couldn't lose. His next two albums, 1993's *In Pieces* and 1994's *The Hits* sold 8 and 10 million copies respectively. His four NBC television specials produced through that time were major ratings winners. But his 1995 album, *Fresh Horses,* was seen as a failure for selling only 6 million copies.

Capitol Concerns

After *Fresh Horses,* Brooks had grave concerns about Capitol's ability to market his work. Those concerns led to a three-month delay in release of *Sevens* in 1997, and replacement of the label's president, Scott Hendricks. *Sevens* was originally timed for release to coincide with the HBO television special *Garth Live from Central Park* on August 7, 1997. The special drew the largest concert audience ever in New York's Central Park, and was the highest-rated original program on HBO in 1997, drawing 14.6 million viewers.

But "by the beginning of June [1997]," Melinda Newman wrote in *Billboard,* "Brooks felt he had no decision but to pull the album, knowing full well that he was missing the opportunity of a lifetime by not coinciding the release with [the concert in] Central Park." Brooks explained, "In 1992, I negotiated and worked real hard to gain the right [in my contract] that if I didn't think things were right during the time of release, I didn't have to release the record. And in my opinion, things were definitely not right." He feared that without the proper marketing plan,

Sevens would "fall on its face, and it would be over for me."

As the situation dragged on, Brooks considered the possibility that the album would never be released. "My thinking in July is that I'm history," he told Newman. "They've got my head under water, and I'm trying to remain calm, and maybe they'll let my head up, and I'll snatch a breath, but it's getting to where I'm thinking I'm going to die down here." Eventually, all Brooks' demands were met, and *Sevens* was released on November 25, 1997. In seven weeks, it sold 3.7 million units, the same number it took *Fresh Horses* more than two years to sell. Never before had a performer wielded that kind of power on Music Row, and it made some industry executives nervous. "It's like having a gorilla in the chicken pen," former Capitol Nashville president Jimmy Bowen told Newsweek's Schoemer. "Some of the chickens are gonna get stomped on. And the ones that don't are gonna be nervous."

Critics say that in his quest to become history's biggest star, he has become ruthless and manipulative." Brian McCollum also wrote in the Detroit Free Press, "sure, he wears his heart on his sleeve, they say. But that's just so nobody notices his hand on his wallet." However, Brooks told Ray Waddell of *Amusement Business* magazine, "that is the only true representation of success in this business, when people give up their money and their time. You can win award after award, and if you're not selling tickets, the awards don't mean anything. Tickets and CD sales can't be hyped, and we take them both very seriously."

In 1998, Capitol Nashville ceased production of Brooks' first six albums to boost their sales as a boxed set. *The Limited Series*—so named because only 2 million copies were manufactured— created controversy among specialty retailers who would have seen greater profits from individual sales of the artist's back catalog. The record company announced plans to re-release the albums individually on the 10th anniversary of the original release dates. Quoted in *Billboard,* Brooks said, "It's just letting the catalog go, and hopefully when it comes back out, it will be an event. And we'll probably do the same thing, bring it back out, and not service it for a while and then bring it back out again, following the Disney [video] model."

Music's Home Run Hitter

1998's *Garth Double Live* was preceded by a publicity blitz that included a multi-million dollar advertising campaign, an appearance with Jay Leno the night before release, a closed circuit performance beamed to 2,400 Wal-Marts the day of release, and three consecutive television specials —each of which aired live on NBC— the second day of release. The goal was to sell one million units the first day, but it took a week to sell 1,085,373 copies. There was speculation that *Double Live* would push Brooks over the 100 million sales mark.

"The 100 million thing has been so focused on in the public that if it happens, so be it," Brooks told Melinda Newman of *Billboard*. "But truthfully, how I'd love the 100 million thing to work is I'd love to feel for the industry, for country music, what Mark McGwire felt from the sports industry on chasing the 70 home runs. I'd love to see us all enjoy and celebrate it and feel like it's all ours and move forward from there and remember that the numbers aren't what's important. It's the trip that gets you there."

Ironically, the baseball diamond was where Brooks chose to watch for the 100 million milestone. Planning a year off from touring, he joined the San Diego Padres for spring training in 1999 to fulfill a lifelong dream and boost support for his children's charity, "Touch 'Em All: Teammates for Kids." The foundation asked major leaguers to pledge a donation for each play in a chosen category, such as home runs, to be matched by both a corporation and an entertainer. If a player pledged $1,000 for every home run, the final donation would add up to $3,000. Quoted on planetgarth.com, Brooks told ESPN, "I want to change people's lives. I want it to give opportunities to kids that do not have it. Those kids go on to do something with their lives that changes the world for a better place."

Selected discography

Garth Brooks, Capitol, 1989.
No Fences (includes "The Thunder Rolls"), Capitol Nashville, 1990.
Ropin' the Wind (includes "Rodeo"), Capitol Nashville, 1991.
Beyond the Season (includes "The Old Man's Back in Town"), Liberty, 1992.
The Chase (includes "We Shall Be Free"), Liberty, 1992.
In Pieces (includes "That Summer"), Capitol, 1993.
Fresh Horses (includes "The Beaches of Cheyenne"), Capitol, 1995.
Sevens (includes "Long Neck Bottle"), Capitol, 1997.
Double Live (includes "It's Your Song"), 1998.

Sources

Books

McCloud, Barry, and contributing writers, *Definitive Country: The Ultimate Encyclopedia of Country Music and Its Performers*, Perigee, 1995.

Periodicals

Amusement Business, Nov. 16, 1998.
Billboard, Jan. 31, 1998; April 11, 1998; Oct. 24,1998.
Country Weekly, July 28, 1998.
Detroit Free Press, Nov. 15, 1998.
Entertainment Weekly, Oct. 2, 1992; Dec. 25, 1992.
Newsweek, March 16, 1998.
USA Today, Nov. 17, 1998.

Online

The Artists—Garth Brooks, Country.com, http://www.country.com.
Brooks' foundation a hit with big leaguers— and kids, planetgarth.com, http://www.planetgarth.com.

Additional information was provided by Capitol Records publicity materials, 1998.

—*Shari Swearingen Garrett*

Brooks & Dunn

Country vocal duo, songwriters

Arista. Reproduced by permission.

Mixing two elements can sometimes cause an explosive reaction that results in something completely new, something greater than the sum of its parts. When Kix Brooks and Ronnie Dunn teamed up, two little-known solo artists who struggled for decades were transformed into overnight superstars, becoming country's top vocal duo. Their debut album, *Brand New Man*, remained on *Billboard*'s Top Country Albums charts for more than five years and is the best-selling album by a country duo in music history. Since their 1991 breakthrough, the duo's standout songwriting and performances have continued to win critical acclaim and every major industry award—as well as an enthusiastic audience, evidenced by record-breaking tours and album sales topping 17 million. "There's never been a male pairing that's turned into this kind of sociological phenomenon," Country Music Association director Ed Benson told *Entertainment Weekly.* "They have an electricity and a camaraderie together that's infectious."

The energetic Kix Brooks—who earned his nickname before he was born—began his musical journey in Shreveport, Lousiana. At six years old, he started playing the ukelele. At age 12, he gave his first performance, during a birthday party for country legend Johnny Horton's daughter, who lived down the street. By the time he began college at Louisiana State University, Brooks was a regular on the club circuit. He recalled a New Orleans joint where flying fists and beer bottles filled the air. "I got a blank pistol," he told *People.* "When they'd get too wild, I'd pop a cap, and they'd be looking for bullet holes in themselves and running for cover." Dunn added, "It took us about 40 years combined, but we finally got out of those danged bars."

After traveling to Alaska to work on the pipeline and to Maine to work in advertising, Brooks moved to Nashville, where a former classmate worked for Charlie Daniels' publishing company. Brooks became a staff writer at Tree Publishing, where he penned hits for John Conley, Nitty Gritty Dirt Band, Highway 101, Sawyer Brown, The Oak Ridge Boys and Ricky Van Shelton. He also continued pursuing a solo career, releasing albums on Avion and Capitol, with only minor success.

Meanwhile, Ronnie Dunn grew up performing with his father's band in west Texas. He was later forced to choose between music and the Baptist ministry while at Abilene Christian College. Moonlighting in honkytonks was not an approved part of the curriculum for psychology and theology students.

Confronted with the choice, Dunn quit school and moved to Tulsa, Oklahoma, with his parents. After years of

For the Record . . .

Members include Leon Eric "Kix" Brooks III (born May 12, 1955, Shreveport, LA); married; wife's name, Barbara; children: Molly, Eric; *Education:* Studied speech and drama at Louisiana State University. Ronnie Gene Dunn (born June 1, 1953, in Coleman, TX); married; wife's name, Janine; children: [first marriage] daughter Whitney, son Jesse, [current marriage] daughter Haley); Education: Studied psychology and theology at Abilene Christian College.

Partnership suggested by Arista executive Tim DuBois; signed to Arista Records, 1990; recorded *Brand New Man,* Arista, 1991, *Hard Workin' Man,* 1993, *Waitin' on Sundown,* 1994, *Borderline,* 1996, *The Greatest Hits Collection,* 1997, *If You See Her,* 1998; highest certified country duo of all time with more than 17 million albums sold.

Awards: Top vocal duet, Academy of Country Music, 1991-96; top vocal duet or group, Academy of Country Music, 1997; top new vocal duet or group, Academy of Country Music, 1991; album of the year, Academy of Country Music, 1992; single record of the year, Academy of Country Music, 1992, for "Boot Scootin' Boogie;" entertainer of the year, Academy of Country Music, 1995 and 1996; favorite band, duo or group, American Music Awards, 1997; rising star award, A.M.O.A. Jukebox Awards, 1992; songwriter of the year (Ronnie Dunn), *Billboard* Entertainment Award, 1995; favorite country album by a duo or group, *Billboard* Entertainment Award, 1998; favorite country duo or group artist, Blockbuster Entertainment Awards, 1995; favorite country album by a duo or group , Blockbuster Entertainment Awards, 1998; songwriter of the year (Ronnie Dunn), BMI Country Awards, 1996 and 1998; vocal duo of the year, Country Music Association, 1992-98; album of the year, Country Music Association, 1994; entertainer of the year, Country Music Association, 1996; video group/duo, Country Music Television, 1997; best country performance by a duo or group with vocal, Grammy Awards, 1993; best country performance by a duo or group with vocal, Grammy Awards, 1997; vocal duo of the year, TNN/Music City News Awards, 1993-98.

Addresses: *Record company*—Arista/Nashville, 7 Music Circle North, Nashville, TN 37203.

playing clubs in Texas and Oklahoma, he won the Marlboro Talent Search. His prizes included recording sessions with producers Barry Beckett and ScottHendricks. It was Hendricks who later brought Dunn to the attention of Arista executive Tim DuBois. Dunn moved to Nashville and signed with Tree Publishing, where Brooks was also on staff.

DuBois noticed similarities in Brooks' and Dunn's music, introduced the two over lunch in 1990, and suggested they try writing together. Brooks told *People,* "Ronnie and I were the most unlikely duo candidates. We had always held onto single egos." When they first paired up, Brooks told David Zimmerman of *USA Today* that,"these songs kept poppin' out," adding that the duo hoped Alan Jackson would include one of their songs in his next project.

DuBois told Zimmerman, "The first song they brought me that they'd written together was 'Brand New Man.' I knew we had something special there. It was obvious I had to convince them that they were an act. They both wanted solo careers very badly and had pursued it for so long. It's not the same thing when you're having to share that spotlight with someone else. I think there was that element of letting go of that dream." Determined to succeed, they cast their chances together. Dunn told Dana Kennedy of *Entertainment Weekly* the duo's success was a result of "sheer blind determination. Psychotic need. There are a lot of people who make it who don't have a thimbleful of talent. They just want it more than anybody else. That's what it takes."

Their debut album, *Brand New Man,* was released in 1991. The album proved the duo had what it took. Kennedy wrote, "Their appeal stems from the way they mix styles—the music is part lonesome-hearted country, part stomping rock & roll, overlaid with a '70s singer/songwriter sensibility."

Their sophomore effort, 1993's *Hard Workin' Man,* left no doubt about the duo's star status. Ted Drozdowski wrote in *Rolling Stone, "Hard Workin' Man* is a smooth-running machine, fueled by Dunn's burr-edged lead vocals, the duo's strong harmonies and choruses built on hooks heavy enough to pierce even the heartiest Saturday night honky-tonker. And that's what hits are made of on anyone's assembly line." *USA Today's* Zimmerman wrote, "Leave the weepy ballads to Vince Gill and the message songs to Garth Brooks (no relation to Kix); the duo's sole aim is to scar up those hardwood dance floors with the gotta-dance tug of songs like ... 'Hard Workin' Man' and the career-making 'Boot Scootin' Boogie,' the dance-hall classic that even invaded disco clubs."

In 1996, the release of *Borderline* marked what Ronnie Dunn called "a little bit of a left turn for us," according to imusic.com. " I felt like it was time for us to kind of veer off the most traveled path. It sure doesn't hurt, in today's climate, to step just a little bit over into what the traditionalists might call 'progressive.'" "Dunn's range and persuasion as a singer have perhaps never been better showcased than on 'My Maria,'" noted imusic.com, "the thrilling remake of a B.W. Stevenson hit of yesteryear that practically jumps out of the grooves at you." Brooks told Tamara Saviano of *Country Weekly*, "We use everyone's input to decide which songs to cut. And of course, Ronnie has such a great voice and radio is really locked into it. As a result, he sings most of the singles. We keep that in mind when we're making the record."

The duo's 1998 album, *If You See Her,* included the 1966 Roger Miller classic "Husbands and Wives." "Cutting that was just a whim," Dunn told Saviano. "I was in the studio, and we had a little bit of down time, and I looked at [producer Don] Cook and said, 'Do you remember that Roger Miller song? Does anybody know the lyrics? I want to cut it while we have a minute." The song eventually went to number one.

The album's title track, "'If You See Him/If You See Her,' [sung with Reba McEntire] was the result of an unprecedented alliance between two superstar acts and their label chiefs, managers, producers and promotion and marketing teams," wrote *Billboard*'s Chet Flippo. "One song became a single for two acts on two different labels, as well as a video. The song also anchors the new album for each act, and the albums themselves are named after the song. A joint tour with McEntire and Brooks & Dunn is powering the whole venture." During that co-headlining tour with McEntire, the two acts took turns going on first. At times, the question of who would open in what city was settled by a simple coin toss. "After a month or so," Dunn joked, "the only argument we had was over who'd go on last. We both wanted to be the opening act!"

In 1998, Brooks and Dunn were ranked the fourth highest-grossing tour for joint dates with McEntire, according to *Amusement Business* magazine, and ninth for the shows they headlined. The duo's performance style has evolved to gain them coveted entertainer of the year awards from both the Academy of Country Music and the Country Music Association. They are the only duo ever to have achieved this honor. "A dynamo in concert," *People* noted, "Brooks likes to jump into the audience, while his laid-back foil packs his energies into the vocals." *USA Today*'s Zimmerman wrote, "In concert,

... Dunn is the less flamboyant of the two, but his vocal intensity somehow matches Brooks' manic leaps, duck-walks and near-violent guitar work." "I come from the school where you just stand there and sing," Dunn told *USA Today*. "I was real shocked when I first saw Kix jumping all over the place and running to the end of the stage."

Their contrasting styles seem to be the secret of the duo's success. "I really don't know why we work so well together," Dunn was quoted in imusic.com. "It must be because we are such opposites, in image and stuff like that and even in our approach to music. ... I think the freedom we give each other has a lot to do with it. We each kind of do our own thing then bring it all together."

In a biography from Arista, Dunn explained, "Kix and I really give each other room to stretch. The two of us are just very different musically, in terms of what we like to hear and write. We accept that. We basically meet in the middle. There's never been a rift, and it keeps things fresh." Brooks told imusic.com, "I'm not much good at analyzing it. We just do what we do and thank God that a lot of folks are into it. I think the public just sees us for what we are: a couple of buddies making music together that obviously has a fun factor to it. We really have fun at what we're doing ... ." But, he explained further in the Arista biography, "I think it's the fear factor that really keeps us going. Our career will have to go on for a lot longer for Ronnie and I to get comfortable with our success or merely take it for granted. We've been scared to death since the day we got together. We know this whole big fun thing that we do all revolves around that next hit. That's a wolf that never stops barking at you."

Brooks summarized on imusic.com: "It goes through your mind sometimes how long all this is going to last.... That tremendous rush we feel when we hit the stage, or when we lay down final vocal tracks in the studio, is still there. It's something I can't imagine losing.... And we hope to keep doing it for a long, long time."

Selected discography

Brand New Man (includes "Boot Scootin' Boogie"), Arista, 1991.
Hard Workin' Man, Arista, 1993.
Waitin' on Sundown, Arista, 1994.
Borderline (includes "My Maria"), Arista, 1996.
The Greatest Hits Collection, Arista, 1997.
If You See Her (includes "Husbands and Wives"), Arista, 1998.

Sources

Books

McCloud, Barry, and contributors, *Definitive Country: The Ultimate Encyclopedia of Country Music and Its Performers,* Perigee, 1995.

Periodicals

Billboard, June 27, 1998, p. 36.
Country Weekly, January 5, 1999, p. 14.
Entertainment Weekly, October 21, 1994.
People, March 29, 1993, p. 51.
Rolling Stone, May 13, 1993, p. 107.
USA Today, March 10, 1993, p. 1D.

Online

Artist showcase, Brooks & Dunn, imusic.com.

Other

Additional information was provided by Arista/Nashville publicity materials, 1998.

—Shari Garrett

Foxy Brown

Hip hop singer

Hip hop/rap artist Foxy Brown's distinctive style combines the street sounds and lyrics of rap with rhythm-and-blues tinged hip-hop, along with a persona borrowed from actress Pam Grier's portrayal of the strong, black, tomboyish film character Foxy Brown in in the film of the same name. Her career reached fruition at the young age of 17 when she made her first musical appearance on LL Cool J's remix of "Who Shot Ya" on *Mr. Smith.* Subsequent appearances included being featured on Jay-Z's hit "Ain't No Nigga," Silk's remix of "Hooked On You, Total's remix of "No One Else," Case's "Touch Me Tease Me," and several songs on Nas's releases. Brown released her platinum debut album, *Ill Na Na,* in 1996 at the age of 18 to critical acclaim within the rap and hip-hop community, and released *Chyna Doll* in 1999. The *Village Voice*'s Evelyn McDonnell wrote, "The actress discovered at the soda fountain is now the 19-year old daughter of a single mother schoolteacher in Park Slope (Brooklyn). Ladies and Gentlemen, Foxy Brown."

Part Filipino, Foxy Brown was born Inga Fung Marchand on September 6, 1979 and was raised in the Prospect Park section of Brooklyn by a single mother who worked as a teacher. She demonstrated talent, initiative, and ambition at an early age. During the winter of 1994, at the age of 15, she was picked from a Brooklyn talent show audience to freestyle rap on stage. Soon after, she was featured rhyming over the track of "I Shot Ya" on LL Cool J's album *Mr. Smith,* and collaborated with the TrackMasters production team, which included Tone and Poke. She also contributed musically to the single "I'll Be," which also featured Jay Z, on the *Mr. Smith* release. In 1997, she was included in the blues *Smokin' Grooves* tour along with Cypress Hill, Erykah Badu, George Clinton, The Roots, Brand New Heavies, Pharcyde, and Outkast in House. Brown eventually pulled out of the tour after missing several dates, but soon collaborated with Mia X, Master P, and Dru Hill on "Big Bad Mamma" from The Party Don't Stop. She also contributed a guest appearance to Puff Daddy's release *No Way Out* on the singles "Fried" and "Release Some Tension".

Brown was included in a group of rap and hip-hop musicians called The Firm, which included Nas Escobar, AZ, and Nature (Nature replaced Cormega). The group released a CD titled *Nas Escobar, Foxy Brown, AZ, and Nature Present The Firm; The Album* on Uni/Interscope in November of 1997. The release entered the *Billboard* Hot 200 Albums at number one in November, and featured guest appearances by Dr. Dre, Pretty Boy (Gavin, Foxy Brown's brother), Miss Jones, Half-A-Mil, Noriega, and Canibus. Brown was featured a month later in the rap magazine *The Source.* She also appeared

For the Record . . .

Born Inga Fung Marchand on September 6, 1979; raised in the Prospect Park section of Brooklyn in; mother worked as a teacher; brother Gavin a musician named "Pretty Boy."

picked from a Brooklyn Talent show audience to freestyle rap on stage at the age of 15, 1994; featured rhyming over the track of "I Shot Ya" on LL Cool's album *Mr. Smit;* collaborated with the TrackMasters production team, which included Tone and Poke; contributed musically to the single I'll Be" which also featured Jay Z, on the *Mr. Smith* release; collaborated with Mia X, Master P, and Dru Hill on "Big Bad Mamma" from *The Party Don't Stop;* contributed a guest appearance to Puff Daddy's release *No Way Out* on the singles "Fried" and "Release Some Tension;" part of a group of rap and hip-hop musicians called The Firm, which included Nas Escobar, AZ, and Nature (Nature replaced Cormega); The Firm released a CD titled *Nas Escobar, Foxy Brown, AZ, and Nature Present The Firm; The Album,* Uni/Interscope, November of 1997; appeared on the *Def Jam's Greatest Hits,* 1997, on the singles "Touch Me, Tease Me," "Get Me Home," and "The Promise;" released debut CD *I'll Na Na,* Def Jam Records 1996 and ; released *Chyna Doll,* Def Jam Records, 1999.

Awards: Platinum status for *I'll Na Na,* 1996.

Addresses: *Record company*—Def Jam Records, 652 Broadway, New York, NY 10012 (212) 229-5200.

---

on the *Def Jam's Greatest Hits* release in 1997, on the singles "Touch Me, Tease Me, Get Me Home," and "The Promise". The soundtrack to the Warner Brothers release *Jackie Brown* in 1997 also featured a guest appearance by Brown.

Brown's debut release, *Ill Na Na,* went platinum soon after its release in 1997. McDonnell wrote, "Scandal can be a starlet's best friend. Flashing flesh helped the so-so *Na Na* grab press and go platinum.... In her eyes, Brown wasn't doing anything Mae West and Madonna hadn't done before. Grier jiggled *and* kicked butt; Foxy wanted to do the same." Brown's idols Roxanne Shante and Salt-n-Pepa had also combined sex appeal with rap music, but Brown's debut at the age of 17 happened to

coincide with a trend in hip-hop and rap toward a tomboyish female approach." McDonnell continued, "Wrapped in furs, constantly deferring to male patrons, and luxury-obsessed, she wasn't doing much for any of your favorite socialist feminist animal rights-activist causes." Brown, young and unapologetically exuberant, used both the criticism and sex appeal to her advantage, propelling her album forward in the process. She also railed against the sexual double standards for men and women in her music, pointing out that men are lauded for being promiscuous and flashy. Part of Brown's appeal is to be true to her own instincts. McDonnell further wrote, "Brown reminds me of Tupac (Shakur). She has the same Hamlet-like combo of Thanatos and Eros, recklessness and introspection."

Brown released her sophomore CD, *Chyna Doll,* at the age of 20 in 1999. She wrote the lyrics for all of the tracks and produced three of them herself. On the autobiographical single "My Life," Brown said she never wanted to be born, she wished her father had used a prophylactic, and she wished she hadn't sought her father's love by dating "thugs." She wrote, "My life, do you feel what I feel" My life, a black girl's ordeal". Brown sings about her personal experience and flatly sing-speaks the chorus. McDonnell described "My Life" as "black-and-white 8mm compared to the melismatic octave-cartwheeling Technicolor we've come to expect." Brown knows how to tell a compelling story through music, and is equally adept at creating a compelling public persona. *Chyna Doll's* "My Life" also addresses a broken friendship with rap artist Li'L Kim, a friendship that Brown concedes in the song was lost due to overblown pride. The two women were close friends before they became famous, and even charted their early course to fame together.

Brown has collaborated with or performed alongside a wide array of rap and hip-hop musicians over the course of only a few years, and her career began to flourish in earnest after her debut release. Brown's combination of artful and gripping storytelling, spotlight-grabbing glamour, natural beauty, gritty realism, and urban sound buttressed her early success, and her discernible vulnerability and youthful boasting further endeared her to fans. Pam Grier met Foxy Brown in 1998 and the two women became friends. The mythical heroine of the silver screen after whom Brown named herself turned out to be the ideal moniker for Brown, as Brown is just as headstrong, courageous, and larger-than-life as the original Foxy Brown. Although Brown shuns the tough, tomboy style of many other female hip-hop and rap artists, her inner strength and choice of stage names reveal the ultimate tomboy: an independent woman with talent, who alone decides what she will or won't exploit.

Selected discography

Nas Escobar, Foxy Brown, AZ, and Nature Present The Firm;
    The Album, Uni/Interscope, 1997.
Ill Na Na, Def Jam, 1996.
Chyna Doll, Def Jam, 1999.

Sources

Periodicals

The Source, December 1997.
Vibe, May 1996.
The Village Voice, February 9, 1999.

Online

http://www.geocities.com/Sunsetstrip/3937/foxy.html
http://www.t2.technion.ac.1L/wc1272122/foxy.html
http://www.Vibe.com/archive/may96/docs/foxy.html

—B. Kimberly Taylor

Deana Carter

Country singer, songwriter

AP/Wide World Photo. Reproduced by permission.

Minneapolis Star-Tribune reporter Bruce Fuller asks, "What music coming out of Nashville these days seems suitable for early mornings with a cup of expectations, for twilight on a doubtful summer evening, for that midnight hour between disappointment and dreams?" The answer? The real, honest, bare-footed performer, Deana Carter. From her bittersweet, "Strawberry Wine" to her ironic "Did I Shave My Legs For This?" Carter burst onto the country music scene in 1996, just as her Dad nicknamed her, with a "Little Bit of Sunshine."

Deana Kay Carter was born on January 4, 1966 in Goodlettsville, Tennessee. Named after famous crooner, Dean Martin, Carter and her two brothers, Ronnie and Jeff were raised by their practical mother Anna, a homemaker, and their musician father, Fred Carter, Jr. Carter told *People* magazine that "there was always music in our house. At family gatherings, you either found a harmony part or washed dishes. I chose the harmony part." Carter also recalled working for Nugget, her Dad's record label: "I lived in that place, packing 45s and labeling them in the back room with my brothers and my mom. It's just something I love." As Carter saw her father become a studio musician legend—playing guitar on, according to Carter's website, "over 90% of all recording sessions in Nashville" throughout the 1960s and 1970s, including Roy Orbison, Simon & Garfunkel, and Elvis Presley—she too longed for a career in music. At age 17, Carter tried to land a record deal, but failed. Carter told *Country Standard Time* reporter Robert Loy that, "it didn't work out because I wasn't ready. Plain and simple at 17 you've just haven't lived enough."

Carter began "living enough" by attending the University of Tennessee where she earned a degree in Rehabilitation Therapy. After working a year and half with stroke and head injury patients, however, she quit. As she told Loy, "It just broke my heart everyday. I had a couple patients that died." Carter told *People*, "I don't take death well." Thus, she fell back into music by playing in Nashville clubs, but supported herself and paid back her student loans through waitressing and other odd jobs.

In 1991, Carter landed her first record deal with Capitol; however, her first album was only released in Europe. Soon after, as she remembered in *People*, "I was dropped, picked up and dropped again [by Capitol].... I just wrote more songs." As Loy wrote, Carter "made a difficult task [songwriting] even harder by refusing to settle for writing anything less than the perfect, definitive song." Carter further told Loy, "I wanted to write a song that was credible enough to have depth and meaning . I ended up sabotaging myself cuz I was trying to write deep, murky, dark stuff, trying to be creative—which means I was just faking it. And it doesn't resonate if it's not real."

By the middle 1990s, Carter's career and personal life took an up turn. In 1994, Carter finally received her big break. After hearing her demo tape, Willie Nelson invited her to sing at Farm Aid—the only solo woman to perform that year. In 1995, Carter wed musician and video art director, Chris DiCroce. That year she also resigned with Capitol records, even though she was 45 minutes late to her audition with Capitol's president Jimmy Bowen. Bowen seemed not to notice Carter's tardiness because, "he was screaming and cussing on the phone with Tanya Tucker's dad." Carter, with just a guitar, played Bowen a song—in between his refusing to take phone calls—and Carter recalled, "he liked it, but needed time." Carter knew that Bowen had worked with her father, and as she told *Country Spotlight's* Elianne Halbersberg, "at least his credibility was impeccable," so she brazenly told Bowen, "You need to decide today because I'm not taking a phone call." Bowen said, "I guess we got a deal."

In 1996, Capitol released Carter's debut album, *Did I Shave My Legs For This?* Carter's imprint on the album went beyond her singing. She co-wrote six of the album's songs, and was the inspiration behind its unusual 3D-hologram cover art. As she told *Atlanta Journal* reporter Miriam Longino, "country music honestly has the most boring album covers I thought, 'Let's broaden our horizons a little bit. Let's try a new idea.'" However, there was some indecision on what should be the first single. Capitol had planned to release "I've Loved Enough to Know," but Carter, playing showcase concerts for radio stations, received a stronger reaction from radio programmers with another song, "Strawberry Wine." Programmers told Carter, as she recalled to *LosAngeles Times* reporter Michael McCall, "Why are you trying to introduce yourself slowly to radio? Why not come out with that killer song?" But Carter felt that her killer song would not get support from Capitol. "They're never going to go for it," she told McCall. "The fears were: It's a waltz, the subject matter of the song, and, as a first single, it being a slow song For a new artist and the first single, it was swan diving." Capitol eventually did go for it and "Strawberry Wine" was released. Reviewing a concert in support of *Did I Shave My Legs For This? Los Angeles Times* reporter Robert Hilburn wrote that Carter "injects a song with the seemingly natural intimacy that is sometimes hard to spot in the entertainment-conscious razzle-dazzle of the pop and country worlds." Thus, "Strawberry Wine," became Carter's breakthrough hit. In 1997, Carter and "Strawberry Wine" received the Country Music Association's (CMA) award for Song and Single of the Year.

Carter's next single was the album's title tune, a song that Halbersberg described as "the result of a gripe session over her philandering, freeloading ex-boyfriend, whom she supported for almost two years by working three jobs." Thus, "Did I Shave My Legs For This?"—a funny rant about a man's total ignorance of his wife's attempt to grab his attention—showed Carter's ability to not only sing bittersweet melancholy, but also playful irony. However, Carter told McCall that, "Music is a very serious business with me. It's something I hold up high and respect. If I'm writing a funny song or a parody, it still has to hold weight and have credibility. You can have fun with what you're doing, but don't let the music suffer."

Carter's success continued in 1998 with the release of her second album, *Everything's Gonna Be Alright*. The title song, written in 1971 by Carter's father for his sister who had been diagnosed with breast cancer, is "a message that I think can make a difference in people's lives. It offers a bright ray of hope." Carter has remained, as country.com's Shannon Wayne Turner stated, "adamant about maintaining personal and professional integrity, choosing to make music that reflects her own life and, she hopes, those of her listeners as well."

Everything's Gonna Be Alright spotlighted Carter's growth, both musically and lyrically. She told *Country Weekly Online* that "by digging a little deeper, more of my different tastes have surfaced [and] there's not one song that's alike or similar to anything else on the radio it's shedding more skin—skin I didn't know I could shed." From the title track, the Southern rock band Lynyrd Skynrd influenced, "The Train Song" to the cover of 1960s singer Melanie's "Brand New Key", *Everything's Gonna Be Alright* again hit all the right notes with country music radio programmers and fans. Carter believes that her audience once again connected to the honesty and integrity of her music: "I never try to do music to please somebody else," she told Turner. "I just don't. I do it for the honesty and the way it comes out of me. I follow my heart, and that's just the way I live my life."

Selected discography

Did I Shave My Legs For This? (includes "Strawberry Wine"), Capitol, 1996.
(Contributor) *Anastasia* (soundtrack), Atlantic Records, 1997.
Everything's Gonna Be Alright (includes "Absence of the Heart"), Capitol, 1998.
(Contributor) *Hope Floats* (soundtrack), Capitol, 1998.
(Contributor) *Touched By An Angel* (soundtrack), Sony Music, 1998.

Sources

Periodicals

Atlanta Journal-Constitution, September 21, 1997.
Country Spotlight, January 1, 1997.
Country Standard Time, November 1996.
Los Angeles Times, February 2, 1997; March 15, 1997.
Minneapolis Star-Tribune, February 9, 1997.
People, February 24, 1997.

Online

www.deana.com
www.country.com
www.countryweekly.com

—Ann M. Schwalboski

Mary Chapin-Carpenter

Singer, songwriter

Mary Chapin Carpenter was formally accepted by the Nashville music industry after stealing the show at the nationally televised 1990 Country Music Awards. Performing her song, "(You Don't Know Me) I'm the Opening Act," she won the praise of many of country music's brightest stars, some of whom inspired Carpenter to write the song. The song itself pokes fun at the big egos of the industry was a risky move because it was a critical commentary of Nashville from someone on the outside—a nobody. She told Leslie Aun of the *Washington Business Journal,* "I was sitting next to Tammy Wynette, and she held my hand and told me this wonderful story about how years prior, when she was just starting out, how some guy treated her like dirt...That's when it really hit me. You could be a nobody like me or be Tammy Wynette, and you could relate to that song. That's why it went over." As a Nashville recording artist by label only, Carpenter has gone on to record numerous hits, win several Grammy awards, and generate high record sales. However, she would always walk the thin line between artistic expression and commercial appeal.

Carpenter's origins are far east of Nashville. Born in Princeton, New Jersey, February 21, 1958, she learned to play the guitar while living in Japan with her father who worked for the Asian Edition of *Life* magazine. The family moved to Washington, D. C. in 1974.

Although she graduated from Brown University with a degree in American Civilization, her father encouraged her to take to the stage at an open mike session at a local bar. She made forty dollars the first night she was hired and excitedly began to consider making her hobby a career.

Carpenter's lyrics often speak of life experiences, winning and losing, and staying true to her ideals. Her ability to connect with personal themes made her popular with both men and women. In 1987, Carpenter released her folksy debut album, *Hometown Girl* for CBS. The album contained long ballads that revealed her talents as a gifted songwriter, but received mostly college radio airplay. Her second album, *State of the Heart,* was released in 1989 and was well received by critics. The album also made her a commercial success. The album went gold, and two songs, "Never Had It so Good" and "Quittin' Time," made *Billboard*'s top ten list. The album also earned major awards for the Top New Female Vocalists by the Academy of Country Music and a Grammy award nomination for Best Country Vocal Performance/Female.

In 1990, Carpenter hit platinum with her album *Shooting Straight In The Dark.* The song "Down at the Twist and Shout" reached number one and won her a Grammy award for Best Country Vocal Performance/Female. However, it was the song "Middle Ground" that captured a theme and made her a darling of the 30-something single group. The song was really about a conversation she had with her sister on searching for a middle ground—and avoiding the extreme highs and lows of life with work, relationships, and friends. Carpenter told Susan Korones Gifford of *Cosmopolitan,* "If you're not married and you don't have kids, it's like you're swimming, but you're not sure if you're gonna drown the next minute. So the song's really about a lot of people in our generation." Carpenter would go on to win four Grammy awards from 1991-94, the most by any artist.

Come On Come On, her 1992 release, moved Carpenter into the stratosphere of the country music scene. The album went triple platinum, received three Grammy awards, had seven hit singles, and spent two years at the top of the *Billboard*'s charts. Her 1994 release, *Stones In The Road,* debuted in the number one position on *Billboard*'s Top Country Albums and remained there for five weeks. The songs contained deeply personal and serious themes that reveal moments of love and loneliness. She told Dana Kennedy of *Entertainment Weekly,* "I feel like I came real late to the party ... (*Stones In The Road*) is about the sorrow I feel that we've forgotten our commitment to more than just material possessions. And it's about me trying to figure out what I've missed."

The tour to support the album was documented in Carpenters book *The Road Tour Book 1995,* which includes essays by Carpenter, augmented by photographs from *Time* magazine's photojournalist William Campbell. All proceeds from the book sales were donated to the CARE Foundation, which is committed to improving the global community. The tour was also documented in the PBS series *In the Spotlight*.

A Place in The World, Carpenter's 1996 release, was a search for self. She told K. T. Oslin of *Entertainment Weekly,* "Place is connected to identity, and identity is connected to self and worth, and together these songs make artistic spiritual sense. I'm always trying to figure out where I fit." One song, "Let Me Into Your Heart," was written for the sound track to the Kevin Costner movie, *Tin Cup.* Carpenter also wrote music for such films as *Fly Away Home* and *Dead Man Walking.* The album achieved gold status and earned her another Grammy nomination for the single "Let Me Into Your Heart."

Carpenter used her commercial success to draw attention to many national issues. The SonyNashville.com web site quotes Carpenter; "I think writing, if you really work at it, has the ability to show you things you might not see otherwise, in yourself and the world around you. I just let my mind run free and see where it goes." Carpenter also wrote an essay for the book *A Voice Of Our Own: Leading Women Celebrate the 75th Anniversary of Women's Suffrage.* She has penned two bedtime stories for children, *Dreamland: A Lullaby* and *Halley Came To Jackson.* Proceeds from her book *Dreamland* were donated to the Voiceless Victims Project of the Institute for Inter cultural Understanding. Carpenter performed at the UNICEF's fiftieth anniversary concert in 1997. She accompanied Defense Secretary William S. Cohen to Bosnia to perform a Christmas Eve concert for the soldiers stationed there.

Selected discography

Hometown Girl, CBS, 1988.
State of the Heart, (includes "Quittin' Time" and "You Never Had It So Good"), CBS, 1989.
Shooting Straight in the Dark , (includes "Down at the Twist and Shout"). CBS, 1991.
Come On Come On, Columbia, 1992.
Stones in the Road, Columbia, 1994.
A Place in The World, Columbia, 1996.

Sources

Periodicals

Billboard, November 19, 1994; September 21, 1996.
Booklist, November 1, 1996.
Cosmopolitan, April 1991.
Entertainment Weekly, July 17, 1992; November 11, 1994; September 27, 1996.
People, November 6, 1995.
Publishers Weekly, August 12, 1996; August 10, 1998.
Time, November 11, 1996.
Washington Business Journal, March 11, 1991.

Online

"Mary Chapin Carpenter," January 8, 1999, http://www.servtech.com
"Mary Chapin Carpenter," Country Weekly Online, January 8, 1999, http://www.countryweekly.com

"Mary Chapin Carpenter," January 8, 1999, http://www.sonynashville.com

—*Tige Cosmos*

Dick Clark

Rock music promoter, producer

Dick Clark doesn't play a musical instrument, has written a few bad songs, and made one record that sunk without a trace, but he has been a prevailing force in the music and television industry for more than 40 years. Branded America's oldest teenager, this industrious television host and radio announcer turned high-powered executive achieved fame and fortune with his youthful looks and productions aimed at adolescents. Clark has been credited with introducing some of rock and roll's brightest stars and he is considered one of rock's most influential promoters. In addition to 33 years of hosting *American Bandstand,* one of America's longest-running television entertainment shows, Clark has hosted and produced thousands of hours of television and radio programming ranging from game shows to awards shows to television films. He has also built an entertainment empire that includes, Dick Clark Productions, a leading independent producer of television programming, and Unistar Communications Group, which distributes his radio shows.

Richard Wagstaff Clark was born on November 30, 1929 in Mount Vernon, New York, to Richard Augustus and Julia Clark. Growing up in Bronxville, New York, Clark spent his childhood listening to the radio and was likely influenced a great deal by his father's work as a radio station manager at WRUN in nearby Utica. Clark recalls a deep admiration for radio voices and characters such as Arthur Godfrey, Steve Allen, and Dave Garroway. When his brother, Bradley, was killed in World War II, Clark used such radio programs as *Make Believe Ballroom* and *Battle of the Baritones* as an antidote for his depression. He soon joined the school dramatics club and served as his high school class president.

The summer before Clark entered Syracuse University as an advertising major and radio minor, his father hired him to work in the mailroom at WRUN. He was only 17 when, in between e as a disc jockey at WAER-FM, Syracuse University's student-run radio station.

Rock 'n Roll History

Clark is proud of his success in radio. He has only had four jobs in an industry renowned for high turnover. Shortly before graduating from college, he gained experience working as a country-western and popular music announcer at WOLF in Syracuse. When he graduated in 1951, Clark returned to Utica where he got a job as a television news anchorman at WKTV. Clark saw more opportunity at a larger station, so he moved to Philadelphia in 1952 and became an announcer for WFIL radio, where he began to host the local radio show *Bandstand.*

For the Record . . .

Born Richard Wagstaff Clark, November 30, 1929, (in Mount Vernon, NY); son of Richard Agustus (a salesman and radio-station manager) and Julia Clark; married Barbara Mallery, 1952 (divorced, 1961); married Loretta Martin (a secretary), 1962 (divorced, 1971); married Kari Wigton, 1977; children: (first marriage) Richard Agustus, II; (second marriage) Duane, Cindy. *Education*: Graduated from Syracuse University in 1951, majored in advertising.

Worked in the mailroom of radio station WRUN, Utica, NY, 1945; disc jockey at WAER, and news announcer and disc jockey at WOLF, both in Syracuse, NY, 1946-51; worked as news announcer, music-show host, and various other positions at WKTV, Utica, NY, 1951; music-show host, WFIL Radio, Philadelphia, 1952-56; host of *Bandstand* on WFIL-TV, Philadelphia, 1956; host of ABC's *American Bandstand*, 1956-1989; host of various game shows and television programs, including *$25,000 Pyramid* and *TV's Bloopers & Practical Jokes*; formed Dick Clark Productions, 1956; co-founder and principal owner, United States Radio Network; founder of SRO Artists, Sea Lark, January Music, Swan Records, and Dick Clark's Caravan of Stars; producer of television series, television specials, various annual award programs, television movies, and syndicated radio programs.

Awards: Daytime Emmy Awards for *$25,000 Pyramid*, 1978, 1984, 1985; Emmy for Best Children's Entertainment Special for co-producing *The Woman Who Willed a Miracle*, 1982; Emmy for Special Achievement of Outstanding Program Achievement for executive producing *American Bandstand*, 1982; inducted into the Academy of Television Arts and Sciences Hall of Fame, 1993.

Addresses: *Home*—Malibu, CA; *Office*—Dick Clark Productions, 3003 W. Olive Ave., Burbank, CA 91505.

WFIL TV had an afternoon dance show similar to the rock and roll dance shows on local stations across America. It was called *American Bandstand*. In 1956, when the show's host was arrested for driving under the influence—an image not well associated with a wholesome show for impressionable teens—the station approached the then twenty-something Clark as a replacement.

Clark had hosted the show for nearly a year before he convinced the American Broadcasting Corporation (ABC) television network to put *American Bandstand* on television screens around the country. ABC purchased the show, and it premiered nationally on August 5, 1957 when Clark introduced Billy Williams, who sang "I'm Gonna Sit Right Down and Write Myself a Letter." The 90-minute show featuring dancing teenagers and musical guests was televised live on weekday afternoons and, briefly that year, on prime time. Dance crazes such as the twist, the watusi, and the stroll were started on the show. *American Bandstand* appeared as a weekly one-hour taped show that ran on Saturday mornings from 1963-87.

Clark grew older in those 33 years, but his youthful appearance and cult status made him an accessible figure to the two generations that grew up with the show. The longest-running musical show in television history, *American Bandstand* featured nearly every pop musician imaginable with the exception of the Beatles, the Rolling Stones, and Elvis Presley. In 1987, when ABC asked him to cut the show back to half an hour, Clark pulled out of the network and put the show into syndication. By 1989, Clark had replaced himself with a new host, 26-year-old David Hirsch, and went behind the scenes to work as executive producer. However, *American Bandstand* had finally exhausted itself as a weekly syndicated production and soon disappeared from television.

With Fame Came Wealth

American Bandstand may have faded from American television sets, but its legacy left Dick Clark an American icon, as well as a very rich man. Clark resourcefully used the show as the bedrock of his entertainment empire. He became a very wealthy man as a result of his shrewd involvement in other business ventures. As a producer and founder of Dick Clark Productions, he provided 170 television programming hours a week by 1985. His company produced made-for-TV movies, game shows, award shows, beauty pageants, and "reality" programs. Clark created *The American Music Awards* in 1974 and has produced the show ever since. His company has also produced such notables as *The Academy of Country Music Awards*, *The Soap Awards*, *The Daytime Emmy Awards*, *The Golden Globe Awards*, and, in 1996, "The 48th Annual Emmy Awards." His made-for-TV-movie credits include *The Man in the Santa Clause Suit"*(1978,; *The Birth of the Beatles* (1979), *Elvis* (1979), and *The Woman Who Willed a Miracle* (1984), which won Clark an Emmy as co-producer. He also tried his hand, somewhat unsuccessfully, at full-length, full-screen motion pictures with a 1985 release of the $4 million, four-year production of *Remo Williams: The Adventure Begins.*

Besides *American Bandstand,* Clark is probably best known as the man who counts down the seconds to the New Year every New Year's Eve in New York's Times Square. Dick Clark Productions has provided ABC with the *New Year's Rockin' Eve* television spectacular every year since 1972. Clark, however, hasn't always found success in television production. Some of his game show ideas have proven less than extraordinary. These include *The Object Is* (ABC, 1963), *Missing Links* (ABC, 1964), *The Krypton Factor* (ABC, 1981), and *Scattergories* (NBC, 1989).

Clark went through a difficult time professionally when he was brought before the House Committee on Legislative Oversight in 1960. The Committee was investigating "payola" in the record and radio industry. (This was the practice of those in the business accepting bribes and favors to promote records.) Clark was eventually cleared of all suspicions, but he was forced to divest himself of some of his business ventures since his holdings in the music business were considered a conflict of interest.

His Face was Everywhere

Clark spent a lot of time and money behind the scenes, but his youthful persona didn't disappear from television screens altogether. While he was hosting *Bandstand,* Clark continued to emcee a number of awards telecasts and host television game shows and half-hour variety shows, including *$25,000 Pyramid,* for which he won three Emmy Awards in 1978, 1984 and 1985; and *TV's Bloopers and Practical Jokes.* At the time, he was the only person to have shows on all three American television networks with NBC's *Bloopers,* ABC's *Bandstand,* and CBS's *$25,000 Pyramid.* Clark has also appeared onscreen playing himself in film and television cameos, as well as original performances in two episodes of the 1964 series *Burke's Law* and, around the same time, an episode of *Perry Mason.* He made his silver screen debut in 1960's *Because They're Young* in which he played a teacher. In 1961 he played a doctor in *The Young Doctors,* a popular soap opera.

Though Clark moved into television broadcasting with *Bandstand,* he didn't abandon music and radio. He hosted *Countdown America,* a Top 40 radio show, as well as *Dick Clark's Rock, Roll & Remembers.* Both were syndicated as weekly shows to more than 1,800 radio stations around the U.S. by Unistar Communications. In 1993, Unistar's merger with Infinity Broadcasting gave the company upward of 3,000 affiliates. His company has also entered the home video and compact disc market with the release of *Dick Clark's Best of Bandstand* videocassettes and *Dick Clark's All-Time Hits* line of CDs. Clark seems to possess an unending supply of energy, not to mention an unrelenting motivation for the success of his enterprise. His influence on the American entertainment industry will doubtlessly continue into the 21st Century as will his status as an icon of American pop culture history.

Sources

Business Wire, February 12, 1999.
Chicago Tribune, May 25, 1989.
PR Newswire, January 20, 1999.
Record, September 29, 1985.
Rocky Mountain News, January 6, 1998.
Washington Times, January 12, 1999.

—*Kelly M. Cross*

Randy Crawford

Singer

What was predicted for Randy Crawford in 1977 has come true more than two decades later. "If consistency is an indication of professionalism," Gary Vercelly wrote in a *Downbeat* portrait of the then-24-year-old singer, "Randy Crawford's stable performance record proves that she is well on her way toward establishing herself, not only as a singer of great sensitivity, but also as a mature woman of sincere, honest expression". Since then Randy Crawford has released over 15 albums and had several international multi-platinum hits. And if she still goes relatively unrecognized in her native land, she has become one of the world's most successful popular singers of the late 1990s. Since her hit interpretation of Bernard Igner's *Everything Must Change*, the secret of Crawford's popularity has changed little. "Regardless of the mode she chooses," Vercelly wrote, "the bottom line of Randy's appeal clearly lies in her ability to bring any tune to life, giving lyrics new meaning and melodies fresh dimensions. Randy has the necessary tools to carry off a sustained cry, creating a religious aura. Even at her most soulful moments, however, her flexible delivery never sounds forced. Her

Photograph by Daniel Ray. Courtesy of Atlantic Records.

For the Record . . .

Born Veronica Crawford, February 18, 1952 in Macon, GA.

Performed on the American and European club circuit at age 15; released first single "If You Say the Word" at age 20; shared stages with jazz musicians Cannonball Adderly, George Benson, and Quincy Jones, 1973-75; signed with Warner Bros., released first album *Everything Must Change*, 1976; first international hit "Street Life" with Crusaders, 1978; released sophmore album *Miss Randy Crawford*, 1978; world tour with Crusaders, 1979; early 1980s albums included *Secret Combination* and *Nightline*; duet "Taxi Dancing" with Rick Springfield, 1984 from the soundtrack *Hard to Hold*; "Almaz" on *Abstract Emotions* became international hit in 1986; released *Rich and Poor*, 1989, includes cover of Bob Dylan's "Knockin' On Heaven's Door"; duet with Italian star Zuccero at the Kremlin, performed at the Vatican Christmas 1991; released *Through The Eyes Of Love* and *Don't Say It's Over*, Warner Bros., 1992-93; dined with South African President Nelson Mandela in 1993; *Naked and True* produced and released in Europe; "Give Me The Night" number one hit in United States in 1995; Warner Bros. released Best Of Randy Crawford, 1996; "Street Life" was used on the soundtrack to the 1997 movie Jackie Brown directed by Quentin Tarentino; released Every Kind of Mood—Randy, Randi, Randee, Wea/Atlantic, 1998; released Love Songs, WEA, 1998.

Addresses: *Record company*—Atlantic Recording Corporation, 1290 Avenue of the Americas, New York, NY 10104.

approach to any music, soul, country, or jazz, is one without dilution."

The art of interpreting songs, as the great popular singers of old did, seems to be going out of fashion more and more. It is Crawford's strength. She is willing to interpret any style of song—jazz, soul, rhythm & blues, pop melodies, smooth ballads or funk—as long as she feels connected to the music and lyrics at a certain time. The pieces she selects are transformed by her pure, warm tone and her emotional vibrato, together with their light and breezy jazz and funk arrangements. "Before you know it, regardless of whatever category the tune was at its inception, it is a Randy Crawford song," wrote

Sonia Murray in *Atlanta Journal and Constitution*, describing the "refashioning" that happens when Crawford interprets a song.

Crawford has toured extensively throughout the world, performed at Europe's best known jazz fests and shared stage with renowned jazz artists like Ray Charles, Al Jarreau, and Joe Sample. Some of her most memorable live performances took place in unusual places such as the Vatican and the Kremlin, at a United Nations benefit concert in Croatia, or a benefit show for Nelson Mandela in South Africa. Despite this apparent globe-trotting, though, she isn't a flashy performer. On stage, she rarely speaks and she moves about very little. Her showmanship seems completely internalized, something displayed in every note she sings. Randy Crawford is not a performer to be seen, she is a singer who has to be heard.

"Street Life"

Crawford grew up with five brothers and sisters in Cincinnati, Ohio. Her parents loved singing themselves and encouraged all their children to sing at home and in the church choir. Asked about early influences, Crawford told Vercelly, "Aretha Franklin was the only person who really touched me deeply as a child." She especially liked Franklin's early recordings made for the Columbia label before she became a star with Atlantic. By the time she was 15, Crawford was singing in night clubs in the United States and Europe with her father acting as her chaperon. Soon she learned to read music and play piano, performed in a group with bassist William "Bootsy" Collins, and later in a jazz band. When she was 20, she released her first single "If You Say the Word."

Within a few years the young singer had shared stages with famous jazz musicians such as Cannonball Adderley, George Benson, and Quincy Jones. According to Vercelly, the late Cannonball Adderley especially valued Crawford's "rare ability to wed strength and emotion in a natural, spontaneous manner" and in 1975, he selected her for the role of Carolina in the folk musical *Big Man: The Legend of John Henry*—Crawford's first exposure to a national audience. In the same year, Crawford took the stage in front of 5000 jazz enthusiasts at the World Jazz Association's (W.J.A.) annual fundraiser at the Shrine Auditorium in Los Angeles. Accompanied by an orchestra directed by Quincy Jones, Crawford interpreted—at Jones's request—Bernard Igner's "Everything Must Change," the lyrics of which she had seen for the first time only one day before the event. In 1976, Crawford's first album, *Everything Must Change*, was released by Warner Bros. It contained two live recordings from the W.J.A. concert, including the title track, as well as studio recordings in styles ranging from soul to country, by composers such as Lennon/McCartney, Paul Simon, and Keith Carradine, all newly arranged by Larry Carlton of the renowned jazz band Crusaders.

Crawford's second album, 1978's *Miss Randy Crawford,* was also primarily a collection of cover versions of recent hits, leading *Downbeat's* reviewer to comment "as if Randy Crawford was still back there interpreting and needing other people's songs," hoping Crawford's next album would be "her own totally." However, like many reviewers in the meantime, this attitude expressed a deep misunderstanding of Crawford's true gift—to give a second life to every song she takes on.

When the popular instrumental jazz group Crusaders were looking for a vocalist to perform with them for the first time, Bob Krasnow, vice-president of talent at Warner Bros., suggested Randy Crawford. "Street Life," the title track of the Crusader's MCA album, became Crawford's first international hit. In 1979, she toured the United States and Europe with the group; Crawford opened the show with own recordings and joined the Crusaders at the end of the group's show to sing "Street Life."

"One Day I'll Fly Away"

With her early 1980s albums *Secret Combination* and *Night-Line,* Crawford's music became funkier, livelier; however, smooth soul ballads still remained her hallmark, songs like "One Day I'll Fly Away" from 1980, and "Almaz," featured on her 1986 album *Abstract Emotions.* Crawford went on three world tours to promote her albums, playing a number of sold-out concerts. Her 1989 album *Rich and Poor* was one of the United States' most popular jazz albums for almost a year. Its first single, a cover of Bob Dylan's "Knockin' On Heaven's Door" became a hit and was used on the soundtrack of the movie *Lethal Weapon 2.*

Crawford started the 1990s with two noteworthy live performances. One was at the Kremlin in1990, with Italian superstar Zuccero whose duet with Crawford, "Diamante," became a hit single in Germany. The other was a Christmas concert for Pope John Paul II at the Vatican in 1991. Crawford's last albums for Warner Brothers were *Through The Eyes Of Love* and *Don't Say It's Over.*

After experiencing difficulties with America record companies who didn't know what to do with an artist who wasn't limited to either the jazz or R&B domain, Crawford got off to a new start in Europe. There the singer had instant success with the album *Naked and True,* released by WEA Germany. Produced by Germany-based Ralf Droesemeyer, the record saw Crawford return to her jazzy soul sound of the 1970s. The initial *Naked and True* tour took Crawford through Europe and South America. The "import," especially Crawford's haunting interpretation of J.J. Cale's song "Cajun Moon," soon won the hearts of jazz and adult contemporary station listeners in the United States. As a result the Atlantic label, Bluemoon, reissued and distributed the album in the United States. In addition to covers of the Patrice Rushen hit "Forget Me Nots" and the Prince classic "Purple Rain," it included a cover of George Benson's multi-format hit "Give Me the Night," which became number one on Smooth Jazz/National AC radio charts. The album remained in the top ten on R&R's NAC album charts for 20 consecutive weeks. 250,000 copies of *Naked and True* were sold in the United States and over half a million worldwide. Awash in newfound popularity, Crawford hit the road again and toured extensively all over the world.

In 1996, in the wake of Crawford's second wave of success, Warner Bros. released *Best Of Randy Crawford* with 14 of Crawford's greatest hits from 1976-95. Crawford's comeback won her new fans—not only those who grew up with black music classics of the sixties and seventies, but also younger people into acid jazz, retro funk and groove samplers.

Crawford's 1998 album *Every Kind of Mood—Randy, Randi, Randee* contained an updated remake of "Almaz", one of Crawford's biggest international hits, as well as covers of trip-hop pioneers Massive Attack's "Hymn of the Big Wheel" and Rose Royce's classic ballad "Wishing on a Star." The album was produced by Mousse T. who had worked on tracks by Prince, U2, Michael Jackson, and Jens Krause, who gave "Give Me The Night" its great sound. Mario Tarradell, reviewing the album for the *Dallas Morning News,* called Crawford a "song stylist" who "can sing anything with elegance, emotion and warmth." And that's all Crawford intends to do in the future. "I will always sing," she told her new record company Atlantic in 1998. "I don't want to do anything else." In the late 1990s, Crawford resided in Europe, enjoying the star-status that her native land refused her.

Selected discography

Singles

"Are You Sure," 1997.
"Give Me the Night," 1997.
"Silence," 1998.

Albums

Everything Must Change, Warner Bros., 1976, reissued, Musicrama, 1997.
Miss Randy Crawford, Warner Bros., 1978.
Now We May Begin, (includes "One Day I'll Fly Away"), 1980, reissued, Musicrama, 1997.
Secret Combination, Warner Bros., 1981, reissued Wea/Warner Bros., 1987.
Nightline, 1983, reissued, 1994, reissued, Musicrama, 1997.
Abstract Emotions, 1986, reissued, Wea, 1994, reissued, Musicrama, 1997.
*Rich And Poor, (*includes "Knockin' On Heaven's Door"), Wea/Warner Bros., 1989.
*Through The Eyes Of Love, Wea/*Warner Bros., 1992.
*Don't Say It's Over, Wea/*Warner Bros., 1993.
Very Best of Randy Crawford, Fly, 1993, reissued, 1999.
Naked And True, (includes "Give Me the Night") WEA/Atlantic, 1995.
*Best Of Randy Crawford, Wea/*Warner Bros., 1996.
Raw Silk, Musicrama, 1997.

Every Kind of Mood—Randy, Randi, Randee, Wea/Atlantic, 1998.
Love Songs, Wea, 1998.

Sources

Periodicals

Atlanta Journal and Constitution, January 29, 1998, p. E4.
Billboard, May 26, 1979, p. 39; October 28, 1995, p. 29.
Dallas Morning News, August 28, 1998, p.71; September 3, 1998, p. 37A.
Downbeat, March 24, 1977, p.30; October 11, 1978, p. 26.
Essence, August 1990, p. 48.

Online

http://home.earthlink.net/~thesonics/Crawford.html
http://imusic.com/showcase2/urban/music/randycrawford.html
http://www.amazon.com
http://www.atlantic-records.com
http://www.contemporaryjazz.com/reviews/crawford.html
http://www.jazzimprov.com/r_crwfr1.htm
http://www.netcetera.nl/crawford.html

—Evelyn Hauser

Damon and Naomi

Psychedelic rock duo

Damon and Naomi, described by *Ptolemaic Terras cope* as "an eerily incandescent pairing of melancholy souls who carved a niche for themselves," is the latest musical incarnation of Damon Krukowski and Naomi Yang. What began as the rhythm section of Galaxie 500 has evolved into this band, named for it's members and seeking musical self expression rather than fitting neatly into any one musical genre. Although their career is still young, Damon and Naomi have carved out a serious following among fans of dreamy ambient psychedelic folk, a genre which has few members but owes much of it's roots to these musicians.

Both Krukowski and Yang were born in New York City and grew up in musical homes. Damon's mother was a jazz singer whose taste leaned heavily on classical jazz artists such as Billie Holiday and Jimmy Rushing. Krukowski counts his mother's friends among the first to teach him to play the piano and guitar. He never practiced either instrument much until he "picked up the drums and finally found an instrument free from written music (he has since) returned to the guitar, but (thinks of himself) as playing the 'composers' guitar (using it primarily to accompany his voice)".

Yang, also found practicing tiresome as a child. Her father played "heavy Bach chorales" on the cello, and both parents listened only to classical music "but the did

have a Beatles record or two lurking in their collection which (she) found right away." When asked about her musical past she commented "maybe my musical taste can be traced to an early exposure to Bach and *The Beatles* [the White Album]".

Musical influences for the duo are wide ranging and always changing. Damon lists folk singers such as Bob Dylan, Robin Williamson [of The Incredible String Band], Tom Rapp [of Pearls Before Swine], Sandy Denny and Bridget St. John. Both of them express great admiration for Robert Wyatt, as a drummer and as a vocalist. "At any given time", Naomi explains, "Damon and I are listening to music that relates to what we are thinking about music and our instruments. I used to listen mostly to what the bass player was doing and it was the rhythm section that was important to me.... But these days, singing has become so important to us ... we are listening to vocal music much more carefully and focusing on the fact that the voice is really a powerful instrument."

Yang, Krukowski and Dean Wareham met in high school. While at Harvard, Wareham and Krukowski formed a punk cover band. After college the two decided to form a "real" band and recruited Yang as their guitarist after finding no suitable candidates from a *Village Voice* ad. The band was called Galaxie 500 after a sixties Ford muscle car model. Their debut album, *Today*, was described by *Melody Maker* as "an astonishing debut by anybody's standards." The album launched what would become a brief but legendary career, gaining acclaim for their unique music, unlike much of the "alternative" music of the late eighties. The liner notes to the reissue of *Today* describes Galaxie's music as having "incredible, supple beauty ... spun like straw ... so sweetly melancholic that it smothered you. Damon's drums drift with the simmering presence of jazz classicism, Naomi's bass is rich with dreamy emotional content, Dean's guitar completes the landscape painting begun by '60-era Sterling Morrison ... there is not one false note struck on *Today*". Galaxie 500, forged new roads in alternative "ambient rock". After cutting three albums the band suddenly parted ways in 1991 after Wareham called it quits. Wareham went on to form Luna, and Damon and Naomi continued to make music on their own.

Upon the initial breakup of Galaxie 500, Damon and Naomi were rejected by most members of the music industry because they had been viewed as just a rhythm section. The notable exception to that rule was Kramer, founder of Shimmy Disc. It was his insistence that they returned to making music with *More Sad Hits*.

Shortly after the release of *More Sad Hits,* they briefly joined Magic Hour with Wayne Rogers and Kate Biggar.

Musically very different from either Galaxie 500 or Damon and Naomi, the band played mostly long drawn out structured improvisations. Reception for the band was uneven at best, with many audiences and reviewers responding negatively to it. The group toured extensively and attracted a small loyal following. During this time, Damon and Naomi expanded their music to more heavily reflect the influences of classic psychedelic artists like Can, The Soft Machine, and Robert Wyatt. Practicing as Magic Hour became increasingly difficult and the group parted on amicable terms.

According to Damon in an interview with *Ptolemaic Terrascope,* "*More Sad Hits* was intended as a swansong.... We figured we'd wait a little and see how we felt. As it happened, it took a couple of years before we wanted to do another ... but during that time we were playing with Kate and Wayne." Although they had recorded their first album as Damon and Naomi, the duo had never performed live. When Kramer asked them to join him in a tour of Japan, he insisted they perform not only with him but as Damon and Naomi as well. Uncomfortable at first, they slowly adapted to being front and center stage. After recording *The Wondrous World of Damon and Naomi,* they toured by themselves to promote the album. The duo recorded *Playback Singers* in their own living room.

Taking the name of *Playback Singers* from Indian musicals where the playback singers are the musicians who record the soundtrack off stage and unseen by the audience, Damon and Naomi recorded this album alone without a producer or audience. "Compromising quality of recording for the sake of nostalgia" is a slogan which is only half true, this is an album of high musical quality. Step by step, the former "rhythm section" for Galaxie 500 have rewritten themselves with their own brand of warm, sincere "psychedelic folk."

Selected discography

(as Pierre Etoile), "This Car Climbed Mt. Washington", Rough Trade, 1990, reissued Elefant, 1997.
More Sad Hits, Shimmy Disc, 1992, reissued, Sub Pop, 1997.
The Wondrous World of Damon & Naomi, Sub Pop, 1995.
(Damon & Naomi with Tom Rapp), "I Shall Be Released", CD accompanying *Ptolemaic Terrascope Terrastock Special Issue,* 1997.
(on *Terrastock Benefit EP),* "14 Auspicious Dreams," Enraptured, 1997.
"The Navigator," Earworm, 1997.
"Spirit of Love," EP, 1997.
Playback Singers, Sub Pop, 1998.

with Galaxie 500

Today, Aurora, 1988, reissued Rykodisc, 1997.
"Tugboat", Aurora, 1988.
On Fire, Rough Trade, 1989, reissued, Rykodisc, 1997.
This Is Our Music, Rough Trade, 1990, reissued, Rykodisc, 1997.
Copenhagen (rec. 1990), Rykodisc, 1997.
Box Set, Rykodisc, 1997.
The Portable Galaxie 500 (rec. 1988-90), Rykodisc, 1997.

with Magic Hour

No Excess Is Absurd, Twisted Village, 1993.
Will They Turn You On or Will They Turn On You, Twisted Village, 1994.
Secession '96, Twisted Village, 1995.
"Sunrise Variations," Flydaddy, 1996.

Sources

Periodicals

Boston Phoenix, May, 1997.
Musician, September, 1997
Ptolemaic Terrascope, June, 1997.
Riverfront Times, June, 1997.

Online

www.terrascope.org
www.subpop.com
www.aald.demon.co.uk/galaxie/galaxie-500-faq.txt

Additional information was obtained through interviews with Damon Krukowski and Naomi Yang and the liner notes to Galaxie 500 *Today*.

—*Jim Powers*

Marlene Dietrich

Actress, singer

AP/Wide World Photo. Reproduced by permission.

Marlene Dietrich's recording career extended over half a century for singing was always part of her acting career. Her first songs, for the German movie *Es liegt in der Luft,* (*There's Something in the Air*), were recorded in 1928 and the soundtrack of her last film *Just a Gigolo,* which included her last musical offerings, was released in 1978. Although she first became famous as an actress, this fame made it easy for Marlene Dietrich to start a second career as chanteuse while she was in her fifties and film offers were becoming scarce. Capitalizing on her image as femme fatale, she performed in night clubs and theaters around the world for over two decades, and her musical work was documented in numerous recordings.

Dietrich's voice, with a range of a mere one-and-a-half-octaves, was not that of a great singer. However, she made up for her technical limitations through inventive phrasing and by avoiding sustained notes. She dramatized her shows with theatrical elements such as extraordinary costumes, lighting and movement. "Her dusky, accented vocals complemented the heavy-lidded character she assumed on stage," wrote Colin Escott in the liner notes to *My Greatest Songs.* She flirted with "the limits of on-stage eroticism, ... hinting at a strangely androgynous sexuality," wrote Escott. With her mixture of intelligence and eroticism, Dietrich created a modern female prototype with a good deal more independence than the traditional stereotype. And she was versatile. One of her less well known musical skills was her ability to play various songs on a saw with a violin bow.

Born in Berlin in 1901 as Marie Magdalene Dietrich into a well-to-do family, Dietrich received a good education. At the young age of 13, Dietrich merged her two names into Marlene and created her stage name. Her father Louis, an officer in the Royal Prussian Police, died while Dietrich was still in school. Her mother Wilhelmina remarried, but her new husband, Colonel Eduard von Losch, died from wounds received in World War I when Dietrich was 17.

In 1919, Dietrich enrolled at the Weimar Konservatorium and began studying violin. She loved the music of Johann Sebastian Bach and eagerly practiced his solo sonatas. Was it because of a wrist injury, or because she was not accepted for further study at the Weimar Academy, or was it an offer to join the chorus line in a burlesque revue? Whatever the reason, Dietrich moved back to Berlin and dived into the Berlin theater scene where she encountered Claire Waldoff, a lesbian entertainer who performed in men's clothes. When she was 21, Dietrich married Rudolph Sieber, the casting director for a German movie in which she played a bit part. A year later, she gave birth to her daughter Maria.

Born Maria Magdalene Dietrich December 27, 1901, in Berlin, Germany; died May 6, 1992, in Paris, France; daughter of Louis Erich Otto (police officer) and Wilhelmina Elisabeth Josephine Felsing; second of two daughters; married Rudolf Sieber (casting director), 1923; daughter Maria (born 1924); became American citizen in 1939; *Education:* attended Auguste Victoria School for Girls, 1906-18; studied violin at the Weimar Konservatorium, 1919; attended Max Reinhard Drama School beginning in 1922; studied violin at the Weimar Konservatorium, 1919; returned to Berlin and studied acting under innovative director Max Reinhard in Berlin.

Joined Reinhard's theater company and played minor roles in 17 German movies, 1922-29; cut her first record, 1926; got her first starring role in *Ship of Lost Men*, directed by Maurice Tourneur, 1927; became an international star as nightclub singer Lola-Lola in *The Blue Angel,* directed by Josef von Sternberg, 1930; Academy Award nomination for her acting in *Morocco,* 1930; moved to Hollywood with von Sternberg and worked with him in six more movies 1931-1935; acted in numerous movies under various directors for Paramount, Universal Pictures, Columbia Pictures, and other production firms, 1936-43; performed in war bond tours and worked on radio broadcasts for war effort, 1943; first performed "Lili Marlene" during North Africa U.S.O. tour, 1943; performed over 500 times before Allied troops, 1943-46; appeared in various movies, 1946-1961, including *A Foreign Affair,* 1948, *Stage Fright,* 1950, *Witness for the Prosecution,* 1957, *Judgment at Nuremberg,* 1961; performed first show as night club singer at Hotel Sahara in Las Vegas, 1953; toured as a concert and cabaret singer until 1975: toured Germany and Israel, 1960; Russia in 1964; Broadway in 1967; and the World Exposition in Montreal June, 1967; oother activities during the 1960s and 1970s included: narrator in Hitler-documentary *The Black Fox,* 1962; first TV special *I Wish You Love* directed by Alexander Cohen, 1972; withdrew from public life after a stage accident in Sydney, Australia, 1975; last appearance in the movie *Just a Gigolo,* 1978; Dietrich's autobiography published in Germany, 1987; English version *Marlene* published in the United States, 1989.

Awards: Légion d'Honneur, France; Medal of Freedom, American Defense Department; honored on a German postage stamp in 1997.

Dietrich had minor roles in 17 movies before film director Josef von Sternberg choose her to co-star with Emil Jannings in the American/German co-production *The Blue Angel.* That role as seductive nightclub singer Lola Lola lures a conservative schoolteacher to ruin, panted the seed for her future image as an actress—and as a person. One of Lola's songs, "Falling in Love Again" composed by Frederick Hollander, was Dietrich's first and most legendary song.

Dietrich the Hollywood Star

Sternberg could see Dietrich's potential as a new type of sex symbol and, after Paramount offered her a two-movie deal based only on a screen test, he persuaded her to go to Hollywood with him. From von Sternberg Dietrich learned about moviemaking and the importance of her image. She was an instant hit in America. She continued to wear men's clothing occasionally as she had done in Berlin. At first it was considered scandalous, but before long it became fashionable among American women. Dietrich was nominated for an Academy Award for her role in *Morocco,* another von Sternberg production, but did not win the coveted Oscar. Dietrich acted in six more von Sternberg movies until 1935. The last few flopped. In 1937, Paramount canceled Dietrich's contract and, before a year was out, she had been labeled "box-office poison." Marlene Dietrich's Hollywood career seemed to be over.

With the rowdy western *Destry Rides Again* from 1939, produced by Universal's Joe Pasternak, Dietrich's image took a radical turn. Once the stylish super-mannequin image Sternberg had created for her was no longer in demand, Dietrich made her comeback as a comedienne. In her role as a bartender, she earned less than twenty percent of what she had earned just two years earlier and sang several of her later most successful songs, such as "See What the Boys in the Back Room will Have." After her revival as a comedienne, Dietrich played various film roles until 1942.

Entertained the Troops

The same year Hitler started World War II, Dietrich became an American citizen. After Allied troops began fighting the Nazis in World War II, Dietrich, starting in 1943, went on tours organized by the United Service Organizations (U.S.O.), dedicated to providing entertainment and recreation for American servicemen in the field. On her North African tour in 1943, she introduced one of her most famous songs. "Lili Marlene" was originally a German marching song which the British Eighth

Army had adopted as their own, for which Dietrich later wrote new lyrics. Dietrich found creative ways to boost the morale of the troops she was entertaining. For example, she would judge who had the best legs of the soldiers she was performing for, or she would play the "musical saw." Dietrich also helped in base hospitals and soldiers' mess halls. She also participated in radio broadcasts aimed against Germany.

In February of 1945, "at battle lines, with the Ninth Army, ... she ignored every discomfort, insisted on the common soldier's diet and clothes, and was a source of endless comfort and pride to the troops," wrote Donald Spoto in *Falling in Love Again*. Dietrich entered Germany with the Allied troops and eventually met her mother again in Berlin. Despite Dietrich's packages of food and medicine, her mother died of heart failure in November of 1945. For her unprecedented work during the war, Dietrich was honored with the French *medal Légion d'Honneur* and with the Medal of Freedom, the highest award a civilian could receive from the American Defense Department.

The Chanteuse

After World War II, Dietrich acted again, more or less successfully, in various movies. She made *A Foreign Affair* with Billy Wilder in 1948, a film which included some unvarnished scenes of the post-war black market. The film also produced some of Dietrich's most famous songs such as "Black Market," and "Illusions." Like many of her songs since the 1930s, they were composed and accompanied by Frederick Hollander. In 1950, Dietrich worked with Alfred Hitchcock in his comic thriller *Stage Fright*. As a singing actress with an international reputation, she interpreted the Cole Porter song "The Laziest Gal in Town" and Edit Piaf's "La Vie an Rose." Finally, after *playing* a nightclub singer many times, Dietrich *became* one herself. Her work entertaining the soldiers had proven her ability to perform live on stage. In 1953, after Dietrich served as Master of Ceremonies in one of her daughter's charity galas at Madison Square Garden, she received an offer to perform at the Las Vegas Hotel Sahara. In 1954, she played the Café de Paris in London, where doctor Alexander Fleming, the inventor of penicillin, watched her show. In 1957, she made her second movie with Billy Wilder, *Witness for the Prosecution*, which was a great success. After that, she returned to stage for a tour of South America.

Dietrich soon expanded her night-club act into a complete one-woman revue. In the first half of her shows Dietrich often performed in a sexy outfit that would appeal to the men, while in the second half she wore a tuxedo, bow tie, top hat and either slacks or tights. "She caressed the microphone as if she were making love to it, and she did a sexy high-kicking dance with a chorus line," described Bill Davidson in *McCalls*.

In August of 1959, *Dietrich in Rio* was recorded on Columbia Records at a Rio de Janeiro performance. Thousands welcomed Dietrich at the Paris airport when she arrived in November of 1959. As she was coming off the airplane, Dietrich carried a box as small as a jewel case which she later explained held the costume for her show, a remark covered by every Paris newspaper, according Bill Davidson in *McCalls*. A male observer called Dietrich's dress "a flesh-colored nothing studded with gold specks and diamonds," reported *Newsweek*. After three weeks of performing a show every night in Paris, Dietrich returned to the United States to perform once again in Las Vegas and Lake Tahoe, Nevada. Her $30,000 a week salary made Dietrich "the highest paid nightclub entertainer in the world," according to Davidson.

In the following years, Dietrich performed on stages all over the world, in Scandinavia, France, Netherlands, Spain, North Africa, Australia, and Japan. In May of 1960, Dietrich went to Berlin for three shows at Berlin's Titania Palast, her first public appearance in Germany since 1930. Surprised by the unfriendly reception given her by some Berliners and some Berlin newspapers, Dietrich told *Newsweek* "They knew I was there in uniform with the American Army during the push through Germany. If that means I'm a traitor, then let them call me a traitor. I became an American citizen because of Hitler...But I'm going there as a singer and entertainer—not as a politician." Nonetheless, Dietrich signed Berlin's Golden Book for Mayor Willy Brandt. Four years later, Time *reported* that Dietrich was celebrated by the Russian press as a "fighter against Fascism" when she performed in a sold-out variety theater in Moscow. "The reason I love you is because you have no lukewarm emotions—you are either very sad or very happy," told Dietrich the 1,350 Russians in the audience according to *Time*, adding "I am proud to say I think that I have a Russian soul myself."

Dietrich's "in concert" shows were directed until 1964 by young composer Burt Bacharach, who helped her assemble her repertoire, arranged her songs, conducted her shows and was at the same time her friend and advisor. "I've never been very self-confident, either in films or on the stage," wrote Dietrich in her memoirs. "On the stage, Burt Bacharach's praise gave me a much-needed feeling of security." In 1967, she debuted her one-woman show on Broadway in the Nine O'Clock

Theater at the Lunt-Fontanne, for which she wore a new dress worth about $30,000. She continued to perform throughout the world, although less frequently, in part because the frequent deaths of many of her loved ones made her unhappy, in part because of several stage accidents she suffered. On September 29, 1975, Dietrich broke her leg on stage in Sydney, Australia. After a long period of medical treatment the seventy-four year old recovered, but she never returned to stage nor to public life. In June of 1976, Dietrich's husband died at age 79.

In 1986, a documentary about Dietrich's life by renowned film director Maximilian Schell—one of her admirers—was released. Although Dietrich refused to talk to journalists after her complete withdrawal from public life at the end of the 1970s, Schell managed to interview Dietrich several times in her Paris apartment, but the star—already in her mid-80s—refused to appear on camera. The interviews were used as voice-over in the documentary which consisted of clippings from Dietrich's movies, shows, and other public appearances. Dietrich's autobiography written in German and titled *Ich bin, Gott sei Dank, Berlinerin*—"I am, Thank God, a Berliner"—was first published in Germany in 1987. Two years later, the English translation came out in the United States as *Marlene*. Dietrich lived alone in Paris until her death in 1992. She is buried in Berlin.

Selected films

The Blue Angel, 1930.
Morocco, 1930.
Blonde Venus, 1932.
Shanghai Express, 1932.
The Devil is a Woman, 1935.
Desire, 1936.
Destiny Rides Again, 1939.
A Foreign Affair, 1948.
The Monte Carlo Story, 1956.
Witness for the Prosecution, 1957.
Touch of Evil, 1958.
Judgment at Nuremberg, 1961.
Just a Gigolo, 1978.
Marlene, (documentary about Dietrich's life and career by Maximilian Schell), 1986.

Selected discography

Marlene Dietrich, Decca, 1949.
Marlene Dietrich at the Café de Paris, (accompanied by George Smith), PHILIPS, Great Britain, 1954.
Marlene Dietrich in Rio, CBS, Brazil, 1959.
Wiedersehen mit MARLENE, Capitol, 1960.

My Greatest Songs, MCA, 1991.
1928-1933 Marlene Dietrich, Asv Living Era, 1992.
The Cosmopolitan Marlene Dietrich, Sony Music, 1993.
Falling In Love Again, MCA, 1998.
Marlene Dietrich, Lili Marlene, MCA.
Wiedersehen Mit Marlene, (Marlene Dietrich in Germany), EMI/Electrola, Germany.
The Legendary Marlene Dietrich, (songs from classic films), MFP/EMI, Great Britain.
Marlene Dietrich in London, (recorded at the Queen's Theatre), Columbia.
Marlene Dietrich singt Alt-Berliner Lieder, AMIGA, Germany.

Selected Writings

Ich bin, Gott sei Dank, Berlinerin (autobiography in German), Ullstein Verlag, 1987.
Marlene (translation of autobiography), Grove Press, 1989.

Sources

Books

Dietrich, Marlene, *Marlene* (translated from German by Salvator Attanasio), Grove Press, 1989.
Higham, Charles, *Marlene: The Life of Marlene Dietrich*, W.W.Norton & Company, 1977.
Spoto, Donald, *Blue Angel: The Life of Marlene Dietrich*, Doubleday & Co., 1992.
Spoto, Donald, *Falling in Love Again, Marlene Dietrich*, Little, Brown and Company, 1985.
Walker, Alexander, *Dietrich*, Harper & Row, 1984.

Periodicals

Biography, June 1998.
Look, October 24, 1961.
McCalls, March 1960.
Newsweek, May 2, 1960.
Time, May 29, 1964.

Online

http://hersalon.com/shrine/marlene/marlene.htm
http://amazon.com
http://www.dpag.de
http://www.pcs.sk.ca/sjk/dietrich/mdbio.htm
http://www.snafu.de/~fright.night/marlene-dietrich-lps.html

Additional information obtained from the liner notes of *My Greatest Songs*, 1991.

—Evelyn Hauser

Celine Dion

AP/Wide World Photo. Reproduced by permission.

From the time she was a child, Celine Dion knew her destiny. Surrounded by a family of musicians, she began entertaining audiences in her parents' piano bar at the age of five. By the time she turned 30, she had cemented her place in the highest levels of pop stardom. With such megahits as "The Power of Love," "Because You Loved Me," and "My Heart Will Go On," Dion maintained a fast-paced and prolific career throughout the 1980s and 1990s. "The girl has a star over her head—she's that lucky," her manager and husband Rene Angelil explained to E. Kaye Fulton in *Maclean's*.

Celine Dion was born the youngest of 14 children to Adhemar and Therese Dion in Charlemagne, Quebec, Canada. When Dion was just a baby, her family formed a singing group called Dion's Family and toured Canada. Therese Dion played the violin, and Adhemar Dion played the accordion. Later, her parents opened a piano bar called Le Vieux Baril. When she was just five years old, she jumped up on a table to sing Ginette Reno songs. Soon, customers were coming back, asking the little girl with the big voice to sing again and again. Even then, Dion relied on the strength of her family. "My family is my foundation," she told Jean-Noel Bassior in *McCalls*. "We never had a lot of money, but we had a wealth of love, joy, and affection."

When Dion was 12 years old, she recorded a demo tape of a song her mother had written for her. Therese Dion wrapped the tape with a red ribbon and sent it off to Canadian manager/producer Rene Angelil, who had previously managed Canadian singer Ginette Reno. Celine's mother enclosed a note with the tape that read: "This is a 12-year-old with a fantastic voice. Please listen to her. We want her to be like Ginette Reno." Angelil let the package sit on his desk for weeks before Dion's brother Michael met with him and convinced him to listen to the tape.

Rose to Canadian Stardom

Once he heard her voice, Angelil invited her to meet with him and perform for him in person. He signed her immediately, with the understanding that he would have complete control over her career. When he couldn't find a label to sign the 12-year-old Dion, he mortgaged his house to finance her first album, which was completely in French. Soon, the young Dion's French albums earned her notoriety in Canada, and she became known as *La P'tite Quebecoise* (the little girl of Quebec).

By the time she was 15 years old, Dion decided to make music her only priority and dropped out of school. "It was taking me away from music, from my happiness, from

For the Record . . .

Born March 30, 1968, in Charlemagne, Quebec; daughter of Adhemar and Therese Dion; youngest of 14 children; married: Rene Angelil, December 17, 1994.

Signed management contract with Rene Angelil, 1980; released seven French language albums in Canada, 1980-1990; released U.S. debut album, *Unison*, 1990; released five albums with Epic Records, 1991-1996, including *Celine Dion*, 1992; *The Colour of My Love*, 1993; *The French Album*, 1995; *Faling Into You*, 1996; *Let's Talk About Love*, 1997; *These Are Special Times*, 1998; reached worldwide success with "My Heart Will Go On," selling more than 50 albums worldwide from both the *Titanic* soundtrack and *Let s Talk About Love*, 1997.

Awards: Grammy Award for Best Album of the Year and Best Bop Album, 1996.

Addresses: *Record company*—Epic Records, P.O. Box 4450, New York, NY 10101-4450

my dreams," Dion told Charles P. Alexander in *Time*. Around the same time, Angelil had divorced his second wife and focused the majority of his time on Dion and her career. After releasing nine French albums, the 18-year-old Celine Dion had grown tired of her little girl image, and decided to make a major change. She had seen singer Michael Jackson perform on television, and told Angelil that she wanted to have the kind of success Jackson had.

In an effort to embark on the path of global superstardom, Celine Dion took a year off of recording,during which she had caps put on her teeth, had a complete makeover, and learned English. She spent the next two years working on a English language album and an American record contract. She also continued to perform throughout Canada. In 1988, Dion and Angelil began to develop a romance, but because of their 26-year age difference, they kept their relationship a secret.

Grew Seedlings of Greater Success

In 1990, Dion released her English debut, *Unison*, on Epic Records in the U.S. The album included the top five single "Where Does My Heart Beat Now," and sold more than a million copies worldwide. Renowned producer David Foster produced five songs on the album. "Celine exceeds the boundaries of talent," Foster told Fulton. "I don't know if she will reach the heights of Barbra Streisand, but there's nobody else in the race."

During the tour for *Unison*, Dion had a scare. She lost her voice before one of her performances and had to cancel part of the tour. Her doctors told her that her vocal chords were severely inflamed, and she had to stay completely silent for three weeks. By the end of her break, she had regained her voice and designed a plan to take better care of herself and preserve her voice. She set a rigid schedule for herself on tour, stopped talking three days before beginning a new album, and kept silent before performances until late in the afternoon.

By 1991, Rene Angelil and Celine Dion had become engaged. "When I met Rene, I loved him, but as a child," Dion told Bassior. "The more I got to know him over all the years we worked together, the more I fell in love with him."

Later that year, Dion released another French language album called *Dion Chante Plamondon*, on which she performed the songs of Canadian composer Luc Plamondon. In 1992, she released her sophomore English album titled simply *Celine Dion*. The album included the hit single "Beauty and the Beast," a duet with Peabo Bryson that was also the title song for the Disney film. The song won both a Grammy award and an Oscar award. She also had a number-one hit with the track "If You Asked Me To" from the same album. *Celine Dion* became her first gold-selling album in the United States and sold more than 12 million copies worldwide. As a result of this success, she was able to embark on her first headlining tour in the U.S.

Experienced Personal Tragedy and Bliss

Dion had even more success with the release *The Colour of My Love* the following year, which included the hit singles "The Power of Love" and "When I Fall in Love," the latter was a duet with Clive Griffin that also appeared on the soundtrack for the film *Sleepless in Seattle*. Peter Galvin wrote in his *New York Times* review, "Ms. Dion exudes a pleasing mixture of innocence and soulfulness throughout the album ... endowing even the slickest songs with palpable passion."

Beyond her growing popularity, Celine Dion also experienced a personal tragedy in 1993. Her niece, Karine

Menard, had died in Dion's arms after a lifelong battle with cystic fibrosis. After thatmoment, Dion made it her personal crusade to raise money for cystic fibrosis among other children's charities. She wrote the song "Vole" in memory of her niece. It appeared in French on her *D'eux* album and in English as "Fly" on her *Falling Into You* album. Dion explained the effect Karine's death had on her to Dennis Hensley in *Cosmopolitan*, "We take a lot for granted. The air we breathe, the ability to walk and talk. When we're happy, it's easy to forget how lucky we are."

Dion's own happiness grew even greater on December 17, 1994, when she married Rene Angelil at a ceremony at Montreal's Notre Dame Basilica in front of 500 guests. The wedding, which cost more than $500,000, was televised nationwide in Canada. Instead of wedding gifts, the couple asked for donations to the Canadian Cystic Fibrosis Foundation and raised $200,000.

Dion released another French album in 1995 called *D'eux*, which was also released in the United States as *The French Album*. It included songs by French pop composer Jean-Jacques Goldman, and became the world's best-selling French language album of all time. The following year, she released her next hit album *Falling Into You*. She reached number-one on the charts with the single "Because You Loved Me," which also appeared on the soundtrack for the film *Up Close and Personal*. *Falling Into You* sold more than ten million copies in the United States alone and won Grammy awards for Best Album of the Year and Best Pop Album.

Achieved Global Domination

In 1997, Celine Dion reached her greatest success ever, becoming a household name all over the world. The catalyst was the song "My Heart Will Go On" from the soundtrack for the award-winning film *Titanic*. The number-one hit was also released on her next album, *Let's Talk About Love*. The song was credited with selling more than 50 million albums worldwide, counting both the soundtrack and *Let's Talk About Love*. For six weeks, the two albums held the number-one and number-two positions on *Billboard*'s album charts.

Let's Talk About Love also included a duet with Dion and her musical hero Barbra Streisand called "Tell Him." Streisand released the song on her own album, *Higher Ground*, as well. "Celine is all anyone could ask for in a singing partner—professional, easygoing, generous," Streisand told Bassior. "Her amazing voice is surpassed only by her kind and gentle heart." Dion also recorded a duet with opera singer Luciano Pavarotti called "I Hate You Then I Love You."

By this time, Dion had no doubt that she had reached the success she dreamed about as an 18-year-old girl watching Michael Jackson on television. "When I was a smaller kid, I wanted to be in show business, and I was holding on to that dream," Dion told Karen S. Schneider and Jeanne Gordon in *People*. "I don't want to hold on to that dream anymore. I want to hold on to the real things."

On April 30, 1998, Celine Dion received the National Order of Quebec, the province's highest honor, then was inducted as an Officer of the Order of Canada the very next day. In August of 1998, she headed out on an extensive 14-country tour that ended by ringing in the new millennium in Montreal on December 31, 1999. In September of 1998, Dion released another French language album titled *S'il Suffisait D'Aimer* (translated *If Only Love Could Be Enough*). She also released a holiday album called *These Are Special Times* in November of 1998, which included the hit "I'm Your Angel," a duet with R. Kelly. By the end of the year, *Forbes* had named her the twelfth highest paid entertainer, with her 1998 pre-tax income estimated at $55.5 million. By the end of the decade, she had sold more than 100 million albums worldwide. "The grace with which she's handled all of this is extraordinary," Sony Music International President Robert M. Bowlin told Chuck Taylor in *Billboard*. "She's really under a microscope, and yet you'd be hard pressed to find much criticism, considering how hard she works and how many records she sells. It speaks volumes about how professional she is."

After her massive world tour, Dion decided to take some time off in the year 2000. She and Angelil decided work on having a family instead of another album, giving Dion's career a bit of a break. "I get paid a lot of money to be on this schedule, but it's okay to want to stop," Dion told Jeremy Helligar in *People*. "And I prefer to stop at the top of my career rather than when no one wants to hear me anymore." Of course, given her lifelong success, Dion won't likely have to worry about that for many years to come.

Selected discography

Unison, Epic Records, 1990.
Dion Chante Plamondon, Epic Records, 1991.
Celine Dion, Epic Records, 1992.
The Colour of My Love, Epic Records, 1993.
The French Album, Epic Records, 1995.
Falling Into You, Epic Records, 1996.

Let's Talk About Love, Epic Records, 1997.
S'il Suffisait D'Aimer, Epic Records, 1998.
These Are Special Times, Epic Records, 1998.

Sources

Periodicals

Billboard, October 17, 1998.
Cosmopolitan, July 1998.
Entertainment Weekly, April 17, 1992; November 12, 1993; June 24, 1994; May 29, 1995; March 15, 1996; March 29, 1996; December 4, 1998.
Interview, March 1999.
Ladies Home Journal, November 1997.
Maclean's, June 1, 1992; December 28, 1992; March 10, 1997; August 4, 1997; April 6, 1998; May 11, 1998; March 8, 1999.
McCalls, June 1998.
New York Times, April 3, 1994.
People Weekly, February 28, 1994; June 13, 1994; March 18, 1996; March 3, 1997; December 8, 1997; January 18, 1999; March 1, 1999.
Time, March 7, 1994; November 24, 1997.
Variety, December 14, 1998.

Online

The Official Celine Dion Website, http://www.celinonline.com (April 4, 1999).

—Sonya Shelton

DMX

Singer, songwriter

AP/Wide World Photo. Reproduced by permission.

Within a year, rapper DMX rose from the streets of Yonkers to become one of hip-hop's most popular and prolific stars. His raw, aggressive lyrics focus on strength and survival, keys to overcoming the adversity of life on the streets. DMX provided an alternative to the glamorous images and tunes of contemporary rap artists like Puff Daddy, he gained a formidable following with his first debut album, *It's Dark and Hell is Hot*. He increased his audience exponentially with his immediate follow-up album, *Flesh of My Flesh, Blood of My Blood*. Both albums reached number one on the *Billboard* charts in their first week, making DMX the first recording artist in music history to have his first two albums reach number one within a year. DMX toured throughout the country with various hip-hop festivals, helping to establish himself as a rap icon with the power and prestige of Tupac Shakur and the Notorious B.I.G.

Born Earl Simmons in the School Street Projects of Yonkers, New York, DMX, also known as Dark Man X, was a lonely boy. Despite his five sisters, the future-rap star was often left alone to walk the streets of his neighborhood, to entertain himself and find his own answers. From this, he says, came his inner strength and his penchant for examining his world, inside and out, an ability that would later be the primary appeal in his candid lyrics about ghetto life. In his solitude, DMX also learned to befriend dogs, developing such a strong bond with his canine friends that he had the name of his former pet, Boomer, tattooed on his back after he was struck and killed by a car. DMX currently owns two pit bulls and often employs dog imagery in his lyrics, exemplified by his smash debut single "Get At Me Dog."

Still an unknown quantity when he signed to Columbia Records in 1992, the new rapper was given very little attention from the label, and his promotional single "Born Loser" came and went unnoticed. DMX protested the label's neglect and was let out of his contract. *The Source* magazine was, in this case, the only source for predicting DMX's bright future by bestowing upon him, in 1991, the prestigious "Unsigned Hype" award a year before he signed with Columbia.

In the years following DMX's failed first attempt, he honed his rugged-voiced and gritty beat by appearing on the singles of several of his contemporaries. He appeared on LL Cool J's "4,3,2,1" and Mic Geronimo's "Usual Suspects." He also wrote and performed an impressive rap, "Money, Power, Respect," for fellow Yonkers recording artist The Lox. He also appeared on Mase's "24 Hrs. to Live," Ice Cube's "We Be Clubbin' (Remix)," and Onyx's "Shut 'em Down," all the while creating a name for himself and building the hype surrounding his debut album. *It's Dark and Hell is Hot*

For the Record . . .

Born Earl Simmons in Yonkers, NY.

Signed deal with Columbia Records, 1992; released promotional single "Born Loser," 1992; signed deal with Ruff Ryders/Def Jam Records, 1997; released debut album *It's Dark and Hell is Hot*, 1998; released single "Get At Me Dog," 1998; arrested, tried, and cleared of charges of rape, sodomy, and unlawful imprisonment against a Bronx exotic dancer; performed with hip-hop package festival tour Survival of the Illest, starred in Hype Williams' movie *Belly*, recorded music for animated cartoon "South Park," 1998; performed with hip-hop tour Hark Knock Life, released second album, *Flesh of My Flesh, Blood of My Blood*, 1999.

Awards: Unsigned Hype award by *The Source*, 1991

Addresses: *Record Company*—Def Jam Records, 160 Varick St. 12th floor, New York, NY, 10003.

was released in May of 1998 by Ruff Ryders/Def Jam Records, whom he had signed with in 1997. The album, promoted by the hugely popular single "Get At Me Dog," shot up the *Billboard* charts to number one and sold over a quarter of a million copies in its first week.

To support the release of his first album, DMX was scheduled to join the "Survival of the Illest" tour with fellow hip-hop artists Onyx and Def Squad. Before the tour could begin in June of 1998 in Roanoke, Virginia, he was forced to return to New York, where he was arrested on charges of rape, sodomy, and unlawful imprisonment, filed by an exotic dancer . He posted bail and rejoined the tour. The allegations followed him until August, when he was cleared of the charges after the results of a judge-ordered DNA test came back negative.

Cleared of the allegations, DMX continued the remarkable year that transformed him from unknown Yonkers MC to worldwide hip-hop hero. He teamed with video director Hype Williams to star in the controversial film "Belly," which was shut down in mid-production for several months because of the excessive violence used to portray urban life. Williams said of DMX in an interview with MTV in July of 1998, "I had heard his vocals and lyrics for many, many years, and I knew he was a tremendous talent. I just didn't know how big of a talent and I didn't know how big of an actor he would be. In

actuality, in my opinion, he's a better actor than a rapper, and people are really going to get a real strong sense of that come November 4." The film debuted, earned little financially, and continued to rouse criticism, but DMX was already hard at work on his follow-up album.

Released in December of 1998, *Blood of My Blood, Flesh of My Flesh* didn't disappoint his fans. It reached number one, like its predecessor, and disappeared from the shelves at record speed. DMX recorded this album in the tradition of his debut, intending to convey the raw, personal trials and obstacles of ghetto life. "I want *Flesh of My Flesh* to be like my connection to the community," he told Def Jam Records. "I want to say what's on my peoples' minds, soak up all their pain. I've learned that when I take it all in, I can make one brotha's pain be understood by the world."

With his follow-up success, DMX became the first recording artist in music history to have his first two albums reach number one within a year, according to *Billboard*. "I wrote fast," DMX told MTV in January of 1999. "I wrote 'The Prayer,' 'Ready to Meet Him' [quickly]. I wrote a lot of joints, you know, but I still got joints to just pick from. I could put out an album right now with joints I've already done, and they're blazin'."

DMX continued to make hip-hop history as part of the "Hard Knock Life" tour, organized by himself and fellow rap artists Jay-Z, Method Man, and Redman. The tour, perhaps the largest and most powerful of its kind, launched in March of 1999. Regardless of DMX's future, he already claimed his place as a prominent figure in music history. "I think society is finally ready to deal with reality," DMX told Def Jam Records in February of 1998. "So for that reason I ain't got no choice but to blow!"

Selected discography

"Born Loser," Columbia, 1993.
It's Dark and Hell is Hot, Ruff Ryders/Def Jam, 1998.
"Get At Me Dog," Ruff Ryders/Def Jam, 1998.
Flesh of My Flesh, Blood of My Blood, Ruff Ryders/Def Jam, 1998.

Sources

Online

"DMX's Hip Hop's Hottest Artist since 2pac," *Yahoo! Music: DMX*, http://artist.music.yahoo.com/muze/performer/DMX.html, (March 7, 1999).

"DMX," *MTV News Gallery*, http://www.mtv.com/news/gal-lery/d/dmx.html, (March 15, 1999).

"DMX," *Def Jam*, http://www.defjam.com/artists/dmx/dmx.html, (March 7, 1999).

"Dark Man X," *DMX*, http://members.tripod.com/~dragon-black/biography.html, (March 7, 1999).

—Karen Gordon

Jimmy Driftwood

Singer, songwriter

Jimmy Driftwood was one of the most prolific and influential folk artists in music history. He penned more than 5,000 songs, and although many of these were recorded and made popular by other artists, he received the fame, recognition, and financial compensation he deserved. Driftwood's distinguished role in the folk genre is even more impressive considering the unique path he took to stardom. While interest in folk music was on the rise in the 1950s, Driftwood was composing folk songs in a classroom in Arkansas. He had trained as a high school teacher, and in his frustration to find an effective method to teach history to his students, he began putting the story and the facts to music, resulting in many of his most popular hits. Most notable of these is "The Battle of New Orleans," a song covered by Johnny Horton which topped both the country and pop charts, received a Grammy award, and spurred Driftwood's success.

Born James Corbett Morris in Mountain View, Arkansas, the future folk singer and songwriter was quickly dubbed "Driftwood" when his father played a joke on his grandmother, wrapping a piece of driftwood in a blanket and passing it off as Jimmy. Driftwood grew up surrounded by music—his father, a local folk singer, taught him to play the fiddle and passed on his repertoire of tunes, and his mother and grandmother shared their folk music with him, too. Driftwood's grandfather gave him a gift he would use throughout his life—a homemade fiddle made from the headboard of a bed and a fence rail. Geographically, Driftwood's town in the Ozark Mountains possessed a rich musical heritage, a combination of both Native American and white cultures. Singing and playing music were as natural to Driftwood as breathing.

Along with his love for music, Driftwood had always wanted to be a teacher, and after graduating high school he earned his teaching degree from Arkansas Teachers College in Conway, later known as the University of Central Arkansas. Despite the economic hardship of the 1930s brought on by the Great Depression, Driftwood found a position teaching history in an elementary school in Snowball, at the age of 29. His students were not eager to learn, however, and after trying several methods unsuccessfully, he called on his childhood appreciation for writing poetry and his musical background, rich in storytelling. Combining the two, he began threading history lessons into folk songs and teaching them to his students. The formula was successful and the children began learning. Driftwood took his songs with him to other schools where he taught, and soon word of mouth had elevated him to something of celebrity status in the region, specifically the towns of Snowball, Mountain View, and Timbo.

Still, Driftwood's songs were but a means to an end, and he continued to teach throughout the 1940s and live quietly with his wife, Cleda Azalea Johnson, a former student whom he had married in 1936. Meanwhile, popular culture had begun to take an interest in folk music, and by the 1950s Driftwood was a valuable commodity among members of academia interested in the rich history of the genre. In the mid-1950s, two musicians who appeared regularly on Red Foley's "Ozark Jubilee," Porter Wagoner and steel guitar player Don Warden, founded their own music publishing company. When they began to search for other artists to supplement their business, Warden's friend Hugh Ashley mentioned Driftwood.

Driftwood, who couldn't be contacted because he didn't own a phone, received word by mail and offered to meet the businessmen in Nashville and perform his music in person. Wagoner and Warden were enticed by "The Battle of New Orleans," a song set to the melody of the fiddle tune "The Eighth of January." Driftwood had written it years earlier in an effort to teach his students about the War of 1812 and it had now gotten him a recording contract with Wagoner and Warden's label, RCA Victor. Driftwood recorded his first album, *Newly Discovered Early American Folk Songs*, in 1957, and it was released early in 1958 seeing modest sales and little airplay.

For the Record . . .

Born James Corbett Morris, June 20, 1907, in Mountain View, AR; (died July 12, 1998, Fayetteville, AR). *Education:* Arkansas State Teachers College.

Married Cleda Azalea Johnson, 1936; wrote "Battle of New Orleans" to teach his high school history students, 1941; signed to RCA Victor and completed first recording session, 1957; released first album, *Newly Discovered Early American Folk Songs*, 1958; gained notoriety when Johnny Horton's recording of "Battle of New Orleans" became a hit, topping both country and pop charts; released second album, *The Wilderness Road*, appeared regularly with Grand Ole Opry and on *Ozark Jubilee*, 1959; ended recording career after six albums, 1961; created Rackensack Folklore Society and held first Arkansas Folk Festival, 1963; established Ozark Folk Center in Mountain View, AR, 1973; built Driftwood Barn and Folklore Hall of Fame, 1982; died of heart attack after being hospitalized in Fayetteville, AR for a stroke.

Awards: Grammy Awards for "The Battle of New Orleans," "Wilderness Road," "Songs of Billy Yank and Johnny Reb," and "Tennessee Stud;" received honorary doctorate in American folklore from Peabody College in Nashville, Tennessee, 1959.

But late one night a country singer named Johnny Horton heard Driftwood's "The Battle of New Orleans" on the radio and decided he wanted to cover it. He eventually convinced his record label, Columbia, to allow him to record the song, and cut it on January 27, 1959. Shortly after its release the tune became a hit, topping both the pop and country charts and remaining there for 21 weeks. Driftwood's songs were hot and his follow-up album, *The Wilderness Road*, was far more successful than his debut, earning him a Grammy award. His songwriting skills were not only making stars of numerous artists, but they were also paving the road for other historically oriented songs. Horton's similarly themed "Sink The Bismarck" and "Johnny Reb" became huge hits not long after.

While "The Battle of New Orleans" was gaining popularity in 1959, Driftwood was still teaching in Arkansas. But his success could not be ignored, especially after he won his first Grammy award for his hit single. In 1959 alone, he performed with the Grand Ole Opry around the world, at Carnegie Hall in New York City, at various folk festivals, at the National Education Association jamboree, and at the United Nations. He also received an honorary doctorate in American folklore from Peabody College in Nashville, Tennessee, and continued writing hit songs like "Tennessee Stud," which boosted singer Eddy Arnold's career and won Driftwood another Grammy.

Once Driftwood began receiving profits from his music, he used his popularity and financial leverage to educate the country on the beauty of Arkansas folk culture. He founded the Rackensack Folklore Society in the 1970s and visited universities to lecture on the importance of folk music. Living in Arkansas' Ozark Mountains as he had for most of his life, he established the annual Arkansas Folk Festival in 1963 and helped find funding for the Ozark Folk Center in 1973. In the early 1980s, he established the Driftwood Barn and Folklore Hall of Fame, where folk musicians perform regularly. He also successfully fought the damming of the Buffalo River in Arkansas and assisted in having it deemed a National River. On July 12, 1998, at age 91, Driftwood suffered a fatal heart attack while in the hospital recovering from a stroke. His songwriting contributions and his efforts to educate on the value of folk music made him as one of the most influential folk artist in music history.

Selected discography

Newly Discovered Early American Folk Songs, RCA Victor, 1958.
Wilderness Road, RCA Victor, 1959.
The Westward Movement, RCA Victor, 1959.
Tall Tales in Song, RCA Victor, 1960.
Songs of Billy Yank and Johnny Reb, RCA Victor, 1961.
Driftwood at Sea, RCA Victor, 1962.
Voice of the People, Monument, 1963.
Down in the Arkansas, Monument, 1965.
Americana, Bear Family, 1991.
The Best of Jimmy Driftwood, Monument, 1966.

Sources

"Jimmy Driftwood," *All-Music Guide*, http://www.allmusic.com (February 13, 1999).
"Jimmy Driftwood," *Bill Slater's Website*, http://billslater.com/driftwood.htm (February 13, 1999).
"Jimmy Driftwood," *Fuller Up, The Dead Musician Directory*, http://elvispelvis.com/jimmiedriftwood.htm (February 13, 1999).
"The Battle of New Orleans," *Tom Simon's Rock and Roll Page*, http://www.crl.com/~tsimon/battle.htm (February 13, 1999).

—*Karen Gordon*

Dru Hill

Vocal Group

Natives of Baltimore, Maryland, the four members of Dru Hill have combined their smooth, R&B vocal stylings with the intention of putting "Baltimore on the map." Unlike many of their contemporaries, the group relay a positive message, focusing their lyrics on life and love, rather than the harsh street grit of most hip-hop and rap. This, combined with their four-part vocal harmonies, have led to a hugely successful first single, "Tell Me," and their first debut album, *Dru Hill*. With several hit singles following, a series of tours, and a hit follow-up album *Enter the Dru*, released in 1998, they have established themselves as leading musical artists in R&B and hip-hop, as well as a crossover success in the mainstream. They have indeed put their hometown on the map.

The four members of Dru Hill—Mark "Sisqo" Andrews, Tamir "Nokio" Ruffin, James "Woody" Green, and Larry "Jazz" Anthony—were still in high school when they met in 1994, as summer employees at Baltimore Harbor's Fudgery. The quartet soon began singing together, offering the patrons of the Inner Harbor free performances

AP/Wide World Photo. Reproduced by permission.

Members include **Mark Andrews** (Sisqo), lead vocals, keyboards, bass, production; **Larry Anthony** (Jazz), second tenor vocals, keyboards, trumpet, piano; **James Green** (Woody, left band, March 1999), born, vocals, drums, keyboards, melody; **Tamir Ruffin** (Nokio), baritone vocals, lyrics, trumpet, keyboard, piano.

Group formed when the four were still in high school, won local version of Apollo Theater's Amateur Night, placed third at Apollo Theater's National Competition, New York, 1994; performed at pool party for Black Entertainment Television's "Rap City," met with Island Black Music President Hiriam Hicks, recorded "Tell Me," for *Eddie* soundtrack, 1995; released first hit single "Tell Me," 1996; released debut album *Dru Hill,* Island Records, 1996; released hit single "In My Bed," 1996; set out on first national tour with Mary J. Blige, released "We're Not Making Love No More," 1997; joined Puff Daddy's "No Way Out" tour, performed for pay-per-view special "Breaking Out-The Concert," opened up for Boyz II Men tour, released second album *Enter the Dru,* Island Black Music, 1998; became trio when Woody left group to pursue solo career in gospel music, headlined tour of North America, 1999.

Addresses: *Record company*— Def Jam, 160 Varick St., 12th Fl., New York, NY 10013-1220, (212) 229-5224, fax (212) 229-5295. *Dru Hill Fan Club*—712 2nd St., NE DC 20002. *Website*—http://www.ubl.com/ubl/cards/010/6/89.html.

of their gospel-influenced harmonizing. All Baltimore natives, they named themselves after Druid Hill Park, what they affectionately refer to as "the spot." Soon they were gaining popularity and entering competitions and talent contests. They won first place twice in the local Apollo Theater's Amateur Night, and went on to place third at the Apollo Theater's National Competition in New York.

Building on their first taste of stardom in 1995, they performed at a pool party for Black Entertainment Television's "Rap City." Island Black Music President Hiriam Hicks saw their show and arranged a meeting with them. The timing was right, and Dru Hill was in the studio later that afternoon, recording the song "Tell Me" for the *Eddie* soundtrack, which was in mid-production at the time. "Tell Me" became the group's first hit single, peaking at number five on the *Billboard*'s Hot R&B Singles chart, drawing national acclaim for the quartet, and becoming the biggest hit on the soundtrack. Dru Hill's debut album, *Dru Hill*, debuted in 1996, peaking at number five on *Billboard*'s Top R&B Albums chart and at number 23 on the *Billboard* 200, and selling more than 1.5 million copies.

But none of their success could have been possible without the group's varied talents and interests. Jazz, as his name suggests, is a jazz fan. With a passion for the blues and his roots in the church, his music has the heart of gospel and the edge of improvisation. He fills the role of Dru Hill's second tenor vocals, as well as contributing keyboards, trumpet and piano to the mix. Sisqo spent most of his childhood in the church singing gospel, but has since developed a love for popular music. His appreciation ranges from classical to hip-hop, but he admits to always being a fan of what's hip. He sings lead vocals for the group, plays keyboards and bass, and assists in arrangement and production. Nokio, an acronym for Nasty On Key In Octave, has his heart in production and the business side of music, feeling most at home in the studio. He is Dru Hill's baritone, singing lyrics he himself often writes and sometimes accompanies with classical trumpet, keyboard and piano. Woody is the melody-maker and the spirited father figure of the group. His roots are also in gospel, as evidenced by his soulful lyrics. He, like the rest, is not just a singer, but also a drummer and keyboardist.

Contributing to the success of their first multiplatinum effort, Dru Hill released hit singles off the album, "In My Bed" and "Never Make a Promise," both of which reached number one on the *Billboard*'s Hot R&B Singles chart. "We're Not Making Love No More," written by singer Babyface, reached number two. By the time they were ready to release a second LP, Dru Hill had established a substantial and loyal fan base.

But since it had been some time since their first full-length release, Island Records released their single "How Deep Is Your Love," from the "Rush Hour" soundtrack on Def Jam Records in September of 1998. Follow-up album *Enter the Dru* was released the following month, a testament to the slight image and style changes made by the group. "We owe it to our fans to give them something different," said Andrews in an interview with *Billboard* magazine for their October 3, 1998 issue. "I watch Michael and Janet [Jackson] and how they alter their images slightly [each time they have a new album]. When we perform, we never do the same show twice." The album features songs written by each member of the group, as well as co-production credit to Andrews and Ruffin.

The first single off the album, "These Are The Times," continued to garner fans for the now nationally famous quartet. Despite the huge number of new groups, Dru Hill has risen above as something unique. According to Angela Thomas, senior VP of Island Black Music, in an interview with *Billboard* magazine in the October 3, 1998 issue, "Dru Hill set the standard ... This group has original songs with no sampling," an important distinction between the group and their contemporaries.

Supplementing their success in the recording studio with live appearances, Dru Hill toured with Mary J. Blige, joined Puff Daddy's "No Way Out" Tour, performed for the pay-per-view special "Breaking Out-The Concert" and opened up for Boyz II Men on their tour. But the quartet was brought down to a trio when Woody decided to leave in March of 1999 to pursue a solo career in gospel. The band mates remained on amicable terms. "He's always been the one that pulled us together [with] the prayer, you know," Nokio told MTV News in an article on March 19, 1999. "[He] prayed for everybody when we had hard times. And I don't know, it's just that when you get a calling like that, you just got to go with it." The remaining Dru Hill members headlined their own tour of North America for the first time in the spring of 1999. As their sophomore effort continues to make its way up the charts, the only sentiment that comes to mind is that "These Are The Times" indeed.

Selected discography

Dru Hill, Island Records, 1996.
"Tell Me", Island Records, 1996.
"In My Bed", Island Records, 1996.
Enter The Dru, Island Black Music, 1998.
"How Deep Is Your Love", Def Jam, 1998.

Sources

Periodicals

Billboard Magazine, October 3, 1998.

Online

"Dru Hill," *MTV News Gallery*, http://www-mtv-d.mtvnodn.com/news/gallery/d/druhill.html (April 4, 1999).
"Dru Hill Page," *IMUSIC*, http://imusic.com/showcase/urban/druhill.html (April 4, 1999).
"Dru Hill Page," *Island Records*, http://www.ubl.com/ubl/cards/010/6/89.html (April 4, 1999).

—Karen Gordon

Jermaine Dupri

Producer, rap artist

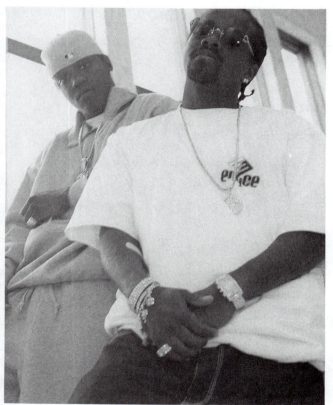

Long before Jermaine Dupri released his debut album in 1998, *Jermaine Dupri Presents: Life in 1472*, he was the man behind the scenes of a host of R&B chart-toppers. Talents like Usher, Da Brat, MC Lyte, Johnny Gill, Lil' Kim, TLC (whose Dupri-produced record *CrazySexyCool* went ten times platinum) and Mariah Carey, among others, had benefited from his work as a producer on their records. Dupri started in the business at an early age, discovering and promoting the young rap duo Kriss Kross while he was still a teenager himself.

Dupri, whose real last name is Mauldin, was born in North Carolina but raised in Atlanta, Georgia. His father, Michael Mauldin, was an Atlanta talent manager, and coordinated a Diana Ross concert in 1982. Little Jermaine managed to get onstage and dance with her. In the following years, he appeared with Herbie Hancock and Cameo before he got his start dancing on the Fresh Fest rap tour with L.L. Cool J., Whodini, Run-D.M.C., Grandmaster Flash and Slick Rick in 1985. At the age of 14, he started his career as a producer by producing a record for the group Silk Tymes Leather and securing a recording contract for them. Then he discovered Kriss Kross. He saw the child duo performing at a local shopping mall and proceeded to design their image and launch them into momentary stardom. In 1992, Columbia Records took on his record label, So So Def, as a subsidiary. Dupri headquartered So So Def in his hometown of Atlanta, a known hotbed of R&B talent. His success also worked to benefit his family—his mother, Tina Mauldin, ran his production company and his father became president of black music division at Columbia.

Dupri the producer and label head had a one-track mind. "I do [music] 100 percent," he told *Time* in 1998. "Ain't nothing else going on in my life. Everybody else got kids, families. It's completely music for me." His home, which he shared with his mother, was tailored to meet all his professional and recreational needs. He had a home studio and often attended So So Def meetings via speakerphone. The gold and platinum records he wrote or produced for the likes of Mariah Carey, TLC and Usher adorned his walls, and he had several full-size video games in his den.

Dupri's talent as a producer became somewhat of a burden to him. After a string of successful records, most notably for R&B man Usher, it seemed he had the magic touch, and everyone wanted to be part of it. Speaking of artists who looked to him to give their careers a little boost, Dupri told *Rolling Stone*, "It's almost like they coming to me looking for a magic trick. It'd be stupid for me to believe that what I did with Usher I can do with Joe Blow. Usher got talent that I can't take away from him. I just had to bring it out."

For the Record . . .

Jermaine Dupri, born Jermaine Mauldin, 1972, in NC; son of Tina and Michael Mauldin.

Started as a dancer on the Fresh Fest tour, 1985; discovered rap duo Kriss Kross as a teen; his label So So Def became Columbia Records subsidiary, 1992; produced and/or remixed for Kriss Kross, Immature, TLC, Run DMC, Xscape, Bobby Brown, DaBrat, El Debarge, Shanice, Da Bush Babees, Bad Boys, Mariah Carey, Puff Johnson, So-so Def Bass All-Stars, Braxtons, Aaliyah, MC Lyte, New Edition, Whodini, Richie Rich, Johnny Gill, Lil' Kim, Roberto Torres, Michael Bolton, Usher, Mase, LSG, Dru Hill, Aretha Franklin, Monica, Jay Z, Keith Sweat, Caught Up, from 1992-1998; released debut *Life in 1472*, 1998.

Addresses: *Record company*—So So Def, 685 Lambert Dr. NE, Atlanta, GA 30324-4125.

In 1998, Dupri stepped out from behind the curtain, front and center, to release his own record. *Jermaine Dupri Presents: Life in 1472,* released on So So Def, was hard-core gangsta rap and it meant something—Dupri had been 14 years in the music business and was born in 1972. The music and lyrics, true to the gangsta rap ethic, were hard-edged. "Like so much great urban music these days, *Life in 1472* is also a disturbing document—a brash and lurid depiction of the gigolo or 'jiggy' lifestyle," *The Village Voice* wrote in a review of the album. *Time* said the record was "tainted with misogyny."

Jermaine Dupri Presents: Life in 1472 was likened to Quincy Jones' *Back on the Block* in several reviews in that, for a solo album, it boasted a long list of guest artists. Those included on the record were among the hottest names in hip-hop and R&B, all of whom just happened to be his friends. Mariah Carey, Nas, Jay-Z, Slick Rick, Too Short, Mase, Lil' Kim, and Snoop Doggy Dogg all appeared on the release. "In an era when no rap album is complete without a cornucopia of guest stars," wrote *Rolling Stone* in a review of *Life in 1472*. "J.D.'s long guest list still stands out." Of Dupri's talents as an MC, *Rolling Stone* said, "J.D.'s own rhymes smoothly straddle that fine line between healthy braggadocio and low-grade megalomania." That was saying a lot for a hard-core rap artist at the time, as many artists of the genre were notorious for not recognizing that fine line, and more for boldly ignoring it.

As if his influence wasn't spread far enough, Dupri wanted to make an accompanying movie for his record, called *Jermaine Dupri Presents: The City of 1472*. Dupri said it was like a hip-hop version of *The Wizard of Oz*, starring himself as the Wizard. He said people would come to his city to make things happen for them in their lives. He likened the city to his real work with artists, his habit for success, and how that seemed to put him in his own world, separate from the rest.

At 26, Dupri maintained that *Jermaine Dupri Presents: Life in 1472* would be his first and last release as a performer. Production is where he wanted to stay, but not because he felt his talents as an MC were at all second rate. "If I was to let producing go and be a full-fledged rapper, I would be one of the best rappers in the game," he told *Rolling Stone*'s Mark Binelli in 1998. "I would be one of them rappers that y'all keep talking about, like Jay-Z, Method Man, Nas. I would be up in that range." And in an uncharacteristically humble comment to *Jet*, Dupri said, "I don't consider myself a star. I create stars."

Selected discography

Jermaine Dupri Presents: Life in 1472, So So Def/Columbia, 1998.

Sources

Periodicals

Rolling Stone, August 6, 1998; December 24, 1998.
The Village Voice, July 28, 1998.
Time, July 20, 1998.
Jet, July 13, 1998.

Online

"Jermaine Dupri," *All-Media Guide*, http://www.allmusic.com (January 5, 1999).

Additional information was provided by Columbia publicity materials, 1999.

—Brenna Sanchez

Antonin Dvorak

Composer

Corbis. Reproduced by permission.

Considered the greatest composer that the Czech nation ever produced, Antonin Dvorak wrote a career's worth of classical works for orchestra, symphony, and choir that survive as some of the most majestic and acclaimed works of nineteenth-century Romantic music. Dvorak's most lasting legacy to musical history, however, is the way in which he infused his work with melodies and elements from Bohemian folk tunes, Gypsy rhythms, and even African-American spirituals. The freshness of spirit and sense of delight that are hallmarks of Dvorak's music, according to many scholars, are considered emblematic of the composer's pleasant, unassuming personality and lifelong devotion to both family and a beloved home in the Czech countryside.

Dvorak was born in Nelahozeves, Bohemia in 1841, a village about 45 miles north of Prague. He was the first of eight children born to Frantisek Dvorak, a second-generation butcher who also ran a local drinking establishment. The elder Dvorak was musically inclined and proficient on the zither and violin, thus little Antonin was exposed to music at an early age, and was reportedly a keen participant in the traditional folk dances that were an integral part of village social life. As a child, Dvorak sang in the church choir and was a student at the village school. The local organist, a man named Josef Spitz, taught Dvorak the violin, and his gifts gained him a place as a junior member Nelahozeves's village band.

Around the age of eleven Dvorak was sent to another town to learn the butcher's trade. The following year, in 1853, he arrived in the town of Zlonice to study German—Bohemia was part of the Austro-Hungarian Empire, and German was the language of government, trade, and commerce. Dvorak was fortunate enough to find a language teacher, Antonin Liehmann, who was also an accomplished musician, and Liehmann began training him on the organ, piano, and viola; he also gave him a solid grounding in musical theory. But understandably, the youth was not learning a great deal of German, and so Dvorak's father, still convinced of his son's destiny as a butcher and tavern keeper, sent him to a more rigorous school. He returned to Zlonice upon completion, and with Liehmann's help convinced his father to send him to Prague for further musical study. An uncle offered to pay the tuition.

Gained Early Renown in Prague

At the age of 16, Dvorak entered Prague's Organ School. He graduated two years later in 1859. He began playing in local ensembles in Prague, but was too poor to buy musical scores; he did not even have his own piano and spent a great deal of time in a friend's quarters.

Born September 8, 1841, in Nelahozeves, Bohemia (now Czech Republic); died May 1, 1904, in Prague; son of Frantisek (a butcher and innkeeper) and Anna Zdenek Dvorak; married Anna Cermakova, November, 1873; children: Otakar, Otilie Suk, Aloisie, Anna, Antonin, Magda. Education: Prague Organ School, 1857-59.

Violinist and viola player in National Opera Orchestra of Prague, 1862-71; wrote first symphony, 1865; private music teacher in Prague, 1861-1878; organist at St. Adalbert's, Prague, 1874; professor of composition, Prague Conservatory, 1891, and director, 1901-04; National Conservatory of Music, New York City, director, 1892-95.

Awards: Prizewinner in Austrian State Stipendium competition, 1874, 1876, and 1877; Order of the Iron Crown, Austro-Hungarian empire, 1889; elected member of Czech Academy of Sciences and Arts, 1890; honorary doctorates from Prague University, Cambridge University, 1891; first musician to be named to the Austrian House of Lords, 1901.

In 1862 he began playing in a small orchestra which evolved into the Provisional Theatre Orchestra. Dvorak became its principal violinist, but also played the viola over the next decade for this leading Prague ensemble. In 1866 Bedrich Smetana, considered the first great composer to emerge from Bohemia, became the orchestra's conductor as well as a mentor to Dvorak, encouraging him to write music based on traditional folk tunes.

During the 1860s Dvorak played in cafes and theaters, and also taught music privately. He wrote his first symphony, *No. 1 in C Minor, The Bells of Zlonice,* in 1865, and also began to write for the opera. Much of this early work was reminiscent of the heavy, somber compositions of Richard Wagner and Johannes Brahms, the most famous living German composers of this era. But it was an 1872 setback that forced Dvorak to re-examine his inspirations: with the Prague Philharmonic, Smetana conducted the overture for an opera Dvorak had written, but *King and Charcoal Burner* was deemed too complicated for staging. Depressed, Dvorak destroyed some of his older compositions, but in the end rewrote *King and Charcoal Burner* and used far more Bohemian melodies and themes. It debuted successfully in Prague in November of 1874.

In 1873 Dvorak took a post as the organist at St. Adalbert's in Prague. He also married Anna Cermakova, one of his former students, that same year. His first true success also came in 1873 when a choral work, *Heirs to the White Mountain,* was enthusiastically received at its initial performance in March. He had based the work on a patriotic poem recalling a Czech defeat in 1620. The following year, with a newfound sense of confidence in his abilities, Dvorak entered the Austrian State Stipendium competition. Brahms sat on its jury, and was greatly impressed by the young Czech and his ability to integrate Bohemian folk melodies into a serious classical opus. Dvorak was awarded a respectable prize that year, and Brahms helped him find a publisher for his music.

In 1878 the music for Dvorak's *Slavonic Dances* was published and these eight Bohemian folk melodies, based on the polka and similar dances from his native area, were immediately praised for their originality. The spirit of the work also fit well with the emergence of Czech nationalist sentiment in this era, as its people struggled to maintain an identity separate from the Empire. *Slavonic Dances* were originally written as a piano work, but Dvorak later orchestrated them; their first public performances took place the following year in Hamburg, Germany and Nice, France. The continued good reception that greeted performances across Europe brought the composer great acclaim. Dvorak finally began to gain some measure of financial stability, and was able to purchase a home for his growing family in the Czech countryside at Vysoka.

In 1877, one of the Dvorak's children died in infancy, and in grief Dvorak—a devout Roman Catholic—he began writing his *Stabat Mater.* This was a Latin poem from the early 14th century that several other well-known composers had also set to music. Dvorak's version was first performed in 1880, and its debut in England nearly three yeas later marked the beginning of Dvorak's successful liaison with British audiences and the London Philharmonic. His works became extremely popular there, and Dvorak frequently sailed there to debut new works.

A Staunch Nationalist

Dvorak continued to write operas based on Czech lore. *The Jacobin* and *Dimitrij,* both of which emerged during the 1880s, were well received. *Kate and the Devil* (1898) won him a prize of two thousand kroner from the Czech Academy of Sciences and Arts. *The Cunning Peasant* (1877) enjoyed numerous performances across Europe over the course of several years, though for some years a debut in Vienna—the center of the opera world—was stymied by nationalist sentiment inside the Austro-Hungarian Empire. Officials at the Vienna Opera had declined to stage Dvorak's Czech operas, and requested that he write a German-language work. He balked at the insult, and felt to do so would be a betrayal of his Czech pride. Yet Dvorak continued to enjoy great success abroad during the 1880s. His cantata, *The Spectre's Bride,* was well received at its debut in 1884, though the composer often dreaded the task of conducting this four-to-five hour performance himself. *St. Ludmilla* was a similar choral work that debuted in London in 1886 with a 350-member choir, based on the Slavic saint and her conversion to Christianity.

In 1891 Dvorak became a professor of composition at the Prague Conservatory, but left the following year when he was hired by the National Conservatory of Music in Manhattan to serve as its director. His generous $15,000 a year salary was paid by Jeanette Thurber, one of the school's founders, but her family fortune soon declined as a result of Wall Street financial crises, and she grew arrears in his salary. At the conservatory, he was expected to take a light teaching load and serve as a composer in residence. During this time he became greatly enamored of African-American and Native American music, and began writing his best known work, *Symphony from the New World, No. 9 in E Minor,* during this period. First performed at Carnegie Hall in December of 1893 by the New York Philharmonic, it made its European debut—conducted by Dvorak during a trip home—in October of 1894 in Prague at its National Theater.

Died in Poverty

In parts of *Symphony from the New World* can be heard melodies Dvorak borrowed from indigenous American sources, which fascinated him as much as the rustic peasant dances of his native Bohemia once had. "Fierce debate raged about whether Dvorak had used Negro and American Indian tunes as the basis for this most loved of symphonies, or whether it was a Czech work that had captured the spirit of American national melodies," noted Jeremy Nicholas in *The Classic FM Guide to Classical Music.* "A century later it seems hugely unimportant when we are swept along with Dvorak's masterly orchestration and his unforgettable themes." Nicholas also noted that in England a few bars from Dvorak's *No. 9* became indelibly associated with a brand of brown bread after it they were used in a memorable television advertisement.

From 1892 to 1895 Dvorak lived on E. 17th Street in New York City, and spent summers in Iowa in a small town founded by Bohemian immigrants called Spillville. He also traveled to the Chicago World Exhibition in 1893, and conducted an orchestra there on Czech Day. But he was homesick for the Bohemian countryside, the house in Vysoka, and his family so despite the debt still owed him by Thurber, he ended his ties with the Conservatory in 1895 and returned home.

Dvorak returned to his professorship at Prague Conservatory, and became its director in 1901. That same year he was honored in his homeland on the occasion of his sixtieth birthday, and became the first musician ever to be named to the Austrian House of Lords. He devoted his last years to working on an opera, *Armida,* but despite his international recognition he had achieved, he lived in relative poverty as a result of unfavorable contracts with his music publishers. The composer was diagnosed with a kidney disease and contracted influenza after *Armida*'s first ill-fated performance. He died several weeks later on May 1, 1904. A national day of mourning was declared, and Dvorak was honored with a burial in Vysehrad Cemetery, where many prominent Czechs are also buried.

Selected discography

Dvorak: No. 1 in C Minor, The Bells of Zionice, with Berliner Staatskapelle, Berlin Classics, 1979.

Dvorak: Stabat Mater, Psalm 149/Jiri Belohlavek and the Czech Philharmonic Orchestra, Chandos, 1991.

Dvorak: The Greatest Hits, Reference Gold, 1993.

Dvorak: Overtures, Vanda, Carnival, Othello, My Home, Naxos, 1994.

Dvorak: Symphony from the New World, No. 9 in E Minor, BBC Radio, 1995.

Dvorak: Opera Overtures and Preludes/Robert Slankovsky, Marco Polo, 1996.

Slavonic Dances/Berliner Philharmonic conducted by Lorin Maazel, EMI Classics, 1997.

Dvorak: Rusalka/Mackerras, Fleming, Heppner, et al., London/ Decca, 1998.

Dvorak: Slavonic Dances Op. 46 & 72/Yoel Levi, Atlanta Symphony Orchestra, Telarc, 1999.

Sources

Books

Nicholas, Jeremy, *The Classic FM Guide to Classical Music,* Pavilion, 1997.

Sadie, Stanley, editor, *The New Grove Dictionary of Music and Musicians,* Macmillan, 1980.

Soleil, Jean-Jacques, and Guy Lelong, *Musical Masterpieces,* Chambers, 1991.

Periodicals

American Record Guide, September/October 1996, p. 115;
September/October 1998, pp. 83-101.

—*Carol Brennan*

Sleepy John Estes

Country blues singer

Sleepy John Estes was one of the most individual of all recorded blues singers. He sang with phrasing that fairly dripped with expressiveness in a high crying tone that seemed often like he was speaking to the listener. The songs he wrote were well suited to this treatment, dealing frequently with his and his neighbors' lives in Brownsville, Tennessee. Estes recorded from the late 1920s through the 1930s when he was one of the most popular artists on the Decca label, until 1941 when his brand of country blues, the down-home music of rural blacks, had become something of an anachronism. His discovery by the fold revivalists of the 1960s rescued him from poverty and gave him a second musical career that lasted nearly 15 years, during which he again became one of the most popular and best-loved bluesmen.

John Adam Estes was born near Ripley, Tennessee on January 25, 1904. His parents were sharecroppers who had sixteen children. Like his brothers and sisters, Estes grew up working his parents' fields. There was little time for school. The most traumatic event of his childhood occurred during a baseball game when a stone struck him in the eye. He lost his vision completely in one eye and his other grew worse and worse until, by his fifties, he was left completely blind. Some say his poor eyesight gave him the appearance that led his friends to nickname him "Sleepy;" others say it was just his penchant for falling asleep on the bandstand during his gigs.

Estes' father, who played guitar, was probably the first musician he ever heard. His father showed Estes a few chords, let him play his guitar occasionally, and taught him his first song, a ditty called "Chocolate Drop." Before long Estes had built his own cigar-box instruments on which he practiced. In 1915 the Estes family moved to Brownsville where John hooked up with David Campbell, a local musician who showed him a little more about playing the guitar. Before long Estes was playing local fish fries, frolics, and house parties in the area. A decisive influence was another local musician, Hambone Willie Newbern. Newbern has won a minor place in blues history as the composer of "Roll and Tumble," which became a blues standard eventually recorded by postwar Chicago artists such as Baby Face Leroy and Muddy Waters, and even the British rock group Cream. Newbern took Estes under his wing and before long they were performing together up and down the Mississippi, hitting points as far-flung as Como, Mississippi, down in the Delta.

Despite all his blues schooling, Estes' guitar playing remained rudimentary at best. It never reached the expressiveness, invention, or power of Charlie Patton, Robert Johnson, or Bukka White. It was merely a convenient vehicle to accompany his singing. But it was his singing that propelled his career. Estes' voice produced a high, plaintive cry that was ageless—it could have been a decrepit old man singing or a teen whose voice had not yet broken. It was a wail, full of pain and pathos. Its sound alone articulated everything the blues represented: loss, despair, loneliness, hurt.

By 1919 he was a popular performer around Brownsville. Reason enough, when his father passed away, for Estes to walk away from the farming he despised. Though Estes wasn't a particularly strong instrumentalist, he managed to surround himself with others who were. He met James "Yank" Rachell around 1920 when he heard another musician was playing a frolic he had expected to be his. His intention was to run off the newcomer. Instead he liked what he heard, and he and Rachell teamed up and started playing square dances and house parties around town, for whites and blacks alike. Rachell had been playing guitar when Estes first heard him, but he soon switched to his second instrument, mandolin.

Later in the 1920s Estes met harmonica player Hammie Nixon, an important figure in the development of blues harmonica. Nixon learned to play from Noah Lewis, the first great modern harp player, and went on to teach James "Sonny Boy" Williamson, one of the first to adapt the harp to urban blues. Estes and Nixon traveled and played together occasionally in the early and mid-

For the Record . . .

Born John Adams Estes, January 25, 1904, in Ripley, TN; one of about sixteen children; parents were poor sharecroppers; married with five children; died June 5, 1977.

Learned guitar from street musicians in Brownsville, in particular David Campbell and Hambone Willie Newbern; played parties and other occasions in and around Brownsville with mandolinist James "Yank" Rachell, harmonica player Hammie Nixon, and guitarist Son Bonds; teamed up with Yank Rachell and Jab Jones as the Three J's Jug Band around 1928; cut first records with Rachell and Jones for Victor, 1929; recorded for Decca and Bluebird, 1934, 1937, 1938, 1941; toured with the Rabbit Foot Minstrels, 1939; recorded or auditioned for Sun Records, 1948; rediscovered by filmmaker David Blumenthal, 1962; played numerous concerts and festivals throughout the 1960s and 1970s, in particular the 1964 Newport Folk Festival; appeared in two films, David Blumenthal's *Citizen South, Citizen North*, 1962, and Samuel Charters's *The Blues*, 1963; continued recording until his death in 1977.

1920s. Around the same time Estes met Son Bonds, a Brownsville guitarist. Estes would use these three men on virtually all of his records, up into the late 1960s in the case of Nixon and Rachell.

Every autumn Estes made it a point to play in Memphis, when the city was overflowing with money from the harvest. On one trip, he and Rachell teamed up with Jab Jones, an occasional member of the Memphis Jug Band, to cash themselves in on the jug band fad. They formed the Three J's Jug Band, with Estes singing and playing guitar, Rachell on mandolin, and Jones blowing jug. They were good enough to catch the attention of Jim Jackson, one of the most popular musicians in Memphis. Jackson offered to act as their agent around Memphis. For reasons known only to them—perhaps they were worried that Jackson would cheat them—they refused the offer, preferring to fend for themselves.

When the jug craze petered out toward the end of the 1920s, Jones switched back to his first instrument, piano. That was how they recorded at Estes' first session in 1929 with the Victor label. The music they made is some of the most unique and interesting in country blues. Jones' deft piano provided the foundation of the music. Rachell soared above on his mandolin, with Estes in between with his keening voice and solid double-time strumming on guitar. It was, in the words of Don Kent's liner notes to *I Ain't Gonna Be Worried No More*, "a session of masterpieces." It produced a cover of a blues chestnut, "Milk Cow Blues," but Estes version never got around to mentioning the cow! It produced an Estes original, "Street Car Blues," possibly the only blues ever written on the subject. Estes' version of Newbern's "Roll and Tumble," entitled "The Girl I Love She Got Long Curly Hair," was Estes' first single and turned out to be one of his most popular as well. The three musicians were reportedly paid $300 each for the session, a royal sum at the time for most any musician. They pocketed the cash and headed straight to the notorious river town, West Helena, Arkansas, where they quickly squandered all of it on drinking, gambling, and general carousing. Rachell had to pawn his watch to get back to Brownsville.

Estes' records were popular and their sales were good, at least until the Depression deepened and the poor could no longer afford luxuries like phonograph records. Estes made his base in Brownsville where he continued to live and perform, while making regular sorties into Arkansas and Missouri. He went up to Chicago occasionally as well and even claimed to have played for gangster Al Capone, who Estes said was crazy about blues. Despite the popularity of his 1929 records, Estes was not able to record again during the first three years of the 1930s. When he heard that Nixon and Son Bonds had just returned from recording in Chicago, he persuaded Nixon to return to the Windy City and set up a session for him. Finally, in 1934 Estes returned to the studio with Hammie Nixon to record for the Decca label. At the session Estes cut "Someday Baby" and "Drop Down Mama," songs that went on to become blues standards, recorded by the likes of Big Joe Williams, Big Maceo, Big Boy Crudup, and Muddy Waters.

After the 1934 session Estes moved to Chicago where he lived for most of the 1930s. His popularity grew. In 1937 his photo graced the cover of Decca's race record catalog. At his next sessions Estes' song-writing style, in which he would sing directly of his own life and that of his Brownsville friends and neighbors, began to take shape. In 1937 he recorded "Floating Bridge," about being swept off a bridge by a raging river and rescued at the last minute by Hammie Nixon. In 1938 he wrote "Fire Department Blues" about his neighbor Martha Hardin. "She's a hard-working woman, her salary is very small/Then when she pay up her house rent, that don't leave anything for insurance at all/Now I wrote Martha a letter, five days later it returned back to me/You know little Martha's house done burned down, she done moved over Bedford Street."

His last session in 1941 saw his musical chronicle of Brownsville in full flower. He sang about a local lawyer, Mr. Clark, who worked as hard for the poor who couldn't pay as much as for the rich who could. He sang about little Laura whose sexual fantasies had a way of all coming true. And he sang about how machines were pushing sharecroppers off the land around town.

That session was Estes' last for some 20 years. Times were changing, not only down on the farm, but in music too. By the 1940s Estes was a vestige of a music—the pure country blues—that had all but died out and been replaced by more sophisticated blues, the so-called "urban blues." Estes disappeared back down into Tennessee. He and Hammie Nixon reportedly made a trip to Memphis to record for Sam Phillips Sun label in 1948, but little came of it.

Sleepy John Estes was all but forgotten until the folk revivalists of the 1950s set out to track down as many of the old recording artists as they could find. Unfortunately, inaccurate rumors about Estes abounded. In his biography, *Big Bill Blues*, Big Bill Broonzy wrote that as a child he had seen Estes play at a railroad camp. Estes was 20 years older than he was, Broonzy wrote, and long dead. Imagine the surprise when filmmaker David Blumenthal finally found Estes, tracked down on a tip from Big Joe Williams via Memphis Slim. He looked like a man in his seventies, but he was only 58—eleven years *younger* than Broonzy! He was found in a ramshackle shack on an abandoned farm with his wife and five children, "living in harsh poverty that was deeply disturbing to see," wrote Samuel Charters in *Sweeter Than The Showers Of Rain*.

Estes' career somehow picked up where it had left off. Producer Bob Koester took over, setting up appearances at festivals. The most important was the 1964 Newport Folk Festival, when he was reintroduced to the world. He went on to tour Europe twice in 1964 and 1968 with the American Folk Blues Festival. He was a celebrated guest at the Ann Arbor Blues Festival in 1969. And in November, 1974 he became the first country bluesman to perform in Japan. Estes made records regularly, up to his death practically, the best being three he did for the Delmark label in Chicago. He frequently worked with his old partners, Yank Rachell and Hammie Nixon, in the 1960s. Sleepy John Estes died on June 5, 1977.

Selected discography

I Ain't Gonna Be Worried No More, Yazoo.
First Recordings, JSP.
1935-1938, Black & Blue.
The Legend of Sleepy John Estes, Delmark.
Broke & Hungry, Delmark.
Brownsville Blues, Delmark.

Sources

Books

Charters, Samuel, *Sweeter Than The Showers Of Rain*, Oak Publications, 1977.
Cohn, Lawrence, editor, *Nothing But The Blues*, Abbeville Press, 1993.
Davis, Francis, *The History of the Blues*, 1995.
Harris, Sheldon, *Blues Who's Who*, Arlington House, 1979.

Online

http://www.blueflamecafe.com/.

Additional information provided by liner notes from Kent, Don, *I Ain't Gonna Be Worried No More*.

—Gerald E. Brennan

Faith Evans

Singer

For a woman who was perhaps known more for being the wife of the infamous rapper, the late Notorious B.I.G., Faith Evans managed to become a musical success in her own right. Evans was born in Lakeland, Florida to an Italian musician father, Richard Swain, who left her before she was born, and an African-American, blues-singing mother, Helene Evans. Raised by her mother and grandparents in Newark, New Jersey, Evans got her start singing in the church. At age four, she caught the attention of the congregation of the Emmanuel Baptist Church in Newark when she sang "Let the Sunshine In."

Her grandparents' influence served her well—Evans was an honor student at University High School, appeared in musicals there, and was named Miss New Jersey Fashion Teen. "I was raised in a very, very Christian home," Evans told *i-D* magazine in a 1998 interview. "It was church, school, church, school. I could hardly go to the corner of my block. It was strict." At 18, she won a scholarship to Fordham University in New York City to major in marketing. After a year, she left to have her first child, a daughter, Chyna, fathered by producer Kiyamma Griffin. She then moved to Los Angeles to pursue her singing career, and did so with her mother's blessing. "I felt she could always go back to school," Helene Evans told *People* in 1998. "Because her mind wasn't going to be there. It was going to be on her music." She was in LA doing backup vocals and working with Al B. Sure!, Mary J. Blige and Pebbles when she caught the ear of famed R&B producer Sean "Puffy" Combs, a.k.a. Puff Daddy. It's said that when he first heard Evans sing, he described her voice as feeling "like rain." He signed her to his label, Bad Boy, in 1994 as the label's first female artist.

Evans met then-up-an-coming gangsta rapper Christopher Wallace, a.k.a. Notorious B.I.G., and even better known as Biggie Smalls, at a photo shoot in August, 1994. Both barely 21, they married nine days later. "He was charming and funny," Evans told *People* in 1998. "We both said 'I want to marry you,' and did it." And from that moment on, the two were plagued by controversy. First, there was the misconception that Evans rode her husband's coattails to fame. In truth, she'd already signed the Bad Boy record deal, but her debut, *Faith* , was released months after his in 1995. Then, Wallace's flaunted infidelities with rapper Lil' Kim, and rumors—which Evans maintained were false—of romance between Evans and rapper Tupac Shakur, which Shakur made claims to on an album. "He was a good person but definitely not ready for marriage," Evans said in the same *People* interview. "I tried my best to be a good wife for as long as I could take the disrespect."

Evans' debut met critical success. She was likened to Minnie Riperton and Chaka Khan. Her influences were gospel singers like Shirley Murdock and Karen Clark-Sheard of the Clark Sisters. "Where some of R&B's male players sound like medieval courtiers with their carefully scripted protestations of adoration," *i-D* magazine wrote in 1998, "Faith's generous and easy meditations of love feel unconditional." In 1995, *Faith* went platinum.

In 1996, Evans and Wallace split up. Early in 1997, he was gunned down in Las Vegas drive-by shooting. Ironically, the two had seen each other earlier that same night, but hadn't spoken. The last time they did speak was on the telephone and that ended with the two hanging up on each other. The next time she saw him, it was to identify his body at the morgue. "I don't even remember my reaction," Evans told *People* of the killing. "It was just blank. But I pulled it together and dealt with it with dignity." Although she had three tracks completed for her follow-up release at the time of Wallace's death, she was too burdened by estate and legal issues, as well as giving birth to the couple's son, Christopher Jr., to spend any time in the studio. At age 24, the newly widowed mother of two had her own, and her late husband's, business to attend to.

Evans' next musical project turned out to be a collaboration between herself, Combs, and the group 112, also

Born 1973 (in Lakeland, FL); daughter of Helene Evans and Richard Swain, raised in Newark, NJ; married rapper Christopher Wallace, a.k.a. Biggie Smalls or Notorious B.I.G., August 1995; widowed March 1997; children: Chyna, born 1992, Christopher Jr.(with Biggie Smalls), and Joshua born 1998. *Education:* Attended Fordham University in NY.

Moved to Los Angeles, 1992, to pursue singing career; signed by Sean "Puffy" Combs' record label, Bad Boy Entertainment, 1994; released debut, *Faith,* 1995; released *Keep the Faith,* 1998.

Awards: Platinum certification for *Faith,* 1996; Grammy award for "I'll Be Missing You," with Combs and 112, 1997.

Addresses: *Record company*—Bad Boy Entertainment, 8 W. 19th St., 9th floor, New York, NY 10011-4206.

on Bad Boy. It was a multi-million selling tribute to Notorious B.I.G. called "I'll Be Missing You." The single topped *Billboard's* Hot 100 and R&B charts and won the 1997 Grammy award for best rap performance by a duo or group.

By the fall of 1998, "Rap's most famous widow," as she was called by *Ebony,* was ready to release her second album. *Keep the Faith* was released in October and met with mostly critical success. *Newsweek's* Allison Samuels called it a "lush mixture of thoughtful love songs and boogie downbeats. Evans' edgy churchchoir voice and soulful delivery make it clear she was born to sing the blues." And Lynn Norment of *Ebony* was just as positive: "Evans continues to let her honey-coated voice and

hear-felt lyrics tell her stories of love and loss and triumph over heartache and adversity." Craig Seymour's 1998 review of *Keep the Faith* for the *Village Voice* was glowing, as well. "Faith's airy yet strong soprano sounds like the dreams you believe in standing at the altar, committing yourself before God," although he did go on to say that her self-written songs from her first album suited her voice better.

"Faith Evans is about as close as these letters are pressed together to breaking bad as the next really big thing in R&B and pop," wrote Chuck Taylor for *Billboard* in 1999. And that seemed to echo industry sentiment from all around—Puff Daddy had given her a strong start, but Faith Evans seemed primed to blaze her own trail.

Selected discography

Faith, Bad Boy, 1995.
Keep the Faith, Bad Boy, 1998.

Sources

Periodicals

Billboard, October 3, 1998; November 7, 1998; January 16, 1999.
Ebony, March 1998; January 1999.
i-D Magazine, December 1998.
Newsweek, November 9, 1998.
People, October 26, 1998; November 16, 1998.
Time, November 8, 1998.
Village Voice, December 1, 1998.

Online

"Faith Evans," *All-Media Guide,* http://www.allmusic.com (January 5, 1999).

—Brenna Sanchez

Milton Gabler

Producer, author

Archive Photos, Inc. Reproduced by permission.

Music surrounds people everyday—in cars, elevators, grocery stores, doctor offices, and homes. But do people listen or just hear this music? Listening to music is a record producer's job, and one of the most successful, but unknown record producers was Milt Gabler. In 1938, Gabler founded Commodore, the first independent jazz record label. Gabler once said, "Just as New Orleans was the cradle of jazz, Commodore Records was the iron lung." And at the helm of this iron lung was Gabler, a man with a sharp ear for talent who really *listened* to music, and who the *Encyclopedia of Rock* called, "one of the record industry's unsung greats."

Milton (Milt) Gabler was born on May 20, 1911 in Harlem, New York. Gabler's Austrian born father owned the Commodore Radio Corporation, a popular radio and speaker supply store. In 1924 Gabler began working at the store while still in high school. One day, to get people's attention, he hooked up a loudspeaker over the shop's door and tuned in a radio station. Customers hearing the music would stop at the store and ask Gabler if he sold records. After having to explain to one too many customers that the shop only carried radios and speaker supplies, Gabler finally convinced his father to begin selling records. Gabler told Dan Morgenstern in *Reading Jazz* that his father told him to flip open the yellow pages and call the "phonograph record companies," which he did, ordering, as he put it, "whatever was coming out." Jazz, though, was what truly interested Gabler.

By 1934, the now renamed store—the Commodore Music Shop—became as *High Fidelity*'s Michael Ullman stated, "the country's most important source of Jazz 78s and a meeting ground for fans and musicians." As shop manager Jack Crystal told Nat Hentoff in *Listen to the Stories*, the store also became "a nondescript shrine for jazz buffs from everywhere." What brought these jazz buffs into the store was the music—music hand selected by Gabler himself—even though, as Hentoff says, "[Gabler] was not a musician, but years of listening had taught him the difference between hot and hokum."

Also in 1934, Gabler began something new. He bought boxes of out-of-print jazz recordings from major record companies who had no plans to re-release them. Therefore Gabler, by selling these recordings at his store, became the first person to sell reissued records. However, this was not his only "first." Gabler was the first to print the names of all participating musicians on a jazz record, thus giving recognition to the all too often unnamed musicians. Gabler compiled these lists himself and could easily name the musicians because, as he told Morgenstern, "You recognize a man by the tone of

For the Record . . .

Born Milton Gabler on May 20, 1911, (in Harlem, NY); son of an American mother and Austrian father who owned a radio supply store. *Education:* attended City College New York, NY for two years.

While still in high school, worked at Commodore Radio Corporation, his father's store; after many customer requests for records, founded the Commodore Music Shop in 1926; reissued out-of-print jazz records in 1934; co-founded United Hot Clubs of America (UHCA), the first mail-order record label; published *Hot Discography*, a jazz music collector's reference list; founded Commodore, first independent jazz record label and began producing records including early albums for jazz greats Jelly Roll Morton, Louis Jordon, and Billie Holiday, in 1938; hired by Decca Records in 1941; as Vice-President of Decca, produced a variety of records for jazz, country, and rock performers such as Ella Fitzgerald, Louie Armstrong, Duke Ellington, and Bill Haley and the Comets; retired in 1971; founded the National Academy of Recording Arts and Sciences (NARAS).

Awards: elected into the Rock and Roll Hall of Fame, 1993.

Address: Home—New York, NY.

his voice. You can recognize a musician by the way he blows his notes." Gabler eventually collected these lists into *Hot Discography*, a reference book of jazz musicians and recordings. Another Gabler first was the co-founding of the United Hot Clubs of America (UHCA), the first mail-order record label. In 1938, after moving the Commodore Music Shop closer to New York City's nightclubs, Gabler began producing jazz records.

Produced Jazz Stars

Over the next 12 years, Gabler produced many great jazz records. His first major success was the legendary jazz singer Billie Holiday's protest song, "Strange Fruit." This song was controversial, and according to Ullman, "many great sessions came to Gabler because of his reputation and daring." Columbia Records, Holiday's record company, had refused to record the song because it told the horrible truth about the commonplace lynchings in the South during the 1940s. Gabler's proved his daring reputation by recording "Strange Fruit" which became Commodore's first big hit.

Throughout the late 1930s and 1940s, success continued for Gabler. The *New Yorker*'s Whitney Balliett wrote that he produced "almost ninety Commodore dates, using over a hundred and fifty musicians and singers." Jazz singers like Holiday and swing musicians like Jelly Roll Morton, pianists like Mel Powell and Joe Sullivan, and many others loved to work with Gabler. Why? One musician, as quoted by Balliett, said, "A ray comesout of him [Gabler]. You can't help doing something the way he wants. Here is this guy, can't read a note of music and he practically tells you what register you're going to play in just by the position of your head." Thus, the musicians trusted Gabler—the non-musician with a gifted ear.

Gabler's Commodore recording sessions, according to the *Boston Globe*'s Bob Blumenthal, fell into three types. The first, "typified the Commodore sound Nicksieland jazz." This sound was made popular by Eddie Condon—a rhythm guitarist whose "propulsive time, command of the chord changes, and catalytic impact on his [band] mates" drove the Chicago jazz sound. However, Condon's music, Blumenthal continued, was not "always viewed favorably by later generations of listeners—in part because most of the musicians were white." The second type of Gabler's Commodore recording sessions was the solo piano sessions. Gabler, according to Ullman, "was lucky with pianists" and he recorded many of them including the "greatest swing pianist of them all, Art Tatum." The third type of session, as categorized by Blumenthal was the "streamlined combos, usually involving black musicians" including electric guitarist Eddie Durham, saxophonist Leon (Chu) Berry, and trumpeters Roy Eldridge and Hot Lips Page.

Rocked Around the Clock

Gabler's success was not unnoticed by the press. In the early 1940s, *Life* not only featured one of Gabler's recording sessions with Paul Whiteman's jazz band, Teagarden, but also included Gabler's Top 30 list of jazz collectors' must-have records. Gabler's success was also picked up by radio stations—who started buying Gabler's records—and by major record labels. In 1941 Decca Records hired Gabler, although he continued to produce records for Commodore until 1950. However, as Blumenthal wrote, "he was determined to avoid [recording] conflicts with Decca."   Gabler even went so far as to avoid recording major jazz artists on smaller independent labels

Gabler's success continued at Decca and in 1954, he signed rock and roll pioneers Bill Haley and the Comets. That year, Gabler produced Haley and the Comets' smash hit, "Rock Around the Clock". Yet, Gabler said that he had done nothing new for Haley. Gabler told *Rolling Stone* that "all the tricks I used [ten years earlier] with Louis Jordon, I used with Bill Haley. The only difference between [them] was the way we did the rhythm. On Jordon, we used a perfectly balanced rhythm section from the swing era . but on rock and roll, what Bill did, he had the heavy back beat."

Gabler retired from Decca Records in 1971. He did not, however, relax: he founded the National Academy of Recording Arts and Sciences (NARAS) which honors all types of musicians and singers each February with Grammy Awards. Moreover, in 1991, Gabler finally received public recognition when he was inducted into the Rock and Roll Hall of Fame.

Selected writings

Hot Discography, 1938.

Selected discography

"Strange Fruit," Billie Holiday, 1939.
"Rock Around the Clock," Bill Haley and the Comets, 1954.

Sources

Books

ASCAP Biographical Dictionary, 4th ed., 1980.
Gottlieb, Robert, Editor. *Reading Jazz: A Gathering of Autobiography, Reportage, and Criticism from 1919 to Now*, Pantheon Books, 1996.
Hardy, Phil and Dave Laing. *Encyclopedia of Rock*, Shirmer Books.
Hentoff, Nat. *Listen to the Stories*, HarperCollins, 1995.

Periodicals

Boston Globe, February 11, 1990.
High Fidelity, January, 1989.
New Yorker, November 26, 1990.
Rolling Stone, February 4, 1991.

—*Anna Schwalboski*

Garbage

Alternative pop band

When a group of three full-time producers and part-time musicians decided to find a singer and make a record, the name "Garbage" had, unbelievably, not yet been used by any other band with a wry sense of humor. The singer they found was a Scottish woman with the equally unlikely name of Shirley, and their 1995 debut sold a million copies in its first year and earned the band a Grammy nomination for Best New Artist. Jason Cohen, writing in *Rolling Stone,* called Garbage's genesis "a tale of friendship, experimentation, and a fateful symbiosis of music and personalities," and Shirley Manson concurred. "If I wasn't in this band, I would go, `Yeah, right, three producers and a girl,'" Manson told Cohen. "But we found a chemistry that I don't think you can predetermine. It was just absolute luck."

"Manson's stardusted glamour seemed out of place when Garbage arrived in 1995, but then everything about them did," wrote another *Rolling Stone* scribe, Rob Sheffield. *Newsweek*'s David Gates would liken them to "a self-consciously corrupted `90s version of Fleetwood Mac." The band's origins lie in the Madison,

Corbis View. Reproduced by permission.

Wisconsin warehouse that is home to Smart Studios, a successful enterprise founded in 1984 by Butch Vig and Steve Marker. Vig and Marker had met at Madison's University of Wisconsin, where Vig majored in film but spent a great deal of time composing soundtracks. With another friend, Duke Erikson, Vig had enjoyed minor local success with a band called Spooner. When they disbanded in 1987 after three records, they occasionally played in another group called Firetown, but devoted their time to producing records for other bands.

Discovered Singer on MTV

Vig's star would rise as a producer, especially when a number of bands from America's West Coast like Killdozer and Tad began trekking to Wisconsin to work with him; his resume would eventually include several stellar, platinum-selling alternative records, including Nirvana's *Nevermind*, and *Siamese Dream* from the Smashing Pumpkins. The Vig-Erikson-Marker trio also loved to work on creating barrages of samples and found noise, which they worked into, remixes for the likes of U2 and Nine Inch Nails. Eventually they had so much leftover

material that they finally decided to merge it with their occasional one-night live projects and force a real live pop band into existence. Yet since they all were less than enthusiastic about fronting a band after spending so many years behind the scenes, they knew they would have to find a singer.

One Sunday night in Madison, they saw a video for an obscure Scottish band called Angelfish on MTV's Sunday night alternative video showcase *120 Minutes,* and decided to contact its redheaded singer. They found Shirley Manson, then under contract to Radioactive Records with her band, living in Edinburgh and extended an invitation to audition for them in Madison. "I was in way over my head," Manson recalled to Jancee Dunn in *Rolling Stone* of the first takes she did in their studio. She was nervous and felt inept as a singer, and they were shy. They would leave her in a sound room and go to the mixing consoles on another floor. "And they were like, 'Make up some words,'" Manson said. "I'd never officially written anything with people, so to ask me to ad-lib was a living nightmare."

Unexpected Success

A native of Edinburgh, Manson had dropped out of school at the age of 15 to work in a clothing store. She was a self-described rebel who came of age in the early 1980s and was, as a teen, a huge Siouxsie and the Banshees fan. "At the time, I felt totally inadequate, totally inarticulate," Manson said in another chat with Dunn. "I felt things but couldn't put them into words. Then I heard one of her records, and she was saying it for me." She got involved in music herself when she joined a band simply because she had a crush on its lead singer. She wound up dating him and staying ten years in Goodbye Mr. MacKenzie, a decade that "gave me no satisfaction. Zero," Manson told Dunn. She had little creative input, and relationship with the lead singer soon became a trauma because of his constant infidelity. "It literally broke me," she recalled in *Rolling Stone.*

Manson formed her own band, Angelfish, around 1994, and it was their video for the song "Suffocate Me" and its sole spin on MTV, that put her in touch with the three guys in Madison. Despite the rough beginning, the quartet clicked and Manson began a long and involved process of writing lyrics and recording with her new best friends. Though they often kept the first takes, there were many willful clashes. "That creative tension is ultimately what winds up on the track," Vig told Cohen in *Rolling Stone.* The result was an eponymous pink-covered CD from a group of unknowns with an almost corny name. But *Garbage* contained a passel of songs that became alternative-radio staples throughout 1995 and 1996, including "Stupid Girl," "I'm Only Happy When It Rains," and "Vow." Not surprisingly, the first track was titled "Supervixen," and the redheaded Manson became an object of mass adoration almost overnight.

Garbage's music also earned accolades, despite their lack of pop pretensions. *Rolling Stone*'s Sheffield declared that the band transforms "subcultural energy into pop flash with a fabulously twitchy singer." Cohen declared that Garbage's team of four "have masterminded a confident collection of emotionally sharpshooting songs, a daring record that scrambles postindustrial crunch with New Wave gloss and grand pop payoffs with techno wizardry." Originally, the Scot and the three producers had no plans to take their project live, but found themselves surprised by the album's overwhelming critical and commercial success. When they made the video for "Vow," "we played live, and after the first take, the crew was clapping," Vig told Dunn. Erikson also remembered that day as a turning point: "I don't know that the applause was really ecstatic or anything, but we felt really good about it," he told Dunn.

Version 2.0

Garbage embarked on a heavy tour schedule in support of their debut over the next two years, and wrote new material in their spare time. Manson also returned to Edinburgh and married her longtime boyfriend. In Scotland, as elsewhere, she had become an instantly recognizable semi-celebrity, but in her hometown, as Dunn noted, people leave her alone. "I get a genuine sense that in America, people like to see people do well," Manson told Dunn in *Rolling Stone.* "Where I come from, it's quite the opposite. People think success is vulgar."

After a three-year hiatus, Garbage's much-anticipated follow-up was released, which they impertinently titled *Version 2.0.* It was met with somewhat mixed reviews, but found assured commercial success with alternative-radio-friendly singles like "Push It" and "I Think I'm Paranoid." Again, the producer-majority talents who wrote much of *Version 2.0*'s music infused it with samples borrowed from the Beach Boys to the Beatles to the Pretenders. "They root through goth, techno and hip-hop, swipe whatever they can use and leave the rest on the floor," declared Sheffield.

Though *Time*'s Christopher John Farley found a few tunes structurally "weak," and a reliance on studio wizardry he deemed "at times, overbearing," he conceded that "*Version 2.0* boasts a unique, expansive sound that fills the speakers and the ears. The songs are hormonal yet thoughtful, mostly morose but always energetically so." Though Sheffield also faulted the electronic artistry that made *Version 2.0* pulse, "it's rare to hear a rock record so carefully put together that still sounds so fresh and playful." Manson was again the focus of much of the critical attention. Writing for *Stereo Review,* Brett Milano faulted the singer for her emotional range, which he declared could be characterized by two attitudes: "sexy and sexier." Milano also remarked that "it would be tempting to dismiss Garbage for making pure ear candy, if only the band weren't so good at it."

Village Voice writer Rob Tannenbaum found praise for the singer and her varying persona: "In her cool chrome voice, Manson declares herself to be: a bonfire, a vampire, a demon, an addict, a lunatic, pregnant, angry, not like the other girl, complicated, and `mental.' She nearly distills songwriting to its exhibitionist essence." In the end, Tannenbaum declared that the second record treaded the same ground as the first. "If Garbage were honest, they' call this *Version 1.1* instead of *Version 2.0,* because it's a better rendition of the first record, a classic upgrade rather than a dramatic reinvention."

Full Circle

The band toured for *Version 2.0* throughout 1998, and some wondered how the heavily produced songs on the record would work into live translation. Judy Coleman reviewed a Los Angeles performance for *Spin,* and found it worked well. "Despite the complex beauty of Garbage's textured sounds, this concert made it difficult to deny that rock is the heart and soul of both albums," Coleman declared. "Even the poor sound quality at the Palladium ... could not muddle the undeniably searing riffs of `Push It' and `Stupid Girl.'"

In 1999 the band opened for Alanis Morissette across North America after picking up two Grammy nominations, for best rock album and album of the year. Manson spoke of the new level of celebrity she and her bandmates seemed to have achieved in an interview with *New Musical Express*'s Victoria Segal. Madonna was in the audience at a recent show in New York, for instance, and Siouxsie Sioux sent them note before a London concert that summer. "It was unbelievably, mind-bogglingly thrilling!" Manson told Segal. "I tried to remember what it was like being 14 years old and watching Siouxsie Sioux at Edinburgh Odeon and imagining if someone had come up to me and whispered in my ear, `When you're 30 years old and in a rock 'n' roll band, she's gonna come and see you play."

Selected discography

Garbage, Almo Sounds, 1995.
Version 2.0, Almo Sounds, 1998.

Sources

New Musical Express, July 11, 1998.
Newsweek, June 1, 1998.
Rolling Stone, October 5, 1995; October 17, 1996; November 13, 1997; May 28, 1998.
Spin, September 1998.
Stereo Review, August 1998.
Time, May 25, 1998.
Village Voice, May 19, 1998.

—Carol Brennan

Erroll Garner

Piano, composer

Jazz innovator, pianist, and composer Erroll Garner was a notably distinctive pianist who recorded with Charlie Parker and was one of the most frequently seen jazz musicians on television in the 1950s and 1960s. Although Garner never learned to read music, and taught himself how to play and compose, his unique virtuoso technique attracted many imitators and ardent fans. His technique included a four-beat fixed pulse of blocked chords in the left hand, using wide-spaced voicings similar to swing rhythm-guitar playing, and he often "kicked" the beat in a style similar to a swing drummer. Strong and bouncy left-hand rhythms and beautiful melodies were the trademarks of Garner's music. He is best known as the composer of "Misty," now an American standard featured in the 1971 film *Play Misty for Me,* and his impact as a jazz innovator rivals his legacy as a successful composer. Paul Conley, who wrote and produced a show about Garner for National Public Radio (NPR), described Garner as, "one of the most original, intuitive and exciting pianists to emerge during the modern jazz era." Garner's influences include "novelty rag" musicians from the 1920s such as Zez Confrey, in addition to Pittsburgh native Earl Hines, Count Basie guitarist Freddie Green, Fats Waller, and classical recordings. *Down Beat*'s Ralph J. Gleason wrote in 1995, "It would be hard to pick out 10 jazz pianists today in whose work Garner would not be justified in calling attention to his own influence."

Garner was born Erroll Louis Garner on June 15th, 1921, in Pittsburgh, Pennsylvania. He and his twin brother Ernest were the youngest of six children and were raised in a musical environment. His older brother, Linton, became a noted musical accompanist and pianist. Garner was playing the piano by the age of three, although he never had any formal training throughout his long career. His mother was born in Staunton, Virginia, and graduated from Avery College in Pittsburgh. She had a remarkable contralto voice and sang in a church choir with Garner's father. Garner's father had aspired to be a concert singer, but he suffered from asthma. At bedtime, Garner's mother would play recordings for her children on the Victrola, and the next morning a young Garner would pull himself up on the piano stool and play exactly what he had heard the night before.

A woman named Miss Madge Bowman taught piano to the Garner family, and Garner began taking lessons from her at age six. She gave up on him shortly thereafter when she realized he was playing all of her assignments by ear instead of learning to read notes. Garner's childhood friend, bassist Wyatt "Bull" Ruther, took piano lessons from Garner's sister, and Conley reported that Ruther remembered how easily Garner picked up music at a young age. At age seven, Garner began to play regularly on Pittsburgh's KDKA radio station with a group called The Candy Kids, and by the age of eleven he was playing on Allegheny riverboats. His high school band teacher recognized Garner's innate ability and encouraged him not to take music lessons in order to preserve his unusual talents, and Garner eventually dropped out of high school to play with Leroy Brown's orchestra. He learned to play the "novelty rag" styles of musicians such as Zez Confrey from the 1920s by listening to old 78 records, and this particular style was marked by steady left hand chord rhythms supporting loose, right-hand melodic interpretations.

Garner traveled to New York City in 1939 as an accompanist for night club singer Ann Lewis, and soon returned to serve as a substitute for Art Tatum in Tatum's trio with guitarist "Tiny" Grimes and bassist "Slam" Stewart. Garner stayed on when the trio became the Slam Stewart Trio in 1945. He had developed an extraordinary style that was uniquely his own, and it was around this time in New York City that he met pianists Billy Taylor and George Shearing, and bassist John Levy while playing at Tondelayo's on 52nd Street. He also played at the Melody Bar on Broadway, at the Rendezvous, and at Jimmy's Chicken Shack uptown. While playing in Los Angeles, Garner met and recorded *Cool Blues* with Charlie Parker, which was released in 1947.

Born Erroll Louis Garner on June 15, 1921 (died January 27, 1977), in Pittsburgh, PA; youngest of six children, raised in a musical environment played piano by the age of three, never had any formal training throughout his long career; mother sang in a church choir with Garner's father, who had aspired to be a concert singer, but suffered from asthma as a child; twin brother named Ernest, older brother Linton became a noted musical pianist and composer.

Played regularly on Pittsburgh's KDKA radio station with a group called The Candy Kids at age seven; played on Allegheny riverboats by age of eleven; high school band teacher recognized Garner's innate ability and encouraged him not to take music lessons in order to preserve his unusual talents; Garner dropped out of high school to play with Leroy Brown's orchestra; early influences include "novelty rag" musicians from the 1920s such as Zez Confrey, along with Pittsburgh native Earl Hines, Count Basie guitarist Freddie Green, Fats Waller, and classical recordings; traveled to New York City in 1939 as accompanist for night club singer Ann Lewis; returned to serve as a substitute for Art Tatum in Tatum's trio with guitarist "Tiny" Grimes and bassist "Slam" Stewart; remained when the trio became the Slam Stewart Trio in 1945; recorded *Cool Blues* with Charlie Parker, released in 1947. Released "Laura," 1946; appeared on the *Tonight Show*; released *Cocktail Time*, 1947; released *The Elf*, 1949; released *Afternoon of an Elf*, 1955; solo recital at the revered Cleveland Music Hall, 1950; became the first and only jazz artist to perform under classical impresario Sol Hurok; released *Body and Soul*, 1952; released *Too Marvelous for Words*, 1954; released *Misty*, 1954; made first live recording, *Concert By The Sea*, in 1956; released *Feeling is Believing*, 1956; released *Paris Impressions*, 1958; scored the music for the film *A New Kind of Love*, 1963; released *That's My Kick*, 1967; single "Misty" featured prominently in the thriller *Play Misty for Me*, 1971; released *Gemini*, 1972; released *Magician*, 1974, released double album *Play It Again Erroll*, 1974; diagnosed with lung cancer; died at the age of 55, 1977; much of his early music was lost because it had not been written down, but his later works were taken down by arrangers as he composed them.

Garner released his romantic version of "Laura" in 1946, which sold a half million copies. He also captured the media's attention, and appeared on the *Tonight Show,* then hosted by Steve Allen, which further catapulted him into the public eye. *Cocktail Time* was released in 1947, followed by *The Elf* in 1949 and *Afternoon of an Elf* in 1955. Garner forged new ground in 1950 with a solo recital at the revered Cleveland Music Hall, a venue for traditionally classical concerts, and later in 1950 gave a concert at New York City's Town Hall. Garner became the first and only jazz artist to perform under classical impresario Sol Hurok, and recitals and recording sessions gradually replaced his nightclub performances. *Body and Soul* was released in 1952, and *Too Marvelous for Words* in 1954. It was his original song "Misty," however, that sealed his stardom; he released the album *Misty* in 1954 along with *Mambo Moves Garner.* Conley wrote, "'Misty' is still one of the most recognized and requested jazz tunes (in 1999)". Both Sarah Vaughn and Johnny Mathis enjoyed hits with the song "Misty."

Garner's first live recording was *Concert By The Sea* in 1956, and since it featured almost every nuance of his artistry, the release was the biggest selling jazz artist on the Columbia label. Garner also released *Feeling is Believing* in 1956, followed by *Paris Impressions* in 1958. He scored the music for the film *A New Kind of Love* in 1963, and released *That's My Kick* in 1967. His single "Misty" was featured prominently in the thriller *Play Misty for Me* in 1971. Garner then released *Gemini* in 1972, followed by *Magician* in 1974, and then the double album *Play It Again Erroll* in 1974. Garner was capable of sitting down, unprepared, and composing and recording two albums in the course of one day. He was remarkably prolific, and as the 20th century came to a close, there were still previously unreleased recordings of Garner's to be brought to the public's attention.

Garner traveled and toured throughout the 1960s and 1970s, and continued to release material as well. He added Latin rhythms to his repertoire, and sold out concerts around the globe. As he aged, he devoted most of his time to composing scores for movies, Broadway shows, ballets, concerts and recording sessions. He earned over a quarter of a million dollars annually. Failing health forced him to stop touring in 1975 and he was soon diagnosed with lung cancer. He died on January 2, 1977 at the age of 55. Much of his early music was lost because it had not been written down, but his later works were taken down by arrangers as he composed them. When Garner played his own compositions with an orchestra, the orchestra worked from the arranger's score while Garner played strictly from memory.

Conley wrote, "There exists in Erroll Garner's playing an emotional infectiousness from which no one with the slightest affinity for music is immune.... Listen to any Erroll Garner recording and you realize, above all else, this man loved to play piano. If you were lucky enough to see him, you also know he loved to share that joy with his audience." Musician Billy Taylor told Conley, "(Garner) was able to be tremendously popular without compromising his integrity as a musician." Conley added, "Such is the joy of a genius."

Selected discography

Cocktail Time, Dial Records, 1947.
The Elf, Savoy, 1949.
Body and Soul, Columbia, 1952.
Too Marvelous for Words, Vol. 3, EmArcy, 1954.
Erroll Garner Collection, Volumes 4 & 5: Solo Time!, EmArcy, 1954.
Mambo Moves Garner, Mercury, 1954.
Misty, Mercury, 1954.
Afternoon of an Elf, Mercury, 1955.
Concert by the Sea, Columbia, 1955.
Feeling is Believing, Columbia, 1956.
Other Voices, Columbia, 1956.
Paris Impressions, Columbia, 1958.
Erroll Garner Plays Gershwin and Kern, Mercury, 1965.
Dancing On The Ceiling, EmArcy, 1965.
Easy to Love, EmArcy, 1965.
That's My Kick, MGM Records, 1967.
Gemini, London Records, 1972.
Magician, London Records, 1974.
Play It Again Erroll, Columbia, 1974.

Penthouse Serenade, Complete Records, 1993.
Serenade to Laura, Complete Records, 1993.
Separate Keyboards: Erroll Garner/Billy Taylor, Complete Records, 1993.

Sources

Books

Balliett, Whitney; *American Musicians--56 Portraits in Jazz,* New York, Oxford
University Press, 1986.
Doran, James M.; *Erroll Garner: The Most Happy Piano,* Scarecrow Press, 1985.

Periodicals

Down Beat, November 1995.

Online

http:alevy.com/garner.html
http://personal.bna.bellsouth.net/bna/w/i/willbp/garner.html
http://www.geocities.com/BourbonStreet/1542/garner.html
http://www.hyperion.advanced.org/10320/Garner.html
http://www.imvs.com/scripts/iMS_AS
http://www.jazzonln.com/feature/garner.html
http://www.npr.org/programs/jazzprofiles/garner.html
http://www.traditionrecords.com/tradition/trcat010.html

—B. Kimberly Taylor

Golden Gate Quartet

Vocal group

The Golden Gate Quartet were pioneers in performing and recording close-harmony black spirituals, accentuated with jazz undertones and rhythmic verve. The group reached its pinnacle of fame in 1956 after forming in the early 1930s and were the best known "jubilee gospel quartet" among a large number of similarly popular a cappella groups in the 1930s and 1940s. Their first performances were in high school as well as at a local barber shop in Norfolk, Virginia, and eventually at Carnegie Hall. A favorite group of Eleanor Roosevelt, the Golden Gate Quartet made several appearances at the White House. By 1956 only bass tenor Orlandus Wilson remained from the original quartet; other members included tenors Clyde Riddick, Clyde Wright, baritone J. Caleb Ginyard, and pianist Emel Burgess. Original members included bass vocalist Robert "Peg" Ford, tenor A.C. "Eddie" Griffin, baritone Willie Johnson, and tenor Henry Owens. Griffin left the band in 1935 and was replaced by first tenor Willie Langford. Ford left the band in 1936 and was replaced by bass tenor Orlandus Wilson.

The group originated in the Norfolk suburb of Berkeley, where barber shop owner A.C. "Eddie" Griffin, a tenor singer, and Robert "Peg" ford, a bass vocalist, recruited two Booker T. Washington High School glee club members: tenor Henry Owns, and baritone Willie Johnson. Together the four formed a quartet to sing gospel music in the then-new "Jubilee" style that was beginning to sweep through churches in Virginia. They called themselves the Golden Gate Quartet and soon became popular throughout the state. Unlike the older Alabama gospel tradition with its trademark reliance on formal song structure and straight-ahead harmonies, Virginia's gospel music was looser, more rhythmic, and provided more room for experimentation. Adopting several techniques used by the Mills Brothers, such as the vocal imitation of musical instruments, the quartet's musical career flourish quickly and without much planning. They also were influenced by the swinging jazz of the Three Keys, and the emotional pleading and wailing of area pulpit preachers. The youthful energy of jubilee gospel music was something new and exciting for the band's members.

The Golden Gate Quartet performed for their first radio broadcast while still in high school, and soon after they graduated, they signed a contract for a radio program in Charlotte, North Carolina. Although they purposely imitated the close-knit harmonies and other techniques used by the Mills Brothers, their material was decidedly different and consisted almost entirely of "jubilee" gospel tunes. As a result, the group was also referred to as "The Golden Gate Jubilee Quartet." Many black a cappella groups had enjoyed a resounding success within the confines of church audiences for many years, but the Golden Gate Quartet added an element of commercial polish and flair that garnered much wider recognition and a more diverse audience. By 1935 Griffin's modest ambitions for his musical career had been more than fulfilled, and he felt more certain about his haircutting business than his singing career, so he retired from the quartet. He was replaced by tenor William Langford, a veteran of several local singing groups. In 1936, Orlandus Wilson, then 16, replaced the elderly and ailing Ford. The new line-up was posed to set traditional gospel music on its ear.

By 1937 the group was being heard nationwide on NBC's *Magic Key* program and was widely considered to be the hottest gospel group in the country. On August 4, 1937, Bluebird talent scout/producer Eli Oberstein recorded the Golden Gate Quartet in a field recording session at the Charlotte Hotel. The group completed 14 tracks in just two hours, and all but two songs required only one take. The release of their debut featuring their signature song, "Golden Gate Gospel Train," brought immediate recognition to the quartet. In 1938 promoter John Hammond placed them on a bill along with Count Basie, Benny Goodman, Big Joe Turner, and James P. Johnson, for the history-making "Spirituals to Swing" concert at Carnegie Hall. The Carnegie Hall performance

For the Record . . .

Members included **Robert "Peg" Ford** (left band, 1936), bass; **A.C. "Eddie" Griffin** (left band 1935), tenor; **Willie Johnson,** baritone; **Willie Langford** (replaced Griffin 1935), **Henry Owens,** first tenor; **Orlandus Wilson** (replaced Ford, 1936), bass tenor.

Band formed in 1934 in Norfolk, VA suburb of Berkeley with Ford, Griffin, Johnson, and Owens; Johnson and Owens were high school glee club members; Ford and Griffin were barber shop owners/workers with an interest in gospel "jubilee" music; band reached its pinnacle of fame in 1956; appeared at the Roosevelt White House inauguration, 1941; appeared at Carnegie Hall; made cameo appearances during the 1940s in numerous films, including *Star-Spangled Rhythm, Hollywood Canteen,* and *A Song Is Born*; by the 1940s, band consisted of Willie Johnson, Willie Langford, Henry Owens, and Orlandus Wilson; by 1956 only Orlandus Wilson remained from the original quartet and other members included pianist Emel Burgess, baritone J. Caleb Ginyard, and tenors Clyde Riddick and Clyde Wright; group retired to France during the 1950s.

Addresses: *Record company—BMG/RCA Records,* 1540 Broadway, New York, NY 10038; (212) 930-4000.

led to a weekly radio show on CBS, as well as to a long-term run at New York City's Cafe Society club where the quartet was heard by numerous celebrities, including Franklin D. Roosevelt. President Roosevelt was so impressed with the Golden Gate Quartet that he invited the group to entertain at his January 1941 inaugural gala at Constitution Hall, a place where lauded African-American singer Marion Anderson had been forbidden to perform just two years earlier by the hall's owners, the conservative Daughters of the American Revolution.

In June of 1940, the group made a milestone—and final—RCA recording with legendary folk and blues singer Leadbelly. The fruits of their collaboration appeared on RCA's *Leadbelly: Alabama Bound*. Soon after that recording session, singer William Langford left the band to form a group called the Southern Sons. The Southern Sons released *I Hear Music In the Air* for RCA, and Langford's place in the Golden Gate Quartet was taken by his longtime friend, Clyde Riddick, who had

been an early replacement for Griffin even before Langford joined the group in the he 1930s. During the 1940s, the Golden Gate Quartet made cameo appearances in numerous films, including *Star-Spangled Rhythm, Hollywood Canteen,* and *A Song Is Born*. The group continued to record for Mercury and Columbia, and in 1948 Willie Johnson exited the group. The group was well-able to deal with Johnson's departure as well as that of Owens when he left the group in the 1950s to become an evangelist preacher.

During the 1950s the group went through several more personnel changes; the advent of rhythm-and-blues and then rock-and-roll somewhat dampened the demand for their music in the Unites States. However, when the group went on a tour of Europe in 1955, they were surprised and delighted to find that there was a new, global audience waiting for them. The members of the group have primarily lived and worked in Europe since the mid-to-late 1950s. Riddick and Wilson anchor the top and bottom of the trademark Golden Gate Quartet sound, with second tenor Clyde Wright, who has been a member of the band, on and off, since 1954, and baritone Paul Brembly, became a member of the group in 1971. The group remained active well into the 1990s.

Selected discography

Travelin' Shoes, BMG/RCA (Bluebird), reissued 1992.
Complete Recorded Works Vol. 1-4, BMG/RCA, reissued 1996.
Meet Me At The Golden Gate, Collector's Edition, reissued 1996.
Radio Transcriptions 1941-1944, Document Records, reissued 1997.
Very Best of Golden Gate Quartet, EMD/Blue Note, reissued 1997.
Kings of Gospel, RCA Victor/Bluebird, reissued 1999.
Golden Gate Quartet: Negro Spirituals, Vol. 1-2, A World of Music, 2000.

Sources

http://members.aol.com/rnbtrain/Gosp-2.html
http://www.cdnow.com/cgi-bin/
http://www.eyeneer.com/America/Gen.../Profiles/golden.gate.quartet.html
http://www.retroactive.com/july98/goldengate.html

—B. Kimberly Taylor

Nina Hagen

Rock singer, songwriter, actress

CorbisView. Reproduced by permission.

Nina Hagen is one of the most controversial rock singers of our time, one that people either love or hate passionately. "Nina Hagen is at once the most outlandish of rock clowns and the most intensely committed and flaked-out female pop visionary since Patti Smith herself," wrote Tim Holmes in *Rolling Stone*, "She sings, mumbles, growls, yelps, shrieks and warbles." On stage as well as in public Hagen loves eccentric appearances. When *Billboard's* Roman Kozak arrived at her New York East Side apartment for an interview before a performance at the Ritz, Hagen received him in her kitchen, "dressed in what looked like a white paper diaper, a black Valkyrie bra, and a leather cap that hid what was left of her cropped red hair." Hagen's career has been a cycle of ups and downs. But her eccentric style which emphasizes her belief in individual freedom, UFO's, and in the divinity of humans hasn't changed much over the years, while her extreme exuberance was in part replaced by political statements and action. After some rather quiet times in the late 1980s, Hagen jumped off to a new start in re-united Germany in the 1990s.

When Nina Hagen was born in March 1955, her parents—script writer Hans Hagen and actress Eva-Maria Hagen—were at the peak of their success in the German Democratic Republic. They divorced when Hagen was two. She stayed with her mother and was heavily influenced by her theater work. When she was about nine, she started taking classes in classical voice, guitar, and piano. Hagen sang in the theater choir and later with the Lacomy singers, a studio background group.

Went West

In the shadow of her mother's fame, Hagen's early rebellion often went unpunished. She was excluded from the communist youth organization, left school after the tenth grade and, when she was 17, failed the admission test for the East German Actors School in Berlin. Instead, she sang along to tapes of Tina Turner and Janis Joplin and went on a trip to Poland where she performed together with a band for the first time. Hagen studied sound engineering in a one-year intensive course at the Studio for Popular Music in East Berlin, which included road-show training. She then performed with several bands at various jazz events in East Berlin and toured East Germany. When her mother's new boyfriend—Wolf Biermann, a prominent singer and songwriter who had publicly criticized the East German regime—was forced to leave the country at the end of 1976, Nina Hagen followed him with her mother to West Germany.

At age 21, Hagen settled in Hamburg and her stepfather helped her to get a recording contract with CBS, giving her time and money to learn about western culture and the music business. After exploring the London reggae and punk scenes, she formed the Nina Hagen Band and, in 1977, gave three sold-out performances in West Berlin. In 1979, her first album *Nina Hagen Band* was released. It included cover versions of the Tubes' "White Punks on Dope," and Norman Greenbaum's "Spirit in the Sky" with German lyrics, and used elements of American new wave similar to Patti Smith or Blondie. Hagen was in high demand and the renowned German news magazine, *Spiegel*, celebrated the band as "one of the hottest European bands since the Sex Pistols." On the way to becoming an international star, however, Hagen dissolved her band because she felt that guitar solos had become more important than her voice to her accompanists. She finished a second album with the band to fulfill her obligation to her record company. *Unbehagen*, released in 1980, was a success throughout Europe. In the meantime, Hagen's extensive European media coverage focused more and more on her scandalous lifestyle rather than on her anti-establishment lyrics and music.

With Dutch guitarist Ferdinand Karmelk, Hagen auditioned musicians for a new Nina Hagen Band in New York and Hollywood and met with Columbia Records executives. A year later, the first Hagen record was released in the United States—a limited edition commercial ten inch EP with two songs each from her first and second album. When Hagen learned that she was pregnant, she moved to Los Angeles alone, where Frank Zappa's manager Bennett Glotzer took over her career. Hagen's first American album *Nunsexmonkrock*—a mixture of hard rock and funk, with elements of Islam and the witch cult of the Middle Ages—was recorded in New York and released in 1982 on the Columbia label. Although it was very controversially received, Hagen toured with her three-piece backing group No Problem Orchestra through England, Canada, and the United States in the summer of 1982.

Hagen's next album *Fearless* was a success. Her "New York, New York" became a top ten dance chart hit. Hagen played with her voice like a "master vocal technician" and sounded "at will like an opera singer, Vincent Price and one of the Chipmunks," wrote Kim Freeman in *Billboard* describing one of Hagen's New York shows. She went on a world tour in 1984, and again a year later after her next album was released in spring 1985.

Nina Hagen in Ekstasy showed once more Hagen's self-esteem. In the title song "Prima Nina in Ekstasy" she sang: "I love myself and I know who I am/I'm Queen of Punkrock/I'm the mother of punk so what the funk." The album included Hagen's interpretations of the Lord's Prayer, Paul Anka's "My Way," and, once again, Norman Greenbaum's "Spirit in the Sky." Hagen was a major act at the 1985 "Rock in Rio" festival and went on a major tour across the United States. "One never knows what to expect from Nina Hagen, except an interesting show," wrote Kathy Gillis about a Hagen performance in New York's Bacon Theatre in *Billboard*. According to Gillis, the show "included a good bit of opera, a hula skirt and a UFO," as well as "a lot of spiritual, social and political talk woven around the songs, all delivered in a dizzying range of voices." In the rock and roll part of the show, Hagen was "prancing around in a lighted bra that looked spectacular when the rest of the stage was dark," and sometimes Hagen sang and spoke French and German in addition to her "lightly accented" English.

Went Political

All of Hagen's later albums sold primarily in Germany. She became more politically articulate, spoke and sang against apartheid in South Africa, and for animal rights. "Don't Kill TheAnimals" became a hit in 1986. *Nina Hagen,* a more rock and roll oriented album, was released in 1989 and that same year she moved to Paris, where fashion designer Jean-Paul Gaultier eliminated her garish makeup and hair colors.

With the title "Gorbachev Rap" on the 1989 album *Nina Hagen* the singer expressed her approval of the political reforms the Soviet Union was undergoing at the time. In the spring of 1990, Hagen performed at a women's festival in Moscow, and went on a Street Party Tour through European cities. In the summer of 1991, her concert in the former East German city of Halle flopped when only 1,200 of 10,000 expected fans showed up.

Besides her solo shows, Hagen acted in the Marianne Rosenbaum comedy "Lilien in der Bank." She also received her own weekly 30-minute talk show on German TV channel RTLplus, and toured Germany in a two-woman Brecht-show with Meret Becker. In May of 1996, Hagen married David Lynn, who was fifteen years her junior, in Los Angeles.

Gave to Charity

Back in the United States in 1998, Hagen participated in an AIDS benefit at the Lust for Life bar in New York City where she sang her classic "New York, New York" along with several new songs accompanied by a four-piece band. Evelyn McDonnell in *Village Voice* found that Hagen's "concoction of punk, funk, reggae, and rock ... sounded stilted, pretentious, weird" twenty years before, but she noted about the 1998 concert: "With her long, dark hair pulled up into ponytails, eyeliner out to her temples, and fluorescent solar systems adorning her pantsuit,...she looked as good as she sounded. Extraterrestrial demon-child is a timeless guise." McDonnell concluded that "Hagen came across not as a blast from the past, but a return of the future."

Hamburg film director Peter Sempel accompanied Hagen for two years with a camera. His documentary *Nina Hagen—Punk and Glory* was presented at the Berlin International Film Festival in February of 1999. At that time, Hagen was planning to perform her charity CD *Om Namah Shivay*, a devotional album with 13 tracks of traditional Hindu songs, in theatres around Germany. She was also planning a big summer tour to promote her new album which was scheduled to hit the shelves in mid-1999.

Selected discography

Nina Hagen Band, (with Nina Hagen Band), UK CBS, 1979.
Unbehagen, (with Nina Hagen Band), CBS, 1980.
Nunsexmonkrock, Columbia, 1982.
Fearless, Columbia, 1984.
Nina Hagen in Ekstasy, (includes "Prima Nina in Ekstasy") Columbia, 1985.
Nina Hagen, German Mercury, 1989.
Love, Polygram, 1990.
Nunsexmonkrock/Nina Hagen Band, Columbia, 1991.
Freud Euch, RCA, 1995.
Bee Happy, RCA, 1996.
14 Friendly Abductions: The Best of Nina Hagen, Columbia/ Legacy, 1996.
Was denn... - Hits '74 - '95, Amiga, 1997.
Om Namah Shivay, 1998.

Sources

Periodicals

Billboard, June 19, 1982, p. 10; February 25, 1984, p. 49; August 24, 1985.
BPI Daily Entertainment Report, January 14, 1999.
Rolling Stone, July 19, 1985, p.90.
Time, July 9, 1990, p. 87.
Village Voice, August 4, 1998, p. 114.

Online

http://archiv.bz-berlin.de/bz/archiv/980220_pdf/BZ006001.htm
http://rhein-zeitung.de/magazin/musik/galerie/ninahagen/main.html
http://trouserpress.com/bandpages/NINA_HAGEN_BAND.html
http://www-2.roughguides.com/rock/entries/entries-h/HAGEN_NINA.html
http://www.amazon.com
http://www.comnet.ca/~rina/nina.html
http://www.munzinger.de

http://www.nina-hagen.com
http://www.totalobscurity.com/nina/album.html

Additional information provided by the liner notes of
The Best Of Nina Hagen, Sony Music Entertainment
Inc., 1996.

—Evelyn Hauser

Herbie Hancock

Piano, keyboards, songwriter

AP/Wide World Photo. Reproduced by permission.

Throughout much of his career, Herbie Hancock was one of the most controversial and revered jazz artists of his time, as was his mentor and friend, the late Miles Davis. His career spanned more than four decades. Besides being a virtuoso pianist and keyboard player, he explored many forms of music, as well as the technological gadgetry that accompanied them. His chameleon ways of changing musical direction to broaden contemporary styles excited and surprised his peers and fans alike. But it came naturally to Hancock, whose boundless creativity formed the music he loved so deeply.

Herbert Jeffrey Hancock was born on April 12, 1940, in Chicago, Illinois to Wayman and Winnie Griffin Hancock. His father was a grocery store clerk, while his mother worked as a secretary. Both parents instilled a love and appreciation for music in all of their children. When Herbie Hancock was a toddler, he was always happy if a piano was near. His love for the piano grew even deeper when his parents bought him an old upright piano for 25 dollars. Instead of getting involved in sports or running the back streets of Chicago with his school friends, Hancock opted to stay home to practice the piano. He used his extra time to pursue his growing interest in science and electronics. However, his interest in music never caused his schoolwork to suffer. His inexhaustible discipline allowed him to skip two grades. During elementary school, his teachers and his mother encouraged him to listen to opera on the radio, which helped his understanding of both music and the piano. At the age of 11, Hancock won a scholastic award for his concert performance of a Mozart concerto with the Chicago Symphony Orchestra.

Delved into Jazz Music

Growing up in Chicago, Hancock was surrounded by the blues, as it echoed through the city during his high school years. Yet, Hancock didn't gravitate toward rhythm and blues, but instead, was moved by the more complex jazz styles. When he heard a classmate play an improvisational piece at a talent show, he was so taken by its freedom that he became devoted to learning all about it. As Lynn Norment noted in *Ebony Magazine*, "He closeted himself for hours alone with Oscar Peterson and George Shearing records, committed their notes to paper and then reproduced them. This tedious exercise led to his ability to analyze and dissect harmonic structures, rhythmic patterns, and choral voicings." After graduating high school, Hancock enrolled at Grinnell College, in Iowa, in 1956 to study engineering. While there, he learned the fundamentals of electronics, which later translated into his own music in the 1970s.

For the Record . . .

Born April 12, 1940, in Chicago, Illinois, son of Wayman Edward and Winnie (Griffin) Hancock; married Gudrun Meixner, August 31, 1986. *Education:* Attended Grinnell College, 1956-60; Roosevelt University, 1960; Manhattan School of Music, 1962; New School of Social Research, 1967.

Performed for the first time at age 11 with the Chicago Symphony Orchestra, 1952; played piano with the Donald Byrd Group, 1960-1963; released debut album *Takin' Off,* 1962; recorded and performed with the Miles Davis Quintet, 1963-1968; formed his own band called, Mwandishi and released a break through fusion album of the same name, 1971; formed acoustic jazz ensemble V.S.O.P., 1977; recorded and released more than 65 solo albums throughout his career.

Addresses: *Record company*—Hancock Records, 825 Eighth Ave., New York, NY 10019

Hancock went on to change his major to music composition and graduated in 1960. He returned to Chicago, and worked with such artists as Coleman Hawkins, Donald Byrd, Dexter Gordon, and Freddie Hubbard.

The following winter, a treacherous snow storm prevented the pianist for Donald Byrd's group from getting to Chicago where they were scheduled to play. Hancock stepped in for the missing pianist. Byrd was impressed by Hancock's performance, and took him under his wing. Byrd took him to New York and introduced him to the jazz establishment, which laid the groundwork for Hancock's 1962 debut album, *Takin' Off,* which included musicians like Dexter Gordon and Freddie Hubbard. A year later, his song "Watermelon Man," was covered by Mongo Santamaria, and subsequently recorded over the years by more than 200 artists.

In 1963, Donald Byrd suggested that Hancock contact Miles Davis. The Davis Group had a philosophy that maintained an environment where the musicians had the freedom to musically express themselves. His meeting with Davis proved very productive. Hancock, Davis, Wayne Shorter, Ron Carter, and Tony Williams, became known as one of the most influential groups in jazz

history. During his time off from The Davis Group, Hancock performed with such jazz greats as Phil Woods, Oliver Nelson, Wes Montgomery, Quincy Jones, and Sonny Rollins.

From Commercials to Commercial Success

In the late 1960s, the once prominent jazz audiences began to thin out as rock and roll gained popularity. To keep working, Hancock wrote commercial jingles for such companies as Chevrolet, Standard Oil, and Eastern Airlines. He also began recording for soundtracks and composing film scores for such films as *Blow Up.* He also wrote the "Fat Albert Rotunda" for comedian Bill Cosby's television special, *Hey, Hey, Hey, It's Fat Albert.*

By 1968, Hancock had left the Davis Group to pursue a solo career. He started playing the electric piano and exploring the technology of electronic instruments and recording equipment. His next album, *Mwandishi,* became one of his first breakthroughs in music technology. In 1973, his work with the Headhunters delved into even more uncharted musical territory. During that time, he continued to play acoustic jazz from time to time with the Davis quintet alumni, while continuing to explore the possibilities of instrumental music through electronics.

In 1983, he moved into a completely different direction with his number-one pop hit, "Rockit." Not only did "Rockit" win a Grammy award for Hancock, but the song raised some eyebrows throughout the industry, primarily because it was one of the few instrumental songs to soar to the top of the charts. Even Hancock was surprised that "Rockit" became such a big hit, and wanted to make a video in order to expose his music to the kids who watched MTV. He hired the video duo Godley and Creme (who had done hit videos for The Police and Duran Duran) to help him.

Hancock recalled the video-making process to Peter Occhiogrosso in *Playboy,* "I told Godley and Creme, 'Look, don't even have me on it, don't have any black people on it—just make it as white as any video they might show by Led Zeppelin or anybody." They laughed. They thought I was joking, but I wanted people to hear the music." Hancock did end up having a cameo, but only on a television screen within the video. When the video for "Rockit" hit the MTV airwaves, it rocketed into heavy rotation. Hancock had jumped another hurdle. Aside from superstars such as Michael Jackson and Lionel Richie, MTV rarely even played videos by black artists in the early 1980s, much less had them in heavy rotation.

Prayer and the Pianist

Throughout his career, Hancock broke through many musical and social barriers without looking back. He attributed his successes and power of positive thinking to his belief in Buddhism, which he began studying in the 1970s. Hancock practiced a sect of Buddhism called Nichiren Shoshu, which involved reciting the prayers of the Lotus Sutra, and chanting the words "Nam-Myoho-Renge-Kyo" (the law of cause and effect through sound). Hancock credited his Buddhist practice for giving him freedom. He explained the feeling to Eric Levin in *People* as, "not being afraid of things that may happen in your life. It's knowing that you can turn all the poison into medicine." He said his Buddhist practice didn't necessarily change his nature, but simply reinforced what he already had.

Hancock has been the quintessential board crosser. He's gone from straight-ahead jazz to opera, from bebop to fusion, from jingles to dance music, from film scores to hip-hop—all while moving between acoustic piano, synthesizers, and emulators. Just when people thought Hancock had settled into the genre of contemporary music, he took another turn in 1992 with a Miles Davis tribute tour. It took Hancock three years to finally process the passing of his friend and mentor, who once said, "Herbie was the step after Bud Powell and Thelonious Monk, and I haven't heard anybody yet who has come after that time."

In the 1990s, Hancock had his fingers on a few other things besides the piano. Continuing to follow the advancing technology, Hancock worked on multimedia projects and cutting-edge Internet audio productions. His past also returned to the forefront, as some of his older works were re-released, including *The Complete Blue Note Sixties Sessions*, a six-CD collection of Hancock's early influential albums. Columbia Records also reissued *An Evening With Herbie Hancock & Chick Corea*, a duet recording from 1978.

Herbie Hancock's recordings in the 1990s stayed true to his chameleon reputation. In 1995, he released *The New Standard*, a translation of songs by artists such as Prince and Peter Gabriel into a jazz style. In 1997, Hancock teamed up with saxophonist Wayne Shorter, who played with Hancock in The Davis Group, for a collaborative album called *1+1* released on Verve Records. Hancock and Shorter, also a practicing Buddhist, had continued their friendship since their days with Miles Davis. The duo followed up the release with a tour that lasted into 1998. Later that year, Hancock reformed the Headhunters to release *Return of the Headhunters* on his own label, Hancock Records. He also released a tribute album to George Gershwin called *Gershwin's World*, with guest appearances by Joni Mitchell, Stevie Wonder, Chick Corea, Kathleen Battle, and Wayne Shorter.

For most of his life, Herbie Hancock let his musical style follow whatever creativity he felt at the time, regardless of genre, then combined it with own his interest in growing technologies. "I want to approach living my life to the fullest," Hancock told Don Heckman in *Down Beat*. "Music isn't any different.... That means the more I learn and the more I am able to experience, the more tools I have to create possibilities of expression that, perhaps, I haven't experienced before. That's what makes me want to go on living and go on striving. That's the best of what life has to offer."

Selected discography

Takin' Off, Blue Note Records, 1962.
Inventions and Dimensions, Blue Note Records, 1963.
My Point of View, Blue Note Records, 1963.
Empyrean Isles, Blue Note Records, 1964.
Maiden Voyage, Blue Note Records, 1965.
Herbie Hancock, Blue Note Records, 1968.
Speak Like A Child, Blue Note Records, 1968.
Fat Albert Rotunda, Warner Bros. Records, 1969.
The Prisoner, Blue Note Records, 1969.
Mwandishi, Warner Bros. Records, 1970.
Crossings, Warner Bros. Records, 1971.
Sextant, Columbia Records, 1972.
Headhunters, Columbia Records, 1973.
Death Wish, One Way Records, 1974.
Thrust, Columbia Records, 1974.
Dedication, CBS/Sony Records, 1974.
Flood, A&M Records, 1975.
Love Me By Name, Arista Records, 1975.
Happy The Man, GB Records, 1976.
Kawaida, Columbia Records, 1976.
Man Child, Columbia Records, 1976.
Secrets, Columbia Records, 1976.
Live In Japan, Columbia Records, 1977.
Sunlight, Columbia Records, 1977.
The Herbie Hancock Trio, Columbia Records, 1977.
Tempest in the Coliseum, Columbia Records, 1977.
V.S.O.P. Quintet, Columbia Records, 1977.
Direct Step, Columbia Records, 1978.
An Evening with Chick Corea and Herbie: Live, Columbia Records, 1978.
The Piano, Columbia Records, 1978.
Live Under the Sky, Columbia Records, 1979.
In Concert: Duets Live, CBS Records, 1979.
Feets Don't Fail Me Now, Columbia Records, 1979.
Jingle Bells Jazz, Columbia Records, 1979.

Hancock Alley, Manhattan Records, 1980.
Mr. Hands, Columbia Records, 1980.
Monster, Columbia Records, 1980.
Magic Windows, Columbia Records, 1981.
Herbie Hancock Quartet, Columbia Records, 1981.
Double Rainbow, Columbia Records, 1981.
By All Means, MPS Records, 1981.
Lite Me Up, Columbia Records, 1982.
Future Shock, Columbia Records, 1983.
Hot and Heavy, Star Jazz Records, 1984.
Sound System, Columbia Records, 1984.
Village Life, Columbia Records, 1985.
Jazz Africa, Live, Verve Records, 1986.
Third Plane, Carerre Records, 1986.
Songs for My Father, Blue Note Records, 1988.
Perfect Machine, Columbia Records, 1988.
Dis Is Da Drum, Mercury Records, 1993.
Jamming, Royalco Records, 1994.
Cantaloupe Island, Blue Note Records, 1995.
New Standard, Verve Records, 1995.
JamminÕ with Herbie, Prime Cuts Records, 1995.
In Concert Live, Tristar Records, 1996.
1+1, Polygram Records, 1997.

Return of the Headhunters, Hancock/Verve Records, 1998.
Gershwin's World, Polygram Records, 1998.

Sources

Periodicals

Down Beat, June 1994, December 1995, April 1996, May 1996, December 1997, September 1998, February 1999.
Ebony, December 1995.
Entertainment Weekly, March 8, 1996, March 15, 1996, October 9, 1998.
Forbes, December 14, 1998.
Knight-Ridder/Tribune News Service, March 3, 1999.
Musician, December 1998.
People Weekly, January 19, 1987.
Playboy, July, 1984.

Online

"Herbie Hancock," *The Ultimate Band List*, http://www.ubl.com (May 1, 1999).

—Sonya Shelton

Lauryn Hill

Singer, songwriter

For Lauryn Hill, gaining a certain level of independence and control as a singer, songwriter, and producer in the predominantly male-centered rap and R&B industry was a formidable struggle. On the first record she ever made, 1993's *Blunted on Reality,* Hill was nothing more than the ultra-hip lead singer and writer of her own raps. By the time *The Score was* released in 1996, Hill was a minor celebrity and object of adoration in the media, a talent so obvious—and with looks so photogenic—that the clamor for her to go solo was incessant. But after gracefully letting her fellow Fugees take that route first, Hill unleashed *The Miseducation of Lauryn Hill* to a platinum sales debut as well as overwhelming critical acclamation and adulation.

In less than six months t, *Miseducation* had sold three million copies. *Spin* named Hill "Artist of the Year, and inside its pages writer Craig Seymour commented upon *Miseducation*'s wide range of fans. "In a fractured musical landscape, it simultaneously united the Sound-Scan masses—from hip-hop heads to frat rats to Lilith Fair maidens," Seymour wrote, and called it "the most

Photograph Marc Baptiste, courtesy of Columbia Records.

For the Record . . .

Born c. 1975, in New Jersey; daughter of Mal a computer analyst) and Valerie (a teacher) Hill; children: Zion David, Selah. *Education:* Attended Columbia University.

Hill joined the Fugees as a teenager in the early 1990s; she also appeared on *As the World Turns* and in the feature films *King of the Hill* and *Sister Act II: Back in the Habit;* made recording debut with Fugees on *Blunted on Reality,* Ruffhouse/Columbia, 1993; 1996's follow-up, *The Score,* Ruffhouse/Colu;mbia, sold 17 million copies; released solo debut, *The Miseducation of Lauryn Hill,* Ruffhouse/Columbia, 1997.

Awards: As a member of the Fugees and co-producer of their second album *The Score,* Hill shared two 1997 Grammy Awards from the National Academy of Recording Arts and Sciences for Best R&B song by a duo or group, for "Killing Me Softly with His Song," and for best rap album; triple platinum certification, November 1998, for *The Miseducation of Lauryn Hill,* Recording Industry Association of America.

Addresses: Record company—c/o Columbia Records, 550 Madison Ave., New York, NY 10022-3211; (212) 833-7080, fax (212) 833-5401.

'feel-good' record of the year, and not just because you can feel good about yourself for liking it. When a black artist brings together people like this, it seems like societal gaps are a little bit narrower."

Hill was born in the mid-1970s and grew up in South Orange, New Jersey, a neighborhood of modest houses on quiet streets that nevertheless was situated not far from a much rougher area with the high-rise buildings of public housing. Her parents were professionals. Her father, Mal, once sang professionally in nightclubs and at weddings, but became a computer analyst, while her mother, Valerie, taught school in nearby Newark. As a child, Hill spent long hours listening to a trove of her mother's old 45s, hundreds of boxes of singles she found stashed in the basement from the likes of Gladys Knight, Curtis Mayfield, and Aretha Franklin from the legendary black music labels Motown, Stax, and Philly International. "One o'clock in the morning, you'd go in her room and you'd see her fast asleep with the earphones on," Valerie Hill told Touré in a 1999 interview for *Rolling Stone.* "This sixties soul that I'd collected just seeped into her veins."

Teen Rapper

Hill made her performing debut on *Showtime at the Apollo* at the age of 13. Her parents rented a van and brought along a group of her friends for the trek to Harlem to hear her sing the Smoky Robinson tune "Who's Lovin' You." But Hill was so afraid of the microphone that she kept her distance from it, and the result was jeers from the merciless audience. Her uncle yelled at her to move closer, "and she grabbed the mike and sang that song with a vengeance, like, `How dare you boo me'," Valerie Hill told *Rolling Stone.* Determined despite her rough start, Hill persevered, pursuing music as well as acting as a teen. She won a role in *As the World Turns* while still in high school, and in 1993, appeared in the Whoopi Goldberg movie *Sister Act II: Back in the Habit.*

Hill had also become acquainted with a friend of her brother's, Prakazrel "Pras" Michel. A Haitian immigrant, Michel formed a rap group and asked Hill to join. The trio became the Fugees-Tranzlator Crew. They danced and rapped in other languages and cut their demo tapes in a basement studio that belonged to Michel's cousin. One day, another cousin of Michel's, Wyclef Jean, came by the studio to hear them. Jean was amazed by Hill's voice and decided to work with them. Later the other female member went off to college, and the trio eventually dropped the "Tranzlator" part and became just the Fugees. Hill herself put off college—though she was accepted by a number of prestigious schools—to take part-time courses at Columbia University.

The Fugees soon attracted attention on the local circuit—in part due to a combination of Hill's stunning looks and her raps—and were signed to the Pennsylvania rap label Ruffhouse. With the Fugees, she recorded *Blunted on Reality,* released in 1993. But the group—still in their teens—felt steamrollered by the whole event, and had been allowed little input into the production process. Their music was given pumped-up, gangsta-style beats by their creative team working on behalf of the label, who wanted to make a standard rap album. The record failed to make a dent in the charts. "Hailed in Europe as a glimpse of the future, *Blunted* was summarily trashed in the American hip-hop press for missing the mark altogether," noted *Rolling Stone*'s Alec Foege.

Scored

However, a New York producer remixed two of *Blunted*'s tracks, the songs became underground club favorites, and suddenly the Fugees—with Hill as their frontperson—were a sensation. For their second album Hill, Jean, and Michel successfully argued with management to gain more creative control, and produced it themselves. *The Score* was released in 1996, a massive success of an album, widely hailed as one of the best of the year and even as a turning point for contemporary African-American music. The record was launched with Hill's lauded vocals on a cover of the 1973 Roberta Flack hit, "Killing Me Softly with His Song," a single that spent five weeks at number one. In the end, *The Score* sold 18 million copies and made the Fugees the best-selling rap act in history. "Rather than reform hip hop, they're re-forming it, with a gumbotic, frenetic amalgam of rock-steady samples, Castilian guitar, and verbal dexterity all over the map," wrote Natasha Stovall in the *Village Voice*. Hill, the critic noted, does "double duty as both rapper and diva. Her book smart-street smart persona and righteous, self-confident presence make her *The Score*'s centrifugal force."

Even early on in her days as a new rap celebrity, Hill was continuously plagued by rumors that she was either about to leave the Fugees and go solo, or speculation about why she had not yet done so. In interviews she stressed the long-time creative relationship she enjoyed with Jean and Michel, and how well they functioned as a team. But then Hill became pregnant in late 1996, and did her first solo song for the soundtrack of a 1997 film with Larenz Tate and Nia Long called *Love Jones*. Meanwhile, Jean recorded and released his own solo album, and Michel was known to be planning one as well. Many assumed Hill's career was stalled indefinitely. Others counseled her against having a child at this crucial point in her life.

Record-Setting Solo Debut

But the pregnancy was a blessing in disguise, for it fueled a huge burst of creativity in Hill. She wrote over two dozen songs, and then recorded them at her home in South Orange and in Kingston, Jamaica, from where the father of her child, Rohan Marley, hailed. Again, she had to fight for the right to produce her own record, though she had shared a Grammy award for *The Score*. Long before *The Miseducation of Lauryn Hill* debuted,

Wyclef Jean had told a reporter that he would be the producer of Hill's solo album, which made Hill roll her eyes later as she remembered hearing of this boast. "You would think that after selling 15 million records that I would be able to produce and write my own joint, but it was a battle," Hill explained to Michael A. Gonzales in a 1998 interview in *The Source.*

The Miseducation of Lauryn Hill debuted in August of 1998 to sales of over 400,000 copies its first week out, setting a record for a black female artist. *Miseducation*'s title mirrored the name of a civil-rights treatise, *The Miseducation of the Negro,* by Carter G. Woodson, but Hill told *Time Out-New York*'s Raquel Cepeda, "it's really about the things that you learn outside of school, outside of what society deems appropriate and mandatory." The record won effusive praise for its honesty, emotional resonance, and panoply of musical styles that interlocked well. Mary J. Blige guested with Hill to sing a duet on "I Used to Love Him," while guitarist Carlos Santana played on "Joy of My World Is in Zion," Hill's tribute to her son.

"Easily flowing from singing to rapping, evoking the past while forging a future of her own, Hill has made an album of often-astonishing power, strength, and feeling," declared *Entertainment Weekly*'s David Browne. He termed the record "infused with African-American musical history," and noted that "every cut, even the apolitical ones, presents a new and unexpected twist, both musically and emotionally." Browne wrote of the dominant "boy's club" vibe of most R&B and hip-hop music, even acclaimed works by women—"the music is as exquisitely manicured as high-cost nails but deeply impersonal," Contrasting such works with *Miseducation,* Browne found Hill's work "infused with the highs and lows of a young woman faced with success and expectations. A cloud hangs over the album, but the effect is human, not programmed."

The Ultimate Revenge

Some of that cloud may have been the result of questions about the future of the Fugees and, in comparison, the less-than-stellar reception to both Jean's and Michel's solo efforts. Label executives stressed that the band was simply enjoying a hiatus and would eventually reconvene in the studio. Some speculated that public-relations finesse was covering up a more serious breach, that Jean's "To All the Girls" was a dig at Hill, and that *Miseducation*'s "Lost Ones" was her response ("my emancipation don't fit your equation," she sings), as was perhaps "Ex-Factor," or even "I Used to Love Him." But Hill downplayed such issues. "The album is not about me bein' upset about a love lost," Hill told Touré. "It's not even really about bein' upset about bein' stabbed in the back."

Before the end of the year, *Miseducation* would sell two million copies and earn Hill eight Grammy nominations. She won five, beating Carole King's 1971 record of four Grammys for her album *Tapestry*. *Spin* named her "Artist of the Year" and *Time* magazine put her on the cover as new face of black music. "Hill isn't out to create bourgeois hip-hop lite," opined its music critic, Christopher John Farley. "She constantly strives to connect her message to the street." Touré declared that the tracks on *Miseducation* evince that Hill has "Joni Mitchell's intense singer-songwriter integrity, Bob Marley's revolutionary spirit and young Chaka Khan's all-natural, Everywoman sensuality." That expressiveness and emotional sincerity came naturally to Hill. "I really don't know any better," as she explained the songwriting process to Melissa Ewey of *Ebony*. "To write something that's too pretentious, that wouldn't feel natural to me. I think the only anxiety that I felt was ... you know that once you release something, it's a reflection of you, and people will beat it up. I knew I'd better do what I had to do to put my best foot forward."

While pregnant with Zion, Hill had worked with Aretha Franklin, writing the track "A Rose Is a Rose" for her 1998 album, and picking up another two Grammy nominations for her production work. She also planned to tour in early 1999, despite the fact that she now had had a second child, daughter Selah, with Rohan Marley. She admitted to Touré that "raising children is a twenty-four-hour job, and making music is a twenty-four-hour job, so I have to be really careful how I do things." Nevertheless, becoming one of the most celebrated female talents of the decade did have its drawbacks. After the Grammy nominations were announced, Hill, her record company and her management team were sued by a quartet of songwriters who claimed they had written and produced some of the songs on *Miseducation* in collaboration with Hill. "If I stopped enjoying this business, I could quit," Hill told *Rolling Stone*'s Kevin Powell. "I never want the industry to drive me; I want to drive it. I want to be a part of a new class of artists who don't have to fall apart to be dope. I'd rather not chronicle my demise."

Selected discography

With the Fugees

Blunted on Reality, Ruffhouse/Columbia, 1993.
The Score, Ruffhouse/Columbia, 1996.

Solo

The Miseducation of Lauryn Hill, Ruffhouse/Columbia, 1998.

Sources

Billboard, May 11, 1996, p. 37; December 12, 1998, p. 6.
Ebony, November 1998, pp. 194-202.
Entertainment Weekly, June 26, 1998; September 4, 1998; October 2, 1998.
Essence, June 1998, pp. 73-76, 156-158.
Harper's Bazaar, April 1998, pp. 204-209.
New York Daily News, August 30, 1998.
People, August 31, 1998; December 28, 1998, pp. 56-57.
Rolling Stone, September 5, 1998, p. 40; September 17, 1998, p. 35; February 18, 1999.
The Source, September 1998, p. 223.
Spin, January 1999, p. 65.
Stereo Review, November 1998, pp. 109-110.
Time, September 7, 1998, pp. 70-72.
Time Out—New York, June 4, 1998.
Us, September 1998.
Village Voice, March 5, 1996, p. 53; April 9, 1996, p. 53; September 1, 1998, p. 57.

—Carol Brennan

Bruce Hornsby

Singer, pianist, songwriter

Archive Photos, Inc. Reproduced by permission.

Bruce Hornsby's illustrious career has included just about every type of success a musician can experience. His musical roles have been varied—lounge musician, unknown pop song writer, successful mainstream musician, Grammy award winner. Audiences are most familiar with Hornsby's work with his band, the Range. "The Way It Is," recorded by Bruce Hornsby and the Range, was one of the most played songs on American radio in 1987. Hornsby embarked on a solo career in the nineties that combined many forms of music and met with critical acclaim. He is known for his acoustic piano playing and honest lyrics intensified by his strong vocals. Hornsby's songs are real life stories about small-town people. His songs are so true to life that the citizens of his hometown, Williamsburg, Virginia, analyze every aspect of each one looking for similarities to their own lives. Hornsby told Jay Cocks of *Time,* "Sometimes they find themselves. Sometimes much to their chagrin."

Hornsby was born in Richmond, Virginia, in 1954 and raised in Williamsburg. He is an avid sports fan and once dreamed of a career in professional basketball after playing on the varsity team for James Blair High School. A few colleges sought after him, but Hornsby didn't think that he could go far in basketball because he averaged only 11 points a game. He still reunites with his old high school teammates for a game of pick-up ball occasionally. He also loves baseball and golf, but it was his love for music that prevailed.

Hornsby practiced piano as seriously as he practiced basketball, even after years of disappointment with his music career. He told Mike D'Orso of *Sports Illustrated,* "I could've easily sacked it in, but I stayed intense. I still am. It goes right back to what I learned on the court." Hornsby studied music at Berklee College in Boston and eventually earned a degree from the University of Miami School of Music in 1977. By 1980 Hornsby had formed a band with his brother Bob. They moved to Los Angeles but suffered through some lean years, which forced Bruce to sign with 20th Century Fox as a songwriter. Hornsby's younger brother, John, co-wrote pop songs with him for 20th Century Fox and is still his songwriting partner.

While in Los Angeles, Hornsby performed in local bars and recorded demo tapes hoping desperately to be signed by a major record company. He did not enjoy writing for other singers and watching his music being altered. Even though celebrities like Huey Lewis tried to help Hornsby, no major labels were taking notice, forcing Hornsby to take a job playing keyboards for Sheena Easton on tour.

In 1984, Hornsby formed Bruce Hornsby and the Range. He recorded a demo tape of his own acoustic music that

For the Record . . .

Born Bruce Randall Hornsby, November 23, 1954, in Richmond, VA; son of Robert Stanley and Lois (Saunier); married Kathy Yankovich, December 31, 1983; children. *Education:* Attended Berklee College in Boston; Bachelor of Arts degree from University of Miami School of Music, 1977.

After college, played in local Virginia clubs; moved to Los Angeles, 1980; signed with 20th Century Fox to write songs for other musicians; toured as keyboard player for Sheena Easton, 1983; formed Bruce Hornsby and the Range, 1984; signed by RCA, 1985; released greatly successful *The Way It Is,* 1986; won first Grammy, 1986; released two more albums with the Range while also songwriting and performing with many other famous musicians, 1988-1990; toured as keyboardist with the Grateful Dead, replacing Brent Mydland, 1990-1992; released first solo album, *Harbor Lights,* 1993; released second solo album, *Hot House,* 1995; released double album *Spirit Trail,* 1998; continued to tour and perform with other distinguished musicians.

Awards: Grammy awards for Best New Artist, 1986, Best Bluegrass Recording, 1989, Best Pop Instrumental Performance, 1993; *Down Beat* Reader's Poll Beyond Album of the Year, 1994; Double platinum certification for *The Way It Is;* platinum certification for *Scenes from the Southside;* ASCAP Song of the Year for "The Way It Is," 1987; Emmy award for Best Original Score, 1987.

Addresses: *Home*—P.O. Box 3545 Williamsburg, VA 23187-3546. *Website*—www.bruce-hornsby.com.

drew major attention from the industry. By 1985, Hornsby and his band were signed by RCA. In 1986 they released *The Way It Is* to critical and popular acclaim. Nicholas Jennings of *Maclean's* wrote, "Its warm, robust sound is something of a novelty in an age of synthesizers." *The Way It Is* spawned three major hits: the title song "The Way It Is," which reached number one on the pop chart, "Mandolin Rain," and "Every Little Kiss." *The Way It Is* earned Bruce Hornsby and the Range a Grammy award for Best New Artist and introduced the public to Hornsby's style of tempo change-ups, stiletto fingering and right-hand piano runs. The

album sold over two million copies and raised the social consciousness about racism with the lyrics for "The Way It Is."

Hornsby and his band followed up their first album with *Scenes from the Southside* in 1988. Although not as mainstream as their first effort, they scored a top ten hit with "The Valley Road." Ralph Novak of *People* raved, "Most surprising and satisfying are the big splashes of jazz piano improvisations that Hornsby injects into such tracks as 'The Valley Road' and 'The Road Not Taken.'" Hornsby later re-recorded "The Valley Road" for a Nitty Gritty Dirt Band album titled *Will the Circle Be Unbroken, Volume II.* That version of the song earned Hornsby another Grammy in 1989 for Best Bluegrass Recording.

Hornsby's piano playing has been labeled everything from country to jazz to blues to swing. He fuses together a variety of styles in every song, and he has earned much admiration from musicians. Over his career, Hornsby has written songs and performed on over 70 albums with artists like Bob Dylan, Don Henley, Branford Marsalis, and Bonnie Raitt, among many others. In 1990 Bruce Hornsby and the Range released *A Night on the Town,* which reached number 20 on the pop chart and included the single "Across the River." This album diverged from the first two musically and was not a huge mainstream success. In the meantime, Hornsby wrote and performed on a successful Don Henley hit, "The End of the Innocence." In 1990 he toured with the Grateful Dead for nearly two years after their keyboard player, Brent Mydland, died in July of that year. He performed over 100 shows with the group until 1992.

In 1992 Hornsby decided to disband the Range and go solo. He released his first solo album in 1993 titled *Harbor Lights.* Hornsby recorded the album in his home in Williamsburg to enable him to help his wife Kathy with their twin sons. The album went gold, and according to Jennings it represented "a welcome move away from Hornsby's mainstream pop sound." What amazed music critic Vic Garbarini of *Playboy* was "Hornsby's skill at threading a folk-based melody through knotty rhythms, his rippling solo lines on folk-funk-jazz workouts like 'Rainbow Cadillac' and the strong lyrics on 'Talk of the Town.'" Hornsby toured as a solo artist, performing with distinguished musicians. In 1993 he won his third Grammy award for Best Pop Instrumental Performance for "Barcelona Mona" with Branford Marsalis, recorded for the Olympics held in Barcelona.

Hornsby continued his solo career in 1995 with the release of *Hot House.* The album contained songs longer than the four-minute standard in pop music. When Melinda Newman of *Billboard* mentioned to Hornsby that radio programmers might not understand him, he replied, "I've never been easily slotted. I've never been part of a movement or part of a new trend. I like that. My whole thing is about trying to find my own voice." His songs always tell stories of small-town people. Hornsby told Newman, "I have a friend who seems to be the gossip line of our town. I've gotten more songs from this guy riding around in his pick-up truck." Guest performances on the album included Jerry Garcia, Bela Fleck, and Chaka Kahn. Hornsby was later nominated with Chaka Kahn for a Grammy for "Love Me Still," a song for the "Clockers" movie soundtrack.

Hornsby did not release another solo album until *Spirit Trail* in 1998. It did not include theusual list of famous guest stars that his other albums boasted. Hornsby wanted his own music to be the focus of the album. *Spirit Trail* started out as a single album, but Hornsby couldn't choose favorites from the 20 songs he created. He told *Rolling Stone,* "The record is very Southern so there are a lot of songs about race, religion, judgment and tolerance." *Down Beat* reported, "Though Hornsby's piano is less of a presence, his playing has never sounded better. Several tracks feature ringing, lyrical piano codas, which upstage the songs." Hornsby continues to tour and perform and has remained true to his bluegrass roots.

Selected discography

(with The Range) *The Way It Is* (includes "The Way It Is," "Mandolin Rain," and "Every Little Kiss"), RCA, 1986.
(with The Range) *A Night on the Town* (includes "Across the River"), RCA, 1990.
Harbor Lights (includes "Rainbow Cadillac" and "Talk of the Town"), RCA, 1993.
Hot House, RCA, 1995.
Spirit Trail, RCA, 1998.

Sources

Periodicals

Billboard, June 10, 1995; October 14, 1995.
Down Beat, February, 1999.
Maclean's, May 10, 1993.
People, May 9, 1988.
Playboy, June, 1993.
Sports Illustrated, April 2, 1990.
Time, May 24, 1993.

Online

The All-Media Guide web site.
Rolling Stone Network web site.

—*Christine Morrison*

Whitney Houston

Singer

AP/Wide World Photo. Reproduced by permission.

Pop singer Whitney Houston is known and admired for the use of her fluid, soaring vocal technique in soul, disco, and R&B music. Her self-titled debut release in 1985, *Whitney Houston*, sold more than 13 million copies and spawned three hit singles— "Saving All My Love For You," "How Will I Know," and "The Greatest Love of All." The multiplatinum album became the best-selling debut of all time by a female solo artist. The single "Saving All My Love for You" garnered Houston the first of five Grammy awards. Her 1987 release, *Whitney*, was the first album by a female to enter the charts at number one, and the album made her the first artist in history to score seven consecutive number one hits.

Houston's foray into movie soundtracks proved equally impressive. *The Bodyguard* earned more than $400 million worldwide and was the most successful soundtrack ever released, with more than 33 million units sold. The soundtrack's overwhelming success was due to Houston's rendition of the Dolly Parton song "I Will Always Love You." Her duet single with Mariah Carey, "When You Believe," for the movie *The Prince of Egypt* was released in 1998 on the same day as her fifth album, *My Love is Your Love,* which featured Missy Elliott, Faith Evans, Wyclef Jean, and Lauryn Hill. With *My Love is Your Love* in 1999, Houston began fusing hip hop with rhythm and blues in a revitalizing career move. Arista president Clive Davis told *Billboard*'s Melinda Newman, "She certainly shows here that she can work at hip-hop and cutting-edge music. ... If anyone has underestimated the magnitude, the breadth of her incredible talent, they're going to be surprised."

Houston, the daughter of successful R&B backup singer Cissy Houston and the cousin of pop and soul singer Dionne Warwick, was deeply involved in music growing up in the Newark, New Jersey area. She sang in the New Hope Baptist junior choir, where her mother served as minister of music for many years. It was watching her mother that made Houston want to become a performer. By the time Houston was eleven, it was clear that she was destined for more than backup singing. When she took center stage to sing a solo, the power of her church-inflected soprano voice moved many in the congregation to tears. As a teenager, Houston sang backup vocals for Chaka Khan and Lou Rawls, and dabbled successfully in teen modeling, gracing the covers of *Seventeen* and *Glamour*. She also studied acting and dancing, appeared in television commercials and sitcoms, and performed occasional singing dates. Her family was grooming her for eventual global superstardom, as her combination of extraordinary talent and exceptional beauty promised to offer a bright career.

For the Record . . .

Born August 9, 1963, in Newark, NJ; daughter of John (head of music management company) and Cissy (R&B backup singer); cousin of Dionne Warwick (pop and soul singer). Married Bobby Brown (R&B singer) in 1992; daughter, Bobbi Kristina.

Sang backup vocals for Chaka Khan and Lou Rawls as a teen; modeled; appeared in television commercials and sitcoms including *The Merv Griffin Show*, *Silver Spoons*, and *Gimmie a Break;* signed with Arista Records in 1985; released *Whitney Houston*, 1985; released *Whitney* in 1987; sang the "Star Spangled Banner" at 1990 Super Bowl, 1990; released *I'm Your Baby Tonight*, 1990; lead role in feature film *The Bodyguard*, 1992; appeared in *Waiting to Exhale*, 1995; starred in *The Preacher's Wife*, *1997;* teamed with singer Mariah Carey to record the theme song "When You Believe" for *The Prince of Egypt*, 1998; released *My Love is Your Love*, 1998.

Awards: Emmy Award for Outstanding Individual Performance in a Variety of Music Program, 1986; Grammy Award for Best Pop Vocal Performance Female, 1987; People's Choice Award for Favorite Female Musical Performer, 1987; People's Choice Award for Favorite Female Musical Performer, 1988; Emmy Award, 1988; Grammy Award for Best Pop Vocal Female, 1989; People's Choice Award for Favorite Female Musical Performer, 1993; People's Choice Award for Favorite Female Musical Performer, 1993; Grammy Award for Record of the Year, 1993; Grammy Award for Best Pop Vocal Performance Female, 1993; Grammy Award for Album of the Year and Best Pop Vocal Performance Female, 1993; NAACP Image Award for Best Female Artist 1997; NAACP Image Award for Best Gospel Album, 1997; NAACP Image Award for Best Artist, 1997; NAACP Image Award for Best Actress, 1997.

Addresses: *Record company*—Arista Records, Arista Building, 6 West 57th Street, New York, NY 10019 (212) 489-7400; 8370 Wilshire Boulevard, 3rd Floor, Beverly Hills, CA 90211 (213) 655-9222.

Shortly after her 18th birthday, Houston began to develop her material and to cement record industry contracts.

She signed with Arista Records in 1985, because the label's president, Clive Davis, had a reputation for picking hits for his singers and for allowing artists to take their time to develop. Houston's debut cemented her career. Her 1985 release, *Whitney Houston*, had three number one singles, was a record-breaking debut, and earned her a Grammy award for "Saving All My Love for You." She spent the next two years touring to support the release, appearing on television shows, and working on material for her next release, *Whitney*, in 1987. *Whitney* entered the charts at number one, and Houston's dynamic MTV videos further ingratiated her to fans. She was chosen to sing the "Star Spangled Banner" at the 1990 Super Bowl and released *I'm Your Baby Tonight* the same year.

After touring strenuously for five years, Houston took time off in the early 1990s to rest and enjoy her success. In 1992 she married R&B artist Bobby Brown before 800 people, and had a daughter, Bobbi Kristina. She appeared in the movie *The Bodyguard* in 1992 as the lead romantic female role opposite Kevin Costner, and sang the movie's theme song, "I Will Always Love You." In 1995 Houston appeared in the movie *Waiting to Exhale,* and she contributed to the soundtrack as well. Her third film appearance in a remake of *The Preacher's Wife* opposite Denzel Washington didn't fare as well at the box office, but did permit Houston to get back in touch with her gospel roots. Houston's shift from superstar singer to box office draw was successful, and placed her in the category of American icon along with other musical film performers such as Diana Ross, Madonna, Elvis Presley, and Dolly Parton.

Houston performed at a White House dinner honoring Nelson Mandela, and is known for her philanthropic endeavors. She has made significant contributions to the United Negro College Fund, the Children's Diabetes Fund, St. Jude's Children's Hospital, and AIDS-related organizations. She also established the Whitney Houston Foundation for Children, Inc., a nonprofit organization established to assist homeless children and children with cancer and AIDS. In August of 1998 Houston teamed up with singer Mariah Carey to record the theme song "When You Believe" for the animated DreamWorks movie *The Prince of Egypt,* which tells the story of Moses. Rumors that the two singers were competitive abounded, so the duo appeared together at the MTV Video Music Awards in September of 1998 wearing identical dresses to present Will Smith with the Best Male Video Award.

The Prince of Egypt soundtrack appeared in stores on the same day in 1998 as Houston's solo album, *My Love is Your Love*. It was her first full-length studio recording in eight years. The single "When You Believe" appeared on *My Love is Your Love,* the *Prince of Egypt* soundtrack, and Carey's 1998 greatest hits release. *Rolling Stone*'s Rob Sheffield wrote of *My Love is Your Love,* "Whitney Houston's first album in eight years is her most consistent ever—in fact, it's her first consistent album....The former ingenue has some grown-up scars now, singing the marital blues with a bite in her voice that she's never come close to before." Esther Iverem of the *Washington Post* wrote, "Whitney Houston may well be heir to the diva mantle passed down by the likes of Aretha Franklin and Diana Ross. Her singing cannot really be said to clone any of her inspirations. With a wide range and undeniable vocal power ... she can obviously belt out a song."

Selected discography

Whitney Houston, Arista, 1985.
Whitney, Arista, 1987.
I'm Your Baby Tonight, Arista, 1991.
The Bodyguard (soundtrack), 1992.
My Love is Your Love, Arista, 1998.

Compilations/Soundtracks

One Moment in Time (1988 Summer Olympics Album), Arista, 1988.

A Very Special Christmas, A&M, 1990.
Bobby Brown: Bobby, MCA, 1992.
A Tribute to Curtis Mayfield, Warner Brothers, 1994.
Ultimate Dance Party, Arista, 1997.
Ultimate Christmas, Arista, 1998.
The Prince of Egypt (soundtrack), DreamWorks, 1998.

Sources

Periodicals

Billboard, October 31, 1998.
New York Daily News, November 29, 1998.
New York Post, November 12, 1998.
Rolling Stone, January 21, 1999.
USA Today, August 20, 1998.

Online

http://www.cdnow.com.
http://www.entertainmentweekly.com.
http://www.geocities.com.
http://www.wallofsound.go.com.
http://www.whitney-fan.com.

—B. Kimberly Taylor

J. Geils Band

Rock artists

Wedding a wealth of classic rock influences — including blues, doo-wop, pop, and R&B—to a lively stage show, the J. Geils Band were attention-getters when they burst onto the New England music scene in the late-1960s. While it took them more than a decade to get widespread commercial success, when the band peaked, it did so as it did everything else—in a big, splashy way. As Gary Graff noted in *MusicHound Rock: The Essential Album Guide,* "[d]uring its 18 years together, the Geils gang was always painfully inconsistent ... [which] was always frustrating for fans, because Geils had a loaded arsenal of talent.... When it clicked, few could beat Geils, and its concerts were usually 'til-we-all-drop marathons."

The band formed in Boston in 1967 after the Hallucinations—a group that included singer, painter, and disc jockey Peter Wolf and drummer Stephen Jo Bladd—broke up, and the pair joined another local act, the J. Geils Band (named for founder and guitarist Jerome Geils). The J. Geils Band, founded as a trio, consisted of its namesake, harmonica player Magic Dick (Dick

Members include **Peter Wolf** (born Peter Blankfield, March 1946, Bronx, NY, left group, 1983), vocals; **Stephen Jo Bladd** (born July 13, 1942, Boston, MA), drums; **Magic Dick** (born Dick Salwitz, May 13, 1945, New London, CT), harmonica; **J. Geils** (born Jerome, February 20, 1946, New York, NY), guitar; **Seth Justman** (born January 27, 1951, Washington, D.C., joined band, 1968), keyboards (and vocals, 1983-1985); **Danny Klein** (born May 13, 1946, New York, NY), bass.

Group formed in Boston, 1967; released self-titled debut on Atlantic, 1971; signed with EMI America and released *Sanctuary* (first gold record), 1978; earned first number one single ("Centerfold") with *Freeze-Frame,* 1981; replaced Wolf with Justman on vocals, 1983; disbanded, 1985.

Addresses: *Record company*—Mercury (for Wolf), World Wide Plz., 825 Fifth Ave., New York, NY 10019; Rounder (for Buestime), One Camp St., Cambridge, MA 02140.

Salwitz), and bass player Danny Klein. With the addition of composer and producer Seth Justman (an organist who became the band's keyboardist) in 1968, the outfit was complete.

By 1971, the band had landed a recording contract with Atlantic and released a self-titled debut that produced a minor Top 40 hit in the single "Looking for a Love." The album won positive notices for its mix of blues and R&B, and prompted *Rolling Stone* to name the J. Geils Band the most promising new act. During the same period, Wolf was enjoying recognition of a different variety, having caught the interest of film star Faye Dunaway. The pair dated for two years before marrying in 1974, a union that lasted four years.

For the J. Geils Band, stardom seemed elusive. In spite of regular touring and recording, the band failed to become pop chart staples, having to settle instead for the occasional small hit. Given the loyal following the band's reportedly energetic stage shows garnered, its third album, 1972's *Full House,* was, appropriately, a live album recorded during a concert in Detroit. A string of albums followed, with the band even renaming itself "Geils" for 1977's *Monkey Island,* which the band produced by itself.

That was all to change in the early 1980s, though. Following the success of 1978's *Sanctuary* (which went gold), the band embarked on a massive 1980 tour in support of the album *Love Stinks,* which also went gold and included minor hits in the title track and "Come Back." Benefiting from heavy MTV airplay and catchy singles, the band's next record, 1981's *Freeze-Frame,* was its biggest ever, and made top ten hits out of the title track and "Centerfold," which spent six weeks at number one on the Billboard pop chart (making it one of the biggest hits of the year). The album earned the band some positive critical notices as well. As Stephen Thomas Erlewine observed in the *All Music Guide to Rock,* on *Freeze-Frame,* "[g]ood-time rock 'n' roll remains at the core of the group's music, but the sound of the record is glossier, shining with synthesizers and big pop hooks."

The sudden commercial success, however, could not heal tensions brewing within the band—particularly those between songwriters Wolf and Justman. After the success of *Freeze-Frame,* the band only recorded one more record, 1982's live album *Showtime!.* When the band allegedly refused material Wolf had written with R&B vocalist Don Covay and Michael Jonzun of the hip-hop act the Jonzun Crew, Wolf left the band for a solo career. The split was a bitter one. As Wolf recalled to Marc Bernardin for a 1997 *Entertainment Weekly* article, "Basically, they threw me out [of the band]."

Justman took Wolf's place as lead singer, and the band released *You're Gettin' Even While I'm Gettin' Odd* in 1984. Without the colorful, rapping Wolf as the band's focal point, however, the new version of the J. Geils Band failed to stir up the excitement of the former unit. Unable to recapture its commercial glory, the band dissolved the following year.

Wolf, on the other hand, initially benefited from the separation, scoring several Top 40 hits from his danceable first solo outings (1984's *Lights Out* and 1987's *Come as You Are*). But Wolf's stardom as a solo artist proved to be nearly as short-lived as the heyday of his former band. After the lackluster reception to 1990's *Up to No Good,* Wolf largely retreated from the rock 'n' roll limelight and found solace in painting, which he had enjoyed dating back to his teens (and which he studied for a time at the Boston Museum School of Fine Arts). It was years before he would attempt another album—and when he did, it was a different Wolf who emerged. His 1996 release, *Long Line,* was a more personal and thoughtful effort than his previous works had been. A collection of soulful rock songs and ballads, it also included two collaborations with singer/songwriter Aimee Mann, formerly of the band 'Til Tuesday.

The late 1990s found an older, more introspective Wolf recording songs that reflected that maturity. As he told David Sprague for a 1996 article in *Billboard,* "I'm not one to slip on the glasses and wax pseudo-intellectual, but I needed to redefine myself and do something that's relevant to who I am now. There's a part of rock 'n' roll that's pure adolescence, but it's not only that. I've gotten rid of that albatross: I don't feel like I'm a gerbil in a cage anymore." As of 1997, Wolf was reported to be working on a memoir, slated to be titled *Further Tales from the Vinyl Jungle.*

Wolf's next album, 1998's *Fool's Parade,* was hailed by *Rolling Stone* writer Anthony DeCurtis as "easily the best work of his solo career—a moving, impassioned statement of rock and roll commitment." For Wolf, the album offered an opportunity to delve deeper into himself and his musical roots. As he told DeCurtis in 1998, *"Fool's Parade* was the first time I felt the composure to take myself more seriously. I really, truly feel that I'm a late bloomer, and this is the most focused effort I've made to express the journey I've been on."

Meanwhile, some of his former bandmates were pursuing a different musical path. Around the time of the dissolution of the J. Geils Band, Geils (billing himself as "Jay") and Magic Dick assembled a roots-oriented blues band called Bluestime, which released a self-titled debut on Rounder in 1994 with Michael "Mudcat" Ward on bass, Steve Ramsay on drums, and Jerry Miller on guitar. A follow-up, *Little Care of the Blues,* appeared in 1996.

Selected discography

J. Geils Band, Atlantic, 1971.
The Morning After, Atlantic, 1972.
Full House, Atlantic, 1972.
Bloodshot, Atlantic, 1973.
Ladies Invited, Atlantic, 1973.
Nightmares (And Other Tales from the Vinyl Jungle), Atlantic, 1974.
Hot Line, Atlantic, 1975.
Blow Your Face Out, Atlantic, 1976.
(As Geils) *Monkey Island,* Atlantic, 1977.
Sanctuary, EMI America, 1978.
Love Stinks, EMI, 1980.

Freeze-Frame, EMI, 1981.
Showtime!, EMI, 1982, reissued, BGO, 1995.
You're Gettin' Even While I'm Gettin' Odd, EMI, 1984.
Flashback: Best of the J. Geils Band, EMI, 1985.
The J. Geils Band Anthology: Houseparty, Rhino, 1993.

Peter Wolf solo

Lights Out, EMI, 1984.
Come as You Are, EMI, 1987.
Up to No Good, MCA, 1990.
Long Line, Reprise, 1996.
Fool's Parade, Mercury, 1998.

Bluestime

Bluestime, Rounder, 1994.
Little Care of the Blues, Rounder, 1996.

Sources

Books

DeCurtis, Anthony and James Henke, editors, *Rolling Stone Album Guide,* Random House, 1992.
DeCurtis, Anthony, and James Henke, editors, *Rolling Stone Illustrated History of Rock & Roll,* Random House, 1992.
Erlewine, Michael, executive editor, *All Music Guide to Rock, 2nd Edition,* Miller Freeman Books, 1997.
Graff, Gary and Daniel Durchholz, editors, *MusicHound Rock: The Essential Album Guide,* Visible Ink, 1999.
Jakubowski, Maxim, executive editor, *Music Television (MTV) Who's Who in Rock Video,* Zomba Books, 1983.
Romanowski, Patricia and Holly George-Warren, editors, *New Rolling Stone Encyclopedia of Rock & Roll,* Fireside, 1995.
Whitburn, Joel, *Billboard Book of Top 40 Hits,* Billboard Books, 1996.

Periodicals

Billboard, April 13, 1996; September 12, 1998.
Entertainment Weekly, May 17, 1996; August 1, 1997; August 7, 1997.
Musician, December 1998.
Rolling Stone, July 12, 1990; October 29, 1998; November 12, 1998.

—K. Michelle Moran

Alan Jackson

Singer, songwriter

AP/Wide World Photos. Reproduced by permission.

Traditions are sometimes forgotten in favor of the new and improved. In the early 1980s, the weeds of a fad—the synthesized pop music of the urban cowboy, had trampled country music's roots. However, in 1989 a new group of country singer/songwriters including a tall, white-hatted Georgia boy, Alan Jackson, tore out those weeds and planted a new tradition. Over the next ten years, Jackson would hit number one on the country music charts over 20 times and win over 45 awards, nearly losing his twenty-year marriage to his high school sweetheart, Denise along the way. However, Jackson remained humble, telling *twangthis.com* that he was "just a guy who sings [and who] hopes I'm keeping a little bit of traditional country music alive for the next generation so they'll know what it is."

Alan Eugene Jackson was born on October 17, 1958 in Newnan, Georgia. His father, Eugene, an autoworker, and mother, Ruth, a homemaker married in 1952 and moved into Eugene's dad's 12 foot by 12 foot tool shed. As their family expanded to seven—Alan and his sisters Diane, Connie, and twins Cathy and Carol—so did the tool shed. While still in high school, Jackson met his future wife, Denise at a Dairy Queen. He married his sweetheart in 1979. Soon after, they moved to Nashville so Jackson could pursue his music career. While Denise worked as a flight attendant, Jackson worked odd jobs including used car salesman and mailman for cable TV's The Nashville Network (TNN). During his lunch breaks Jackson would study what type of country music hit the charts, what fans liked and what they were buying.

In the early 1980s, country music fans seemed to like and buy the bland, "pop-ified" country music of the urban cowboy while everyone else seemed to be riding bucking broncos in bars, wearing cowboy boots, hats, and tight blue jeans. Country music, according to *Country Weekly* reporter Gerry Wood, "got very plasticized strings everywhere . traditional roots were just getting ground under like plowed ground." As the 1980s urban cowboy fad cooled off, as stated by Ken Kragen on TNN's *The Life and Times of the All-star Class of '89*, "country music started to retrench and almost as a reaction against this popularizing of country music, traditionalists came along." One of these new traditionalists was Alan Jackson. However, it would be Denise, Jackson's wife, not Jackson himself who found his big break. On one of Denise's flights, she ran into country superstar Glen Campbell. She told him about Jackson's desire to be a country singer/songwriter and asked Campbell for advice. Campbell gave Denise the name of his company's manager, Marty Gamblin, and told Jackson to call. Soon after, Gamblin hired Jackson to write songs for Glen Campbell Enterprises. Thus, a

For the Record . . .

Born Alan Eugene Jackson on October 17, 1958 in Newnan, GA; son of Eugene (an autoworker) and Ruth Jackson; sisters: Diane, Connie, and twins Cathy and Carol; married Denise, December 15, 1979; children: Mattie (born June 19, 1990), Alexandra (born August 23, 1993) and Dani (born August 28, 1993).

Grew up in a 12' by 12' tool shed; hired by Glen Campbell Enterprises as a songwriter until he signed to Arista Records in 1989; released first album *Here in the Real World*; 1990, the title song becomes number one hit; became member of the Grand Ole Opry, 1991; success continued over the next 10 years with eight more albums which included a total of over twenty number one hits such as "Midnight in Montgomery," "Chattahoochee," "Little Bitty," and "I'll Go on Loving You;" opened the Alan Jackson Showcar Café in Pigeon Forge, TN, 1998.

Awards: Academy of Country Music (ACM) Top New Male Vocalist, 1990; TNN/Music City News Star of Tomorrow, 1991; ACM Country Music Album of the Year, 1991; Country Music Association (CMA) Music Video of the Year, 1992; CMA Single of the Year, 1993; ASCAP Songwriter of the Year, 1993, 1994, 1998; American Music Awards (AMA) Favorite Album, 1994; CMA Entertainer of the Year, 1995; ACM Male Vocalist of the Year, 1995, 1996, TNN/Music City News Entertainer of the Year, 1996, 1997.

Addresses: *Home*—Nashville, TN. *Fan Club*—P.O. Box 121945, Nashville, TN. *Web site*—ajackson.com.

chance meeting on an airplane had started Jackson's career.

Icing On The Cake

By the late 1980s, country music fans had had enough of the synthesized pop that was passing for country music. A new class of country music superstars—musicians who sounded a lot like country music legends Hank Williams, Faron Young, Merle Haggard, and George Jones—emerged, led by Randy Travis. In 1989, seeing this return to tradition, record labels signed their own "new traditionalists" including Clint Black, Travis Tritt, Vince Gill, Garth Brooks, and Alan Jackson. In 1990, along with the birth of his first daughter, Mattie, Jackson's first album, *Here in the Real World* was released on Arista Records. *Here in the Real World* produced four number one singles including the title track, "Wanted," "Chasin' That Neon Rainbow," and "I'd Love You All Over Again." Jackson also won two major awards that year: TNN/Music City News Song of the Year for "Here in the Real World," and the Academy of Country Music (ACM) for Top New Male Vocalist.

In 1991, Jackson released his second album, *Don't Rock the Jukebox*. Five songs, four of which Jackson wrote or co-wrote, topped the country music charts: "Someday," "Dallas," "Love's Got a Hold on You," "Midnight in Montgomery," and the title track. In two of these number one hits, Jackson paid respect to his musical inspirations—Hank Williams and George Jones. "Midnight in Montgomery" honors the legendary country singer/songwriter Williams. In "Don't Rock the Jukebox," Jackson wrote what *Country Music Culture*'s Curtis W. Ellison called, "a homage to George Jones—another Hank Williams admirer—and to honky tonk music, a statement against rock and roll in favor of country music." Jackson won four awards that year including TNN/Music City News Star of Tomorrow and Album of the Year, and ACM's Country Music Single and Album of the Year.

In 1992, Jackson's success continued with two new albums: *Honky Tonk Christmas* and *A Lot 'Bout Livin' (and a Little 'Bout Love)*, the latter producing five number one hit singles including "Chattahoochee." Jackson not only won five awards that year including CMA Music Video of the Year, ASCAP Song of the Year, and TNN/Music City News Male Artist, Single, and Album of the Year, but also welcomed another baby daughter, Alexandra.

In 1994, Jackson's fifth album, *Who I Am* was released. This album, according to *Entertainment Weekly* music reviewer Alanna Nash, seemed to "show him to be more emotionally vulnerable." With hits like "Let's Get Back to Me and You" and "Job Description," Nash believed that "seldom has a star made his life away from home sound so lonely." Thus, for the first time, Jackson seemed to be feeling the pressures of success. Jackson told *People* magazine that "[My career] is like a movie or something [and my home] is more like the real world for me, in the woods with my family." He further commented that "[he was] realizing that all those things that you wanted so bad aren't gonna make you happy or keep you happy." In the same vein, Jackson told *People* that he realized that "my life is really like a fairy tale [and] you gotta be happy with yourself and with your spouse and with your life. All the rest is just icing on the cake." Jackson won 10 awards in 1994 including ASCAP Song and Songwriter of the Year as well as ACM Top Male Vocalist and American Music Awards Favorite Album and Single of the Year.

Separated, Reconciled, and "High Mileage"

Throughout the mid-to-late 1990s, Jackson's star continued to burn brightly. In 1995, Jackson released his *Greatest Hits* album and won eight major awards including CMA Entertainer of the Year. In 1996 Jackson released his seventh album, *Everything I Love*, his first album of all new material in three years. This album included the number one single "Little Bitty," written by songwriting great Tom T. Hall, which told people to enjoy life "because it goes on only for a little bitty while." Speaking on his approach to music, Jackson told *twangthis.com* that "I just try to have fun with it and pick songs and write songs that I like. I don't really worry about what's going to happen to it commercially." Country music fans loved what Jackson liked and awarded him TNN/Music City News Entertainer of the Year in 1996 and 1997. Dani, Jackson's third daughter was also born in 1997. Thus, Jackson's music career and home life seemed to be on a solid ground, however, what Jackson loved most—his family—was crumbling.

In February 1998, *USA Today* announced that Jackson and Denise had separated. Jackson told *USA Today*'s Brian Mansfield that "what was happening was, I couldn't be happy. I kept trying to let everything else make me happy. Maybe that's why I'm successful. I worked so hard to get all this stuff to make me happy." Jackson continued, "Then that didn't do it. It actually got worse. This career added other problems to it. I isolated myself more." After months of therapy, Jackson and Denise reconciled and renewed their wedding vows on December 15, their nineteenth wedding anniversary. Denise told *Life* that "I see that separation as a gift. It forced us to put our attention back on our relationship." Jackson told *Life* that "I realize what makes you happy: It's having someone to love and someone who loves you."

In September 1998, Jackson released his eighth album, *High Mileage*. *Life* called this album, "an ode to marriage" while *country.com* stated that "the album is Jackson's take on life's latest chapter both the home runs and the curve balls as it came rushing to him." *High Mileage*'s first single, "I'll Go On Loving You," written by Kieran Kane, "is sure to set tongues wagging," Mansfield said, because, "[it] is a markedly different sound for Jackson [who] recites much of the song's intimate lyrics in which the singer watches his lover step out of her dress, yet speaks of a love that will last after the passing 'pleasures of the flesh.'" After 10 years in country music, which *Chicago Sun-Times* reporter Dave Hoekstra described as, "like a new snakeskin boot. You have to grow into it," Jackson had not only grown a successful music career that helped revive traditional country music, but had grown into a happy man, as well. As he told *People*, "You can have everything, but if you ain't' got nobody to enjoy it with, it ain't no fun."

Selected discography

Here in the Real World, Arista Records, 1990.
Don't Rock the Jukebox, Arista Records, 1991.
Honky Tonk Christmas, Arista Records, 1992.
A Lot 'Bout Livin' (and a Little 'Bout Love), Arista Records, 1992.
Who I Am, Arista Records, 1994.
Greatest Hits, Arista Records, 1995.
Everything I Love, Arista Records, 1996.
High Mileage, Arista Records, 1998.

Sources

Books

Ellison, Curtis, *Country Music Culture: From Hard Times to Heaven*, University Press Of Mississippi, 1995.

Periodicals

Chicago Sun-Times, September 21, 1998.
Entertainment Weekly, July 7, 1998.
Good Housekeeping, June 1995.
Life, February 1999.
People, Special Issue, 1994.
USA Today, February 20, 1998; September 1, 1998.

Online

twangthis.com
country.com
geocities.com
ajackson.com

Additional information provided by *The Life and Times of the All-Star Class of '89*, a TNN special program broadcast January 25, 1999, and from liner notes from Alan Jackson's albums.

—Ann M. Schwalboski

Jewel

Singer, songwriter

AP/Wide World Photo. Reproduced by permission.

Pop superstar Jewel combined original musical compositions with a beguiling, heartfelt voice and a charming, honest demeanor. Within the span of four years, Jewel went from living in a van in the San Diego, California area and performing for customers in local coffeehouses to selling more than 10 million copies of her 1995 debut release, *Pieces of You.* Jewel also received a two million dollar advance for a book of her intensely personal poetry titled, *A Night Without Armor,* which became a mainstay on the *New York Times* bestseller list. Her sophomore release, *Spirit,* was released in mid-November of 1998 and had already been certified as triple platinum by January 1, 1999. *Entertainment Weekly's* Jeff Gordinier described Jewel as, "The beautiful and beatific muse of positivity (who has) won a worldwide audience." He described *Spirit* as "a collection of 'spiritual' ballads; it's as downy-tufted and low-angst as a basket of napping puppies."

Born Jewel Kilcher on May 23, 1974 in Payson, Utah, as one of three children to singer/songwriters Atz Kilcher and Nedra Carroll. Jewel was raised on an 800-acre ranch in Anchorage, Alaska that had no running water, no locks on the doors, and no television. Jewel could play the piano before she could read, and spent much of her childhood tending horses, gardening, baling hay, and singing. Her parents performed throughout Alaska and began to include Jewel in their shows after her sixth birthday. Jewel's parents divorced when she was eight, and her mother relocated to San Diego while her father remained in Alaska. Jewel continued touring with her father until the age of 15, when she received a vocal scholarship to the Interlochen Arts Academy in Michigan for her junior and senior years of high school. The scholarship covered only 70 percent of the tuition at Interlochen, so Jewel raised the remaining 30 percent by performing a solo concert and through the donations of the people of Homer, Alaska. Jewel's first solo performance, at 15 was for Tom Bodet's *End of the Road* show.

Jewel began playing the guitar and writing songs during her senior year of high school. She also studied dance, sculpture, and drama. She had originally intended to pursue a career in opera but had a change of heart. After graduating from high school, Jewel moved to San Diego to live with her mother and took jobs as a waitress and a secretary to support herself. To save money, Jewel and her mother decided to move out of their home and to live in separate vans. Jewel kept a knife handy in case she was ever bothered at night while sleeping.

She began performing in coffeehouses around the San Diego area, and landed a regular Thursday evening slot at the Innerchange cafe in Pacific Beach, CA. It was there that she caught the ear of an Artists & Repretoire

Billboard Top 200. Her single "Who Will Save Your Soul" was re-released in 1996, and between 1996-98, she appeared on *The Tonight Show with Jay Leno, Saturday Night Live, Late Night with Conan O'Brien, The David Letterman Show,* and *Live with Regis and Kathie Lee.* The single "Who Will Save Your Soul" peaked at number eleven on the *Billboard* singles chart in September of 1996, and "You Were Meant For Me" was then re-released in 1996. Jewel performed at Lilith Fair in July of 1997, which generated a lot of publicity and favorable reviews. By the end of 1997, "You Were Meant for Me" had set the record for the longest charting single on the *Billboard* Hot 100—over 60 weeks. In addition, *Pieces of You* became the second most popular album of 1997, selling over 4.3 million copies and going platinum more than eight times in the U.S. By the end of 1997, Jewel had attained superstar status.

Jewel received a $2 million advance in 1998 to publish a book of poetry—some of the poetry dating back to her high school year, including *A Night Without Armor.* The book spent weeks on the *New York Times* bestseller list and was in its twentieth printing at the start of 1999. Jewel's 1998 sophomore release, *Spirit,* reached number four on the *Billboard* 200 albums chart a month after it was released. *Spirit* featured soulful ballads and poignant lyrics, combined with Jewel's clear, melodic vocals. The release was produced by Patrick Leonard, noted for his work with Madonna, and featured Flea from the Red Hot Chili Peppers on bass.

Through the years 1997-98 Jewel's presence had become nearly impossible to ignore. She performed for Pope John Paul II in December of 1998, along with the vocal group Manhattan Transfer, British trio Cleopatra, and other musicians. She graced the cover of *Time* in July of 1997, the cover of *Rolling Stone* twice in 1998, and appeared on the covers of *Details, Interview, Vogue, People,* and *Entertainment Weekly.* Jewel made her acting debut in 1998 in director Ang Lee's Civil War drama, *Ride With The Devil.* Vainshtein had worked with Carroll when making managerial decisions concerning Jewel's career. A month before Jewel began shooting *Ride With The Devil* in February of 1998, she fired Vainshtein and named Carroll her sole manager. Vainshtein responded with a $10 million lawsuit for breach of contract.

Jewel received an American Music Award in 1997 for Best New Artist, a Blockbuster Entertainment Award for Favorite CD in May of 1998 for *Pieces of You*, and was nominated for three MTV Video Music Awards and for an MTV Viewer's Choice Award in 1997. Speaking about her commercial success, she told Gordinier, "I don't want to get on my deathbed and look back at my life and realize I worried about what just doesn't matter.... I really don't

(A&R) woman for Atlantic Records named Jenny Price, as well as future manager Inga Vainshtein. Price told Gordinier, "We saw Jewel and our mouths just dropped. She was ... this little wildflower that had so much raw talent, and she was in some kind of purple jumper, and she was yodeling. The next day I called my boss at Atlantic, and I said, 'We have to sign this girl.' It was so clear to me." Jewel grew in popularity at the Innerchange and played as many as four shows a day. She met and worked with Steve Poltz, the lead singer of The Rugburns. They wrote the singles "You Were Meant For Me" and "Adrian" together.

In March of 1994, Jewel signed to Atlantic Records, and soon recorded four sets of live material at the Innerchange, including "Pieces of You" and "Little Sister," which made it on to her 1995 debut album, *Pieces of You.* The album received favorable reviews but did not sell well initially. It was produced by Ben Keith, who was noted for his work with Neil Young and James Taylor, and featured Neil Young's band, the Stray Gators. Jewel toured and opened for other bands around the country, and then 14 months later her debut release reached the think I'm going to care that I sold ten million records, or what people thought of my poetry book."

Selected discography

Pieces of You, Atlantic Records, 1995.
Spirit, Atlantic Records, 1998.

Sources

Books

Kilcher, Jewel: *A Night Without Armor,* HarperCollins, 1998.

Periodicals

Details, July 1998.
Entertainment Weekly, January 15, 1999.
Interview, July 1998.
People, January 18, 1999.
Rolling Stone, December 3, 1998; May 15, 1998.
Time, July 21, 1997.

Online

http://www.atlantic-records.com
http://www.cs.mun.ca/~colins/jewel/html
http://www.endor.org/jewel
http://www.eonline.com
http://www.geocities.com/SunsetStrip/Backstage/9849/frames1229.html
http://www.jeweljk.com/main/
http://www.listen.to/ggta
http://www.rl.sonicnet.com/news/archive/singlestory.jhtml?id=510144

—B. Kimberly Taylor

Kiss

Rock band

AP/Wide World Photo. Reproduced by permission.

For over 25 years, Kiss have been thrilling and entertaining audiences all over the world. Concert crowds have been comprised mostly of rabidly adoring fans, who are known as the Kiss Army. This popular success was no simple feat for a band that has been universally derided, dismissed or ignored by rock critics and music journalists.

The band got its start when bassist and vocalist Gene Simmons started jamming with another musical acquaintance of his, guitarist and vocalist Paul Stanley. The two of them met when they were working on other musical projects. Simmons and Stanley decided to complete the line up with the addition of another guitarist and a drummer. They scoured the advertisements in various music and entertainment presses, looking for musicians who might be interested in hooking up with them and sharing in Simmons's and Stanley's visions for music, theatrics, and success. They found drummer Peter Criss through an advertisement he had placed in *Rolling Stone* magazine. They contacted their soon-to-be lead guitarist Ace Frehley through an advertisement he placed in *Village Voice*.

They played a number of gigs throughout 1973 and were signed by Casablanca Records in early 1974. In February of that year, they released their self titled debut album, *Kiss*. The LP would eventually go on to sell enough copies in America to earn the band their first gold record for album sales. Toward the end of the year, Kiss released their second album, *Hotter Than Hell,* which also went gold.

Two more albums were released during the following year. *Dressed to Kill* came out in the spring of 1975 and at the close of the year, Kiss released their first live concert album, *Alive!* Both albums were certified gold the year of their initial release. The album *Alive!* even managed to reach the top ten of the American album charts.

Around this time, the Kiss Army—the band's official fan club—was formed. The popularity of the band was increasing rapidly as legions of young fans sought to worship at the crass heavy metal altar of their heroes. According to Brock Helander in *The Rock Who's Who*, the wild and crazy success of Kiss was due, in no small part, to the fact that they "combined elements of glitter rock and heavy metal, garish costuming, and make up, [which when combined with] an extensive media campaign by their record company and near constant touring [which was laden with] spectacular on stage special effects...[served to] nonetheless endear [Kiss] to legions of prepubescent fans with gimmicks such as blood spitting, fire breathing, explosions, dry ice fogs and

For the Record . . .

Members include **Eric Carr** (born July 12, 1950 in Brooklyn, NY, died November 24, 1991 in New York, NY; joined the band, 1980), drums, vocals; **Peter Criss** (born Peter Crisscoula, December 20, 1947 in Brooklyn, NY; left the band, 1980), drums, vocals; **Ace Frehley** (born Paul Frehley, April 27, 1951 in Bronx, NY; left the band 1982), guitar, vocals; **Bruce Kulick** (joined the band, 1985), guitar; **Gene Simmons** (born Chaim Klein, August 25, 1949 in Haifa, Israel), bass, vocals; **Eric Singer** (joined the band, 1982), drums; **Paul Stanley** (born Paul Stanley Eisen, January 20, 1952 in Queens, NY), guitar, vocals; **Vinnie Vincent** (born Vincent Cusano; joined the band, 1982, left the band, 1984), guitar.

Group formed in New York City, 1973; signed to Casablanca and released *Kiss*, 1974; released *Hotter Than Hell*, 1974; released *Dressed to Kill*, 1975; released *Alive!*, 1975; released *Rock and Roll All Over*, 1976; released *Love Gun*, 1977; released *Alive II*, 1977; released *Double Platinum*, 1978; released *Dynasty*, 1979; released *Kiss Unmasked*, 1980; released *Music From the Elder*, 1981; released *Creatures of the Night*, 1982; signed to Mercury and released *Lick It Up*, 1983; released *Animalize*, 1984; released *Asylum*, 1985; *Crazy Nights*, 1987; released *Smashed, Thrashes, and Hits*, 1988; released *Hot in the Shade*, 1989; released *Revenge*, 1992; released *Alive III*, 1993; released *MTV Unplugged*, 1996; released *Psycho Circus*, 1998.

Awards: Gold certification for *Kiss*, 1974; gold certification for *Hotter Than Hell*, 1975; gold certification for *Dressed to Kill*, 1975; gold certification for *Alive!*, 1975; gold certification for *Lick It Up*, 1983; platinum certification for *Destroyer,* 1976; platinum certification for *Rock and Roll All Over*, 1976; platinum certification for *Love Gun*, 1977; platinum certification for *Alive II*, 1977; platinum certification for *Double Platinum*, 1978; platinum certification for *Animalize*, 1984.

Addresses: *Record company*—Mercury Records, 825 8th Avenue, 27th Floor, New York, NY 10019.

common denominator of their audience, when they emphasizing the theatrics and spectacle of the show over the music which was "barely competent over-loud guitar based music." The theatrics at a Kiss concert drove Kiss Army members wild and the fans started to emulate the distinctive individual appearance of their heroes. Criss was the cat, Frehley was the space creature. Simmons was the demon, and Stanley the star child.

The hard work and dedication Kiss poured into their near constant touring began to pay high dividends in 1976. Their next album, *Destroyer*, became their first platinum selling album. In December of that same year, Kiss finally had their first top ten hit single in America when the ballad "Beth" shot to the top of the pop singles charts. Before the year ended, Kiss released another platinum selling album, *Rock and Roll All Over*. In 1977 the platinum selling albums *Love Gun* and *Alive II* were released, the latter yet another live concert release.

During the following year, Kiss released a two-record set of their greatest hits entitled *Double Platinum*, an album which essentially lived up to its name. At the height of their popularity, in October of 1978, the four members of Kiss simultaneously released their individual self titled debut solo albums. All four of them managed to make it into the top fifty of the American album charts.

Further solidifying their tremendous popularity in America, the band was featured in an animated cartoon called "Kiss Meets the Phantom of the Park." They were also marketed and merchandised on practically everything imaginable. In 1979, Kiss released their next studio album, *Dynasty*, which was their first album of new material in over two years. Just like its predecessors were, *Dynasty* was certified platinum.

At the dawn of the 1980s, all was not well within the Kiss camp. Citing musical differences, Criss left the band to pursue a solo career and was replaced by Eric Carr. The band went on to release *Kiss Unmasked*, which was their first album that did not reach the top thirty of the American album charts. The next year saw the release of the concept album entitled *Music From the Elder*, an album that failed to match the success of the previous Kiss albums. 1982 saw the release of *Creatures of the Night*. Also that year, witnessed the addition of Vinnie Vincent to the Kiss lineup as he replaced Frehley, who had quit the band after he was involved in a serious automobile accident.

A new stage in the history of Kiss occurred in 1983, when the band decided to forgo their makeup and over the top and outlandish stage costuming they had been using for

rocket firing guitars in performance. Kiss was "universally attacked by critics" according to Helander because of their tendency to pander to the lowest the previous decade. Kiss also signed to Mercury Records that year and released their maiden Mercury album *Lick It Up*. The first post-makeup Kiss album was certified gold.

The following year, Vincent was fired and was replaced by Mark St. John. Later in 1984, Kiss released *Animalize*, which not only made it into the top 20 on the American album charts but was certified platinum as well. *Asylum* came out in 1985 and Bruce Kulick replaced St. John on guitar. Another American top 20 album, *Crazy Nights*, surfaced in 1987. The next year, Kiss released another greatest hits compilation called *Smashes, Thrashes, and Hits*. This was followed by *Hot in the Shade*, in late 1989.

The single "Forever" was released in 1990, the first Kiss top ten single in America in nearly 15 years. In late 1991, Carr died of cancer and was replaced by Eric Singer on drums. Kiss then went on the create their first top ten American album since 1979 with the release of the 1992's *Revenge.* A third live album, *Alive III,* was released in 1993.

Over the next few years, the band toured the globe before the original lineup reunited in New York City to record and tape a segment for *MTV Unplugged*. The resulting album was released as *MTV Unplugged*, in the spring of 1996. Around this time, the reunited original band announced plans to tour again in full makeup and costumes. The resulting tour was a tremendous success. Kiss then released *Psycho Circus*, the original band's first album of new material since *Kiss Unmasked* in 1980.

Commenting on their phenomenal success and longevity in the music industry, Simmons told *People*'s Mike Flaherty in 1994 that "we've been reviled, hated by anyone who writes about music. But for 20 years we've been stubborn and committed to our vision, even though it meant going totally against fashion. Perhaps that's why we've lasted."

Selected discography

Kiss, Casablanca, 1974.
Hotter Than Hell, Casablanca, 1974.
Dressed to Kill, Casablanca, 1975.
Alive!, Casablanca, 1975.
Rock and Roll All Over, Casablanca, 1976.
Love Gun, Casablanca, 1977.
Alive II, Casablanca, 1977.
Double Platinum, Casablanca, 1978.
Dynasty, Casablanca, 1979.
Kiss Unmasked, Casablanca, 1980
Music From the Elder, Casablanca, 1981.
Creatures of the Night, Casablanca, 1982
Lick It Up, Mercury, 1983.
Animalize, Mercury, 1984
Asylum, Mercury, 1985.
Crazy Nights, Mercury, 1987.
Smashed, Thrashes, and Hits, Mercury, 1988.
Hot in the Shade, Mercury, 1989.
Revenge, Mercury, 1992.
Alive III, Mercury, 1993
MTV Unplugged, Mercury, 1996.
Psycho Circus, Mercury, 1998.

Sources

Books

Helander, Brock, ed. *Rock Who's Who*, second edition, Schirmer, 1996.
Rees, Dayfdd, and Crampton, Luke, *Encyclopedia of Rock Stars*, DK, 1996.

Periodicals

People, June 27, 1994.

—*Mary Alice Adams*

Mark Knopfler

Guitar, songwriter

A brief look through Mark Knopfler's career, and there's no question: the man loves his job. Starting out as the singer, guitarist, and songwriter for the hit 1980s rock group Dire Straits, Knopfler branched out into producing other artists and composing music for film. To fill in the gaps, he played guitar for such major artists as Eric Clapton, Bob Dylan, Joan Armitrading, and Randy Newman. He approached every aspect of his career with the utmost dedication and motivation, mixed in with a whole lot of fun.

Born August 12, 1949, in Glasgow, Scotland, Knopfler moved to Newcastle, England as a young child. His father, originally from Hungary, was an architect, and his mother was a school teacher. Knopfler's interest in music was sparked by his uncle's piano playing. He recalled his inspiration to Dan Forte in *Guitar Player*, "I heard my uncle Kingsley playing boogie woogie on the piano when I was about eight or nine, and I thought that those three chords were the most magnificent things in the world—still do."

As a teenager, Knopfler's father tried to encourage his musical interest by giving him a Fender electric guitar. Unfortunately, his father didn't know he also needed an amplifier to play it. Instead of crushing his dad's excitement, Knopfler attempted to amplify the guitar through his family's radio, completely destroying it.

Knopfler left home to attend journalism school at the age of 17. After graduation, he landed a job as a reporter and music critic at the *Yorkshire Evening Post*, where he stayed for two years. From there, he pursued an English degree at Leeds University, where he graduated in 1973. He later used his education in literature as the influence for some of his lyrics, and his favorites included William Shakespeare, Raymond Chandler, and a list of metaphysical poets.

After graduating from college, Knopfler moved to London to pursue a career in music. A struggling musician, he moved into a room that had no heat and slept on an ambulance stretcher instead of a bed. Finally, he decided to get a job teaching English part-time at Loughton College for a more stable income, and he worked there until 1977. During this time, he met bass player John Illsley, who worked at a lumber yard. The two formed what became Dire Straits with Knopfler's brother David on rhythm guitar and Pick Withers on drums.

The group convinced a local disc jockey to play a song from their demo called "Sultans of Swing," which resulted in a record deal with Phonogram's Vertigo label. In 1978, Dire Straits released their self-titled debut. The following year, after Dire Straits released their second album, *Communique*, Knopfler played guitar on Bob Dylan's album *Slow Train Coming* and Steely Dan's *Gaucho*.

Mark Knopfler hit a rough spot in 1980 when he and his brother David began having creativedifferences. Mark accused David of not having enough of a commitment to the band and the friction resulted in David's departure from the band before the release of their next album, *Making Movies*. Dire Straits replaced David Knopfler with guitarist Hal Lindes and recruited keyboardist Alan Clark. "David was under a lot of strain," John Illsley told Ken Tucker and David Fricke in *Rolling Stone*. "Mark felt very responsible for David and didn't quite know what to do. But once *Making Movies* was out and David had left, it seemed to lift a tremendous strain. Mark felt very freed."

Dire Straits continued to perform and record between Mark Knopfler's other projects. They released *Love Over Gold* in 1982, *Twisting by the Pool*, an EP, in 1983. They also released *Alchemy: Dire Straits Live* in 1984. Then, the group hit huge worldwide success in 1985 with the release of *Brothers in Arms*. The album and the single "Money for Nothing" soared to the top of the charts all over the world, and the album sold more than 15 million copies. The band won several awards for the album, single, and video. Their notoriety landed Knopfler and John Illsley an invitation to perform in the fourth annual Prince's Truse Grock Gala concert in London, with such

For the Record . . .

Born August 12, 1949, in Glasgow, Scotland; married: Lourdes Salamone. *Education:* Leeds University, 1973.

Formed Dire Straits and signed a record contract with Vertigo Records, 1977; signed U.S. contract with Warner Bros. and released self-titled debut, 1978; released six albums and two EPs, 1979-1988; composed first film score for *Local Hero*, 1982; Dire Straits announced breakup, 1988; collaborated with Notting Hillbillies and Chet Atkins, 1990; Dire Straits reformed for *On Every Street*, 1991; released debut solo album, *Golden Heart*, 1996.

Addresses: *Record company*—Warner Bros. Records, 3300 Warner Blvd., Burbank, CA 91505-4694

artists as Eric Clapton, Phil Collins, Paul McCartney, Elton John, and Tina Turner.

After Dire Straits had become a global success, Knopfler announced their breakup in 1988. "A lot of press reports were saying we were the biggest band in the world," he told Rob Tannenbaum in *Rolling Stone.* "There's not an accent then on the music; there's an accent on the popularity. I needed a rest." He reunited with John Illsley and another incarnation of Dire Straits one more time in 1991 for the release of *On Every Street.*

Knopfler also expanded his pursuits into film music in the early eighties. He made his film composing debut in 1983 with the movie *Local Hero*. The score won a British Academy of Film and Television Award. Knopfler's song "Going Home" as single from the soundtrack album, also won the award for Best Film Theme or Song at the 1984 Ivor Novello Awards. His work in film music continued through the years with such films as *Cal* in 1984, *Comfort and Joy,* also in 1984. He also wrote the soundtracks to *The Color of Money* in 1986, *The Princess Bride* in 1987, *Last Exit to Brooklyn* in 1990, *Wag the Dog* in 1998, and *Metroland* in 1999. His scores were in such demand that *Screenplaying*, a sampling of his music for motion pictures was released in 1993.

Knopfler continued performing and recording with other artists after the breakup of Dire Straits, as well. He collaborated with his long-time friends, singer/guitarist

Steve Phillips, keyboardist Guy Fletcher, and singer/guitarist Brendan Croker to form the Notting Hillbillies in 1990. The group released *Missing ... Presumed Having a Good Time* on Warner Bros. Records, and embarked on a small club tour. The band grew out of informal jam sessions among its members. "We were having so much fun, it became a band by accident," Knopfler told Tannenbaum. That same year, Knopfler also recorded an album of duets with guitarist Chet Atkins called *Neck and Neck.* The album won Grammy Awards for Best Country Vocal Collaboration and Best Country Insturmental Performance.

In 1996, Knopfler launched his own solo career after nearly 20 years of collaborations. He recorded his debut, *Golden Heart,* in Nashville, Tennessee, and Dublin, Ireland. He invited guest musicians to contribute to the album, including country artist Vince Gill and the Chieftain's Sean Keane and Derek Bell. The first single, "Darling Pretty," also appeared on the soundtrack for the film *Twister.*

After more than two decades of writing, performing, and recording music, Knopfler ashowed no signs of slowing down. After all, he loves his job. "My enjoyjment of making records has increased with age," he said in his record company biography. "I love to write. Being inspired, for want of a better word, is one of the best feelings you can have…. It's a huge, glorious adventure for me, and I love being a part of it."

Selected discography

Screenplaying, Warner Bros. Records, 1993.
Golden Heart, Warner Bros. Records, 1996.

with Dire Straits

Dire Straits, Warner Bros. Records, 1978.
Communique, Warner Bros. Records, 1979.
Making Movies, Warner Bros. Records, 1980.
Love Over Gold, Warner Bros. Records, 1982.
Twisting by the Pool, Warner Bros. Records, 1983.
Alchemy: Dire Straits Live, Warner Bros. Records, 1984.
Brothers in Arms, Warner Bros. Records, 1985.
Money for Nothing, Warner Bros. Records, 1988.
On Every Street, Warner Bros. Records, 1991.

with others

(with Notting Hillibillies) *Missing ... Presumed Having a Good Time,* Columbia Records, 1990.
(with Chet Atkins) *Neck and Neck,* Warner Bros. Records, 1990.

Sources

Books

Rees, Dafydd and Luke Crampton, *Rock Movers & Shakers,*
Billboard Books, New York, 1991.

Periodicals

Billboard, May 19, 1990
Entertainment Weekly, March 29, 1996.
Guitar Player, September 1984; June 1992; July 1996.
People, September 2, 1985; April 15, 1996.
Rolling Stone, November 21, 1985; April 5, 1990; December
1990; October 1991.
Stereo Review, June 1980.

Online

"Mark Knopfler: The Story," *Warner Bros. Records,* http://
www.wbr.com/markknopfler, (September 18, 1998).
"Mark Knopfler: Interviews, *Warner Bros. Records,* http://
www.wbr.com/markknopfler, (September 18, 1998).

—*Sonya Shelton*

kd Lang

Singer, songwriter

Corbis. Reproduced by permission.

Trying to maintain a creative existence on the edge of what was considered socially acceptable was never easy. Excelling and successfully thriving on the periphery of the popular music frontier was almost unheard of at all. For the critically acclaimed and award winning Canadian chanteuse kd Lang, the aforementioned scenario was just her modus operandi.

She was born Katherine Dawn Lang on November 2, 1961, in the tiny prairie town of Consort, Alberta, Canada. Lang was the youngest of the four children born to Audrey and Fred Lang. She grew up in a musical family, where her mother would drive the children to music lessons which were located in a town over an hour away, regardless of the weather. Desiring to study music and art, Lang left Consort in order to attend school at Red Deer College, which was located some 90 miles south of the province's capital of Edmonton. While there, Lang dabbled in performance art while increasingly growing disenchanted with her studies. She eventually dropped out of school in order to concentrate more fully on her musical performances.

Musically, Lang was drawn to country, she even claimed to be the modern day embodiment of Patsy Cline, the famous country crooner who had died in the early 1960s, at the height of her popularity. Stylistically, however, Lang defied categorization and conventions. Her costumes and stage appearances were an eclectic mix of punk and country with her short closely cropped hair, long square dance skirts, chunky boots, and bulky socks.

Lang got a job as the singer of an Edmonton based country swing band, in 1982. The group disbanded shortly thereafter. Undaunted, Lang decided to form her own band and called them the Reclines, in honor of Patsy Cline. In 1984, Lang and the Reclines released their debut effort, *A Truly Western Experience*, on the Canadian independent label Bumstead. She toured across Canada and managed to find a spiritual home in Toronto where audiences there loved her eclectic and quirky style of mixing rockabilly and country. Her appearance did not bother them at all. Lang's avante garde nature even managed to impress Seymour Stein of Sire Records who signed her and the band to a recording contract. Her first major label album, *Angel With a Lariat*, was released in 1986. It netted her a Canadian Juno Award for the Best Country Vocalist the very next year. Her sophomore effort, *Shadowland* was released in 1988. Both of the albums featured Lang and the Reclines funky "cowpunk" melodies and vocals that highlighted Lang's impassioned croonings and torch song stylings.

Increasingly, Lang began to amass a large fan base and win over critics. She won her first Grammy in 1988 for

Born Katherine Dawn Lang, November 2, 1961 in Consort, Alberta, Canada; *Education:* attended Red Deer College.

Formed kd Lang and the Reclines c. 1983; signed to Bumstead and released *A Truly Western Experience*, 1984; signed to Sire and released *Angel With a Lariat*, 1986; released *Shadowland*, 1988; released *Absolute Torch and Twang*, 1989; went solo and released *Ingenue*, 1992; released *Even Cowgirls Get the Blues*, (soundtrack), 1993; released *All You Can Eat*, 1995; released *Drag*, 1997.

Awards: Juno Award (Canada) for Best Country Female Vocalist, 1987; Grammy Award for Best Country Vocal Collaboration for "Crying," 1988; Juno Award for Canadian Country Music Entertainer of the Year 1989; Grammy Award for Best Country Female Vocal for *Absolute Torch and Twang*, 1990; Gold certification for *Absolute Torch and Twang*, 1990; Gold certification for *Shadowland*, 1992; American Music Award for Favorite New Artist Adult Contemporary, 1993; Platinum certification for *Ingenue*, 1993; Grammy Award for Best Pop Female Vocal for "Constant Craving," 1993; Juno Award for Album of the Year for *Ingenue*, 1993; Juno Award for Songwriter of the Year, 1993; Juno Award for Producer of the Year, 1993; MTV Video Music Award for Best Female Video for "Constant Craving," 1993; BRIT Award (England) for Best International Female Artist, 1995; received the Officer of the Order of Canada, 1997 .

Addresses: *Record company*—Sire Records, 75 Rockefeller Plaza, New York, NY 10019.

the Best Country Vocal Collaboration for her duet with Roy Orbison on the song "Crying." She won her second Juno Award in 1989 for the Country Music Entertainer of the Year. Despite all of the critical accolades, Lang was ostracized by the country music establishment in Nashville. Commenting on this, she told the *London Observer*'s Alan Jackson that, "I guess they don't think a girl should look or act they way I do. Nashville is very much a white male Christian society, and if you don't play by its rules, you don't really exist."

Her third album, *Absolute Torch and Twang* was released in the summer of 1989. The following year, Lang won a Grammy for Best Country Female Vocal Performance for *Absolute Torch and Twang*. Later that same year, 1990, *Absolute Torch and Twang* was a certified gold selling album in America.

Despite all of the additional critical success Lang garnered for her music, the Nashville country music establishment continued to ignore her. As a result, Lang started to focus her attention and musical skills in other areas, most notably pop jazz and torch song crooning. Commenting on her change in focus, Lang told the *New York Times*' Michael Specter that, "country music was a part of my life. Now it isn't. We had a good relationship, really, but we wanted each other at arm's length. The people in Nashville didn't want to be responsible for my looks or my actions. But they sure did like the listeners I brought."

1992 saw *Shadowland* certified gold in America. It also marked the release of the first non-country influenced album by Lang. *Ingenue* was the first album wholly credited to Lang, not Lang and the Reclines. It was a lounge-tinged collection of torch songs and sweeping ballads. The pop cabaret stylings of *Ingenue* won Lang new legions of fans, especially among the adult contemporary music aficionados. Critics as well were fond of the album and the new incarnation of Lang.

Her new approach to music was amply rewarded in 1993 as Lang won the Favorite New Adult Contemporary Artist prize at the American Music Awards. She also landed her third Grammy for the Best Pop Female Vocal for the top ten adult contemporary smash hit single, "Constant Craving." *Ingenue* was certified platinum in America, in March of 1993. Lang also won Juno Awards for Album of the Year for *Ingenue*, Songwriter of the Year, and Producer of the Year. The video for "Constant Craving" earned Lang the 1993 MTV Video Music Award for Best Female Video. Toward the end of that award winning year, Lang released the soundtrack for the film "Even Cowgirls Get the Blues."

Lang kept her profile relatively low key until early 1995 when she was named the Best International Artist at the BRIT Awards in London. In the autumn of that same year, she released her next album *All You Can Eat*. It was another two years before she released another album, the lounge and jazz inspired *Drag*. In 1997, Lang was bestowed with the honor of the Office of the Order of Canada.

Discussing her success with the *Chicago Tribune*'s Jack Hurst, Lang said, "I'm a living example of success via the media. I've never had radio airplay. I'm a media thing."

Selected discography

(with The Reclines) *A Truly Western Experience,* Bumstead, 1984.
(with The Reclines) *Angel With a Lariat,* Sire, 1986.
(with The Reclines) *Shadowland,* Sire, 1988.
(with The Reclines) *Absolute Torch and Twang,* Sire, 1989.
Ingenue, Sire, 1992.
Even Cowgirls Get the Blues (soundtrack), Sire, 1993.
All You Can Eat, Sire, 1995.
Drag, Sire, 1997.

Sources

Books

Magill, Frank, ed. *Great Lives From History: American Women Series,* volume 3, Salem Press, 1995.
Rees, Dayfdd, and Crampton, Luke, *Encyclopedia of Rock Stars,* DK, 1996.

Periodicals

Chicago Tribune, February 7, 1988.
Interview, September, 1997.
London Observer, May 27, 1990.
New York Times, July 23, 1992.

—Mary Alice Adams

Little Willie John

R&B singer

Perhaps the most overlooked R&B and soul pioneer, singer Little Willie John was a stellar performer and strong force in the history of music. Nicknamed "Little" for his height and age, the barely five-foot-tall John had his first huge hit at the age of 18. With his wide-ranging and emotionally rich voice, John recorded a string of hits between 1953 and 1962 that not only transformed him into a star but provided the material for many artists who covered his songs. The most notable of these tunes was "Fever," first recorded by John in 1956 and since covered by Peggy Lee, the McCoys, Rita Coolidge, and Madonna. Although he received far less recognition, John is often held in the esteemed company of James Brown, Sam Cooke, and Clyde McPhatter.

Born in Cullendale, Arkansas, on November 15, 1937, and raised in Detroit, Michigan, John began his singing career in a church choir like many of his contemporaries. His family formed a gospel quintet, The United Four, in which he sang, but he would soon step out on his own. He was only 14 years old when he was first discovered at a talent contest in Detroit sponsored by Johnny Otis. However, King Records' Syd Nathan, who was in the audience that night, signed another talent contest performer, Hank Ballard, instead. In the years following, John, who was barely into his teenage years, sang with Count Basie and Duke Ellington, and recorded for Savoy Records. When he was 16, he recorded a Christmas album, but it went unnoticed. His sister Mabel was also a recording artist on the Stax label and a vocalist in Ray Charles' Raelettes, but her career would pale next to that of her brother.

Bandleader Paul "Hucklebuck" Williams met John and took him on tour with his orchestra for a year. But John liked to live big, and Williams had no patience to discipline the rebellious singer. When the tour was in New York City, Williams fired John, but he would soon be discovered by King Records' Henry Glover. When King Records finally signed John in 1955, he didn't disappoint. He scored a hit with his debut recording, a cover of Titus Turner's "All Around the World," recorded on June 27, 1955. The hit, a unique blues version wholly unlike Turner's comical rendition of the tune, hit number six on the R&B charts. John followed up with "Need Your Love So Bad," another hit further establishing his stardom.

In an attempt to repeat the success of his first hit, he released "I'm Sticking With You Baby," but it wasn't until 1956 that he recorded his most popular hit "Fever," co-written with Eddie Cooley and recorded on March 1 in Cincinnati. The single reached number one on the R&B charts and became a huge pop crossover hit. John is known as the first person to record the tune, which would become an R&B standard. Most of the artists who covered the song had bigger hits, especially Peggy Lee, whose cover in 1958 propelled her to stardom and reached number eight on the pop charts, shadowing John's version, which only reached the top 30.

To promote "Fever," John performed on tour with his own revue, featuring James Brown and his Famous Flames as the opening act. John followed up his chart success with a string of R&B hits, including "Talk To Me, Talk To Me," recorded in New York City on January 4, 1958, which reached number five on the R&B charts and number 20 on the pop charts. "Sleep," a unique cover of an old song made popular in 1924 by Fred Waring's Pennsylvanians, also scored in the top 20 on the pop charts. The ballad "Let Them Talk," and "Heartbreak," which was inspired by James Brown, also charted, but not as well. John continued to record his intimate, emotional vocals on charters "Suffering With the Blues," and "Need Your Love So Bad," helping to etch his slot in music history. In 1959 he hit both the R&B and pop charts with "Leave My Kitten Alone," which was written by John and Titus Turner, and later recorded by the Beatles on a BBC radio show.

John, unlike many other African-American artists, crossed over to the pop charts regularly. But although John saw great success in his professional career, having earned a total of 14 hit singles on both the R&B and pop charts, his personal life was quite turbulent.

After the release of "Take My Love," his last recording to chart, the lack of attention began to affect him and his behavior worsened. He was an alcoholic with a penchant for violence, and it was not uncommon for him to carry a knife. At the height of his fame, he brought a gun with him to perform at the Apollo Theater in Harlem.

In 1964, at an after-show party in a private home in Seattle, Washington, John got into a fight with ex-convict Kevin Roundtree over stealing a chair from one of the women John was with. Roundtree hit John, and in response John fatally stabbed him. Two years later, in May of 1966, he was convicted of manslaughter and sentenced to 8 to 20 years in the Washington State Prison in Walla Walla. He was admitted to the prison on July 6, 1966, and two years into his term, on May 26, 1968, he died. The cause of John's death is uncertain— the press were told it was pneumonia, his death certificate says he died of a heart attack.

John gained prominence at a young age and died young too, but not completely without recognition. Soul singer James Brown, who also recorded for King Records, dedicated an album to John entitled *Thinking of Little Willie John and a Few Nice Things*. Little Willie John was also featured as one of the primary artists in Rhino Records' King reissues series. Although still relatively unknown to mainstream listeners, the music industry has acknowledged his stature as a primary influence on soul music. In 1996, John was inducted into the Rock and Roll Hall of Fame.

Selected discography

Fever, King, 1956.
The Sweet, The Hot, The Teenage Beat, King, 1961.
Come On and Join Little Willie John, King, 1962.
These are My Favorite Songs, King, 1964.
Little Willie Sings All Originals, King, 1966.
Free At Last, Bluesway, 1970.
Grits and Soul, Charly, 1985.
Mister Little Willie John, King, 1987.
Little Willie John Sings All Originals, Deluxe, 1988.
Sure Things, King, 1990.
Fever: The Best of Little Willie John, Rhino, 1993.
All 15 of His Chart Hits 1953-1962, King, 1996.
Greatest Hits, King, 1996.

Sources

Books

Romanowski, Patricia, ed., *The New Rolling Stone Encyclopedia of Rock & Roll*, Rolling Stone Press, 1995.

Online

"Little Willie John," *All-Music Guide,* http://www.allmusic.com (February 15, 1999).
"Little Willie John," *The Rock and Roll Hall of Fame*, http://www.rockhall.com (February 15, 1999).
"Little Willie John," Tom Simon's Rock and Roll Page, http://www.crl.com/~tsimon/lwjohn.htm (February 15, 1999).

—Karen Gordon

Nils Lofgren

Rock guitarist, vocalist

Though he is undoubtedly better known for his work backing other, more famous musicians—most notably Bruce Springsteen and Neil Young—guitarist Nils Lofgren has had a reasonably impressive solo career in rock as well, having recorded more than a dozen solo albums since 1975. He has also enlivened his concerts with daring jumps and flips while playing guitar.

Born in Chicago in 1952, Lofgren grew up in Maryland, close to Washington, D.C. His musical education began with the accordion at the age of five, but by the time he hit 15, Lofgren, won over by the likes of The Beatles and Jimi Hendrix, found himself drawn to rock and roll—and the guitar. It was reportedly after seeing Hendrix in concert that Lofgren left school and fled to New York's Greenwich Village, where, as a 16-year-old, he recorded a single for Sire Records with the band Dolphin.

By the late 1960s, Lofgren was fronting his own band, Grin, which he formed with drummer Bob Berberich and bass player Bob Gordon. Lofgren's brother Tom later joined the band on guitar. It was Grin's growing notoriety

Corbis View. Reproduced by permission.

Born 1952, Chicago, IL. Married to Cis.

Formed Grin with Bob Gordon (bass) and Bob Berberich (drums), 1969; sang and played piano on Neil Young's 1970 album *After the Gold Rush;* released self-titled debut with Grin on Spindizzy, 1971; released last album with Grin, *Gone Crazy,* on A&M, 1973; released first solo album *Nils Lofgren* on A&M, 1975; replaced guitarist Little Steven Van Zandt in Bruce Springsteen's E Street Band, 1984-1991; member of Ringo Starr's All-Starr Band, 1992.

Addresses: *Record Company*—The Right Stuff, 1750 N. Vine St., Hollywood, CA 90028. *Website*—www.rawks.com/nils.

that drew the attention of Neil Young, who invited Lofgren to work with him on Young's *After the Gold Rush* (1970), to which Lofgren contributed vocals and piano. Lofgren nearly joined Young's band Crazy Horse, as well, after contributing to the band's 1971 debut.

Instead Lofgren pursued a rock future with his own band. But while Grin's first two albums, 1971's *Grin* and *1 + 1* in 1972, earned strong critical praise, their commercial fortunes were disappointing. After 1972's *All Out,* Lofgren headed out on the road with Young. He returned to record Grin's 1973 album *Gone Crazy,* but that turned out to be the band's swan song. Facing financial woes and little prospect of attracting the audience some critics felt they deserved, Grin disbanded in 1974. "We were getting better than we had ever been, but the record company said, 'Hey, you're not selling enough albums, so you can't make records anymore,'" Lofgren recalled to Jas Obrecht in *Guitar Player.* "We didn't want to go back to doing Top 40 in nightclubs. We didn't want to stagnate forever and live in the past. It was sad to break up, but other than that, the whole era and life of Grin itself was a very positive, exciting thing."

Having toured with Young on the *Tonight's the Night* tour in 1973, Lofgren was a logical choice to join Young in the studio for the 1975 album of the same name. Lofgren also released his first solo recording in 1975, a self-titled effort that included "Keith Don't Go," a nod to Keith Richards of the Rolling Stones, and a cover of Carole King's "Goin' Back." *Nils Lofgren* is considered by a

number of critics to be among his strongest efforts. Commenting on the album in the *Rolling Stone Album Guide,* Paul Evans called it "an absolute delight: solid rock delivered with infectious energy and great self-confidence." After that auspicious debut, Lofgren apparently stumbled somewhat on his next release, 1976's *Cry Tough,* produced by Al Kooper. Some critics noted that while his musicianship was impressive, his vocals were decidedly less so.

If *Cry Tough* got mixed notices, the following year's *I Came to Dance* apparently fared even worse critically. After 1977's double live album *Night After Night,* it was two years before Lofgren released another record. The wait was worth it, as 1979's *Nils* was hailed as a strong return. The album featured three songs co-written with Lou Reed, who included another trio of the pair's collaborative compositions on his own *The Bells* (1979). The single "Shine Silently," while never a chart hit, earned particular praises.

After inking a deal with Backstreet Records, Lofgren released *Night Fades Away* in 1981, followed by *Wonderland* in 1983. However, a week after *Wonderland's* release, Lofgren said in a 1991 *Rolling Stone* article that after a new president took over the label, Lofgren was promptly dropped. "'I had to look for a new deal, and to my horror I couldn't get one,'" Lofgren told John Swenson in that story.

Lofgren again found refuge as a sideman, hitting the road with Young for the 1983 *Trans* tour. He then joined Springsteen's E Street Band in 1984, replacing Little Steven Van Zandt. The union proved to be a solid one, with Lofgren remaining a member of the band until Springsteen opted to work without the group in 1991. The mid-1980s thus saw few solo releases from Lofgren, aside from two compilations and 1985's *Flip,* which yielded a minor hit in the UK with the single "Secrets in the Street."

The recording break was apparently a welcome one for Lofgren, though. As he told David Simons in a 1998 article in *Musician,* "When I worked with Bruce, he completely removed that whole animal of making records and competing in the commercial world. . . . And that pause let me come back to my own music refreshed, feeling like my batteries were recharged, and ready for the next record."

After the lengthy stint as a Springsteen sideman, Lofgren toured with Ringo Starr as part of his All-Starr Band before focusing again on his solo career. For 1991's *Silver Lining,* Lofgren's musical friends returned the favor. The album featured the talents of Starr, Clarence Clemons, Levon Helm, Billy Preston, and Springsteen, who lent harmony vocals to the single "Valentine." As Swenson noted, the album reflected Lofgren's maturation while maintaining "the high-energy guitar playing that Lofgren has been known for."

His maturation was in evidence in his next release, 1992's *Crooked Line,* as well. Reviewing the album for *Entertainment Weekly,* Jim Farber called it the "toughest-sounding power-pop record since Matthew Sweet's *Girlfriend,* not to mention the truest." Helping out this time was Young, who lent backing vocals and harmonica to "You" and played electric guitar on "Drunken Driver."

For a performer who has made his mark as player, it is perhaps fitting that Lofgren's late 1990s efforts included two live records: 1997's *Code of the Road: Greatest Hits Live!* and 1998's *Acoustic Live.* While he never became the type of rock superstar he played backup for, by the 1990s Lofgren said he had learned to take comfort in playing live, which he likened to "therapy at this point" in a 1996 interview with Gregory Isola in *Guitar Player.* "I've had a real up-and-down career—that hit record has been elusive—but the audience has kept me going," he told Isola. "They don't care what chart position you're in or how many units you didn't sell or what some executive thinks of you. They let you know instantly if you've knocked 'em out—that's liberating."

Selected discography

Nils Lofgren, A&M, 1975.
Cry Tough, A&M, 1976.
I Came to Dance, A&M, 1977.
Night After Night, A&M, 1977.
Nils, A&M, 1979.
Night Fades Away, Backstreet, 1981.
Wonderland, Backstreet, 1983.
Flip, Columbia, 1985.
The Best of Nils Lofgren, A&M, 1985.
Classics Volume 13, A&M, 1989.
Silver Lining, Rycodisc, 1991.
Crooked Line, Rycodisc, 1992.
Damaged Goods, Pure, 1995.

Code of the Road: Greatest Hits Live!, The Right Stuff, 1997.
Acoustic Live, The Right Stuff, 1998.

With Grin

Grin, Spindizzy, 1971.
1 + 1, Spindizzy, 1972.
All Out, Spindizzy, 1972.
Gone Crazy, A&M, 1973.
Best of Grin, Epic, 1985.

With Neil Young

After the Gold Rush, Reprise, 1970.
Tonight's the Night, Reprise, 1975.
Trans, Geffen, 1982.

Sources

Books

Buckley, Jonathan and Mark Ellingham, eds., *Rock: The Rough Guide,* Rough Guides, 1996.
DeCurtis, Anthony and James Henke, eds., *The Rolling Stone Album Guide,* Random House, 1992.
Erlewine, Michael, executive editor, *All Music Guide to Rock, 2nd Edition,* Miller Freeman Books, 1997.
Graff, Gary and Daniel Durchholz, eds., *musicHound Rock: The Essential Album Guide,* Visible Ink, 1999.
Romanowski, Patricia and Holly George-Warren, eds., *The New Rolling Stone Encyclopedia of Rock & Roll,* Fireside, 1995.

Periodicals

Billboard, June 1, 1991.
Entertainment Weekly, Sept. 4, 1992.
Guitar Player, December 1985; June 1991; March 1996.
Musician, December 1998.
Oakland Press (Michigan), February 28, 1999.
Rolling Stone, Sept. 29, 1983; July 4, 1985; March 7, 1991; May 30, 1991.

—*K. Michelle Moran*

Nick Lowe

Singer, songwriter

Mention Nick Lowe to any fan of the new wave and punk rock movements of the late 1970s and early 1980s and you will most likely send them into a nostalgic journey. There is Nick Lowe the English singer, songwriter, bass guitarist, and band member of the pioneering British pub-rock group Brinsley Schwartz; Nick Lowe the ground breaking solo artist; and of course Nick Lowe, record producer extrodinare, godfather of all that was new wave. Lowe lead the pack when punk rock and new wave came alive in the late 1970s, the genius behind the legendary production company Stiff Records with artists that included Elvis Costello, Graham Parker, the Pretenders, and the Damned. Artists as varied as Johnny Cash, Rod Stewart, and Curtis Stigers have recorded his songs. As a musician he has managed to reinvent himself several times over his career, never allowing himself to run out of new ideas or new musical interests.

Lowe first hit the stage with a group called Kippington Lodge in 1965. Lowe was the primary songwriter and bass guitarist of the band, which included his friend, guitarist Brinsley Schwartz. Kippington Lodge released five singles on Parlaphone before evolving into Brinsley Schwartz in 1969. The group was at ground zero when London pub-rock exploded onto the scene in the early 1970s. It was with Brinsley Schwarz that Lowe first worked with Dave Edmunds. Edmunds produced the group's 1974 album, *The New Favorites of Brinsley Schwarz* and, as The Electricians, played with the group on the soundtrack to David Bowie's 1974 film, *Ziggy Stardust*.

By the mid-70s Lowe was a veteran of the London pub-rock scene and ready to focus his talents on production. In 1976, Lowe formed Stiff Records with Jake Riviera and Dave Robinson. He told Margit Detweiler of *Philadelphia City Paper Interactive* that he got the "job at Stiff Records as a producer because, simply, out of the three people who started it, I'd had more studio experience." Lowe would use his own talents as a musician, songwriter, and singer while honing his engineering and production skills. On any typical day at Stiff, he told Detweiler, "The door would open and in would come who knows what. They would maybe only have a title or a snatch of a tune, but, generally, they had bags of attitude. So I'd get the guitar out and work their thing up into some kind of demonstration of what they could do."

Stiff's—and Lowe's—first release, "Heart of the City"/ "So it Goes" sold out of its first pressing. Lowe's studio productions and original songs would carry the label through its nascent stages. Most notable among his protegees was Elvis Costello, whose first five albums were produced by Lowe. Lowe turned the dials during the recording of Graham Parker's first album, *Stop Your Sobbing* by the Pretenders, and British punk pioneers the Damned's *Damned Damned Damned*. It was the initial success of Stiff's first singles that helped spawn the large independent label industry in London. Major labels were scrambling thereafter to catch up with the new British Punk Rock and new wave mania and profit from its new stars.

In 1977, Lowe and Edmunds co-founded the near super group Rockpile. The band became a popular touring band in Great Britain and the United Sates, opening for Elvis Costello, Blondie, and the Cars. As a warm up band they tended to overshadow the featured artists. Lowe told Detweiler, "We had so much of a better time than the groups we were opening for. They'd tell us, 'You're going down too well.' So we'd have to play shorter. Well, they couldn't have done anything worse, we just took out our two rather crappy tunes and hit the ground running with our full-on blasting sets for 20 minutes."

Due to contractual obligations, Rockpile's several recorded works were released as either Lowe or Edmunds solo albums. The band garnered both critical and popular acclaim with their heady brew of rock influences. But when the band seemed on the verge of stardom, Lowe would explain to Mim Udovitch of *Esquire*, "I ran a mile." Lowe's other talents in production allowed him to escape stardom. He told Udovitch "There's no more exciting time than being just about to make it. Not being known is not much fun, and being famous and well known isn't much fun. But just being on that cusp is great. Whatever you can do to extend that, it's the best place to be."

In 1977, Riviera left Stiff, and Lowe and Costello formed the Radar Label. The debut release of the newly formed label was Lowe's first solo album, *Jesus of Cool* in England and *Pure Pop For Now People* in the United States. The album, more or less Rockpile's debut release, was widely praised by critics, and ushered in the burgeoning "power-pop" rock sub-genre. The album produced the British smash hit "I Love The Sound Of Breaking Glass." He followed the firstalbums success with the 1979 release of *Labour of Lust* which yielded his only top 40 hit in the United States, "Cruel to Be Kind," and the British hit "Cracking Up."

Lowe's studio style earned him the nickname "Basher" for his proclivity towards borrowing from past artists. Lowe, however, would later explain to Michael Gelfand of *Musician* that "no one can get to the source of it all. Not even Ray Charles or Bob Dylan or Johnny Cash—you know, the signpost artists. They got it from someplace else. It goes back and back and back. Everyone's just doing reruns of their own influences." After a busy decade of producing, writing tunes, and touring with bands, Lowe married country singer Carlene Carter— daughter of Johnny Cash—in 1979.

In the early 1980s, Lowe continued producing for the likes of John Hiatt, Paul Carrack, the Fabulous Thunderbirds, and his wife Carlene Carter. For most of the

decade, Lowe was known more for his production credits than his solo releases. His solo efforts seemed rushed as he devoted more and more of his time to producing. Personally he was increasingly frustrated with his own music, telling Udovitch "I was only operating on two or three cylinders, and if I tried to get serious, then I didn't like it." While operating one or two cylinders short, Nick Lowe only increased his catalogue of flop albums in the 1980s. His slump would actually help him get back to the more relaxed independent labels that he knew and enjoyed. Lowe told Detweiler that his label, Warner Brothers, just said "'Have some money and go away,' which was fantastic." Lowe was uncomfortable with the blitz of public appearances that are associated with major record label releases.

In the 1990s, Lowe began to regain his perspective explaining to Detweiler, "OK, I've got my little pop star thing out of the way, learned a thing or two, but now its time for me to do something that's actually good." Lowe released *The Impossible Bird* in 1994, arguably his best work to date. The album includes his own rendition of "Beast in Me," a song he had written for Johnny Cash. Lowe's biggest financial success to date came when Curtis Stigers covered his song "(What's So Funny 'Bout) Peace, Love and Understanding," for the soundtrack to the Kevin Costner and Whitney Houston film, *The Bodyguard*. Lowe received millions of dollars in royalties for the song, which hit paydirt the first time when Costello recorded it in 1979.

In 1998, Lowe released his tenth solo album, *Dig My Mood.* The album explores a range of styles from blues, jazz, soul, and country. Coupled with his 1994 release, *Impossible Bird,* it marked a new direction for Lowe. As the new lounge movement was heading into the mainstream the now silver- haired Lowe found himself once again at the lead. As to the secret of his long term success, he told Udovitch, "I haven't done my best stuff yet," and reflects, "There's not many (artists from the 1970's) where you feel that their story is still unraveling somehow."

Selected discography

With Brinsley Schwarz

Brinsley Schwartz, 1970.
Despite It All, 1971.
Silver Pistol, 1972.
Nervous on the Road, 1972.
Please Don't Ever Change, United Artists, 1973.
The New Favorites of Brinsley Schwarz, United Artists, 1974.
(As The Electricians) *Ziggy Stardust* (soundtrack), 1974.

Brinsley Schwarz, Capitol, 1978.
Fifteen Thoughts of Brinsley Schwarz, United Artists, 1978.

With Rockpile

Seconds of Pleasure, Columbia, 1979.

Solo albums

Pure Pop for Now People (includes "So it Goes" and "Marie Provost"), Columbia, 1978; released in England as *Jesus of Cool,* Radar, 1978.
Labour of Lust (includes "Cruel To Be Kind"), Columbia, 1979.
Nick the Knife, Columbia, 1982.
The Abominable Showman, Columbia, 1983.
Nick Lowe and His Cowboy Outfit, Columbia, 1984.
16 All-Time Lowes, Demon, 1985.
The Rose of England (includes "I Knew the Bride"), Columbia, 1985.
Pinker and Prouder Than Previous, Columbia, 1988.
Party of One, Warner Brothers, 1990.

Impossible Bird, 1994.
Dig My Mood, 1998.

Sources

Periodicals

Down Beat, August 1998.
Esquire, July 1998.
Guitar Player, July 1998.
Musician, December 1998.
Rolling Stone, August 20, 1998.

Online

City Paper Interactive, June 6, 1998; www.cpcn.com
CDNOW, January 8, 1999; www.cdnow.com
Rounder Records, January 8, 1999; www.rounder.com

—Tige Cosmos

Martha and the Vandellas

R&B vocal group

AP/Wide World Photo. Reproduced by permission.

What Martha Reeves and the Vandellas might have become had it not been for Diana Ross and the Supremes is anyone's guess, but to hear Reeves tell it, the group would have almost certainly been a larger player for a longer period on the R&B scene. Even though the vocal group's peak occurred for but a few years early in its career in the 1960s, the hit singles produced by Martha and the Vandellas—including "Dancing in the Street," "Heat Wave," and "Nowhere to Run"—are among the most enduring in Motown and pop music history, having found their way onto soundtracks, radio playlists, and commercials decades after they were originally recorded. And in an era of sweet, sound-alike girl groups, the act distinguished itself as gutsier and grittier than most. Dubbing them "one of Motown's edgiest outfits," Paul Evans said of the group in the *Rolling Stone Album Guide* that their "best songs are all bass, brass, and thunder—the singers have to fight hard just to keep up."

Reeves chronicled her humble beginnings in the autobiography *Dancing in the Street: Confessions of a Motown Diva,* co-authored with writer Mark Bego in 1994. She was the third oldest in a family of 12 children, and the first daughter. She was born July 18, 1941 in a house on Washington Street in Eufala, Alabama, where a midwife assisted her mother because the family couldn't afford a doctor. Reeves didn't remain in Alabama for long, however. She was just under a year old when the entire family pulled up stakes and moved to Detroit, where they lived with relatives who had relocated earlier in search of employment.

Reeves' vocal talent was evident at a very young age. At the age of three, she and older brothers Benny and Thomas won a church talent contest. In her autobiography, she recalls being entranced by the entertainers she saw on stage and screen at the Paradise Theater in Detroit, where her godmother, Beatrice Lockett, took her to see the likes of Cab Calloway and others.

In 1960, Reeves (who also sang professionally around this time as "Martha LaVaille") joined a group called the Del-Phis, which included Michiganders Annette Beard, Gloria Williamson, and Rosalind Ashford. The vocal group recorded the single "I'll Let You Know" for Chess subsidiary Checkmate Records, but the single went nowhere. In her autobiography, Reeves blamed the label, accusing it of not supporting the act.

It was a mixture of luck and circumstance that brought Reeves and her Del-Phis to the attention of the Motown powers-that-be. After a chance encounter at Detroit's Twenty Grand nightclub, Reeves got a job as secretary of Motown A&R director William "Mickey" Stevenson. While at work one day, she learned that background

Members include **Martha Reeves** (born July 18, 1941, Eufala, Alabama), lead vocals; **Rosalind Ashford** (born September 2, 1943, Detroit, Michigan; left group, 1969), vocals; **Annette Beard** (left group, 1963), vocals; **Betty Kelly** (born September 16, 1944, Detroit; joined group, 1963), vocals; **Lois Reeves** (born Sandra Delores, April 12, 1948, Detroit), vocals; **Sandra Tilley** (died 1981), vocals; **Gloria Williamson** (left group c. 1962), vocals.

Reeves joined Del-Phis with Ashford, Beard, and Williamson, 1960; discovered by Motown's William "Mickey" Stevenson c. 1962; recorded first Holland-Dozier-Holland song, "Heat Wave," 1963; disbanded between 1969 and 1971; reformed with Lois Reeves and Tilley, 1971; disbanded again, 1972; filed suit against Motown for back royalties, 1989; settled suit favorably with Motown, 1991.

Awards: Inducted into Rock and Roll Hall of Fame, 1995.

Addresses: *Record company*—Motown, 825 Eighth Avenue, 28th Floor, New York, NY 10019.

---

vocalists were needed immediately for a recording session with Marvin Gaye. When other vocalists weren't able to come to the studio, Reeves and her fellow Del-Phis were enlisted to sing backup on Gaye's "Hitch Hike" and "Stubborn Kind of Fellow." Then, when fellow Motown singer Mary Wells reportedly failed to appear for a recording session, Reeves and the Vandellas found themselves in the studio recording a single of their own, "I'll Have to Let Him Go"—but not as the Del-Phis. Instead, the group was called Martha and the Vandellas, with "Vandella" taken from a merger of Van Dyke (a Detroit road near Reeves' parents' home) and singer Della Reese, a favorite of Reeves'. Martha and the Vandellas was thus officially formed in 1962. However, Williamson opted not to sign a contract with Motown and reportedly left the act at that point.

When another Martha and the Vandellas single, the ballad "Come and Get These Memories," cracked the Top 40 in 1963, the powerful Motown songwriting and production trio of Brian Holland, Lamont Dozier, and Eddie Holland offered their song "Heat Wave" to the group. It became one of the band's biggest hits, peaking at number four on the Billboard pop chart and topping the R&B chart for several weeks in 1963.

For several years thereafter, the hits continued to pour in for Martha and the Vandellas. "Quicksand" entered the Top 40 at the end of 1963, and later made its way into the Top 10, followed by what is probably the band's best-known and biggest hit, 1964's "Dancing in the Street," which spent 11 weeks in the top 40 (including two weeks at number two).

Some critics today say Martha and the Vandellas' popularity was at least partially due to the songs that the act received from Holland-Dozier-Holland, a conclusion that is borne out by the commercial and chart success of the band. The Holland-Dozier-Holland collaborations with Martha and the Vandellas turned out to be the most fruitful for the group, and occurred at the height of its popularity.

But, when Holland-Dozier-Holland left Motown in the late-1960s (after landing 28 songs in the top 20 for various artists, 12 of which hit number one between 1963 and 1966 alone), it turned out to be the beginning of a downturn for Martha and the Vandellas. As Joe McEwen and Jim Miller wrote in an essay on Motown in the *Rolling Stone Illustrated History of Rock & Roll,* the "best Vandellas records were made with H-D-H [Holland-Dozier-Holland], but after the atypically infectious 'Jimmy Mack' in early 1967, the two teams went their separate ways. The result for Martha and the Vandellas was little short of disastrous." Although Martha and the Vandellas scored two more top 40 hits after the top ten smash "Jimmy Mack" (a number one R&B hit)--including the number 11 hit "Honey Chile," recorded under the name Martha Reeves and the Vandellas in 1967--those turned out to be the band's last big hits.

The latter part of the band's career was fraught with more change. While Beard had left the band in 1964 (to be replaced by former Velvelette Betty Kelly), the entire group was dormant between 1969 and 1971. When Reeves reformed the unit in 1971, it included her sister, Lois Reeves, and Sandra Tilley (another former Velvelette, albeit for a short stint). That incarnation was a brief one, though, and by 1972 Reeves had embarked on a solo career. Meanwhile, Lois joined the female vocal trio Quiet Elegance, organized by Temptations Melvin Franklin and Otis Williams. Martha Reeves and the Vandellas played its final show at Detroit's Cobo Hall on December 21, 1972, according to the Reeves autobiography. Tilley died nearly a decade later, in 1981, during brain tumor surgery.

At the same time that the Vandellas' popularity was waning, Reeves developed substance abuse problems from tranquilizers and uppers. She also bore a child out of wedlock to an abusive man she had dated only briefly. In her autobiography, she called her son, Eric Jermel Graham (born onNovember 10, 1970), "the greatest gift to me in this whole wide world" and "a reason to live a purposeful life." Early in her solo career, Reeves was also briefly married to a disc jockey named Willie Dee. After that rocky period, a 1988 *Ebony* magazine article reported that the singer experienced a "religious rebirth" in 1977.

Although the heyday of the Vandellas was over, Reeves remained active as a singer, both with and without various Vandellas. In addition to touring, she recorded several solo albums, starting with a self-titled release in 1974. She joined female vocalists such as Brenda Lee, Leslie Gore, and Mary Wells for "The Legendary Ladies," a 1987 special on the Cinemax cable network, and toured with Mary Wells and Temptations David Ruffin and Eddie Kendricks the same year. Then, in 1989, Reeves recruited Ashford and Beard for a reunion Vandellas concert in Manchester, England; the three have periodically played and toured together since then. The three also filed suit against Motown Records in 1989 for back royalties for the song "Heat Wave;" Reeves wrote in her autobiography that they had not received any royalty checks for the music since 1972. In 1991, the suit was settled in favor of Reeves and the Vandellas after a settlement was reached between Motown founder Berry Gordy Jr. and Reeves. "He [Gordy] said he was sorry it had gone so far," Reeves told *Jet* magazine in 1991. Terms of the settlement were not made public.

There was some renewed interest in the group during the 1990s, a period that saw the release of several compilations of hits and singles. In 1995, Martha Reeves and the Vandellas were inducted into the Rock and Roll Hall of Fame during a ceremony in New York. Recalling her career in a 1988 *Ebony* article, Reeves said, "I sang because it made me happy *and* helped me to help my family. It allowed me to develop from a little girl in the ghetto to someone who could pay my bills . . ."

Selected discography

Come and Get These Memories, Gordy, 1963.
Heat Wave, Gordy, 1963.
Dance Party, Gordy, 1965.
Martha & the Vandellas Greatest Hits, Gordy, 1966.
Watchout! (includes "Jimmy Mack"), Gordy, 1966.
Martha & the Vandellas Live!, Gordy, 1967.
Ridin' High, Gordy, 1968.
Sugar n' Spice, Gordy, 1969.
Natural Resources, Gordy, 1970.

Black Magic, Gordy, 1972.
Martha Reeves & the Vandellas Anthology, Motown Records, 1974.
Martha Reeves & the Vandellas: Motown Superstar Series, Volume 11, Motown Records, 1980.
Martha Reeves & the Vandellas: Compact Command Performance (CD only), Motown Records,1986.
Martha Reeves & the Vandellas/Live Wire!: The Singles, 1962-1972, Motown Records, 1993.
Martha Reeves & the Vandellas: Motown Legends, Motown Records, 1993.
Motown Milestones, Motown Records, 1995.
Martha Reeves: Produced by Richard Perry, MCA, 1974.
The Rest of My Life, Arista, 1976.
We Meet Again, Fantasy, 1978.
Gotta Keep Moving, Fantasy, 1980.
*Martha Reeves: The Collection*Object Enterprises, 1986.

Sources

Books

DeCurtis, Anthony and James Henke, editors, *Rolling Stone Album Guide,* Random House, 1992.
DeCurtis, Anthony, and James Henke, editors, *Rolling Stone Illustrated History of Rock & Roll,* Random House, 1992.
Erlewine, Michael, executive editor, *All Music Guide to Rock, 2nd Edition,* Miller Freeman Books, 1997.
Graff, Gary and Daniel Durchholz, editors, *MusicHound Rock: The Essential Album Guide,* Visible Ink Press, 1999.
Palmer, Robert, *Rock & Roll: An Unruly History,* Harmony Books, 1995.
Reeves, Martha, and Mark Bego, *Dancing in the Street: Confessions of a Motown Diva,* Hyperion, 1994.
Romanowski, Patricia and Holly George-Warren, editors, *New Rolling Stone Encyclopedia of Rock & Roll,* Fireside, 1995.
Whitburn, Joel, *Billboard Book of Top 40 Hits, Sixth Edition,* Billboard Books, 1996.

Periodicals

Booklist, August 1994; February 15, 1995.
Ebony, February 1988.
Entertainment Weekly, August 26, 1994.
Jet, July 17, 1989; April 8, 1991; January 30, 1995.
People, August 10, 1987; September 12, 1994.
Publishers Weekly, July 4, 1994.

Online

"Martha and the Vandellas," Rock and Roll Hall of Fame and Museum,http://www.rockhall.com/induct/vandella.html.

—*K. Michelle Moran*

Pietro Mascagni

Composer, conductor

Pietro Mascagni was a prolific Italian composer who completed more than 15 operas in his 82 years. The most memorable of these was *Cavalleria Rusticana*, a tempestuous love story set in a small Sicilian town. The one-act opera won the Sonzogno Competition, and its highly successful premiere in 1890 marked the early climax of Mascagni's career. The string of operas that followed produced several popular arias, but none achieved the status of *Cavalleria*. In contrast, his close friend Puccini, composer of the much revered *La Bohème*, achieved great success, which caused tension between the two and eventually led to the dissolution of the relationship. Toward the end of Mascagni's life, he became affiliated with fascist Italy, composing operas for Mussolini and numerous political gatherings. As a result, he lost the relationships of many of his musical peers and died poor and alone in Rome.

Pietro Antonio Stefano Mascagni was born on December 7, 1863, in Livorno, Italy, the son of a baker. When Mascagni was ten, his mother died, and three years later, against his father's wishes, he began studying music under the tutelage of Alfredo Soffredini, a composer, teacher, and musical reviewer. In 1881 he composed his first cantata, *In Filanda*. The composition was entered in a contest in Milan and won a handsome sum from Count Florestano de Larderel, a prize which made it financially possible for him to study at the Milan Conservatory. At the school he studied alongside Boito,

Ponchielli, and Saladino and roomed with the famous Puccini. In 1883 Mascagni derived *Pinotta* from the previously composed *In Filanda*, and attempted to enter it into the Conservatory's musical contest, but his registration was too late.

In April 1885, after losing interest in the routine of his daily studies, Mascagni left the Conservatory. He found a position immediately with the company of Dario Acconci, and soon after toured the country as a conductor in the operette companies of Vittorio Forlì, Alfonso and Ciro Scognamiglio, and Luigi Arnaldo Vassallo. In 1886 Mascagni met Luigi Maresca and his future wife, Lina. He accompanied them to Cerignola, where he accepted a position as master of music and singing at the local philharmonic society.

By the following year, he and Lina were married and expecting their first child, Domenico. In 1882, Mascagni discontinued work on his opera *Guglielmo Ratcliff* so that he could focus his attention on the composition of *Cavelleria Rusticana* for the Sonzogno music competition. The opera triumphed over the other 72 entries by composers like Bossi and Giordano to win first place. On May 17, 1890, the *Cavelleria* premiered at the Costanzi Theater in Rome. Its success was unparalleled, and soon it was playing at theaters in Florence, Palermo, Venice, Hamburg, Petersburg, Dresden, Buenos Aires, and Vienna. But the rest of Mascagni's career, though long, diverse, and fruitful, would never again reach the level of success that *Cavelleria* achieved.

Mascagni followed his massive success with the 1891 opera *L'amico Fritz*, a lyrical composition yielding such popular numbers as Cherry Duet. The comedy premiered on October 31, 1891, at the Costanzie Theater in Rome, successful because its melodic strength, though here combined with more refined harmony, was not unlike that in *Cavelleria*. In an attempt to increase his audience, Mascagni began conducting outside Italy, where he earned a strong reputation in Vienna, Paris, and London. On November 10, 1892, Mascagni premiered *I Rantzau* at the La Pergola Theater in Florence. The incestuous love story was received quite favorably by audience and critics alike, touted for its orchestration and the performances of its singers. Three years later Mascagni premiered the finally-finished *Guglielmo Ratcliff* on February 16 at the Teatro alla Scala in Milan. *Silvano*, a rushed opera written to fulfill a contract with Sonzogno, premiered at the same theater on March 15. *Guglielmo* achieved moderate success, but *Silvano* was a terrible critical and popular failure.

Beginning in 1895, Mascagni worked as director of Liceo Musicale of Pesaro for several years. His one-act opera

For the Record . . .

Born Pietro Antonio Stefano Mascagni, December 7, 1863, in Livorno, Italy; died August 2, 1945, in Rome, Italy. *Education:* Studied with Alfredo Soffredini, 1875. Enrolled in Milan Conservatory and studied with Ponchielli and Saladino, left without completing studies, 1885.

Began regular music studies with Alfredo Soffredini, 1876; composed first cantata, *In Filanda,* and won first place in musical contest in Milan; moved to Milan and enrolled in Milan Conservatory, where he met Puccini, 1882; left Milan without completing studies, toured as conductor in the operette companies of Forli, Scognamiglio, and Vassallo, 1885; met Luigi Maresca, 1886; left company of Maresca to become master of music and singing in philharmonic of Cerignola, 1887; finished composition of *Cavalleria Rusticana,* 1889; won Sonzogno contest for *Cavalleria Rusticana,* premiered the opera in Costanzi Theater in Rome, opera played throughout Italy, 1890; premiered *L'Amico Fritz* at Costanzi Theater in Rome, 1891; premiered and directed *I Rantzau* at La Pergola Theater in Florence, 1892; premiered *Guglielmo Ratcliff* and Silvano, both at Teatro alla Scala in Milan, 1895; premiered *Iris* at Costanzi Theatre in Rome, 1898; toured Russia, 1900; premiered *Le Maschere* in six Italian theatres, conducted the late Verdi's Requiem in Vienna, 1901; toured United States, 1902-1903; became director of Scuola Musicale Romana, in Rome, 1903; premiered *Amica* in Monte Carlo, 1905; premiered *Le Maschere,* 1908; toured South America, premiered *Isabeau* in Buenos Aires, 1911; premiered *Parisina* in Milan, 1913; premiered *Parisina* in Livorno and Rome, 1914; premiered *Lodoletta* in Rome, 1917; premiered *Il Piccolo Marat* in Rome, 1921; conducted *La Boheme* as homage to late Puccini, 1930; premiered *Pinotta* in San Remo, 1932; premiered *Nerone* in Milan and Livorno, 1935; participated in celebration of 50-year anniversary of *Cavalleria Rusticana,* recorded in studio under Mascagni's direction, 1940; last appearance at La Scala for *L'Amico Fritz,* 1943;

Awards: First place in Sonzogno Competition for *Cavalleria Rusticana,* 1890.

Zanetto was performed there in 1896. Two years later, on November 22, *Iris* premiered, a collaboration with Luigi Illica, at the Constanzi Theater in Rome. The composition was another moderate success, initiating the popularity of fin-de-siecle exotic opera. On January 17, 1901, *Le maschere* premiered at six Italian theaters and was unsuccessful at all of them. By 1902 Mascagni chose to resign his position at Liceo Musicale so he could tour the United States, where he performed in New York, Philadelphia, Boston, and San Francisco.

Amica premiered with a libretto by Choudens in Monte-Carlo on March 16, 1905. It was better received than *Le maschere,* but still not widely popular, a point of tension between Mascagni and Puccini that led to their dispute the same year. In 1910 the two temporarily rekindled their friendship, and the following year Mascagni's career was on an upswing with the premiere of the romantic opera *Isabeau,* received warmly by Italians in Buenos Aires and similarly embraced in Milan and Venice. However, critics noted that the romantic style of the opera lacked originality and suggested Mascagni might have lost his creativity. This idea was only reaffirmed by the resounding failure of *Parisina,* a collaboration with D'Annunzio.

In 1910 Mascagni began an affair with Anna Lolli, and by 1913 his wife remarried the musician Guido Farinelli. This change in his personal life was perhaps mirrored in his professional life with the premiere of *Lodoletta* in Rome on April 30, 1917. The composition was a marked return to the lyrical genre that attempted to rival Puccini's *La rondine.* Two years later, on December 13, Mascagni premiered his operette *Sì* in Rome. Finding success with a balance of lyricism and drama gave Mascagni confidence to compose *Il piccolo Marat,* which premiered in 1921 but failed in comparison to the two previous compositions.

Around 1927 Mascagni began to realize that his career was languishing and he went into seclusion, moving to the Albergo Plaza in Rome, where he would remain until his death. His brief public appearances thereafter were politically attached to the fascist party in Italy, signified by the 1932 premiere of *Pinotta* in San Remo. Three years later Mascagni premiered *Nerone* in Milan, his last work, written with Mussolini in mind, as a final attempt to battle the inevitable modernism surrounding him.

Mascagni made his final appearance in April of 1943 at the La Scala Theater for a performance of *L'Amico Fritz.*

His fascist associations left him friendless and poor at the time of his death on August 2, 1945. Mascagni remains a prominent figure in the history of Italian opera, and *Cavelleria Rusticana* an enduring favorite.

Selected operas

Cavalleria Rusticana, 1890.
L'amico Fritz, 1891.
I Rantzau, 1891.
Guglielmo Ratcliff, 1895.
Silvan, 1895.
Zanetto, 1896.
Iris, 1898.
Le Maschere, 1901.
Amica, 1905.
Isabeau, 1911.
Parisina, 1913.
Lodoletta, 1917.
Si, 1919.
Il Piccolo Marat, 1921.

Pinotta, 1932.
Nerone, 1935.

Sources

Books

Rosenthal, Harold, and John Warrack, eds., *The Concise Oxford Dictionary of Opera*, Oxford University Press, 1979.
Sadie, Stanley, ed., *The New Grove Dictionary of Opera*, Macmillan Press Limited, 1992.

Online

"Pietro Mascagni," *HNH*, http://www.hnh.com/composer/mascagni.htm (March 7, 1999).
"Pietro Mascagni," *Erik Bruchez's Mascagni Home Page*, http://rick.stanford.edu/opera/Mascagni/ (March 7, 1999).
"Evening at Pops," *WGBH*, http://www.pbs.org/wgbh/pops/progintermezzo.html (March 7, 1999).

—*Karen Gordon*

Tommy McClennan

Blues singer

For a short time, Tommy McClennan had the world of blues in the palm of his hand. Tracked down in rural Mississippi by Bluebird Records, the most prestigious blues label of the day, signed to a recording contract, and brought to Chicago, McClennan escaped the grueling existence of a black farm hand almost effortlessly. In Chicago, he met all the leading blues musicians of the time, including the Chicago blues "Godfathers," Big Bill Broonzy and Tampa Red. In just over two years with Bluebird, he recorded 40 songs. Then abruptly McClennan's alcoholism gained the upper hand. After February of 1942, he never recorded again. Over the next ten years he performed sporadically in clubs and on the streets. Eventually he vanished so completely into Chicago's poor, black underclass that his death has never been confirmed. The 40 songs he left behind, however, reveal the unique talent of a powerful blues singer.

Little is known about Tommy McClennan's early life. He was born sometime in April 1908 in Yazoo County, Mississippi, probably on the J.F. Sligh farm, where he was raised. It is assumed that he started playing guitar as a teenager. He performed on the streets of Yazoo City, nine miles from the Sligh farm, in the 1920s. After working the farm all week, he spent weekends in the city, playing pool and suckling the alcoholism that would later ruin his musical career. Before long he was playing with other local musicians. Booker Miller remembered traveling with McClennan in the late 1920s. Mississippi singer-guitarist David "Honeyboy" Edwards played with McClennan around the town of Greenwood, Mississippi. "He was playing house parties like I was," Edwards told researcher Pete Welding in an interview quoted in the liner notes of *Tommy McClennan: The Bluebird Recordings*, "so I was learning under Tommy." McClennan also played house parties regularly enough in Itta Bena, Mississippi, with Robert Petway that Edwards would later say the two men had the same style.

Sometime in the late 1930s, Big Bill Broonzy, a Mississippi bluesman then based in Chicago, told Lester Melrose about McClennan. Melrose was a white music store owner and music publisher who ran the Chicago offices of RCA Victor's Bluebird label. Melrose became so enthusiastic about recording McClennan that he made up his mind to drive down to Yazoo City and bring him back to Chicago to record. Before he left, Melrose was warned by Broonzy not to go to the Sligh farm himself looking for the singer. He should stay in Yazoo City and send a local black to the farm to prevent the white owners from thinking that Melrose was trying to make off with one of their farm hands. Once in Mississippi, however, Melrose ignored Broonzy's advice. When he arrived and asked for McClennan, the riled white owners chased him away in such short order, that he had to flee without his car.

Somehow Melrose managed to get McClennan up to Chicago. The new Bluebird artist was a small man with a compact frame. The one surviving photo of him shows a man dressed in a stylish suit with wide lapels, a striped silk tie, a Panama hat tilted at a jaunty angle, who peers off camera without a trace of emotion. McClennan's first Bluebird session was held on November 2, 1939. It was just Tommy and his guitar. The session produced stark discordant music that was very much out of character for the label that had produced smooth, accomplished, almost pop performances by musicians like Jr. Gillum, Fats Waller, and Tampa Red.

Later writers seem to have a hard time finding good things to say about Tommy McClennan's musicianship. In his groundbreaking book *The Country Blues*, Samuel Charters characterized McClennan as "a limited guitar player and his voice was flat and harsh." Tony Russell, in *The Blues—From Robert Johnson to Robert Cray*, described McClennan's records as "raucous juke-joint music without much technical subtlety." But a lack of subtlety has never been a stranger to the blues. In many ways, McClennan's sloppy, moving music foreshadows the exciting early days of postwar Chicago electric blues, whose guitars are frequently mistuned and whose drummers often cannot hold the beat, but which have an undeniable excitement. McClennan's primitive instru-

Born April 8, 1904, near Yazoo City, MS; raised on J.F. Sligh farm; probably died in late 1950s or early 1960s in Chicago.

Began playing guitar as teenager in Mississippi; performed in streets and at house parties in Mississippi in late 1920s and 1930s; brought to Chicago by Lester Melrose to record for Bluebird Records early 1939; had five sessions at Bluebird, on November 22, 1939, May 10, 1940, December 12, 1940, September 15, 1941, and February 20, 1942; performed only sporadically in clubs and on the streets of Chicago afterwards.

mental technique heightens his primitive energy, his jangly, misshapen guitar amplifies the force of his rich, raw voice.

McClennan cut some of his most popular numbers at that first session, including "Whiskey Head Woman" and "New Shake 'Em On Down," closely modeled on Bukka White's hit, "Shake 'Em On Down." Another tune he cut at the first session was the controversial "Bottle Up And Go." One verse, about a card game between a black and a white, twice uses the word "nigger," an epithet that was common among Southern blacks but deeply resented by blacks in the North. Bill Broonzy warned McClennan that the song would get him into trouble. According to Broonzy, quoted in the *Bluebird Recordings* liner notes, McClennan replied "hell no, I'll never change my song." That evening Broonzy took Tommy to a party and eventually the guests wanted to hear Bluebird's newest artist sing something. Broonzy had warned him not to sing the controversial song, but McClennan did anyway. When he finished the third verse, the offensive one, the other guests were so riled Big Bill had to push McClennan out a window to escape their wrath. Five blocks later, fortifying themselves in a bar, McClennan said he had to go back for his guitar. Broonzy told him not to bother as he still had part of it hanging around his neck.

Over the next two years, McClennan performed four more sessions for Bluebird, in May and December 1940, and September 1941. At the latter, he recorded "Cross Cut Saw Blues," later covered by numerous artists. His final session at Bluebird took place on February 20, 1942 in Chicago. He cut eight tracks—the number he always cut—with the same forceful singing and rough n' ready

guitar he had displayed on other outings. When his session was over, Tommy joined his old friend Robert Petway who was recording in the same studio just afterwards. He took the vocal on Petway's "Boogie Woogie Woman." It was destined to be his last appearance on record. Bluebird dropped him from their roster of artists not much later. His drinking had made him too unreliable.

Cut loose by his record company, McClennan declined deeper into alcoholism over the next decade. He performed less and less. After a while he simply disappeared into the black slums of Chicago. According to blues researcher Gayle Wardlow, McClennan died destitute in the early 1960s. It is impossible to say for sure as no death record exists. As Samuel Charter wrote that "Tommy McClennan seems to have died when he stopped singing."

Tommy McClennan represented the end of a line—the rough and tumble country blues musician accompanied by his own acoustic guitar. By the end of the 1940s, that sound, the sound of Charley Patton, Son House, and Robert Johnson, was overtaken by a new sound. It was just as raw but played on electric guitars. McClennan's legacy was his influence on later artists like Muddy Waters and the songs he left behind.

Selected discography

Tommy McClennan: The Bluebird Recordings 1939-1942, RCA, 1997

Sources

Books

Barlow, William, *Looking Up At Down: The Emergence of Blues Culture*, Temple University Press, Philadelphia, 1989.

Charters, Samuel, *The Country Blue,* Da Capo, New York, 1975.

Davis, Francis, *The History of the Blues*, New York, 1995.

Harris, Sheldon, *Blues Who's Who.* Arlington House: New Rochelle, NY, 1979.

Russell, Tony, *The Blues—From Robert Johnson to Robert Cray.* Schirmer Books, New York, 1997.

Additional information obtained from the liner notes from *Tommy McClellean: The Bluebird Recordings 1939-1942* written by Mary Katherin Aldin.

—*Gerald E. Brennan*

Clyde McPhatter

Singer

A prominent singer in rock history, Clyde McPhatter's short life was marked by a steady stream of chart-topping hits and unprecedented success. McPhatter achieved mainstream popularity in the early 1950s as the lead singer for Billy Ward & His Dominoes, applying the intensity of his well-trained gospel tenor to the secular love songs of the group. This winning combination reached beyond McPhatter's personal success to become a basic formula in R&B and soul music. Feeling stifled under the constraints of the Dominoes, McPhatter left in 1953 to form the Drifters. His unparalleled vocal style and name recognition helped create one of the most notable vocal groups in R&B. After being drafted in 1954 and serving a short stint in the Army, McPhatter embarked on a solo career. Although he continued to record hits like "A Lover's Question" and "I Never Knew," his alcoholism eventually eclipsed his distinctive and magical sound and led to his death from a heart attack in 1972. Although neglected at the time of his death and unaware of his influence on music history, McPhatter had become one of the pioneer voices in rock.

Born a minister's son in Durham, North Carolina, on November 15, 1932, and raised in New Jersey, McPhatter spent much of his childhood in church, singing gospel in the choir and mastering the passion of the music. At 18, McPhatter was asked to join vocal group Billy Ward & His Dominoes, the first consequential move of his career. Reservations about bringing the religious dramatics of gospel to the sexy, romantic secular tunes of the group led McPhatter to initially bill himself as Clyde Ward, claiming to be Billy's brother. From 1950 to 1952, the group scored with hits "Do Something For Me," "I Am With You," and "Sixty-Minute Man," one of the first R&B singles to also score on the pop charts; "Have Mercy Baby," reached number one on the R&B charts for ten weeks in 1952.

In 1953, however, McPhatter grew resistant to Ward's inflexibility and left the band with encouragement from Atlantic Record's Ahmet Ertegun, who promised him top billing and a recording contract with his own act. McPhatter tapped his former gospel group, The Mount Lebanon Singers. Band members included William Anderson, James Johnson, David Baughn, and David Baldwin, who chose the name "the Drifters" from a bird book. The group signed with Atlantic Records, but when the chemistry failed to emerge, McPhatter regrouped with Bill Pinkney of Jerusalem Stars, Andrew and Gerhart Thrasher of Thrasher Wonders, and Willie Ferbie. The combination proved successful and their first debut hit "The Way I Fell," reached number one on the R&B charts and sold in the millions. The group went on to record several other hits, including "Money Honey" and "White Christmas." Just before the release of the successful hit "Honey Love" in May of 1954, McPhatter was drafted to the Army.

In July 1955 McPhatter returned from his short time in the Army and left the Drifters to go solo. The group continued a long and successful career without McPhatter, whose stardom was still holding throughout the second half of the decade. His first hit after returning from military service was a duet with Ruth Brown called "Love Has Joined Us Together," which reached the top ten on the R&B charts. His releases continued to chart consistently during the next several years, among them "Come What May," "Long Lonely Nights," "Just to Hold My Hand," "Seven Days," "Without Love (There is Nothing)," and "A Lover's Question," one of the biggest hits of his career and an R&B classic. Singles like "You Went Back on Your Word," and "Lovey Dovey" hit the top 20, but the climax of McPhatter's career had already passed.

In early 1960, McPhatter switched from Atlantic to MGM, and later switched again to Mercury. Though he was still headlining venues like the Apollo Theater in Harlem, he was beginning to lose his battle against alcoholism. He moved to England in 1968 and toured heavily, but his top 20 singles, including "Ta Ta" on the Mercury label and "I Never Knew," were already behind him. After two years and little success, he returned to the U.S., where he recorded an LP for the record label Decca. McPhatter died of a heart attack related to his excessive drinking in 1972 in Teaneck, New Jersey.

Although McPhatter never reached the stardom of Smokey Robinson, Jackie Wilson, or Elvis Presley, his distinct and passionate vocal style heavily influenced these artists. The profound effect of McPhatter's role in rock

Selected discography

Clyde McPhatter & the Drifters, Atlantic, 1958.
Love Ballads, Atlantic, 1958.
With Billy Ward & the Dominoes, King, 1958.
Let's Start Over Again, MGM, 1959.
Clyde, Atlantic, 1959.
Ta Ta, Mercury, 1960.
May I Sing for You, Mercury, 1960.
Lover Please, Mercury, 1962.
Rhythm and Soul, Mercury, 1963.
Clyde McPhatter's Greatest Hits, Mercury, 1963.
Songs of the Big City, Mercury, 1964.
Live at the Apollo, Mercury, 1965.
Welcome Home, Decca, 1970.
A Tribute to Clyde McPhatter, Atlantic, 1973.
Bip Bam, Edsel, 1984.
Deep Sea Ball—The Best of Clyde McPhatter, Atlantic, 1991.
Meet Billy Ward & His Dominoes, Fat Boy, 1996.
Forgotten Angel, 32 Jazz, 1998.

Sources

Books

Romanowski, Patricia, ed., *The New Rolling Stone Encyclopedia of Rock & Roll,* Rolling StonePress, 1995.
Warner, Jay, *Billboard's American Rock 'n' Roll in Review,* Schirmer Books, 1997.

Online

"Clyde McPhatter," *All-Music Guide,* http://www.allmusic.com (January 19, 1999).
"Clyde McPhatter," The Rock and Roll Hall of Fame, http://www.rockhall.com (January 19, 1999).

—*Karen Gordon*

Memphis Jug Band

Blues/jug band

The Memphis Jug Band was the first good-time band of the blues era. Putting on one of their records is still like unleashing a slightly tipsy, slightly unruly party in your living room. Some bluesmen had better technique; some had greater intensity, or more fanatic fans. But for sheer pleasure it is difficult to outdo the Memphis Jug Band at its best. The grunt of the jug, the honk of the kazoo, the half-drunk sounding harmonies, the alternately plaintive or rollicking harmonica—all these improbable elements add up to music that is unique and magical.

The Memphis Jug Band created the jug band craze in the late 1920s, and for a few years it had incredibly broad appeal. Black audiences bought their records and listened to them play on Beale Street in Memphis, Tennessee. Well-to-do white residents of the city often hired them to play at their parties and social events. Memphis's Mayor Crump, the boss of the city's political machine, used them at his rallies. And the Jug Band just kept getting better—only the Great Depression and the fickle taste of the public finally spelled its end.

The Memphis Jug Band was the brainchild of Will Shade. Shade founded the group, wrote and arranged its songs, found gigs, prepared it for recording sessions, and played harmonica and banjo. He was the one constant through the Jug Band's many incarnations. Shade was born in Memphis, TN on February 5, 1898 The son of Will

Shade Sr. and Mary Brimmer, he was raised by his maternal grandmother, and her friends and neighbors took to calling him Son Brimmer. The moniker stuck and Shade's friends knew him as Son. Shade spent his youth in and around Beale Street, the center of the Memphis music scene. As a teenager, he started following a street musician named Tee-Wee Blackman around, trying to figure out how he fingered his guitar. After a while Blackman took Shade aside and gave him lessons. He showed Shade how to play "Newport News Blues," a song the Jug Band would later record, in the keys of E and A. In his book *The Bluesmen*, Samuel Charters relates that Shade figured he knew enough and ended the lessons—until he realized he could not figure out other key positions on the guitar on his own.

Once he had a few licks down, Shade started playing guitar in the streets of Memphis. Within a few years he had joined a medicine show, a traveling variety show that toured the countryside entertaining and selling patent medicine to country folk. Shade learned how to play harmonica with the medicine shows, and probably other pick-up instruments like washtub bass and washboard.

He was back in Memphis with his wife Jennie, Shade told Charters, and they were performing in a bar when a man named Roundhouse came in. He asked if he could play along with them. They agreed. Roundhouse produced a large bottle and started blowing it. The crowd went wild, shouting "Jug band! Jug band!" The next day Shade made up his mind to organize his own jug band. The idea had been brewing in his mind for some time, ever since he had first heard the Louisville, Kentucky group, Clifford Haye's Jug Blowers. Despite their name, however, the Jug Blowers' was a jazz band. Shade's group would end up defining what we today consider jug band music, folksy music played by a group using instruments like guitar, harmonica, kazoo, washboard, banjo, violin, and mandolin. And of course jug, which one doesn't really "blow" but buzzes into with the lips.

The Jug Band would change line-up at virtually every performance and recording session. The first Shade put together was with himself on guitar and harmonica, Ben Ramey on kazoo, Will Weldon on guitar, and Charlie Polk on jug, with each taking turns singing. While they were playing in Beale Street, the Jug Band caught the attention of Ralph Peer, who ran Victor Records in Memphis. After an audition, Peer told them to prepare four songs for a recording session.

The session was held on February 24, 1927. Charters relates that they were nervous after rehearsing all night the night before. But undoubtedly being poor blacks entering the domain of Southern white businessmen also contributed to their case of nerves. Peer applied the standard remedy of the times, a bottle of whiskey, and soon they were relaxed and ready to play. Maybe whiskey was all they needed though—Tony Russell in *The Blues—From Robert Johnson to Robert Cray* quotes a Jug Band contemporary "When they don't get drunk there's not much pep in them."

Victor liked the sides the band cut and called them back to the studio in June of 1927. The session was held in Chicago, Illinois. While there they played the Grand Central Theater and made such an impression that Ma Rainey, probably the most famous blues artist of the day, asked them to appear at her show in Gary, Indiana. Unfortunately their performance ended disastrously when a snake they used escaped and the terrified audience bolted for the exits. In the end, the serpent was captured and no one was hurt. But Ma Rainey was upset—she had leapt atop the piano—and wasn't likely to hire the Jug Band again soon.

In October of 1927, the band had its third Victor session, this time in Atlanta, Georgia. Sometime after that, Will

Shade met Charlie Burse. Burse was born on August 25, 1901 in Decatur, Alabama, one of Robert and Emma Burse's fifteen children. He learned music as a boy playing a banjo he made himself. When Shade met him he was playing guitar, however, on Beale Street. Shade was impressed and asked him to join the Jug Band. He did. It was the beginning of a deep friendship that would endure for the rest of both men's lives.

"The heart of the Memphis Jug Band," Charters wrote in *The Country Blues*, "was the musicianship and the enthusiasm of Son [Shade] and Burse." Shade's harmonica was one hallmark of the Jug Band's music. "He embroidered the texture of the band's blues numbers with poignant passages that provided a musical counterpoint to the lead vocal's lines," wrote William Barlow in *Looking Up At Down: The Emergence of Blues Culture*, "[there was] a gentle and melodic quality to his sound." Burse didn't record with the Jug Band until September 1928. What he contributed, in addition to his musicianship, was an unrestrained exuberance. Engineers reportedly had problems recording him—he tapped his foot too loudly. Exuberance fairly drips from the numbers Burse sang, pieces like "Insane Crazy Blues" and he always swept the rest of the band up along with him.

By February of 1928 the band, in Charter's words, "had style, a sense of professionalism ... the band that Charlie Burse came into was a tight musical group with a uniqueness and raw musicality in everything they did." They had developed a broad repertoire that included dance tunes, rags, sentimental ballads, minstrel songs, and blues. They even recorded two instrumental waltzes. Their superb vocal harmony was showcased on two of their most popular tunes "Stealin' Stealin'" and "K.C. Moan." The constantly changing personnel virtually guaranteed that no two Jug Band sessions would sound alike. In the seven years the band was together it used at least fifteen different musicians. The musicians who played with the Memphis Jug Band at one time or another formed a who's who of Memphis talent: Walter "Shakey" Horton (harmonica), Furry Lewis (guitar), Memphis Minnie (guitar), Bo Carter (guitar), Charlie Nickerson (piano), Milton Robie (violin), Hambone Lewis (jug), Hattie Hart (vocals), Vol Stevens (mandolin/banjo), Jab Jones (piano/jug), Charlie Pierce (violin), Robert Burse, Charlie's brother, (washboard), and even Shade's first guitar teacher, Blackman.

The Jug Band's style was largely the result of Will Shade's dedication and attention to detail. Peer would contact him about two months before a recording session had been scheduled. Shade wold then line up the material and musicians, arranging the music, and rehearsing the band. He practiced every song 10 to 15 times, until the band had the song and the timing down— the length of the song was determined by what could fit on a 78-rpm record. The remarkable thing is that Shade never rehearsed the chaotic energy out of the band. They almost always sound like they've just been dragged off Beale Street into a party.

Once Shade had proven his reliability, Ralph Peer started paying him a regular weekly 25 dollar advance on his composer royalties. Those royalties could be as high as six cents per record. Shade was flush with cash, bought a house, and let Peer persuade him to invest in Victor common stock. The band received $50 per side, which was divided among the musicians. The Jug Band unleashed a jug band craze in Memphis. Within a year a plethora of other bands, like Cannon's Jug Stompers, the South Memphis Jug Band and the Beale Street Jug Band, were formed. The Memphis Jug Band was so popular, according to William Barlow, that for a time it split into two units in order to handle all the bookings. They were in constant demand to entertain at white parties and at Mayor Crump's political rallies. They played Mardi Gras in New Orleans every year.

As the Great Depression dragged on from 1929 into the 1930s recording dates in Memphis became fewer and fewer. At first the Memphis Jug Band seemed immune— they had nine sessions in 1930, far more than any other jug band, and released so many records that Victor saw fit to issue some under other names, such as "Carolina Peanut Boys" and "Memphis Sheiks." On November 28, 1930 Victor pulled the plug on music in Memphis. Ralph Peer held the last recording sessions, in rented studios because Victor's own had already been closed. The Memphis Jug Band, in four years, had recorded 54 songs for the company.

After losing their Victor contract, Shade and Burse carried on as musicians. They had to, they didn't know how to do anything else! In 1932, with Vol Stevens and Jab Jones, they cut five sides for the Champion label, which went under shortly afterwards. They had to scrounge by with club and party dates and by playing in the street until their last record session in 1934 for OKeh. The session produced some of the Memphis Jug Band's finest music, including "Gator Wobble," a virtuoso harmonica piece, and "Little Green Slippers," a virtuoso jug blowing performance.

Afterwards it was downhill. The Depression had ruined investments everywhere and Shade was forced to sell his Victor stock for a fraction of what he had paid. He and Jennie lost their house. With no demand for jug band music and no other profession to fall back on, Shade fell deeper and deeper into poverty. When Charters tracked him down in 1956 he was living in a slum tenement near Beale Street, not far from Burse. Shade was working only intermittently but nonetheless planning his musical comeback. Burse had been a little more fortunate, continuing to work as a musician until into the 1940s.

In 1956, thanks to Charters, Burse and Shade recorded a few pieces for the Folkways label. In 1958 they appeared together on a TV special about W.C. Handy that aired locally in Memphis. They died within a year of each other, Burse on December 20, 1965, Shade on September 18, 1966. Their long slide into oblivion calls to mind the words of an early Memphis Jug Band song, "What's The Matter:" "My mother taught me, my father taught me too/ Son, that thing in Memphis gonna be the death of you."

Selected discography

Memphis Jug Band, Yazoo 1067
Memphis Jug Band, The Complete Recordings in Chronological Order, Volumes 1-3, Document Records

Sources

Barlow, William. *Looking Up At Down: The Emergence of Blues Culture*, Temple University Press, Philadelphia, 1989.
Charters, Samuel. *The Country Blues*, Da Capo, New York, 1975.
Charters, Samuel, *Sweeter Than The Showers Of Rain*, Oak Publications, New York, 1977.
Cohn, Lawrence, editor, *Nothing But The Blues*, Abbeville Press, New York, 1993.
Davis, Francis, *The History of the Blues*, New York, 1995.
Harris, Sheldon, *Blues Who's Who*, Arlington House, New Rochelle, NY, 1979.
Russell, Tony, *The Blues—From Robert Johnson to Robert Cray*, Schirmer Books, New York, 1997.

—*Gerald E. Brennan*

Memphis Minnie

Archive Photos, Inc. Reproduced by permission.

For nearly three decades, Memphis Minnie was one of the most influential blues artists in the United States. From the early 1920s until she retired in the mid-1950s, she released more than 180 songs, in addition to those released after her death in 1973. Minnie's songwriting and performances thrived in a genre dominated by men. Unlike most female blues singers of the time, Minnie also wrote her own songs and played guitar. She cemented her place in blues history with such classics as "Bumble Bee," "Hoodoo Lady," and "I Want Something for You." Her repertoire included country blues, urban blues, the Melrose sound, Chicago blues, and postwar blues.

Born Lizzie Douglas in Algiers, Louisiana, Memphis Minnie was the eldest of Abe and Gertrude Wells Douglas' 13 children. Throughout her childhood, her family always called her "Kid." When she was seven years old, the Douglas family moved to Wall, Mississippi, just south of Memphis. The following year, she received her first guitar for Christmas. She learned to play both the guitar and banjo and performed under the name Kid Douglas.

In 1910, at the age of 13, she ran away from home to live on Beale Street in Memphis, Tennessee. Throughout her teenage years, she would periodically return to her family's farm when she ran out of money. The majority of the time, she played and sang on street corners. Her sidewalk performances eventually led to a tour of the South with the Ringling Brothers Circus.

Still performing under the name Kid Douglas, she returned to Memphis and became embroiled in the Beale Street blues scene. At the time, women were highly valued—along with whiskey and cocaine—and Beale Street was one of the first places in the country where women could perform in public. In order to survive financially, most of the female performers on Beale Street were also prostitutes, and Minnie was no exception. She received $12 for her services—an outrageous fee for the time.

Beyond the buzz she created as a performer, she also developed a reputation as a woman who could take care of herself. "Any men fool with her, she'd go for them right away," blues guitarist/vocalist Johnny Shines told Paul and Beth Garon in *Woman With Guitar.* "She didn't take no foolishness off them. Guitar, pocket-knife, pistol, anything she got her hands on, she'd use it; y'know Memphis Minnie used to be a hell-cat."

During the 1920s, she reportedly married Will Weldon, also known as Casey Bill. However, some historians claim the two didn't meet until their first recording sessions together in 1935 and never married. If she did

Born Lizzie Douglas on June 3, 1897, in Algiers, LA (died August 6, 1973); married: Will Weldon (a.k.a. Casey Bill), circa 1920s; Joe McCoy, 1929-1934; Earnest Lawlars (a.k.a. Little Son Joe), 1939.

Began performing on the streets of Memphis, Tennessee, 1910; signed recording contract with Columbia Records, 1929; released more than 180 songs on various labels until her retirement in 1953, including Columbia Records, Vocalion, Decca, Bluebird, Okeh, and Checker.

marry Weldon, she had left him within the decade, and married guitarist Kansas Joe McCoy in 1929. Minnie and McCoy often performed together and were discovered by a talent scout from Columbia Records that same year. They went to New York City for their first recording sessions, and it was then that she changed her name to Memphis Minnie.

McCoy and Minnie released the single "When the Levee Breaks" backed with "That Will Be Alright," but McCoy performed all the vocals. Two months later, they released "Frisco Town" and "Going Back to Texas." Minnie sang alone on "Frisco Town" and sang a duet with McCoy on "Going Back to Texas."

In 1930, Minnie released one of her favorite songs "Bumble Bee," which led to a recording contract with the Vocalion label. Later that year, she and McCoy released "I'm Talking About You" on Vocalion. The couple continued to produce records for Vocalion for two more years, then left the label and decided to move to Chicago. It didn't take long before Minnie and McCoy had become a part of the city's blues scene, and they had introduced country blues into an urban environment.

Divorce Expanded Musical Horizons

McCoy and Minnie recorded songs together and on their own for Decca Records until they divorced in 1934. According to several reports, McCoy's increasing jealousy of Minnie's fame and success caused the breakup. The two-part single "You Got To Move (You Ain't Got To Move)" was the last record issued by the couple.

Back on her own, Minnie began to experiment with different styles and sounds. She recorded four sides for the Bluebird label in 1935 under the name Texas Tessie.

They included "Good Mornin'," "You Wrecked My Happy Home," "I'm Waiting on You," and "Keep on Goin'." In August of that year, she returned to the Vocalion label to record two songs in tribute to boxing champion Joe Louis: "He's in the Ring (Doing That Same Old Thing" and "Joe Louis Strut." Columbia later released "He's in the Ring" on the collection The Great Depression: American Music in the '30s in 1994.

In October of 1935, Minnie recorded with Casey Bill Weldon for the first time on "When the Sun Goes Down, Part 2" and Hustlin' Woman Blues." It was about this time that Minnie had teamed up with manager Lester Melrose, the single most powerful and influential executive in the blues industry during the 1930s and 1940s. By the end of the 1930s, Minnie had recorded nearly 20 sides for Decca Records and eight sides for the Bluebird label. In 1939, she returned to the Vocalion label. She had also met and married her new musical partner, guitarist Earnest Lawlars, also known as Little Son Joe.

Minnie and Little Son Joe also began to release material on Okeh Records in the 1940s. Their earliest recordings together included "Nothin' in Ramblin'" and "Me and My Chauffeur Blues." The couple continued to record together throughout the decade. In 1952, Minnie recorded a session for the legendary Chess label, when it was just two months old. Singles from the session included "Broken Heart" and a re-recording of "Me and My Chauffeur Blues." The following year, she released her last commercial recording after 24 years in blues music, "Kissing in the Dark" and "World of Trouble" on the JOB label.

Within the next few years, Minnie's health began to fail. She retired from her music career and returned to Memphis. She performed one last time at a memorial for her friend, blues artist Big Bill Broozny in 1958. Periodically, she would appear on Memphis radio stations to encourage younger blues musicians. As the Garons wrote in Woman with Guitar, "She never laid her guitar down, until she could literally no longer pick it up." In 1960, Minnie suffered from a stroke and was bound to a wheelchair. The following year, Little Son Joe passed away. The trauma provoked Minnie to have a second stroke.

Illness Forced Retirement

By the mid-1960s Minnie had entered the Jell Nursing Home and she could no longer survive on her social security income. The news of her plight began to spread, and magazines such as Living Blues and Blues Unlimited appealed to their readers for assistance. Many fans quickly sent money for her care, and several musicians held benefits to help her. On August 6, 1973, Memphis Minnie died of a stroke in the nursing home. In true blues fashion, she was buried in an unmarked grave at the New Hope Cemetery in Memphis.

In 1980, Memphis Minnie was one of the first 20 artists inducted into the Blues Hall of Fame. Her work was featured on several blues compilations throughout the 1980s and 1990s. Compilations of her own work also continued to surface, including *I Ain't No Bad Girl* in 1989 and *Queen of the Blues* in 1997.

Selected discography

Singles

"When the Levee Breaks"/"That Will Be Alright," Columbia, 1929.

"Frisco Town"/"Going Back to Texas," Columbia, 1929.

"Bumble Bee," Columbia, 1930.

"Stinging Snake Blues," Vocalion, 1934.

"You Got to Move (You Ain't Got to Move)," Decca Records, 1934.

"He's in the Ring (Doing That Same Old Thing)," Vocalion, 1935.

"When the Sun Goes Down, Part 2," Bluebird, 1935.

"Hustlin' Woman Blues," Bluebird, 1935.

"Me and My Chauffeur Blues," Okeh Records, 1941; re-released, Chess Records, 1952.

"Joe Louis Strut," Vocalion, 1935.

"In My Girlish Days," Okeh Records, 1941.

"Looking the World Over," Okeh Records, 1941.

"Broken Heart," Chess Records, 1952.

"Kissing in the Dark"/"World of Trouble," JOB, 1953.

Albums

I Ain't No Bad Girl, Portrait/CBS Records, 1989.
Queen of the Blues, Sony Music, 1997.

Sources

Books

Garon, Paul and Beth, *Woman with Guitar: Memphis Minnie's Blues*, Da Capo Press, New York, 1992.
Periodicals
American Heritage, September 1994.
Down Beat, May 1995, March 1998.
High Fidelity, April 1989.

Online

http://www.blueflamecare.com/Memphis_Minnie.html (September 23, 1998).
http://www.memphisguide.com/music2/blues/bluesartists/minnie.html (September 23, 1998).

—*Sonya Shelton*

Natalie Merchant

Singer, songwriter

AP/Wide World Photo. Reproduced by permission.

A celebrated pop performer over two decades, Natalie Merchant began her career as the lead singer for the band 10,000 Maniacs, then branched out into a solo career focused on messages of politics and women's issues. Merchant attempted to blend her own style of social consciousness and spirituality into music that encompassed folk-pop and moody ballads.

The daughter of Anthony and Ann, Natalie Ann Merchant was born the third of four children on October 26, 1963, in Jamestown, New York. In an interview with Drew DeSilver in *Vegetarian Times*, Merchant said, "When I was growing up, the town was the center of the universe, like home towns always are when you're a kid. In 1974, we won an 'All-America City' award, and it made everybody in school feel proud."

However, Merchant's childhood didn't resonate with the perfect harmony of a child at the center of the universe. At the age of seven, her parents divorced. Around that same time, she realized that her hometown suffered the same difficulties as other cities. She watched many people lose their jobs as companies shut down or moved elsewhere. She found isolation in an already isolated community. Merchant wrote a song called "Maddox Table," on the 10,000 Maniacs album *The Wishing Chair*, which was about the events she saw taking place in the furniture-making capital of Jamestown. "I met an old man who used to work at Maddox Tables," she told DeSilver in *Vegetarian Times*. "I told him I'd written a song about the company, and I gave him a copy of the record. I never thought I'd meet someone like the person in the song."

After her parents divorce, Merchant primarily lived with her mother. She found a group of friends she felt she could communicate with when her mother remarried and moved the family to a commune in upstate New York. "I fell in love with those people!" Merchant told Nisid Hajari in *Entertainment Weekly*. "They were artists. They were ladies that didn't shave their legs. They lived alone and fed the wood stove in the winter, and they were strong."

At the age of 16, Merchant made several changes to her life, one of which was deciding to become a vegetarian. She discovered new worlds of nutrition, diet, ecology, and medicine, which had been around for centuries. Although Merchant was proud of her decision, her family did not share her joy. They continued to prepare meat dishes at home, and forced her to eat around the meat. Her vegetarian ideas were not completely dismissed, however. Her stepmother later became a vegetarian and her father cut down on eating meat due to a heart condition.

Committed to Maniacal Music Style

Merchant consistently made life decisions in the blink of the eye, and once she made up her mind, nothing could stop her. One such decision was when she decided to quit high school and go straight to college. While there, she pursued an associate's degree and worked odd jobs. Merchant's career in music began almost purely out of circumstance. In 1980, she met keyboardist Dennis Drew and bassist Steve Gustafson, who worked as disc jockeys at her college radio station. Early the following year, Drew and Gustafson enlisted guitarist Robert Buck to form a band called Still Life. In need of a singer, her friends asked her to join them, as well. After they added guitarist John Lombardo, the group changed their name to 10,000 Maniacs.

Merchant told *People*, "The first five times I went to see 10,000 Maniacs [in 1981], I wasn't in the band. But they saw me sitting there and said, 'C'mon up and sing.' So I did that for the next five shows. They kept luring me up onstage, and I kind of liked it. It was pretty exciting, and Jamestown as a whole was pretty boring."

The 10,000 Maniacs differed quite a bit from the other bands playing around town. While these other bands were doing cover tunes of top 40 bands, the 10,000 Maniacs were doing covers of alternative bands from Europe, like Joy Division, and Reggae groups, such as The Mighty Diamonds. College disc jockeys started giving the band their copies of import records, which they eagerly incorporated into their playlist. Soon, the band started writing their own material: peppy, pop-folk songs flavored with bluegrass and Italian folk music.

In 1983, the band released its first album, *Secrets of the I-Ching*. Their subsequent albums gained popularity, and the 10,000 Maniacs became a success. By 1989, the feel-good vibe of the band began to fade. The release of their fourth album, *Blind Man's Zoo*, did not fair well with many critics because of its "stiff-collared preachiness." The band even stopped playing cuts off the album in concert as a result of low responses from their audiences.

Embarked on Flowering Solo Career

In 1993, after 12 years with 10,000 Maniacs, Natalie Merchant decided to leave the band and pursue a solo career. Two years later, she released her solo debut, *Tiger Lily,* which entered the *Billboard* album chart at number. 13 just two weeks after its release, and eventually went triple-platinum. With the help of 10,000 Maniacs producer, Paul Fox, Merchant wrote and recorded the 11 tracks on *Tiger Lily* in only five months. During that time, she refused to let record company executives hear any of the music until the album was mixed.

"A lot of people at the [Elektra Records] company really had preconceived notions of what my solo record should sound like, and I didn't even want to hear them," she later told *Entertainment Weekly*. Merchant claims that she initially financed studio time with a loan, then Elektra Records paid her back. According to some reviews, *Tiger Lily* explored a sadness between poignant and maudlin, depending on the listener's point of view.

The song "River," which appeared on the album, was a tribute to the late actor River Phoenix, who she had a brief friendship with and spoke to mostly by phone. "I feel I am most successful as a songwriter when I just look at the people and tell their stories," Merchant explained to Jeremy Helligar in *People*. "I didn't know River Phoenix that well, but his death struck me powerfully. I thought, 'There's someone who was a kindred spirit. Somebody whom I always wanted to spend time with but never got to.' The few times we spent together, he inspired me to push out boundaries. He had such a vibrant personality. I felt cheated when he died."

Explored the Dark Side

In May of 1998, Merchant released her next album, *Ophelia*, which explored the seasons, angst, and joys of a woman's life. Right after its release, it debuted at number eight on the *Billboard* album charts. *Ophelia* presented full orchestral arrangements, layered vocal harmonies, keyboards, horns, and guest performances by more than 30 musicians. Merchant's lyrical inspiration on *Ophelia* returned to Shakespeare's doomed *Hamlet* heroin with traces of "the heart is a lonely hunter" theme. In addition to releasing the album, Merchant collaborated with directors Mark Seliger and Fred Woodward to produce a companion 23-minute video of the same name. In the video, Merchant played the roles of seven different characters (complete with dubbed-in Italian and Swedish accents) ranging from a Depression-era suffragette to a Mob moll.

In 1998, Merchant co-headlined the Lilith Fair summer festival with fellow pop singer Sarah McLachlan. Away from the studio and off the road, Merchant spent much of her time as a liberal activist, which earned her many accolades and a reputation as a media crusader. Merchant returned to her hometown in 1998 for a special appearance with 300 children at the Jamestown Boys and Girls Club. That same year, she donated $30,000 to the "Way to Go" program at the club, and another $15,000 each to the YMCA and the YWCA. The programs earmarked Merchant's donations to help prevent teen pregnancies. Natalie Merchant also took high-profile stands on such issues as commercial logging, animal rights, and abortion, but refrained from using her music as a vehicle for her activism. She insisted that the inspiration for her songs would continue to come from her personal experiences, memories, and observations. "I write songs about the things that are important to me," she told Andy Steiner in *Utne Reader*. "I guess you find whatever you can in your own experience that will be meaningful to other people."

Selected discography

Tigerlily, Elektra Records, 1995.
Ophelia, Elektra Records, 1998.

Sources

Periodicals

Buffalo News, April 18, 1998.
Entertainment Weekly, October 29, 1993; May 26, 1995; July 21, 1995; May 29, 1998.
Mother Jones, January 1999.
National Catholic Reporter, July 31, 1998.
Newsweek, June 1, 1998.
People Weekly, May 23, 1988; July 3, 1995.
Time, May 25, 1998.
Utne Reader, November/December 1998.
Vegetarian Times, March 1989.

Online

"Natalie Merchant," *Wall of Sound*, http://wallofsound.go.com/artists/nataliemerchant/home.html (May 1, 1999).
"Natalie Merchant," *Elektra Records*, http://www.elektra.com (May 1, 1999).

—Sonya Shelton

Morcheeba

Trip-hop group

Coribs View. Reproduced by permission.

In the late '90s, any group that created ethereal tones over soft hip-hop beats and was fronted by an other-worldly sounding female vocalist was termed "trip-hop." For a while, it seemed any artist associated with the genre was guaranteed to sell records. Groups like Lamb, Olive, Gus Gus, and Portishead all sold well within this genre. Paul and Ross Godfrey formed Morcheeba with singer Skye Edwards and became trip-hop sensations.

Brothers Paul and Ross Godfrey Edwards at a party in London in late 1994, while all three in their mid-to-late twenties. The two brothers had been fooling around with music together practically all their lives, but once they met Edwards, it gelled. "We never really had the focus to do anything until we met Skye," Paul Godfrey told Britt Robson of *Request* in 1996. The Godfrey's write and play all of Morcheeba's music, but it's Edwards' sweet vocal intonations that fans recognize. In 1998, *Rolling Stone*'s Kara Manning said "Edwards is a gifted stylist who knows how to elevate the simplest lyric to a ravaged revelation or a wicked kick in the ass."

The first single off Morcheeba's debut record *Who Can You Trust?*, "Trigger Hippie," is typical of the somewhat cynical tone of many the trio's songs. "Trigger Hippie" was written about a passive, new-age, Earth-loving friend of Ross' who got drunk one night, smashed up a bar and beat up a police officer. Some of their other songs—about the dirty side of the music industry and bank robberies gone wrong—come from a mix of group's jaded sense of things with it's laid-back attitude.

Despite the fact that they don't depend on electronic-based instruments—actual guitar and drums can be heard on their songs and they only sample sparingly from other records—Morcheeba still was lumped under the market-savvy trip-hop label. As much as they didn't feel it was an entirely accurate tag, they did acknowledge that it helped their career. "To begin with, it did help us get a record contract, a recording studio, a world tour, and the press on our side," guitarist/keyboardist Ross Godfrey told *Billboard* in 1998. "So, I can't say that I hate it from the bottom of the heart, because obviously it's done a lot for us as a band. In that sense, it's great. We kind of came in through the back door, which helped us out. And now we're in the position to do whatever we like." Brother Paul has a less-than-sanguine outlook on the label. "That tag is just total bollocks," he told Ben Thompson of *Spin*, "There's nothing psychedelic about our music whatsoever. It's just instrumental hip-hop made by middle-class people who can afford all the equipment but don't know any rappers."

The credits on their CD sleeves are proof of Morcheeba's only mild interest in electronica. Musicians' names—

For the Record . . .

Members include **Skye Edwards**, vocals, lyrics, guitar; **Paul Godfrey**, arrangements, lyrics, drums; and **Ross Godfrey**, guitar, keyboards.

Formed late 1994 in London, England; released debut, *Who Can You Trust?*, Warner Brothers' Discovery Records, 1996; toured with Live and Fiona Apple, 1997; released *Big Calm*, Sire, 1998; headlined the Lilith Fair second stage, 1998.

Address: *Record company*—Warner Music International, 75 Rockefeller Plaza, 7th Floor, New York, NY 10019.

and not sampled songs from other artists—are listed. That's where they differ from their trip-hop brethren. "I took my hands off and [the music] became more organic," Paul Godfrey told Michael Gelfand of *Musician* in 1998. "I let musicians do more of their own thing, rather than just sitting there like a Fascist with a sampler."

After *Who Can You Trust?*, Morcheeba was approached by former Talking Heads' frontman David Byrne to do some production work on his next release. The band ended up producing nine tracks for Byrne, six of which ended up on his 1997 release, *Feelings*. They were thrilled to be working with the music industry legend, and were surprised to find that they got along so well. "We pretty much had an instant spacey rapport with him," Paul told *Raygun* in 1997. "We grew up listening to the Talking Heads, so we kind of couldn't believe this all was happening. It's just very, very inspiring. He's been through it all and we're about to go through it all. It's a great place for two artists to meet."

Aside from working with Byrne, touring was pretty much all Morcheeba had time for after the release of *Who Can You Trust?* But the trio had no interest in trying to recreate their studio sound on a live stage. "The amount of bands that I've seen that are just so static onstage because they're relying on their equipment and the technology more than their ability to actually entertain makes us not want to go anywhere near that road," Ross told Gelfand. Edwards continued, "If we wanted it to sound the same we could just stick on a DAT [digital audio tape] and then mime to it." Ross adds: "It's all about energy, really. And the audience is generally into the visual aspect of things."

The trio wasted no time and worked to get their second release, *Big Calm*, out in 1998. Gelfand noted that, unlike other "next big thing" bands, who make a big hit with their debuts and then fizzle with the follow-up release, Morcheeba pushed even farther forward with *Big Calm*. "Morcheeba backed up all the hype that had been slathered on them by delivering an enticing collection of songs built on ingenious sample loops, trip-hop beats, insidious instrumental hooks and cool-jazz vocals," wrote Gelfand. With *Big Calm*, Morcheeba also broke away from the trip-hop pack. "Haunting dub rhythms and vintage spy-movie themes still provide the backdrop for this London trio, but on its second disc Morcheeba sounds remarkably ripe," wrote the *San Francisco Examiner-Chronicle* in 1998. "With [the CD's] mesmeric rhythm-and-blues tracks the group can finally put all those Portishead comparisons to rest."

During the first four years of Morcheeba's existence, Edwards gave birth to two children. The first, Jaeger, to whom *Who Can You Trust?* was dedicated, went with the band on their first U.S. and European tours. *Big Calm* and its supporting tour was scheduled for March of 1998, pegged to give Edwards one month's maternity leave after the birth of her second child. Edwards' status as a mother extended the band's reach into an even more diverse market than their varied music did. Women's magazines, for whom a British trip-hop trio would normally have been of little interest, profiled the band using the angle of Edwards as new-age rock mother.

The group had a strong appeal for women. During the summer of 1998, Morcheeba was the must-see second stage headliner of the Lilith Fair, the immensely successful female-based touring festival, led by pop songstress Sarah Mclaughlin. "Mixmaster Paul Godfrey's strong rhythms combined with his brother Ross' guitar work to produce a sound that was simultaneously lazy and edgy," wrote the *Washington Times*, in a 1997 review of Lilith. "Lead singer Skye Edwards' soothing voice and swaying stage persona rounded out what was one of the most pleasant surprises of the festival."

Their sound comes from three very different musicians, three very different personalities. Godfrey, Godfrey and Edwards find a comfortable balance in their divergent musical tastes. "Because the musical differences between us are so big, it's very easy to collaborate," Ross told Gelfand. "If we were closer, we'd be stepping on each other's toes. We're all completely in our own corners, and the music that comes out isn't forced and flows along nicely." There's a balance of temperaments that the three find, as well. "It's easy," Edwards told Thompson. "Paul is a control freak and Ross just wants to lie on the sofa smoking all day—so I just slot in the middle."

Selected discography

Who Can You Trust?, Discovery, 1996.
Big Calm, Sire, 1998.

Sources

Periodicals

Alternative Press, February 1997.
Billboard, October 5, 1996; February 21, 1998; April 4, 1998.
Everybody's News, September 19, 1997.
Musician, December 1998.
New York Times, December 16, 1996.
Request, December 1996.
Rolling Stone, April 18, 1998.
Time Out NYC, March 19-26, 1998.
USA Today, November 5, 1996.
Venice, January 1997.
Village Voice, April 15, 1997; April 22, 1997; May 12, 1998.

Online

"Morcheeba," *All-Music Guide*, http://www.allmusic.com (January 5, 1999).

Additional information was provided by Warner Music International publicity materials, 1999.

—*Brenna Sanchez*

Fats Navarro

Brief careers are sometimes difficult to characterize, but since Fats Navarro was such a key figure in bridging the gap between the original bebop musicians—Gillespie, Parker, Monk, Powell—and the so-called hard bop school, his brief career deserves examination. And his music must be listened to. Despite the fact that trumpet styles frequently overlap and sometimes blur, Navarro's sound and his conception of trumpet playing remain clearly identifiable nearly a half century after his death at age 26.

Theodore Navarro was born of Cuban parentage in Key West, Florida on September 24, 1923. Little has been written about his early life, but we do know that he began studying piano at age six, then tenor saxophone somewhat later. It was on the saxophone that his first professional dates, with the Walter Johnson band in Miami, were noted. He began his trumpet studies at age 13 and it was on this horn that he broke in with the Snookum Russell band in 1941. "Fats Navarro and I left home together," trumpeter Idrees Sulieman told Ira Gitler for his *Swing to Bop*. "We were good friends. And I remember the night I left home was the Monday after Easter, in '41. J.J. [Johnson] was with Fats in Snookum Russell's band, and we had a big jam session in Orlando, the three of us." At that time Navarro was favoring the style of trumpeter Dud Bascomb from the Erskine Hawkins orchestra. He also played in other territory bands, sometimes doubling on tenor sax.

Navarro's first national notice, as well as the notice of other influential musicians, began when he joined the Andy Kirk band in 1943. Andy Kirk and His 12 Clouds of Joy was a popular traveling and recording band dating back to 1936. Navarro soon met another trumpeter, Howard McGhee, who was to influence his playing and contribute in a major way to his musical development and recording career. After nearly two years with Kirk, Navarro enjoyed his first major exposure to the movers and shakers of the early bop movement.

Dizzy Gillespie, long acknowledged as the trumpet guru of the bop era, had been playing in the trumpet section of singer Billy Eckstine's band. Gillespie had been moving and shaking not only the members of that band and its leader, but the entire jazz community. Gillespie's totally fresh, innovative solos, developed largely through interaction with the Minton's group, which included alto saxophonist Charlie Parker and pianists Bud Powell and Thelonious Monk, had energized fellow musicians as well as eager listeners. But Gillespie was restless and needed to move on to the role of leader. Having heard Navarro, he recommended the younger trumpeter to Eckstine as his eventual replacement. As the leader told Leonard Feather for his *New Encyclopedia of Jazz*, "A

AP/Wide World Photo. Reproduced by permission.

week or two after [Navarro] had joined us, you'd hardly know Diz had left the band. His ideas and feelings were the same and there was just as much swing."

Navarro remained with Eckstine's band for about 18 months. In 1946 he was replaced by another young trumpet phenomenon, Kenny Dorham. Of this period, Budd Johnson, tenor saxophonist/writer/arranger, told Ira Gitler, author of *Swing to Bop*, "I remember when Fats Navarro first heard Diz he said, Oh, man, that's the way I want to play. That's where it is ...When Dizzy left the band then I took over as musical director, but Fats stayed. They were in the band together. So all of that rubbed off on him there, and he was struggling with it until he really got it. And he played pretty good saxophone too." Two other bandmates also told Gitler of Navarro's dedication at this time. Saxophonist Don Lanphere said, "He was after musical perfection and I think this is something he let be known to people. He worked hard at achieving this." And his friend Sulieman related, "Fats would practice all day long. Sit in the bed with his mute and practice all day." Navarro then settled in New York, which became the center of his activities for the last four years of his life.

As Frank Tirro wrote in his *Jazz: A History*, "Bebop was teaching trumpeters to play in a new way, and the technical excellence of Dizzy Gillespie led others to follow in his stylistic footsteps." Navarro, through his diligence, had achieved comparable technical excellence and at the same time a fatter, warmer tone quality. Most critics, fellow musicians and listeners noted then, and still celebrate, Navarro's clean articulation of notes in the speediest of passages, combined with a beauty of tone quality. Also, he played exciting ideas. It was these attributes that led to his pairing with drummer Kenny Clarke, tenor giants Coleman Hawkins, Eddie Lockjaw Davis, Sonny Rollins, and Illinois Jacquet, among other, for recordings and club dates between 1946-47. During this period, Fats also met Tadd Dameron, a pianist better respected for his writing and arranging skills.

Dameron and Navarro collaborated on a six-piece band from September, 1947, to April, 1949. Two recording sessions on Blue Note and one on Capitol during this period produced some of Navarro's best recorded work. Dameron, an innovative writer and arranger, fit in well with the emerging bebop style, utilizing its unique language in ways most writers could not master. Such originals as "The Chase," "Our Delight," and "Dameronia" became excellent vehicles for Navarro's solo work. Another pairing that produced recorded fireworks was the one with trumpeter Howard McGhee, Navarro's former Andy Kirk bandmate. Originally an admirer of the trumpet style of Roy Eldridge, McGhee had, since 1943, become one of the foremost practitioners of the bebop style. His October, 1948, collaboration with Navarro on Blue Note found both horn men at the top of their game. Their interaction on such tunes as Double Talk is remarkable.

Navarro eventually fell into a trap that caught so many of the jazz musicians of the 1940s. Following in the footsteps of Charlie Parker, the acknowledged leader of the bebop school, Navarro became addicted to heroin. The trumpeter got caught up in the need to satisfy his addiction and began neglecting his health. He eventually developed a serious case of tuberculosis. Bassist Charles Mingus, in his *Beneath the Underdog*, recalled an experience with Navarro after Fats joined the Lionel Hampton band in 1948: "The tour continued and Fats began to complain that he didn't feel good, he hurt all over and he wanted out. [I] thought it was just an excuse because they were all tired of the strenuous one-nighters. One day on the bus Fats began coughing up blood. When they got to Chicago he quit the band and left for New York."

Navarro's sickness did not diminish the fire in his playing until the end. Mingus also recalled an incident just after Fats joined the Hampton five-man trumpet section. Navarro had been hired strictly for his solo work, a fact which drew a comment from one of the other trumpeters who complained that the newcomer couldn't even read. Mingus wrote, "Fats laughed, grabbed the musician's part, eyed it and said, 'Schitt, you ain't got nothin' to read here!' And he sight-read from the score impeccably for the entire last show." A session he recorded with the fabulous Bud Powell and a young Sonny Rollins in August, 1949, contains some of the finest Navarro work on record, including "Bouncing with Bud" and "52nd Street Theme."

In an odd melding of talents, Navarro recorded one side with the King of Swing, Benny Goodman, in 1948. They did an old Fats Waller tune and Goodman favorite, "Stealin' Apples." The last recorded evidence of Navarro's talent came at New York's Birdland, in a gig with Charlie Parker, Bud Powell and others. Though the recording is somewhat rough, and Fats was only weeks from death and at times sounds tired, the brilliance still shines through.

Nearly every critic and musician has spoken of Navarro's place in jazz history. Joachim E. Berendt, in his *The Jazz Book*, noted: "Just as all trumpeters of traditional jazz come from Armstrong, so do all modern trumpeters stem from Gillespie. The four most important in the forties were Howard McGhee, Fats Navarro, Kenny Dorham, and young Miles Davis. The early death of Fats Navarro was as lamented by the musicians of his generation as Bunny Berigan's and Bix Beiderbecke's passing had been mourned by the musicians of the Swing and Chicago periods. Fats' clear, assured playing was a forerunner of the style practiced by the generation of hard bop since the late sixties...." And Dizzy Gillespie, in his *to BE or not to BOP*, wrote: "I believe in this parallel between jazz and religion. Definitely! Definitely! The runners on the trumpet would be Buddy Bolden, King Oliver, Louis Armstrong, Roy Eldridge, me, Miles, and Fats Navarro, Clifford Brown, Lee Morgan, Freddie Hubbard—they're the runners. They created a distinctive style, a distinctive message to the music, and the rest of them follow that. Our Creator chooses great artists."

Selected discography

Bird and Fats—Live at Birdland, 1950, Cool and Blue, 1950.
(With Kenny Dorham and Sonny Stitt) *Fats Navarro Memorial, 1946-47*, Savoy, 1993.
(With others) *Fats Navarro and Tadd Dameron, The Complete Blue Note and Capitol Recordings of, 1948-49*, Blue Note, 1995.

Sources

Books

Berendt, Joachim E., *The Jazz Book: From Ragtime to Fusion and Beyond,* Lawrence Hill & Company, 1892.
Carr, Ian, Digby Fairweather and Brian Priestley, *Jazz: The Rough Guide,* The Rough Guides, 1995.
Feather, Leonard, *The New Edition of the Encyclopedia of Jazz,* Bonanza Books, 1965.
Gillespie, Dizzy, with Al Fraser, *to BE or not to BOP,* Doubleday & Company, 1979.
Gitler, Ira, *Swing to Bop,* Oxford University Press, 1985.
Holtje, Steve and Nancy Ann Lee, *Music Hound Jazz: The Essential Album Guide,* Visible Ink Press, 1998.
Mingus, Charles, *Beneath the Underdog,* Alfred A. Knopf, 1971.
Taylor, Arthur, *Notes and Tones: Musician to Musician Interviews,* Perigee Books, 1977.
Tirro, Frank, *Jazz: A History,* W.W. Norton & Company, 1977.

Periodicals

Coda, October, 1950.

Additional information provided by the album notes of *Fats Navarro and Tadd Dameron: The Complete Blue Note and Capitol Recordings of,* notes by Carl Woideck, Blue Note, 1995.

—Robert Dupuis

'N Sync

Pop group

After winning over hordes of young listeners in Europe in the late 1990s, the five member vocal outfit 'N Sync returned to their native America to meet equal, if not greater, approval. Along with fellow crooners Backstreet Boys, 'N Sync spearheaded a resurgence of boyish singing acts specializing in smooth harmonizing, with an eye towards the teen market. While 'N Sync's efforts were widely scoffed at by critics, who found the band's appeal to be limited to their pin-up good looks, a legion of fans nevertheless pushed the quintet's self-titled 1998 debut album to the top of sales charts. Hot on the heels of *'N Sync*, the group created an equally successful holiday album, *Home for Christmas.*

Unlike many groups marketed toward teens, 'N Sync's origins stem not from a savvy talent agent's orchestration, but from a growing circle of friends' appreciation for singing. However, 'N Sync do share the wholesome, innocent image that a number of "boy groups" project, a fact evident from their earliest occupations. The initial momentum towards the formation of 'N Sync began in 1995 when Chris Kirkpatrick, an employee at the Universal Studios family theme park in Orlando, Florida,

AP/Wide World Photo. Reproduced by permission.

For the Record . . .

Members include **Lance Bass** (born May 4, 1979, in Laurel, MS), vocals; **Joshua Scott "JC" Chasez** (born August 8, 1976, in Washington, D.C.), vocals; **Joey Fatone** (born January 28, 1977, in Brooklyn, NY), vocals; **Chris Kirkpatrick** (born October 17, 1971, in Clarion, PA), vocals; **Justin Timberlake** (born January 31, 1981, in Memphis, TN), vocals.

Group began in 1995 by Kirkpatrick in Orlando, FL, where he and Timberlake crossed paths at the Universal Studios theme park; signed to Ariola, the domestic branch of the German label BMG and release self-titled debut album in Europe, 1996; toured extensively throughout Europe, Asia, and Africa, 1996-98; signed by BMG's American label, RCA, who re-released *'N Sync* in the U.S.; release seasonal album *Home for Christmas* on RCA, 1998; launch major tour, 1999.

Addresses: *Record company*—RCA, 1133 Avenue of the Americas, New York, NY, 10036. *Fan club*—'N Sync Official Fan Club, P.O. Box 5248 Bellingham, WA, 98227.

befriended two ex-members of television's *Mickey Mouse Show*, Justin Timberlake and JC Chasez. Next came Brooklyn-born thespian Joey Fatone, who was also on Universal Studio's payroll, and had appeared in front of the camera as a bit player in the 1993 spoof of science fiction films, *Matinee*. The final link in the group's circle was provided when Timberlake's vocal coach steered the foursome in the direction of high school senior Lance Bass, a day care worker and ex-choirboy from Mississippi, who relocated to Orlando after initial reluctance.

In addition to an instant vocal compatibility, the five singers quickly discovered a strong harmony at the level of friendship. Reflecting both of these qualities—as well as the last letters of the quintet's first names—Timberlake's mother Lynne Harless christened the group 'N Sync. However, while the fledgling act had quickly forged a sound and a group identity, they were a far cry from stardom, and soon sought a manager who could deliver them to an audience. Before long, 'N Sync were taken under the wings of Johnny and Donna Wright. A husband and wife team, the Wrights had previously managed another popular ensemble of teen heartthrobs during the 1980s, New Kids on the Block, and had recently helped form Backstreet Boys, a five piece vocal combo with whom 'N Sync would later be extensively compared.

By the fall of 1996, the Wrights maneuvered 'N Sync into a contract with the BMG/Ariola label, and soon recorded their catchy debut single, "I Want You Back." However, it was not in the U.S. but in Europe that 'N Sync were first embraced with open arms, and the band spent the next two years extensively touring overseas. As Johnny Wright shrewdly assessed, European audiences had been generally more enthusiastic than Americans towards sugary pop groups such as Take That and Bros. Countries such as Germany proved no exception to the rule, sending "I Want You Back" and the follow-up single "Tearin' Up My Heart" high on sales charts. Additionally, the intense sojourn abroad allowed 'N Sync to hone their live performance skills before their return home. As Bass recounted to *Billboard*'s Wolfgang Spahr in 1997, the quintet "rehearse[d] in and old warehouse which doesn't have any air conditioning, and when you have to jump around in 40-degree [Celsius]heat three to four hours four times a week, it makes you pretty strong."

In the meantime, the public mood in the U.S. had shifted. Since the early 1990s, aggressive, guitar based acts with alternative and heavy metal roots held a virtual tyranny over sales charts, and record executives became sheepish about signing many groups with a light pop appeal. However, this trend of angst-ridden expression tended to alienate many music lovers—crucially, those in early adolescence. "People forgot that most of the kids in America aren't particularly happy and would relate to music that said life can be good," quipped record industry scout Steven Greenberg in *Rolling Stone*. "Everyone was aiming at an audience college age and above and hoping that the music would trickle *down*. The younger audience had no choice but to listen to music that was created for a much older audience." Apparently, this suppression built up a hearty appetite amongst teenagers, and suddenly the U.S. devoured young outfits like Backstreet Boys and Hanson. Within this setting, 'N Sync made their triumphant return to their own shores.

In the spring of 1998, 'N Sync's debut album was finally released in America on RCA, nearly two years after the same disc had been pressed overseas. After gaining initial momentum from the high powered dance single "I Want You Back," it did not take long before the quintet came into their own on the American sales charts. However, while record buyers embraced 'N Sync's mixture of catchy harmonizing and ballads of teen love gone awry, critics were generally unforgiving. "If all it takes for pop stars to win adolescent hearts and minds these days is the adequate abilities and pallid hooks of this bunch," decried a reviewer for the *Los Angeles Times*, "then every other semi-attractive singing, dancing young man in America should take heart." In addition, 'N Sync was also besieged with allegations of stealing the sound of Johnny Wright's other runaway success, Backstreet Boys. While 'N Sync themselves acknowledged the apparent similarities with their crooning contemporaries, they viewed such press with a grain of salt. "People try to make a feud out of everything," Timberlake explained to *Rolling Stone* on the subject. "And we didn't even see it that way."

'N Sync subsequently took their highly choreographed stage show across the United States, and like a number of youth-targeted groups before them, the quintet decided to perform in rather unconventional venues—in this case, roller skating rinks. As in Europe, the five singers soon found it commonplace to be physically bombarded onstage by enthusiastic female fans. Not surprisingly, such appeal was capitalized on by a number of publishers who created an onslaught of 'N Sync posters, fan magazines, and hastily written paperbacks, but the band remained remarkably humble. "When we read teen magazines and they're like 'These Fab Five hotties," Fatone mused to *People*, "we're like, 'Wrong!'" Still, critics remained skeptical as to how much of 'N Sync's mass appeal was due to teen hormones rather than vocal virtuosity. The sudden release of the full length *Home for Christmas* album (given the secular title *Winter Album* in markets outside of the US) did not prove to be a radical departure from 'N Sync's bubble-gum style.

Selected discography

'N Sync, RCA, 1998.
Home for Christmas, RCA, 1998.

Sources

Periodicals

Billboard, June 21, 1997.
People, February 8, 1999.
Rolling Stone, November 12, 1998.

Online

http://www.paradox2010.com

—Shaun Frentner

Stevie Nicks

Singer, songwriter

A trailblazer for women in rock music, singer Stevie Nicks was one of the first female performers to maintain a feminine stage persona in the masculine world of rock and roll. She reached international recognition in the mid-1970s singing for the band Fleetwood Mac, and her flowing, chiffon-draped, gypsy costumes later became trend-setting fashion. Nicks embarked on a solo career in 1981 and continued writing and recording her own music long after her departure from Fleetwood Mac. "Stevie Nicks is more than a rock icon," Rob Sheffield wrote in Rolling Stone. "She's the high priestess of her own religion, ruling a world of prancing gypsies, gold-dust princesses, and white-winged doves, all without going anywhere near a sensible shoe."

Born Stephanie Nicks in 1948, she grew up migrating from one city to another throughout the western United States. Her father, Jesse Seth Nicks, was a business executive who kept moving his wife Barbara and their family as he changed jobs. "Our father would always be getting promoted and transferred, so we never grew up in any one place," Nicks' brother Christopher told Timothy White in Rolling Stone. "We moved from Phoenix to New Mexico to Texas to Utah to Los Angeles to San Francisco."

Stevie Nicks' interest in music began early, and she received her first guitar when she was 13 years old. While she was in high school in Palo Alto, California, she met guitarist Lindsey Buckingham and the two became both musically and romantically involved. In 1968, Nicks' family moved to Chicago, but she stayed behind to play with Buckingham in the band Fritz. Within a couple of years, the band moved to Los Angeles. Buckingham and Nicks moved in together, and she worked as a waitress to support them. "Lindsey thought it would be selling out for him to work at a restaurant like that, so I did," Nicks told Jancee Dunn in Harper's Bazaar.

Twirled Onstage with Fleetwood Mac

By 1973, Stevie Nicks and Lindsey Buckingham had split with Fritz and released their own album on Polydor Records called Buckingham/Nicks. It was this album that grabbed the attention of a British band called Fleetwood Mac, which included drummer Mick Fleetwood, bassist John McVie, and keyboardist Christine McVie. The band wanted Lindsey Buckingham to join them, but he wouldn't agree unless Stevie Nicks was included in the agreement. "Buckingham/Nicks had to bite the bullet for Fleetwood Mac," Nicks later wrote in the liner notes for her box set Enchanted. "We'll never quite know exactly what would have happened if we'd gone the other way.... But it would have been a whole other life."

The new version of Fleetwood Mac released their self-titled album in 1975. It sold approximately three million copies, and the band embarked on a successful tour. It was the beginning of a legendary rock formation, but the band faced several challenges almost immediately. "We were a strange group of three English people and two American people," Nicks told Sarah McLachlan in Interview, "and that was very hard on the road, because we were just so different."

The following year, Fleetwood Mac began recording their next album, Rumors. During this time, the band went into a period of personal chaos. Buckingham and Nicks were in the middle of a turbulent break up, John and Christine McVie were in the process of divorcing, and Mick Fleetwood was also divorcing his wife. The emotional commotion came through loud and clear in the group's songwriting, resulting in a hugely successful album. Rumors ended up selling 18 million albums in the U.S. alone, and remained on Billboard's album charts for nearly nine years. "Probably the reason people love Rumors so much is because they say that great art comes out of great tragedy," Nicks told Joe Benson in Off the Record.

Despite the turmoil in their personal lives, Fleetwood Mac continued to work together professionally. They released their next album, Tusk, in 1979, along with a live album recorded on tour, Fleetwood Mac Live, in 1980. By

For the Record . . .

Born Stephanie Nicks on May 26, 1948, in Phoenix, AZ; daughter of Jesse Seth and Barbara Nicks; married Kim Anderson, 1983; divorced 1984.

Began performing with Lindsey Buckingham, 1966; released *Buckingham/Nicks* on Polydor Records, 1973; joined Fleetwood Mac, 1974; released first solo album, *Bella Donna*, 1981; released a total of seven albums with Fleetwood Mac, 1975-90; left Fleetwood Mac for full-time solo career, 1993; reunited with Fleetwood Mac for *The Dance*, 1997.

Addresses: *Record company*—Modern/Atlantic Records, 75 Rockefeller Plaza, New York, NY 10019.

this time, Stevie Nicks had established herself as the centerpiece of Fleetwood Mac's live performances. She danced, spun, and twirled on stage like a magical princess in a fairy tale. "When I walk up on that stage, I give people a little bit of an escape into fairyland," said Nicks in *Glamour*. "I'm the only one in the group who's free to sprinkle stardust here and there."

Ventured Out on Solo Flight

Nicks decided to spread her musical wings beyond the confines of Fleetwood Mac in the early 1980s. She released her first solo album, *Bella Donna*, on Atlantic Records in 1981. The album climbed to the top of the charts and quickly reached platinum sales. Nicks remained a member of Fleetwood Mac, but felt the need to open up another avenue for her music. "'Bella Donna' is a term of endearment I use, and the title is about making a lot of decisions in my life, making a change based on the turmoil in my soul," Nicks explained to Timothy White in *Rolling Stone*.

Bella Donna included several hits, including a duet with singer Tom Petty called "Stop Draggin' My Heart Around." Nicks said recording the album helped her learn to take more responsibility for her work as a songwriter and performer. "For *Bella Donna*, I had to learn to stand up and lead," Nicks told Jon Pareles in *Mademoiselle*. "I had to learn to do this alone."

Stevie Nicks returned to the studio with Fleetwood Mac to record *Mirage*, which was released in 1982. Then, she continued her solo career with *Wild Heart*, which included the singles "Nightbird" and "Enchanted." Around this same time, she married Kim Anderson, the widowed husband of her best friend Robin Stucker, who died of leukemia. The marriage lasted a short eight months.

Traumatized by Personal Turmoil

Nicks continued her fast-paced recording and touring schedule with another solo album in 1985 called *Rock A Little*. Unfortunately, she couldn't maintain her rock and roll stride without the help of a multi-million-dollar cocaine habit that ultimately burned a hole through the cartilage in her nose. In 1986, her addiction became so bad that she entered into a 28-day rehab program at the Betty Ford Center in Rancho Mirage, California. "But after I quit cocaine, things got even worse," Nicks recalled to Todd Gold and Steve Dougherty in *People*.

After Fleetwood Mac released *Tango in the Night* in 1987, Lindsey Buckingham decided to leave the band. During the same time, Stevie Nicks decided to see a psychiatrist about her cocaine addiction. The doctor prescribed a powerful tranquilizer called Klonopin and Nicks was on her way to another drug addiction. She released the solo album *Other Side of the Mirror*, but through the haze of drugs, remembered very little of the tour that followed. Despite her addiction, Stevie Nicks continued to write, record, and perform on her own and with Fleetwood Mac. Fleetwood Mac released *Behind the Mask* in 1990, and the following year, Nicks released a greatest hits album, called *Timespace*, which included three new songs.

In 1993, Stevie Nicks began to turn her life around. She left Fleetwood Mac. And after she fell into a fireplace and gashed her head, she entered a 45-day detox program to help her drug addiction. The following year, she released her fifth solo album entitled *Street Angel*. "I've earned my place as an enduring woman in rock 'n roll, and I'm not about to give it up. Not as long as I still feel inspired by the music," Nicks told Larry Flick that year in *Billboard*. But as her tour ended the following year, Stevie Nicks put all that aside and vowed never to sing in front of people again. "Singing is the love of my life, but I was ready to give it all up because I couldn't handle people talking about how fat I was," Nicks explained to Steve Dougherty and Todd Gold in *People*.

Between her increasing weight and constant fatigue, Stevie Nicks decided to have her breast implants that she had received in 1976 removed. She discovered that both implants were "totally broken" and a possible factor in her health problems. After her surgery, her energy and health began to return and her weight slimmed down. This led to her renewed outlook about performing again. She recorded the songs "Somebody Stand By Me" for the *Boys on the Side* soundtrack in 1995 and "Twisted" for the *Twister* soundtrack in 1996.

Created Renewals and Reunions

The following year, the members of Fleetwood Mac reunited for a three-month, sold-out tour and recorded the album *The Dance*, which commemorated the twentieth anniversary of the band's benchmark album *Rumors*. The CD includedlive renditions of their previous hit songs, plus four new tracks. "We didn't all enjoy it very much the first time because we were too high and too uptight," Nicks told Chris Willman in *Entertainment Weekly*. Fleetwood Mac reunited on stage again in 1998 for their induction into the Rock and Roll Hall of Fame.

Stevie Nicks also released her first greatest hits boxed set, *Enchanted*, that same year. "It was like looking at a great book report of my life, good and bad," Nicks told Ray Rogers in *Interview*. "Each song tells me exactly who I was in my life when I wrote it." Nicks also contributed two songs—"If You Ever Did Believe" and "Crystal"—to the *Practical Magic* soundtrack.

At the age of 50, Nicks was still combating the division between her stage persona and her offstage personality. "The girl onstage is glamorous and movie star-esque," Nicks told Barbara Stepko in *McCalls*. "The thing is, when the makeup, the clothes, and the glitter come off, some people still treat me like her. In real life, I'm normal, practical, and 50 years old. A grown-up person who could be a grandmother."

However, Stevie Nicks insisted that despite her age, she would continue to record and perform rock music for as long as there were people who wanted to listen. "As long as I can play a song and people are still sitting there at the end of it," Nicks told Jeremy Helligar in *People*, "I won't worry about my music losing value."

Selected discography

Bella Donna, Atlantic Records, 1981.
Wild Heart, Atlantic Records, 1983.
Rock a Little, Atlantic Records, 1985.
Other Side of the Mirror, Atlantic Records, 1989.
Timespace, Atlantic Records, 1991.
Street Angel, Modern/Atlantic Records, 1994.
Enchanted, Modern Atlantic Records, 1998.

with Fleetwood Mac

Fleetwood Mac, Warner Bros. Records, 1975.
Rumors, Warner Bros. Records, 1977.
Tusk, Warner Bros. Records, 1979.
Fleetwood Mac Live, Warner Bros. Records, 1980.
Mirage, Warner Bros. Records, 1982.
Tango in the Night, Warner Bros. Records, 1987.
Behind the Mask, Warner Bros. Records, 1990.
The Dance, Warner/Reprise Records, 1997.

Sources

Periodicals

Billboard, March 26, 1994; August 29, 1998; September 5, 1998.
Boston Globe, April 24, 1998.
Entertainment Weekly, May 24, 1996; May 1, 1998; May 8, 1998.
Glamour, December 1981.
Harper's Bazaar, November 1997.
ICE, February 1998.
Interview, March 1995, July 1998.
Mademoiselle, August 1982.
McCalls, January 1999.
New York Times, June 19, 1998.
Off the Record, September 6, 1998.
People, December 29, 1980; October 5, 1981; June 13, 1994; January 19, 1998; May 18, 1998.
Rolling Stone, September 3, 1981; September 22, 1994; May 14, 1998.
San Francisco Chronicle, April 26, 1998.
Teen, March 1983.
Time, October 24, 1983.
Toledo Blade, May 18, 1998.

Online

The Nicks Fix, http://nicksfix.com (September 23, 1998).

—Sonya Shelton

Danilo Perez

Pianist, composer

Even though he is new to the Latin jazz music scene, Panamanian-born Danilo Perez is considered one of the finest contemporary pianists and jazz composers. Born in 1966 in Panama, his father, dance band singer Danilo Sr., wasted no time in starting his son on his musical path. At three , he gave Danilo Jr. his first set of bongos. Perez now holds a degree in jazz composition from Boston's Berklee College of Music and serves as professor at the New England Conservatory of Music.

While growing up in Panama, Perez's early influences included Gershwin, Duke Ellington, John Coltrane, and his mentor in spirit and composition Thelonious Monk. Perez's album for Impulse! records, *PanaMonk,* is a study of and tribute to Monk.

When Perez went to the United States to study jazz, his knowledge of jazz musicians expanded immensely. Living jazz legends played key roles in the shaping of the young pianist. Wynton Marsalis asked Perez to tour Poland with his band in 1995. The young Perez was the first Latin artist to perform with Marsalis. For the 1996 Summer Olympics, Perez and Marsalis played together again.

Perhaps Perez's biggest influence in terms of style and thought was Dizzy Gillespie. Perez performed with Gillespie and his United Nations Orchestra from 1989 until the band leaders death in 1992. "One of the things Dizzy taught me was to learn about my own heritage even more than I knew already. He said it was more important for jazz for you to get to what your roots are, than to learn about other things," Perez told Phil Johnson of the *Independent.*

It was shortly after that, in 1993, when Perez released his first album, *Danilo Perez,* on the Novus label. In 1994, at the age of 27, Perez released what is considered his most personal album, *The Journey,* a musical account of the torturous trip African slaves made across the oceans in the hulls of the slave ships. The album made it to the top ten jazz lists of New York's *Village Voice,* the *New York Times, Billboard Magazine,* and the *Boston Globe.* It also allowed Perez to become a recognizable name in the jazz community.

Critics have hailed *The Journey,* Perez's second recording, for its quality of composition and incorporation of Afro-Cuban influences into a jazz context. Perez set up the album as a dream series tracing the route of slaves, stolen or sold from their homes and transported across the sea. *The Journey* begins with "The Capture," makes it way through the "The Taking," "Chains," The Voyage," and finishes with "Libre Spiritus." Renowned saxophonist David Sanchez and percussionist Giovani Hildalgo play on the album, which was recorded in two days at the Power Station in New York City.

According to Minstrel Music Network, "On *The Journey,* Perez ... seeks to blur the distinctions between musical styles, through his all-encompassing vision, and (by implication) to eradicate the distinctions between those people native to the Americas, and the Africans and Europeans who mixed with them to cast the alloy of multiculturalism."

On his third album, *PanaMonk,* Perez paid tribute to Thelonious Monk as well as all the other musicians he had been in contact with up to that point. An almost entirely wordless album, *PanaMonk* lets the music speak for itself. A listener can hear the appreciation and love Perez has for improvisational playing and composing, all of which Monk was revered for. Perez told *JazzTimes Magazine,* "His (Monk's) music was the epitome of small group playing, the epitome of jazz music. If you really want to know about jazz and swing, he's one of the best to go to."

After an extensive world tour, Perez released *Central Avenue* in 1998. In this album, his fourth, "Perez is pausing to re-examine his roots, sum up his discoveries and chart his future path," wrote Fernando Gonzalez in the liner notes for the album. *Central Avenue* is a blend of blues, folk songs, a sprinkling of Caribbean influence and some Middle Eastern melodies thrown in for added spice. Tommy LiPuma, who worked with Perez on *PanaMonk,* produced the album.

The album is, according to Perez, the combination of all the cultures he would see on any major thoroughfare in any big city. "*Central Avenue* is a street in Panama, which is like a melting pot of many cultures. As a child, I could see people from all over the world there, from all social levels. The new album is like *Central Avenue,* because I was trying to find common musical ground between my own culture and the music I discovered when I came to the United States," he explained to Steve Graybow in a 1998 *Billboard* interview.

He arranged a worthy ensemble, including bassists John Pattutucci and Avishai Cohen, and drummer Jeff "Tain" Watts, whom he played with on *PanaMonk.* His inspiration for a multicultural band came from Gillespie's United Nations band. Recorded in New York, most songs on the album were done in one take, so as not to lose the spontaneity and freshness of the session.

The only song not done in one take was "Panama Blues." For that song, which features Panamanian folk singer Raul Vital, Perez recorded the folksinger and his chorus of mejorana singers in the mountain regions of Panama and then brought the recording back to New York where he and his ensemble added their musical touch. Mejorana is an improvisational style of singing where the singers can go on for hours, especially when supplied with alcohol. Perez told Graybow of *Billboard,* "[I heard] the blues in their voices, much like the blues down in Mississippi," and instantly wanted to record them. But, Perez didn't want to take the singer out of his environment and thus lose the influence.

"When I brought the mejorana tape to New York, everyone was freaking out," Perez told Graybow. "It sounded good by itself, but matching up instruments with it was a challenge. Mejorana singers improvise while drinking, and the rhythms move back and forth, flowing like the waves on the sea. But God was on our side, and we were able to complete the song."

For a relatively young man, Perez has been privy to some important and prominent people. He performed as a special guest at President Clinton's Inaugural Ball, and played the piano on the Bill Cosby theme song. He has also worked on film scores, having created the soundtrack for *Winter in Libson,* a 1990 European film staring Dizzie Gillespie. Perez, it seems, is a on his way to becoming his own living legend.

Selected discography

Danilo Perez, Novus, 1992.
The Journey, Novus, 1993.
PanaMonk, Impulse!, 1996.
Central Avenue, Impulse!, 1998.

Sources

Periodicals

Billboard, October 3, 1998.
Independent, October 23, 1998.
Los Angles Times, December 10, 1998.

Online

"Critics Choice: Danilo Perez/PanaMonk," Billboard Reviews & Previews Online, http://www.billboard-online.com (February 12, 1999).
"Danilo Perez: New Artist Biography," Jazz Central Station, http://www1.jazzcentralstation.com (January 15, 1999).
"Liner Notes," Impromptu, http://www.impulserecords.com (January 18, 1999).
Minstrel Music Network, http://home.m2n.com (January 18, 1999).
www.allmusic.com.

Additional information was provide by Impulse! publicity materials.

—*Gretchen Van Monette*

Phish

Rock band

Phish calls Burlington, Vermont, its hometown. The rock quartet of Trey Anastasio, Page McConnell, Mike Gordon, and Jon Fishman have become one of the most successful rock groups ever. Phish has sold well over three million albums and have earned over $10 million on tours alone in 1997. The band is a modern anamoly in the rock music scene, growing to stardom without the assistance of MTV or commercial radio.

The fans and the music of Phish are most often compared to the Grateful Dead. Like the Deadheads before them, Phish Heads grew in number as a result of the group's live shows, as the band toured constantly in the mid 1980s to mid 1990s. Phish Heads fill the venue's parking lot a day before the show, establishing a temporary community, selling tie die t-shirts, playing hacky-sack, juggling, playing music, and dancing. True Phish Heads will live this carnival life and follow the band from city to city until tours end. Musically, the band's shows are mostly improvisational jam sessions, and Phish Heads will never hear the same show twice. Their musical menu serves up a wide range of styles including rock, jazz, blues, funk, Latino, classical, calypso, and folk. The often fantastical lyrics that accompany the myriad of rhythms are influenced by J.R. Tolkien's *The Hobbit,* Lewis Carroll's *Alice's Adventures in Wonderland,* Kipling's *The Jungle Book,* Dr. Seuss, and *Sesamie Street.* Phish's drummer, Jon Fishman, described the band's style of music to Parke Puterbaugh of *Rolling Stone* magazine; "We all have a certain desire to honor the roots and traditions of music, but there's also this persistent desire to find out what else we can do rather than the common forms, the things you always hear."

Phish came together in 1983, when two University of Vermont students, freshman Trey Anastasio and sophomore Jeff Holdsworth, began playing their guitars together in dorm lounges. They both shared an interest in the Grateful Dead, the Allman Brothers, Frank Zappa, and Led Zeplin. The two fledging band members found their first recruit in University of Vermont freshman Jon "Fish" Fishman. Fishman told Puterbaugh, "He [Anastasio] and a friend were having a conversation about who looked like they belonged there and who didn't. I came walking by, and they both fell down laughing. They pegged me from a hundred yards in a crowd of people, going, 'He doesn't look like he belongs here'." A few days after their first meeting, Anastasio would burst into Fishman's dorm room, after following the sounds of his drumming, and encourage him to join the group. With two guitarists and a drummer, the band needed a bass player. A few days later Anastasio posted a sign for a bass player and Mike Gordon responded. They derived their name from Fishman's nickname. Fishman's appearance made him a regular campus character that the band enjoyed. One journalist described Fishman after meeting him for the first time as "something out of the Lord of the Rings." (*Go Phish;* Dave Thompson). Subsequently, Fishman's short, bearded, and bespectacled appearance helped identify the bands offbeat persona.

Holdsworth got the band their first gig after seeing a flyer for an ROTC party on campus. They used hockey sticks for mike stands. The band was given the boot after their fourth song. The DJ blasted Michael Jackson's *Thriller,* and the once empty dance floor quickly filled up. The band took the not so subtle hint and left the stage. However, the band's first show was not a completeloss; they gained their first official fan, Amy Skelton, who now works as the band's merchandising manager.

After a year of playing in campus dorms, the band felt they were ready to hit the city of Burlington. They became regulars at Nectar, a popular downtown restaurant and bar. It was at Nectar that the band experimented with their music and put together an original stage show. Fishman told Puterbaugh, "Basically, the crowd was our guinea pig." The band slowly developed a community with the audience. They interacted with the audience, allowing fans to read poetry or perform strange acts on stage. "All music is conversation," Fishman explained to Charles Hirshberg and Nubar Alexanion of *Life.* They would signal the audience to rise or fall, or shout a line in a song. It was this early inside communication the

For the Record . . .

Members include **Trey Anastasio** (born Ernest Anastasio, September 30, 1964, in Fort Worth TX. *Education:* Goddard College), guitar, lead vocals, songwriter; **Jon Fishman** (born February 19, 1965, in Philadelphia, PA. *Education:* Goddard College), drums, vocals; **Mike Gordon** (born June 3, 1965, in Boston, MA. *Education:* University of Vermont), bass, vocals; and **Page McConnell** (born May 17, 1963, in Philadelphia. *Education:* Goddard College), keyboards, vocals.

Group formed on October 30, 1983, in Burlington, VT; played in bars and small concert halls for five years; self-released debut album, *Junta*, 1988; reissued on Elektra, 1992; released, *Lawn Boy*, Absolute A-Go-Go Records, 1990; signed with Elektra, 1992; released *Picture of Nectar*, 1992; *Rift*, 1993; *Hoist*, 1994; *A Live One*, 1995; *Billy Breathes*, 1996; *Slip Stitch and Pass*, 1997; *The Story of Ghost*, 1998; first studio produced video produced in the spring of 1994.

Addresses: *Record company*—Elektra records, 75 Rockefeller Plaza, New York, NY 10019; *Email*—info@phishnet; *Website*—rec.music.phish.

band developed with the audience that linked their fans to them so dearly.

For the next two years, the band plays regular gigs at Nectar and various Burlington bars. In 1985, Phish picked up a fifth member after performing at the Goddard Springfest at Goddard College. Page McConnel, a student at Goddard College, was the organizer of the event. McConnel not only convinced the band they needed a keyboard player, he also managed to convince Anastasio, Holdsworth, and Fishman to transfer to Goddard College. He lured them with Goddard College's more liberal academic policies. The college rewarded McConnell with fifty dollars for recruiting each of the band's members. Gordon, however, remained at the University of Vermont to study film.

In 1986, the band lost one band member when Holdworth became a born again Christian and followed the tele-evangelist Jimmy Swaggart. Despite the loss of Holdworth, the band continued playing and developing their music and stage show. From 1988 to 1990, the band had two independent releases, *Junta* and *Lawn Boy*.

Rumblings Came From the Underground

The band's big recording break came while playing a show at Manhattan's Marquee club. A Talent Scout from Elektra Entertainment, Sue Drew, caught their act and was intrigued not only by the sound, but also by the strange community that surrounded them. Drew gave her pitch outlining the great success to come with the band's signing to Elektra Entertainment. The band just listened, politely disinterested. She told Hirshberg and Alexanion, "They could not have cared less." Phish members did not want to become tied to commercial success. The band enjoyed their freedom to experiment and create unpredictable music. Phish encouraged fans to tape their shows and would even set up sound boards to give their fans high quality recordings at their shows. Elektra was not pleased with the bands policy of allowing fans to tape the show, but relented.

A Picture of Nectar was released in 1992. Their first major release was a tribute to the old venue in Bulington. The single "Chalkdust Torture" was distributed to radio stations to support the album sales. Although the album was more structured than their previous independent releases, critics felt the it was too scattered and did not fit together well. The album show cased the band's wide musical taste with tracks covering bluegrass, jazz, Latin, and casual instrumentals to furious punk. The album received moderate success.

On the road in 1992, the band was gaining exposure. Phish played four shows on the first HORDE tour. The radio play and large outdoor amphitheaters gave the band a much wider audience, which began to cause some stirrings from their once underground fan base. Phish Heads were concerned the band would be discovered, and the community would be destroyed.

In 1993, *Rift* was released by Elektra. Legendary producer Barry Becket assisted with the album. It was the first time the band had ever worked with a producer. Beck's production credits included Bob Dylan's *Slow Train Coming* and Dire Straits' *Communiqué*. The addition of a producer helped give the album more focus and achieved Elektra's goal of increasing album sales. Oddly, the ballad "Fast Enough for You," was selected as the single for radio play. The song received play mostly on adult-contemporary formats.

Appeared on MTV

Things really began to move when the band released *Hoist* in March of 1994. Gordon, the film school graduate, directed the bands only studio-style video release for the single track "Down with Disease." Phish called on Paul Fox to produce the third Electra release. Paul Fox's previous credits included tracks for XTC, 10,000 Maniacs, and the Sugar Cubes. Phish invited some friends to the recording sessions—Bela Fleck, Allison Krauss, the Tower of Power horn section, the Ricky Grundy Chorale, Rose Stone, and Jonathan Frakes. Album sales doubled for Elektra, and the video received play on MTV. Again Phish Heads were not happy with the growing success, and the band was concerned about being chained to hit songs and losing there spontaneity.

In the fall of 1994, a new tradition was established. Phish played the entire Beatle's *White Album* in costume for their second set of a three set concert in Glen Falls, New York. Later, the band would continue these costume sets at various shows. At the end of 1994, Phish was one of the top 50 grossing acts of the year as ranked by Pollstar. The band played over 100 shows to over 600,000 fans.

Four Albums and a Book

In 1995, the band released a double album, *A Live One,* which was recorded live at the Clifford Ball, in 1994. The album reached number 15 on *Billboard* 200. It captured the spirit of their show and received the approval of true Phishianados. The band's 1996 release, *Billy Breathes,* peaked at number 7 on the *Billboard* 200. The band released *Slip Stitch and Pass* in 1997, another live album that was recorded at a show in Hamburg, Germany. The album peaked at number 17. In 1998, Phish released their ninth album, *The Story of Ghost.* Phish also published a book, *The Phish Book,* in 1998. The book is as unconventional as the band's music, covering a year in the life of Phish on the road from 1996 to 1997.

With the growing commercial success of their albums and sell out concerts, Phish is not afraid of becoming imprisoned by record companies or new fans. Anastasio told David E. Thigpen of *Time* magazine, "It's too late for commercial success to ruin us."

Selected discography

Untitled Studio Session, unreleased, 1985.
The White Album, unreleased, 1987.
The Man Who Stepped into Yesterday, unreleased, 1988.
Junta, original release, 1988, reissued, Elektra, 1992.
Lawn Boy, Absolute A-Go-Go Records, 1990, reissued, Elektra, 1992.
Picture of Nectar, Elektra, 1992.
Rift, Elektra, 1993.
Hoist, Elektra, 1994.
A Live One, Elektra, 1995.
Billy Breathes, Elektra, 1996.
Slip Stitch and Pass, Elektra, 1997.
The Story of Ghost, Elektra, 1998.

Sources

Books

Dean Budnick, *The Phishing Manual,* Hyperion, 1996.
Dave Thompson, *Go Phish,* St. Martin's Griffin, 1997.

Periodicals

Amusement Business, July 27, 1998.
Billboard, October 3, 1998.
Entertainment Weekly, November 1, 1996.
Guitar Player, May, 1996.
Life, June, 1996.
People Weekly, November 27, 1998.
Rolling Stone, February 20, 1997.

Online

"Phish: The Official Web Site," http://www.phish.com (January 7, 1999).
"CD Now," http://www.cdnow.com (January 22, 1998).

—*Tige Cosmos*

The Platters

Vocal group

The Platters, like their predecessors The Ink Spots, were the most popular African-American vocal group of their decade, topping both the R&B and pop charts, and often beating out covers by white artists, a feat previously unaccomplished by a black recording artist. A typical doo-wop group in Los Angeles in the early 1950s, the group's humble beginnings were soon turned around when they were introduced to Samuel "Buck" Ram, then manager of singer Linda Hayes, sister of group member Tony Williams. As producer, manager, songwriter, and vocal coach, Ram transformed original members David Lynch, Alex Hodge, Herb Reed, and Williams into the biggest pop sensation of the1950s. Famous for their smooth harmonies and romantic lyrics, The Platters maintained a series of hits throughout the decade, introducing into our culture such classics as "The Great Pretender," "My Prayer," "Smoke Gets in Your Eyes," and "Twilight Time." The group's line-up was modified considerably after its inception, most notably when lead singer Williams left to pursue a solo career in 1961.

In 1953, under the tutelage of Ram, The Platters polished their stylized sound and entered the studio to produce their first recordings for Federal Records, an R&B subsidiary of King. Unhappy with the current line-up, Buck replaced Hodge with baritone Paul Robi and hired Zola Taylor, formerly of Shirley Gunter and The Queens. The more diverse vocal combination recorded debut release "Only You (And You Alone)," but the song was poorly produced and failed to chart. Although The Platters had released several songs in 1953 and 1954, including "Give Thanks," and "Shake It Up Mambo," the group failed to realize any chart success. Buck, however, focused his energies on the club circuit and consistently provided the group with well-paying gigs. The Penguins, the Los Angeles vocal group behind the smash hit "Earth Angel," noted The Platters' steady work and financial success and signed on with Ram. Ram approached Mercury Records with a package deal—one group a hit-maker, the other a protégé—and successfully signed both the Penguins and The Platters to the label in 1954.

While it became clear that the Penguins were a one-hit-wonder, The Platters' re-recorded Mercury debut "Only You" reached number five on the charts in November of 1955. As a follow-up to their first hit, Ram wrote "The Great Pretender," thus named because he had promised another hit before the song had even been written. His confidence was merited, however, when the single hit number one on the pop and R&B charts, marking the group's crossover into pop success and securing their star status. Shortly thereafter The Platters released the million-seller "You've Got the Magic Touch," which again supported their status as a crossover group, reaching number four on both the pop and R&B charts. To augment the popularity of their smooth and sexy harmonies, they released their first album *The Platters* in July of 1956. The same year the Platters debuted in the United Kingdom, they released a record with "Only You" and "The Great Pretender," which debuted at number five on the charts.

In 1957 Williams tried his powerful warbling singing solo, but The Platters, at the height of their fame, shadowed him. The act had become an international sensation, touring the world in the late 1950s, dubbed by Mercury Records as "international ambassadors of goodwill." In 1958 The Platters appeared on "Dick Clark's Saturday Night TV Show", earned another million-selling single with "Out of My Mind," and recorded what was one of the first music videos ever, a promotional clip of their fourth chart-topping R&B single, "Twilight Time," performed on "American Bandstand." And, before the year was through, they produced "Smoke Gets In Your Eyes" in Paris, France during an extended European tour.

"Smoke Gets In Your Eyes" reached number three on the R&B charts and topped the pop charts, becoming another classic hit to enter into our culture's collective repertoire. However, the fortunes turned for the group in the summer of 1959, leading to bad publicity for The Platters and hurting their popularity. Four members of the group were arrested in Cincinnati, Ohio for engaging in sexual

For the Record . . .

Members include **Sandra Dawn** (1962-65, born New York , NY), contralto vocals; **Alex Hodge** (1953-55), baritone vocals; **David Lynch** (born 1929, St. Louis, MO, died January 2, 1981), tenor vocals; **Nate Nelson** (1962-65, born April 10, 1932, New York , NY, died June 1, 1984), baritone vocals; **Herbert Reed** (born 1931, Kansas City, MO), bass vocals; **Paul Robi** (1955-62, born 1931, New Orleans, LA, died February 1, 1989), baritone vocals; **Zola Taylor** (1954-62, born 1934), contralto vocals; **Sonny Turner** (1961-65, born ca. 1939, Cleveland, OH), lead vocals; **Tony Williams** (1953-60, born April 15, 1928, Roselle, NJ, died August 14, 1992), lead vocals.

Formed in Los Angeles, CA and signed to Federal Records, 1953; Zola Taylor joined group, 1954; Hodge fired by manager Buck Ram and replaced with Paul Robi, 1955; group signed to Mercury Records, 1955; "Great Pretender" hit number one, band appeared in rock films *The Girl Can't Help It* and *Rock Around the Clock*, 1956; recorded "Smoke Gets in Your Eyes," first hit single produced in a foreign country (Paris, France), 1957; male members of group arrested in Cincinnati, OH for allegedly engaging in improper sexual relations, some radio stations pulled singles; released last Top Ten hit "Harbor Lights," 1960; Williams left band to pursue solo career, replaced by Turner, 1961; Taylor and Robi left band, replaced by Dawn and Nelson respectively, 1962; 45s previously unissued released by Mercury, 1964; brief success on Musicor label, 1966; returned to Mercury, 1974.

Awards: Inducted into Rock and Roll Hall of Fame, 1990.

Addresses: *Management*—Regina Wilson, Roewill Entertainment Group, (941.575.8272); Dan Sawyer, Sawyer Productions, (702.876.2334*); Website*—w w w . a w e b s t a t i o n . n e t / p l a t t e r s ; *E m a i l*—roewil@mindspring.com.

The Platters' last Top Ten hit came in 1960 with single "Harbor Lights," which reached number eight on the pop charts. Several Platters singles charted in the Top 40 the same year, including "Red Sails in the Sunset" and "To Each His Own," and the compilation album *Encore of Golden Hits* was certified gold. The group's popularity was starting to wane, though, and in 1961 Williams left the group to pursue a solo career, signing with Reprise Records. But the public was not very receptive to Williams without his vocal counterparts and he achieved only moderate success, even when covering Platters originals.

The replacement of Williams with lead vocalist Sonny Turner instigated discontent from Mercury Records, who refused to release singles led by Turner and instead continued to release old Williams-led singles. Ram and The Platters filed a lawsuit to contest the decision. More personnel changes took place in 1962 when Robi and Taylor left and were replaced by Sandra Dawn and Nate Nelson, formerly of Flamingos. The group ended its relations with Mercury Records and scored its last Top 100 with the release of "It's Magic."

Switching to the Musicor label, The Platters experienced limited success with "I Love You 1000 Times" and "With This Ring," both scoring in the Top 40 on the pop and R&B charts. Before disbanding in 1970. For much of the 1970s, Ram fought in court for the legal rights to the name Platters and won, but his numerous lawsuits didn't prevent the countless vocal groups from calling themselves the Platters, each with its own combination of former Platters members. The original Platters were inducted into the Rock and Roll Hall of Fame in 1990, commemorating their far-reaching effect as one of the most successful African-American pop groups in music history.

Selected discography

The Platters, Bella Musica, 1955.
The Fabulous Platters, Mercury, 1956.
Flying Platters, Mercury, 1958.
Pick of Platter, Mercury, 1959.
Reflections, Mercury, 1960.
Song for Only the Lonely, Mercury, 1962.
Christmas with the Platter, Mercury, 1963.
The New Soul of the Platters, Mercury, 1965.
I Love You 1,000 Times, Musicor, 1966.
Going Back to Detroit, Musicor, 1967.
Only You, Charly, 1968.
Smoke Gets in Your Eyes, Instant, 1968.
The Best of the Platters, Mercury, 1973.

relations with four 19-year-old women, three of whom were white. The media picked up on the scandal, and although the men were found innocent, public reaction was decidedly negative and many radio stations discontinued play on their new singles.

The Great Pretender, Trace, 1974.
Precious Moments, Philips, 1975.
Platterama, Mercury, 1982.
The Magic Touch: An Anthology, Mercury, 1991.
The Musicor Years, Kent, 1995.
You'll Never, Never Know, PolyGram, 1998.
The Golden Sides, Pair, 1998.

Sources

Books

Rees, Dafydd, *Encyclopedia of Rock Stars,* DK Publishing, Inc., 1996.

Romanowski, Patricia, editor, *The New Rolling Stone Encyclopedia of Rock & Roll,* Rolling Stone Press, 1995.

Warner, Jay, *Billboard's American Rock 'n' Roll in Review,* Schirmer Books, 1997.

Online

"The Platters," *All-Music Guide,* http://www.allmusic.com (January 19, 1999).

"The Platters," *The Rock and Roll Hall of Fame,* http://www.rockhall.com (January 19, 1999).

—*Karen Gordon*

Lloyd Price

Singer, songwriter

Lloyd Price, a prominent, influential, and multi-talented musical artist, contributed extensively to R&B and early rock and roll. As a singer and songwriter in the 1950s, he recorded American classics "Lawdy Miss Clawdy," "Personality," and "Stagger Lee," all of which hit the R&B and pop charts. As a record producer, club owner, and shrewd businessman, he founded several successful record labels and the New York City club Turntable. Unlike many other successful artists at the time, Price wrote his own material, and nearly all of his hits were originals. He applied his New Orleans roots in blues music to writing and performing catchy tunes that crossed over onto the pop charts and warranted his status as a major influence in rock history.

Born in Kenner, Louisiana on March 9, 1933, Price, like many of the successful R&B artists of the 1950s, trained his voice singing gospel in the local church choir. By 1950, the teenage Price was leading a vocal quintet and playing gigs at local clubs. Not content to merely sing songs, Price soon began writing and performing commercial jingles for his local radio station, WBOK. One of these jingles, "Lawdy Miss Clawdy," became so popular that Price decided to take it to Imperial Records in an attempt to secure a recording contract. The label turned him down, signing Fats Domino instead. The two became friends, and soon after Price was signed to the Specialty label, he re-recorded his jingle as a full-length song with Domino playing piano.

The single hit number one on the R&B charts, remaining there for a full seven-week run. In an attempt to achieve similar fame, several artists, Elvis Presley among them, copied Price's song, but with less success. Two more top five R&B hits followed that same year—"Oooh, Oooh, Oooh" and "Restless Heart." In 1953, Price's well-known hit "Ain't It a Shame" reached number eight on the R&B charts in February, and reappeared at number eight again in December, establishing the song as a unique case in chart history and Price as a successful vocalist. But the talented musician also possessed an acute business sense. He urged Little Richard to send a tape to a subsidiary of Specialty Records, thus starting Little Richard's recording career.

Price's career was interrupted in 1953 when he was drafted to the Army to serve in the Korean War. Unable to leave his music behind, however, he formed a band abroad and performed for troops in the Far East. When Price was discharged from the Army in 1956, he relocated to Washington, D.C. and founded his own label, Kent Record Company. In order to retain control of his material but ensure that it would be distributed nationally, the keen businessman leased his songs to ABC-Paramount. "Just Because," the first release on his own label, reached number 29 on the pop charts. In 1959, Price rewrote the folk song "Stack-O-Lee," giving it a more R&B, pop sound and changing its name to "Stagger Lee." It reached the top of the pop charts and charted at number seven in the UK, becoming his first million seller. Price's style was shifting from his New Orleans roots in blues to a more mainstream pop sound.

Later that year, he joined an R&B package tour in Virginia called "Biggest Show of Stars" for seven weeks, where he performed with peers Clyde McPhatter and Bo Diddley, among others. This was a bustling year for Price, who went on to produce the hit song "Personality," a bluesy rock ballad which reached number two on the pop charts and topped the R&B chart, earning Price the nickname "Mr. Personality." In September, "I'm Gonna Get Married" peaked at number three on the pop charts, and was Price's final number one hit on the R&B charts. Augmenting these successful releases were: "Where Were You (On Our Wedding Day), "Wont'cha Come Home, and "Come Into My Heart," which reached number 20 on the pop charts and served as a triumphant ending to a year that would become the height of Price's career.

In 1960 Price continued to record, scoring his biggest hit of the year with "Lady Luck," which reached number 14 on the pop charts, while its B-side, "Never Let Me Go," reached a low number 82 on the charts. In May, the tune "For Love" climbed to number 43 on the pop charts and its reverse side, "No Ifs No Ands," reached number 40

For the Record . . .

Born March 9, 1933, in Kenner, LA.

Led R&B vocal group in New Orleans, LA, wrote and performed commercial jingles for local radio station WBOK, including future hit "Lawdy Miss Clawdy," 1950; signed to Specialty Records and re-recorded "Lawdy Miss Clawdy," which reached top of the R&B charts, followed up with two more R&B top five hits, 1952; drafted to US Army to serve in Korean War, 1953; discharged from Army and founded Kent Record Company in Washington, D.C., 1956; "Stagger Lee" hit US at number one and the UK at number seven, "Personality" hit number one on R&B charts and number two on pop charts; "I'm Gonna Get Married" hit number one on R&B charts and number three on pop charts, 1959; founded Double-L label with friend Harold Logan and issued first solo recording by Falcons vocalist Wilson Pickett, 1963; established college scholarship fund for black students, 1964; moved to New York City and established new label Turntable, opened club by same name, 1969; released *To the Roots and Back* on GSF label, 1972; created three-day *Zaire Music Festival* in Africa with boxing promoter Don King, 1974; formed LPG label with King, 1976.

Awards: received Pioneer Award at sixth annual Rhythm and Blues Foundation ceremony, 1995; inducted into Rock and Roll Hall of Fame, 1998.

Addresses: *Website*—http://onlinetalent.com/ Lloyd_Price_homepage.html; *email*— agent@onlinetalent.com

Releases "Just Call Me (And I'll Understand)" and "(You Better) Know What You're Doin'" both charted within the top 100, and the hit "Question" reached the top 20.

By 1963, Price was no longer scoring hits with the same frequency, and he put his energies starting another label, Double-L, with friend Harold Logan. Price's first release on this label was a cover of Errol Garner's "Misty" which would be his first single in three years to reach the top 100. "Billie Baby" followed in 1964, but by this time Price was busying himself establishing a college scholarship fund for African-American students. In 1969, Price's

Double-L partner Logan was found murdered in their New York City office, a Price album playing in the background. Price then went on to found Turntable, his new label, and a club by the same name, both in New York City where he was now based. This year was also notable for his final chart hit "Bad Conditions," which peaked at 21.

With the exception of Price's album release *To The Roots and Back* in 1973, and *The Nominee* in 1978, the 1970s were not too eventful for him. In 1976, he collaborated with boxing promoter Don King to promote a three-day music festival in Zaire, Africa, and later that year the two founded the record label LPG in New York. The various covers of "Stagger Lee" still charting in 1972 showed his continued force in the industry. In 1995 the Kenner City Council honored Price when they renamed 4th Street to Lloyd Price Avenue. Later that year he received the Pioneer Award from the Rhythm and Blues Foundation, and in 1998 he was inducted into the Rock and Roll Hall of Fame.

Selected discography

To The Roots and Back, GSF, 1972.
The Nominee, LPG, 1978.
Lloyd Price, Specialty, 1986.
Personality Plus, Specialty, 1986.
Walkin' the Track, Specialty, 1986.
Greatest Hits, Curb, 1990.
Lawdy!, Specialty, 1991.

Sources

Books

Rees, Dafydd, *Encyclopedia of Rock Stars*, DK Publishing, Inc., 1996.
Romanowski, Patricia, editor, *The New Rolling Stone Encyclopedia of Rock & Roll*, Rolling Stone Press, 1995.
Warner, Jay, *Billboard's American Rock 'n' Roll in Review*, Schirmer Books, 1997.

Online

"Lloyd Price," *The Rock and Roll Hall of Fame*, http://www.rockhall.com (February 15, 1999).
"Lloyd Price," *Tom Simon's Rock and Roll Page*, http://www.crl.com/~tsimon/price.htm (February 15, 1999).

—*Karen Gordon*

Giacomo Puccini

Composer

Corbis View. Reproduced by permission.

Giacomo Puccini was the last of Italy's great opera composers, a lineage that began in the seventeenth century with Claudio Monteverdi and progressed through Gioacchino Rossini and Giuseppe Verdi. But unlike his predecessors, Puccini wrote lighter works in a new, realistic style that gained popularity in the late nineteenth century. His operas were notable for their delightful melodies and three-dimensional female heroines. His three great works—*La Bohème, Madama Butterfly,* and *Turandot*—remain some of the most popular standards in the opera repertoire.

Born in 1858, Puccini was the eldest boy of several children in a musically gifted family in Lucca, Italy, where several generations of Puccinis had already achieved minor local renown. When his father died when he was just six, Puccini's formidable mother asked the authorities to decree that the father's post as organist at the Church of San Martino be passed on to her son when he came of age; his uncle, Fortunato Magi, assumed the post in the interim. Puccini began music study with Magi, and then took classes from Carlo Angeloni at Lucca's Pacini Institute; both men had been taught by the elder Puccini. When he reached the age of 14, he began working as organist at San Martino.

It is said that around 1876, Puccini, then about 18, walked 13 miles to a theater in Pisa to hear *Aida,* the great Verdi opera, and immediately decided to become an opera composer as well. Serious study, however, would be needed, and with this in mind he secured a stipend from a grand-uncle, and then a scholarship to the Conservatory in Milan. He arrived in late 1880, and studied diligently for the next three years. He learned composition in the class of Amilcare Ponchielli, the composer of the opera *La Gioconda.* Ponchielli's lighter style was a great influence on Puccini.

The first of Puccini's works to be performed was *Capriccio sinfonico,* a piece written for his examinations, at the Conservatory in 1883. It was also accepted for publication, and premiered later that year at the famed La Scala with an orchestra. Completed in 1778, La Scala is considered the virtual heart of Milan and is one of the world's top opera venues. Upon graduation, Puccini decided to enter an opera competition for young Italian composers sponsored by music publisher Sonzogno. Ponchielli found a librettist to help, but the entry, *Le Villi,* did not fair well; however, other influential Milanese music-lovers secured it a production at the Teatro del Verme theater in May of 1884. It premiered at La Scala the following year.

Around this time Puccini met a Lucca woman named Elvira Gemignani. She eventually left her merchant husband for Puccini. Though they never married, they had a son in 1886 and spent the rest of their lives together. Puccini's first early successes in Milan led to a commission from La Scala to write an opera. He was given an advance and a stipend, and wrote *Edgar,* which was a complete failure at its premiere in April of 1889. His third attempt fared much better: *Manon Lescaut* was deemed a great success at its premiere in Turin's Teatro Regio theater in February of 1893. Based on a well-received French novel and play, its London production caused the playwright and drama critic George Bernard Shaw to hail Puccini as the successor to Verdi.

Manon Lescaut was produced in Philadelphia and then Paris. While in Paris Puccini began writing an opera based on the book *Scenes de la Vie de Bohème* by Henri Murger. He then heard that another Italian composer, Ruggiero Leoncavallo, was writing a similar work, and finished his quickly. The result was *La Bohème,* which premiered at the Teatro Regio in February of 1896. Set in Paris's Left Bank in the 1830s, it tracks the romances of a group of young bohemians. It premiered to mixed reviews, but was restaged in Palermo later in 1896 and fared much better; the audience refused to leave the concert hall until the final death scene was repeated for an encore. *La Bohème* would be the first of Puccini's works in the *verismo* style, a backlash against heavy symbolism and mythological themes common to most operas of the era. Taken from the Italian root for "truth" or "reality," verismo operas were set in the present or recent past, and featured accessible themes and characters. Leoncavallo's *I Pagliacci* was one of the first in this style.

The success of *La Bohème* would earn Puccini the lifelong enmity of Leoncavallo. It also made him famous and exceedingly wealthy. With the earnings he built a villa on Florence's Lake Massaciuccoli that he named Torre del Lago. Puccini was famously handsome and charming, but he also possessed a melancholic side that he drew on to give depth to his characters. He was wholly uninterested in religion or politics, and enjoyed racing sports cars on his property and gambling at cards.

Tosca and Madama Butterfly

Puccini wrote slowly. His next work, *Tosca,* premiered four years after *La Bohème* at the Teatro Constanzi theater in Rome in January of 1900. Set in the same city exactly one hundred years before, its title character was an opera singer attempting to bargain for the release of her political dissident lover in a time of Napoleonic political strife in Rome. Her foe was the sadistic aristocrat police chief who wanted to see Tosca humiliated. The work premiered at the New York Metropolitan Opera a year later, and quickly became a classic.

The composer was nearly killed in automobile accident in 1903, but managed to finish one of his most popular works during his convalescence. *Madama Butterfly* premiered at La Scala in February of 1904, but its storyline—a Japanese woman who falls in love with an American navalofficer—brought jeers from the audience. It is believed that hecklers were hired by composers who were jealous of Puccini's success.

On the advice of his friend, the great Italian conductor Arturo Toscanini, Puccini revised *Madama Butterfly,* and a new version premiered in Brescia in May of 1904 to a much better reception. For its Metropolitan Opera premiere, Puccini traveled to the United States for first time in 1906. The Met commissioned his next work, *La Fanciulla del West,* ("The Girl of the Golden West"), set during the California gold rush of the 1840s, but Italian singers play-acting as Wild West characters failed to enchant audiences or critics. Enrico Caruso sang at its Met premiere in 1910, but *La Fanciulla* was soon forgotten.

Scandal and War

For a time, Puccini stopped composing as the result of personal misfortunes. A scandal in his household was salaciously chronicled in the press: a servant girl died, and at first her death was thought to be a suicide. But reports that Elvira Gemignani had accused her of a relationship with Puccini surfaced. An autopsy ruled the death suspicious and implicated Gemignani, but later evidence suggested that the Gemignani family had actually harassed the girl.

Puccini's next work, *La Rondine,* premiered at Monte Carlo in March of 1917. He then premiered a trilogy of one-act operas, *Il Trittico,* at the Metropolitan Opera in December of 1918. Its American premiere was largely the result of the war in Europe, just recently ended. *Il Trittico* consists of the drama *Il Tabarra* ("The Cloak"), the religious piece *Suor Angelica,* and the comic work *Gianni Schicchi.*

Puccini and his family moved from Torre del Lago and settled in Viareggio. It was there that Puccini began work on *Turandot,* his final opera. In 1924 he was diagnosed with throat cancer, and underwent radiation treatment in Brussels. While there, he suffered a heart attack on November 29. The announcement of Puccini's death halted a performance of *La Bohème* at La Scala. Benito Mussolini gave a eulogy at his funeral. He was buried at Torre del Lago.

Puccini Endures

Turandot premiered at La Scala in April of 1926, conducted by Toscanini. On that night, the action and music froze just where Puccini had left it, and Toscanini turned to the audience with tears in his eyes and said, "Here the Maestro put down his pen." Like *Madama Butterfly, Turandot* employs an Asian setting and female lead, and remains one of Puccini's most enduring works. A composer named Franco Alfano was later hired to complete the third act. In September of 1998, *Turandot* was staged in Beijing, China, in a $15 million production conducted by Zubin Mehta that attracted opera fans from around the world.

La Bohème later became the basis for the hit musical *Rent,* which premiered on Broadway to massive box-office receipts in 1996. Its creator, Jonathan Larson, used the setting and action of Puccini's work and gave it an even more "verismo" feel by placing it in contemporary New York City, specifically the artists' enclave of the East Village.

Selected discography

Manon Lescaut, Deutsche Grammophon, 1987.
Tosca, Deutsche Grammophon, 1992.
Turandot, BMG/RCA Victor, 1996.
Madama Butterfly, Vox, 1996.
Favorite Puccini: 20 Best-Loved Arias, EMI Classics, 1996.
La Bohème, Opera d'Oro, 1997.
The Best of Puccini, Naxos, 1997.

Sources

Books

Plotkin, Fred, *Opera 101: A Complete Guide to Learning and Loving Opera,* Hyperion, 1994.
Sadie, Stanley, ed., *The New Grove Dictionary of Music and Musicians,* Macmillan, 1980.

Periodicals

Fortune, October 12, 1998, p. 44.
Opera News, March 1999, p. 82.
Rolling Stone, May 16, 1996, p. 54.
Stereo Review, April 1996, p. 100.
Time, March 4, 1996, p. 71.

—Carol Brennan

Puff Daddy

Producer, singer, songwriter

AP/Wide World Photo. Reproduced by permission.

Producer, songwriter, singer, and entrepreneur Puff Daddy, or Sean "Puffy" Combs, founded Bad Boy Records in 1991, and sold more than 12 million albums in three years, including five platinum and ten gold albums. His hit single "No Way Out" rose to number one on six *Billboard* charts for12 weeks; the multi-platinum single was the best-selling single of the year, and captured audiences in Europe as well. As founder of Bad Boy Records, he contributed to or oversaw the music and careers of Notorious B.I.G., Mase, Ginuwine, The Lox, Foxy Brown, Black Rob, Lil' Kim, Twista, Busta Rhymes, Carl Thomas, Faith Evans, 112, Jay-Z, Shyne, Fuzzbubble, Tanya Blount, Total, Q-Tip, Mariah Carey, and numerous other hip-hop and rap artists. In 1999, he started a clothing line called Sean John, and founded Bad Boy Films production company, which released the film *No Way Out*. The film starred Combs and was produced and directed by him as well. No other record label founder to date has been more in the limelight than Puff Daddy, and none have contributed as much musically for the artists. The sometimes controversial Puff Daddy is a generational leader, selling a lifestyle rather than a record label, and—like the Motown and Def Jam founders before him—managed to capture the spirit of his time in music and marketing.

Sean Combs was born on November 4, 1970 in the Harlem section of New York City as the first of two children born to Melvin and Janice Combs. His mother, an aspiring model, raised the two children. His father was a street hustler who was fatally shot in Central Park when Combs was three years old. He discovered this at a later at the age of thirteen when perusing old newspaper clippings in the library. He lived in Harlem until the age of twelve, where he enjoyed block parties that featured hip-hop and rap music, and musical rhyming contests in Central Park. His family moved to Mount Vernon, NY, when he was twelve and he attended the all-male private school Mount St. Michael's Academy. He was thin in high school and earned the nickname "Puffy" while playing football for Mount St. Michael's Academy, because he would puff out his chest in an attempt to look bigger. In 1988, he went to Howard University and stayed for a year and a half. While at Howard, he demonstrated his knack for entrepreneurial enterprise by selling term papers and old exams, and promoting house parties and campus concerts.

Feeling unsettled, he left Howard eager to enter the work force and make a name for himself. He contacted Andre Harrell, then president of Uptown records in New York City, and asked to work as an intern for the label. Harrell was so fond of Combs that he gave him room and board and a small salary in return for his promotional skills. Combs' efforts soon eclipsed those of entire departments at Uptown and his contributions to hit singles by artists such

---

Born Sean Combs on November 4, 1970 in the Harlem section of New York City; first of two children born to Melvin and Janice (an aspiring model) Combs;father fatally shot in Central Park when he was three; children: two sons: Justin (born mid-1990s) and Christian Casey (born 1999). *Education:* Attended Howard University in 1988 for a year and a half.

Started as an intern at Uptown records in New York City; due to superb promotional efforts and producer contributions was promoted to vice-president of the Promotion Department; founded Bad Boy Records,1991; sold more than 12 million albums in three years, including five platinum and ten gold albums; hit single "No Way Out" rose tonumber one on six *Billboard* charts for twelve weeks; contributed to the releases of and/or oversaw the music and careers of Notorious B.I.G., Mase, Ginuwine, The Lox, Foxy Brown, Black Rob, Lil' Kim, Twista, Busta Rhymes, Carl Thomas, Faith Evans, 112, Jay-Z, Shyne, Fuzzbubble, Tanya Blount, Total, Q-Tip, Mariah Carey, KRS-One, LL Cool J, Busta Rhymes, Brian McKnight, SWV, Boyz 11 Men, Q-Tip, Beck, Whitney Houston, and others; released and was featured in the film *No Way Out,* which he produced and directed; released the single "Can't Nobody Hold Me Down," 1996 with rapper Mase; released "I'll Be Missing You," as a tribute to slain friend and rapper Notorious B.I.G., 1997; performed with other Bad Boy Records artists on the *No Way Out* Tour, 1998; opened a soul food restaurant in Manhattan, mid-1990s; founded a charity called Daddy's House Social Programs, a non-profit organization for local underprivileged children; created a Sean John clothing line and a Bad Boy Films production company in 1999; released a gospel album titled *Thank You* in 1999.

Awards: ASCAP'S Songwriter of the Year Award, 1997.

Addresses: *Record company*—Bad Boy Records,/Arista, 6 West 57th Street, New York, NY 10019; (212) 489-7400.

event was so popular it became overcrowded and eventually violent—the audience, impatient to leave, broke into a stampede and nine people were killed as a result. The event's poor organization and lack of security were attributed to Combs, and he was devastated by the experience. This early tragedy tested his resiliency and resolve, but he emerged optimistic and much stronger.

Publicized Feud

While at Uptown Records, Combs produced multi-platinum releases for Jodeci and Mary J. Blige. Blige's debut CD, *What's the 411?,* proved to be a seminal example of hip-hop and R&B fusion. His success with these efforts prompted Combs to consider founding his own label within Uptown, and the first artist he wanted to sign was a Brooklyn-based rapper named Biggie Smalls who performed under the name Notorious B.I.G. (born Christopher Wallace). Combs was given Notorious B.I.G.'s tape by an editor at *The Source* and he became captivated by Notoriouw B.I.G.'s vivid lyricism and distinct New York sound. In order to lure Notorious B.I.G. away from his already lucrative street-hustling lifestyle, Combs offered him a hefty advance and instant recognition on the soundtrack for the film *Who's The Man,* as well as an offer to collaborate on a song with Mary J. Blige. The offer worked, and Notorious B.I.G.'s career skyrocketed.

In 1993, Combs was fired from Uptown Records, reportedly because he was overconfident in the eyes of his coworkers, who felt threatened by his success. Combs then negotiated a $15 million deal to relocate Bad Boy Records to Arista Records, retaining complete creative control with full support from Arista. He produced several number one hits withCraig Mack and Notorious B.I.G., and his involvement in the artists' videos and on their songs and remixes heightened his own profile. As Combs and Notorious B.I.G. were meeting with success on the east coast, Suge Knight and his Death Row Records artists—Tupac Shakur, Dr. Dre, and Snoop Doggy Dogg—were flourishing on the west coast. Combs and Knight were friends until Shakur was wounded in November of 1994 by a gunshot in the lobby of a Times Square recording studio. Shakur blamed the assault on Combs and B.I.G., both of whom were, coincidentally, in the building at the time.

The feud between Knight and Combs escalated; Knight made a veiled yet pointed remark about Combs at *The Source* Awards.Knght also offered to sign to Death Row Records those artists who didn't want a label's CEO appearing in their videos and on their releases. A friend of Knight's was then shot, and Knight blamed the shooting on a member of Combs 'entourage. In March of

as Jodeci, Mary J. Blige, and others rendered him invaluable to the label. Within a year, he was promoted to vice-president of the Promotion Department. At the close of 1991, Combs organized a charity celebrity event at New York's City College basketball auditorium. The

1996, there was a stand-off in the parking lot of the Soul Train Awards between the Combs faction and the Knight faction; guns were drawn, but none were shot. In September of that year, Shakur was gunned down in Las Vegas. Shortly after, Combs, then a nascent vocalist, released the single "Can't Nobody Hold Me Down" with newfound rapper Mase. NotoriousB.I.G. released *Life After Death* the same year, and the title single reached number one on the charts. In March of 1997, Notorious B.I.G. was fatally shot after a Soul Train Awards party. Combs was in the car ahead of B.I.G.'s when he was shot, and rushed his best friend to the hospital. After Notorious B.I.G.'s death, Combs released "I'll Be Missing You," as a tribute to him, which featured the melody and hook from the Police hit of 1983 titled "Every Breath You Take." The single immediately reached number one on the charts, as did Notorious B.I.G.'s single "Mo' Money, Mo' Problems" from his posthumously-released CD *No Way Out* featuring Combs and Mase. The release sold more than four million copies.

Combs and the rest of the Bad Boy Records family took center stage on the first *No Way Out* Tour, bringing together a diverse audience. It was the second biggest concert of the year, after the Rolling Stones Tour. Along with his astounding artistic and financial success, Combs has had to grapple with producer, artist, and DJ detractors who claimed his reliance on obvious samples such as Grandmaster Flash's "The Message" on *Can't Nobody Hold Me Down*, the Police hit on "I'll Be Missing You," and David Bowie's "Let's Dance" on *Been Around the World* detracted from the general artistry and creativity of rap and hip-hop music. His admirers felt these obvious samples were a choice and a message, and part of a larger, successful commercial picture.

Selling a Lifestyle

After the birth of Combs' first son, Justin, in the mid-1990s, he felt a deeper sense of permanency and responsibility in his life. He opened a soul food restaurant in Manhattan and named it after Justin. His second son, Christian Casey, was born on April 1, 1999. Combs, who is noted for working as much as 20 hours a day and for partying just as hard, founded a charity called Daddy's House Social Programs, a non-profit organization for local underprivileged children. The program provides children with access to computer camps, social clubs, and other

beneficial outlets. In addition to creating a Sean John clothing line and a Bad Boy Films production company, he released a gospel album titled *Thank You* to inspire the generation to turn to God.

Combs has produced music for KRS-One, Mariah Carey, LL Cool J, Busta Rhymes, Brian McKnight, SWV, Boyz 11 Men, Q-Tip, Beck, Whitney Houston, and all of the artists at Bad Boy Records. He transcended the role of label CEO, producer, and recording artist to achieve what few have achieved before him: the role of generational lifestyle leader, always in sync with and frequently defining the times.

Selected discography

Albums

No Way Out, Bad Boy, 1997.
Thank You, Bad Boy Records, 1999.

Compilations/Soundtracks

Diana, Princess of Wales: A Tribute, Columbia, 1997.
Funkmaster Flex Presents The Mix Tape, Volume 2, RCA, 1997.
In Tha Beginning...There Was Rap, Priority, 1997.
Chef Aid: The South Park Album, American, 1998.

Sources

Periodicals

The Source, September, 1998.

Online

http://puffmase.simplenet.com/home.html
http://mohan2m.8m.com/puffdaddy/mam.html
http://tmone.simplenet.com/puffy.com
http://www.wallofsound.go.com/artists/puffdaddy/home.html
http://www.ewsonline.com/badboy/index.html
http://www.geocities.com/area51/cavern
http: www.geocities.com/SunsetStrip/Studio/7253
http:www.mp3dda.com/evolve/evolve.cgi'37
http://www.nj.com/spotlight/puffy/

—*B. Kimberly Taylor*

Rammstein

German techno-metal band

A sextet of Germans who sing about death, blood, and sexual trauma entirely in their own language, backed by thunderous metal guitar chords twinned with the synthesizers of dance music, would seem an unlikely act to find an audience in North America. But Rammstein merged several disparate elements going on inside the European music scene and achieved huge success there as a result; a spectacular stage show involving numerous pyrotechnic stunts also added to their reputation and helped create a buzz about them overseas. Though extremely successful in Germany and across Europe's northern lands, Rammstein has been criticized in the press as a "fascist" band, a charge they vehemently reject.

Rammstein took their name from an infamous 1988 airshow disaster in Germany that killed several onlookers. Its members—guitarist Richard Kruspe, singer Till Lindemann (a onetime Olympic swimmer), drummer Christoph Schneider, bassist Oliver Riedel, second guitarist Paul Landers, and keyboardist Flake Lorenz—all hail from the Berlin and Schwerin area. With the exception of Riedel, all were well into their twenties in 1989 when the Berlin Wall came down as the Communist bloc collapsed. The following year ceremonies were held that officially rejoined the states of the former Communist-bloc East Germany with those in its affluent European Union counterpart in West Germany. An array of new social ills was the unexpected result, and the resentment simmering on both sides led to a rise in the number of violent right-wing groups. Their fury found a target in Germany's large immigrant population. Numerous incidents of terrorism and violence carried out by a well-organized network of fascists of varying stripes and allegiances became a staple of the nightly news. Western Germans commonly blamed the disenfranchised youth of the former eastern lands for Germany's shameful new reputation as an emerging neo-fascist land, but the skinhead movement was not without disenchanted teens on the other side as well.

Rammstein grew out of such social and economic ills, and their huge commercial success as well as vilification in the media owe to this divide. When they formed in Berlin in early 1994, they were already seasoned musicians in the thriving German metal-goth-industrial scene. In an interview with Christopher Pearson for the *Dartmouth Review,* the band noted that before they coalesced as Rammstein, "we were each playing in different bands but we found that each of us was frustrated in their band. We couldn't express what we wanted to express musically in our old bands."

The members of Rammstein liked the hard, synthesizer-based music of contemporary bands like KMFDM—a sound very popular in Germany and referred to as "EBM," for "electronic body music"—but shared a passion for metal as well. When they were teens, it was extremely difficult to obtain rock records in the heavily-censored climate of East Germany. As Kruspe told Paul Gargano in an interview for *Metal Edge,* "You didn't have records at all.... You had to make tapes from second or third copies. KISS, for example, was an absolute phenomenon. They represented capitalism in its purest sense, and every child was KISS infected because they were so big." Kruspe also recalled that to even write the band's name on one's notebook at school could be grounds for expulsion. "I used to have a poster of them in my room," Kruspe told Gargano, "and when I was 12 years old my stepfather tore it down and into a thousand pieces. I was up all night trying to put it back together, and you can be sure it was hanging the next day."

Conquest of Europe

Rammstein was taken on by a management company in the spring of 1994, and signed with Germany's Motor Music, a part of Polygram Records, in early 1995. In March of that year they traveled to Sweden to record their first album, *Herzeleid.* The first single, "Du riechst so gut" ("You smell so good") was released in Europe in August of 1995, and the entire LP the following month. They then toured Germany with a popular EBM act, Project Pitchfork, and in early 1996 opened for the Ramones. They spent the following summer playing the massive open-air festivals that are an integral part of the German alternative music scene, and found success in countries like Holland, Sweden, and Norway.

The seeds for Rammstein's invasion of the American alternative/metal scene were planted when two of their songs appeared on the soundtrack to the 1997 David Lynch film, *Lost Highway*. When it came time to do their first video, as the band told the *Dartmouth Review*, "we thought of whom we would most want to direct it and we came up with the name of David Lynch. All of us like his work a lot. Then we contacted him and sent him one of our tapes, asking if he would be willing to direct our video." Lynch was busy with his film at the time, but liked Rammstein's sound so much he included two songs, "Heirate mich" and "Rammstein," on the soundtrack to his film, which, like other odd works of his, was a hit with disaffected youth.

By this point Rammstein were a huge commercial success in Germany, but were critically disparaged in the music press. Assumed to be right-wing Ossies, some of the band's pronouncements and imagery played into such rumors, but much of their music revolved around nonpolitical themes of sexual lust and dysfunction. Guitarist and spokesperson Kruspe even went to far as to term the German media irresponsible when he was interviewed by *NY Rock.* "Accusing a band of having fascistic tendencies attracts a fascistic audience even if the band is not fascistic at all," Kruspe said, comparing it with the far less wary reception they received in America. "Germany can be really uptight about things ... a show with a lot of pyrotechnics is simply that—a good show. Not everything is political, but it is a very German thing to try and find the proverbial fly in the soup. Plus we're German. So, of course, they can't like us," Kruspe joked. Rammstein also became infamous for its treatment of the media in return: in one reported incident, the band taped an MTV Europe employee to a chair and set off a smoke bomb near him before a show in Germany.

After the *Lost Highway* songs attracted a cult fan base overseas, it was decided to release *Sehnsucht* ("Longing"), their second LP, as Rammstein's debut in North America. *Sehnsucht* was already a huge success in Germany. It debuted in the States in early 1998, and by the following summer had sold over 100,000 copies and broken the Billboard Top 100. Perhaps most surprising of all was the amount of radio play its first single, "Du Hast" ("You Hate"), received on both rock and alternative stations. The group was also beginning to court controversy Stateside as well: a video clip for "Du Hast," roughly based on the Quentin Tarantino film *Reservoir Dogs,* was initially rejected by MTV because of its heavy gore content.

Hit a Nerve with U.S. Teens

Rammstein made their U.S. concert debut at the College Music Journal (CMJ) Marathon, an insider convention well-known for launching new bands, in New York City in September of 1997. They returned to Germany and played numerous shows that year, and in December of 1997 came back to North America for another brief tour. By the time they came back for a third visit, in the spring of 1998, *Sehnsucht* had been selling well and the media was ready, fed by rumors of an unbelievable live show in which Lindemann set himself afire in a special 140-pound chain-mail suit coated with a flammable paste. As he erupts, the singer makes reference to the air-show disaster as he intones, "Rammstein is the place where hope crashed to the ground." Such sentiments sound particularly ominous delivered in the German language in a deep voice. Even more enthralling to Rammstein's growing number of fans were the mock sado-masochistic and homoerotic rituals that band members perform on one another.

Yet again, the media were anything but complimentary. In one of his milder statements, *New York Times* writer Ben Ratliff called Rammstein "a prolonged, not-so-clever caricature of the German temperament's dark side, all severity and kinkiness." Ratliff termed them a Teutonic send-up of Gwar, the theatrical metal band, "but Rammstein isn't nearly as loony or inventive." *Village Voice* writer Sia Michel also reviewed the same sold-out show at the Roxy in New York and lauded the band for their marketing savvy, for "without the smoke and s/m hijinks, no one would pay much attention to yet another bunch of angry young men combining cockrock riffage with pedestrian techno-industrial flourishes, especially ones who sing solely in German," declared Michel.

Their American label, London, asked them to re-record one track in English, and they did so because they just wanted to hear what it would sound like. Yet in a surprising turn, the radio DJs preferred to play the German version. Kruspe told *NY Rock* that during their live shows, he was "really surprised how many people could sing along. But, you know, most of us grew up behind the iron curtain. When we started to listen to music, and especially American music, we didn't understand the lyrics and it wasn't really important. I think the feeling they get from the songs is what is really important. Maybe hearing them in another language helps to add some mystery."

Selected discography

Herzeleid, Motor Music/Polygram, 1995.
Sehnsucht, London Records, 1998.

Sources

Billboard, July 19, 1997, p. 56.
Dartmouth Review, December 15, 1998.
Metal Edge, January 1999.
New Musical Express, October 14, 1998.
New York Times, May 8, 1998, p. E24.
NY Rock, November 1998.
Village Voice, May 19, 1998, p. 146.

—Carol Brennan

Maurice Ravel

Composer

CorbisView. Reproduced by permission.

One of France's greatest musical geniuses, Maurice Ravel is best known as the composer of the riveting orchestral piece *Boléro,* perhaps the most universally recognized of all classical melodies. Music scholars deem Ravel one of the century's best orchestrators for his ability to create a kaleidoscopic array of sounds within an orchestra, but he also wrote several superb, technically difficult works for the piano.

Maurice Joseph Ravel was born on March 7, 1875, in Ciboure, a town in the Pyrenees region of France near the border with Spain. His mother, Marie Delouard, was of Basque heritage, and his father was an engineer of Swiss birth whose family was originally of French origins. From his father he inherited a sincere passion for the arts, while his mother was fond of singing Spanish folk songs to him as a child; many of Ravel's compositions would draw upon the musical heritage of that country. With their infant son, the Ravels moved to Paris, and he would later be joined by a younger brother, Edouard. The family lived in the bohemian neighborhood of Montmartre, and Ravel began piano lessons at the age of seven with a respected composer of the time, Henri Ghis.

By the time he was eleven, Ravel was studying harmony, and a few years later easily passed the entrance examinations to the rigorous Paris Conservatoire. He would remain there for over a dozen years, and was an excellent and disciplined student; though sometimes at odds with his instructors for the avant-garde bent of his compositions as an adult student. His first pieces for the piano were written at the age of 18, and almost all of his later work would be composed on the instrument. Gabriel Fauré, an esteemed French composer of the day, was one of Ravel's teachers, and the sole one to provide him with encouragement to explore the creative possibilities outside the traditional training given at the Conservatoire.

Ravel's first published work, *Menuet Antique,* appeared in 1895. He also wrote a Spanish-themed work for two pianos, *Habanera,* that year, with his good friend, the pianist Ricardo Vines, whom he knew from the Conservatoire for several years. Both had Spanish mothers, and Vines would go on to an acclaimed concert career. *Habanera* was not published until a few years later, when Ravel included it as part of *Les Sites Auriculaires,* which premiered at the first public performance of a Ravel composition in March of 1898. Later he would orchestrate the *Habanera* work into his *Rhapsodie Espagnole* from 1908.

Sheherazade was Ravel's first work for orchestra, and was performed in Paris at the Societe Nationale de Musique in May of 1899, which he also conducted. His

For the Record . . .

Born Maurice Joseph Ravel, March 7, 1875, (died December, 1937) in Ciboure, Basses-Pyrenees, France; died December 28, 1937, in Paris, France; son of Pierre Joseph (an engineer) and Marie (Delouard) Ravel. *Education:* Studied at Paris Conservatoire, 1899-1905.

First published work, *Menuet Antique,* 1895; first performance of a composition with *Les Sites Auriculaires,* Paris, 1898; first work for orchestra, *Sheherazade,* performed as conducted by Ravel in Paris, 1899; founding member, Societe des Apaches, c. 1900; first opera, *L'heure espagnole,* premiered in Paris, 1911; ballet, *Daphnis et Chloé,* premiered at Ballet Russe de Monte Carlo, 1912.

Awards: French legion d'honneur (declined), 1920; honorary doctorate in music from Oxford University, 1928.

originated at an Apache evening, and its five movements were dedicated to different members of the group. Vines gave its first public performance.

Ravel met with continued success in the early years of the century. His chamber piece *Quartet in F major,* first performed in March of 1904, met with tremendous critical success and would become a favorite with audiences as well. Still, the accolades and financial bounties showered upon Ravel also provoked professional jealousy inside the competitive Parisian music scene, and in 1905 he was declared ineligible to compete for the prestigious Prix de Rome, the most important award for young composers in France, and a Conservatoire-affiliated competition that he had entered thrice before. The judges of the Conservatoire were evidently biased against him, and one in particular wished to promote the works of his own pupils. But several other musicians and musicologists rallied around Ravel and publicly condemned the panel. A great war in the press followed, and even came to be known the Ravel Affair. In the end, the director of the Conservatoire was forced to resign.

An Enforced Rivalry

Another furor erupted in 1907 with the premiere of Ravel's *Histoires Naturelles,* which consisted of satirical verse about animals set to his equally biting music. The critics derided it, especially the highly regarded Pierre Lalo, who termed Ravel a plagiarist of Claude Debussy. For weeks a debate raged in the press over the attributes of each. Ravel's ultimate revenge, however, came with the extremely successful premiere of his *Rhapsodie espagnole* for the orchestra, first performed in Paris in 1908, to enthusiastic applause and critical accolades.

Less favorable was the reception of his first opera, *L'heure espagnole* ("The Spanish Hour"), which premiered at the Opera Comique in Paris in May of 1911. However, after World War I, the one-act comedy found surprising success both in Europe and abroad. It premiered in Chicago in 1920 and at the New York Metropolitan Opera five years later. The musical tale, set in a clockmaker's shop in Spain several generations before, showcased Ravel's talent for orchestration, as various instruments were cleverly utilized to re-create the sounds of this particular enterprise.

piano piece, *Pavane pour une infante défunte,* was published that same year and proved extremely popular upon its debut at another Societe concert in 1902. The concerts made him a rising star in the competitive music scene in Paris. Another work performed that same evening, *Jeux d'Eau* ("Fountains"), would also receive a strong critical reception. An essay on Ravel in *Composers Since 1900* called *Jeux d'Eau* "remarkable for its unusual resonances, extraordinary exploitation of piano sonorities, and its brilliant use of the upper register of the keyboard.... It opened a new world of haunting sounds and timbres for piano writing; certainly it opened them for Debussy who, from the moment he became acquainted with it, began to write for the piano in an entirely new manner."

The Apaches

Around 1900, Ravel formed the Societe des Apaches with Igor Stravinsky, Manuel de Falla, Florent Schmitt and other progressive composers and musicians of the day in Paris. Their name reflected their renegade attitude toward the staid conservatism of the Parisian musical world, and they strove to write and promote innovative and fresh works. One controversial effort they rallied behind was Claude Debussy's opera *Pelleas et Melisande.* Ravel's demanding piano masterwork, *Miroirs,*

Worked with Diaghilev

Along with his fascination with Spain, Ravel was also intrigued by the Viennese waltz. His eight *Valses Nobles et Sentimentales w—valse* being the French term for the dance—drew upon the form and remain "highly representative of clear, forceful writing, marked by a condensing and a hardening of the system of chords that they obey," noted Jean-Jacques Soleil and Guy Lelong of the 1911 work in *Musical Masterpieces.* Ravel also began to collaborate with the choreographer Sergei Diaghilev, who staged arrangements of Ravel's piano suite *Ma Mère l'Oye* ("Mother Goose"), a work based on several French fairy tales. Diaghilev then commissioned from Ravel the impressionistic ballet *Daphnis et Chloé,* which premiered with the Ballet Russe de Monte Carlo—with the famed Nijinsky dancing the lead—in 1912. The tale of two young shepherds and thwarted love, based on a work from early Greek literature, at first received a mixed reception from critics, but would later be termed "one of the major symphonic works in French music of the twentieth century," according to Soleil and Lelong. "An important orchestral effect is created by rarely-used instruments: alto flute in G and clarinet in E flat among others. A mixed choir of four voices blends in at times, with closed mouths, to the sounds of the orchestra."

When World War I erupted, Ravel—though nearly 40—attempted to enlist in the French Army, but was rejected. Instead he served in the motor corps near the front lines, which aversely affected his nerves for a time. Furthermore, his mother, with whom he had been especially close, was in poor health, and she died not long after the war. During this somber time of his life, Ravel wrote the piano work *Le Tombeau de Couperin,* which commemorated the war dead. It premièred in Paris in 1920, and was orchestrated by himself as well for another debut that same year.

Refused Legion d'honneur

For 1920's *La Valse,* Ravel returned once more to the waltz, this time basing it on the works of Johann Strauss the Younger. *La Valse* was a huge success, but Ravel was still at odds with the more conservative music establishment despite his acclaim. The French government attempted to award him its prestigious Legion d'honneur in 1920, which he declined. The following year he retired to the Ile-de-France countryside, to a villa called Le Belvedere. There he wrote—though less prolifically than in his earlier career—and enjoyed gardening and entertaining his beloved Siamese cats. Ravel was also known as an elegant dresser, and was allegedly the first man in France to wear pastel-hued shirts. He had impeccable manners and was an entertaining storyteller, but never married, believing that the artistic temperament was unsuited to the institution.

Ravel continued to write chamber works, such as the *Sonata for Violin and Cello,* and penned another opera,

this one in collaboration with the illustrious French writer Colette. *L'enfant et les sortilèges* ("The Child and the Enchantments"), the stage fantasy of a young child beset by singing objects, had its premiere in Monte Carlo in March of 1925. In 1928 the composer toured America for the first time, and was deeply moved by a standing ovation given one of his works in New York City, remarking that such applause had never greeted his premieres in his own Paris.

The Stirring *Boléro*

Later that year Ravel created what would become his signature piece, a work for the orchestra that was an immediate and resounding success, and an enduring one as well. *Boléro* was commissioned by the dancer Ida Rubinstein, and for her Ravel provided a simple piece of music, fantastically orchestrated, with the premise of a gypsy dancer at a Spanish tavern intoxicating four men with her dance. *Boléro* is simply the same passage repeated for seventeen minutes, a few bars of lilting music first played by the flute section, and then allowing the instruments to take their turns until a rousing crescendo. "Built on a single theme in two sections, *Boléro* is a stunning tour de force with an inescapable kinetic appeal as the melody grows in dynamics and changes in orchestral color, until a thunderous climax erupts in full orchestra," declared *Composers Since 1900.*

Premiered at Paris Opera in November of 1928, and not long afterward in the United Sates under the baton of Arturo Toscanini with the New York Philharmonic, *Boléro* was a great sensation at the time. Nearly every symphony added the piece to its repertoire, and recorded versions of it were also popular. It is assumed to be the most often performed piece ever written for the orchestra. It was used in the Dudley Moore/Bo Derek film *10* in 1979, a comic look at a midlife crisis that posited that *Boléro* was remarkably suitable as background music for a private act.

A British scientific study, published in 1997, presented the theory that *Boléro's* repetitive nature may have been symptomatic of the early onset of Alzheimer's disease. By the early 1930s Ravel was noticing a precipitous drop in his motor skills, originally thought to have been brought on by a 1932 taxicab accident in Paris. He became unable to write music or even letters, and his last missive written to a childhood friend in 1934 noted that it took him over a week to complete. His speech abilities also began to falter, and a 1937 operation to remove a supposed brain tumor found nothing. He went into a coma a few days later, and died in December of 1937.

The street in Ciboure on which Ravel was born was renamed in his honor, as the street of Le Belvedere, is now a museum dedicated to his life and work. He remains one of France's most exalted composers. Music scholar Arbie Orenstein called Ravel "an exponent of that careful, precise workmanship, elegance, and grace he so admired in the music of Mozart," he declared in *American Scholar*. "His work, however, was a monument to the dignity and precision that even now all worthy musicians should strive for and that French music has at its best always captured."

Selected discography

Orchestral Works, PGD/London Classics, 1988.

Ravel Conducts Ravel: Boléro, Piano Concerto, Pearl/Koch, 1992.

Boléro, Daphnis, Ma mère l'oye, Valses nobles, Naxos, 1992.

Le Tombeau de Couperin, Sonatine, Miroirs, Musique D'Abord, 1993.

Valses nobles et sentimentales, etc., Chandos, 1993.

Ravel: Complete Piano Works/Philippe Entremont, Sony Music, 1994.

Rapsodie espagnole, Pavane, etc., Naxos, 1994.

Ravel: Complete Solo Piano Works/Louis Lortie, Chandos, 1994.

Ravel: Greatest Hits (Leonard Bernstein, Branford Marsalis, New York Philharmonic Orchestra, English Chamber Orchestra), Sony Music, 1994.

L'Heure Espagnole, Stradivarius, 1995.

Ravel en Espagne: L'Heure Espagnole, etc., Pearl/Koch, 1997.

Boléro, Madacy Records, 1997.

L'enfant et les sortilèges, etc., PGD/Deutsche Grammophon, 1997.

Ravel: Boléro, La Valse, Spanish Rhapsody, etc., I Love Classics, 1999.

Ravel: Piano Concertos, etc., PGD/Deutsche Grammophon, 1999.

Sources

Books

Ewen, David, editor, *Composers Since 1900: A Biographical and Critical Guide,* H. W. Wilson, 1969.

Nicholas, Jeremy, *The Classic FM Guide to Classical Music,* Pavilion, 1997.

Sadie, Stanley, editor, *The New Grove Dictionary of Music and Musicians,* Macmillan, 1980.

Soleil, Jean-Jacques, and Guy Lelong, *Musical Masterpieces,* Chambers, 1991.

Periodicals

American Scholar, Winter 1995, pp. 91-102.

—*Carol Brennan*

Joshua Redman

Saxophone

AP/Wide World Photo. Reproduced by permission.

Ever since saxophonist Joshua Redman burst onto the jazz scene in 1991, he has displayed the maturity and skill of a veteran, earning immediate recognition from critics and colleagues alike. As the winner of a prestigious talent competition in his early twenties, this "young lion" astounded listeners with a richness and technical precision, and has honed his ability over the years to become more soulful as well. His first album, *Joshua Redman,* was released on the Warner Brothers label in 1993, and since then, his output has continued to bring accolades. One of the so-called New Emotionalists, Redman's works aim to convey a raw power rather than an intellectual experience. "Music doesn't come from music, music comes from life," he outlined to Jim Macnie in *Down Beat.* "That means taking walks, hanging out, going to parties, reading, playing sports ... the list is endless, right?" Redman's approach has helped to popularize jazz to a wider audience. But not only is Redman an outstanding musician, he has a fascinating background, too. He had won a full scholarship to Harvard, graduated summa cum laude, and was set to enter law school when he decided to defer his education in order to concentrate on music for a while. Jazz became his permanent career, and he went on to release a number of albums as a leader, as well as appearing as a sideman on others. In 1998, he released his sixth major effort, *Timeless Tales (For Changing Times).*

Redman was born on February 1, 1969, in Berkeley, California. His mother, Renee Shedroff, is the daughter of Eastern European Orthodox Jewish immigrants. She was an amateur dancer and artists' model who now works as a librarian. His father is Dewey Redman, a jazz saxophonist who worked with experimental jazz legend Ornette Coleman. His parents met in San Francisco during the mid-1960s and never married. Redman's father, who quit his job as a teacher in Texas to play jazz, was already working in New York with Coleman when his son was conceived on a visit from Shedroff. In fact, he had moved east in 1967 with another woman, but Shedroff was intent on having a child with him. After Redman was born, she left her modeling job in order to raise him, surviving on welfare in a one-bedroom apartment in Berkeley. Redman's mother passed along her passion for music, and her son showed talent from a young age. When Redman was just two-and-a-half years old, his mom took him to a concert featuring an Indian instrument called the gamelan, and when they returned home, he mimicked it by lining up pots and pans in order of the tones they produced. He also could play the recorder and clarinet.

When Redman was ten, he began playing tenor saxophone, thanks to a school program that loaned instruments to low-income students. He was influenced by his mother's extensive record collection featuring the likes of Charlie Parker, Sonny Rollins, John Coltrane, and Cannonball Adderly. In addition, he went with his mother to see his father play in concert about once a year when he came to town, although he has noted that he was not emulating his father by taking up the sax. His father was not involved in his upbringing, but Redman harbors no ill will. He told Stephen J. Dubner in *New York,* "I have a good relationship with my dad—it's just not a father- son relationship. It's more of a buddy relationship, a mentor-student relationship." In fact, Redman took note of his father's relative obscurity in the music industry and decided from a young age that he would pursue other roads. "I wanted to make sure that even if I ended up in music, I would never be forced to do something that runs counter to my artistic instincts in order to put food on the table," Redman explained to Zan Stewart in *Down Beat.*

Though Redman became a soloist with the prestigious Berkeley High School Jazz Ensemble, he never wavered from his scholarly pursuits. After graduating as valedictorian of his class in 1986, he won a full scholarship to Harvard University, where he considered becoming a doctor before majoring in urban studies, planning on a career in law. "I was very interested in addressing the social problems of the city—poverty, racism, homelessness," Remand related to Dan Ouellette in *Down Beat.* "I thought being a lawyer would give me the best background to make a difference." As a respite from his studies, Redman continued to enjoy music, joining the jazz band at Harvard and playing gigs during his summers off from school. In 1989, in fact, he performed at the Village Vanguard in Manhattan with his father. After graduating summa cum laude and Phi Beta Kappa in 1991 with a grade point average of 3.87, he took his law school entrance exams and received a perfect score. He was accepted at Harvard and Stanford as well as his first choice, Yale, but decided to take a one-year hiatus from academia in order to play music full-time.

After moving to New York, Redman rented a place with four friends in Brooklyn, not far from where his father lived, and they began seeing each other regularly for the first time and collaborating. They performed together and after about a year, released an album, *Choices,* for a small label out of Europe called enja. Becoming weary of the confusion surrounding why he and his father did not share a surname, Redman changed his last name. In 1991, after some prodding from his friends, he entered the Thelonious Monk International Jazz Instrumental Competition in Washington, D.C. The respected event was judged by big names Benny Carter, Branford Marsalis, Jackie McLean, Jimmy Heath, and Frank Wess, and offered a first prize of $10,000. Redman won it with his renditions of Jerry Valentine's *Second Balcony Jump,* the ballad *Soul Eyes* by Mal Waldron, and Monk's *Evidence.* As Dan Ouellette put it in *Down Beat,* "He blew the rest of the saxophonists off the stage."

Initially skeptical of the idea of a competition, Redman felt music was too subjective to be ranked, but later he was pleased to have had the opportunity to showcase his talent. He remarked to Geoffrey Himes in the *Washington Post* that competitions are "great for the cause of jazz, because Americans love competition, and that hook will get the public interested in young musicians they might never listen to otherwise." Winning the competition sparked Redman's career. He began receiving calls from luminaries like Pat Metheny and Charlie Haden; he was given the chance to work with people he respected. And, as part of his first prize, he was the featured performer at the Blues Alley club. Soon, record companies were dashing to sign him. A scout for Warner Brothers had seen him play at the Vanguard and again at the Monk competition, and knew he had found a gem. Warner Brothers signed Redman in 1992, and in 1993, after just a four-hour recording session, he released *Joshua Redman.* The album contained six original tunes and some covers of classic hits like *Salt Peanuts, Body and Soul,* and *I Got You (I Feel Good).*

Overall, critics were amazed that such a young, new musician could have such talent. "Jazz is about improvisation," Redman told Paul Keegan in *GQ.* "When I practice, I just pick up the horn and play through a song, taking the song to different keys, trying different improvisational ideas, experimenting with it." His approach worked, winning him comparisons to much more seasoned musicians, such as Sonny Rollins, and an outpouring of admiration. Stewart noted in *Down Beat,* "Listening to the album, you're grabbed by Redman's sound. It's rich, weighty, and deep. And this fellow makes the music move, creating heat and interest, be it on a sultry blues or a come-hither ballad." Gene Seymour in *Newsday* remarked that *Joshua Redman* "is simply the most startlingly assured debut album by a young jazz artist in memory." In *Time,* David E. Thigpen commented, "It's been a long time since jazz produced a saxophonist with Redman's fearless improvisational skill and mature melodic sense." Some critics were somewhat less enthusiastic, claiming that Redman's style was a bit too reserved, but overall, praise was universal. The album sold more than 30,000 copies during its first four months—a remarkable amount for a jazz recording—and was nominated for a Grammy Award.

Once word got out, other musicians desired Redman as a sideman. He played with veteran traditionalists such as Milt Jackson and Joe Williams, while also winning respect from eclectic players like Pat Metheny. He even performed in June of 1993 on the White House lawn with Illinois Jacquet and President Bill Clinton. In August of that year, he was a standout at a jam session at the Lincoln Center, showing up jazz greats like David Murray and George Coleman, then toured with the Lincoln Center Jazz Orchestra in 1994. In the meantime, he was collecting a slew of awards, being named the best new artist by the *Jazz Times,* 1992, hot jazz artist by *Rolling Stone,* 1993, and number one tenor saxophonist (talent deserving of wider recognition) in the *Down Beat* critics' poll, 1993.

Redman's second release, *Wish,* released in September of 1993, was recorded live and featured an all-star lineup including Metheny on guitar, Charlie Haden on bass, and Billy Higgins on drums. The foursome rehearsed for only a few hours in order to capture that spontaneity that Redman cherished, and again, it was a success. *Wish* sold more than 90,000 copies in the United States and won the *Down Beat* readers poll for album of the year in 1994; Redman also won jazz artist of the year honors and narrowly missed being named best tenor sax player (Joe Henderson squeaked past). Still, some observers pointed out that Redman had not yet developed a distinctive style, one that would identify him by his unique sound. However, this was not held against him, especially in light of the fact that his talent, charisma, and attractiveness seemed to be welcoming a wider audience to the world of jazz. Another facet that endeared him to wider audiences was his use of popular songs remade as jazz tunes, such as Eric Clapton's *Tears in Heaven* and Stevie Wonder's *Make Sure You're Sure.* Redman's next effort, *Mood Swing,* 1994, captured even more listeners, selling 104,000 copies. Some critics found it to be his finest work up to that point.

The mid-1990s found Redman on the road more than at home. In 1995, he released another album, but not from the studio. The double-CD set *Spirit of the Moment: Live at the Village Vanguard* included originals and covers, and infused a bluesy feel that popularized Redman's music even more. He later expounded to Macnie in *Down Beat,* "People have found my music to be accessible, and that's been both a blessing and a curse.... Some have said that because my music is accessible, I must be compromising it—conforming it: to appeal to people. Implicitly that means it lacks substance.... I am who I am and I play the way I play, and the way I play has been and will be honest and from my soul.... To a lot of people, there's a natural opposition between great art and success. That's a dangerous mindset."

As Redman's star rose, his reputation only blossomed. Britt Robson in the Minneapolis *StarTribune* wrote, that although "there are moments when Redman still can fall prey to crowd-pleasing gimmickry," he "deserves credit for refusing to rest on his laurels, showing constant improvement over the past four years. His trademark has become clipped phrases that are deftly strung together to create irresistibly swinging songs, brimming with tonal variation and creative turns." In 1996, Redman released *Freedom in the Groove,* which also proved to be fast-seller, and in 1998, he came out with *Timeless Tales (For Changing Times).* This collection boasted an interesting melange of pop tunes, including the Beatles' *Eleanor Rigby,* Bob Dylan's *The Times They Are A-Changin',* and other songs by artists ranging from Cole Porter, Rodgers & Hammerstein, and the Gershwins to Prince, Joni Mitchell, and Stevie Wonder.

Redman was married in 1997 and moved from his midtown Manhattan home to a New York City suburb.

He enjoys reading and going to art museums, and likes the television show *Star Trek*. He was the first jazz musician to have a clothes designer—Donna Karan—as a corporate sponsor. Redman also appeared in director Robert Altman's 1996 film *Kansas City,* about the rise of the jazz scene there, as well as the criminal and political arenas, during the 1930s. As for Redman's outlook on the future of jazz, he responded that he has no idea what to expect: "That's what makes it exciting," Redman remarked to Martin Gayford in the *Daily Telegraph.* "If I knew what it was going to look like, I wouldn't be so excited to be a part of it. Jazz is a music of surprise; it's a music of spontaneity. I think jazz musicians live—I know I do—for being surprised and not knowing what's going to come next."

Selected discography

Joshua Redman, Warner Bros., 1993.
Wish, Warner Bros., 1993.
Mood Swing, Warner Bros., 1994.
Spirit of the Moment: Live at the Village Vanguard, Warner Bros., 1995.
Freedom in the Groove, Warner Bros., 1996.
Timeless Tales (For Changing Times), Warner Bros., 1998.

Contributor

Dewey Redman, *Choices,* enja, 1992.
John Hicks, *Friends Old and New,* RCA, 1992.
Bob Thiele Collective, *Louis Satchmo,* Red Baron, 1992.
Danny Gatton and Bobby Watson, *New York Stories,* Blue Note, 1992.
Elvin Jones, *Youngblood,* enja, 1992.

Sources

Books

Contemporary Musicians, volume 12, Gale Research, 1994.

Periodicals

Daily Telegraph, October 31, 1998, p. 8.
Dallas Morning News, February 28, 1997, p. 30.
Down Beat, June 1993, p. 26; December 1994, p. 28; January 1996, p. 10; May 1996, p. 16; January 1999, p. 24.
Economist, January 22, 1994, p. 94.
Entertainment Weekly, September 30, 1994, p. 59; September 15, 1995, p. 106.
Essence, November 1994, p. 64.
GQ, June 1994, p. 93.
Los Angeles Times, November 1, 1997, p. F12.
Newsday, April 1, 1993, p. 67; October 7, 1993, p. 84; September 14, 1994, p. B7.
New York, January 24, 1994, p. 36.
Star Tribune (Minneapolis, MN), May 7, 1995, p. 1F; February 7, 1996, p. 1E; February 8, 1996, p. 4B.
Time, November 22, 1993, p. 76; November 30, 1998, p. 128.
Toronto Star, October 8, 1998.
Washington Post, December 3, 1993, p. N25.

Online

"Joshua Redman," Yahoo! Music, http://musicfinder.yahoo.com (February 4, 1999).

Geri Speace

R.E.M.

Alternative rock band

When four college guys started a garage band together in Athens, Georgia in 1980, they had no idea they'd go on to sign a historically lucrative record deal, see the end of their band as they knew it, and reign as one of the most influential bands of their era. University of Georgia students drummer Bill Berry, guitarist Peter Buck, bassist Mike Mills and vocalist Michael Stipe formed R.E.M. When they started, punk rock was mostly what was being played in garages by angst-ridden youth across America, but R.E.M. (named for the "rapid eye movement" phase of sleep) was busy making catchy guitar pop. R.E.M. signify the point at which all that misdirected, avant-garde, "alternative" music was driven out of the garage and into heady commercial success.

At the start R.E.M. was a driven college rock band, often playing two or three shows a night, five nights a week, three weeks a month. They applied the post-punk D.I.Y. (do it yourself) mentality to what they were doing and just played tirelessly. All the experience and exposure showed up well on their first single, "Radio Free Europe" and "Sitting Still," which was released on their

AP/Wide World Photos. Reproduced by permission.

Members include **Bill Berry** (born William Thomas Berry, July 31, 1958, Duluth, MN), 1980-97, drums; **Peter Buck** (born Peter Lawrence Buck, December 6, 1956, Berkeley, CA), guitar; **Mike Mills** (born Michael Edward Mills, December 17, 1958, Orange, CA), bass, vocals; **Michael Stipe** (born John Michael Stipe, January 4, 1960, Decatur, GA), vocals.

Group formed in Athens, Georgia, 1980; signed to IRS Records, 1982; released debut EP *Chronic Town*, 1982; released *Murmur*, 1983; released *Reckoning*, 1984; released *Fables of the Reconstruction*, 1985; released *Life's Rich Pageant*, 1986; released *Document*, 1987; signed a five-record, $10-million record deal with Warner Brothers, 1988; released *Green*, 1988; released *Out of Time*, 1991; released *Automatic for the People*, 1992; released *Monster*, 1994; signed a five-record, $80-million record deal with Warner Brothers, 1996; released *New Adventures in Hi-Fi*, 1996; drummer Bill Berry left band, October, 1997; released *Up*, 1998.

Awards: Four Grammy awards.

Addresses: *Record company*—Warner Brothers, 75 Rockefeller Plaza, New York, NY 10019.

---

local Hib-Tone record label in 1981. "Radio Free Europe" earned them a cult following which led to their first EP, *Chronic Town*, on IRS records in 1982.

It wasn't until 1983 and the release of *Murmur* that anyone besides critics—and those hip to the Georgia underground—took to R.E.M. But because R.E.M.'s haunting style of folk and rock clashed with the synthetic early '80s new-wave sound, more people sat up and listened. *Murmur* peaked at number 136 on the album charts, but *Rolling Stone* selected it as album of the year and R.E.M. as band of the year. With their 1984 release, *Reckoning*, the sound was still unlike anything else being played at the time and the push behind R.E.M. became even stronger, as did record sales. With at least one release per year on IRS from 1985's *Fables of the Reconstruction* to 1988's greatest hits collection *Eponymous*, the band gained more and more critical acclaim, fans, and record sales. Their 1987 release *Document* did the unthinkable, reaching the top ten, and produced

a hit single, the anti-love song called "The One I Love." But in 1988, R.E.M. grew up.

In 1988, R.E.M. officially earned the right to be called "sell-outs" by their purist fans. After R.E.M. signed a five-record, ten-million-dollar deal with Warner Bros., people could call them whatever they wanted to, but they had to acknowledge the band as a commercial success. Once they were on top, though, R.E.M. did not fail to look back down and got involved with grassroots political and environmental causes. Stipe spoke out on behalf of Greenpeace, animal rights, and the homeless. After their first release for Warner Bros., *Green*, R.E.M. had become the world's most popular band.

After an exhaustive tour to support the release of *Green*—during which Stipe cursed *Green*'s hit single "Stand," which had the entire country humming it, as the worst song they'd ever written—the band went on a touring hiatus. They hibernated up for three years until the much-anticipated release of *Out of Time* in 1991. R.E.M. blossomed on *Out of Time*, both instrumentally and commercially. They used a more exotic selection of instruments, including horns and mandolins. The release sped to number one on the album charts, and went quadruple platinum. Its hit singles "Losing My Religion" and "Shiny Happy People," a duet with Kate Pierson of the B-52's, were the summer anthems of 1991. On 1992's *Automatic for the People*, R.E.M. dug deep inside and pulled out a somber, introspective collection of songs. Its hits were "Drive," "Man on the Moon," and "Everybody Hurts."

When *Monster* was released in 1994, it seemed geared to be played loudly. R.E.M. rocked harder on this record than on any before. *Monster* included rockers with reverb-laded guitars and distorted vocals alongside more trademark-sounding songs. The album hit number one almost immediately although it produced a lukewarm first single, "What's the Frequency, Kenneth?" which peaked at number 28. To support *Monster*, the band geared up for its first tour in five years, but canceled it after a few weeks in March 1995 when drummer Bill Berry suffered a near-fatal double brain aneurysm in Switzerland.

The small-town boys from Georgia made music-industry history in 1996, signing a five-record, $80 million deal with Warner Music, the largest record contract ever awarded at the time. The deal came at the end of a bidding war, with DreamWorks, Sony, Capitol and MCA offering $35 to $50 million. "R.E.M. embodies everything important about this company," Warner Bros. president Steven Baker told the *Los Angeles Times*. "They are a tremendously hard-working, successful band with integrity and vision." Two weeks later, the band released *New Adventures in Hi-Fi*, which, although it debuted at number two, wasn't very well received and enjoyed only lukewarm sales.

In early October of 1997, on the first day of rehearsals, drummer Berry decided to leave the band. "Rock drummers are like car tires: they're regularly replaced, but you don't get far if you're missing one," wrote *Time* in 1998. This was especially true for R.E.M. The band was always known for working as a democracy—every decision in their 17 years together had been made unanimously. All members received songwriting credit on their albums, drummer Berry included. "I put it to the guys," Berry told *Rolling Stone*. "I don't want to do this anymore." "I was just consumed by Bill's departure," Michael Stipe told *Rolling Stone* in 1998.

For the band's first release after Berry's departure, 1998's *Up*, all ears were tuned to hear the sound of a new R.E.M. "The pulsing drum machine that opens *Up* hints at what skeptics may have feared: The Berry-less (but not drummerless) R.E.M. may have bought a floor ticket to music's latest overplayed trend, electronica," Ann Powers wrote in *Rolling Stone* in 1998. "But the mellotron, harpsichord and other groovy effects on *Up* never overwhelm the band's mighty sense of self." Or as David Fricke wrote in *Rolling Stone*, "*Up* is the record that Michael Stipe, Peter Buck and Mike Mills would have made with or without departed drummer Bill Berry."

Up also was a first for Stipe as lyricist: for the first time, his enigmatic song lyrics were printed on the CD's insert. *Stereo Review* noted in a 1998 review of *Up* that Stipe, known for mumbling his often cryptic verse, seemed to be trying to make himself a little clearer. "The most interesting aspect [of *Up*] is Michael Stipe's lyrical openness; he has never been more nakedly self reve-latory, nor has he enunciated his lyrics with such delib-erate precision." The reviews for *Up* were wildly mixed, from speculation that it was the group's best record ever, to *Billboard*'s 1998 review of it as a "record that sounds as if the group was sulking all the way through it." In a year-end interview with *Rolling Stone* in 1998, Stipe had this response: "If this record dropped out of the sky by a three-piece band that nobody had heard of, people would be in the street shouting at the top of their lungs, naked, about it."

Selected discography

Chronic Town, IRS, 1982.
Murmur, IRS, 1983.
Reckoning, IRS, 1984.
Fables of the Reconstruction, IRS, 1985.
Life's Rich Pageant, IRS, 1986.
Document, IRS, 1987.
Dead Letter Office, IRS, 1987.
Green, IRS, 1988.
Out of Time, Warner Brothers, 1991.
Automatic for the People, Warner Brothers, 1992.
Monster, Warner Brothers, 1994.
New Adventures in Hi-Fi, Warner Brothers, 1996.
Up, Warner Brothers, 1998.

Sources

Books

Gary Graff and Daniel Durcholz, editors, *MusicHound Rock: The Essential Album Guide*, Visible Ink Press, 1998.
Romanowski, Patricia and Warren, Holly George, editors, *The Rolling Stone Encyclopedia of Rock & Roll*, Fire-side/Simon & Shuster, 1995.

Periodicals

Billboard, October 30, 1998.
Newsweek, October 26, 1998.
New York Times, October 28, 1998.
Rolling Stone, December 11, 1997; September 3, 1998; November 12, 1998; December 24, 1998
Stereo Review, December 1998.
Time, October 26, 1998.
Village Voice, November 3, 1998.

Online

"R.E.M.," *All-Media Guide*, http://www.allmusic.com (Janu-ary 5, 1999).
SVS Internet Services, http://www.svs.com/rem/news/wb.text (January 5, 1999).

—*Brenna Sanchez*

Chris Rice

Christian contemporary musician

After Christian pop artist Michael W. Smith started his own independent record label, Rocketown Records, he knew which artist he wanted to be Rocketown's first. Chris Rice, who'd been traveling the country for more than a decade with his youth ministry, was the chosen one. So after Rice's debut release on Rocketown, *Deep Enough to Dream*, in 1997, the Christian songwriter had to add touring to promote his record to his already-packed schedule of youth camps and retreats.

Rice was raised in Maryland by his parents, who were Christian bookstore owners. He was known for his gift with kids—talking, listening, singing, playing ball with them—and was somewhat hesitant about signing a record contract that would obligate him to time away from his youth ministry. "After 12 fruitful years of full time teaching, singing and worship leading in youth and college retreat settings, I wondered how my life would change this year with the release of *Deep Enough to Dream*," Rice wrote in his bio. But his recording career only served to extend his outreach. In his contract with Rocketown, he stipulated that 15 weeks a year be reserved for his youth ministry. *Billboard* called *Deep Enough to Dream* "one of the most successful new releases ... in the Christian music industry." Releasing a record did change things for Rice—he was more accessible than ever. He started receiving letters and e-mail daily from students and adults from as far away as Thailand, Indonesia, Australia, New Zealand and Korea.

Although *Deep Enough to Dream* was Rice's first release, he had experience and success at songwriting for other Christian artists, Kathy Trocolli most notably. He began his songwriting career in the 1980s and was named the *American Songwriter* Christian Songwriter of the Year in 1995 for Kim Boyce's "By Faith." After his own release, Rice immediately was referred to as Christian music's James Taylor, which accurately described his folksy guitar style and sweet voice. But his songwriting was based on years of experience answering kids' questions, which made his songs unique. "Rice isn't afraid to confront the Big Questions—How do we get to know God? Why such suffering if there's a great and loving God? etc.," said Eugene, Oregon's *Register-Guard* in 1998. "But [he] still has a common touch, putting existentialist flesh on divine queries." Rice came across in interviews as distinctly down to earth and likable. Another review that painted Rice as a quiet and humble thirty-something songwriter was found in the *Dayton Daily News*: "Rice's lyrics show why he is so popular with teens—he's genuine, and he doesn't talk down to anybody."

The first release was a charm for Rice and *Deep Enough to Dream* earned six Gospel Music Association Dove

For the Record . . .

Born in MA, to Christian bookstore owners.

Started singing in Christian youth ministries, 1985; signed to Rocketown Records, 1996; released debut record *Deep Enough to Dream*, 1997; earned six nominations at Gospel Music Association Dove Awards, 1998; released *Past the Edges*, 1998.

Awards: *American Songwriter* magazine's Songwriter of the Year, 1995.

Address: *Record company*—Rocketown Records, 404 Bridge St., Franklin, Tennessee 37064-9040.

Award nominations in the spring of 1998 including New Artist, Male Vocalist, Pop/Contemporary Album, and as both artist and songwriter for Inspirational Recorded Song of the Year. He wasn't awarded any Doves, but during a performance in Tulsa, Oklahoma, the week after the awards ceremony, the crowd chanted "oh for six!" and awarded him an honor of their own—a talking parrot stuffed animal they called "The Parrot Award."

Rice's first release as a recording artist was also Rocketown's first release as an independent record label, and a lot was proved in their first joint outing. In starting the label, founder Michael W. Smith told the *Tennessean* in 1997, "We said, 'Let's be small. Let's create something the way it used to be... If it fails, I'd rather go down as an independent than sell it. To me it doesn't matter about the money, what matters is the vision." And Smith's vision, as he stated it in the early days of Rocketown, was family. He wanted the business to be like a family, based on relationships. Which was why Rice found so comfortable a home with the label. "They are so focused on really helping me and with what I am doing rather than turning me into some big star," Rice told *The Tennessean* in 1997. "It's more relationship oriented. They're really interested in what I'm doing in my life and enhancing that rather than taking me out of that." Rice's success with Rocketown allowed the label family to take on some new members—a band called Watermark signed on after Rice's debut and was preparing to release its debut as Rice was preparing for his second.

Despite being a self-proclaimed slow writer, Rice was ready with his second release in the fall of 1998—just a year after his first. With *Past the Edges* Rice moved away from "the folky sound of the first album into a more aggressive, acoustic pop vein," wrote *Billboard* in 1998. "Rice has a warm, accessible voice, but his calling card is his poignant lyrics, which reflect universal questions and concerns."

With added horns, synthesizers, strings, and the occasional accordion, *Past the Edges* was even called funky. Rice came across on this release more as everyman—and that's how he approached writing it. "I take the stance in some of these songs of a nonbeliever because I don't want to just feel like an answer man," Rice told *Billboard* in 1998. "I want to identify with both believers and nonbelievers Even as a Christian, there is a lot of stuff I'll never figure out, and it's okay to not have the answers, but it's not okay to drop everything and not question and not think." Rice's producer, Monroe Jones, concurred in the same article. "He doesn't approach things from a cliché," he said. "He doesn't approach it from 'I know it, so you need to know it.'"

Although Rocketown enjoyed the widespread coverage of Sony distribution, Rice kept things very personal with fans. He joined Michael W. Smith and the husband-and-wife duo Wilshire on Smith's two-month "Live the Life" tour in the fall of 1998. The tour was planned so that Rice and Wilshire, co-openers for Smith, could have time before the show in many cities to meet with concertgoers in the parking lot.

Selected discography

Deep Enough to Dream, Rocketown, 1997.
Past the Edges, Rocketown, 1998.

Sources

Periodicals

Billboard, August 15, 1998; October 24, 1998.
CBA Marketplace, November 1998.
Church Musician Today, January 1999.
Dallas Morning News, September 19, 1998.
Dayton Daily News, October 8, 1998.
Register-Guard, November 6, 1998.
The Tennessean, February 11, 1997.
Times-News Weekender, February 28, 1998.

Online

"Chris Rice," *All-Media Guide*, http://www.allmusic.com (January 5, 1999).

Additional information was provided by Rocketown publicity materials, 1999.

—*Brenna Sanchez*

Run DMC

Rap group

Run DMC emerged as one of the most innovative rap groups on the American musical scene in the early 1980s. While not the inventors of the rap music genre, Run DMC was most definitely its pioneer with distinctively sparse beats and a savvy penchant for incorporating rock and heavy metal lyrical samples and music into their highly acclaimed and wildly popular pop cultural vignettes. Run DMC's street-wise rhymes helped to not only set the tone but also the stage for such influential followers as Boogie Down Productions, Chuck D, Public Enemy, Ice Cube and N.W.A.

The tremendous success of Run DMC also helped to transform the economic structure of rap music. Before the emergence of Run DMC, rap music was marketed for the sale of singles. The group changed all of that when they released albums that were not solely comprised of a single or two surrounded by substandard filler material. In direct opposition to this, Run DMC released solidly cohesive albums which rivaled many of the rock and pop albums of the day in consistency and quality of the songs.

AP/Wide World Photo. Reproduced by permission.

Members include **DMC** (born Darryl Mc Daniel, May 31, 1964 in Hollis, Queens, NY), vocals; **Jam Master Jay** (born Jason Mizell, January 21, 1965 in Hollis), turntables; **Run** (born Joseph Simmons, November 14, 1964 in Hollis), vocals.

Group formed c.1982; signed to Profile Records and released "It's Like That/Sucker MCs," 1983; "Hard Times/ Jam Master Jay," 1983; "Rock Box," 1984; "30 Days," 1984; *Run DMC,* 1984; *King of Rock,* 1985; *Raising Hell,* 1986; *Tougher Than Leather,* 1988; *Back From Hell,* 1990; *Together Forever,* 1991; and *Down With the King,* 1993.

Awards: Platinum certification for *Raising Hell,* 1986; platinum certification for *Tougher Than Leather,* 1988; gold certification for *Down With the King,* 1993.

Addresses: *Record company*—Profile Entertainment, 740 Broadway, 7th Floor, New York, New York 10003.

The middle class New York City borough of Hollis, Queens, was the birthplace of Run, DMC, and their turntable-spinning friend, Jam Master Jay. In the early 1980s, Run started to rap over breakbeats with his school friend DMC. On the advice of Run's brother, Russell Simmons, who had recently co-founded the burgeoning record label Def Jam, Run and DMC began to practice their raps and rhymes in earnest. After they graduated from high school in 1982, Run and DMC invited their friend Jam Master Jay to scratch records on the turntables over which both Run and DMC would trade rhymes.

In 1983, Run DMC signed a recording contract with Profile Records and released their first single "It's Like That/Sucker MCs." According to one of their many web sites, "the single sounded like no other rap at the time— it was spare, blunt, and skillful, with hard beats and powerful, literate, and daring vocals, where Run and DMC's vocals overlapped as they finished each other's lines. It was the first new school hip hop recording." "It's Like That" eventually lodged itself in the top 20 of the American rhythm and blues (R&B) chart. This was also where Run DMC's follow up single, "Hard Times/Jam Master Jay," found a home.

Early 1984 saw the release of two more Run DMC singles, "Rock Box" and "30 Days." Both of these singles were also R&B hits. The sound of "Rock Box" indicated things to come as the group sought to incorporate the rock sound of the electric guitar in the song. Run DMC eventually released their self-titled debut album later that same year.

Always striving to break new ground by using different structural elements in their songs, Run DMC aspired to be the kings of rock music. By 1985, their vision of cross-genre domination was not far from being realized. With the release of their follow up album, *King of Rock,* Run DMC became the most celebrated, acclaimed, and successful rap group in the United States.

Run DMC's tremendous success was due, in no small part, to the beats they rhymed over. The once solid divisions between rock and rap music were now starting to break down. The sound of the group was an eclectic mix of solid thumping loops of funky drum beats combined with thunderous heavy metal guitar riffs. The album *King of Rock* spawned a trio of R&B hits which included the title track, "You Talk Too Much," and "Can You Rock It Like This." Also during 1985, Run DMC made their film debut in the rap movie "Krush Groove."

Run DMC entered mainstream American music in 1986. Their next single, the top ten R&B smash hit "My Adidas," elevated the shoes in question to hip hop cult status. Their third album, *Raising Hell,* unified both rockers and rappers with their cover of the old Aerosmith song, "Walk This Way." The genre-busting success of the song was clear when it peaked at number four on the pop charts. The success of the single catapulted *Raising Hell* to the number one spot on the R&B album charts, which, at the time, was a first for a rap group. On the pop charts it made it into the top ten and helped to push sales of the album to over a million copies, earning Run DMC the distinction of having the first rap album to have ever achieved platinum certification. Run DMC was also the first rap group to have a video aired on MTV. Other hit singles culled from the album included "You Be Illin" and "It's Tricky."

Tougher Than Leather was the 1988 platinum successor to *Raising Hell.* That same year Run DMC also starred in a movie by the same name. By this time, the climate in rap music had begun to change as the socially savvy raps and rhymes of the street-wise gangsta subgenre started to erode the popularity of Run DMC.

With the 1990 release of *Back From Hell,* Run DMC began to incorporate some of the politics of gangsta rappers, but the change of pace failed to ignite album sales. The following year their greatest hits package, *Together Forever,* was released. Run DMC managed a bit of a comeback with the gold selling 1993 album, *Down With the King*. The title track made it into the top ten of the R&B singles charts. The album also included Run DMC's first large number of collaborations with some of the more current stars and performers in hip hop.

According to Ira Robbins in the *Trouser Press Guide to 90s Rock,* Run DMC wasn't the first (or even the best) rap group around, but superb rhyming skills, diverse subject matter, artistic integrity, and unprecedented imagination made the Hollis crew early leaders of '80s rap. The group's use of electric guitar leads and reggae music added to their distinctive sound and helped establish them as pioneers of the rap music genre.

Selected discography

"It's Like That/Sucker MCs," Profile, 1983.
"Hard Times/Jam Master Jay," Profile, 1983.
"Rock Box", Profile, 1984.
"30 Days", Profile, 1984.

Run DMC, Profile, 1984.
King of Rock, Profile, 1985.
Raising Hell, Profile, 1986.
Tougher Than Leather, Profile, 1988.
Back From Hell, Profile, 1990.
Together Forever, Profile, 1991.
Down With the King, Profile, 1993.

Sources

Books

Robbins, Ira, ed., *Trouser Press Guide to 90s Rock*, Fireside, 1997.

Online

"The Biography," http://home.earthlink.net/tgmoren/rundmc/bio.html (January 24, 1999).
"Music News of the World," http://sonicnet.com/news/archive/sto...ZLAACGITUIDIAKCFEQ ?id502833&pid=503778 (January 24, 1999).

—*Mary Alice Adams*

Pee Wee Russell

Clarinetist, saxophonist

From the beginning, Pee Wee Russell was an enigma, an unclassifiable jazz musician whose unique style graced uncounted live and recorded jazz sessions. Bent on developing a singular voice, Russell consistently surprised both fellow musicians and fans with his recognizable solos. Though he became proficient on several reed instruments and a good reader of music, and though he could blend well with an ensemble with fine tone quality, Russell always preferred smaller groups to larger ones and developed a clarinet style that utilized growls, squeaks, swoops, whispers, and shouts to express his daring musical personality. Most critics and fellow musicians regard him as one of the truly inventive, expressive voices in jazz. Categorized for most of his career as a Dixieland or Chicago-style jazzman, Russell in his later years embraced, and was embraced by, many listeners and musicians of more modern bent.

The late and only child of the father for whom he was named and Ella Ballard Russell, Pee Wee was born in the Maplewood section of St. Louis on March 27, 1906. By his own testimony and that of friends, he was fawned upon by his parents who, while not affluent, dressed him finely and bought him whatever he seemed to desire, including his first musical instruments. Initially, his parents called him by his middle name, Ellsworth, to avoid confusion around the house. His father worked at a variety of jobs—clerical, managerial, sometimes entrepreneurial—and was usually upwardly mobile. The family moved to Okmulgee, then to Muskogee, Oklahoma just as Russell was about to enter elementary school. He began taking piano lessons, later switching to drums, xylophone, and other instruments provided by his indulgent parents. Next came the violin, at which the boy showed some proficiency. That career ended, however, at about age 12, when his mother accidentally sat on the violin.

As Russell's biographer, Robert Hilbert, wrote in his *Pee Wee Russell: The Life of a Jazzman*, "But his interest in music was far from over. One night in 1918, his father took him to an Elks event he had arranged [Russell's father managed the Elks lodge].... Alcide "Yellow" Nunez [a clarinetist] was holding forth with his band, the Louisiana Five. Nunez, one of the first prominent white jazzmen in New Orleans ... was a charter member of the Original Dixieland Jazz Band [ODJB] in Chicago.... But the aspect of Nunez's playing that held young Russell enthralled was the thrill of the unexpected: improvisation." Forty years later Russell expressed his still-remembered excitement at this event and throughout his career free-wheeling improvisation remained the hallmark of his playing.

Immediately, the youngster began begging for a clarinet, soon provided by his parents, along with lessons

For the Record . . .

Born Charles Ellsworth Russell, March 27, 1906, in St. Louis, MO; died February 15, 1969, in Alexandria, VA; son of Charles Ellsworth Russell (a clerk, store manager, and broker) and Ella Ballard; married Mary Chaloff, March 11, 1943, in New York.

Original inspiration was from New Orleans musicians; first clarinet teacher was Charles Merrill in Muskogee, OK; began playing professionally at local events in 1919; attended high school, Western Military Academy, in 1921; began playing on Mississippi riverboats, 1922; left St. Louis as a home base to play in Mexico with the band of Herbert Berger; made first records in 1922; beginning in 1923, played a variety of dance jobs; called to Houston, TX area to play with the band of pianist Peck Kelley that included clarinetist Leon Rappolo and trombonist Jack Teagarden; met and befriended cornetist Bix Beiderbecke in St.Louis; moved to New York to record with the band of cornetist Red Nichols, 1927; recorded extensively in New York with various bands in late 1920s through 1930s; joined trumpeter-leader Louis Prima at New York's Famous Door, beginning a 30-year stint in various clubs and studios, 1935; recorded widely with a variety of partners; veered away from Dixieland and Chicago-style in later years, playing with many modernists.

Connected with Legends

As Russell told biographer Hilbert, "I learned one thing: how to get where you re going on time." He also learned enough from his music teachers in his one year there to advance to the first chair of the clarinet section of the band before leaving the Academy, and probably ending his formal education. At this point Russell moved back to St. Louis with his family, finding a Prohibition-era city bursting with social clubs energized by ragtime and jazz. Among the groups causing a stir was the first version of the Mound City Blues Blowers, headed by the irrepressible vocalist and player, Red McKenzie. The young clarinetist played with Thomas Sonny Lee, an accomplished trombonist from Texas who would later become a star with many big bands and in New York studios. He also met Henry Allen, the great trumpet stylist, and began playing jobs on Streckfus Line Mississippi riverboats.

Although he stood nearly six feet tall, Russell weighed only about 125 pounds and soon acquired the nickname "Pee Wee." In 1922 he began traveling the upper Midwest, by now a reasonably accomplished dance band musician. At this point, Russell joined the band of Herbert Berger in Juarez, Mexico from where the group traveled to Hollywood before returning to St. Louis. A trip to New York with Berger's band saw Russell cutting his first records in 1922. Bigger things were in the offing.

Legendary pianist Peck Kelley worked with his popular band almost exclusively in the Houston area. Upon the recommendation of Sonny Lee, Kelley sent for Russell in the summer of 1924 to fill the clarinet chair. With Kelley and master trombonist Jack Teagarden as his guides, Russell developed the resolve to become a jazz musician, one who would build upon the individualized approach of his leader and bandmate. The summer job ended and Russell returned to St. Louis and mostly society dance jobs until called by hot trumpeter Wingy Manone to join his band for a job in San Antonio. Another return to St. Louis in the spring meant more dance jobs and a reprise with the Berger orchestra, complete with regular radio broadcasts. It was at this point in 1925 that Russell met two of the most influential musicians in jazz and in his career, cornetist Bix Beiderbecke and saxophonist Frank Trumbauer.

Both players had already achieved a degree of fame, Beiderbecke from his recordings with the Wolverines. As Russell told Whitney Balliett for his profile titled *Even His Feet Look Sad*, "We [Beiderbecke and I] hit it right off. We were never apart for a couple of years—day, night, good, bad, sick, well, broke, drunk." They played together in Trumbauer's band and they listened to all

from Charles Merrill, one of the few professional clarinetists in Muskogee, who played in the pit orchestra of the Broadway Theater. Turned on as he was by the new instrument and the sounds of the new music—jazz—Russell practiced and listened devotedly. He was caught by the records of the ODJB that featured clarinetist Larry Shields. Within a year, Russell was playing his first professional gig, albeit for meager pay, with a local park band. Shortly after entering Central High School in 1919, Russell was already addicted to two things—jazz music and alcohol. He often skipped classes in favor of girls, good times, and devilment, which sometimes included sampling what his father dispensed as the Elks club bartender. When his father caught him sneaking out to play a riverboat job on the Arkansas River with the Deepriver Jazz Band, the budding musician was transferred in September, 1920, from his high school to the Western Military Academy in Alton, Illinois, for discipline.

manner of music, including that of some of the more modern classical composers. The band's extended summer engagement at the Blue Lantern in Hudson Lake, Indiana became famous, attracting musicians from Chicago, such as Benny Goodman, reedman Bud Freeman and cornetist Jimmy McPartland as spectators. When the gig ended, Beiderbecke and Trumbauer-joined Gene Goldkette's orchestra and Russell once again resigned himself to dance jobs in St. Louis. The influence of Beiderbecke, especially his unusual note selection in improvising, would be forever with Pee Wee Russell, jazzman.

Called to New York by cornetist/leader Red Nichols, Russell arrived on August 14, 1927 and recorded with Nichols Five Pennies the next morning. Through that late summer and fall the clarinetist began a parade of recording dates that continued throughout much of his career. Often the group contained the same or similar personnel, with only the designated leader's name changing. Good jazz jobs were not plentiful, but Russell's growing reputation earned him a large share of them throughout 1928, and in October he began a coast-to-coast tour with the band of Paul Hagan. As the band worked its way back from Hollywood, Russell dropped out in St. Louis, where for the next six months he honed his clarinet style. When Nichols called him back to New York in the summer of 1929, not only could he play all manner of dance and commercial jobs, but Russell's jazz voice was now clearly identifiable.

Nichols controlled several groups, including recording and pit orchestras for Broadway shows. Russell recorded with breakthrough tenorman Coleman Hawkins and Jack Teagarden and played in theaters with the likes of Glenn Miller and Benny Goodman; this group was once directed by George Gershwin. As the Depression pressed in, jobs became more scarce, but Russell's reputation was such that legitimate bookers and jazz players alike were anxious to take advantage of the reedman's skills. He played in clubs and recorded on occasion with Teagarden, Red Allen, Red McKenzie, and others during the early 1930s, but as with most musicians, Russell scuffled for enough jobs to maintain. When he met Bobby Hackett on a summer job in 1933, Hackett was playing guitar and violin. Russell encouraged him to pursue the cornet; it was on that instrument and the trumpet that Hackett earned worldwide recognition.

Survived the Depression

During a good part of this 1930s period he had a live-in arrangement with Lola, whom many assumed was his wife, and who may have been related to his first clarinet teacher in St. Louis. But as the work lessened Russell began to drink more and his relationship with Lola deteriorated, then ended. Basically shy, on his own since his early teen years, and deeply into drinking, Russell took poor care of his physical needs, even his clarinet, and often looked disheveled and in need of food and sleep. His body began to rebel during this period.

By 1935 Russell was playing on 52nd Street at the Famous Door with the band of the popular trumpeter Louis Prima, with whom he traveled to Los Angeles. The band was featured in short films by Paramount and Vitaphone and was a hit in clubs. In 1936 Prima enlarged from five to 12 pieces and did some recording for Brunswick. When they moved to Chicago the big band bombed and Russell developed pleurisy and was unable to play for two months. After playing a few local jobs in Chicago, he returned to New York in 1937, stepping into a Dixieland band being formed by Red McKenzie at Nick Rongetti's famous restaurant with Eddie Condon, Bobby Hackett, and drummer Johnny Blowers. Soon Hackett took over the leadership chores of the band which drew celebrities and bohemians as fans.

Russell was the mainstay at Nick's for nearly a decade, though he was often fired and rehired by the owner. Concurrently, the ever-changing group recorded regularly, particularly with Milt Gabler's Commodore label. Largely promoted and arranged by Condon, Life magazine featured the Hackett band in a generous spread, complete with photos, in August, 1938. Pee Wee, thanks to his expressive, wrinkled face almost as much as his music, had become famous. As Warren W. Vache described in his *Jazz Gentry: Aristocrats of the Music World*, "Many people more famous than Pee Wee could walk down a New York street without anybody's taking the trouble to say hello. New Yorkers are used to seeing the faces of the stars in all fields of endeavor. But there was something about Pee Wee that made everybody, even those who only knew him by reputation, greet him as an old friend wherever he went." Russell was even doing promotional work for Conn clarinets. He took a short stint as a leader, then agreed to join a big band being formed by Hackett. This short-lived venture produced some recordings, but came to a halt for Russell in mid-1939, when he returned to Nick's to play in the band organized by Condon, but now fronted by tenor man Bud Freeman, soon to become known as the Summa Cum Laude band. They broke up in Chicago in June, 1940 as a live group, although they etched a Columbia session under the name Bud Freeman's Chicagoans a month later.

Experienced Highs and Lows

Russell managed to keep up a steady stream of work: recordings, private parties, club dates, radio broadcasts, and the growing number of events called jam sessions that were not spontaneous, but staged. In mid-1940 Russell joined cornetist McPartland in Chicago, became ill for a while, then returned to Nick's with cornetist Wild Bill Davison at the helm. In 1942, Condon--the effervescent leader of the Chicago school, guitarist, promoter, wise-crack artist, writer--began a series of concerts that eventually centered in the series at Town Hall. These concerts continued through 1960, with Russell often the star soloist. Russell expressed some sorrow about that time to Hilbert: "Those guys made a joke of me, a clown, and I let myself be treated that way because I was afraid. I didn't know where else to go, where to take refuge."

The same year was significant in another important way. In the spring, Russell met Mary Chaloff, three years his junior, and soon moved into her apartment. They were married at New York's City Hall on March 11, 1943. A bright, beautiful woman from an accomplished family, Mary brought a kind of stability to her husband that he had not known, even though she initially could not comprehend his music. As Hilbert related, "They had a special closeness that had developed out of their bantering relationship.... While Pee Wee had developed a dependency on Mary, she was anything but a doormat.... She was a strong-willed, independent woman when it was not considered "proper" to be one. She supported Pee Wee's fragile ego and attempted to give him the personal confidence he often lacked. She made a home for him."

The pattern had long been established: club dates, jam sessions, studio and live recordings, drinking, traveling, late hours, poor nutrition—always playing and being sought out by other players. Having survived Prohibition, the Great Depression, and World War II, Russell had yet a few more hurdles to surmount. Bebop reared its head, becoming a serious challenge to the Dixieland-style of music that the clarinetist had become so well associated with; Dixieland and Swing were under attack. During this period, a feud resulted in Russell's switching from his principal base of Nick's to the new night club, Eddie Condon's. Not the least of the new hurdles was his health. As Russell told Balliett, "For ten years I couldn't eat anything. All during the forties.... I lived on brandy milkshakes and scrambled-egg sandwiches. And on whiskey. The doctors couldn't find a thing.... It began to affect my mind...." Sometime in 1949, he jockeyed between the east coast and Chicago, a period which for him remained a blank, then to San Francisco where he was hospitalized for nine months with pancreatitis. With his weight at 73 pounds, he nearly died.

Thanks to the help of influential friends in the media, fellow musicians who played benefits, and fans who donated blood and money, Russell survived the charity ward of the hospital and was able to return to New York, still hospitalized. He was away from Mary for nearly three years; she reclaimed him in 1951. In 1952 Russell resumed an association with promoter/musician George Wein at his Boston Storyville club and formed a band that included the great cornetist Ruby Braff, who had become as inventive a musician as Russell. Wein originated the famous Newport Jazz Festivals in 1954, at which Russell played in a band fronted by Hackett. It was here that Russell first teamed with a progressive musician, as Stan Kenton and he jammed together. This began what eventually developed into an entirely different phase of Russell's career. As Wein told Hilbert, "[Russell] never met anybody else's terms. He just kept playing as well as he could play. He was listening to new things all the time and absorbing it all in his ear...."

Flirted with the Modernists

Through his relationship with Wein, Russell began to play in concerts and on record with a variety of musicians, including pianist Thelonious Monk, one of the founders of the bebop school, and the innovative, multitalented Gerry Mulligan. He and modern clarinetist Jimmy Giuffre performed a duet that became the talk of the jazz world. Many think this modernist, along with Kenny Davern and Bobby Gordon, most resembles Russell in his playing. In December, 1957 Russell played in what has become one of the treasured television performances in jazz, *The Sound of Jazz*, hosted by John Crosby. It featured many of the masters of the Swing era as well as more modern players. Not that Russell had turned completely modern: he continued through the mid- and late-1950s to play and record with such stalwarts as trumpeter Buck Clayton and trombonist Vic Dickenson. And Ruby Braff became one of his favorite partners because of his unclassifiable inventiveness.

This period also saw a transformation in Russell's personal life. Not that he quit drinking and became a buttoned-down icon, but Mary managed to bring a degree of moderation to his antics, and he was experiencing some of the fame and true regard that his long career deserved. Musicians of every stripe and critics recognized that in his unique way Russell was a true voice of jazz. As noted critic Stanley Dance wrote in

Metronome of a 1960 recording: "Taste is important to both Pee Wee and Buck Clayton, and basically this is therefore a good marriage. Pee Wee, with his sincere approach, tortured lyricism, and ear for harmonies that please and satisfy, seems to fall on he contemporary scene like manna on the desert.... He has long been appreciated in many quarters, but it required the current critical climate for his talents to bereverently labeled as Art with a capital." And tenor patriarch Coleman Hawkins added, "For thirty years, I've been listening to him play those funny notes. He used to think they were wrong, but they weren't. He's always been way out, but they didn't have a name for it then."

An established regular at the Newport Jazz Festivals, Russell in April, 1961 accompanied promoter Wein on a European tour to Essen, Berlin, Copenhagen, and Paris. Russell's reputation had preceded him and the reception buoyed his spirits. A dark note marred the tour, however. He and Mary both experienced some physical problems. Upon their return, Russell immediately stepped into a flurry of recording and television appearances, some of which had popular appeal. But because he was paired with some of his old mates and typecast into playing "Muskrat Ramble" and "When the Saints Go Marching In," for the zillionth time, Russell began to rebel. He began to select his gigs more carefully and laid plans to form a more modern quartet with trombonist Marshall Brown. It included bassist Russell George and drummer Ron Lundberg--pianoless like the Gerry Mulligan Quartet; they debuted in October, 1962 after a long period of rehearsal. With both live and recorded performances, critical and popular reception was mixed. He continued to travel on his own, closing 1963 by winning the Down Beat critics poll and beginning 1964 with preparations for a trip to Australia, New Zealand, and Japan with Eddie Condon's All-Stars.

Discovered a New Talent

That trip was especially gratifying for Russell as he was received enthusiastically everywhere. Upon his return, he again played in an increasing number of jazz festivals, frequently thrilling the audiences with his own composition, "Pee Wee's Blues." In September he again toured Europe with Wein and a band that included Braff and Bud Freeman. He then tacked on a solo visit to England, his first, in which he played with a variety of British bands. Following his somewhat acrimonious breakup with Marshall Brown and the quartet, Russell was finding renewed pleasure in playing some of the more standard repertoire, although he frequently sat in with modernists at the various festivals.

A surprising side of Russell emerged in 1965. At Mary's urging, he took up oil painting and brought to it the same degree of inventiveness and improvisation that informed his music. Bud Freeman acted as a kind of agent for Russell's paintings and told Hilbert, "He was so good that people around the world identified more with the idea that he was a famous painter than a clarinet player. So he sold something like 54 paintings for not less than seven hundred dollars a painting." With recognition on two fronts now his, Russell entered into a period of relative stability, undergirded by his loving, watchdog wife. He was accepting fewer jobs and spending more time at home with Mary and with his painting. He revisited Mexico on a tour arranged by Wein and played at the Montreal Expo 67. However, in May Mary was admitted to St. Vincent's Hospital suffering from a long-standing undiagnosed internal disorder. Pancreatic cancer was the final diagnosis; Mary died on June 7, 1967. Biographer Hilbert wrote: "Without Mary, Pee Wee's life—even his music—suddenly meant nothing to him. Just when he at last seemed happy and secure, fate made his worst fear a reality: the self-styled loner finally had to face his demons by himself."

Russell resorted to his familiar answeralcohol and general neglect of his health. Though he continued to play with some regularity, particularly in the Washington area, his music activity was diminishing. At the insistence of a friend, he entered Alexandria Hospital in February, 1969. Russell died on February 15 from chronic pancreatitis and cirrhosis of the liver. Many have tried to describe Russell's sound and his approach to music. In his *The Swing Era*, Gunther Schuller wrote, "...there is something inherently vocal about Russell's performance. It is as if clarinet and human voice—some remarkably extended voice, to be sure—are welded into one." And biographer Hilbert observed, "His was the pure flame. Hot, gritty, profane, real. No matter what physical or mental condition Russell was in, night after night he spun wondrous improvisations. No matter how disjointed his life, how scrambled his mind, how incomprehensible his speech, his music remained logical and authoritative, elegant and graceful, haughty and proud."

Selected discography

Portrait of Pee Wee, Esoteric, 1958.
Jazz Reunion (with Coleman Hawkins and Bob Brookmeyer), Candid, 1961.
Ask Me Now!, Impulse!, 1965.
Eddie Condon in Japan, Chiaroscuro.
Giants of Jazz: Pee Wee Russell, Time-Life.

Sources

Books

Balliett, Whitney, *American Musicians: 56 Portraits in Jazz,* Oxford University Press, 1986.

Erlewine, Michael, et al, editors, *All Music Guide to Jazz,* Miller Freeman Books, 1996.

Hilbert, Robert, *Pee Wee Russell: The Life of a Jazzman,* Oxford University Press, 1993.

Holtje, Steve and Lee, and Nancy Ann, editors, MusicHound Jazz: *The Essential Album Guide,* Visible Ink Press, 1998.

Vache, Warren W., *Jazz Gentry: Aristocrats of the Music World,* The Scarecrow Press, 1999.

Periodicals

Coda, March 1969.

Down Beat, April 3, 1969.

New York Times, February 16, 1969.

—*Robert Dupuis*

Camille Saint-Saëns

Composer, pianist

Corbis View. Reproduced by permission.

A piano prodigy in his youth but an estimable personage in French music as an adult, Camille Saint-Saëns is one of the few great musical names associated with a country better known for its contribution to the visual arts. Saint-Saëns was renowned for his breathtaking skill as a pianist—he was compared to Mozart as a child and Beethoven later—but his compositions for the symphony, ballet, and concerto ensemble are a legacy of his formidable intelligence and talent. They are considered quintessentially French pieces: clear, ordered, and intellectually profound.

Saint-Saëns was born in Paris in 1835 at home at 3 rue de Jardinet in the Latin Quarter. His father was a clerk at the Ministry of the Interior, but died of consumption before Camille was a year old. Their unusual family name came from their hometown, which had been known once in Latin as Sanctus Sidonius. The death of his father was not the only setback Saint-Saëns suffered at an early age—he was a sickly child, and tuberculosis threatened him as well. He lived with his mother and her aunt, Charlotte Masson, who began teaching him piano at the age of two. A precocious child, he wrote his first work for the instrument at the age of three.

Madame Clemence Saint-Saëns, a devoted mother and great influence upon her son well into his adulthood, soon recognized the necessity for serious lessons, and after just a few years of formal training Camille debuted in his first formal performance. The event took place in 1846 at Paris's Salle Pleyel. At the close of the performance, the ten-year-old offered to play any of Mozart's piano concertos by memory. In addition to such startling musical skill and memory, Saint-Saëns proved to be gifted academically. As a teen he excelled in Latin and mathematics at school and loved the intellectual challenges of science and philosophy, as well. He was thirteen when he entered the prestigious Paris Conservatory for further musical training, where he studied the organ and began classes in composition. His *Ode a Sainte-Cecile,* a homage to the patron saint of music, won him his first competition award in 1852 from a Paris musical society.

Saint-Saëns wrote his first symphony at the age of 18, and it was presented anonymously in a Paris performance two years later. Such accomplishments brought an array of prominent admirers to Saint-Saëns' recitals, and both Gioacchino Rossini and Louis-Hector Berlioz were counted among his early supporters. In 1853, after finishing his studies at the Conservatory, Saint-Saëns was hired as a church organist at St. Severin in Paris, but in 1857, at the age of just twenty-two, he became organist at the Church of the Madeleine. This was Paris's most fabled church of the modern era, and it was an illustrious appointment for Saint-Saëns that added much

For the Record . . .

Born Charles Camille Saint-Saëns, October 9, 1835, in Paris, France, (died December 16, 1921 in Algiers, Algeria); son of Jacques Joseph Victor (a government clerk) and Clemence Franchise Collin Saint-Saëns; married Marie Laure Emile Truffot, 1875 (separated, 1881); two children died in infancy. *Education:* Studied at the Paris Conservatory, 1848-52.

Made formal debut at Salle Pleyel, Paris, 1846; wrote first symphony at the age of 18 and performed in public two years later; served as church organist, 1853-57; organist at the Madeleine, 1857-76; Ecole Niedermeyer, teacher, 1861-65; co-founder of Societe Nationale de Musique, 1871; wrote first opera, *La princesse jaune,* 1872.

Awards: Legion d'honneur, France, 1868; received honorary doctorate from Cambridge University, 1893; made commander of the Victorian Order of the British Empire, 1901.

to his fame. It was at the Eglise Sainte-Marie-Madeleine, as it was known then, that Saint-Saëns met the great Hungarian composer and pianist Franz Liszt, who happened by the church one day and heard Saint-Saëns improvising. Liszt, who influenced a generation of classical pianists, called the young Frenchman the greatest organist in the world.

Impressed Wagner

Early on in his career Saint-Saëns was considered part of a new and modern vanguard of musicians and composers, though later his views would grow considerably orthodox. As a young man, he was a disciple of Richard Wagner, whose early works were met with critical derision. Saint-Saëns defended both *Tannhaueser* and *Lohengrin* as important masterpieces, and a century later they remain two of Wagner's most famous and revered operas. In return, Wagner recognized Saint-Saëns as a gifted keyboardist prodigy. Once Saint-Saëns was visiting Wagner with a mutual friend, and the latter two were speaking German, a language in which Saint-Saëns was not conversationally fluent. Bored, he picked up a manuscript of Wagner's—the unfinished score for *Siegfried*—and began playing it *prima vista,* "on first sight." Wagner was astounded.

In Paris, Saint-Saëns was a celebrity, known as a talented composer and gifted performer. He also began to win acclaim from abroad, and was invited to play before for Queen Victoria. From 1861 to 1865 he taught at the Ecole Niedermeyer, and influenced several rising young church organists and composers, including Gabriel Faure. He would effect even more decisive influence upon French music as a founder—with Romain Bussine—of the Societe Nationale de Musique in 1871. At the time, German music and German composers dominated much of the classical world, and the Societe's motto, *Ars Gallica,* reflected its mission to encourage young French composers and promote their works to the public. The Societe premiered early works of Claude Debussy and Maurice Ravel, among many others.

Saint-Saëns was of course a prolific composer himself. His 1863 *Introduction and Rondo capriccioso in A Minor* (Op.28) would become a standard performance piece for violinists. *Piano Concerto No. 2 in G Minor* was written in just 17 days in 1868, but is nevertheless considered by scholars as exemplary of his talents in piano composition. Like Liszt, Saint-Saëns also began writing symphonic poems. *Le Rouet d'Omphale* was the first of these, published in 1872, and *Danse macabre,* dating from 1874 is perhaps the most well known of his symphonic poems. The eerie music is based on poem by Henri Cazalis that finds the specter of death playing a violin for skeletal figures on a dark winter night.

A Disastrous Marriage

Saint-Saëns lived with his mother well into his twenties, and was famous in Paris for his short stature, odd walk, and lisp, all of which were caricatured in the press. In 1875, nearing forty, he entered into a disastrous marriage with Marie Laure Emile Truffot—a young woman nearly half his age—with whom he had two sons. Tragically both sons died within six weeks of each other—one from an illness and the other after falling out of a window. For the latter death Saint-Saëns blamed his wife, and when they went on vacation together in 1881 he simply disappeared one day. A separation order was enacted, but they never divorced.

During the 1870s Saint-Saëns gained increasing recognition as a composer. His opera *Samson et Delilah* is the only one of his dozen operas to remain in the performing repertoire a century later. Rather unusual when it debuted in Weimar in 1877 for its biblical themes, it would not be performed in France for another 15 years. Two works that Saint-Saëns wrote in 1886 would define his style. The first, commissioned by the London Royal Philharmonic Society, was his *Symphony No. 3 with Organ in C Minor*

(Op. 78). Written for a large orchestra—It requires three flutes, three trumpets, three kettledrums, as well as organ and piano—Is considered an outstanding example of Saint-Saëns' style and remains a popular favorite with classical audiences. Part of its finale was even used in the score of the 1995 film *Babe.*

Another work from 1886, *Le carnaval des animaux,* was written while on holiday, and Saint-Saëns did not wish that any part of this lighthearted work be associated with his name, for he considered it frivolous. The only part he allowed was a cello piece called "The Swan." Ironically, it would become one of the most beloved works in his repertoire when it debuted in its entirety a year following his death.

Became Increasingly Eccentric

When Madame Clemence Saint-Saëns died in 1888, her son plummeted into a deep depression, and even considered suicide. He began to write less and travel more, taking with him his beloved dogs and a dedicated servant. His visited many exotic locales, and was especially fascinated by life and customs in North Africa and Egypt. His work *Africa,* dating from 1891, reflects this passion, while *Fifth Piano Concerto* (1896) is sometimes referred to as the "Egyptian." During a visit to South America, Saint-Saëns was commissioned to write a national anthem for Uruguay. He also traveled to Russia, and became friends with Peter Tchaikovsky. On a visit to America in 1915, Saint-Saëns was hailed as greatest living French composer. The British sovereign Edward VII made him a commander of the Victorian Order in appreciation of the 1901 coronation march that Saint-Saëns penned.

Saint-Saëns was also the first established composer to score a film, *L'assassinat du Duc de Guise,* dating from 1908. Despite his visionary talents and legendary energies, he grew increasingly eccentric and cranky in his old age, and was sometimes derided in the press for his strong opinions. He conducted a campaign against the work of Debussy at one point, and called for a suppression of all German music during World War II. But he also wrote prolifically on a variety of non-musical topics, and published literary criticism and essays on art antiquities. He died in Algeria in 1921.

Selected discography

Symphonies 1-5 /Jean Martinon, ORTF, EMI Classics, 1989.
Concertos /Ma, Licad, Lin, Maazel, et al, Sony, 1991.
Organ Symphony, Bacchanale, etc./Gunzenhauser, Naxos International, 1992.
Samson et Dalila /Barenboim, Domingo, Deutsche Grammophon, 1992.
Chamber Works /The Banff Camerata, Summit, 1994.
Saint-Saëns Vol. 2 /Geoffrey Simon, London Philharmonic, Cala, 1994.
Greatest Hits: Saint-Saëns, Sony, 1995.
Le Carneval des Animaux, Symphony No. 3, Point Classics (Eclipse), 1996.
Saint-Saëns: Symphony No. 3, Danse macabre, etc./Maazel, Sony, 1996.
The Best of Saint-Saëns, Naxos International, 1997.
Cello Concertos, etc./Kliegel, Monnard, et al., Naxos International, 1997.
Africa, Symphony No. 2, Symphony in F Major, Bis, 1997.

Sources

Goulding, Phil G., *Classical Music: The 50 Greatest Composers and their 1,000 Greatest Works,* Fawcett Columbine, 1992.
Nicholas, Jeremy, *The Classic FM Guide to Classical Music,* Pavilion, 1997.
Sadie, Stanley, editor, *The New Grove Dictionary of Music and Musicians,* Macmillan, 1980.
Soleil, Jean-Jacques, and Guy Lelong, *Musical Masterpieces,* Chambers, 1991.

—Carol Brennan

Erik Satie

Composer

Only decades after his 1925 death was French composer Erik Satie hailed as a genius of contemporary classical music. His work was extremely simple in structure, yet innovative and marked by a characteristic wit. His reliance on unusual harmonic configurations was a reaction against the heavy, symbol-rich music of his era, a time when the works of Romantic European composers like Richard Wagner were still very much in vogue. Satie left a relatively scarce body of work behind, most of it written for the piano. But his groundbreaking use of bitonal or polytonal notes would become a hallmark of twentieth-century modernist music.

Satie was born Erik Alfred Leslie Satie in 1866 in Honfleur, near Le Havre, France. Both his father and his uncle—known as "Uncle Seabird," who instilled in him a love a theater and a disdain for the conventional—were ship brokers. Satie's mother Jane was Scottish and wrote her own pieces for the piano. She died when he was just six.

Satie was left with his grandparents in Honfleur by his widowed father. They had Satie re-baptized in the Roman Catholic faith. His musical ability was already in evidence, and he began lessons with the local organist, a man named Vinot, who introduced him to Gregorian plainsongs, the serenely monophonic religious chants dating back to music of the 13th century. Satie later showed a marked preference for such constructions in his own compositions, and was deeply interested in medieval music for much of his early career.

In 1878, he moved to Paris with his father, who remarried the following year. Satie disliked his stepmother, another musically gifted individual named Eugenie Barnetsche, who favored the Romantic compositions of Felix Mendelssohn, Frederic Chopin and other popular composers of the time. It was likely her influence, however, that led Satie to take up study at the rigorous, but conservative Paris Conservatoire. He was a mediocre student who made up his own piano exercises and was eventually dismissed. The first two pieces Satie wrote for the piano, *Valse-Ballet* and *Fantaisie-Valse,* were published in 1885. Instead of subtitling them in the usual style using "Opus 1" to indicate the first entry in his catalog, Satie demonstrated his wry sense of humor and used "Op. 62."

Satie was conscripted into the military in 1886, but fell ill with bronchitis and was discharged. During his recuperation he read a great deal by Josephin Peladan, the leader of a mystical artistic society called Rose et Croix, also known as the Rosicrucians. In 1890 he met Peladan, and became the society's unofficial composer. The work lasted until around 1895. He grew increasingly immersed in medieval music and Gothic art during this period, and a set of four piano pieces, *Ogives* (whose name refers to the rib vaults of Gothic architecture) was written during this era and published in 1886. Around this same time Satie befriended a Spanish symbolist poet known as Contamine de Latour, who claimed a kinship with Napoleon as well as a right to the French throne. Satie began setting some of Contamine's mediocre verse to music and his compositions *Elégie, Les anges, Les fleurs, Sylvie* and *Chanson* date from this time.

With S*arabandes* in 1887, "Satie now turned his back on the Middle Ages and the organum-like, petrified movement of *Ogives* and instead wrote music with a kind of solemn dance character, constantly shifting between immobility and movement, between melodic expressivity and vibrant chords," wrote Olof Höjer in the liner notes for a 1996 CD of Satie's piano works. "The harmonic language is very advanced, presenting sequences of unprepared, dissonant and unresolved chords." A saraband was a stately baroque dance with origins in Asian female fertility dance and was considered sexually suggestive.

Gained Renown

Satie sometimes paid for the publication of his music out of his own pocket. Ironically, his father and stepmother had begun a music publishing firm, and his next work,

Gymnopedies in 1888, was included in the firm's *La musiques des familles* catalog. These three piano pieces took their name from a celebratory rite thought to have been performed by naked youths in ancient Greece, The subject of the pieces earned Satie some notoriety in bohemian Paris.

For *Gnossiennes,* three more piano pieces, Satie was inspired by the excavations on Crete of a great palace at Knossos being carried out at the time. The title may have been also been a pun that referred to the Greek term *gnosis,* or "knowledge." Gnosticism was an integral part of Rosicrucianism, and as Höjer wrote, "In the Gnossiennes there is no clear-cut beginning, nor any indisputably logical ending. In theory, the music could begin in any of a series of places, continue for any amount of time and end in many different places. It has been said that this music seems to spiral around itself." This latter quality may have inspired Satie to gradually abandon the use of bar lines in his compositions.

By all accounts Satie lived an eccentric life. Until 1898 he had quarters on the Rue Cortot in Montmartre, a place where he was a familiar neighborhood figure. He wrote his works in Montmartre cafes, and was always seen with bowler hat and umbrella. Reportedly he never used soap, but rather a pumice stone, and wore only gray velvet suits. At one point after he inherited some money, Satie founded his own church. He never went anywhere except on foot, even after he moved to a working-class neighborhood in the southern section of Paris called Arcueil. He even walked home in the middle of the night from the piano-playing jobs he took at cafes and music halls like Chat noir, Auberge du clou, Le lapin agile. It was at the Auberge de clou he met Suzanne Valadon, a former trapeze artist, artist's model, and painter. Their romance lasted a good part of 1896, but after its dissolution Satie remained a bachelor.

Around 1891 Satie met Claude Debussy, a man who would eclipse him as one of the greatest French composers, and helped sway Debussy toward a fresher style. Darius Milhaud, another renowned French composer, also befriended Satie and drew great inspiration from his radical ideas about tone and form.

Vexations

Satie became famous for his brief piano piece he titled *Vexations,* published in 1893. "To play this motif 840 times in succession, it would be advisable to prepare oneself beforehand, in the deepest silence, by serious immobilities," he wrote at the top of the score. Later musicians interpreted this statement to mean that the piece should be played, literally, 840 times, an arduous challenge that was only undertaken first in September of 1963 by the modernist composer John Cage. It took a relay team of ten pianists over 18 hours to perform.

Satie's move to Arcueil had marked the onset of a lonely, impoverished time for him, but he revived when he enrolled at well-regarded Schola Cantorum in 1905. After three years of study he earned diploma marked "tres bien." He began writing again after a few years' hiatus, and gave his works whimsical titles like *Desiccated Embryos, Flabby Preludes for a Dog,* and *Three Pieces in the Shape of a Pear.* The last name was the result of criticism that Satie's music had "no form." With such compositions Satie included similarly whimsical instructions: not *forte* or "loud," but "light as an egg" or "with astonishment."

Satie also wrote and sketched. His *Memoirs of an Amnesiac,* culled from his journals, was published in 1953. In satirical verse he discussed such topics as the rigor's of a composer's life, his bizarre diet of only white foods, and the intelligence of animals. "That animals have intelligence cannot be denied," Satie wrote. "But what is Man doing to improve the mental condition of his resigned fellow-creatures?.... Homing pigeons have absolutely no preparation in geography to help them in their job; fish are excluded from the study of oceanography; cattle, sheep and calves know nothing of the rational organization of a modern slaughter-house, and are ignorant of the nutritive role they play in the society Man has made for himself."

Found Favor with New Generation

Satie began to gain recognition from other composers and artists in the years prior to World War I. French composer Maurice Ravel performed his *Sarabandes* at a concert of the Societe Musicale Independante in 1911, and his earlier works were finally published and began to earn him a modest income. The Surrealist poet and filmmaker Jean Cocteau became a great fan. With Cocteau and Pablo Picasso, Satie wrote *Parade,* a ballet performed by Serge Diaghilev's Ballet Russes in May of 1917. Its realistic setting and anti-war sentiment were met with scandalized reviews, and Satie sent a postcard to one critic that was deemed imprudent, for which he was sentenced to eight days in prison. Only the good connections of a friend got him off. But the publicity brought a new generation of composers and musicians near to Satie, and a group of young French composers known as Les Six proclaimed themselves his heirs, and strove to write music that was as austere as Satie's.

Satie began working on the symphonic drama *Socrate* around 1917, a composition he hoped would be "white and pure like antiquity," according to *The New Grove Dictionary of Music and Musicians.* "The result was a creation in which his restricted means came into perfect focus and balance." It was not performed publicly until 1920. Two festivals of Satie's works were held that same year.

Work Foreshadowed Movie Soundtracks

As he entered his sixties, Satie grew increasingly eccentric. One of his last works was *Musique d'ameublement,* or "Furnishing Music." The painter Henri Matisse had coined the term to describe music that would make up the background of another artistic event, and therefore was to be regarded as utterly unimportant. Satie wrote some pieces that premiered at an art opening in March of 1920, and reportedly became unnerved that patrons paid attention to the music. Later such music would become commonplace in contemporary films. He also worked with painter Francis Picabia and filmmaker Rene Clair on a joint ballet/film project called *Relache* ("Theater closed"), which closed after one night.

A heavy drinker for much of his life, Satie suffered health problems and friends in Paris began looking after him. He died on the first day of July in Paris in 1925 of sclerosis of the liver. No one had seen his Arceuil apartment since he had moved there in 1898. After his death his friend Milhaud found that it contained nothing more than a bed, chair, table, and piano whose pedals had to be pulled by string.

Only in the mid-twentieth century, several decades after his death, did Satie's works begin to attract serious scrutiny. *Vexations* was periodically resurrected, and a solo pianist once tried to play it in its entirety, but stopped after fifteen hours, the result of recurring hallucinations. On its centenary in honor of Satie's birth, it was again performed in New York City by a team of pianists. Alex Ross reviewed the performance for the *New York Times* and wrote that "the imposed repetition has the virtue of focusing attention on the revolutionary nature of this music, its defiance of harmonic order.... Sketchy, diminished chords alternate in hypnotic succession, with brief melodic shapes drifting through the upper lines and a chaconnelike theme churning in the bass."

Selected discography

3 Gymnopedies & Other Piano Works, PGD/London Classics, 1987.
Music of Erik Satie, Collins Classics, 1991.
Erik Satie, WEA/Atlantic/Erato, 1993.
Satie Favorites, Denon, 1993.
Erik Satie: The Complete Piano Music/Olof Höjer, Vols. 1-4, Prophone Records, 1996-98.
Satie: Gnossiennes; Gymnopedies; Ogives; Petite Ouverture a Danser; Sarabandes, Philips, 1996.
After the Rain: The Soft Sounds of Erik Satie, PGD/London Classics, 1996,
Satie on Accordion, Winter & Winter, 1998.
Erik Satie: Encore!, Bis, 1998.
Satie: Gnossiennes/Gymnopedies, Glossa, 1998.

Sources

Books

Sadie, Stanley, ed., *The New Grove Dictionary of Music and Musicians,* Macmillan, 1980.

Periodicals

New York Times, May 20, 1993.
Stereo Review, December 1996.

Other

"Le Gymnopédiste," by Olof Höjer, for the notes to *Erik Satie: The Complete Piano Music,* Vol. 1, Prophone Records, 1996.

—*Carol Brennan*

Peggy Seeger

Folk singer

Peggy Seeger is considered by many to be *the* female folksinger, responsible for the continuous upswing of folk music popularity. It is a fitting title, considering Peggy was living and breathing folk music since before she was born. Brought into musical history by Roberta Flack in the late 1970s, "First Time Ever I Saw Your Face," one of the most stirring love ballads was penned in Seeger's honor, by the late Scottish songwriter/folk singer, Ewan MacColl.

Born into a family already well immersed in the folk culture, Seeger and her siblings were raised with music surrounding them. Her mother and father, Charles and Ruth Seeger, were accomplished musicians and teachers, and they brought their business home with them, filling their homes in New York and Maryland with music and musicians and from cultures around the world. Their business was cataloging folk music for the Archive of American Folk Songs of the Library of Congress. According to Seeger, "They had me analyzing and transcribing tunes for an anthology at age eleven." Her parents often entertained the musicians they were cataloging, and Seeger was right along side, listening and learning. "We had always sung as a family, but when Mike and I learned folk banjo and guitar, the singsongs became weekly events," she reminisced on her website. According to Kristin Baggelaar in *Folk Music—More than a Song*, "it was through listening to other musicians and field recordings of singers and instrumentalists from all over the United States that she absorbed the folk idiom and developed her singing and playing techniques."

Their parents' profession also influenced the rest of her siblings. Her brother Pete Seeger was a well-known political-protest folk musician who, while coming of age during the changing decades of the 1930s and 1940s, toured with Woody Guthrie. Her brother Mike also performed and wrote music. Seeger recorded the album *Three Sisters*, with her sisters, Penny and Barbara.

Seeger was gifted with the ability to learn musical instruments amazingly fast. Learning first on the piano at the age of seven and then moving on to other instruments, including the guitar, five-sting harp, string banjo, autoharp, Appalachian dulcimer and the English concertina. Her formal musical education took place at the prestigious Radcliffe College in Cambridge, Massachusetts, where she began using her voice as an instrument. She carried on her parents' work by singing traditional songs.

After college, Seeger spent a lot of time touring the world, including living in Holland. She learned Russian and began adventuring to eastern countries like the former Soviet Union, China, and Poland. She also ventured through Europe and parts of Africa. In the mid 1950s Seeger was asked to perform in a London television production of *Dark of the Moon*. After becoming a British subject, she met the person who would become her biggest influence—and her future husband—Ewan MacColl. MacColl saw Seeger while rehearsing with a band called the Ramblers, and later penned his signature tune "First Time Ever I Saw Your Face."

After marrying in 1958, the couple went on to write, compose, sing, play and tour together for almost 30 years until MacColl's death. Seeger is often quoted giving thanks to her husband who "helped me to crystallize a singing style and, most important, showed me who 'the folk' really are." Shortly after marrying MacColl, Seeger began writing her own folksongs. "Songwriting," quotes her website, "helps me to live in the present, 'at the same time as myself,' as Ewan MacColl used to say. It is my way of trying to let tomorrow's people know part of what it was like to be alive today."

Considered to be one of North America's finest singers of traditional songs, Seeger is credited with reviving the British folk music scene. Seeger has more than 100 recordings bearing her name, and over a three dozen solo albums, for numerous British and American labels. Her most recognized folksong "If I was an Engineer," was recorded in 1970 for the British Festival of Fools, as an ode to feminism. Seeger and MacColl, as the London

For the Record . . .

Born Margaret Seeger, June 17, 1935 New York; daughter of Charles and Ruth Singer; sister of Pete Seeger; married folk singer, songwriter Ewan MacColl, 1958. *Education:* Ratcliffe College.

Recorded dozens of albums, as a solo artist and with various performers including MacColl, Irish songwriter Irene Scott, and various siblings; released *American Folk Songs for Children*, Smithsonian/Folkways Records, 1957; *Almost Commercially Viable*, Golden Egg, 1992; *An Odd Collection*, Rounder Records, 1996; returned to the United States in the 1990s.

Addresses: *Record company*—Camp St. 1, Cambridge, MA 02140; (617) 354-0700; *Email*—info@rounder.com

Critics Group, were the forces behind the annual festival. "If I Was An Engineer" was on *At the Present Moment*, released by Rounder Records in 1973.

Seeger traveled upon the more political and social side of folk music, staying with the traditions of Leadbelly, the Guthries and her own brother Pete. Many of her songs dealt with politically charged issues. "Seeger's distinctly clear and very pretty voice especially lends to the optimism, even when singing on darker subjects such as wife abuse, abortion and death," wrote Chris Speek for the *Chapel Hill News*.

After her husband's death from heart problems in 1989, Seeger decided to go on the road and toured most of Australia and the United States. She also began collaborating with a close friend, Irish singer Irene Scott. Together, performing under the name No Spring Chickens, the duo released *Almost Commercially Viable* for Golden Egg in 1992. The album was named after a comment a record company professional made. Album title notwithstanding, according to Andy Malkin in *Stirrings*, in 1998, "both Peggy and Irene's voices are really fresh, despite their combined ages of over a century."

In 1994, Seeger returned to the United States. She continued to record albums, and began compiling material for her as yet unpublished songbooks. In 1996, Seeger released *An Odd Collection* for Rounder. "Seeger rather resembles Simon and Garfunkel sans harmonies, or a more historically and politically conscious Peter, Paul and Mary," wrote Speek. Her feminist views were

easily displayed on the album with subjects ranging from housewife duties to nuclear pollution to unionism. It was on this album that Seeger finally got the chance to pay tribute to her husband—"On This Very Day" recalls the day she and MacColl met.

Seeger's 1998 release, *Period Pieces*, is a collection of her songs from the 1960s through the 1980s. It is a wonderful collection of the themes she had sung about throughout the decades. The difference, wrote Chris Morris for *Billboard* in 1998, lies in her song's arrangements. "The majority (of songs on the album) are characterized by a buoyancy and humor not usually associated with political song." Seeger also was able to pay tribute to her mother with her 1998 release *American Folk Songs For Children*. Released a number of times since she first recorded it in 1950s, the album is a dedication to her mother. Her mother originally collected all the materials on the album.

Along with recording albums of folk anthems, Seeger has also published various print collections including *The Peggy Seeger Songbook, Warts and All,* and *The Essential Ewan MacColl Songbook*. In her own songbook, Seeger included nearly 150 songs and one poem, arranged in chronological order. As Faith Petric wrote in *The Folknik* in 1998, "Let's just say she is the consummate song writer, absolutely one of the very, very best. If it's in our lives, Peggy has written a song about it." As Seeger told *Billboard*, "The trick is to make music that men and women can respect but which is presented in a feminine way... I do not want to intimidate or to make men think I'm hostile. It's a tricky business."

Selected discography

American Folk Songs For Children, Smithsonian/Folkways Records, 1957.
Peggy Alone, Argo Records, 1967.
At the Present Moment, Rounder Records, 1973.
The Angry Muse, Argo Records, 1968.
Almost Commercially Viable, Golden Egg, 1992.
Folkways Years, 1955-92: Songs of Love and Politics, Smithsonian/Folkways 1992.
An Odd Collection, Rounder 1996.

Sources

Books

All Music Guide.
Baggelaar, Kristin, *Folk Music—More Than A Song*, Thomas Crowell Co., NY, 1976.

Penguin Encyclopedia of Popular Music, 1989.
Strambler, Irwin and Landon, Grellun, *The Encyclopedia of Folk, Country and Western Music*, St. Martins Press, 1969.
The Guinness Encyclopedia of Popular Music, 1992.

Periodicals

Billboard, October 3, 1998.
Chapel Hill News, April 3, 1998.

Online

www.pegseeger.com.
www.allmusic.com

—*Gretchen Van Monette*

Bruce Springsteen

Singer, songwriter

AP/Wide World Photo. Reproduced by permission.

Rock and Roll Hall of Fame inductee and rock legend Bruce Springsteen framed the working man's concerns with a combination of muscular, hard-driving rock and a poet's sensitive flair for phrasing. *Time* and *Newsweek* magazines ran simultaneous, competing cover stories on him in 1975, and like Elvis Presley before him in the 1950s, Springsteen transcended music to embody rock and roll in the American culture of the 1980s. His 1984 release, the multi-platinum *Born in the U.S.A,* was a rock landmark which featured on the cover the back of a man standing before a U.S. flag wearing a white T-shirt and blue jeans, with a red bandanna tucked into his back pocket. This Springsteen album cover was a cultural image as familiar to 1980s America as then-president Ronald Reagan. It was one of the biggest selling records in history, and launched seven top ten singles.

Springsteen won an Oscar and four Grammy Awards for his haunting ballad "Streets of Philadelphia," which was penned for the film *Philadelphia* in 1993, and in 1995 he won a Grammy Award for Best Contemporary Folk Album for *The Ghost of Tom Joad.* He was inducted into the Rock and Roll Hall of Fame on March 15, 1999. A reviewer for *Billboard* described Springsteen as, " a veteran who has successfully juggled the roles of rock star, pop icon, folk hero, social activist, and everyman. As devoted as his fans are to him, the "Boss" is just as committed to them, keeping their wishes uppermost in mind at every step in his illustrious career."

Springsteen was born in Freehold, NJ, in 1949; his mother, Adele, worked as a secretary and his father, Douglas, took odd jobs and was noted for being a superb pool player. Although Springsteen is a Dutch name, he was also Italian, and his ancestors lived in the Neapolitan region of Italy. Both of his parents wanted him to pursue a career route other than music, and his father was particularly strident about the topic. As a result, Springsteen and his father often experienced a clash of wills. Some of Springsteen's material would later reflect their battles: the fury evident in "Adam Raised A Cain" from *Darkness on the Edge of Town,* the wistful parting in "Independence Day" from *The River,* and the touching reconciliation in "Walk Like A Man" from *Tunnel of Love.* Springsteen told *Billboard*'s Melinda Newman about the time his mother bought an electric guitar for him, "Standing outside that music store, the guitar was $60. That was an enormous, enormous amount of money at the time.... So (buying) the guitar was a great, a a very meaningful gesture of faith at that time from her." Springsteen never wavered from his goal to be a musician and joined his first rock band at the age of 16 in 1965. The band was called The Castiles. Springsteen's parents relocated to California when he was 15, but he chose to remain behind in

For the Record . . .

Born 1949 in Freehold, NJ; mother, Adele, (a secretary); father, Douglas, (took odd jobs and was noted for being a superb pool player); married Julianne Phillips in 1987; married Patti Scialfi in 1991; three children with Scialfi: Evan, Jessica, Sam. *Education:* briefly attended classes at Ocean County Community College.

Joined his first rock band, The Castiles, 1965; began playing in different bands in the seaside town of Asbury Park, NJ, and in New York City; led a variety of groups in the late 1960s and early 1970s, including Steel Mill, The Rogues, Dr. Zoom and the Sonic Boom, and the Bruce Springsteen Band; released *Greetings From Asbury Park, NJ,* 1973; released *The Wild, the Innocent, and the E Street Shuffle,* 1973; released *Born to Run,* 1975; featured simultaneously on the covers of both *Newsweek* and *Time,* 1975; released *Darkness on the Edge of Town* in 1978; released *The River,* 1980; *The River* reached number one on *Billboard* album chart; released *Nebraska,* 1982; *Nebraska* reached number three on the *Billboard* album chart; released the multi-platinum *Born in the U.S.A.,* 1984; it was one of the biggest-selling releases in rock history, featuring seven top ten singles, including "Dancing in the Dark," which peaked at number two on the *Billboard* singles chart; released 3-CD set *Bruce Springsteen and the E Street Band: Live 1975-1985,* the set entered the *Billboard* charts at number one, 1986; released *Tunnel of Love,* 1987; simultaneously released *Human Touch* and *Lucky Town,* 1992, both recorded without the E Street Band, they entered the charts at number two and number three; recorded the theme song "Streets of Philadelphia" for the film *Philadelphia,* 1993; released *Greatest Hits* in 1995; released *The Ghost of Tom Joad,* 1995; followed the album's release with his first solo acoustic tour; 4-CD box set titled *Tracks* released in 1998.

Awards: Oscar and four Grammy Awards for the title theme song, "Streets of Philadelphia," for the film *Philadelphia,* 1993; Grammy Award for Best Contemporary Folk Album for *The Ghost of Tom Joad,* 1995; inducted into the Rock and Roll Hall of Fame, March 15, 1999.

Addresses: *Record company*—Columbia Records, 2100 Colorado Avenue, Santa Monica, CA 90404 (310) 449-2100; 51 W. 52nd Street, New York, NY 10019 (212) 833-4321.

New Jersey. He briefly took classes at Ocean County Community College, and had some poems published in the school's literary magazine, but his heart was in performing and playing music. He began playing in Asbury Park, New Jersey, and in New York City and led a variety of groups in the late 1960s and early 1970s, including Steel Mill, The Rogues, Dr. Zoom and the Sonic Boom, and the Bruce Springsteen Band—which is how he met many of the musicians who would later comprise his E Street Band.

In 1972 at the age of 23, Springsteen signed a management deal with a fledgling songwriter/producer named Mike Appel and his partner Jim Cretecos. The contract was signed outside in a parking lot at night, and although it helped Springsteen in the short run and started his career, it also hindered him severely in the long run. Appel, a man perceived by others to be a contentious and abrasive manager, was nevertheless whole-heartedly devoted to Springsteen's career and fought to have Springsteen's material played over the radio and to provide Springsteen with the largest concert audiences possible. Apple set up an audition for Springsteen with legendary Columbia Records Artist and Repretoire (A&R) executive John Hammond, the man who signed Bob Dylan. Hammond was so uncharacteristically impressed with Springsteen and his material that he signed him on to the label. Springsteen told Newman, "I just stood up and sang the best songs I had. I was incredibly excited. I felt very confident about what I was doing and being there, and nervous at the same time."

Springsteen released *Greetings From Asbury Park, NJ,* in 1973. Sales and airplay were minimal, and reasons range from DJs feeling resistant to or put off by his marketing moniker, "the New Dylan," to in-fighting and stubborn corporate politics at his record label. A few critics, however, noted and publicized Springsteen's early talent. When *The Wild, the Innocent, and the E Street Shuffle* was released later in 1973, the critics raved even more, and the DJs played the second release even less. In the meantime, Springsteen's concerts were growing more and more popular, and he was learning how to connect with and energize his audiences.

After seeing a show at Cambridge's Harvard Square Theatre, music critic Jon Landau penned the memorable line, "I saw rock and roll future and its name is Bruce Springsteen" in *The Real Paper.* Landau's review was placed in a Boston concert venue/bar's window, and after Landau stumbled upon Springsteen out in the cold one day, shivering as he read the review, the two became friends. Springsteen wanted Landau to co-produce *Born to Run* in 1975, which displeased and displaced Appel. *Born to Run* was an immensely popular record and, as a result of its popularity, Springsteen was featured simultaneously on the covers of both *Newsweek* and *Time* in 1975. *Born to Run* featured a Phil-Spector-like "wall of sound" production, combined with his earlier brand of rich, urbane lyricism. Springsteen followed the album's release with tours in the United States, the United Kingdom, and Sweden. Springsteen also sued to break his contract with Appel because he wanted to regain control of his finances and his songs. Appel countersued to keep Springsteen from recording with Landau, and the lawsuits kept Springsteen away from the studios for two years. Springsteen won his case, Landau became his manager and producer, and Springsteen was in control of his catalogue and career.

Springsteen released *Darkness on the Edge of Town* in 1978, followed by *The River* in 1980, and *Nebraska* in 1982. The hit single "Hungry Heart" was included on *The River,* and it became his first album to reach *Billboard*'s number one spot. Springsteen's all-acoustic *Nebraska,* however, featured the stories that Springsteen held dear in his heart: bleak, haunting, wistful tales of those alienated from the American dream. He told Newman, "I enjoyed making *Nebraska* so much, I pursued it before I went back to making *Born in the U.S.A.*" *Nebraska* reached number three on the *Billboard* album chart. The multi-platinum *Born in the U.S.A.* was released in 1984 and was one of the biggest-selling releases in rock history; it spawned seven top ten singles, including "Dancing in the Dark," which peaked at number two on the *Billboard* singles chart. The album's success led to sold-out tours, the release of the 3-CD set *Bruce Springsteen and the E Street Band: Live 1975-1985,* which entered the *Billboard* charts at number one in 1986. Springsteen wed model/actress Julianne Phillips in 1986, released *Tunnel of Love* in 1987, and then became romantically involved with backup singer/guitarist Patti Scialfa. After leaving Phillips, Springsteen had a son with Scialfa named Evan in 1990, and married her in 1991.

In 1992, he simultaneously released *Human Touch* and *Lucky Town,* both recorded without the E Street Band. The albums entered the charts at number two and number three. In 1993, Springsteen recorded the theme song "Streets of Philadelphia" for Jonathan Demme's film *Philadelphia,* which starred actor Tom Hanks. The haunting, poignant ballad earned Springsteen an Oscar and four Grammy Awards. He released *Greatest Hits* in 1995, which included three new songs recorded with the E Street Band.

The first incarnation of the E Street Band was formed in 1972 and included saxophone player Clarence Clemons, organist Danny Federici, drummer Vini Lopez,

keyboard player David Sancious, and bassist Garry Tallent. Federici and Lopez had also played with Springsteen in the band Steel Mill. The E Street Band was named after a street in Belmar, NJ, where the band rehearsed in Sancious' parents' basement. Lopez left the band first, followed by Sancious, and they were replaced by keyboard player Rolf Bilton and drummer Max Weinberg. The E Street Band broke up in 1989, but continued to play with Springsteen on and off throughout the 1990s.

Springsteen released *The Ghost of Tom Joad* in 1995, an album reminiscent of his earlier acoustic release, *Nebraska.* The album won a Grammy Award for Best Contemporary Folk Album and its single, "Dead Man Walking," was nominated for a Grammy Award for Best Male Rock Vocal Performance. He followed the album's release with his first solo acoustic tour. Springsteen attended his 30th high school reunion in 1997 at the Holiday Inn in Tinton Falls, NJ, underscoring his reputation as an "average guy".

Springsteen released a four CD box set titled *Tracks* in November of 1998. *Tracks* was the first box set to ever debut at number one on the *Billboard* charts. The set features 66 songs, 56 of them had never been released. *Tracks* provided an opportunity for listeners to be in on his creative process. Springsteen had once helped induct Bob Dylan into the Rock and Roll Hall of Fame, and his turn came on March 15, 1999, when he was formally inducted himself. Springsteen told Newman, "Hopefully when I go into my work, there are things that help my fans sort through their own struggles and their own issues. You know, that's just what I've always tried to do, and that's what I still try to do."

Selected discography

Greetings from Asbury Park, NJ, Columbia, 1973.
The Wild, the Innocent, & the E Street Shuffle, Columbia, 1973.
Born to Run, Columbia, 1975.
Darkness at the Edge of Town, Columbia, 1978.
The River, Columbia, 1980.
Nebraska, Columbia, 1982.
Born in the U.S.A., Columbia, 1984.
Live: 1975-1985, Columbia, 1986.
Tunnel of Love, Columbia, 1987.
Chimes of Freedom, Columbia, 1988.
Lucky Town, Columbia, 1992.
Human Touch, Columbia, 1992.
Philadelphia, Epic, 1993.
Greatest Hits, Columbia, 1995.

The Ghost of Tom Joad, Columbia, 1995.
Tracks, Columbia, 1998.

Sources

Periodicals

The Advocate, May 1996.
Billboard, November 7, 1998.
CD Review, April 1996.
Esquire, December 1988.
Guitar World, October 1995.

Mojo, May 1998; June 1994.
Musician, July 1995; November 1992.
New Music Express, March 1996.
Newsweek, October 27, 1975.
Q Magazine, August, 1992.
The Real Paper, May 22, 1974.
Time, October 27, 1975.

Online

http://home.theboots.net/theboots/books/musn1192.html
http://wallofsound.go.com

—*B. Kimberly Taylor*

Richard Strauss

Composer, conductor

Considered one of the greatest in Germany's long line of musical giants, Richard Strauss was an innovator early in his career. His work was influenced by both Franz Liszt and Richard Wagner, and in mid-career he became famous for operas that at the time were considered quite daring. In his elder years, Strauss fell into disgrace for his somewhat inadvertent associations with the Nazi Party.

Strauss was born into a wealthy and accomplished Munich family in 1864. His mother was an heiress of the Pschorr brewing dynasty, a famous name in German beer, and his father Franz was a well-regarded horn player in the Munich Symphony Orchestra. The elder Strauss, however, had also become famous for his tirades against the music of Richard Wagner, a revered name in Germany music during the era; he even forbid his son to listen to Wagner's operas or compositions. Strauss began learning piano by the age of four, taking lessons from colleagues of his father's, and began to compose around the age of six. He gave piano recitals as a teen, and attended the University of Munich for a time to study philosophy and esthetics. When he was just 18, Strauss premiered his first symphony in Dresden, Germany. The conductor of the Munich Symphony Orchestra, Hans von Buelow, allowed him to make his conducting debut—without rehearsal—in Munich in 1884 leading the orchestra through his *Suite for Winds in B Flat.*

In 1885 Strauss became conductor of the Meiningen Court Orchestra, and one of its violinists, Alexander Ritter, became a great influence. Ritter was a composer and poet, married to Wagner's niece, and introduced Strauss to the music of both Liszt and Wagner.

In 1886 Strauss became assistant conductor of the Munich Court Opera, and traveled to Italy that same summer. The following year, he broke from the traditional form and began working in what he called the "tone poem." Other composers, such as Liszt, generally used the term "symphonic poem," but both phrases describe a piece of program music based on an extramusical idea. The work, *Aus Italien,* used discord and ignited a controversy—half the premiere audience cheered, while the other half booed. Another tone poem, *Don Juan,* premiered in Weimar, Germany, in 1889 to a more favorable reception. Music scholars consider *Don Juan* Strauss's first mature work, and its success made an important figure in German music seemingly overnight. Another tone poem, *Tod und Verklärung* ("Death and Transfiguration"), also met with critical approval when it debuted in 1889.

Till Eulenspiegels lustige Streiche ("Till Eulenspiegel's Merry Pranks"), a 1894 comic tale of arogue, and *Also*

Corbis. Reproduced by permission.

Sprach Zarathustra ("Zarathustra Spoke")—based on a book by German philosopher Friedrich Nietzsche and debuted in 1896—would become Strauss's most enduring works for the orchestra. The *Zarathustra* melody gained even greater recognition when film director Stanley Kubrick used them in his classic film *2001: A Space Odyssey.* Another tone poem from this era, *Ein Heldenleben* ("A Hero's Life") in 1898 featured the composer himself as hero, the music critics as foes. "All were well received and consolidated his position as the outstanding composer of his day, regarded as the arch-fiend of modernism and cacophony because of the huge instrumental forces, the innovatory design and the naturalistic effects employed in these masterpieces," noted an essay on Strauss in the *New Grove Dictionary of Music and Musicians.*

Strauss fell ill for a time, and wintered in Egypt in 1892. He was busy writing his first opera, *Guntram,* during this period. It premiered at the Weimar *Hofttheater* in May of 1894. Its Munich debut was a spectacular failure. The Munich Orchestra actually the petitioned the local authorities to censor it, and it closed after one performance. The composer felt the sting of this treatment in his native city keenly, and would later extract his own creative revenge.

Strauss met soprano Pauline de Ahna in 1887, a famously tempestuous performer, and they married in September of 1894. During this time, his career as both a composer and conductor was progressing splendidly. He found favor with Wagner's widow Cosima, who oversaw the annual Bayreuth Festival of Wagner's operas, and directed some of its productions. In 1896 he was hired as chief conductor of the Munich Opera, and composed his second opera, *Feuersnot,* in the final years of the century. It premiered in Dresden in November of 1901, a medieval tale set in Munich that mocked the city's conservative strain. By this time he was serving as music director for the Berlin Royal Opera, a post he held until around 1910.

Strauss was a enigmatic persona in his day. Many disliked him, though some appreciated his genius. At times he was condemned as vulgar and preoccupied with money and fame. "Not many people would have written an enormous and deafening symphonic poem about his own home life, including an embarrassingly boastful five minutes depicting his sexual prowess; and fewer would have been happy to conduct it in a department store and brag about the enormous fee afterwards," remarked Philip Hensher in the *Spectator.* The work that Hensher referred to was the *Symphonia domestica,* which premiered in America in 1904. But Strauss also campaigned determinedly to revise German copyright law, and after a seven-year fight, music royalty laws were amended to be more favorable to composers, rather than the publishing firms.

Strauss ignited even more controversy with his 1905 opera *Salome,* based on Oscar Wilde's titillating play. It premiered in December of 1905 at the Dresden Royal Opera, and was vilified in the press as erotic, vulgar, and altogether repulsive, but audiences still flocked to see it. Its title character was a minor figure from the biblical account of the death of John the Baptist. Salome is the teenage stepdaughter of Herodes, the tetrarch who has imprisoned the apostle—here called Jochanaan—for his belief in Christ. Bewitching but spoiled, Salome is fascinated by the prisoner, and angers when he spurns her advances. She performs the "Dance of the Seven Veils" for her stepfather, then demands the head of Jochanaan as her reward for this erotic moment. In the opera's final scene, she rapturously kisses Jochanaan's bloody severed head.

For years to come, productions of *Salome* had to include a ballerina performing the Seven Veils dance, since the female opera singers steadfastly refused. Strauss's own father proclaimed the opera "perverted music," and even Kaiser Wilhelm II had words of caution for him. But Strauss's *Salome* was staged 50 times around the world over the next two years, and the success provided Strauss with funds to build a villa in the mountainous area of Bavaria called Garmisch-Partenkirchen. Despite its worldwide success, the production of *Salome* at the New York Metropolitan Opera in 1907 was plagued by internal strife at the organization, and the production was canceled after opening night.

Strauss followed this success with another violence-driven opera that featured an unbalanced woman, *Elektra*, which made its debut in January of 1909 at the Dresden Royal Opera. It was Strauss's first work with a new librettist, the Austrian poet Hugo von Hofmannsthal. Their collaboration would prove a prolific and successful one over the next two decades.

Strauss's work suddenly became more conservative with the period comic opera *Der Rosenkavalier.* Debuting in Dresden in 1911, it greatly pleased audiences; it used the waltz as a recurring musical theme and was quite Mozart in spirit. It remains Strauss's most enduringly popular work. Other operas written with Hofmannsthal included *Ariadne auf Naxos* ("Ariadne on Naxos"), 1912; *Die Frau ohne Schatten* ("The Woman without Shadows"), 1919; *Die agyptische Helena* ("The Egyptian Helena"), 1928; and *Arabella*, 1933.

By World War I, Strauss—then in his fifties—was a preeminent figure in German music. He co-founded the Salzburg Festival in 1917 with Hofmannsthal and Max Reinhardt, and from 1919 onward served as joint director at the famed Vienna Staatsoper. But the rise of Germany's National Socialist Party and Adolf Hitler would irrevocably affect Strauss and his musical legacy. Upon coming to power in 1933, the Nazis created a state music bureau, the *Reichsmusikkammer,* and made him president without asking; it was largely a ceremonial office bestowed on him as the leading German composer, but Strauss also remained silent about new Nazi laws that excluded composers and musicians of Jewish heritage from this and other organizations, including all the leading orchestras. In 1933, Arturo Toscanini resigned in protest from the Bayreuth Festival over the Nazis' tactics, and Strauss was invited to take over as conductor. Though Nazi propaganda trumpeted Strauss's works as exemplarily "German," the composer opposed the Party when he attempted to premier another opera, *Der Schweigsame Frau,* with a libretto written by Stefan Zweig, a Jewish writer. Strauss objected when Zweig's name was omitted from the bill, and it enjoyed a brief run in Dresden before the Nazis shut it down. Strauss and his family were then placed under house arrest in Vienna, his music banned for a time, and all access to their assets blocked. But Strauss complied with these terms in order to protect his son's wife, who was Jewish, and their child. After the war, he and his family were allowed to emigrate to Switzerland.

After the war, Strauss was cleared of any collaborationist charges for holding Nazi office, and premiered a lament for 23 strings, *Metamorphosen,* in Zurich in early 1946. An elegiac piece, the 81-year-old composer wrote it after learning that all of Germany's great opera houses had been destroyed by Allied bombs. A 1947 London festival organized by Sir Thomas Beecham in his honor marked his final absolution, and his final work, *Four Last Songs,* premiered posthumously in 1950. He died in Garmisch-Partenkirchen on September 8, 1949. While gravely ill, he famously uttered the words, "Dying is just as I composed it in *Tod and Verklärung,*" according to *Grove.*

Selected discography

Also Sprach Zarathustra, Telarc, 1988.
Der Rosenkavalier, PGD/Deutsche Grammophon, 1988.
Die Schweigsame Frau, PGD/Deutsche Grammophon, 1994.
Salome, PGD/Deutsche Grammophon, 1994.
Don Juan, Prestige/Applausi, 1996.
Ariadne auf Naxos, Gala, 1997.
Elektra, Gala, 1997.
Strauss: The Complete Music for Winds, Hyperion, 1997.
Symphonia Domestica, BMG/RCA Victor, 1998.
Four Last Songs/15 Lieder, PGD/London Classics, 1999.

Sources

Books

Plotkin, Fred, *Opera 101: A Complete Guide to Learning and Loving Opera,* Hyperion, 1994.
Sadie, Stanley, ed., *The New Grove Dictionary of Music and Musicians,* Macmillan, 1980.

Periodicals

American Record Guide, September 1995.
Opera News, March 30, 1996.
Spectator, January 30, 1999; February 13, 1999.

—Carol Brennan

Supertramp

Rock band

The history of Supertramp stretches over three decades and despite an interruption in the 1990s, the power of their creations still pulled thousands of loyal fans to their concerts in the late 1990s. With eight albums to their credit—one platinum four gold—that generated over $50 million in sales worldwide, the British band secured itself a place in the late 20th century's gallery of rock legends. Their most successful album, *Breakfast in America,* sold over 18 million copies worldwide. "Their music—self-dubbed 'sophisto-rock'—is a carefully arranged, generally medium-tempo amalgam of ethereal art-rock sonorities; power drumming; whiffs of R&B-ish sax; steady jabs of electric piano," wrote Jon Pareles in *Rolling Stone* at the peak of Supertramp's success, "either [Rick] Davies' bluesy, nasal vocals or Roger Hodgson's reedy, ingenuous ones; and some of the most tenacious riffs in rock."

It all began in the late 1960s when 25-year-old Rick Davies, an English drummer for the club band Joint living a modest life in Munich, Germany, made the acquaintance of Stranley August Miesegaes, a young Dutch millionaire who was interested in sponsoring the band. After the Joint dissolved in 1969, Miesegaes, who strongly believed in Davies' potential, encouraged him first to switch from drums to piano and singing, and then offered financial backing for a band that Davies assembled. Hundreds of musicians showed up to audition in response to Davies' ad in *Melody Maker.* One of them was Roger Hodgson, a young man who had just left a private boarding school. He exchanged ideas with Davies during a break and they soon became friends. Davies and Hodgson started out writing songs for the band together. From Supertramp's third album on, they basically wrote and sang their own songs but shared the credits for them. While blue-collar child Davies' hallmark was his rather cynical lyrics, the well-educated optimist Hodgson wrote mostly about dreams and aspirations.

Supertramps Never Cried

First named Daddy, the band was soon renamed Supertramp, a name band member Richard Palmer drew from the title of one of his favorite novels. By June 1970, the new band had secured a contract with British A&M. Supertramp's first albums, *Supertramp* and *Indelibly Stamped,* which were recorded in 1970 and 1971 respectively, were commercial failures. As a result, , their rich sponsor withdrew his financial support but nevertheless paid the group's equipment bills totaling some $100,000. However, the band finally fell apart after the second album proved to be a failure. Hodgson and Davies, who had in the meantime become close friends, decided to stay together.

The two remaining "Supertramps" put another group together in 1973. Joining the new band were bassist Dougie Thomson and saxophonist John Heliwell, both former members of the British R&B group Alan Bown. Californian drummer Bob C. Benberg from the popular pub-rock formation Bees Make Honey also joined the band. A&M Records in England gave Supertramp a second chance. They paid a small salary to the band members and the rent on an old Englishfarmhouse, where the band moved with their families and pets. The outcome of this communal living experiment was the material for their next three albums and the re-emergence of Supertramp as "a totally unified force," as A&M manager Derek Green told *Rolling Stone.*

Pushed the Limits

Within five years, by the latter half of the 1970s, Supertramp managed to become a top band with an international reputation, and they performed that feat without a frontman, without creating a special image for themselves, and even without much media spectacle. *Crime Of The Century,* Supertramp's third album dedicated to their former sponsor, was released in 1974 and became an instant success in England and Canada, led by the debut hit "Dreamer." "Bloody Well Right," another song from the album, made it into the American top 40.

In 1975, Supertramp toured the United States for the first time, visiting 25 cities and filling 2000-seat venues. When the tour ended, Supertramp went to Los Angeles to record *Crisis? What Crisis?* However, the band did not become really popular in America until two years later, with the release of their fifth album *Even In The*

Quietest Moments. "Give a Little Bit," the album's first track with it's catchy acoustic guitar intro became an international hit, although not a major one.

That changed with 1979's *Breakfast In America*. Four of its tracks—"The Logical Song," "Take The Long Way Home," "Goodbye Stranger," and the title song—became international top hits. The album was a multi-platinum success. Several songs went to number one in the charts in Europe, Australia and the United States, and the band was able to sell out stadiums. Supertramp's live show lasted over two hours. Superior sound combined with films, slides and a computer-controlled light show were given priority over the individuals in the band. This perfectionism, with Hodgson its main driving force, caused critics to complain about the band's overly polished sound. However, a rawer edge was added when their roadies joined them on stage as the Trampettes to sing falsetto backup for the tune "Hide in Your Shell." A live album recorded at a November 1979 show in Paris before some 8,000 people was released in 1980.

Never Gave Up

Famous Last Words, Supertramp's next studio album, was released three years after *Breakfast in America*, in 1982. David Fricke's review for *Rolling Stone* described its content as "light, glistening melodies ... cushioned like crown jewels in rich, sensuous arrangements," but at the same time noted a "sense of emotional helplessness and blasé surrender at the heart of these songs." The album's title became the band's fate. Unhappy with the heavy blues influence, founding member Roger Hodgson left one year after its release, and Rick Davis took over the song-writing and singing. *Brother Where You Bound* from 1985 was dominated by R&B schemes and featured Pink Floyd's David Gilmour on the title track. The 1987 album *Free as a Bird* with its brassier, pop oriented sound was the band's last studio recording of the 1980s. After a tour in 1988, the group only performed occasionally together.

Some Things Never Change, Supertramp's first studio album in ten years, was released in 1997. Produced with the help of studio musicians from Los Angeles, the album kept the slow pace typical for Supertramp, but with a stronger emphasis on jazz elements. Their 1997 world tour which brought them to the United States again was well covered by the media. But—as Ernesto Lechner noted in a concert review for the Los Angeles Time—the American audience was not impressed by the new songs, even if they were supported visually by computer-generated images. Only when Davis sang the good old pieces, did people start moving. "The night belonged to Davis, who filled the songs with such passion that they didn't seem a touch dated," wrote Lechner. This is proved by their still huge and loyal fan base in Europe which pushed the album into the top ten in many European countries. According to Supertramp's website, the band was planning another release in 1999.

Selected discography

Singles

"Land Ho," A&M, 1974.

Albums

Supertramp, A&M, 1970.
Indelibly Stamped, A&M, 1971.
Crime Of The Century, (includes "Dreamer," "Bloody Well Right") A&M, 1974, reissued 1987.
Crisis? What Crisis?, A&M, 1975, reissued PGD/A&M 1988.
Even In The Quietest Moments, (includes "Give a Little Bit") A&M, 1977, reissued PGD/A&M 1988.
Breakfast In America, (includes "Breakfast in America," "The Logical Song," "Take The Long Way Home," "Goodbye Stranger,") A&M, 1979, reissued PGD/A&M 1987.
Paris, A&M, 1980, reissued PGD/A&M 1987.
Famous Last Words, A&M, 1982.
Brother Where You Bound, A&M, 1985, reissued 1987.
Free as a Bird, A&M, 1987.
Classics Volume 9, PGD/A&M, 1987.
Some Things Never Change, Oxygen, 1997.
Very Best Of Supertramp, Poly, 1994, reissued 1999.

Sources

Periodicals

Dallas Morning News, June 5, 1997.
Independent, September 17, 1997.
Los Angeles Times, August 16, 1997.
Rolling Stone, July 12, 1979; December 9, 1982.

Online

http://huizen.dds.nl/~suptramp/bios.html.
http://www.amrecords.com/.
http://www.microtec.net/~sylvn/tramp/school/history.htm.
http://www.microtec.net/~sylvn/tramp/school/int_bs01.htm.
http://www.microtec.net/~sylvn/tramp/school/int_rh01.htm.
http://www.microtec.net/~sylvn/tramp/school/int_rh02.htm.
http://www.microtec.net/~sylvn/tramp/school/trampfaq.htm.
http://www.microtec.net/~sylvn/tramp/trivia.

—*Evelyn Hauser*

Tampa Red

Slide guitar

Though not widely known or listened to in the 1990s, Tampa Red is one of the seminal figures in blues history. His career spanned the 26 years from 1928 to 1954, the Golden Age of the blues. He cut nearly 230 sides and released more 78s than any other blues artist. He formed a vital link between the country blues of the 1920s and the electric Chicago blues of the postwar era. His songs were popular with the record public and other artists who covered them frequently. His impeccable slide guitar technique influenced blues players like Muddy Waters, Elmore James, and Robert Nighthawk, and rock-era musicians like Ry Cooder. What's more, his help and kindness enabled countless musicians to get a foothold in the Chicago clubs and recording studios of the 1930s and 1940s.

Tampa Red was born Hudson Woodbridge in Southville, Georgia. The date of his birth is uncertain. Tampa himself gave dates varying from 1900 to 1908. The birth date given on his death certificate is January 8, 1904. Just as little is known about his parents, John and Elizabeth Woodbridge. They passed away while Tampa was a child, and he and his brother Eddie were given over to the care of their grandmother, Annie Whittaker. Tampa took her last name as his own and was raised by her in Tampa, Florida.

Tampa's first musical inspiration was his brother, Eddie, who played guitar around the Tampa area. For a while,

according to William Barlow's *Looking Up At Down: The Emergence of Blues Culture*, Tampa followed a musician named Piccolo Pete through the streets of the city. Pete eventually showed Tampa some rudimentary blues licks. Apparently, Tampa also picked up some knowledge from early recordings of women blues singers like Ma Rainey, Bessie Smith, and Ida Cox. "That [1920] record of "Crazy Blues" by Mamie Smith, it was one of the first blues records ever made," Tampa told Martin Williams in an interview quoted in the liner notes to *Tampa Red: The Bluebird Recordings 1934-1936.* "I said to myself, 'I don't know any music, but I can play that.'"

By 1925, Tampa had moved to Chicago and taken to playing the blues in the street. He had also adopted the name Tampa Red, after his Florida home and either his red hair or his light complexion, depending on who one believes. In Chicago, Tampa met Thomas Dorsey. It was an encounter that changed Tampa's life. Dorsey was an accomplished pianist, composer, and arranger who had performed and recorded with the leading female blues singers of the era, in particular the great Ma Rainey. Dorsey introduced Tampa to J. Mayo Williams, the front man for Paramount Records in Chicago. Williams arranged a session at Paramount for Tampa.

His first 78, "Through Train Blues," didn't shake up the world. He had to share the record with Paramount's big star, Blind Lemon Jefferson. But his second record, released in 1928, caused a sensation. The song was called "It's Tight Like That." The song's sexual suggestiveness and infectious rhythm caught the public's fancy in a big way—it sold nearly one million copies. Tampa would later recall people lined up outside record stores waiting to buy it. The song was composed and performed by Tampa and Dorsey, who played blues under the name Georgia Tom. The success of "It's Tight Like That" surprised both men—and delighted them as well--they shared some $4,000 in royalties! "It was just a little old song but they really went for it," Tampa told Jim O'Neal, in an interview quoted in *The Bluebird Recordings 1934-1936.* "'Tight Like That' wasn't no original tune," Dorsey is quoted by William Barlow, "It was just something that popped up at the right time to make some money." The song came about when Mayo Williams heard them playing with a tune, borrowed from a Papa Charley Jordan song, built around the then-popular catch phrase, "Tight Like That." Williams loved it and insisted they record it right away.

The song's popularity spawned a slew of imitators. Even Tampa and Georgia Tom recorded it. Samuel Charters called "It's Tight Like That" the most over-recorded song of its time. It's rapping, half-spoken style gave rise to a new musical category called hokum. Tampa and Georgia

For the Record . . .

Born Hudson Woodbridge in Southville, GA, January 8, 1904; parents John and Elizabeth Woodbridge; following their death, raised with brother Eddie by grandmother, Annie Whittaker; adopted her last name; moved to Chicago in early 1920s; adopted the name Tampa Red; married Francis; died March 19, 1981.

Learned guitar as a boy; performed as a street musician in Tampa and Chicago; met pianist and composer Thomas Dorsey in Chicago around 1927-28; introduced by Dorsey to Paramount's J. Mayo Smith; first recording "Through Train Blues," 1928; with Thomas Dorsey (aka Georgia Tom), released a series of recordings beginning with million-seller "It's Tight Like That;" played on records by Ma Rainey, Madilyn Davis, Lil Johnson, and Frankie "Half Pint" Jaxon, 1928-30; last Paramount session, May 7, 1932; signed by RCA Victor's Bluebird label, 1934; remained with label until 1954, releasing hits like "Give It Up Buddy And Get Going," "Mean Mistreater Blues," "Anna Lee Blues," "Don't You Lie To Me," "Give Me Mine Now," "Cryin' Won't Help You," and "Love Her With A Feeling;" "When Things Go Wrong With You (It Hurts Me Too)" last big hit, 1949; dropped by RCA, 1954.

Tom recorded for a while under the name "The Hokum Boys." Their collaboration did much to establish the piano-guitar combo in blues. More important, it sealed Tampa's future as a blues artist. He was in demand. In 1928 and 1929, besides making their own records, he and Georgia Tom appeared on recordings by Ma Rainey, Madilyn Davis, Lil Johnson, and female impersonator Frankie "Half Pint" Jaxon.

In 1932 Dorsey abandoned blues for gospel music. The Depression was bottoming out too. It looked like Tampa's career might be over. After the frantic recording of 1928-32, he did not have a single session between May 7, 1932 and March 22, 1934. Three events contributed to his resurrection: the repeal of Prohibition, the rise of the jukebox, and Lester Melrose taking over RCA Victor's new Bluebird label. Jukeboxes provided cheap entertainment in the newly legal bars. Lester Melrose recognized their importance for record companies and made sure his artists were well represented in Chicago jukeboxes.

Melrose signed Tampa to a Bluebird contract in 1934. Bluebird was the RCA Victor budget line—its 78s cost only 35 cents, not seventy five cents like most others—and was affordable for the black blues audience. Before long, Tampa was one of Bluebird's leading artists. He helped develop the smooth Bluebird sound, built on a stable of in-house musicians who played on most of the company's releases. During a 20-year association with the label, Tampa recorded a variety of music standards (like "Nobody's Sweetheart,") boogie woogie ("Shake It Up A Little"), swing-flavored tunes ("Mr. Rhythm Man"), and, of course, blues ("Anna Mae Blues").

Tampa became Lester Melrose's right-hand man in Chicago. Tampa's apartment on 35th and State became a meeting point for blues musicians visiting or living in Chicago, a kind of combination rehearsal hall and boarding house. "Melrose'd pay [Tampa] for the lodging," Blind John Davis is quoted in *Nothing But The Blues*, "and Mrs. Tampa would cook for 'em." According to Muddy Waters, later the only way to a contract with Melrose was through Tampa Red.

By the 1940s Tampa's sound had evolved a long way from the hokum of 1928. Cuts like "You're Gonna Miss Me When I'm Gone" and "Mercy Mama Blues" have a much rougher, urban sound, that looks ahead to the blues of Sunnyland Slim and Muddy Waters. In fact, strains of Muddy can already be heard in 1934's "Kingfish Blues." Only the smooth tunefulness of Tampa's singing keeps some of these records from being as raw as any postwar blues. Twenty years after "It's Tight Like That," Tampa had another huge hit. 1949's "When Things Go Wrong With You (It Hurts Me Too)" broke into the new Billboard Rhythm & Blues chart. The song's insistent beat, the harmony singing in the chorus, the interplay of the guitar and piano, Tampa's exquisite phrasing, the "dog" growls, the way the band abruptly cuts out in the last chorus, all combine to make a perfect blues record, as moving as Elmore James's more famous cover version.

In 1954, Tampa's wife Francis passed away. The loss devastated him. Afterwards, he was overcome by a drinking problem which, in William Barlow's words, "left him virtually incapacitated." Except for a brief "rediscovery," he lived out the rest of his days in seclusion on the South Side of Chicago. He died in Chicago's Central Nursing Home on March 19, 1981. He was buried—without a headstone—in Mt. Glenwood Cemetery in Glenwood, Illinois.

Tampa Red's importance to the development of the blues is only now being recognized. RCA's decision to release his complete Bluebird recording is contributing a great deal to this recognition. Tampa melded country blues with pop music and in doing so helped create the urban blues. He was one of the first bluesmen to use an electric guitar. He influenced most of the blues players who followed him. In an interview quoted in *The Bluebird Recordings*, Ry Cooder expressed the thought that Tampa's influence went far beyond the blues: "I really think that it's a straight line from Tampa Red to Louis Jordan to Chuck Berry, without a doubt.... Tampa Red changed it from rural music to commercial music."

Selected discography

Tampa Red: The Bluebird Recordings 1934-1936, RCA, 1997.
Tampa Red: Bottleneck Guitar 1928-1937, Yazoo 1039, 1992.

Sources

Books

Barlow, William, *Looking Up At Down: The Emergence of Blues Culture*, Temple University Press, 1989.
Charters, Samuel, *The Country Blues,* Da Capo, 1975.
Cohn, Lawrence, editor, *Nothing But The Blues*, Abbeville Press, 1993.
Davis, Francis, *The History of the Blues*, 1995.
Harris, Sheldon, *Blues Who's Who*, Arlington House, 1979.
Russell, Tony, *The Blues—From Robert Johnson to Robert Cray,* Schirmer Books, 1997.

Addtional information obtained from Mark Humphrey, *Tampa Red: The Bluebird Recordings 1934-1936,* liner notes.

—*Gerald E. Brennan*

James Taylor

Singer, songwriter

Corbis View. Reproduced by permission.

Long-standing folk and pop singer/songwriter James Taylor ushered in the singer/songwriter movement in the early 1970s, and refined his style over the course of three decades—all the while maintaining the distinct musical craftsmanship that led to his early success. Taylor appeared on the cover of *Time* in 1971 and was touted by the magazine as the originator of the singer/songwriter era. In 1997, twenty- six years later, Bob Kurson of the *Chicago Sun-Times* wrote of a live Taylor performance, "Even the most militant atheist...would have sworn that James Taylor's voice was a gift from God ... Taylor's voice resonates with a thousand personalities." Kurson also wrote of Taylor's guitar playing, "There are guitarists—terrific guitarists—who would gleefully trade their first-borns to play an acoustic like Taylor." Eleven of Taylor's albums reached gold status and four reached platinum; he received a Lifetime Achievement Award at the 1998 *Billboard* Music Awards, and garnered three Grammy Awards over the course of his long and ever-evolving career.

Taylor was born James Vernon Taylor in Boston, Massachusetts, on March 12, 1948, as one of five children born to Dr. Isaac and Gertrude Taylor. His siblings included brothers Alex, Livingston, and Hugh, and sister Kate Taylor. Three years after he was born, the family moved to Chapel Hill, NC, where his father had accepted a position as Dean of the University of North Carolina/Chapel Hill Medical School. Starting at the age of five, Taylor attended the Milton Academy, a prep school located outside of Boston. By the time Taylor was eight, he had already studied cello and expressed a desire to play guitar.

His parents gave him a guitar two years later in 1960, and by 1963—at the age of 15—he played folk songs at local venues on Martha's Vineyard with close friend Danny "Kootch" Kortchmar. He dropped out of the Milton Academy during his junior year and joined a band called The Fabulous Corsairs with his brother Alex and Zach Weisner. Weisner was replaced a few months later with Jerry Burnham. In 1965, at the age of 17, Taylor moved to New York City and soon afterwards, admitted himself for ten months to the McLean Psychiatric Hospital in MA to be treated for depression. His song "Knocking Round the Zoo" was inspired by his stay there. After ten months of hospitalization, he took a trip to Russia.

In 1966, Taylor graduated from high school in the McLean Psychiatric Hospital, and then Kortchmar and O'Brien joined him to form The Flying Machine. Although they created studio recordings at the time, their material was not released until 1971 under the name James Taylor and the Original Flying Machine. The band stayed together for only one year, and Taylor began using heroin in 1968. He moved to London, recorded demos, and was

Born James Vernon Taylor, March 12, 1948, in Boston, MA, on; son of Dr. Isaac (Den of University of North Caroling—Chapel Hill Medical School) and Gertrude Taylor; married singer Carly Simon in 1972 (divorced in 1982); married Kathryn Walker in 1985, (divorced in 1996); children: Ben and Sally (from marriage to Simon).

Studied cello as a child; took up the guitar at age 12; played folk songs at local venues on Martha's Vineyard with close friend Danny "Kootch" Kortchmar as a teen; joined a band called The Fabulous Corsairs with his brother Alex and Jerry Burnham; moved to New York City; formed band The Flying Machine with Kortchmar and O'Brien; released material as *James Taylor and the Original Flying Machine*, 1971; first outside artist signed to Apple Records; released *James Taylor* in the U.K., 1968; *James Taylor* released in the U.S, 1969; reissued on EMI Records, 1991; released *Sweet Baby James*, 1970; released the single "Fire & Rain," 1970; featured on the cover of *Time*, 1971; released the single "Don't Let Me Be Lonely" in 1972; released duet "Mockingbird," 1974 with Simon; released *Gorilla* and "How Sweet It Is (To Be Loved By You)," 1975; played at Carnegie Hall with guests Carole King and David Crosby; released "Shower The People" in 1976; released *Greatest Hits*, 1976; released *James Taylor*, 1977; released *James Taylor Live*, 1993; released *James Taylor Best Live*, 1994; released *Hourglass*, 1997, album peaked at number nine on *Billboard* charts, with more than 70,000 copies sold in the first week of its release; appeared on NBC's *Saturday Night Live* six from 1976-93, and on NBC's *The Tonight Show* six times between 1985-94.

Awards: Grammy Award Best Pop Vocal Performance, Male, "You've Got A Friend," 1972; Grammy Award, Best Pop Vocal Performance, Male for "Handy Man," 1978; Grammy Award Best Children's Recording, *In Harmony Sesame Street*, 1981; . Lifetime Achievement Award at the 1998 *Billboard* Music Awards.

Address: *Record company*—Columbia/Sony, 550 Madison Avenue, New York, NY 10022; (212) 833-8000; or 2100 Colorado Avenue, Santa Monica, CA 90404; (310) 449-2100.

introduced to Paul McCartney by producer Peter Asher. Taylor became the first outside artist signed to the Beatles' record label, Apple Records.

He released *James Taylor* in England with little success, returned to the United States, and admitted himself into the Austin Riggs psychiatric hospital in Maryland, where he was treated for his heroin addiction and depression. A year later in 1969, *James Taylor* was released in America. Taylor signed to Warner Brothers Records and moved to California with Asher. When *Sweet Baby James* was released in 1970, it rose to number one on the charts and became a best seller for two years. The popular single "Fire & Rain" was released in 1970 as well, and *Sweet Baby James* was soon certified as platinum. Taylor performed with Joni Mitchell on a BBC radio show in 1970, and his career was permanently launched.

Singer/Songwriter Era

Taylor was featured on the cover of *Time* magazine in 1971 as the originator of the burgeoning singer/songwriter movement, and *James Taylor and the Original Flying Machine* was released as a nod to his popularity. The hit single "You've Got A Friend" was released in 1971, and Taylor toured 27 cities with his band—which included Carole King—and Kootch's band, Jo Mama. Taylor won a Grammy Award in 1972 for "You've Got A Friend." The song also garnered a Grammy for Carole King for Song of the Year. Taylor released the single "Don't Let Me Be Lonely" in 1972, and married singer Carly Simon, with whom he had a son, Ben, and a daughter, Sally.

Taylor and Simon released the duet "Mockingbird" in 1974, which became a million seller, and was featured on Simon's *Hotcakes* album. Taylor released *Gorilla* and the single "How Sweet It Is (To Be Loved By You)" a year later in 1975, and played at Carnegie Hall with guests King and David Crosby. He released the single "Shower The People" in 1976 and toured with David Sanborn. Later that year the platinum selling *James Taylor's Greatest Hits* was released followed by *James Taylor* a year later, which also went platinum. In 1978, he received a Grammy Award for the single "Handy Man," and Peter Asher won a Grammy for Producer of the Year for his work with Taylor. Taylor won another Grammy in 1981 for Best Children's Recording for his *In Harmony Sesame Street* album. In 1982, Taylor performed for more than a million fans in New York City's Central Park as part of a nuclear disarmament rally, which also included performances by Bruce Springsteen, Jackson Browne, Joan Baez, and Linda Ronstadt. The concert was aired nationally on radio and filmed for *In Our Own Hands*.

Taylor and Simon divorced in 1982, so Taylor's 1981 release, *Dad Loves His Work,* was later viewed as a response to an ultimatum delivered by Simon over the amount of time Taylor spent touring. Three years later he married Kathryn Walker at the Cathedral of St. John the Divine in New York City. Taylor also performed in 1985 at the first rock festival held in Moscow, the highlights of which were shown on the Showtime cable network.

Further Success and Personal Losses

Taylor's 1969 Apple debut was re-released in 1991 by EMI Records followed by *James Taylor Live* in 1993, which sold more than a million copies. *James Taylor Best Live* was released in 1994 and a year later he received an honorary doctorate of music at the Berklee College of Music in Boston. Taylor delivered the college's commencement speech that year, as well. 1996 was a turbulent year for Taylor: he and Walker divorced, his father died at the age of 75, and producer and band member Don Grolnick died of cancer. Taylor's next release in 1997, *Hourglass,* reflected his losses and an acute awareness of the brevity of life. It opened and peaked at number nine on the *Billboard* charts, with more than 70,000 copies sold in the first week of its release. Taylor performed at the VH1 Honors benefit concert in Los Angeles, and performed on the A&E network's *Live By Request* show.
1
Taylor collaborated with a diverse group of musicians throughout his long career, including his ex-wife Simon, King, Mitchell ("California" and "In France They Kiss On Main Street"), Karla Bonoff, Steve Winwood ("Back In The High Life"), Paul Simon and Art Garfunkel ("Wonderful World"), sister Kate Taylor's "It's In His Kiss," Linda Ronstadt ("Gonna Work Out Fine"), George Jones ("Bartender's Blues," a cover of Taylor's own song), Brazilian musician Milton Nascimento, Neil Young (vocals for three songs and banjo on Young's Harvest Moon release), Crosby and Graham Nash, Ricky Skaggs (duet with Skaggs on "New Star Shining"), Jimmy Buffett, and John Hall of Hall & Oates. Taylor appeared on NBC's *Saturday Night Live* six times between 1976 and 1993, and on NBC's *The Tonight Show* six times between 1985 and 1994. In 1998, it was clear that both of Taylor's children with Carly Simon intended to follow in their parents' musical footsteps, as both were preparing to release debut albums. Taylor received the 1998 *Billboard* Lifetime Achievement Award.

Selected discography

James Taylor, Apple Records, 1968, reissued, EMI Records, 1991.
Sweet Baby James, Warner Brothers Records, 1970.
James Taylor and the Original Flying Machine, Euphoria Records, 1971, reissued, Gadfly Records 1996.
Mud Slide Slim & The Blue Horizon, Warner Brothers, 1971.
One Man Dog, Warner Brothers, 1972.
Walking Man, Warner Brothers, 1974.
Gorilla, Warner Brothers, 1975.
In The Pocket, Warner Brothers, 1976.
Greatest Hits, Warner Brothers, 1976.
James Taylor, CBS Records, 1977.
s*Dad Loves His Work,* CBS Records, 1981.
That's Why I'm Here, CBS Records, 1985.
Never Die Young, CBS Records, 1988.
New Moon Shine, Columbia Records, 1991.
James Taylor Live, Columbia Records, 1993.
James Taylor Best Live, Columbia Records, 1994.
Hourglass, Columbia/Sony Records, 1997.

Sources

Acoustic guitar, July/August, 1992.
Boston Herald, June 4, 1998.
Chicago Sun-Times, July 5, 1997.
Chicago Tribune, July 5, 1997.
Frets, December 1987.
Guitar Extra, Spring 1992.
Guitar Player, May 1984.
Life, October 1985.
Musician, April 1988.
New York Times, February 3, 1988; April 8, 1981.
New York Times Magazine, February 21, 1971.
Newsweek, November 4, 1985.
Parade, July 12, 1981.
People, August 24, 1981; October 6, 1980.
Rolling Stone, December 10, 1981; June 11, 1981; July 10, 1980; September 6, 1979; February 18, 1971.
Saturday Review, September 12, 1970.
Stereo Review, January 1978.
Time, October 23, 1985; March 1, 1971.

Online

http://www.james-taylor.com/
http://www.sonymusic.com/artists/JamesTaylor/jt/index.html

—B. Kimberly Taylor

Third Eye Blind

Rock and roll band

The rock band Third Eye Blind released their debut album *Third Eye Blind* in the spring of 1997. One of its singles, "Semi-Charmed Life," reached number one on the modern rock chart by the summer. Since then four more singles from the album were released successfully, postponing talk of one-hit-wonders at least until a new album is recorded. At 34, Stephan Jenkins, the band's handsome and charismatic leader, lived the life of a starving musician long enough to relish his new found fame, but not to put much stock in it. "I'm bemused by my stardom," he told *People*. "But it's fun."

Jenkins produced and recorded *Third Eye Blind* and impressed several record company executives before signing with Elektra/Asylum. He told Elysa Gardner of *Details*, "We always approached record companies by telling them 'don't tell us what to do. We're gonna make the record we wanna make.'" Third Eye Blind's live performances and original fourteen song demo tape are what captured the attention of several record companies. Jenkins had already done some high profile production work while Third Eye Blind was still only a local touring band. Jenkins' lyrics, guitarist Kevin Cadogan's arrangements andr the catchy songs were responsible for hooking their mainly college age listeners, alledged critics. "Balancing a cheery ear for harmonies with a finely honed sense of despair, this clamorous pop band displays deft songwriting...." noted *Entertainment Weekly* writer David Grad.

Jenkins spent some time touring the San Francisco Bay Area as a solo musician before he formed Third Eye Blind. He graduated from the University of California at Berkeley in 1988 with an English degree. His father, a retired professor at Stanford, wanted his son to be a professor or an environmentalist, but Stephan had other ideas. Music was in his blood from the day he started playing pots and pans at age five. After college, Jenkins started performing at the local San Francisco clubs with little success but bottomless drive. He told to *People* that having enough money to eat for a day was his main concern. "In the morning you scrounge up enough dimes and quarters to get coffee'" he said. "You put in thick cream and a lot of sugar, which gives you the calories you need to get to lunch." Jenkins refused to throw in the towel and eventually decided to form a band so he wouldn't have to go it alone.

Jenkins had performed with an array of musicians by the time he formed Third Eye Blind in the early nineties. Guitarist Kevin Cadogan joined the band In 1995. Early in his career, Cadogan took guitar lessons from Joe Satriani. Cadogan was impressed with Jenkins' ambition. He introduced Jenkins to drummer Brad Hargraves, and when bassist Arion Salazar joined the band, Third Eye Blind was complete. The group made a successful tour of the Bay Area. When they opened for Counting Crows and Oasis, they realized that the fans were responding. "I don't wanna make this sound too grandiose," Jenkins told Gardner, " but we had the sense that we were special." The Oasis gig is their most renowned. Opening bands usually serve as target practice for fans at the Bill Graham Civic Auditorium, but when Third Eye Blind performed, they were called back for an encore and ended up receiving double their original fee.

By then the record companies had taken notice. A bidding war broke out but Third Eye Blind eventually signed with Elektra. The band liked Elektra Records CEO Sylvia Rhone, who was willing to give them everything they needed to record their first album—including artistic freedom. She allowed Jenkins to produce the album himself. "As a band, we had really worked for a long time to get to this point." Jenkins told *Interview*. "And this is important: We got all the things we didn't have before—the tools, the studio, the microphones, the time, the budget to buy food—to go in and make the record we wanted to make. And we didn't have the record company on our backs; we were like kids playing." They played with some pretty impressive toys. To record the guitar arrangements for the haunting song "God of Wine," the band used the scoring theater of film producer George Lucas' Marin County production facility. "I looked out into this enormous space and thought, 'My God, this is amazing,'" Kevin Cadogan told James Rotondi of

For the Record . . .

Members include **Kevin Cadogan,** guitar and vocals; **Brad Hargreaves,** drums; **Stephan Jenkins,** vocals and percussion; **Arion Salazar,** bass and vocals.

Group formed in San Francisco in the early nineties after Jenkins spent time touring solo; Kevin Cadogan joined band bringing along drummer Brad Hargreaves, 1995; band toured San Francisco Bay Area, 1995; Jenkins produced the Braids' cover of Queen's "Bohemian Rhapsody," 1995; Third Eye Blind opened for Oasis with great acclaim, 1996; group signed with Elektra and released *Third Eye Blind,* produced by Jenkins, 1997.

Addresses: *Record company*—Elektra Entertainment Group, 75 Rockefeller Plaza, New York, NY 10019; 345 North Maple Drive, Beverly Hills, CA 90210. *Website*—www.thirdeyeblind.net.

Guitar Player. He added, "The recording I'd done in the past was always on a tight budget, where you didn't have time to do the things you wanted, and you knew that you weren't quite getting the right tones. Making this record, I was able to sit down and listen to 20 or 30 amps and guitars to find the right combinations, and get tones that we were completely satisfied with."

The results paid off. *Third Eye Blind* was released in 1997. The first single, "Semi-Charmed Life," a song about a junkie's love of oral sex and the drug crystal-meth was an unlikely pop charmer. "I wrote the song about drugs and f———— and I'm pretty much clean living on the road," Jenkins told *Rolling Stone.* "We can't even believe it got onto the radio." Jenkins credits part of the band's success to certain radio stations like KROQ Los Angeles, KITS San Francisco, and KNDD Seattle with. "Those are the stations that very early on believed in this band," he told *Billboard.* "Semi-Charmed Life" hit number one on the modern rock chart and number four on the pop chart. As Hal Horowitz wrote in the *Music Monitor,* "Seldom has a band with words this smart, music this melodic and cranky hooks this sweet and bumpy taken hold of the masses so quickly."

Another single, "Graduate," was released shortly thereafter and reached number 14 on the modern rock chart. "How's It Going to Be" was the third single released to rave reviews. Its lyrics describe the feeling of a dying

relationship. "I think we all feel violated when we find that a relationship actually has time limits, that it's not unconditional," explained Jenkins to *Billboard.* Every song on *Third Eye Blind* tells a story. When asked by his girlfriend, actress Charlize Theron in the *Interview* article; why he doesn't write books or poetry instead of music lyrics, Jenkins responded, "Music was always the thing that compelled me the most. There's something about a four-minute song that creates this complete world you can step into."

After the release of their debut album, Third Eye Blind left on a world tour for a number of months. Jenkins is happy that Elektra set up tour dates all over the world—one even at the base of Mt. Fuji in Japan. , "That's one of the really cool things Elektra has done," Jenkins told *Billboard.* "They looked at us as a global rock band. It's a dream to go over to Japan and be well received." Third Eye Blind has toured the world twice in two years, the first year opening for the Rolling Stones and U2 for several shows. As an opening act for such superstars, Third Eye Blind played huge arenas where they were well received. Hanging out with Bono was a new experience as well. As Jenkins told *Billboard,* "He shows up in our dressing room with a case of champagne and Guiness to show us how to make Black Velvets. Then he invites us to join him on his jet." Though he misses his girlfriend when he tours, Jenkins knows the importance of hitting the road. "Recording is a fun, intuitive process," he said, "but performing is more communal and is about making the connection."

Third Eye Blind's goal is to release six or seven singles from the debut album and to continue writing new material while touring. "Jumper" is the latest successful single hitting the charts and dominating MTV air time. The song is about a gay friend who kills himself rather than face an intolerant world. MTV has given "Jumper" so much attention that Jenkins wants Third Eye Blind to expand its horizons by becoming more involved in the creation of their videos. The success of their first album, there is plenty of work to keep the band busy.

Selected discography

Album

Third Eye Blind, Elektra, 1997.

Singles; on Elektra

"Semi-Charmed Life."
"Graduate."
"How's It Going to Be."

"Losing A Whole Year."
"Jumper."

Sources

Periodicals

Billboard, December 6, 1997; January 31, 1998.
Details, September, 1997.
Entertainment Weekly, April 25, 1997.
Guitar Player, February, 1998.
Interview, September, 1998.
Palo Alto Weekly, June 6, 1997.
People, October 12, 1998.
Rolling Stone, April 10, 1998.

Online

The All-Media Guide Copyright 1991-1998 by Matrix Software, Inc.
The Music Monitor, 1998.

—*Christine Morrison*

Pam
Tillis

Singer, songwriter

No female performer of the 1990s did more to revitalize country music than Pam Tillis. She pushed the boundaries of the genre by incorporating the pop, jazz, blues, and folk influences of her early career and adding honky-tonk, comedy, torch and ethnic flavor to the mix. From her 1991 breakthrough *Put Yourself in My Place* to her 1998 release, *Every Time*, Tillis has remained one of the most versatile artists on the scene.

"I just get bored easily," Tillis explained to Kimmy Wix of Country.com, "so I like to keep it new. I never like to repeat myself and I always want to be breaking new ground. Yeah, my antennas are always up, and I guess I'm just a musical sponge. I'm just always kinda tuned into the different sounds of life."

The daughter of country legend Mel Tillis, Pam tuned in to those sounds early. As a baby, her father's demo tapes were her lullabies as she napped in a guitar case. She began making up songs to sing for her kindergarten teacher at age four. And she first joined her father on the Grand Ole Opry stage at eight. "Singing and clowning was my way of gaining the acceptance I longed for," Tillis said. "Not much has changed." Tillis began studying classical piano at eight, took up guitar at 11, began writing at 13, and started singing in clubs at 15. "A lot of folks assumed Dad taught me these things, but he was working 300 days of the year," Tillis explained. "I learned from osmosis."

Throughout her education, Tillis said, music was the only thing she took seriously. After two semesters at the University of Tennessee, she recalled, "... instead of continuing to waste my parents' money, I decided to quit and enroll instead in the Music City School of Hard Knocks." She pounded the pavement of Music Row, singing back-up and demos, as well as jingles for Hardee's, Coors, and Country Time Lemonade. She wrote songs for Sawgrass Music, her father's publishing company, before heading to California to "dabble in jazz rock" in 1977.

She focused on songwriting when she returned to Nashville in 1979. Her songs have been recorded by artists as varied as Chaka Khan, Martina McBride, Gloria Gaynor, Conway Twitty, Juice Newton, and Highway 101. Tillis recorded a pop album, *Above and Beyond the Doll of Cutie*, in 1983, during a short stay on the Warner Brothers label. She called it "a time of experimenting, writing and trying to find my sound." She was well on her way to finding that sound when she signed with Arista/Nashville in 1989. "It might have been obvious to everyone else, but it took Pam Tillis two decades to realize she really is a country singer," Alanna Nash wrote in *Entertainment Weekly*. "Pam had twang on her tongue and sawdust in her blood, yet the disco and blues she tried early in her career proved alien to her system."

Produced Own Music

Success quickly followed Tillis' return to her roots. In 1991, *Put Yourself in My Place*, her first completely country album, offered timeless hits like "Maybe It Was Memphis" and "Don't Tell Me What to Do." Both eventually went to number one, and the title track made the top five. Tillis told Country.com, "If a song is a hit, if it has any impact at all, it's not just background music. It gets incorporated into the fabric of people's lives. Audiences are an awfully good barometer. They let you know what they like or don't like. It happens every night. When we launch into 'Maybe It Was Memphis,' you can feel the emotion go across the room. That's the power of a great song. 'Don't Tell Me What to Do' means as much to the fans as when I first released it. Attitude never goes out of style."

On 1992's *Homeward Looking Angel*, Tillis exhibited her playful side in the comedic ditty "Cleopatra, Queen of Denial." The top ten song also won Music Row's Video of the Year. The sassy "Shake the Sugar Tree" went to Number One, while the plaintive "Let That Pony Run" hit the Top Five. "With *Sweetheart's Dance*, Tillis ... placed herself among country's most accomplished modern women," Nash wrote about Tillis' 1994 album. "That she

Born Pamela Yvonne Tillis, July 24, 1957, in Plant City, FL; daughter of Mel Tillis (country singer-songwriter); married Rick Mason, 1978 (divorced); married Bob DiPiero, 1991 (divorced); *Children:* (first marriage) Ben. *Education*—Attended University of Tennessee.

Singer/songwriter, actress; made first stage appearance with father, Mel Tillis, at age eight; staff writer for father's publishing company, Sawgrass Music, 1976-77; member of Freelight jazz band, 1977-78; signed with Warner Brothers, Nashville, 1982; moved to Arista/Nashville, 1989; recorded Put Yourself in My Place, 1991, Homeward Looking Angel, 1992, Sweetheart's Dance, 1994, All of This Love, 1995, Greatest Hits, 1997, Every Time, 1998; only female country artist of 1990s to solo produce her own music, 1995; participated in first all-female country tour with Lorrie Morgan and Carlene Carter, 1996; hosted "Live at the Ryman" television series, 1995; guest starred in "Diagnosis Murder" and "Promised Land" (CBS), 1998; 18 top ten songs.

Awards: Music Row Video of the Year for "Cleopatra, Queen of Denial," 1993; Country Music Association Female Vocalist of the Year, 1994; Country Music Television Top Female Video Artist, 1995.

Addresses: *Record company*—Arista/Nashville, 7 Music Circle North, Nashville, TN 37203. *Management*—Stan Moress, 1209 16th Ave. S., Nashville, TN 37212. *Fan club*—Pam Tillis Fan Network, c/o Johanna Michel, P.O. Box 128575, Nashville, TN 37212. *Website*—Official Pam Tillis World Wide Web Site: www.pamtillis.net. Arista/Nashville site: www.twangthis.com.

can strike this kind of synthesis, both musical and personal, suggests that Tillis, like her father, is in it for the long haul."

In 1995, Tillis took on a role few women of Nashville have —sole producer of her own music—and *All of This Love* was the result. Again, she demonstrated her range with singles such as "The River and the Highway" and "Betty's Got a Bass Boat." Tillis called her *Greatest Hits* record, released in 1997, a turning point. "With it, I closed the first chapter of my career and began the second," she said. Her career gained momentum when the single "All the

Good Ones Are Gone" was nominated for numerous awards, including two Grammys.

Change of Pace

The light-hearted "I Said A Prayer," the first single off 1998's *Every Time*, gained notice as a change of pace for Tillis. "She's been known for the most deeply emotional, heart-wrenching songs around —especially 'All the Good Ones Are Gone,'" Wherehouse Entertainment music buyer Jeff Stoltz told Jim Bessman of *Billboard* magazine. "'I Said A Prayer' is 'more rocking and a big summer song.'" Tillis told Country America, "It's funny, that little song. My son recently drove across the country, and he said he heard it every time he turned on the radio. I said, 'Well, that's because it applies to you.'" The album was released after a year of what Tillis called "'cataclysmic' personal and professional upheaval," Bessman wrote. It was a year that ended both her marriage and her longtime management situation.

Arista/Nashville senior vice president of marketing Fletcher Foster told Bessman, "This album [*Every Time*] is very diverse. Pam has obviously ventured out as an artist." Diversity is a trademark of Tillis' concert performances, too. She told Country.com's Wix, " I think you'll walk away and say, 'I didn't know she did all that.' That's really what I'm all about. I like eclectic and like to really mix it up. You can describe a Shania in one word or you might say 'sexy,' or 'Wynnona is soulful.' But when you say 'Pam Tillis,' you think versatile."

She has toured with Alan Jackson, George Strait, Vince Gill, and fellow second-generation stars Lorrie Morgan and Carlene Carter. In 1998, Tillis fulfilled her lifelong dream of performing with her father, joining him for weekly shows at his Branson, Missouri, theater. "I was adamant about not doing it before I established myself," Tillis told Michael Bane of *Country Music.* "I never wanted to ride on any coattails. And sometimes I'd get impatient, because that would be a drag. There'd be things that'd come up that I'd want to do with Dad, but I just went, 'no way, they won't get it.' The spin doctors, the critics, I just thought they wouldn't get it yet. So I waited."

Acting Repertoire

She felt 1998 was the right time to expand her acting repertoire. She appeared in back-to-back crossover episodes of *Promised Land* and *Diagnosis Murder* on the Columbia Broadcasting System (CBS). "My interest in acting started in 1989 when I starred in Tennessee Repertory's 'Jesus Christ Superstar' as Mary Magdalene," explained Tillis, who has also appeared on *L.A. Law* and hosted *Live at the Ryman*.

Tillis has maintained a rare level of creative control over her career, and plans to keep it that way. "There are people who made it faster and hit it bigger," she told Bane, "but I feel I've been blessed with a consistent career. And, I've gotten to do it on my own terms. I've done each album a little different, not wanting to become my own 'cliche.'"

And as she told Wendy Newcomer of *Country Weekly*, "I love what I'm doing, but I think most artists always feel like they've yet to do their masterpiece. Look at someone like my dad, who's got 50 albums out. I've got a long way to go creatively. My dream is just to keep making music."

Selected discography

Put Yourself in My Place, Arista/Nashville, 1991.
Homeward Looking Angel, Arista/Nashville, 1992.
Sweetheart's Dance, Arista/Nashville, 1994.
All of This Love, Arista/Nashville, 1995.
Greatest Hits, Arista/Nashville, 1997.
Every Time, Arista/Nashville, 1998.
The Prince of Egypt soundtrack, contributor, Nashville/Dream-Works, 1998.

Sources

Books

McCloud, Barry, and contributing writers, *Definitive Country: The Ultimate Encyclopedia of Country Music and Its Performers*, Perigee, 1995.

Periodicals

Billboard, May 23, 1998.
Country America, January 1999.
Country Music, January 25, 1999.
Country Weekly, July 21, 1998.
Entertainment Weekly, May 6, 1994.

Online

"Some 'New Attitude' from Pam Tillis," Country.com, http://www.country.com (June 1998).
"Pam Tillis—Showcase Artist," Country.com, http://www.country.com (March 1996).

Additional information was provided by Arista/Nashville publicity materials, 1998.

—*Shari Swearingen Garrett*

Chucho Valdès

Piano, band leader

Due to the political and social embargo the United States imposed upon Cuba the last half of the 1900s, it is not unusual for many people in the United States to shrug at the mention of Jesus "Chucho" Valdès. Yet throughout the world, the Cuban bandleader is considered one of the most influential pianists of his generation. Valdès began playing piano at the age of three and discovered jazz two years later. His father, prominent jazz pianists Bebo Valdès, encouraged his son's musical path. In fact, the young musician often played with the orchestras his father directed. Age the age of 16 Valdès formed his first jazz trio. He continued to study music and would perform with various jazz groups throughout his early years. While performing with the Orquesta Cubana de Musica Moderna, he decided to form the long enduring and popular group Irakere.

While grooming his son, Chuchito, to take over his role as bandleader, composer and arranger of Irakere, Valdès focused his energies elsewhere. "In Irakere, I developed myself as a composer and arranger, and in the process I let go of the piano a little bit," Valdès told Ben Ratliff in

For the Record . . .

Born Jesus Valdès, 1941 in Cuba, to prominent Latin jazz pianists Bebo Valdès.

Valdès began learning piano at age three; formed first jazz trio at age 16; formed Latin jazz band Irakere, 1973; several prominent Latin jazz musicians, including Paquito D'Rivera, Arturo Sandoval, drummer Enrique Pla and bassist Carlos del Puerto, performed with Irakere, 1973-99; formed Crisol with Roy Hargrove, 1996; released over a dozen albums including *Babalu Aye*, and *From Havana with Love*.

Addresses: *Record company*—Bembe Records, P.O. Box 1792, Redway, CA. 95560.

an on-line article at *latinolink.com*. "I want to play the piano... it's now or never," he explained. Not only revered as incredible jazz musicians, Irakere was considered the best salsa dance band in Cuba. Cuban musician Jose Luis Cortes suggested that Irakere could easily be considered the Rolling Stones of Cuba, referring to the super-star rock band.

Since its formation in 1973, Irakere has made quite an impact on Cuban music. "Irakere is one of the bands that symbolize modern Cuba, one of the most popular bands, very much present as part of the Havana cultural scene and all over the island," said Qbadisc record label owner Neb Sublette during a 1994 National Public Radio interview. Sublette recalls seeing Irakere perform at La Tropical, a giant beer garden in Havana, and watching thousands of "young, mostly black, kids dancing their brains out to this 15-piece band blowing away."

Irakere, meaning forest or woods, refers to an ancient African region where the greatest African percussionists lived and gathered to play. The music traveled to Cuba as it was settled. The band, sensitive to its roots and associations, incorporates traditional African instruments, like bata drums, and folk songs into their musical repertoire. Along with African influences, Valdès also names jazz greats like pianists Bill Evans and Dave Brubeck as musical inspirations. He has played with American jazz mainstays Wynton Marsalis, David Sanchez and Roy Hargrove. As the president of the Havana Jazz Festival, Valdès often invited these musicians, and many others, to play at their annual festival.

During 1996, Valdès and trumpeter Hargrove joined forces to create Crisol, a Cuban-American big band, led by Hargrove. In 1998, Crisol and Valdès won a Grammy in the Latin jazz category. This was Valdès' second Grammy—he and Irakere won a Grammy in 1979 with their album *Live at Newport*.

In 1998, Valdès embarked on his most extensive tour of the United States, playing shows in Philadelphia, Pennsylvania, Washington, DC, Los Angles, California, and St. Paul, Minnesota. That same year, he was asked to perform at the Lincoln Center for the Performing Arts during Cuban music week that year. Valdès has released over a dozen albums with his signature Cuban jazz quality. "Valdès is the musical patriarch of Cuba, and a master pianist, composer and big-band jazz leader.... Valdès exhaled genres with innovative juxtapositions and seamless virtuosity," exclaimed Britt Robson in a 1998 *Minneapolis Star Tribune* concert review.

Because Valdès lived in Cuba he has been unable to sign with an American recording company. But that hasn't stopped him and Irakere from getting their music out. The 1996 release *!Afrocubanismo Live!* was recorded in Canada at the inaugural *!Afrocuabanismo!* Festival in Banff, Alberta, in 1994. Featured on this recording is the legendary Cuban percussionist Jose Luis Quintana Fuerte. *Bele Bele en la Habana,* released by EMI's Blue Note Records in June, 1998, is considered Valdès breakthrough album within the United States. The album is, according to Terry Perkins review for the *St. Louis Post-Dispatch,* "a fiery, challenging set of tunes that encompasses a wide range of Afro-Cuban musical styles. This recording is a must for anyone who's interested in Latin jazz—or great keyboard playing." The *Los Angeles Times'* Don Heckman, however, says the music may throw off some American jazz fans who mightbe expecting continuity of style in the recording. Valdès was never a musician that stuck to any one style of jazz for long, and *Bele Bele en la Habana* is no exception.

Irakere's 1998 release, *Babalu Aye*, was nominated for a 1999 Grammy award. The album features Cuba's premiere folkloric singer, Lazaro Ros, in a 14-minute tribute to the Yoruba orisha (deities) Babaku Aye, in the traditional Cuban call and response song style. Original drummer Enrique Pla keeps the beat for new vocalist Jose Miquel. This combination, the liner notes read "strikes an exquisite balance between youthful fire and accomplished wisdom." While a virtuoso at mixing the musical genres of numerous cultures, Valdès always stayed true to his Cuban heritage. "I'm investigating the African roots of Cuban music. The only way to do it is to stay in Cuba," he told *Time*'s Christopher John Farley. "My work is here. They rhythms are here."

Selected discography

Irakere, CBS, 1979.
Legendary Irakere in London, Ronnie Scott's, 1987.
Irakere, Blue Note, 1992.
From Havana With Love, Westwind, 1995
Afrocubanismo! Live! , Bembe Records, 1996.
Babalu Aye (contains "Babalu Aye"), Bembe Records, 1998.
Bele Bele en La Habana , EMI Music Canada, 1998.

Sources

Periodicals

Los Angeles Times, November 21, 1997; November 23, 1997; June 28, 1998
Minneapolis Star Tribune, June 1998
Newsday, June 1998
St. Louis Post-Dispatch, October 1998
Time, June 22,1998

Online

www.afrocubaweb.com/Chucho
www.bembe.com
www.imnworld.com/Valdès.html
www.latinolink.com

Additional information was provided by the liner notes written by Leonardo Acosta for *Bele Bele en La Habana*, 1998; from liner notes by Jimmy Durchslag to *Babalu Aye*, 1998; and from *All Things Considered*, National Public Radio, November, 11, 1993.

—*Gretchen Van Monette*

Van Halen

Rock group

AP/Wide World Photo. Reproduced with permission.

With groundbreaking musicianship and energetic showmanship, Van Halen dominated the hard rock scene for more than two decades. Guitarist Edward Van Halen was the one constant draw for fans throughout the years, as the band went through three different singers who brought varying styles to Van Halen's music.

Beginning with David Lee Roth in the late 1970s, the group established itself as a powerful musical force. When Roth left the band in 1985, he was replaced by established solo artist Sammy Hagar, who took Van Halen to the top of the album charts for more than ten years. Then, in the late 1990s, former Extreme singer Gary Cherone took center stage with yet another change in style and musical direction. Throughout the changes, Eddie Van Halen continued to forge strong musical partnerships with each of the frontmen and ensured the band's survival by establishing himself as one of the most revolutionary guitarists in rock music. As James Rotondi wrote of Eddie in *Guitar Player*, "He not only redefined electric guitar technique, but he immeasurably changed the sound, structure, and style of the instrument itself."

Eddie and his brother, drummer Alex Van Halen, were both born in Holland and moved to Pasadena, California, in 1962. Their father, Jan Van Halen, played saxophone and clarinet in jazz bands, and encouraged his sons' interest in music. In 1965, the Van Halen brothers formed their first band, the Broken Combs, when Alex was just 13 years old and Eddie was 11. Eddie played piano and Alex played saxophone in the Broken Combs' lunchroom performances at Hamilton Elementary School.

A year after they formed their first band, Eddie decided to buy a drum set with money he made on his paper route. At the same time, Alex bought a guitar and took flamenco guitar lessons. While Eddie was delivering papers, Alex would often play on his drum set, and soon the brothers switched instruments. As teenagers, they formed another band called Revolver, and later performed in a group called Mammoth.

In 1973, Eddie and Alex decided to enroll in Pasadena City College to take classes in music theory. There they met singer David Lee Roth and bassist Michael Anthony. First they convinced Roth to leave his band, the Red Ball Jets, to join Mammoth. At one of their nightclub performances, Anthony's band, Snake, opened the show, and not long after, they invited him to join Mammoth. When they discovered that another band had already trademarked the name, the Van Halen brothers wanted to change the name to Rat Salade. Roth convinced them that Van Halen would make a better choice.

Party Image Grabbed Attention

As the group developed, Eddie and Roth became the center of attention. Eddie would later demand recognition for his brother Alex's musical talent, but Anthony remained in the background throughout his career. "It's a little restricting playing behind a guitarist like Ed," Anthony told JasObrecht in *Guitar Player*, "but it feels good because of who he is."

Van Halen played local clubs and parties for four years before they got the attention of Warner Bros. Records' staff producer Ted Templeman. He saw the band play to a small crowd at the Starwood in Los Angeles and was amazed at their performance. "I saw their sets," Templeman later told Debby Miller in *Rolling Stone*, "and there were like 11 people in the audience, and they were playing like they were at [a large stadium like] the Forum." Templeman convinced label president Mo Ostin to sign the band, and they embarked on the beginning of a long, successful rock career with Warner Bros. Records. Their self-titled debut was released in 1978, and the first single was a cover version of the Kinks' "You Really Got Me." The album went on to sell more than 10 million copies worldwide. "The vision was that we would play whatever kind of music we wanted, regardless of trends, and that we would exhibit our true personalities," Roth told Nancy Collins in *Rolling Stone*. "Then, if people like it, you're going to be a star."

Van Halen went on their first tour, then quickly returned to the studio to record and release *Van Halen II* in 1979. This sophomore effort included the hits "Dance the Night Away" and "Beautiful Girls." The band kept up their fast pace in 1980 with the release of *Women and Children First*, which took only two-and-a-half weeks to record. With hits such as "And the Cradle Will Rock" and "Everybody Wants Some," the album climbed to the top ten on *Billboard*'s album chart just one week after its release.

Eddie was amazed at how fast the group rocketed to the top. "Just three years ago, I was fighting my way up front with the rest of the kids to see Aerosmith," he said to Mikal Gilmore in *Rolling Stone*. "Then, a year later, we were *playing* with them.... I knew I'd always play guitar, but I had no idea I'd be in the position I'm in now."

Rode Through Roller Coaster Years

Sales seemed to have peaked with *Women and Children First* as Van Halen's next two albums—*Fair Warning* and *Diver Down*—sold about half the number of copies of their debut. Eddie later said that he regretted the number of cover songs the band recorded on *Diver Down*, which included the hits "Pretty Woman" and "Dancing in the Streets." "I'd rather bomb making music that comes through me than be in the world's biggest cover band," Eddie explained to Ray Rogers in *Interview*.

Van Halen's slump ended in 1984, and their climb to the top resumed with the release of their number-one single "Jump" and the album *1984*. It was the first time the group used a significant amount of keyboards on an album, and fans responded favorably. The band followed the release with more hit songs from the album, including "Panama" and "I'll Wait," and a successful world tour.

High on the success of *1984*, singer Roth decided to release a solo EP the following year. He recorded four cover tunes on *Crazy from the Heat* and began discussing a possible movie deal with the same title. According to the remaining members of Van Halen, Roth decided he wanted to pursue a solo career in music and an acting career and left the band. Roth explained his side to David Rensin in *Playboy*, "Edward wanted to make music that took more than a year in the studio and play it live for two months. I wanted to make music in half that time and play it twice as much."

Faced with a vacant singer slot in the band, Van Halen began brainstorming for a replacement. They considered recording an album using different singers on each song, then ultimately decided to maintain a group. One day, Eddie was getting his car fixed, and his auto mechanic, Claudio Zampolli, suggested he talk to singer Sammy Hagar. He spoke to Hagar right then from the mechanic's phone and invited him to jam with the band. Eddie had been a fan of Hagar's singing and songwriting when the singer fronted the band Montrose in the mid-1970s. They also worked with the same producer, Ted Templeman.

Soared with Second Singer

Hagar met with the band, rehearsed with them, and by the end of 1985, he became Van Halen's new singer. In the beginning, the new incarnation of Van Halen and Roth continued to talk about each other in the press. "One thing about Roth," Eddie told Steve Dougherty in *People*, "he's not half the singer Sammy is, but he is creative. I'm not slagging him about the music. Onstage he was fine. It was offstage that he made having a human relationship impossible."

Van Halen's first release with Hagar, *5150*, was a huge success and became the band's first of several number-one albums. It included hit songs like, "Why Can't This Be Love," "Best of Both Worlds," and "Dreams." The group sold out every show on their 38-city tour, and constantly boasted about the strong bond between the members. "I don't know what it is about the guy," Alex said in *Rolling Stone*. "You could be having the worst day of your life, but you walk in and there's Sammy. And it just makes my day."

Eddie explained how Hagar freed up his songwriting options, too, in an interview with David Wild in *Rolling Stone*. "From the first second, Sammy could do anything I threw at him," he said. "I'm in heaven because now I can write whatever I want and not worry because Sammy can sing it all."

Van Halen released its second album with Hagar in 1988 called *OU812*. With tracks like, "Finish What Ya Started" and "When It's Love," the album quickly climbed to number one on *Billboard*'s album charts. In the summer of that year, the group headlined the Monsters of Rock tour, which also included Metallica, Dokken, and the Scorpions.

After taking a couple of years off, Van Halen returned with a vengeance in 1991 with the harder-edged, number-one album *For Unlawful Carnal Knowledge*. The CD included the megahit "Right Now," which exposed the band to even wider audiences. "When we first cut 'Right Now,' I almost didn't add a guitar to it because it sounded great with just piano, bass, and drums," Eddie Van Halen

told James Rotondi in *Guitar Player*. "It's not that I care less about the guitar, but the song as a whole means more to me."

Van Halen recorded a socio-political video to accompany the song, which was produced by Carolyn Mayer and directed by Mark Fenske. The video became one of the most requested videos on MTV, and won "Best Video," "Best Art Direction," and "Best Editing" at the MTV Video Music Awards.

In 1993, the band released a live album from the tour for *For Unlawful Carnal Knowledge*, which was called *Van Halen Live: Right Here, Right Now*. Later that year, their longtime manager, Ed Leffler, died of thyroid cancer. This tragic event sent the members of the group into a time of reflection, and eventually was referenced as the turning point that led to the next lineup change.

Their next album, *Balance*, was released in 1995, and debuted at number one on the charts. Eddie explained his impression of the album's title to David Wild in *Rolling Stone*, "I think of it as the balance between the four of us that makes everything work." While recording *Balance*, the band hired a new manager: Ray Danniels, Alex's brother-in-law and longtime manager of Rush. However, the death of Leffler had already began to take its toll on the group. "With Ed dying last year, it was the first time that we have had a reality check in the nine years I've been with the band," Sammy Hagar told Craig Rosen in *Billboard*.

Friction Brought Back the Past

According to Hagar, Danniels' involvement with Van Halen began to cause friction between its members. The group recorded the song "Humans Being" for the *Twister* soundtrack. Alex and Eddie also recorded an instrumental track on their own for the soundtrack called "Respect the Wind." The group was in the process of recording another song for the soundtrack when Eddie and Hagar got into a dispute about the lyrics. Danniels also informed Hagar that the song would instead be used on a greatest hits record, which Hagar was against releasing in the first place.

On June 20, 1996, Hagar was either fired from Van Halen or quit, depending on who's recounting the story. Eddie insisted that Hagar left to pursue a solo career, just as David Lee Roth had in 1985. "I did not quit this band," Hagar told Chris Willman in *Entertainment Weekly*. "I was forced out of this band. And I would be back in this band tomorrow if they got a new manager and wanted me."

Van Halen proceeded with the greatest hits album, and recruited former singer David Lee Roth to record two new songs for the release. *Van Halen: Best of Volume 1* was released with the new tracks "Can't Get This Stuff No More" and "Me Wise Magic," and rumors of a Roth reunion spread like wildfire. When MTV invited Van Halen, with Roth, to present an award at the Video Music Awards, it seemed as if the rumors had been confirmed. However, Van Halen insisted a reunion was never part of the plan.

"I asked him [Roth] to do a song for the *Van Halen: Best of* because I wanted it to have something new," Eddie Van Halen explained to Anthony Bozza in *Rolling Stone*. "Then MTV and everybody else—including him—thought it was a reunion."

After another fallout with the members of his former band, Roth released a public statement on October 2, 1996, explaining his side of the story. "I was an unwitting participant in this deception," he wrote. "It sickens me that the reunion as seen on MTV was nothing more than a publicity stunt.... Those who know me know trickery was never my style."

Created Third Incarnation

During this same time, Danniels had recommended former Extreme singer Gary Cherone as a possible new singer for the band. Danniels was the manager for Extreme before the band broke up the previous year. After meeting with him, Van Halen hired Cherone as the new frontman and began writing songs for a new album. Former singer Hagar returned to his own solo career and released his first album since the breakup in 1997, titled *Marching to Mars*. "I took two weeks to think about what happened," Hagar told Tom Sinclair in *Entertainment Weekly*. "Then I went into the studio and started writing songs." After taking some time to let the dust settle, Hagar also expressed an interest in eventually performing with the group sometime in the future. "If I never walk on stage with Eddie Van Halen again, I'll be really disappointed," he said.

In 1998, Van Halen released their first album with their third singer, appropriately titled *Van Halen III*. On this record, Eddie not only contributed to writing the lyrics, but also sang on the track "How Many Say I?" He described the album to Chris Willman in *Entertainment Weekly* as "heavier than anything we've ever done and deeper on an emotional level; the kind of stuff that gives you goose bumps." However, some critics and fans didn't have the same positive reaction. "Cherone has one speed as a singer on *III*—pained exertion," Greg Kot wrote in *Rolling Stone*, "and longtime bassist Michael Anthony and drummer Alex Van Halen sound as though they're lumbering at any tempo." Tom Sinclair wrote in *Entertainment Weekly*, "Despite the anointing of yet another lead singer, *Van Halen III* is more chunky guitar feast than vocal tour de force."

The members of Van Halen insisted that the album's decrease in sales and increase in criticism was immaterial. "We have to please ourselves first," Eddie told Chris Willman in *Entertainment Weekly*. "And if nobody likes it, don't buy it! Listen to the Roth and Sammy records if that's what you prefer. Nobody's twisting your arm."

At the close of the 1990s, Eddie claimed he was finished with playing musical lead singer in Van Halen. "If Gary ever develops LSD—lead singer disease—I am quitting," Van Halen told Ray Rogers in *Interview*. "No more Van Halen.... Whether everyone likes what I do or not is irrelevant."

Selected discography

Van Halen, Warner Bros. Records, 1978.
Van Halen II, Warner Bros. Records, 1979.
Women and Children First, Warner Bros. Records, 1980.
Fair Warning, Warner Bros. Records, 1981.
Diver Down, Warner Bros. Records, 1982.
1984, Warner Bros. Records, 1984.
5150, Warner Bros. Records, 1985.
OU812, Warner Bros. Records, 1988.
For Unlawful Carnal Knowledge, Warner Bros. Records, 1991.
Van Halen Live: Right Here, Right Now, Warner Bros. Records, 1993.
Balance, Warner Bros. Records, 1995.
Van Halen: Best of Volume 1, Warner Bros. Records, 1996.
Van Halen III, Warner Bros. Records, 1998.

Sources

Periodicals

Billboard, April 17, 1992; September 19, 1992; December 17, 1994.
Entertainment Weekly, October 18, 1996; January 10, 1997; May 23, 1997; March 20, 1998.
Guitar Player, October 1981, May 1993, March 1995, July 1995, February 1997.
Interview, April 1998.
New York, May 11, 1998.
People, February 11, 1985; June 23, 1986; April 6, 1998.
Playboy, August 1987.

Rolling Stone, April 17, 1980; September 4, 1980; June 21, 1984; April 11, 1985; July 3, 1986; March 24, 1988; August 11, 1988; February 18, 1993; March 23, 1995; April 6, 1995; April 2, 1998; April 16, 1998.
Stereo Review, June 1998.
Teen, September 1985.

Online

Van Halen 3, http://www.vanhalen3.com (September 23, 1998).
ÒVan Halen Timeline,Ó *The Official Van Halen Website*, http://www.van-halen.com (September 23, 1998).

—*Sonya Shelton*

Robbie Williams

Singer, songwriter

AP/Wide World Photo. Reproduced by permission.

After five years with the British boy toy band Take That, Robbie Williams left the group and was dismissed and discredited by the music press in the United Kingdom. He proved the critics wrong by winning over new legions of fans and selling more albums than any other artist in the United Kingdom in 1998.

Robert Peter Maximillian Williams was born on February 13, 1974, in Stoke-on-Trent, Staffordshire, England. Williams thrived in the limelight. While in his teens, he joined the Stoke-on-Trent Theatre Company and performed in a number of productions in various minor roles before landing a small part on the English television soap opera, *Brookside*. He dropped out of school at 16 and went to work as a salesperson, a job he hated.

Williams responded to a newspaper advertisement looking for young men who were interested in becoming members of an English boy band that would rival the pop music dominance of America's New Kids on the Block. The advertisement was placed by Nigel Martin Smith, the svengali-like figure behind the band. In 1990, Williams auditioned for the band and was later named the fifth and final member of the Greater Manchester based band, Take That.

For the first year or so, the band traveled across England perfecting and promoting its image and music. They were signed to RCA and had their first big break in 1992 when they released the single, "It Only Takes a Minute." The single cracked the British top ten. It was the first Take That single to do so. Later that same year, they released their debut album, *Take That and Party*. The album debuted at number five on the British album charts. Take That's next single was a cover of the Barry Manilow song, "It Could Be Magic." It climbed to the British top three in January of 1993. The following month, Take That won the BRIT Award for Best British Single for "It Could Be Magic." Take That released their debut album in America in the spring of 1993.

For the remainder of 1993, Take That continued to release chart topping hit singles in the United Kingdom. "Pray" debuted at number one in July. They repeated the achievement in October with "Relight My Fire" and two months later, "Babe" hit the top of the charts. Their sophomore release, *Everything Changes* debuted at number one in October and was certified platinum in the United Kingdom.

At the BRIT Awards in February 1994, Take That took home statues for the Best Single and Best Video for the song "Pray." Their next single, "Everything Changes" also debuted at number one, making Take That the first band to enter the British charts at number one four times

Born Robert Peter Maximillian Williams, February 13, 1974, in Stoke-on-Trent, Staffordshire, England.

Joined Take That in 1990; signed to RCA Records and released *Take That and Party*, 1992; *Everything Changes*, 1993; and *Nobody Else*, 1995. Left Take That and signed to Chyrsalis and released "Freedom 96," 1996; *Life Through a Lens*, 1997; and *I've Been Expecting You*, 1998.

Awards: BRIT Award (England) for Best British Single for "Could It Be Magic," 1993; British platinum certification for *Everything Changes*, 1993; BRIT Award for Best Single for "Pray," 1994; BRIT Award for Best Video for "Pray," 1994; MTV European Music Award for Best Group, 1994; British platinum certification for *Life Through a Lens*, 1998.

Addresses: *Record company*—Chrysalis Records, 1290 Avenue of the Americas, 42nd Floor, New York, NY 10104.

and have four number one singles from their debut album. Their string of consecutive number one debuts was broken in July of 1994 as "Love Ain't Here Anymore" debuted at number three. In October, Take That's next single "Sure" debuted at number one in England. The following month, Take That won the Best Group Award at the inaugural European MTV Music Awards.

"Back for Good" was the next Take That single. Just as many of its predecessors had done,"Back for Good" debuted at number one in Britain in the spring of 1995. In May, the third Take That album *Nobody Else* debuted at number one on the British album charts. Despite the tremendous success of the band, all was not well within the ranks of Take That.

On July 17, 1995, it was announced that Williams was leaving the band, effective immediately. This announcement caused a great deal of animosity between Williams and Martin-Smith when, to Martin-Smith's disapproval, Williams wanted to honor his touring commitments. Williams had begun to grow tired of the highly regimented, pretty boy pop image that Take That had cultivated. He started to sleep with groupies, take drugs, and drink

heavily. His rebelliousness ostracized him from the rest of the band. After cavorting on stage and off with Oasis at the Glastonbury Music Festival, in June of 1995, Williams decided that he wanted out of Take That. Rather than allowing Williams to exit the band gracefully, Martin-Smith, in effect, kicked him out, thus setting into motion a legal suit between himself and Williams.

When he was ousted from the band, Williams immersed himself in alcohol, partying, bitterness and self pity. His previously trim figure ballooned as he drank and ate excessively. He spent the remainder of 1995 and most of 1996 as a professional partygoer, appearing at bars and celebrations everywhere. The British press had a field day with his downward spiral and dismissed Williams as a talentless lout who was full of resentment for his former band and friends.

Williams was unable to record anything until late 1996 due to contract restrictions with RCA. This eventually cost him most of his previous earnings. On June 26, 1996, Williams signed a recording contract with Chrysalis. He released an updated cover of the George Michael song called "Freedom 96" later that year. In comments included at his Geocities web site, Williams called the single, "more a statement than a single. The lyrics tell my story. After this, I'm going to go away and re-invent myself, then come back with my own stuff."

Collaborating with Guy Chambers and sobering up in the process, Williams began to work on his debut solo record. The album, *Life Thru a Lens*, was released on September 29, 1997. Commenting on the songs on the album, Williams said at the Geocities web site that, "they're stories about me and my experiences. It's been really good for me to write them, it's been like having my own counseling sessions." The first single, "Old Before I Die" went to number two on the British singles chart. The album was well received by both critics and fans.

The single "Angels" enraptured both the United Kingdom and Europe and helped to push sales of *Life Thru a Lens* to 300,000 copies in Europe and 1.2 million in the United Kingdom, becoming quadruple platinum in less than one year. In September of 1998, Williams scored his first solo number one single with the song "Millennium," which was taken from his second album, *I've Been Expecting You*, released the following month.

By the end of 1998, Williams had become the highest selling artist in Britain for the year, with sales in excess of two million copies. Commenting about his critics, Williams quipped at the Geocities web site that, "there are still people who can't believe it when they hear me sing. You see them thinking, 'Hey, he actually has a good voice.' People have a preconceived idea if you're in a boy band, they think you have [little] talent. But, it doesn't worry me now, because as far as I am concerned I've proved to myself I have talent."

Selected discography

with Take That

Take That and Party, RCA, 1992.
Everything Changes, RCA, 1993.
Nobody Else, RCA, 1995.

Solo albums

"Freedom 96," Chrysalis, 1996.
Life Through a Lens, Chrysalis, 1997.
I've Been Expecting You, Chrysalis, 1998.

Sources

Books

Rees, Dayfdd, and Luke Crampton, *Encyclopedia of Rock Stars*, DK, 1996.

Periodicals

Billboard, October 3, 1998.
Economist, January 16, 1999.

Online

"Biography," Geocities, wysiwyg://88/http://www.geocities....setStrip/Lounge/8286/Biography.htm (January 19, 1999).

—*Mary Alice Adams*

Trisha Yearwood

Singer

AP/Wide World Photo. Reproduced by permission.

Country singer Trisha Yearwood had long harbored a desire to be a professional singer, but she kept it in check long enough to please her parents. "Even before I sang in front of anybody, I knew I wanted to do this," Yearwood expressed to Kate Meyers in *Entertainment Weekly*. "But I'm from a pretty conservative family and, you know, to say, 'Oh, I'd like to be a country-music star in Nashville' was kind of crazy." So she headed for Nashville, ostensibly to attend college, but in reality to get to the center of country music. "I never had a back-up plan," Yearwood commented to Gaye Delaplane of the *Gannett News Service*. "I always knew I'd go to Nashville and give it a shot. But I didn't tell anybody that." Now, she has the best of both worlds—Yearwood is known in the music world as not only one of the top female stars with a bevy of awards to her name, but also as a business-degree holder who makes all of her own career decisions.

Yearwood's powerful vocal style is sometimes compared to Linda Ronstadt, but she also incorporates pop, folk, and rock nuances into her repertoire. Though she started off her career wearing the typical country outfits and belting straightforward Nashville tunes, she adopted a sleeker, more business-like look and updated musical style in order to broaden the appeal of her genre. Yearwood's professional image is also useful in her off-stage career running her own corporation, Trisha Yearwood, Inc. "The bottom line with me," as she noted to Suzanna Andrews in *Working Woman,* "is that I want to see everything: every contract that goes through, anything to do with my career, my financial statements, personal *and* company." She is obviously doing well for herself, because the Academy of Country Music and the Country Music Association both declared her the top female vocalist of 1997 and 1998, and her albums have sold millions.

Patricia Lynn Yearwood was born on September 19, 1964, to Jack (a banker until his retirement) and Gwen Yearwood, who is retired from teaching the third grade. She grew up on a farm in the small town of Monticello, Georgia, about an hour south of Atlanta. As a youngster, she liked listening to classic country artists like Hank Williams, Patsy Cline, and Kitty Wells. Yearwood and her older sister, Beth, were all-A students in junior high and high school, and Yearwood figured that her talent for numbers suited her for a career in accounting. However, she was growing more passionate about music as she listened to Southern rock bands like the Allman Brothers and the Eagles as well as singers such as Elvis Presley, James Taylor, Gordon Lightfoot, and her favorite, Linda Ronstadt. "She had a power and an emotion in her voice that made you believe every word she sang," Yearwood recounted to Robert Hilburn of the

For the Record . . .

Born Patricia Lynn Yearwood, September 19, 1964, in Monticello, GA; daughter of Jack (a banker) and Gwen (a teacher) Yearwood; married Chris Latham (a musician and songwriter), 1987 (divorced, 1991); married Robert Reynolds (a musician), May 21, 1994. *Education:* Junior college, associate's degree in business; attended University of Georgia; Belmont University, Nashville, TN, B.B.A., 1987.

Worked as an MTM Records, Nashville, TN, receptionist, 1987; demo singer and background vocalist, late 1980s; signed with MCA Records, 1990; released debut album, *Trisha Yearwood*, 1991. Head of Trisha Yearwood, Inc.; celebrity product sponsor for Wild Heart fragrance and Discover card. Film appearances include *The Thing Called Love*, Paramount, 1993.

Awards: Academy of Country Music, top new female vocalist, 1991, top female vocalist, 1997, 1998; American Music Awards, best new country artist, 1992; Country Music Association female vocalist of the year, 1997, 1998; Grammy Award for best country collaboration (with Aaron Neville), for "I Fall to Pieces," 1994, for best country collaboration (with Garth Brooks), for "In Another's Eyes," 1998, and for best female vocal performance, for "How Do I Live," 1998.

Addresses: *Home*—Hendersonville, TN. *Office*—c/o MCA Records, 70 Universal City Plaza, Universal City, CA 91608-1011. TN. *Agent*—William Morris Agency, 151 S. El Camino Dr., Beverly Hills, CA 90212-2775.

Los Angeles Times. "My favorite song was probably 'Love Has No Pride,' but I listened to everything over and over. I knew the albums so well I knew which song it was from the first note."

Yearwood was named outstanding senior girl of the class of 1982 at Piedmont Academy. Though she started performing in church events, school musicals, and talent shows while in school, she pursued a two-year business degree at a junior college after graduation rather than go immediately into show business. However, after one semester at the University of Georgia, she knew she was unhappy with the large campus and yearned to be closer to the heart of countrymusic. In 1986, Yearwood transferred to Nashville's Belmont University, one of the few colleges to offer a major in music business. After promising her parents she would finish college if they sent her to Nashville, she graduated with a bachelor's degree in business administration in 1987, which later was invaluable in helping her to run her own career. While in college, Yearwood interned at MTM Records, the now-defunct studio started by Mary Tyler Moore, and after graduation, became a receptionist there. Aspiring to make her mark, she recorded a demo tape and used it to land jobs working as a backup singer for other hopefuls putting together demo tapes.

Yearwood's reputation spread by word-of-mouth, and she was soon making a living in the studio as a backup singer, as well as performing in a local club. She even worked on a demo in 1989 with up-and-comer Garth Brooks, and their friendship came in handy later when he shot to stardom. Brooks told her he would like to help her out if he succeeded in the music industry, and he introduced her to his producer, Allen Reynolds, who then took Yearwood to producer Garth Fundis. The two began working together, and Fundis helped Yearwood create a slick demo tape. In 1990, Yearwood sang backup on Brooks's *No Fences* album and performed live at a "label showcase," a short concert to show off her skills in front of record labels. She caught the attention of Nashville producer Tony Brown, who signed her to MCA Nashville. Yearwood then appeared as the opening act for Brooks's 1991 tour. "I had done some singing with a few bands, but I never had to carry the show or talk to the audience," Yearwood remarked to Hilburn in the *Los Angeles Times.* "So, I was terrified talking to an audience."

However, the tour stirred up a fan base for her debut album, *Trisha Yearwood,* released on MCA in 1991, shortly before the tour began. The song "She's in Love with the Boy" immediately hit number one on the country charts, the first country female vocal single ever to debut in the top spot. Later, "The Woman Before Me" went to number one as well, and the album hit number two on the country charts. The release had added appeal because Brooks had contributed to two of the tracks. Two million copies were sold, and in 1991 Yearwood was named top new female vocalist by the Academy of Country Music. The next year, she was chosen as best new country artist by the American Music Awards. Though she seemed right on track for future success at that point, Yearwood was unhappy with her management firm of Doyle-Lewis, who was also handling Brooks. She wanted someone to provide more attention to her, so she hired Ken Kragen of Los

Angeles, who also managed Kenny Rogers and Travis Tritt. Though many around Nashville muttered that she was ungrateful and overly ambitious, Yearwood's move led to a much higher profile in the industry. She went on to become the spokesperson for the Wild Heart fragrance for Revlon and made millions doing appearances for the Discover credit card. Talk show hosts like Jay Leno and David Letterman invited her on their shows, and a full-length biography, *Get Hot or Go Home,* came out about her life. Later, she acted in the Peter Bogdanovich film *The Thing Called Love* in 1993, which also showcased her singing talent.

In 1992 Yearwood released *Hearts in Armor* and began working on her image. She shed the down-home look of curly hair, denim shirts, and jeans in lieu of straight hair and designer clothes by Norma Kamali, DKNY, and Anne Klein. "I didn't want the sequins and big hair," Yearwood related to Kate Meyers in *Entertainment Weekly.* "I wanted a classy image because I feel that the music is classy." She added, "If you saw me on the street you wouldn't say, 'I bet she's a country singer.' You might think I was a business executive." *Hearts of Armor* reflected a slight shift in her musical style as well, displaying a more mature sound. Her next album, *The Song Remembers When,* released in 1993, was another hit, boasting an array of tunes tinged with styles from folk ("Hard Promises to Keep") to rock ("If I Ain't Got You") to pop ("Lying to the Moon"). She then released an album of Christmas music, *The Sweetest Gift,* in 1994. After that, 1995's *Thinkin' About You* brought her two number one hits in one year, which is somewhat unusual for a female country artist, and the subsequent *Everybody Knows,* out in 1996, also yielded a number one hit with "Believe Me, Baby (I Lied)."

To wrap up the 1996 Summer Olympics in Atlanta, Georgia, Yearwood sang "The Flame" live to a broadcast of roughly 3.5 billion people after recording it for the *One Voice* Olympic album. She remarked to Chet Flippo in *Billboard,* "I'm not easily moved by things, but that was pretty amazing.... What was so overwhelming was the feeling that this is the only time that the whole world comes together, and you really feel it there." Also that year, she shed 30 pounds off of her five-foot, eight-inch frame, reportedly to get fit after finding out that her father was diagnosed with diabetes. Yearwood believes the fact that she is not perfect endears her to fans. "I think I'm kind of a real role model," she explained to Jennifer Mendelsohn in *USA Weekend,* "rather than something impossible." Her down-to-earth attitude is also appealing, as Mendelsohn noted: "Unassumingly pretty and soft-spoken, she's more like someone you'd chat with over produce at a suburban supermarket than a global superstar."

In spite of having a rash of popular successes, Yearwood was experiencing a dry spell in the arena of honors. She had won a Grammy Award with Aaron Neville in 1994 for best country collaboration for a remake of the Patsy Cline song "I Fall to Pieces," but was not even nominated for a Country Music Association award in 1995. Yearwood hit her stride in 1997 and 1998 with a string of hits and awards. In 1997, she released *Songbook: A Collection of Hits,* containing seven songs that previously reached number one, as well as three new tracks. One of the previously unreleased tunes was "How Do I Live," which was used on the soundtrack for the film *Con Air.* Fellow country star Lee Ann Rimes released a version of the same tune around the same time, fueling a small rivalry, and some radio stations even mixed the two together to create a "duet" effect. Yearwood won a Grammy in 1998 for best female vocal performance for her interpretation of "How Do I Live," as well as another Grammy that year with Garth Brooks for best country collaboration, for "In Another's Eyes."

In addition, Yearwood was also named top female vocalist in 1997 and 1998 by the Academy of Country Music and won the female vocalist of the year award from the Country Music Association both years as well. She also sang with Luciano Pavarotti in the summer of 1998 at his benefit for Liberian children. Though Yearwood has not written any of her own material, she is precise about choosing songs. "I always select music based on emotion, how it makes me feel, even before I made records," Yearwood told Rex Rutkoski of the *Gannett News Service.* She added, "My producer, Garth Fundis, and I have to catch ourselves if we begin to think about recording a song we don't believe in just because we think it might be a hit. We have to ask ourselves: 'Why should we consider it if not for the right reasons?'" The singer has indicated that she does pen tunes, but just has not recorded any of them yet. Her time is curbed severely by her frenetic touring schedule, and she also finds it important to balance her time with her family members and husband.

Yearwood was married in about 1987 to Chris Latham; they divorced in 1991 amid rumors that Yearwood was involved with Brooks (she vehemently denied the claims). She was married on May 21, 1994, to Robert "Bobby" Reynolds, a bass player for the group The Mavericks. They live in a log-and-rock house on an 18-acre wooded lot in Hendersonville, Tennessee, north of Nashville, an area that is so remote they need a four-wheel drive truck to get there. Though their careers call them on the road about 200 days each year, they find ways to stay close by talking on the phone and visiting each other during their tours. When home, they enjoy grocery shopping together, reading biographies, and sipping coffee on the porch of their expansive 4,500-square-foot home. Yearwood encourages people to follow their dreams and not fall prey to letting opportunities slip by. "I came from a very small town, I didn't know anybody in Nashville or the business" she explained to Rutkoski. "I had no connections.... People ask me when I decided to be a singer. I tell them I didn't. I really feel like music chose me."

Selected discography, all on MCA

Trisha Yearwood, 1991.
Hearts in Armor, 1992.
The Song Remembers When, 1993.
The Sweetest Gift, 1994.
Thinkin' About You, 1995.
Everybody Knows, 1996.
Songbook: A Collection of Hits, 1997.

Sources

Books

Contemporary Musicians, volume 10, Gale Research, 1994.

Periodicals

Billboard, July 27, 1991, p. 30; August 17, 1996, p. 25; June 13, 1998, p. 1.
Country Music, January/February 1996, p. 30.
Entertainment Weekly, April 16, 1993, p. 24; August 8, 1997, p. 78.
Gannett News Service, October 28, 1994; July 14, 1995; December 6, 1996.
Los Angeles Times, February 8, 1992, p. F4; October 25, 1992, Calendar, p. 8; February 10, 1998, p. F6.
People, November 16, 1992, p. 105; November 15, 1993, p. 23; October 7, 1996, p. 61.
Star Tribune (Minneapolis, MN), October 6, 1998, p. 1E.
TV Guide, September 19, 1998, p. 28.
USA Weekend, September 20, 1998, p. 8.
Working Woman, August 1995, p. 37.

Online

"CMA Awards and Nominations—Trisha Yearwood," Country Music Association web site,http://www.countrymusic.org (November 5, 1998).

—Geri Speace

Cumulative Indexes

Cumulative Subject Index

Volume numbers appear in **bold**.

Point of Grace **21**
Rice, Chris **25**
Smith, Michael W. **11**
Stryper **2**
Waters, Ethel **11**

Clarinet
Adams, John **8**
Bechet, Sidney **17**
Braxton, Anthony **12**
Byron, Don **22**
Dorsey, Jimmy
See Dorsey Brothers, The
Fountain, Pete **7**
Goodman, Benny **4**
Herman, Woody **12**
Russell, Pee Wee **25**
Shaw, Artie **8**
Stoltzman, Richard **24**

Classical
Ameling, Elly **24**
Anderson, Marian **8**
Arrau, Claudio **1**
Baker, Janet **14**
Bernstein, Leonard **2**
Boyd, Liona **7**
Bream, Julian **9**
Britten, Benjamin **15**
Bronfman, Yefim **6**
Canadian Brass, The **4**
Carter, Ron **14**
Casals, Pablo **9**
Chang, Sarah **7**
Clayderman, Richard **1**
Cliburn, Van **13**
Copland, Aaron **2**
Davis, Anthony **17**
Davis, Chip **4**
Dvorak, Antonin **25**
Fiedler, Arthur **6**
Fleming, Renee **24**
Galway, James **3**
Gingold, Josef **6**
Gould, Glenn **9**
Gould, Morton **16**
Hampson, Thomas **12**
Harrell, Lynn **3**
Hayes, Roland **13**
Hendricks, Barbara **10**
Herrmann, Bernard **14**
Hinderas, Natalie **12**
Horne, Marilyn **9**
Horowitz, Vladimir **1**
Jarrett, Keith **1**
Kennedy, Nigel **8**
Kissin, Evgeny **6**
Kronos Quartet **5**
Kunzel, Erich **17**
Lemper, Ute **14**
Levine, James **8**
Liberace **9**
Ma, Yo Yo **24**
Earlier sketch in CM **2**
Marsalis, Wynton **6**
Mascagni, Pietro **25**
Masur, Kurt **11**
McNair, Sylvia **15**
McPartland, Marian **15**
Mehta, Zubin **11**
Menuhin, Yehudi **11**
Midori **7**
Mutter, Anne-Sophie **23**

Nyman, Michael **15**
Ott, David **2**
Parkening, Christopher **7**
Perahia, Murray **10**
Perlman, Itzhak **2**
Phillips, Harvey **3**
Rampal, Jean-Pierre **6**
Rangell, Andrew **24**
Rostropovich, Mstislav **17**
Rota, Nino **13**
Rubinstein, Arthur **11**
Salerno-Sonnenberg, Nadja **3**
Salonen, Esa-Pekka **16**
Schickele, Peter **5**
Schuman, William **10**
Segovia, Andres **6**
Shankar, Ravi **9**
Solti, Georg **13**
Stern, Isaac **7**
Stoltzman, Richard **24**
Sutherland, Joan **13**
Takemitsu, Toru **6**
Thibaudet, Jean-Yves **24**
Tilson Thomas, Michael **24**
Toscanini, Arturo **14**
Upshaw, Dawn **9**
Vienna Choir Boys **23**
von Karajan, Herbert **1**
Weill, Kurt **12**
Wilson, Ransom **5**
Yamashita, Kazuhito **4**
York, Andrew **15**
Zukerman, Pinchas **4**

Composers
Adams, John **8**
Allen, Geri **10**
Alpert, Herb **11**
Anderson, Wessell **23**
Anka, Paul **2**
Atkins, Chet **5**
Bacharach, Burt **20**
Earlier sketch in CM **1**
Badalamenti, Angelo **17**
Beiderbecke, Bix **16**
Benson, George **9**
Berlin, Irving **8**
Bernstein, Leonard **2**
Blackman, Cindy **15**
Bley, Carla **8**
Bley, Paul **14**
Braxton, Anthony **12**
Brickman, Jim **22**
Britten, Benjamin **15**
Brubeck, Dave **8**
Burrell, Kenny **11**
Byrne, David **8**
Also see Talking Heads
Byron, Don **22**
Cage, John **8**
Cale, John **9**
Casals, Pablo **9**
Clarke, Stanley **3**
Coleman, Ornette **5**
Cooder, Ry **2**
Cooney, Rory **6**
Copeland, Stewart **14**
Also see Police, The **20**
Copland, Aaron **2**
Crouch, Andraé **9**
Curtis, King **17**
Davis, Anthony **17**
Davis, Chip **4**

Davis, Miles **1**
de Grassi, Alex **6**
Dorsey, Thomas A. **11**
Dvorak, Antonin **25**
Elfman, Danny **9**
Ellington, Duke **2**
Eno, Brian **8**
Enya **6**
Esquivel, Juan **17**
Evans, Bill **17**
Evans, Gil **17**
Fahey, John **17**
Foster, David **13**
Frisell, Bill **15**
Frith, Fred **19**
Galás, Diamanda **16**
Garner, Erroll **25**
Gillespie, Dizzy **6**
Glass, Philip **1**
Golson, Benny **21**
Gould, Glenn **9**
Gould, Morton **16**
Green, Benny **17**
Grusin, Dave **7**
Guaraldi, Vince **3**
Hamlisch, Marvin **1**
Hammer, Jan **21**
Hancock, Herbie **25**
Earlier sketch in CM **8**
Handy, W. C. **7**
Hargrove, Roy **15**
Harris, Eddie **15**
Hartke, Stephen **5**
Henderson, Fletcher **16**
Herrmann, Bernard **14**
Hunter, Alberta **7**
Ibrahim, Abdullah **24**
Isham, Mark **14**
Jacquet, Illinois **17**
Jarre, Jean-Michel **2**
Jarrett, Keith **1**
Johnson, James P. **16**
Jones, Hank **15**
Jones, Quincy **20**
Earlier sketch in CM **2**
Joplin, Scott **10**
Jordan, Stanley **1**
Kenny G **14**
Kenton, Stan **21**
Kern, Jerome **13**
Kitaro **1**
Kottke, Leo **13**
Lacy, Steve **23**
Lateef, Yusef **16**
Lee, Peggy **8**
Legg, Adrian **17**
Lewis, Ramsey **14**
Lincoln, Abbey **9**
Lloyd, Charles **22**
Lloyd Webber, Andrew **6**
Loesser, Frank **19**
Loewe, Frederick
See Lerner and Loewe
Mancini, Henry **20**
Earlier sketch in CM **1**
Marsalis, Branford **10**
Marsalis, Ellis **13**
Martino, Pat **17**
Mascagni, Pietro **25**
Masekela, Hugh **7**
McBride, Christian **17**
McPartland, Marian **15**

Tangerine Dream **12**
Tesh, John **20**
Winston, George **9**
Winter, Paul **10**
Yanni **11**

Cornet
Armstrong, Louis **4**
Beiderbecke, Bix **16**
Cherry, Don **10**
Handy, W. C. **7**
Oliver, King **15**
Vaché, Warren, Jr. **22**

Country
Acuff, Roy **2**
Akins, Rhett **22**
Alabama **21**
  Earlier sketch in CM **1**
Anderson, John **5**
Arnold, Eddy **10**
Asleep at the Wheel **5**
Atkins, Chet **5**
Auldridge, Mike **4**
Autry, Gene **25**
  Earlier sketch in CM **12**
Bellamy Brothers, The **13**
Berg, Matraca **16**
Berry, John **17**
Black, Clint **5**
BlackHawk **21**
Blue Rodeo **18**
Boggs, Dock **25**
Bogguss, Suzy **11**
Bonamy, James **21**
Boone, Pat **13**
Boy Howdy **21**
Brandt, Paul **22**
Brannon, Kippi **20**
Brooks & Dunn **25**
  Earlier sketch in CM **12**
Brooks, Garth **25**
  Earlier sketch in CM **8**
Brown, Junior **15**
Brown, Marty **14**
Brown, Tony **14**
Buffett, Jimmy **4**
Byrds, The **8**
Cale, J. J. **16**
Campbell, Glen **2**
Carter, Carlene **8**
Carter, Deana **25**
Carter Family, The **3**
Cash, Johnny **17**
  Earlier sketch in CM **1**
Cash, June Carter **6**
Cash, Rosanne **2**
Chapin Carpenter, Mary **25**
  Earlier sketch in CM **6**
Chesney, Kenny **20**
Chesnutt, Mark **13**
Clark, Guy **17**
Clark, Roy **1**
Clark, Terri **19**
Clements, Vassar **18**
Cline, Patsy **5**
Coe, David Allan **4**
Collie, Mark **15**
Confederate Railroad **23**
Cooder, Ry **2**
Cowboy Junkies, The **4**
Crawford, Randy **25**
Crowe, J. D. **5**
Crowell, Rodney **8**

Cyrus, Billy Ray **11**
Daniels, Charlie **6**
Davis, Linda **21**
Davis, Skeeter **15**
Dean, Billy **19**
DeMent, Iris **13**
Denver, John **22**
  Earlier sketch in CM **1**
Desert Rose Band, The **4**
Diamond Rio **11**
Dickens, Little Jimmy **7**
Diffie, Joe **10**
Dylan, Bob **21**
  Earlier sketch in CM **3**
Earle, Steve **16**
Estes, John **25**
Flatt, Lester **3**
Flores, Rosie **16**
Ford, Tennessee Ernie **3**
Foster, Radney **16**
Frizzell, Lefty **10**
Gayle, Crystal **1**
Germano, Lisa **18**
Gill, Vince **7**
Gilley, Mickey **7**
Gilmore, Jimmie Dale **11**
Gordy, Jr., Emory **17**
Greenwood, Lee **12**
Griffith, Nanci **3**
Haggard, Merle **2**
Hall, Tom T. **4**
Harris, Emmylou **4**
Hartford, John **1**
Hay, George D. **3**
Herndon, Ty **20**
Hiatt, John **8**
Highway 101 **4**
Hill, Faith **18**
Hinojosa, Tish **13**
Howard, Harlan **15**
Jackson, Alan **25**
  Earlier sketch in CM **7**
Jennings, Waylon **4**
Jones, George **4**
Judd, Wynonna
  See Wynonna
  See Judds, The
Judds, The **2**
Keith, Toby **17**
Kentucky Headhunters, The **5**
Kershaw, Sammy **15**
Ketchum, Hal **14**
Kristofferson, Kris **4**
Lamb, Barbara **19**
Lang, kd **25**
  Earlier sketch in CM **4**
Lawrence, Tracy **11**
LeDoux, Chris **12**
Lee, Brenda **5**
Little Feat **4**
Little Texas **14**
Louvin Brothers, The **12**
Loveless, Patty **21**
  Earlier sketch in CM **5**
Lovett, Lyle **5**
Lynn, Loretta **2**
Lynne, Shelby **5**
Mandrell, Barbara **4**
Mattea, Kathy **5**
Mavericks, The **15**
McBride, Martina **14**
McClinton, Delbert **14**
McCoy, Neal **15**

McCready, Mindy **22**
McEntire, Reba **11**
McGraw, Tim **17**
Miller, Roger **4**
Milsap, Ronnie **2**
Moffatt, Katy **18**
Monroe, Bill **1**
Montgomery, John Michael **14**
Morgan, Lorrie **10**
Murphey, Michael Martin **9**
Murray, Anne **4**
Nelson, Willie **11**
  Earlier sketch in CM **1**
Newton-John, Olivia **8**
Nitty Gritty Dirt Band, The **6**
O'Connor, Mark **1**
Oak Ridge Boys, The **7**
Oslin, K. T. **3**
Owens, Buck **2**
Parnell, Lee Roy **15**
Parsons, Gram **7**
  Also see Byrds, The
Parton, Dolly **24**
  Earlier sketch in CM **2**
Pearl, Minnie **3**
Pierce, Webb **15**
Price, Ray **11**
Pride, Charley **4**
Rabbitt, Eddie **24**
  Earlier sketch in CM **5**
Raitt, Bonnie **3**
Raye, Collin **16**
Reeves, Jim **10**
Restless Heart **12**
Rich, Charlie **3**
Richey, Kim **20**
Ricochet **23**
Rimes, LeAnn **19**
Robbins, Marty **9**
Rodgers, Jimmie **3**
Rogers, Kenny **1**
Rogers, Roy **24**
  Earlier sketch in CM **9**
Sawyer Brown **13**
Scruggs, Earl **3**
Scud Mountain Boys **21**
Seals, Dan **9**
Shenandoah **17**
Skaggs, Ricky **5**
Sonnier, Jo-El **10**
Statler Brothers, The **8**
Stevens, Ray **7**
Stone, Doug **10**
Strait, George **5**
Stuart, Marty **9**
Sweethearts of the Rodeo **12**
Texas Tornados, The **8**
Tillis, Mel **7**
Tillis, Pam **25**
  Earlier sketch in CM **8**
Tippin, Aaron **12**
Travis, Merle **14**
Travis, Randy **9**
Tritt, Travis **7**
Tubb, Ernest **4**
Tucker, Tanya **3**
Twain, Shania **17**
Twitty, Conway **6**
Van Shelton, Ricky **5**
Van Zandt, Townes **13**
Wagoner, Porter **13**
Walker, Clay **20**
Walker, Jerry Jeff **13**

Grisman, David **17**
Guthrie, Arlo **6**
Guthrie, Woody **2**
Hakmoun, Hassan **15**
Hardin, Tim **18**
Harding, John Wesley **6**
Hartford, John **1**
Havens, Richie **11**
Henry, Joe **18**
Hinojosa, Tish **13**
Ian and Sylvia **18**
Ian, Janis **24**
Iglesias, Julio **20**
  Earlier sketch in CM **2**
Incredible String Band **23**
Indigo Girls **20**
  Earlier sketch in CM **3**
Ives, Burl **12**
Khan, Nusrat Fateh Ali **13**
Kingston Trio, The **9**
Klezmatics, The **18**
Kottke, Leo **13**
Kuti, Fela **7**
Ladysmith Black Mambazo **1**
Larkin, Patty **9**
Lavin, Christine **6**
Leadbelly **6**
Lightfoot, Gordon **3**
Los Lobos **2**
Makeba, Miriam **8**
Mamas and the Papas **21**
Masekela, Hugh **7**
McKennitt, Loreena **24**
McLean, Don **7**
Melanie **12**
Mitchell, Joni **17**
  Earlier sketch in CM **2**
Moffatt, Katy **18**
Morrison, Van **3**
Morrissey, Bill **12**
N'Dour, Youssou **6**
Nascimento, Milton **6**
Near, Holly **1**
O'Connor, Sinead **3**
Ochs, Phil **7**
Odetta **7**
Parsons, Gram **7**
  Also see Byrds, The
Paxton, Tom **5**
Pentangle **18**
Peter, Paul & Mary **4**
Pogues, The **6**
Prine, John **7**
Proclaimers, The **13**
Rankins, The **24**
Redpath, Jean **1**
Ritchie, Jean, **4**
Roches, The **18**
Rodgers, Jimmie **3**
Sainte-Marie, Buffy **11**
Santana, Carlos **1**
Seeger, Peggy **25**
Seeger, Pete **4**
  Also see Weavers, The
Selena **16**
Shankar, Ravi **9**
Simon and Garfunkel **24**
Simon, Paul **16**
  Earlier sketch in CM **1**
  Also see Simon and Garfunkel
Snow, Pheobe **4**
Steeleye Span **19**
Story, The **13**
Sweet Honey in the Rock **1**

Taj Mahal **6**
Thompson, Richard **7**
Tikaram, Tanita **9**
Toure, Ali Farka **18**
Van Ronk, Dave **12**
Van Zandt, Townes **13**
Vega, Suzanne **3**
Wainwright III, Loudon **11**
Walker, Jerry Jeff **13**
Watson, Doc **2**
Weavers, The **8**
Whitman, Slim **19**

French Horn
Ohanian, David
  See Canadian Brass, The

Funk
Bambaataa, Afrika **13**
Brand New Heavies, The **14**
Brown, James **2**
Burdon, Eric **14**
  Also see War
  Also see Animals
Clinton, George **7**
Collins, Bootsy **8**
Fishbone **7**
Gang of Four **8**
Jackson, Janet **16**
  Earlier sketch in CM **3**
Khan, Chaka **19**
  Earlier sketch in CM **9**
Mayfield, Curtis **8**
Meters, The **14**
Ohio Players **16**
Parker, Maceo **7**
Prince **14**
  Earlier sketch in CM **1**
Red Hot Chili Peppers, The **7**
Sly and the Family Stone **24**
Stone, Sly **8**
  Also see Sly and the Family Stone
Toussaint, Allen **11**
Worrell, Bernie **11**

Funky
Avery, Teodross **23**
Front 242 **19**
Jamiroquai **21**
Wu-Tang Clan **19**

Fusion
Anderson, Ray **7**
Avery, Teodross **23**
Beck, Jeff **4**
  Also see Yardbirds, The
Clarke, Stanley **3**
Coleman, Ornette **5**
Corea, Chick **6**
Davis, Miles **1**
Fishbone **7**
Hancock, Herbie **25**
  Earlier sketch in CM **8**
Harris, Eddie **15**
Johnson, Eric **19**
Lewis, Ramsey **14**
Mahavishnu Orchestra **19**
McLaughlin, John **12**
Metheny, Pat **2**
O'Connor, Mark **1**
Ponty, Jean-Luc **8**
Reid, Vernon **2**
Ritenour, Lee **7**
Shorter, Wayne **5**

Summers, Andy **3**
  Also see Police, The
Washington, Grover, Jr. **5**

Gospel
Anderson, Marian **8**
Armstrong, Vanessa Bell **24**
Baylor, Helen **20**
Boone, Pat **13**
Brown, James **2**
Caesar, Shirley **17**
Carter Family, The **3**
Charles, Ray **24**
  Earlier sketch in CM **1**
Cleveland, James **1**
Cooke, Sam **1**
  Also see Soul Stirrers, The
Crouch, Andraé **9**
Dorsey, Thomas A. **11**
Five Blind Boys of Alabama **12**
Ford, Tennessee Ernie **3**
4Him **23**
Franklin, Aretha **17**
  Earlier sketch in CM **2**
Franklin, Kirk **22**
Golden Gate Quartet **25**
Green, Al **9**
Hawkins, Tramaine **17**
Houston, Cissy **6**
Jackson, Mahalia **8**
Kee, John P. **15**
Knight, Gladys **1**
Little Richard **1**
Louvin Brothers, The **12**
Mighty Clouds of Joy, The **17**
Oak Ridge Boys, The **7**
Paris, Twila **16**
Pickett, Wilson **10**
Presley, Elvis **1**
Redding, Otis **5**
Reese, Della **13**
Robbins, Marty **9**
Smith, Michael W. **11**
Soul Stirrers, The **11**
Sounds of Blackness **13**
Staples, Mavis **13**
Staples, Pops **11**
Take 6 **6**
Waters, Ethel **11**
Watson, Doc **2**
Williams, Deniece **1**
Williams, Marion **15**
Winans, The **12**
Womack, Bobby **5**

Guitar
Abercrombie, John **25**
Ackerman, Will **3**
Adé, King Sunny **18**
Allison, Luther **21**
Allman, Duane
  See Allman Brothers, The
Alvin, Dave **17**
Atkins, Chet **5**
Autry, Gene **25**
  Earlier sketch in CM **12**
Barnes, Roosevelt "Booba" **23**
Baxter, Jeff
  See Doobie Brothers, The
Beck **18**
Beck, Jeff **4**
  Also see Yardbirds, The
Belew, Adrian **5**

Rodgers, Nile **8**
Rush, Otis **12**
Saliers, Emily
  See Indigo Girls
Sambora, Richie **24**
  Also see Bon Jovi
Santana, Carlos **19**
  Earlier sketch in CM **1**
Satriani, Joe **4**
Scofield, John **7**
Segovia, Andres **6**
Sharrock, Sonny **15**
Shepherd, Kenny Wayne **22**
Shines, Johnny **14**
Simon, Paul **16**
  Earlier sketch in CM **1**
Skaggs, Ricky **5**
Slash
  See Guns n' Roses
Springsteen, Bruce **25**
  Earlier sketch in CM **6**
Stewart, Dave
  See Eurythmics
Stills, Stephen **5**
  See Buffalo Springfield
  Also see Crosby, Stills, and Nash
Stuart, Marty **9**
Summers, Andy **3**
  Also see Police, The
Tampa Red **25**
Taylor, Mick
  See Rolling Stones, The
Thielemans, Toots **13**
Thompson, Richard **7**
Tippin, Aaron **12**
Toure, Ali Farka **18**
Towner, Ralph **22**
Townshend, Pete **1**
Travis, Merle **14**
Trynin, Jen **21**
Tubb, Ernest **4**
Ulmer, James Blood **13**
Vai, Steve **5**
Van Halen, Edward
  See Van Halen
Van Ronk, Dave **12**
Vaughan, Jimmie **24**
  Also see Fabulous Thunderbirds, The
Vaughan, Stevie Ray **1**
Wagoner, Porter **13**
Waits, Tom **12**
  Earlier sketch in CM **1**
Walker, Jerry Jeff **13**
Walker, T-Bone **5**
Walsh, Joe **5**
  Also see Eagles, The
Wariner, Steve **18**
Waters, Muddy **24**
  Earlier sketch in CM **4**
Watson, Doc **2**
Weir, Bob
  See Grateful Dead, The
Weller, Paul **14**
White, Lari **15**
Whitfield, Mark **18**
Whitley, Chris **16**
Whittaker, Hudson **20**
Wilson, Brian **24**
Wilson, Nancy
  See Heart
Winston, George **9**
Winter, Johnny **5**

Wiseman, Mac **19**
Wray, Link **17**
Yamashita, Kazuhito **4**
Yarrow, Peter
  See Peter, Paul & Mary
Yoakam, Dwight **21**
York, Andrew **15**
Young, Angus
  See AC/DC
Young, Malcolm
  See AC/DC
Young, Neil **15**
  Earlier sketch in CM **2**
  Also see Buffalo Springfield
Zappa, Frank **17**
  Earlier sketch in CM **1**

Harmonica
Barnes, Roosevelt, "Booba" **23**
Dylan, Bob **3**
Guthrie, Woody **2**
Horton, Walter **19**
Lewis, Huey **9**
Little Walter **14**
McClinton, Delbert **14**
Musselwhite, Charlie **13**
Reed, Jimmy **15**
Thielemans, Toots **13**
Waters, Muddy **24**
  Earlier sketch in CM **4**
Wells, Junior **17**
Williamson, Sonny Boy **9**
Wilson, Kim
  See Fabulous Thunderbirds, The
Wonder, Stevie **17**
  Earlier sketch in CM **2**
Young, Neil **15**
  Earlier sketch in CM **2**
  Also see Buffalo Springfield

Heavy Metal
AC/DC **4**
Aerosmith **22**
  Earlier sketch in CM **1**
Alice in Chains **10**
Anthrax **11**
Black Sabbath **9**
Blue Oyster Cult **16**
Cinderella **16**
Circle Jerks **17**
Danzig **7**
Deep Purple **11**
Def Leppard **3**
Dokken **16**
Faith No More **7**
Fishbone **7**
Ford, Lita **9**
Guns n' Roses **2**
Iron Maiden **10**
Judas Priest **10**
Kilgore **24**
King's X **7**
Kiss **25**
L7 **12**
Led Zeppelin **1**
Megadeth **9**
Melvins **21**
Metallica **7**
Mötley Crüe **1**
Motörhead **10**
Nugent, Ted **2**
Osbourne, Ozzy **3**
  Also see Black Sabbath

Pantera **13**
Petra **3**
Queensryche **8**
Reid, Vernon **2**
  Also see Living Colour
Reznor, Trent **13**
Roth, David Lee **1**
  Also see Van Halen
Sepultura **12**
Skinny Puppy **17**
Slayer **10**
Soundgarden **6**
Spinal Tap **8**
Stryper **2**
Suicidal Tendencies **15**
Tool **21**
Warrant **17**
White Zombie **17**
Whitesnake **5**

Humor
Borge, Victor **19**
Coasters, The **5**
Dr. Demento **23**
Jones, Spike **5**
Lehrer, Tom **7**
Pearl, Minnie **3**
Russell, Mark **6**
Sandler, Adam **19**
Schickele, Peter **5**
Shaffer, Paul **13**
Spinal Tap **8**
Stevens, Ray **7**
Yankovic, "Weird Al" **7**

Inventors
Fender, Leo **10**
Harris, Eddie **15**
Paul, Les **2**
Scholz, Tom
  See Boston
Teagarden, Jack **10**
Theremin, Leon **19**

Jazz
Abercrombie, John **25**
Adderly, Cannonball **15**
Allen, Geri **10**
Allison, Mose **17**
Anderson, Ray **7**
Armstrong, Louis **4**
Art Ensemble of Chicago **23**
Avery, Teodross **23**
Bailey, Mildred **13**
Bailey, Pearl **5**
Baker, Anita **9**
Baker, Chet **13**
Baker, Ginger **16**
  Also see Cream
Barbieri, Gato **22**
Basie, Count **2**
Bechet, Sidney **17**
Beiderbecke, Bix **16**
Belle, Regina **6**
Bennett, Tony **16**
  Earlier sketch in CM **2**
Benson, George **9**
Berigan, Bunny **2**
Blackman, Cindy **15**
Blakey, Art **11**
Blanchard, Terence **13**
Bley, Carla **8**

Ulmer, James Blood 13
US3 18
Valdes, Chuco 25
Vaughan, Sarah 2
Walker, T-Bone 5
Washington, Dinah 5
Washington, Grover, Jr. 5
Weather Report 19
Webb, Chick 14
Weston, Randy 15
Whitaker, Rodney 20
Whiteman, Paul 17
Whitfield, Mark 18
Whittaker, Rodney 19
Williams, Joe 11
Wilson, Cassandra 12
Wilson, Nancy 14
Winter, Paul 10
Witherspoon, Jimmy 19
Young, La Monte 16
Young, Lester 14
Zorn, John 15

Juju
Adé, King Sunny 18

Keyboards, Electric
Aphex Twin 14
Bley, Paul 14
Brown, Tony 14
Chemical Brothers 20
Corea, Chick 6
Davis, Chip 4
Dolby, Thomas 10
Emerson, Keith
    See Emerson, Lake & Palmer/Powell
Eno, Brian 8
Foster, David 13
Froom, Mitchell 15
Hammer, Jan 21
Hancock, Herbie 25
    Earlier sketch in CM 8
Hardcastle, Paul 20
Jackson, Joe 22
    Earlier sketch in CM 4
Jarre, Jean-Michel 2
Jones, Booker T. 8
Kitaro 1
Man or Astroman? 21
Manzarek, Ray
    See Doors, The
McDonald, Michael
    See Doobie Brothers, The
McVie, Christine
    See Fleetwood Mac
Orbital 20
Palmer, Jeff 20
Pierson, Kate
    See B-52's, The
Sakamoto, Ryuichi 19
Shaffer, Paul 13
Sun Ra 5
Waller, Fats 7
Wilson, Brian
    See Beach Boys, The
Winwood, Steve 2
    Also see Spencer Davis Group
    Also see Traffic
Wonder, Stevie 17
    Earlier sketch in CM 2
Worrell, Bernie 11
Yanni 11

Liturgical Music
Cooney, Rory 6
Talbot, John Michael 6

Mandolin
Bromberg, David 18
Bush, Sam
    See New Grass Revival, The
Duffey, John
    See Seldom Scene, The
Grisman, David 17
Hartford, John 1
Lindley, David 2
McReynolds, Jesse
    See McReynolds, Jim and Jesse
Monroe, Bill 1
Rosas, Cesar
    See Los Lobos
Skaggs, Ricky 5
Stuart, Marty 9

Musicals
Allen, Debbie 8
Allen, Peter 11
Andrews, Julie 4
Andrews Sisters, The 9
Bacharach, Burt 20
    Earlier sketch in CM 1
Bailey, Pearl 5
Baker, Josephine 10
Berlin, Irving 8
Brightman, Sarah 20
Brown, Ruth 13
Buckley, Betty 16
    Earlier sketch in CM 1
Burnett, Carol 6
Carter, Nell 7
Channing, Carol 6
Chevalier, Maurice 6
Crawford, Michael 4
Crosby, Bing 6
Curry, Tim 3
Davis, Sammy, Jr. 4
Day, Doris 24
Garland, Judy 6
Gershwin, George and Ira 11
Hamlisch, Marvin 1
Horne, Lena 11
Johnson, James P. 16
Jolson, Al 10
Kern, Jerome 13
Laine, Cleo 10
Lerner and Loewe 13
Lloyd Webber, Andrew 6
LuPone, Patti 8
Masekela, Hugh 7
Menken, Alan 10
Mercer, Johnny 13
Moore, Melba 7
Patinkin, Mandy 20
    Earlier sketch in CM 3
Peters, Bernadette 7
Porter, Cole 10
Robeson, Paul 8
Rodgers, Richard 9
Sager, Carole Bayer 5
Shaffer, Paul 13
Sondheim, Stephen 8
Styne, Jule 21
Waters, Ethel 11
Weill, Kurt 12
Yeston, Maury 22

Oboe
Lateef, Yusef 16

Opera
Adams, John 8
Ameling, Elly 24
Anderson, Marian 8
Baker, Janet 14
Bartoli, Cecilia 12
Battle, Kathleen 6
Blegen, Judith 23
Bocelli, Andrea 22
Bumbry, Grace 13
Caballe, Monserrat 23
Callas, Maria 11
Carreras, José 8
Caruso, Enrico 10
Copeland, Stewart 14
    Also see Police, The
Cotrubas, Ileana 1
Davis, Anthony 17
Domingo, Placido 20
    Earlier sketch in CM 1
Fleming, Renee 24
Freni, Mirella 14
Gershwin, George and Ira 11
Graves, Denyce 16
Hampson, Thomas 12
Heppner, Ben 23
Hendricks, Barbara 10
Herrmann, Bernard 14
Horne, Marilyn 9
McNair, Sylvia 15
Norman, Jessye 7
Pavarotti, Luciano 20
    Earlier sketch in CM 1
Price, Leontyne 6
Sills, Beverly 5
Solti, Georg 13
Sutherland, Joan 13
Te Kanawa, Kiri 2
Toscanini, Arturo 14
Upshaw, Dawn 9
von Karajan, Herbert 1
Weill, Kurt 12
Zimmerman, Udo 5

Percussion
Aronoff, Kenny 21
Baker, Ginger 16
    Also see Cream
Blackman, Cindy 15
Blakey, Art 11
Bonham, John
    See Led Zeppelin
Burton, Gary 10
Collins, Phil 20
    Earlier sketch in CM 2
    Also see Genesis
Copeland, Stewart 14
    Also see Police, The
DeJohnette, Jack 7
Densmore, John
    See Doors, The
Dunbar, Aynsley
    See Jefferson Starship
    Also see Journey
    Also see Whitesnake
Dunbar, Sly
    See Sly and Robbie
Fleetwood, Mick
    See Fleetwood Mac
Hampton, Lionel 6

RuPaul **20**
Sade **2**
Sager, Carole Bayer **5**
Sainte-Marie, Buffy **11**
Sanborn, David **1**
Seal **14**
Seals & Crofts **3**
Seals, Dan **9**
Secada, Jon **13**
Sedaka, Neil **4**
Selena **16**
Shaffer, Paul **13**
Shamen, The **23**
Sheila E. **3**
Shirelles, The **11**
Shonen Knife **13**
Siberry, Jane **6**
Simon, Carly **22**
    Earlier sketch in CM **4**
Simon, Paul **16**
    Earlier sketch in CM **1**
Sinatra, Frank **23**
    Earlier sketch in CM **1**
Smiths, The **3**
Snow, Pheobe **4**
Sobule, Jill **20**
Sonny and Cher **24**
Soul Coughing **21**
Sparks **18**
Spector, Phil **4**
Spice Girls **22**
Springfield, Dusty **20**
Springfield, Rick **9**
Springsteen, Bruce **25**
    Earlier sketch in CM **6**
Squeeze **5**
Stafford, Jo **24**
Stansfield, Lisa **9**
Starr, Ringo **24**
    Earlier sketch in CM **10**
Steely Dan **5**
Stereolab **18**
Stevens, Cat **3**
Stewart, Rod **20**
    Earlier sketch in CM **2**
    Also see Faces, The
Stills, Stephen **5**
Sting **19**
    Earlier sketch in CM **2**
    Also see Police, The
Story, The **13**
Straw, Syd **18**
Streisand, Barbra **2**
Suede **20**
Summer, Donna **12**
Sundays, The **20**
Supremes, The **6**
Surfaris, The **23**
Sweat, Keith **13**
Sweet, Matthew **9**
SWV **14**
Talk Talk **19**
Talking Heads **1**
Taylor, James **25**
    Earlier sketch in CM **2**
Tears for Fears **6**
Teenage Fanclub **13**
Temptations, The **3**
The The **15**
They Might Be Giants **7**
Thomas, Irma **16**
Three Dog Night **5**
Tiffany **4**

Tikaram, Tanita **9**
Timbuk 3 **3**
TLC **15**
Toad the Wet Sprocket **13**
Tony! Toni! Toné! **12**
Torme, Mel **4**
Townshend, Pete **1**
    Also see Who, The
Turner, Tina **1**
Valli, Frankie **10**
Vandross, Luther **2**
Vega, Suzanne **3**
Velocity Girl **23**
Vinton, Bobby **12**
Walsh, Joe **5**
Warnes, Jennifer **3**
Warwick, Dionne **2**
Was (Not Was) **6**
Washington, Dinah **5**
Waters, Crystal **15**
Watley, Jody **9**
Webb, Jimmy **12**
Weller, Paul **14**
Who, The **3**
Williams, Andy **2**
Williams, Dar **21**
Williams, Deniece **1**
Williams, Joe **11**
Williams, Lucinda **24**
    Earlier sketch in CM **10**
Williams, Paul **5**
Williams, Robbie **25**
Williams, Vanessa **10**
Williams, Victoria **17**
Wilson, Brian **24**
    Also see Beach Boys, The
Wilson, Jackie **3**
Wilson Phillips **5**
Winwood, Steve **2**
    Also see Spencer Davis Group
    Also see Traffic
Womack, Bobby **5**
Wonder, Stevie **17**
    Earlier sketch in CM **2**
XTC **10**
Yankovic, "Weird Al" **7**
Young M.C. **4**
Young, Neil **15**
    Earlier sketch in CM **2**
    Also see Buffalo Springfield

Producers
Ackerman, Will **3**
Albini, Steve **15**
Alpert, Herb **11**
Austin, Dallas **16**
Baker, Anita **9**
Bass, Ralph **24**
Benitez, Jellybean **15**
Bogaert, Jo
    See Technotronic
Brown, Junior **15**
Brown, Tony **14**
Browne, Jackson **3**
Burnett, T Bone **13**
Cale, John **9**
Clark, Dick **25**
    Earlier sketch in CM **2**
Clarke, Stanley **3**
Clinton, George **7**
Collins, Phil **2**
    Also see Genesis

Combs, Sean "Puffy" **25**
    Earlier sketch in CM **16**
Costello, Elvis **2**
Cropper, Steve **12**
Crowell, Rodney **8**
Dixon, Willie **10**
DJ Premier
    See Gang Starr
Dolby, Thomas **10**
Dozier, Lamont
    See Holland-Dozier-Holland
Dr. Dre **15**
    Also see N.W.A.
Dupri, Jermaine **25**
Edmonds, Kenneth "Babyface" **12**
Enigma **14**
Eno, Brian **8**
Ertegun, Ahmet **10**
Ertegun, Nesuhi **24**
Foster, David **13**
Fripp, Robert **9**
Froom, Mitchell **15**
Gabler, Milton **25**
Gordy, Jr., Emory **17**
Gray, F. Gary **19**
Grusin, Dave **7**
Hardcastle, Paul **20**
Holland, Brian
    See Holland-Dozier-Holland
Holland, Eddie
    See Holland-Dozier-Holland
Jackson, Millie **14**
Jam, Jimmy, and Terry Lewis **11**
Jones, Booker T. **8**
Jones, Quincy **20**
    Earlier sketch in CM **2**
Jourgensen, Al
    See Ministry
Krasnow, Bob **15**
Lanois, Daniel **8**
Laswell, Bill **14**
Leiber and Stoller **14**
Lillywhite, Steve **13**
Lynne, Jeff **5**
Marley, Rita **10**
Martin, George **6**
Master P **22**
Mayfield, Curtis **8**
McKnight, Brian **22**
McLaren, Malcolm **23**
Miller, Mitch **11**
Osby, Greg **21**
Parks, Van Dyke **17**
Parsons, Alan **12**
Post, Mike **21**
Prince **14**
    Earlier sketch in CM **1**
Queen Latifah **24**
    Earlier sketch in CM **6**
Riley, Teddy **14**
Robertson, Robbie **2**
Rodgers, Nile **8**
Rubin, Rick **9**
Rundgren, Todd **11**
Shocklee, Hank **15**
Simmons, Russell **7**
Skaggs, Ricky **5**
Spector, Phil **4**
Sure!, Al B. **13**
Sweat, Keith **13**
Swing, DeVante
    See Jodeci
Too $hort **16**

Brandy **19**
Braxton, Toni **17**
Brown, James **16**
  Earlier sketch in CM **2**
Brown, Ruth **13**
Brownstone **21**
Bryson, Peabo **11**
Burdon, Eric **14**
  Also see War
  Also see Animals
Busby, Jheryl **9**
C + C Music Factory **16**
Campbell, Tevin **13**
Carey, Mariah **20**
  Earlier sketch in CM **6**
Carr, James **23**
Charles, Ray **24**
  Earlier sketch in CM **1**
Cole, Natalie **21**
  Earlier sketch in CM **1**
Color Me Badd **23**
Commodores, The **23**
Cooke, Sam **1**
  Also see Soul Stirrers, The
Crawford, Randy **25**
Cropper, Steve **12**
Curtis, King **17**
D'Angelo **20**
D'Arby, Terence Trent **3**
Dawn, Sandra
  See Platters, The
DeBarge, El **14**
Des'ree **24**
  Earlier sketch in CM **15**
Dibango, Manu **14**
Diddley, Bo **3**
Domino, Fats **2**
Dr. John **7**
Dru Hill **25**
Earth, Wind and Fire **12**
Edmonds, Kenneth "Babyface" **12**
En Vogue **10**
Evora, Cesaria **19**
Fabulous Thunderbirds, The **1**
Four Tops, The **11**
Fox, Samantha **3**
Franklin, Aretha **17**
  Earlier sketch in CM **2**
Gaye, Marvin **4**
Gill, Johnny **20**
Gordy, Berry, Jr. **6**
Green, Al **9**
Hall & Oates **6**
Hayes, Isaac **10**
Hill, Lauryn **25**
  Also see Fugees, The
Hodge, Alex
  See Platters, The
Holland-Dozier-Holland **5**
Houston, Whitney **25**
  Earlier sketch in CM **8**
Howland, Don **24**
Hurt, Mississippi John **24**
Ike and Tina Turner **24**
Incognito **16**
Ingram, James **11**
Isley Brothers, The **8**
Jackson, Freddie **3**
Jackson, Janet **16**
  Earlier sketch in CM **3**
Jackson, Michael **17**
  Earlier sketch in CM **1**
  Also see Jacksons, The

Jackson, Millie **14**
Jacksons, The **7**
Jam, Jimmy, and Terry Lewis **11**
James, Etta **6**
Jodeci **13**
John, Willie **25**
Jones, Booker T. **8**
Jones, Grace **9**
Jones, Quincy **20**
  Earlier sketch CM **2**
Jordan, Louis **11**
Kelly, R. **19**
Khan, Chaka **19**
  Earlier sketch CM **9**
King, B. B. **24**
  Earlier sketch in CM **1**
King, Ben E. **7**
Knight, Gladys **1**
Kool & the Gang **13**
LaBelle, Patti **8**
Los Lobos **2**
Love, G. **24**
Lynch, David
  See Platters, The
Martha and the Vandellas **25**
Maxwell **22**
Mayfield, Curtis **8**
McKnight, Brian **22**
McPhatter, Clyde **25**
Medley, Bill **3**
Meters, The **14**
Milli Vanilli **4**
Mills, Stephanie **21**
Mo', Keb' **21**
Monifah **24**
Moore, Chante **21**
Moore, Melba **7**
Morrison, Van **24**
  Earlier sketch in CM **3**
Ndegéocello, Me'Shell **18**
Nelson, Nate
  See Platters, The
Neville, Aaron **5**
  Also see Neville Brothers, The
Neville Brothers, The **4**
O'Jays, The **13**
Ocean, Billy **4**
Ohio Players **16**
Otis, Johnny **16**
Pendergrass, Teddy **3**
Peniston, CeCe **15**
Perry, Phil **24**
Pickett, Wilson **10**
Platters, The **25**
Pointer Sisters, The **9**
Price, Lloyd **25**
Priest, Maxi **20**
Prince **14**
  Earlier sketch in CM **1**
Rainey, Ma **22**
Rawls, Lou **19**
Redding, Otis **5**
Reed, Herbert
  See Platters, The
Reese, Della **13**
Reeves, Martha **4**
Richie, Lionel **2**
  Also see Commodores, The
Riley, Teddy **14**
Robi, Paul
  See Platters, The
Robinson, Smokey **1**

Ross, Diana **6**
  Also see Supremes, The
Ruffin, David **6**
  Also see Temptations, The
Sam and Dave **8**
Scaggs, Boz **12**
Secada, Jon **13**
Shai **23**
Shanice **14**
Shirelles, The **11**
Shocklee, Hank **15**
Sledge, Percy **15**
Sly & the Family Stone **24**
Soul II Soul **17**
Spinners , The **21**
Stansfield, Lisa **9**
Staples, Mavis **13**
Staples, Pops **11**
Stewart, Rod **20**
  Earlier sketch in CM **2**
  Also see Faces, The
Stone, Sly **8**
Subdudes, The **18**
Supremes, The **6**
  Also see Ross, Diana
Sure!, Al B. **13**
Sweat, Keith **13**
SWV **14**
Taylor, Zola
  See Platters, The
Temptations, The **3**
Third World **13**
Thomas, Irma **16**
Thornton, Big Mama **18**
TLC **15**
Tony! Toni! Toné! **12**
Toussaint, Allen **11**
Turner, Sonny
  See Platters, The
Turner, Tina **1**
  Also see Ike and Tina Turner
Vandross, Luther **24**
  Earlier sketch in CM **2**
Was (Not Was) **6**
Waters, Crystal **15**
Watley, Jody **9**
Wexler, Jerry **15**
White, Karyn **21**
Williams, Deniece **1**
Williams, Tony
  See Platters, The
Williams, Vanessa **10**
Wilson, Jackie **3**
Winans, The **12**
Winbush, Angela **15**
Womack, Bobby **5**
Wonder, Stevie **17**
  Earlier sketch in CM **2**
Zhane **22**

Rock
10,000 Maniacs **3**
311 **20**
AC/DC **4**
Adam Ant **13**
Adams, Bryan **20**
  Earlier sketch in CM **2**
Aerosmith **22**
  Earlier sketch in CM **3**
Afghan Whigs **17**
Alarm **2**
Albini, Steve **15**
Alexander, Arthur **14**

Walsh, Joe **5**
  Also see Eagles, The
Walsh, Marty
  See Supertramp
War **14**
Warrant **17**
Weezer **20**
Weller, Paul **14**
White Zombie **17**
Whitesnake **5**
Whitley, Chris **16**
Who, The **3**
Wilson, Brian **24**
  Also see Beach Boys, The
Winter, Johnny **5**
Winthrop, Dave
  See Supertramp
Winwood, Steve **2**
  Also see Spencer Davis Group
  Also see Traffic
Wolf, Peter **25**
Wray, Link **17**
Wyatt, Robert **24**
X **11**
Yardbirds, The **10**
Yes **8**
Yo La Tengo **24**
Young, Neil **15**
  Earlier sketch in CM **2**
  Also see Buffalo Springfield
Zappa, Frank **17**
  Earlier sketch in CM **1**
Zevon, Warren **9**
Zombies, The **23**
ZZ Top **2**

Rock and Roll Pioneers
Ballard, Hank **17**
Berry, Chuck **1**
Clark, Dick **25**
  Earlier sketch in CM **2**
Darin, Bobby **4**
Diddley, Bo **3**
Dion **4**
Domino, Fats **2**
Eddy, Duane **9**
Everly Brothers, The **2**
Francis, Connie **10**
Glitter, Gary **19**
Haley, Bill **6**
Hawkins, Screamin' Jay **8**
Holly, Buddy **1**
James, Etta **6**
Jordan, Louis **11**
Lewis, Jerry Lee **2**
Little Richard **1**
Nelson, Rick **2**
Orbison, Roy **2**
Otis, Johnny **16**
Paul, Les **2**
Perkins, Carl **9**
Phillips, Sam **5**
Presley, Elvis **1**
Professor Longhair **6**
Sedaka, Neil **4**
Shannon, Del **10**
Shirelles, The **11**
Spector, Phil **4**
Twitty, Conway **6**
Valli, Frankie **10**
Wilson, Jackie **3**
Wray, Link **17**

Saxophone
Adderly, Cannonball **15**
Anderson, Wessell **23**
Ayler , Albert **19**
Barbieri, Gato **22**
Bechet, Sidney **17**
Braxton, Anthony **12**
Carter, Benny **3**
  Also see McKinney's Cotton Pickers
Carter, James **18**
Chenier, C. J. **15**
Clemons, Clarence **7**
Coleman, Ornette **5**
Coltrane, John **4**
Curtis, King **17**
Desmond, Paul **23**
Dibango, Manu **14**
Dorsey, Jimmy
  See Dorsey Brothers, The
Getz, Stan **12**
Golson, Benny **21**
Gordon, Dexter **10**
Harris, Eddie **15**
Hawkins, Coleman **11**
Henderson, Joe **14**
Herman, Woody **12**
Hodges, Johnny **24**
Jacquet, Illinois **17**
James, Boney **21**
Kenny G **14**
Kirk, Rahsaan Roland **6**
Koz, Dave **19**
Lacy, Steve **23**
Lateef, Yusef **16**
Lloyd, Charles **22**
Lopez, Israel "Cachao" **14**
Lovano, Joe **13**
Marsalis, Branford **10**
Morgan, Frank **9**
Mulligan, Gerry **16**
Najee **21**
Osby, Greg **21**
Parker, Charlie **5**
Parker, Maceo **7**
Pepper, Art **18**
Redman, Joshua **25**
  Earlier sketch in CM **12**
Rollins, Sonny **7**
Russell, Pee Wee **25**
Sanborn, David **1**
Sanders, Pharoah **16**
Shorter, Wayne **5**
Threadgill, Henry **9**
Washington, Grover, Jr. **5**
Winter, Paul **10**
Young, La Monte **16**
Young, Lester **14**
Zorn, John **15**

Sintir
Hakmoun, Hassan **15**

Songwriters
2Pac **17**
Acuff, Roy **2**
Adams, Bryan **20**
  Earlier sketch in CM **2**
Adams, Yolanda **23**
Aikens, Rhett **22**
Albini, Steve **15**
Alexander, Arthur **14**
Allen, Peter **11**
Allison, Mose **17**

Alpert, Herb **11**
Alvin, Dave **17**
Amos, Tori **12**
Anderson, Ian
  See Jethro Tull
Anderson, John **5**
Anka, Paul **2**
Armatrading, Joan **4**
Astbury, Ian
  See Cult, The
Atkins, Chet **5**
Autry, Gene **25**
  Earlier sketch in CM **12**
Bacharach, Burt **20**
  Earlier sketch in CM **1**
Baez, Joan **1**
Baker, Anita **9**
Balin, Marty
  See Jefferson Airplane
Barlow, Lou **20**
Barrett, (Roger) Syd
  See Pink Floyd
Basie, Count **2**
Becker, Walter
  See Steely Dan
Beckley, Gerry
  See America
Belew, Adrian **5**
Benton, Brook **7**
Berg, Matraca **16**
Berlin, Irving **8**
Berry, Chuck **1**
Bjork **16**
  Also see Sugarcubes, The
Black, Clint **5**
Black, Frank **14**
Blades, Ruben **2**
Blige, Mary J. **15**
Bloom, Luka **14**
Bono
  See U2
Brady, Paul **8**
Bragg, Billy **7**
Brandt, Paul **22**
Brickell, Edie **3**
Brokop, Lisa **22**
Brooke, Jonatha
  See Story, The
Brooks, Garth **25**
  Earlier sketch in CM **8**
Brown, Bobby **4**
Brown, James **16**
  Earlier sketch in CM **2**
Brown, Junior **15**
Brown, Marty **14**
Browne, Jackson **3**
Buck, Peter
  See R.E.M.
Buck, Robert
  See 10,000 Maniacs
Buckingham, Lindsey **8**
  Also see Fleetwood Mac
Buckley, Jeff **22**
Buckley, Tim **14**
Buffett, Jimmy **4**
Bunnell, Dewey
  See America
Burdon, Eric **14**
  Also see War
  Also see Animals
Burnett, T Bone **13**
Burning Spear **15**
Bush, Kate **4**

Wagoner, Porter **13**
Waits, Tom **12**
  Earlier sketch in CM **1**
Walden, Narada Michael **14**
Walker, Jerry Jeff **13**
Walker, T-Bone **5**
Waller, Fats **7**
Walsh, Joe **5**
  Also see Eagles, The
Wariner, Steve **18**
Warren, Diane **21**
Waters, Crystal **15**
Waters, Muddy **24**
  Earlier sketch in CM **4**
Waters, Roger
  See Pink Floyd
Watt, Mike **22**
Webb, Jimmy **12**
Weill, Kurt **12**
Weir, Bob
  See Grateful Dead, The
Welch, Bob
  See Fleetwood Mac
Weller, Paul **14**
West, Dottie **8**
White, Karyn **21**
White, Lari **15**
Whitley, Chris **16**
Whitley, Keith **7**
Williams, Dar **21**
Williams, Deniece **1**
Williams, Don **4**
Williams, Hank, Jr. **1**
Williams, Hank, Sr. **4**
Williams, Lucinda **24**
  Earlier sketch in CM **10**
Williams, Paul **5**
Williams, Victoria **17**
Wills, Bob **6**
Wilson, Brian **24**
  Also see Beach Boys, The
Wilson, Cindy
  See B-52's, The
Wilson, Ricky
  See B-52's, The
Winbush, Angela **15**
Winter, Johnny **5**
Winwood, Steve **2**
  Also see Spencer Davis Group
  Also see Traffic
Womack, Bobby **5**
Wonder, Stevie **17**
  Earlier sketch in CM **2**
Wray, Link **17**
Wyatt, Robert **24**
Wynette, Tammy **2**
  Earlier sketch in CM **2**
Yearwood, Trisha **25**
  Earlier sketch in CM **10**
Yoakam, Dwight **21**
  Earlier sketch in CM **1**
Young, Angus
  See AC/DC

Young, Neil **15**
  Earlier sketch in CM **2**
  Also see Buffalo Springfield
Zappa, Frank **17**
  Earlier sketch in CM **1**
Zevon, Warren **9**

Trombone
Anderson, Ray **7**
Brown, Lawrence **23**
Dorsey, Tommy
  See Dorsey Brothers, The
Miller, Glenn **6**
Teagarden, Jack **10**
Turre, Steve **22**
Watts, Eugene
  See Canadian Brass, The

Trumpet
Alpert, Herb **11**
Armstrong, Louis **4**
Baker, Chet **13**
Berigan, Bunny **2**
Blanchard, Terence **13**
Brown, Clifford **24**
Cherry, Don **10**
Coleman, Ornette **5**
Davis, Miles **1**
Eldridge, Roy **9**
  Also see McKinney's Cotton Pickers
Ferguson, Maynard **7**
Gillespie, Dizzy **6**
Hargrove, Roy **15**
Hawkins, Erskine **19**
Hirt, Al **5**
Isham, Mark **14**
James, Harry **11**
Jensen, Ingrid **22**
Jones, Quincy **20**
  Earlier sketch in CM **2**
Jones, Thad **19**
Loughnane, Lee **3**
Marsalis, Wynton **20**
  Earlier sketch in CM **6**
Masekela, Hugh **7**
Matthews, Eric **22**
Mighty Mighty Bosstones **20**
Miles, Ron **22**
Mills, Fred
  See Canadian Brass, The
Navarro, Fats **25**
Oliver, King **15**
Rodney, Red **14**
Romm, Ronald
  See Canadian Brass, The
Sandoval, Arturo **15**
Severinsen, Doc **1**
Terry, Clark **24**

Tuba
Daellenbach, Charles
  See Canadian Brass, The
Phillips, Harvey **3**

Vibraphone
Burton, Gary **10**
Hampton, Lionel **6**
Jackson, Milt **15**
Norvo, Red **12**

Viola
Dutt, Hank
  See Kronos Quartet
Jones, Michael
  See Kronos Quartet
Killian, Tim
  See Kronos Quartet
Menuhin, Yehudi **11**
Zukerman, Pinchas **4**

Violin
Acuff, Roy **2**
Anderson, Laurie **25**
  Earlier sketch in CM **1**
Bell, Joshua **21**
Bromberg, David **18**
Bush, Sam
  See New Grass Revival, The
Carter, Regina **22**
Chang, Sarah **7**
Clements, Vassar **18**
Coleman, Ornette **5**
Cugat, Xavier **23**
Daniels, Charlie **6**
Doucet, Michael **8**
Germano, Lisa **18**
Gingold, Josef **6**
Grappelli, Stephane **10**
Gray, Ella
  See Kronos Quartet
Harrington, David
  See Kronos Quartet
Hartford, John **1**
Hidalgo, David
  See Los Lobos
Kennedy, Nigel **8**
Krauss, Alison **10**
Lamb, Barbara **19**
Lewis, Roy
  See Kronos Quartet
Marriner, Neville **7**
Menuhin, Yehudi **11**
Midori **7**
Mutter, Anne-Sophie **23**
O'Connor, Mark **1**
Perlman, Itzhak **2**
Ponty, Jean-Luc **8**
Salerno-Sonnenberg, Nadja **3**
Shallenberger, James
  See Kronos Quartet
Sherba, John
  See Kronos Quartet
Skaggs, Ricky **5**
Stern, Isaac **7**
Whiteman, Paul **17**
Wills, Bob **6**
Zukerman, Pinchas **4**

Cumulative Musicians Index

Volume numbers appear in **bold**.

Baldwin, Donny
   See Starship
Baliardo, Diego
   See Gipsy Kings, The
Baliardo, Paco
   See Gipsy Kings, The
Baliardo, Tonino
   See Gipsy Kings, The
Balin, Marty
   See Jefferson Airplane
Ball, Marcia 15
Ballard, Florence
   See Supremes, The
Ballard, Hank 17
Balsley, Phil
   See Statler Brothers, The
Baltes, Peter
   See Dokken
Balzano, Vinnie
   See Less Than Jake
Bambaataa, Afrika 13
Bamonte, Perry
   See Cure, The
Bananarama 22
Bancroft, Cyke
   See Bevis Frond
Band, The 9
Bangles 22
Banks, Nick
   See Pulp
Banks, Peter
   See Yes
Banks, Tony
   See Genesis
Baptiste, David Russell
   See Meters, The
Barbarossa, Dave
   See Republica
Barbata, John
   See Jefferson Starship
Barber, Keith
   See Soul Stirrers, The
Barbero, Lori
   See Babes in Toyland
Barbieri, Gato 22
Bardens, Peter
   See Camel
Barenaked Ladies 18
Bargeld, Blixa
   See Einstürzende Neubauten
Bargeron, Dave
   See Blood, Sweat and Tears
Barham, Meriel
   See Lush
Barile, Jo
   See Ventures, The
Barker, Paul
   See Ministry
Barker, Travis Landon
   See Aquabats
Barlow, Barriemore
   See Jethro Tull
Barlow, Lou 20
   Also see Dinosaur Jr.
Barlow, Tommy
   See Aztec Camera
Barnes, Danny
   See Bad Livers, The
Barnes, Micah
   See Nylons, The
Barnes, Roosevelt "Booba" 23
Barnwell, Duncan
   See Simple Minds

Barnwell, Ysaye Maria
   See Sweet Honey in the Rock
Barr, Ralph
   See Nitty Gritty Dirt Band, The
Barre, Martin
   See Jethro Tull
Barrere, Paul
   See Little Feat
Barrett, Dicky
   See Mighty Mighty Bosstones
Barrett, Robert
   See Goodie Mob
Barrett, (Roger) Syd
   See Pink Floyd
Barron, Christopher
   See Spin Doctors
Barrow, Geoff
   See Portishead
Bartels, Joanie 13
Bartholomew, Simon
   See Brand New Heavies, The
Bartoli, Cecilia 12
Barton, Lou Ann
   See Fabulous Thunderbirds, The
Bartos, Karl
   See Kraftwerk
Basehead 11
Basher, Mick
   See X
Basia 5
Basie, Count 2
Bass, Colin
   See Camel
Bass, Colin
   See Chumbawamba
Bass, Lance
   See 'N Sync
Bass, Ralph 24
Batchelor, Kevin
   See Big Mountain
   See Steel Pulse
Batchelor, Kevin
Batel, Beate
   See Einstürzende Neubauten
Batiste, Lionel
   See Dirty Dozen
Batoh, Masaki
   See Pearls Before Swine
Batoh, Masaki
   See Ghost
Battin, Skip
   See Byrds, The
Battle, Kathleen 6
Bauer, Judah
   See Jon Spencer Blues Explosion
Baumann, Peter
   See Tangerine Dream
Bautista, Roland
   See Earth, Wind and Fire
Baxter, Adrian
   See Cherry Poppin' Daddies
Baxter, Jeff
   See Doobie Brothers, The
Bayer Sager, Carole
   See Sager, Carole Bayer
Baylor, Helen 20
Baynton-Power, David
   See James
Bazilian, Eric
   See Hooters
Beach Boys, The 1
Beale, Michael
   See Earth, Wind and Fire

Beard, Annette
   See Martha and the Vandellas
Beard, Frank
   See ZZ Top
Beasley, Paul
   See Mighty Clouds of Joy, The
Beastie Boys 25
   Earlier sketch in CM 8
Beat Farmers 23
Beatles, The 2
Beauford, Carter
   See Dave Matthews Band
Beautiful South 19
Beaver Brown Band, The 3
Bechet, Sidney 17
Beck 18
Beck, Jeff 4
   Also see Yardbirds, The
Beck, William
   See Ohio Players
Becker, Walter
   See Steely Dan
Beckford, Theophilus
   See Skatalites, The
Beckley, Gerry
   See America
Bee Gees, The 3
Beers, Garry Gary
   See INXS
Behler, Chuck
   See Megadeth
Beiderbecke, Bix 16
Belafonte, Harry 8
Belew, Adrian 5
   Also see King Crimson
Belfield, Dennis
   See Three Dog Night
Bell, Andy
   See Erasure
Bell, Brian
   See Weezer
Bell, Derek
   See Chieftains, The
Bell, Eric
   See Thin Lizzy
Bell, Jayn
   See Sounds of Blackness
Bell, Joshua 21
Bell, Melissa
   See Soul II Soul
Bell, Ronald
   See Kool & the Gang
Bell, Taj
   See Charm Farm
Belladonna, Joey
   See Anthrax
Bellamy Brothers, The 13
Bellamy, David
   See Bellamy Brothers, The
Bellamy, Howard
   See Bellamy Brothers, The
Belle, Regina 6
Bello, Elissa
   See Go-Go's, The
Bello, Frank
   See Anthrax
Belly 16
Belushi, John
   See Blues Brothers, The
Ben Folds Five 20
Benante, Charlie
   See Anthrax
Benatar, Pat 8

Booth, Tim
  See James
Boquist, Dave
  See Son Volt
Boquist, Jim
  See Son Volt
Bordin, Mike
  See Faith No More
Borg, Bobby
  See Warrant
Borge, Victor 19
Borowiak, Tony
  See All-4-One
Bostaph, Paul
  See Slayer
Boston 11
Bostrom, Derrick
  See Meat Puppets, The
Bottum, Roddy
  See Faith No More
Bouchard, Albert
  See Blue Oyster Cult
Bouchard, Joe
  See Blue Oyster Cult
Bouchikhi, Chico
  See Gipsy Kings, The
Bowen, Jimmy
  See Country Gentlemen, The
Bowens, Sir Harry
  See Was (Not Was)
Bowie, David 23
  Earlier sketch in CM 1
Bowie, Lester
  See Art Ensemble of Chicago, The
Bowman, Steve
  See Counting Crows
Box, Mick
  See Uriah Heep
Boy Howdy 21
Boyd, Brandon
  See Incubus
Boyd, Eadie
  See Del Rubio Triplets
Boyd, Elena
  See Del Rubio Triplets
Boyd, Liona 7
Boyd, Milly
  See Del Rubio Triplets
Boyle, Doug
  See Caravan
Boyz II Men 15
Bozulich, Carla
  See Geraldine Fibbers
Brad 21
Bradbury, John
  See Specials, The
Bradshaw, Tim
  See Dog's Eye View
Bradstreet, Rick
  See Bluegrass Patriots
Brady, Paul 8
Bragg, Billy 7
Bramah, Martin
  See Fall, The
Brand New Heavies, The 14
Brandt, Paul 22
Brandy 19
Branigan, Laura 2
Brannon, Kippi 20
Brantley, Junior
  See Roomful of Blues
Braxton, Anthony 12
Braxton, Toni 17

Bream, Julian 9
Breeders 19
Brendel, Alfred 23
Brennan, Ciaran
  See Clannad
Brennan, Enya
  See Clannad
Brennan, Maire
  See Clannad
Brennan, Paul
  See Odds
Brennan, Pol
  See Clannad
Brenner, Simon
  See Talk Talk
Brevette, Lloyd
  See Skatalites, The
Brickell, Edie 3
Brickman, Jim 22
Bridgewater, Dee Dee 18
Briggs, David
  See Pearls Before Swine
Briggs, James Randall
  See Aquabats
Briggs, Vic
  See Animals
Bright, Garfield
  See Shai
Bright, Ronnie
  See Coasters, The
Brightman, Sarah 20
Briley, Alex
  See Village People, The
Brindley, Paul
  See Sundays, The
Britten, Benjamin 15
Brittingham, Eric
  See Cinderella
Brix
  See Fall, The
Brockenborough, Dennis
  See Mighty Mighty Bosstones
Brockie, Dave
  See Gwar
Brokop, Lisa 22
Bromberg, David 18
Bronfman, Yefim 6
Brooke, Jonatha
  See Story, The
Brookes, Jon
  See Charlatans, The
Brooks & Dunn 25
  Earlier sketch in CM 12
Brooks, Baba
  See Skatalites, The
Brooks, Garth 25
  Earlier sketch in CM 8
Brooks III, Leon Eric "Kix"
  See Brooks & Dunn,
Broonzy, Big Bill 13
Brotherdale, Steve
  See Joy Division
  Also see Smithereens, The
Broudie, Ian
  See Lightning Seeds
Brown, Bobby 4
Brown, Brooks
  See Cherry Poppin' Daddies
Brown, Clarence "Gatemouth" 11
Brown, Clifford 24
Brown, Donny
  See Verve Pipe, The

Brown, Duncan
  See Stereolab
Brown, Foxy 25
Brown, George
  See Kool & the Gang
Brown, Harold
  See War
Brown, Heidi
  See Treadmill Trackstar
Brown, Ian
  See Stone Roses, The
Brown, James 16
  Earlier sketch in CM 2
Brown, Jimmy
  See UB40
Brown, Junior 15
Brown, Lawrence 23
Brown, Marty 14
Brown, Melanie
  See Spice Girls
Brown, Mick
  See Dokken
Brown, Morris
  See Pearls Before Swine
Brown, Norman
  See Mills Brothers, The
Brown, Rahem
  See Artifacts
Brown, Ray 21
Brown, Ruth 13
Brown, Selwyn "Bumbo"
  See Steel Pulse
Brown, Steven
  See Tuxedomoon
Brown, Tim
  See Boo Radleys, The
Brown, Tony 14
Browne, Jackson 3
  Also see Nitty Gritty Dirt Band, The
Brownstein, Carrie
  See Sleater-Kinney
Brownstone 21
Brubeck, Dave 8
Bruce, Dustan
  See Chumbawamba
Bruce, Jack
  See Cream
Bruford, Bill
  See King Crimson
  Also see Yes
Bruster, Thomas
  See Soul Stirrers, The
Bryan, David
  See Bon Jovi
Bryan, Karl
  See Skatalites, The
Bryan, Mark
  See Hootie and the Blowfish
Bryant, Elbridge
  See Temptations, The
Bryant, Jeff
  See Ricochet
Bryant, Junior
  See Ricochet
Bryson, Bill
  See Desert Rose Band, The
Bryson, David
  See Counting Crows
Bryson, Peabo 11
Buchanan, Wallis
  See Jamiroquai
Buchholz, Francis
  See Scorpions, The

Carr, Eric
 See Kiss
Carr, James **23**
Carr, Martin
 See Boo Radleys, The
Carr, Teddy
 See Ricochet
Carrack, Paul
 See Mike & the Mechanics
 Also see Squeeze
Carreras, José **8**
Carrigan, Andy
 See Mekons, The
Carroll, Earl "Speedo"
 See Coasters, The
Carruthers, John
 See Siouxsie and the Banshees
Cars, The **20**
Carter, A. P.
 See Carter Family, The
Carter, Anita
 See Carter Family, The
Carter, Benny **3**
 Also see McKinney's Cotton Pickers
Carter, Betty **6**
Carter, Carlene **8**
Carter, Deana **25**
Carter Family, The **3**
Carter, Helen
 See Carter Family, The
Carter, James **18**
Carter, Janette
 See Carter Family, The
Carter, Jimmy
 See Five Blind Boys of Alabama
Carter, Joe
 See Carter Family, The
Carter, June **6**
 Also see Carter Family, The
Carter, Maybell
 See Carter Family, The
Carter, Nell **7**
Carter, Nick
 See Backstreet Boys
Carter, Regina **22**
Carter, Ron **14**
Carter, Sara
 See Carter Family, The
Carthy, Martin
 See Steeleye Span
Caruso, Enrico **10**
Casady, Jack
 See Jefferson Airplane
Casale, Bob
 See Devo
Casale, Gerald V.
 See Devo
Casals, Pablo **9**
Case, Peter **13**
Cash, Johnny **17**
 Earlier sketch in CM 1
Cash, Rosanne **2**
Cassidy, Ed
 See Spirit
Catallo, Gene
 See Surfin' Pluto
Catallo, Shris
 See Surfin' Pluto
Cates, Ronny
 See Petra
Catherall, Joanne
 See Human League, The
Catherine Wheel **18**

Caustic Window
 See Aphex Twin
Cauty, Jimmy
 See Orb, The
Cavalera, Igor
 See Sepultura
Cavalera, Max
 See Sepultura
Cave, Nick **10**
Cavoukian, Raffi
 See Raffi
Cease, Jeff
 See Black Crowes, The
Cervenka, Exene
 See X
Cetera, Peter
 See Chicago
Chamberlin, Jimmy
 See Smashing Pumpkins
Chambers, Martin
 See Pretenders, The
Chambers, Paul **18**
Chambers, Terry
 See XTC
Champion, Eric **21**
Chance, Slim
 See Cramps, The
Chancellor, Justin
 See Tool
Chandler, Chas
 See Animals
Chandra, Sheila **16**
Chaney, Jimmy
 See Jimmie's Chicken Shack
Chang, Sarah **7**
Channing, Carol **6**
Chapin Carpenter, Mary **25**
 Earlier sketch in CM 6
Chapin, Harry **6**
Chapin, Tom **11**
Chapman, Steven Curtis **15**
Chapman, Tony
 See Rolling Stones, The
Chapman, Tracy **20**
 Earlier sketch in CM 4
Chaquico, Craig **23**
 Also see Jefferson Starship
Charlatans, The **13**
Charles, Ray **24**
 Earlier sketch in CM 1
Charles, Yolanda
 See Aztec Camera
Charm Farm **20**
Chasez, Joshua Scott "JC"
 See 'N Sync
Che Colovita, Lemon
 See Jimmie's Chicken Shack
Chea, Alvin "Vinnie"
 See Take 6
Cheap Trick **12**
Checker, Chubby **7**
Cheeks, Julius
 See Soul Stirrers, The
Chemical Brothers **20**
Cheng, Chi
 See Deftones
Chenier, C. J. **15**
Chenier, Clifton **6**
Chenille Sisters, The **16**
Cher **1**
 Also see Sonny and Cher
Cherone, Gary
 See Extreme
 See Van Halen

Cherry, Don **10**
Cherry, Neneh **4**
Cherry Poppin' Daddies **24**
Chesney, Kenny **20**
Chesnutt, Mark **13**
Chess, Leonard **24**
Chevalier, Maurice **6**
Chevron, Phillip
 See Pogues, The
Chicago **3**
Chieftains, The **7**
Childress, Ross
 See Collective Soul
Childs, Toni **2**
Chilton, Alex **10**
Chimes, Terry
 See Clash, The
Chin, Tony
 See Big Mountain
Chisholm, Melanie
 See Spice Girls
Chopmaster J
 See Digital Underground
Chrisman, Andy
 See FourHim
Christ, John
 See Danzig
Christian, Charlie **11**
Christina, Fran
 See Fabulous Thunderbirds, The
 Also see Roomful of Blues
Chuck D
 See Public Enemy
Chumbawamba **21**
Chung, Mark
 See Einstürzende Neubauten
Church, Kevin
 See Country Gentlemen, The
Church, The **14**
Cieka, Rob
 See Boo Radleys, The
Cinderella **16**
Cinelu, Mino
 See Weather Report
Cipollina, John
 See Quicksilver Messenger Service
Circle Jerks, The **17**
Cissell, Ben
 See Audio Adrenaline
Clannad **23**
Clapton, Eric **11**
 Earlier sketch in CM 1
 Also see Cream
 Also see Yardbirds, The
Clark, Alan
 See Dire Straits
Clark, Dave
 See Dave Clark Five, The
Clark, Dick **25**
 Earlier sketch in CM 2
Clark, Gene
 See Byrds, The
Clark, Graham
 See Gong
Clark, Guy **17**
Clark, Keith
 See Circle Jerks, The
Clark, Mike
 See Suicidal Tendencies
Clark, Roy **1**
Clark, Steve
 See Def Leppard

Cotrubas, Ileana **1**
Cotten, Elizabeth **16**
Cotton, Caré
  See Sounds of Blackness
Cougar, John(ny)
  See Mellencamp, John
Coughlan, Richard
  See Caravan
Counting Crows **18**
Country Gentlemen, The **7**
Coury, Fred
  See Cinderella
Coutts, Duncan
  See Our Lady Peace
Coverdale, David
  See Whitesnake **5**
Cowan, John
  See New Grass Revival, The
Cowboy Junkies, The **4**
Cox, Andy
  See English Beat, The
  Also see Fine Young Cannibals
Cox, Terry
  See Pentangle
Coxon, Graham
  See Blur
Coyne, Mark
  See Flaming Lips
Coyne, Wayne
  See Flaming Lips
Cracker **12**
Craig, Albert
  See Israel Vibration
Craig, Carl **19**
Crain, S. R.
  See Soul Stirrers, The
Cramps, The **16**
Cranberries, The **14**
Crash Test Dummies **14**
Crawford, Da'dra
  See Anointed
Crawford, Dave Max
  See Poi Dog Pondering
Crawford, Ed
  See fIREHOSE
Crawford, Michael **4**
Crawford, Randy **25**
Crawford, Steve
  See Anointed
Cray, Robert **8**
Creach, Papa John
  See Jefferson Starship
Cream **9**
Creedence Clearwater Revival **16**
Creegan, Andrew
  See Barenaked Ladies
Creegan, Jim
  See Barenaked Ladies
Crenshaw, Marshall **5**
Cretu, Michael
  See Enigma
Criss, Peter
  See Kiss,
Crissinger, Roger
  See Pearls Before Swine
Croce, Jim **3**
Crofts, Dash
  See Seals & Crofts
Cronin, Kevin
  See REO Speedwagon
Cropper, Steve **12**
Cropper, Steve
  See Booker T. & the M.G.'s

Crosby, Bing **6**
Crosby, David **3**
  See Byrds, The
  Also see Crosby, Stills, and Nash
Crosby, Stills, and Nash **24**
Cross, Bridget
  See Velocity Girl
Cross, David
  See King Crimson
Cross, Mike
  See Sponge
Cross, Tim
  See Sponge
Crouch, Andraé **9**
Crover, Dale
  See Melvins
Crow, Sheryl **18**
Crowded House **12**
Crowe, J. D. **5**
Crowell, Rodney **8**
Crowley, Martin
  See Bevis Frond
Cruikshank, Gregory
  See Tuxedomoon
Cruz, Celia **22**
  Earlier sketch in CM **10**
Cuddy, Jim
  See Blue Rodeo
Cugat, Xavier **23**
Cult, The **16**
Cumming, Graham
  See Bevis Frond
Cummings, Burton
  See Guess Who
Cummings, Danny
  See Dire Straits
Cummings, David
  See Del Amitri
Cunningham, Abe
  See Deftones
Cunningham, Ruth
  See Anonymous 4
Cuomo, Rivers
  See Weezer
Cure, The **20**
  Earlier sketch in CM **3**
Curless, Ann
  See Exposé
Curley, John
  See Afghan Whigs
Curran, Ciaran
  See Altan
Currie, Justin
  See Del Amitri
Currie, Kevin
  See Supertramp
Currie, Steve
  See T. Rex
Curry, Tim **3**
Curtis, Ian
  See Joy Division
Curtis, King **17**
Curve **13**
Custance, Mickey
  See Big Audio Dynamite
Cuthbert, Scott
  See Everclear
Cutler, Chris
  See Pere Ubu
Cypress Hill **11**
Cyrus, Billy Ray **11**
D.J. Lethal
  See House of Pain

D.J. Minutemix
  See P.M. Dawn
D'Angelo **20**
D'Angelo, Greg
  See Anthrax
D'Arby, Terence Trent **3**
Dacus, Donnie
  See Chicago
Dacus, Johnny
  See Osborne Brothers, The
Daddy G
  See Massive Attack
Daddy Mack
  See Kris Kross
Daellenbach, Charles
  See Canadian Brass, The
Dahlheimer, Patrick
  See Live
Daisley, Bob
  See Black Sabbath
Dale, Dick **13**
Daley, Richard
  See Third World
Dall, Bobby
  See Poison
Dallin, Sarah
  See Bananarama
Dalton, John
  See Kinks, The
Dalton, Nic
  See Lemonheads, The
Daltrey, Roger **3**
  Also see Who, The
Dammers, Jerry
  See Specials, The
Damon and Naomi **25**
Dando, Evan
  See Lemonheads, The
Dandy Warhols **22**
Danell, Dennis
  See Social Distortion
Daniels, Charlie **6**
Daniels, Jack
  See Highway 101
Daniels, Jerry
  See Ink Spots
Danko, Rick
  See Band, The
Danny Boy
  See House of Pain
Danzig **7**
Danzig, Glenn
  See Danzig
Darin, Bobby **4**
Darling, Eric
  See Weavers, The
Darriau, Matt
  See Klezmatics, The
Darvill, Benjamin
  See Crash Test Dummies
Das EFX **14**
Daugherty, Jay Dee
  See Church, The
Daulne, Marie
  See Zap Mama
Dave Clark Five, The **12**
Dave, Doggy
  See Lords of Acid
Dave Matthews Band **18**
Davenport, N'Dea
  See Brand New Heavies, The
Davidson, Lenny
  See Dave Clark Five, The

Dittrich, John
  See Restless Heart
Dixon, George W.
  See Spinners, The
Dixon, Jerry
  See Warrant
Dixon, Willie 10
DJ Domination
  See Geto Boys, The
DJ Fuse
  See Digital Underground
DJ Jazzy Jeff and the Fresh Prince 5
DJ Muggs
  See Cypress Hill
DJ Premier
  See Gang Starr
DJ Ready Red
  See Geto Boys, The
DJ Terminator X
  See Public Enemy
DMC
  See Run DMC
DMX 25
Doc Pomus 14
Doe, John
  See X
Dog's Eye View 21
Dogbowl
  See King Missile
Doherty, Denny
  See Mamas and the Papas
Dokken 16
Dokken, Don
  See Dokken
Dolby, Monica Mimi
  See Brownstone
Dolby, Thomas 10
Dolenz, Micky
  See Monkees, The
Dombroski, Vinnie
  See Sponge
Domingo, Placido 20
  Earlier sketch in CM 1
Dominici, Charlie
  See Dream Theater
Domino, Fats 2
Don, Rasa
  See Arrested Development
Donahue, Jerry
  See Fairport Convention
Donahue, Jonathan
  See Flaming Lips
Donald, Tony
  See Simple Minds
Donelly, Tanya
  See Belly
  Also see Breeders
  Also see Throwing Muses
Donohue, Tim
  See Cherry Poppin' Daddies
Donovan 9
Donovan, Bazil
  See Blue Rodeo
Doobie Brothers, The 3
Doodlebug
  See Digable Planets
Doors, The 4
Dorge, Michel (Mitch)
  See Crash Test Dummies
Dorney, Tim
  See Republica
Dorough, Bob
  See Pearls Before Swine

Dorough, Howie
  See Backstreet Boys
Dorsey Brothers, The 8
Dorsey, Jimmy
  See Dorsey Brothers, The
Dorsey, Thomas A. 11
Dorsey, Tommy
  See Dorsey Brothers, The
Doth, Anita
  See 2 Unlimited
Dott, Gerald
  See Incredible String Band
Doucet, Michael 8
Doughty, M.
  See Soul Coughing
Doughty, Neal
  See REO Speedwagon
Douglas, Jerry
  See Country Gentlemen, The
Dowd, Christopher
  See Fishbone
Dowling, Dave
  See Jimmie's Chicken Shack
Downes, Geoff
  See Yes
Downey, Brian
  See Thin Lizzy
Downie, Gordon
  See Tragically Hip, The
Downing, K. K.
  See Judas Priest
Doyle, Candida
  See Pulp
Dozier, Lamont
  See Holland-Dozier-Holland
Dr. Dre 15
  Also see N.W.A.
Dr. John 7
Drake, Nick 17
Drake, Steven
  See Odds
Drayton, Leslie
  See Earth, Wind and Fire
Dream Theater 23
Dreja, Chris
  See Yardbirds, The
Drew, Dennis
  See 10,000 Maniacs
Driftwood, Jimmy 25
Droge, Pete 24
Drozd, Stephen
  See Flaming Lips
Dru Hill 25
Drumbago,
  See Skatalites, The
Drumdini, Harry
  See Cramps, The
Drummond, Don
  See Skatalites, The
Drummond, Tom
  See Better Than Ezra
Dryden, Spencer
  See Jefferson Airplane
Dubbe, Berend
  See Bettie Serveert
Dube, Lucky 17
Dubstar 22
Dudley, Anne
  See Art of Noise
Duffey, John
  See Country Gentlemen, The
  Also see Seldom Scene, The

Duffy, Billy
  See Cult, The
Duffy, Martin
  See Primal Scream
Dufresne, Mark
  See Confederate Railroad
Duggan, Noel
  See Clannad
Duggan, Paidraig
  See Clannad
Duke, John
  See Pearls Before Swine
Dukowski, Chuck
  See Black Flag
Dulli, Greg
  See Afghan Whigs
Dumont, Tom
  See No Doubt
Dunbar, Aynsley
  See Jefferson Starship
  Also see Journey
  Also see Whitesnake
Dunbar, Sly
  See Sly and Robbie
Duncan, Bryan 19
Duncan, Gary
  See Quicksilver Messenger Service
Duncan, Steve
  See Desert Rose Band, The
Duncan, Stuart
  See Nashville Bluegrass Band
Dunlap, Slim
  See Replacements, The
Dunn, Donald "Duck"
  See Booker T. & the M.G.'s
Dunn, Holly 7
Dunn, Larry
  See Earth, Wind and Fire
Dunn, Ronnie Gene
  See Brooks & Dunn
Dunning, A.J.
  See Verve Pipe, The
Dupree, Champion Jack 12
Dupree, Jimmy
  See Jackyl
Dupri, Jermaine 25
Duran Duran 4
Durante, Mark
  See KMFDM
Duritz, Adam
  See Counting Crows
Durrill, Johnny
  See Ventures, The
Dutt, Hank
  See Kronos Quartet
Dvorak, Antonin 25
Dyble, Judy
  See Fairport Convention
Dylan, Bob 21
  Earlier sketch in CM 3
Dylan, Jakob
  See Wallflowers, The
D'Amour, Paul
  See Tool
E., Sheila
  See Sheila E.
Eacrett, Chris
  See Our Lady Peace
Eagles, The 3
Earl, Ronnie 5
  Also see Roomful of Blues

Falconer, Earl
  See UB40
Fall, The **12**
Fallon, David
  See Chieftains, The
Fältskog, Agnetha
  See Abba
Fambrough, Henry
  See Spinners, The
Fankhauser, Merrell **24**
Farley, J. J.
  See Soul Stirrers, The
Farndon, Pete
  See Pretenders, The
Farrar, Jay
  See Son Volt
Farrar, John
  See Shadows, The
Farrell, Frank
  See Supertramp
Farrell, Perry
  See Jane's Addiction
Farris, Dionne
  See Arrested Development
Farris, Tim
  See Israel Vibration
Farriss, Andrew
  See INXS
Farriss, Jon
  See INXS
Farriss, Tim
  See INXS
Fatboy Slim **22**
Fatone, Joey
  See 'N Sync
Fay, Johnny
  See Tragically Hip, The
Fay, Martin
  See Chieftains, The
Fearnley, James
  See Pogues, The
Fehlmann, Thomas
  See Orb, The
Feinstein, Michael **6**
Fela
  See Kuti, Fela
Felber, Dean
  See Hootie and the Blowfish
Felder, Don
  See Eagles, The
Feldman, Eric Drew
  See Pere Ubu
Feliciano, José **10**
Fender, Freddy
  See Texas Tornados, The
Fender, Leo **10**
Fennell, Kevin
  See Guided By Voices
Fennelly, Gere
  See Redd Kross
Fenwick, Ray
  See Spencer Davis Group
Ferguson, Jay
  See Spirit
Ferguson, Keith
  See Fabulous Thunderbirds, The
Ferguson, Maynard **7**
Ferguson, Neil
  See Chumbawamba
Ferguson, Steve
  See NRBQ
Ferrell, Rachelle **17**

Ferrer, Frank
  See Love Spit Love
Ferry, Bryan **1**
Ficca, Billy
  See Television
Fiedler, Arthur **6**
Fielder, Jim
  See Blood, Sweat and Tears
Fields, Johnny
  See Five Blind Boys of Alabama
Fier, Anton
  See Pere Ubu
Finch, Jennifer
  See L7
Fine Young Cannibals **22**
Finer, Jem
  See Pogues, The
Fink, Jr., Rat
  See Alien Sex Fiend
Finn, Micky
  See T. Rex
Finn, Neil
  See Crowded House
Finn, Tim
  See Crowded House
fIREHOSE **11**
Fishbone **7**
Fisher, Brandon
  See Superdrag
Fisher, Eddie **12**
Fisher, Jerry
  See Blood, Sweat and Tears
Fisher, John "Norwood"
  See Fishbone
Fisher, Phillip "Fish"
  See Fishbone
Fisher, Roger
  See Heart
Fishman, Jon
  See Phish
Fitzgerald, Ella **1**
Fitzgerald, Kevin
  See Geraldine Fibbers
Five Blind Boys of Alabama **12**
Flack, Roberta **5**
Flaming Lips **22**
Flanagan, Tommy **16**
Flannery, Sean
  See Cherry Poppin' Daddies
Flansburgh, John
  See They Might Be Giants
Flatt, Lester **3**
Flavor Flav
  See Public Enemy
Flea
  See Red Hot Chili Peppers, The
Fleck, Bela **8**
  Also see New Grass Revival, The
Fleetwood Mac **5**
Fleetwood, Mick
  See Fleetwood Mac
Fleischmann, Robert
  See Journey
Fleming, Renee **24**
Flemons, Wade
  See Earth, Wind and Fire
Flesh-N-Bone
  See Bone Thugs-N-Harmony
Fletcher, Andy
  See Depeche Mode
Fletcher, Guy
  See Dire Straits

Flint, Keith
  See Prodigy
Flores, Rosie **16**
Floyd, Heather
  See Point of Grace
Flür, Wolfgang
  See Kraftwerk
Flynn, Pat
  See New Grass Revival, The
Fogelberg, Dan **4**
Fogerty, John **2**
  Also see Creedence Clearwater Revival
Fogerty, Thomas
  See Creedence Clearwater Revival
Folds, Ben
  See Ben Folds Five
Foley
  See Arrested Development
Foo Fighters **20**
Forbes, Derek
  See Simple Minds
Forbes, Graham
  See Incredible String Band
Ford, Lita **9**
Ford, Mark
  See Black Crowes, The
Ford, Penny
  See Soul II Soul
Ford, Robert "Peg"
  See Golden Gate Quartet
Ford, Tennessee Ernie **3**
Fordham, Julia **15**
Foreigner **21**
Forsi, Ken
  See Surfaris, The
Fortune, Jimmy
  See Statler Brothers, The
Fortus, Richard
  See Love Spit Love
Fossen, Steve
  See Heart
Foster, David **13**
Foster, Malcolm
  See Pretenders, The
Foster, Paul
  See Soul Stirrers, The
Foster, Radney **16**
Fountain, Clarence
  See Five Blind Boys of Alabama
Fountain, Pete **7**
Four Seasons, The **24**
Four Tops, The **11**
FourHim **23**
Fox, Lucas
  See Motörhead
Fox, Oz
  See Stryper
Fox, Samantha **3**
Foxwell Baker, Iain Richard
  See Jesus Jones
Frame, Roddy
  See Aztec Camera
Frampton, Peter **3**
Francis, Black
  See Pixies, The
Francis, Connie **10**
Francis, Mike
  See Asleep at the Wheel
Franke, Chris
  See Tangerine Dream
Frankenstein, Jeff
  See Newsboys, The

Giblin, John
  See Simple Minds
Gibson, Bob **23**
Gibson, Debbie
  See Gibson, Deborah
Gibson, Deborah **24**
  Earlier sketch in CM **1**
Gibson, Wilf
  See Electric Light Orchestra
Gifford, Katharine
  See Stereolab
Gifford, Peter
  See Midnight Oil
Gift, Roland **3**
  Also see Fine Young Cannibals
Gilbert, Gillian
  See New Order
Gilbert, Nicole Nicci
  See Brownstone
Gilbert, Ronnie
  See Weavers, The
Gilbert, Simon
  See Suede
Giles, Michael
  See King Crimson
Gilkyson, Tony
  See X
Gill, Andy
  See Gang of Four
Gill, Janis
  See Sweethearts of the Rodeo
Gill, Johnny **20**
Gill, Pete
  See Motörhead
Gill, Vince **7**
Gillan, Ian
  See Deep Purple
Gillespie, Bobby
  See Primal Scream
Gillespie, Dizzy **6**
Gilley, Mickey **7**
Gillian, Ian
  See Black Sabbath
Gillies, Ben
  See Silverchair
Gillingham, Charles
  See Counting Crows
Gilmore, Jimmie Dale **11**
Gilmour, David
  See Pink Floyd
Gin Blossoms **18**
Gingold, Josef **6**
Ginn, Greg
  See Black Flag
Gioia
  See Exposé
Gipp, Cameron
  See Goodie Mob
Gipsy Kings, The **8**
Giraudy, Miquitte
  See Gong
Gittleman, Joe
  See Mighty Mighty Bosstones
Glass, Eddie
  See Fu Manchu
Glass, Philip **1**
Glasscock, John
  See Jethro Tull
Glennie, Jim
  See James
Glitter, Gary **19**
Glover, Corey
  See Living Colour

Glover, Roger
  See Deep Purple
Go-Go's, The **24**
Gobel, Robert
  See Kool & the Gang
Godchaux, Donna
  See Grateful Dead, The
Godchaux, Keith
  See Grateful Dead, The
Godfrey, Paul
  See Morcheeba
Godfrey, Ross
  See Morcheeba
Goettel, Dwayne Rudolf
  See Skinny Puppy
Goffin, Gerry
  See Goffin-King
Goffin-King **24**
Gogin, Toni
  See Sleater-Kinney
Goh, Rex
  See Air Supply
Gold, Julie **22**
Golden Gate Quartet **25**
Golden, William Lee
  See Oak Ridge Boys, The
Golding, Lynval
  See Specials, The
Goldsmith, William
  See Foo Fighters
Goldstein, Jerry
  See War
Golson, Benny **21**
Gong **24**
Goo Goo Dolls, The **16**
Gooden, Ramone Pee Wee
  See Digital Underground
Goodie Mob **24**
Goodman, Benny **4**
Goodman, Jerry
  See Mahavishnu Orchestra
Goodridge, Robin
  See Bush
Gordon, Dexter **10**
Gordon, Dwight
  See Mighty Clouds of Joy, The
Gordon, Jim
  See Traffic
Gordon, Kim
  See Sonic Youth
Gordon, Mike
  See Phish
Gordon, Nina
  See Veruca Salt
Gordy, Berry, Jr. **6**
Gordy, Emory, Jr. **17**
Gore, Martin
  See Depeche Mode
Gorham, Scott
  See Thin Lizzy
Gorka, John **18**
Gorman, Christopher
  See Belly
Gorman, Steve
  See Black Crowes, The
Gorman, Thomas
  See Belly
Gosling, John
  See Kinks, The
Gossard, Stone
  See Brad
  Also see Pearl Jam

Gott, Larry
  See James
Goudreau, Barry
  See Boston
Gould, Billy
  See Faith No More
Gould, Glenn **9**
Gould, Morton **16**
Goulding, Steve
  See Poi Dog Pondering
Grable, Steve
  See Pearls Before Swine
Gracey, Chad
  See Live
Gradney, Ken
  See Little Feat
Graffety-Smith, Toby
  See Jamiroquai
Graham, Bill **10**
Graham, Glen
  See Blind Melon
Graham, Johnny
  See Earth, Wind and Fire
Graham, Larry
  See Sly & the Family Stone
Gramm, Lou
  See Foreigner
Gramolini, Gary
  See Beaver Brown Band, The
Grandmaster Flash **14**
Grant, Amy **7**
Grant, Bob
  See The Bad Livers
Grant Lee Buffalo **16**
Grant, Lloyd
  See Metallica
Grappelli, Stephane **10**
Grateful Dead, The **5**
Gratzer, Alan
  See REO Speedwagon
Gravatt, Eric
  See Weather Report
Gravediggaz **23**
Graves, Denyce **16**
Gray, Del
  See Little Texas
Gray, Ella
  See Kronos Quartet
Gray, F. Gary **19**
Gray, James
  See Blue Rodeo
Gray, James
  See Spearhead
Gray, Luther
  See Tsunami
Gray, Tom
  See Country Gentlemen, The
  Also see Seldom Scene, The
Gray, Walter
  See Kronos Quartet
Gray, Wardell
  See McKinney's Cotton Pickers
Grebenshikov, Boris **3**
Grech, Rick
  See Traffic
Greco, Paul
  See Chumbawamba
Green, Al **9**
Green, Benny **17**
Green, Carlito
  See Goodie Mob

Hardcastle, Paul **20**
Hardin, Eddie
  See Spencer Davis Group
Hardin, Tim **18**
Harding, John Wesley **6**
Hardson, Tre "Slimkid"
  See Pharcyde, The
Hargreaves, Brad
  See Third Eye Blind
Hargrove, Kornell
  See Poi Dog Pondering
Hargrove, Roy **15**
Harket, Morten
  See A-ha
Harley, Bill **7**
Harley,, Wayne
  See Pearls Before Swine
Harms, Jesse
  See REO Speedwagon
Harper, Ben **17**
Harper, Raymond
  See Skatalites, The
Harrell, Andre **16**
Harrell, Lynn **3**
Harrington, Carrie
  See Sounds of Blackness
Harrington, David
  See Kronos Quartet
Harris, Addie "Micki"
  See Shirelles, The
Harris, Damon Otis
  See Temptations, The
Harris, Eddie **15**
Harris, Emmylou **4**
Harris, Evelyn
  See Sweet Honey in the Rock
Harris, Gerard
  See Kool & the Gang
Harris, James
  See Echobelly
Harris, Jet
  See Shadows, The
Harris, Joey
  See Beat Farmers
Harris, Kevin
  See Dirty Dozen
Harris, Lee
  See Talk Talk
Harris, Mark
  See FourHim
Harris, Mary
  See Spearhead
Harris, R. H.
  See Soul Stirrers, The
Harris, Steve
  See Iron Maiden
Harris, Teddy **22**
Harrison, George **2**
  Also see Beatles, The
Harrison, Jerry
  See Talking Heads
Harrison, Nigel
  See Blondie
Harrison, Richard
  See Stereolab
Harry, Deborah **4**
  Also see Blondie
Hart, Chuck
  See Surfin' Pluto
Hart, Hattie
  See Memphis Jug Band
Hart, Lorenz
  See Rodgers, Richard

Hart, Mark
  See Crowded House
Hart, Mark
  See Supertramp,
Hart, Mickey
  See Grateful Dead, The
Hart, Robert
  See Bad Company
Hart, Tim
  See Steeleye Span
Hartford, John **1**
Hartke, Stephen **5**
Hartley, Matthieu
  See Cure, The
Hartman, Bob
  See Petra
Hartman, John
  See Doobie Brothers, The
Hartnoll, Paul
  See Orbital
Hartnoll, Phil
  See Orbital
Harvey, Bernard "Touter"
  See Inner Circle
Harvey, Philip "Daddae"
  See Soul II Soul
Harvey, Polly Jean **11**
Harvie, Iain
  See Del Amitri
Harwood, Justin
  See Luna
Haseltine, Dan
  See Jars of Clay
Hashian
  See Boston
Haskell, Gordon
  See King Crimson
Haskins, Kevin
  See Love and Rockets
Haslinger, Paul
  See Tangerine Dream
Hassan, Norman
  See UB40
Hastings, Jimmy
  See Caravan
Hastings, Pye
  See Caravan
Hatfield, Juliana **12**
  Also see Lemonheads, The
Hauser, Tim
  See Manhattan Transfer, The
Havens, Richie **11**
Hawes, Dave
  See Catherine Wheel
Hawkes, Greg
  See Cars, The
Hawkins, Coleman **11**
Hawkins, Erskine **19**
Hawkins, Nick
  See Big Audio Dynamite
Hawkins, Roger
  See Traffic
Hawkins, Screamin' Jay **8**
Hawkins, Sophie B. **21**
Hawkins, Taylor
  See Foo Fighters
Hawkins, Tramaine **17**
Hawkins, Xian
  See Silver Apples
Hay, George D. **3**
Hayes, Gordon
  See Pearls Before Swine

Hayes, Isaac **10**
Hayes, Roland **13**
Haynes, Gibby
  See Butthole Surfers
Haynes, Warren
  See Allman Brothers, The
Hays, Lee
  See Weavers, The
Hayward, David Justin
  See Moody Blues, The
Hayward, Richard
  See Little Feat
Headliner
  See Arrested Development
Headon, Topper
  See Clash, The
Healey, Jeff **4**
Heard, Paul
  See M People
Hearn, Kevin
  See Barenaked Ladies
Heart **1**
Heaton, Paul
  See Beautiful South
Heavy D **10**
Hecker, Robert
  See Redd Kross
Hedford, Eric
Hedges, Eddie
  See Blessid Union of Souls
Hedges, Michael **3**
Heggie, Will
  See Cocteau Twins, The
Heidorn, Mike
  See Son Volt
Heitman, Dana
  See Cherry Poppin' Daddies
Helfgott, David **19**
Hell, Richard
  See Television
Hellauer, Susan
  See Anonymous 4
Hellerman, Fred
  See Weavers, The
Helliwell, John
  See Supertramp
Helm, Levon
  See Band, The
  Also see Nitty Gritty Dirt Band, The
Helmet **15**
Hemingway, Dave
  See Beautiful South
Hemmings, Paul
  See Lightning Seeds
Henderson, Andy
  See Echobelly
Henderson, Billy
  See Spinners, The
Henderson, Fletcher **16**
Henderson, Joe **14**
Hendricks, Barbara **10**
Hendrix, Jimi **2**
Henley, Don **3**
  Also see Eagles, The
Henrit, Bob
  See Kinks, The
Henry, Bill
  See Northern Lights
Henry, Joe **18**
Henry, Kent
  See Steppenwolf

Huffman, Doug
  See Boston
Hughes, Bruce
  See Cracker
Hughes, Glenn
  See Black Sabbath
Hughes, Glenn
  See Village People, The
Hughes, Leon
  See Coasters, The
Human League, The **17**
Humes, Helen **19**
Humperdinck, Engelbert **19**
Humphreys, Paul
  See Orchestral Manoeuvres in the Dark
Hunt, Darryl
  See Pogues, The
Hunter, Alberta **7**
Hunter, Charlie **24**
Hunter, Mark
  See James
Hunter, Shepherd "Ben"
  See Soundgarden
Hurley, George
  See fIREHOSE
Hurst, Ron
  See Steppenwolf
Hurt, Mississippi John **24**
Hutchence, Michael
  See INXS
Hutchings, Ashley
  See Fairport Convention
  Also see Steeleye Span
Huth, Todd
  See Primus
Hütter, Ralf
  See Kraftwerk
Hutton, Danny
  See Three Dog Night
Huxley, Rick
  See Dave Clark Five, The
Hyatt, Aitch
  See Specials, The
Hyde, Michael
  See Big Mountain
Hyman, Jerry
  See Blood, Sweat and Tears
Hyman, Rob
  See Hooters
Hynde, Chrissie
  See Pretenders, The
Hyslop, Kenny
  See Simple Minds
Ian and Sylvia **18**
Ian, Janis **24**
  Earlier sketch in CM **5**
Ian, Scott
  See Anthrax
Ibbotson, Jimmy
  See Nitty Gritty Dirt Band, The
Ibold, Mark
  See Pavement
Ibrahim, Abdullah **24**
Ice Cube **25**
  Earlier sketch in CM **10**
  Also see N.W.A
Ice-T **7**
Idol, Billy **3**
Iglesias, Julio **20**
  Earlier sketch in CM **2**
Iha, James
  See Smashing Pumpkins
Ike and Tina Turner **24**

Illsley, John
  See Dire Straits
Incognito **16**
Incredible String Band **23**
Incubus **23**
Indigo Girls **20**
  Earlier sketch in CM **3**
Inez, Mike
  See Alice in Chains
Infante, Frank
  See Blondie
Ingram, Jack
  See Incredible String Band
Ingram, James **11**
Ink Spots **23**
Inner Circle **15**
Innes, Andrew
  See Primal Scream
Innis, Dave
  See Restless Heart
Insane Clown Posse **22**
Interior, Lux
  See Cramps, The
INXS **21**
  Earlier sketch in CM **2**
Iommi, Tony
  See Black Sabbath
Iron Maiden **10**
Irons, Jack
  See Red Hot Chili Peppers, The
Isaak, Chris **6**
Isacsson, Jonas
  See Roxette
Isham, Mark **14**
Isles, Bill
  See O'Jays, The
Isley Brothers, The **8**
Isley, Ernie
  See Isley Brothers, The
Isley, Marvin
  See Isley Brothers, The
Isley, O'Kelly, Jr.
  See Isley Brothers, The
Isley, Ronald
  See Isley Brothers, The
Isley, Rudolph
  See Isley Brothers, The
Israel Vibration **21**
Ives, Burl **12**
Ivey, Michael
  See Basehead
Ivins, Michael
  See Flaming Lips
J, David
  See Love and Rockets
J.
  See White Zombie
J. Geils Band **25**
Jabs, Matthias
  See Scorpions, The
Jackson 5, The
  See Jacksons, The
Jackson, Al
  See Booker T. & the M.G.'s
Jackson, Alan **25**
  Earlier sketch in CM **7**
Jackson, Eddie
  See Queensryche
Jackson, Freddie **3**
Jackson, Jackie
  See Jacksons, The
Jackson, Janet **16**
  Earlier sketch in CM **3**

Jackson, Jermaine
  See Jacksons, The
Jackson, Joe **22**
  Earlier sketch in CM **4**
Jackson, Karen
  See Supremes, The
Jackson, Mahalia **8**
Jackson, Marlon
  See Jacksons, The
Jackson, Michael **17**
  Earlier sketch in CM **1**
  Also see Jacksons, The
Jackson, Millie **14**
Jackson, Milt **15**
Jackson, Pervis
  See Spinners , The
Jackson, Randy
  See Jacksons, The
Jackson, Tito
  See Jacksons, The
Jacksons, The **7**
Jackyl **24**
Jacobs, Christian Richard
  See Aquabats
Jacobs, Jeff
  See Foreigner
Jacobs, Parker
  See Aquabats
Jacobs, Walter
  See Little Walter
Jacox, Martin
  See Soul Stirrers, The
Jacquet, Illinois **17**
Jade 4U
  See Lords of Acid
Jaffee, Rami
  See Wallflowers, The
Jagger, Mick **7**
  Also see Rolling Stones, The
Jairo T.
  See Sepultura
Jalal
  See Last Poets
Jam, Jimmy
  See Jam, Jimmy, and Terry Lewis
Jam, Jimmy, and Terry Lewis **11**
Jam Master Jay
  See Run D.M.C.
James **12**
James, Alex
  See Blur
James, Andrew "Bear"
  See Midnight Oil
James, Boney **21**
James, Cheryl
  See Salt-N-Pepa
James, David
  See Alien Sex Fiend
James, David
  See Spearhead
James, Doug
  See Roomful of Blues
James, Elmore **8**
James, Etta **6**
James, Harry **11**
James, Jesse
  See Jackyl
James, John
  See Newsboys, The
James, Onieda
  See Spearhead
James, Richard
  See Aphex Twin

Jones, Stacy
  See Letters to Cleo
  See Veruca Salt
Jones, Steve
  See Sex Pistols, The
Jones, Terry
  See Point of Grace
Jones, Thad 19
Jones, Tom 11
Jones, Will "Dub"
  See Coasters, The
Joplin, Janis 3
Joplin, Scott 10
Jordan, Lonnie
  See War
Jordan, Louis 11
Jordan, Stanley 1
Jorgensor, John
  See Desert Rose Band, The
Joseph, Charles
  See Dirty Dozen
Joseph, Kirk
  See Dirty Dozen
Joseph-I, Israel
  See Bad Brains
Josephmary
  See Compulsion
Jourgensen, Al
  See Ministry
Journey 21
Joy Division 19
Joyce, Mike
  See Buzzcocks, The
  Also see Smiths, The
Judas Priest 10
Judd, Naomi
  See Judds, The
Judd, Wynonna
  See Judds, The
  Also see Wynonna
Judds, The 2
Juhlin, Dag
  See Poi Dog Pondering
Jukebox
  See Geto Boys, The
Jungle DJ "Towa" Towa
  See Deee-lite
Jurado, Jeanette
  See Exposé
Justman, Seth
  See J. Geils Band
K-Ci
  See Jodeci
Kabongo, Sabine
  See Zap Mama
Kahlil, Aisha
  See Sweet Honey in the Rock
Kain, Gylan
  See Last Poets
Kakoulli, Harry
  See Squeeze
Kale, Jim
  See Guess Who
Kalligan, Dick
  See Blood, Sweat and Tears
Kamanski, Paul
  See Beat Farmers
Kaminski, Mik
  See Electric Light Orchestra
Kamomiya, Ryo
  See Pizzicato Five
Kanal, Tony
  See No Doubt

Kanawa, Kiri Te
  See Te Kanawa, Kiri
Kane, Arthur
  See New York Dolls
Kane, Big Daddy 7
Kane, Nick
  See Mavericks, The
Kannberg, Scott
  See Pavement
Kanter, Paul
  See Jefferson Airplane
Kaplan, Ira
  See Yo La Tengo
Karajan, Herbert von
  See von Karajan, Herbert
Karges, Murphy
  See Sugar Ray
Kath, Terry
  See Chicago
Kato, Nash
  See Urge Overkill
Katunich, Alex
  See Incubus
Katz, Simon
  See Jamiroquai
Katz, Steve
  See Blood, Sweat and Tears
Kaukonen, Jorma
  See Jefferson Airplane
Kavanagh, Chris
  See Big Audio Dynamite
Kay Gee
  See Naughty by Nature
Kay, Jason
  See Jamiroquai
Kay, John
  See Steppenwolf
Kaye, Carol 22
Kaye, Tony
  See Yes
Kean, Martin
  See Stereolab
Keane, Sean
  See Chieftains, The
Kee, John P. 15
Keelor, Greg
  See Blue Rodeo
Keenan, Maynard James
  See Tool
Keene, Barry
  See Spirit
Keifer, Tom
  See Cinderella
Keitaro
  See Pizzicato Five
Keith, Jeff
  See Tesla
Keith, Toby 17
Kelly, Betty
  See Martha and the Vandellas
Kelly, Charlotte
  See Soul II Soul
Kelly, Kevin
  See Byrds, The
Kelly, Rashaan
  See US3
Kemp, Rick
  See Steeleye Span
Kendrick, David
  See Devo
Kendricks, Eddie
  See Temptations, The

Kennedy, Delious
  See All-4-One
Kennedy, Frankie
  See Altan
Kennedy, Nigel 8
Kenner, Doris
  See Shirelles, The
Kenny, Bill
  See Ink Spots
Kenny, Clare
  See Aztec Camera
Kenny G 14
Kenny, Herb
  See Ink Spots
Kenton, Stan 21
Kentucky Headhunters, The 5
Kern, Jerome 13
Kerr, Jim
  See Simple Minds
Kershaw, Sammy 15
Ketchum, Hal 14
Key, Cevin
  See Skinny Puppy
Keyser, Alex
  See Echobelly
Khan, Chaka 19
  Earlier sketch in CM 9
Khan, Nusrat Fateh Ali 13
Khan, Praga
  See Lords of Acid
Kibble, Mark
  See Take 6
Kibby, Walter
  See Fishbone
Kick, Johnny
  See Madder Rose
Kid 'n Play 5
Kidjo, Anjelique 17
Kiedis, Anthony
  See Red Hot Chili Peppers, The
Kilbey, Steve
  See Church, The
Kilgallon, Eddie
  See Ricochet
Kilgore 24
Killian, Tim
  See Kronos Quartet
Kimball, Jennifer
  See Story, The
Kimball, Jim
  See Jesus Lizard
Kimble, Paul
  See Grant Lee Buffalo
Kincaid, Jan
  See Brand New Heavies, The
Kinchla, Chan
  See Blues Traveler
King Ad-Rock
  See Beastie Boys, The
King, Albert 2
King, Andy
  See Hooters
King, B.B. 24
  Earlier sketch in CM 1
King, Ben E. 7
King, Bob
  See Soul Stirrers, The
King, Carole 6
  Also see Goffin-King
King Crimson 17
King, Ed
  See Lynyrd Skynyrd

LaPread, Ronald
  See Commodores, The
Larkin, Patty **9**
Larson, Chad Albert
  See Aquabats
Larson, Nathan
  See Shudder to Think
Last Poets **21**
Laswell, Bill **14**
Lataille, Rich
  See Roomful of Blues
Lateef, Yusef **16**
Latimer, Andrew
  See Camel
Laughner, Peter
  See Pere Ubu
Lauper, Cyndi **11**
Laurence, Lynda
  See Supremes, The
Lavin, Christine **6**
Lavis, Gilson
  See Squeeze
Lawlor, Feargal
  See Cranberries, The
Lawrence, Tracy **11**
Lawry, John
  See Petra
Laws, Roland
  See Earth, Wind and Fire
Lawson, Doyle
  See Country Gentlemen, The
Layzie Bone
  See Bone Thugs-N-Harmony
Le Mystère des VoixBulgares
  See Bulgarian State Female Vocal Choir,
  The
Leadbelly **6**
Leadon, Bernie
  See Eagles, The
  Also see Nitty Gritty Dirt Band, The
Lear, Graham
  See REO Speedwagon
Leary, Paul
  See Butthole Surfers
Leavell, Chuck
  See Allman Brothers, The
LeBon, Simon
  See Duran Duran
Leckenby, Derek "Lek"
  See Herman's Hermits
Led Zeppelin **1**
Ledbetter, Huddie
  See Leadbelly
LeDoux, Chris **12**
Lee, Beverly
  See Shirelles, The
Lee, Brenda **5**
Lee, Buddy
  See Less Than Jake
Lee, Garret
  See Compulsion
Lee, Geddy
  See Rush
Lee, Peggy **8**
Lee, Pete
  See Gwar
Lee, Sara
  See Gang of Four
Lee, Stan
  See Incredible String Band
Lee, Tommy
  See Mötley Crüe

Lee, Tony
  See Treadmill Trackstar
Leeb, Bill
  See Front Line Assembly
Leen, Bill
  See Gin Blossoms
Leese, Howard
  See Heart
Legg, Adrian **17**
Lehrer, Tom **7**
Leiber and Stoller **14**
Leiber, Jerry
  See Leiber and Stoller
LeMaistre, Malcolm
  See Incredible String Band
Lemmy
  See Motörhead
Lemonheads, The **12**
Lemper, Ute **14**
Lenear, Kevin
  See Mighty Mighty Bosstones
Lenners, Rudy
  See Scorpions, The
Lennon, John **9**
  Also see Beatles, The
Lennon, Julian **2**
Lennox, Annie **18**
  Also see Eurythmics
Leonard, Glenn
  See Temptations, The
Lerner, Alan Jay
  See Lerner and Loewe
Lerner and Loewe **13**
Lesh, Phil
  See Grateful Dead, The
Leskiw, Greg
  See Guess Who
Leslie, Chris
  See Fairport Convention
Less Than Jake **22**
Lessard, Stefan
  See Dave Matthews Band
Letters to Cleo **22**
Levene, Keith
  See Clash, The
Levert, Eddie
  See O'Jays, The
Leverton, Jim
  See Caravan
Levin, Tony
  See King Crimson
Levine, James **8**
Levy, Andrew
  See Brand New Heavies, The
Levy, Ron
  See Roomful of Blues
Lewis, Hambone
  See Memphis Jug Band
Lewis, Huey **9**
Lewis, Ian
  See Inner Circle
Lewis, Jerry Lee **2**
Lewis, Marcia
  See Soul II Soul
Lewis, Michael
  See Quicksilver Messenger Service
Lewis, Mike
  See Yo La Tengo
Lewis, Otis
  See Fabulous Thunderbirds, The
Lewis, Peter
  See Moby Grape

Lewis, Ramsey **14**
Lewis, Roger
Lewis, Roger
  See Dirty Dozen
  See Inner Circle
Lewis, Roy
  See Kronos Quartet
Lewis, Samuel K.
  See Five Blind Boys of Alabama
Lewis, Shaznay T.
  See All Saints
Lewis, Terry
  See Jam, Jimmy, and Terry Lewis
Lhote, Morgan
  See Stereolab
Li Puma, Tommy **18**
Libbea, Gene
  See Nashville Bluegrass Band
Liberace **9**
Licht, David
  See Klezmatics, The
Lifeson, Alex
  See Rush
Lightfoot, Gordon **3**
Lightning Seeds **21**
Ligon, Willie Joe
  See Mighty Clouds of Joy, The
Liles, Brent
  See Social Distortion
Lilienstein, Lois
  See Sharon, Lois & Bram
Lilker, Dan
  See Anthrax
Lilley, John
  See Hooters
Lillywhite, Steve **13**
Lincoln, Abbey **9**
Lindemann, Till
  See Rammstein
Lindes, Hal
  See Dire Straits
Lindley, David **2**
Linna, Miriam
  See Cramps, The
Linnell, John
  See They Might Be Giants
Lipsius, Fred
  See Blood, Sweat and Tears
Lisa, Lisa **23**
Little Feat **4**
Little, Keith
  See Country Gentlemen, The
Little, Levi
  See Blackstreet
Little Richard **1**
Little Texas **14**
Little Walter **14**
Littrell, Brian
  See Backstreet Boys
Live **14**
Living Colour **7**
Llanas, Sam
  See BoDeans
Llanas, Sammy
  See BoDeans, The
Lloyd, Charles **22**
Lloyd, Richard
  See Television
Lloyd Webber, Andrew **6**
Locke, John
  See Spirit
Locking, Brian
  See Shadows, The

Marley, Bob **3**
Marley, Rita **10**
Marley, Ziggy **3**
Marr, Johnny
  See Smiths, The
  Also see The The
Marriner, Neville
Mars, Chris
  See Replacements, The
Mars, Derron
  See Less Than Jake
Mars, Mick
  See Mötley Crüe
Marsalis, Branford **10**
Marsalis, Ellis **13**
Marsalis, Wynton **20**
  Earlier sketch in CM **6**
Marsh, Ian Craig
  See Human League, The
Marshal, Cornel
  See Third World
Marshall, Jenell
  See Dirty Dozen
Martha and the Vandellas **25**
Martin, Barbara
  See Supremes, The
Martin, Carl
  See Shai
Martin, Christopher
  See Kid 'n Play
Martin, Dean **1**
Martin, Dewey
  See Buffalo Springfield
Martin, George **6**
Martin, Greg
  See Kentucky Headhunters, The
Martin, Jim
  See Faith No More
Martin, Jimmy **5**
  Also see Osborne Brothers, The
Martin, Johnney
  See Mighty Clouds of Joy, The
Martin, Phonso
  See Steel Pulse
Martin, Sennie
  See Kool & the Gang
Martin, Tony
  See Black Sabbath
Martinez, Anthony
  See Black Flag
Martinez, S. A.
  See 311
Martini, Jerry
  See Sly & the Family Stone
Martino, Pat **17**
Marvin, Hank B.
  See Shadows, The
Marx, Richard **21**
  Earlier sketch in CM **3**
Mascagni, Pietro **25**
Mascis, J
  See Dinosaur Jr.
Masdea, Jim
  See Boston
Masekela, Hugh **7**
Maseo, Baby Huey
  See De La Soul
Masi, Nick
  See Four Seasons, The
Mason, Dave
  See Traffic
Mason, Nick
  See Pink Floyd

Mason, Steve
  See Jars of Clay
Mason, Terry
  See Joy Division
Masse, Laurel
  See Manhattan Transfer, The
Massey, Bobby
  See O'Jays, The
Massive Attack **17**
Mastelotto, Pat
  See King Crimson
Master P **22**
Masur, Kurt **11**
Material
  See Laswell, Bill
Mathis, Johnny **2**
Mathus, Jim
  See Squirrel Nut Zippers
Matlock, Glen
  See Sex Pistols, The
Mattacks, Dave
  See Fairport Convention
Mattea, Kathy **5**
Matthews Band, Dave
  See Dave Matthews Band
Matthews, Chris
  See Shudder to Think
Matthews, Dave
  See Dave Matthews Band
Matthews, Eric **22**
Matthews, Ian
  See Fairport Convention
Matthews, Quinn
  See Butthole Surfers
Matthews, Scott
  See Butthole Surfers
Matthews, Simon
  See Jesus Jones
Maunick, Bluey
  See Incognito
Maurer, John
  See Social Distortion
Mavericks, The **15**
Maxwell **22**
Maxwell, Charmayne
  See Brownstone
Maxwell, Tom
  See Squirrel Nut Zippers
May, Brian
  See Queen
Mayall, John **7**
Mayfield, Curtis **8**
Mays, Odeen, Jr.
  See Kool & the Gang
Mazelle, Kym
  See Soul II Soul
Mazibuko, Abednigo
  See Ladysmith Black Mambazo
Mazibuko, Albert
  See Ladysmith Black Mambazo
Mazzola, Joey
  See Sponge
Mazzy Star **17**
MC 900 Ft. Jesus **16**
MC Clever
  See Digital Underground
MC Eric
  See Technotronic
MC Lyte **8**
MC Serch **10**
MC5, The **9**
MCA
  See Yauch, Adam

McAloon, Martin
  See Prefab Sprout
McAloon, Paddy
  See Prefab Sprout
McArthur, Keith
  See Spearhead
McBrain, Nicko
  See Iron Maiden
MCBreed **17**
McBride, Christian **17**
McBride, Martina **14**
McCabe, Nick
  See Verve, The
McCabe, Zia
McCall, Renee
  See Sounds of Blackness
McCarrick, Martin
  See Siouxsie and the Banshees
McCarroll, Tony
  See Oasis
McCartney, Paul **4**
  Also see Beatles, The
McCarty, Jim
  See Yardbirds, The
McCary, Michael S.
  See Boyz II Men
McClary, Thomas
  See Commodores, The
McClennan, Tommy **25**
McClinton, Delbert **14**
McCluskey, Andy
  See Orchestral Manoeuvres in the Dark
McCollum, Rick
  See Afghan Whigs
McConnell, Page
  See Phish
McCook, Tommy
  See Skatalites, The
McCoury, Del **15**
McCowin, Michael
  See Mighty Clouds of Joy, The
McCoy, Neal **15**
McCracken, Chet
  See Doobie Brothers, The
McCready, Mike
  See Pearl Jam
McCready, Mindy **22**
McCulloch, Andrew
  See King Crimson
McCullough, Danny
  See Animals
McCuloch, Ian **23**
McD, Jimmy
  See Jimmie's Chicken Shack
McDaniel, Chris
  See Confederate Railroad
McDaniels, Darryl "D"
  See Run D.M.C.
McDermott, Brian
  See Del Amitri
McDonald, Barbara Kooyman
  See Timbuk 3
McDonald, Ian
  See Foreigner
  Also see King Crimson
McDonald, Jeff
  See Redd Kross
McDonald, Michael
  See Doobie Brothers, The
McDonald, Pat
  See Timbuk 3
McDonald, Steven
  See Redd Kross

Miller, Jerry
  See Moby Grape
Miller, Mark
  See Sawyer Brown
Miller, Mitch **11**
Miller, Rice
  See Williamson, Sonny Boy
Miller, Robert
  See Supertramp
Miller, Roger **4**
Miller, Steve **2**
Milli Vanilli **4**
Mills Brothers, The **14**
Mills, Donald
  See Mills Brothers, The
Mills, Fred
  See Canadian Brass, The
Mills, Harry
  See Mills Brothers, The
Mills, Herbert
  See Mills Brothers, The
Mills, John, Jr.
  See Mills Brothers, The
Mills, John, Sr.
  See Mills Brothers, The
Mills, Mike
  See R.E.M.
Mills, Sidney
  See Steel Pulse
Mills, Stephanie **21**
Milsap, Ronnie **2**
Milton, Doctor
  See Alien Sex Fiend
Mingus, Charles **9**
Ministry **10**
Miss Kier Kirby
  See Lady Miss Kier
Mitchell, Alex
  See Curve
Mitchell, John
  See Asleep at the Wheel
Mitchell, Joni **17**
  Earlier sketch in CM **2**
Mitchell, Keith
  See Mazzy Star
Mitchell, Mitch
  See Guided By Voices
Mitchell, Roscoe
  See Art Ensemble of Chicago, The
Mittoo, Jackie
  See Skatalites, The
Mize, Ben
  See Counting Crows
Mizell, Jay
  See Run D.M.C.
Mo', Keb' **21**
Moby **17**
Moby Grape **12**
Modeliste, Joseph "Zigaboo"
  See Meters, The
Moerlen, Pierre
  See Gong
Moffatt, Katy **18**
Moginie, Jim
  See Midnight Oil
Mohr, Todd
  See Big Head Todd and the Monsters
Molland, Joey
  See Badfinger
Molloy, Matt
  See Chieftains, The

Moloney, Paddy
  See Chieftains, The
Monarch, Michael
  See Steppenwolf
Money B
  See Digital Underground
Money, Eddie **16**
Monifah **24**
Monk, Meredith **1**
Monk, Thelonious **6**
Monkees, The **7**
Monroe, Bill **1**
Montana, Country Dick
  See Beat Farmers
Montand, Yves **12**
Montenegro, Hugo **18**
Montgomery, John Michael **14**
Montgomery, Wes **3**
Monti, Steve
  See Curve
Montoya, Craig
  See Everclear
Montrose, Ronnie **22**
Moody Blues, The **18**
Moon, Keith
  See Who, The
Mooney, Tim
  See American Music Club
Moore, Alan
  See Judas Priest
Moore, Angelo
  See Fishbone
Moore, Archie
  See Velocity Girl
Moore, Chante **21**
Moore, Johnny "Dizzy"
  See Skatalites, The
Moore, Kevin
  See Dream Theater
Moore, LeRoi
  See Dave Matthews Band
Moore, Melba **7**
Moore, Sam
  See Sam and Dave
Moore, Thurston
  See Sonic Youth
Morand, Grace
  See Chenille Sisters, The
Moraz, Patrick
  See Moody Blues, The
  Also see Yes
Morcheeba **25**
Moreira, Airto
  See Weather Report
Morello, Tom
  See Rage Against the Machine
Moreno, Chino
  See Deftones
Moreve, Rushton
  See Steppenwolf
Morgan, Frank **9**
Morgan, Lorrie **10**
Morley, Pat
  See Soul Asylum
Morphine **16**
Morricone, Ennio **15**
Morris, Keith
  See Circle Jerks, The
Morris, Kenny
  See Siouxsie and the Banshees
Morris, Nate
  See Boyz II Men

Morris, Stephen
  See Joy Division
  Also see New Order
  Also see Pogues, The
Morris, Wanya
  See Boyz II Men
Morrison, Bram
  See Sharon, Lois & Bram
Morrison, Claude
  See Nylons, The
Morrison, Jim **3**
  Also see Doors, The
Morrison, Sterling
  See Velvet Underground, The
Morrison, Van **24**
  Earlier sketch in CM **3**
Morrissett, Paul
  See Klezmatics, The
Morrissey **10**
  Also see Smiths, The
Morrissey, Bill **12**
Morrissey, Steven Patrick
  See Morrissey
Morton, Everett
  See English Beat, The
Morton, Jelly Roll **7**
Morvan, Fab
  See Milli Vanilli
Mosbaugh, Garth
  See Nylons, The
Mosely, Chuck
  See Faith No More
Moser, Scott "Cactus"
  See Highway 101
Mosher, Ken
  See Squirrel Nut Zippers
Mosley, Bob
  See Moby Grape
Moss, Jason
  See Cherry Poppin' Daddies
Mothersbaugh, Bob
  See Devo
Mothersbaugh, Mark
  See Devo
Mötley Crüe **1**
Motörhead **10**
Motta, Danny
  See Roomful of Blues
Mould, Bob **10**
Moulding, Colin
  See XTC
Mounfield, Gary
  See Stone Roses, The
Mouquet, Eric
  See Deep Forest
Mouskouri, Nana **12**
Mouzon, Alphonse
  See Weather Report
Moye, Famoudou Don
  See Art Ensemble of Chicago, The
Moyet, Alison **12**
Moyse, David
  See Air Supply
Mr. Dalvin
  See Jodeci
Mudhoney **16**
Mueller, Karl
  See Soul Asylum
Muir, Jamie
  See King Crimson
Muir, Mike
  See Suicidal Tendencies

Nyro, Laura **12**
O'Brien, Darrin Kenneth
  See Snow
O'Brien, Derek
  See Social Distortion
O'Brien, Dwayne
  See Little Texas
O'Brien, Ed
  See Radiohead
O'Brien, Marty
  See Kilgore
O'Bryant, Alan
  See Nashville Bluegrass Band
O'Connell, Chris
  See Asleep at the Wheel
O'Connor, Billy
  See Blondie
O'Connor, Daniel
  See House of Pain
O'Connor, Mark **1**
O'Connor, Sinead **3**
O'Day, Anita **21**
O'Donnell, Roger
  See Cure, The
O'Hagan, Sean
  See Stereolab
O'Hare, Brendan
  See Teenage Fanclub
O'Jays, The **13**
O'Reagan, Tim
  See Jayhawks, The
O'Riordan, Cait
  See Pogues, The
O'Riordan, Dolores
  See Cranberries, The
Oak Ridge Boys, The **7**
Oakes, Richard
  See Suede
Oakey, Philip
  See Human League, The
Oakley, Berry
  See Allman Brothers, The
Oasis **16**
Oates, John
  See Hall & Oates
Ocasek, Ric
  See Cars, The
Ocasek, Ric **5**
Ocean, Billy **4**
Oceans, Lucky
  See Asleep at the Wheel
Ochs, Phil **7**
Odds **20**
Odetta **7**
Odmark, Matt
  See Jars of Clay
Ofwerman, Clarence
  See Roxette
Ofwerman, Staffan
  See Roxette
Ogino, Kazuo
  See Ghost
Ogletree, Mike
  See Simple Minds
Ogre, Nivek
  See Skinny Puppy
Ohanian, David
  See Canadian Brass, The
Ohio Players **16**
Oje, Baba
  See Arrested Development
Olafsson, Bragi
  See Sugarcubes, The

Olander, Jimmy
  See Diamond Rio
Olaverra, Margot
  See Go-Go's, The
Oldfield, Mike **18**
Oldham, Jack
  See Surfaris, The
Oldham, Sean
  See Cherry Poppin' Daddies
Olds, Brent
  See Poi Dog Pondering
Oliver, Joe
  See Oliver, King
Oliver, King **15**
Olson, Jeff
  See Village People, The
Olson, Mark
  See Jayhawks, The
Olsson, Nigel
  See Spencer Davis Group
Onassis, Blackie
  See Urge Overkill
Ono, Yoko **11**
Orange, Walter "Clyde"
  See Commodores, The
Orb, The **18**
Orbison, Roy **2**
Orbital **20**
Orchestral Manoeuvres in the Dark **21**
Orff, Carl **21**
Orlando, Tony **15**
Örn, Einar
  See Sugarcubes, The
Örnolfsdottir, Margret
  See Sugarcubes, The
Orr, Benjamin
  See Cars, The
Orr, Casey
  See Gwar
Orrall, Frank
  See Poi Dog Pondering
Orzabal, Roland
  See Tears for Fears
Osborne, Bob
  See Osborne Brothers, The
Osborne Brothers, The **8**
Osborne, Buzz
  See Melvins
Osborne, Sonny
  See Osborne Brothers, The
Osbourne, Ozzy **3**
  Also see Black Sabbath
Osby, Greg **21**
Oskar, Lee
  See War
Oslin, K. T. **3**
Osman, Mat
  See Suede
Osmond, Donny **3**
Ostin, Mo **17**
Otis, Johnny **16**
Ott, David **2**
Our Lady Peace **22**
Outler, Jimmy
  See Soul Stirrers, The
Owen, Randy Yueull
  See Alabama
Owens, Buck **2**
Owens, Campbell
  See Aztec Camera
Owens, Henry
  See Golden Gate Quartet

Owens, Ricky
  See Temptations, The
Oyewole, Abiodun
  See Last Poets
P.M. Dawn **11**
Page, Jimmy **4**
  Also see Led Zeppelin
  Also see Yardbirds, The
Page, Patti **11**
Page, Steven
  See Barenaked Ladies
Paice, Ian
  See Deep Purple
Palmer, Bruce
  See Buffalo Springfield
Palmer, Carl
  See Emerson, Lake & Palmer/Powell
Palmer, Clive
  See Incredible String Band
Palmer, David
  See Jethro Tull
Palmer, Jeff **20**
Palmer, Keeti
  See Prodigy
Palmer, Phil
  See Dire Straits
Palmer, Richard
  See Supertramp
Palmer, Robert **2**
Palmer-Jones, Robert
  See King Crimson
Palmieri, Eddie **15**
Paluzzi, Jimmy
  See Sponge
Pamer, John
  See Tsunami
Pankow, James
  See Chicago
Panter, Horace
  See Specials, The
Pantera **13**
Papach, Leyna
  See Geraldine Fibbers
Pappas, Tom
  See Superdrag
Parazaider, Walter
  See Chicago
Paris, Twila **16**
Park, Cary
  See Boy Howdy
Park, Larry
  See Boy Howdy
Parkening, Christopher **7**
Parker, Charlie **5**
Parker, Graham **10**
Parker, Kris
  See KRS-One
Parker, Maceo **7**
Parker, Tom
  See Animals
Parkin, Chad
  See Aquabats
Parks, Van Dyke **17**
Parnell, Lee Roy **15**
Parsons, Alan **12**
Parsons, Dave
  See Bush
Parsons, Gene
  See Byrds, The
Parsons, Gram **7**
  Also see Byrds, The

Plant, Robert **2**
　Also see Led Zeppelin
Platters, The **25**
Ploog, Richard
　See Church, The
Pogues, The **6**
Poi Dog Pondering **17**
Poindexter, Buster
　See Johansen, David
Point of Grace **21**
Pointer, Anita
　See Pointer Sisters, The
Pointer, Bonnie
　See Pointer Sisters, The
Pointer, June
　See Pointer Sisters, The
Pointer, Ruth
　See Pointer Sisters, The
Pointer Sisters, The **9**
Poison **11**
Poison Ivy
　See Rorschach, Poison Ivy
Poland, Chris
　See Megadeth
Polce, Tom
　See Letters to Cleo
Police, The **20**
Pollard, Jim
　See Guided By Voices
Pollard, Robert, Jr.
　See Guided By Voices
Pollock, Courtney Adam
　See Aquabats
Polygon Window
　See Aphex Twin
Pomus, Doc
　See Doc Pomus
Ponty, Jean-Luc **8**
　Also see Mahavishnu Orchestra
Pop, Iggy **23**
　Earlier sketch in CM **1**
Popper, John
　See Blues Traveler
Porter, Cole **10**
Porter, George, Jr.
　See Meters, The
Porter, Tiran
　See Doobie Brothers, The
Portishead **22**
Portman-Smith, Nigel
　See Pentangle
Portnoy, Mike
　See Dream Theater
Posdnuos
　See De La Soul
Post, Louise
　See Veruca Salt
Post, Mike **21**
Potts, Sean
　See Chieftains, The
Powell, Baden **23**
Powell, Billy
　See Lynyrd Skynyrd
Powell, Bud **15**
Powell, Cozy
　See Emerson, Lake & Palmer/Powell
Powell, Kobie
　See US3
Powell, Paul
　See Aztec Camera
Powell, William
　See O'Jays, The

Powers, Kid Congo
　See Cramps, The
　See Congo Norvell
Prater, Dave
　See Sam and Dave
Prefab Sprout **15**
Presley, Elvis **1**
Pretenders, The **8**
Previn, André **15**
Price, Alan
　See Animals
Price, Leontyne **6**
Price, Lloyd **25**
Price, Louis
　See Temptations, The
Price, Mark
　See Archers of Loaf
Price, Ray **11**
Price, Rick
　See Electric Light Orchestra
Pride, Charley **4**
Priest, Maxi **20**
Prima, Louis **18**
Primal Scream **14**
Primettes, The
　See Supremes, The
Primus **11**
Prince **14**
　Earlier sketch in CM **1**
Prince Be
　See P.M. Dawn
Prince, Prairie
　See Journey
Prine, John **7**
Prior, Maddy
　See Steeleye Span
Proclaimers, The **13**
Prodigy **22**
Professor Longhair **6**
Prong **23**
Propatier, Joe
　See Silver Apples
Propes, Duane
　See Little Texas
Prout, Brian
　See Diamond Rio
Public Enemy **4**
Puccini, Giacomo **25**
Puente, Tito **14**
Puff Daddy
　See Combs, Sean "Puffy"
Pullen, Don **16**
Pulp **18**
Pulsford, Nigel
　See Bush
Pusey, Clifford "Moonie"
　See Steel Pulse
Pyle, Andy
　See Kinks, The
Pyle, Artemis
　See Lynyrd Skynyrd
Pyle, Pip
　See Gong
Q-Tip
　See Tribe Called Quest, A
Quaife, Peter
　See Kinks, The
Quasi
Queen **6**
Queen Ida **9**
Queen Latifah **24**
　Earlier sketch in CM **6**

Queensryche **8**
Querfurth, Carl
　See Roomful of Blues
Quicksilver Messenger Service **23**
R.E.M. **25**
　Earlier sketch in CM **5**
Rabbitt, Eddie **24**
　Earlier sketch in CM **5**
Rabin, Trevor
　See Yes
Radiohead **24**
Raffi **8**
Rage Against the Machine **18**
Raheem
　See GetoBoys, The
Rainey, Ma **22**
Rainey, Sid
　See Compulsion
Rainford, Simone
　See All Saints
Raitt, Bonnie **23**
　Earlier sketch in CM **3**
Rakim
　See Eric B. and Rakim
Raleigh, Don
　See Squirrel Nut Zippers
Ralphs, Mick
　See Bad Company
Rammstein **25**
Ramone, C. J.
　See Ramones, The
Ramone, Dee Dee
　See Ramones, The
Ramone, Joey
　See Ramones, The
Ramone, Johnny
　See Ramones, The
Ramone, Marky
　See Ramones, The
Ramone, Ritchie
　See Ramones, The
Ramone, Tommy
　See Ramones, The
Ramones, The **9**
Rampal, Jean-Pierre **6**
Ramsay, Andy
　See Stereolab
Ranaldo, Lee
　See Sonic Youth
Randall, Bobby
　See Sawyer Brown
Raney, Jerry
　See Beat Farmers
Rangell, Andrew **24**
Ranglin, Ernest
　See Skatalites, The
Ranken, Andrew
　See Pogues, The
Rankin, Cookie
　See Rankins, The
Rankin, Heather
　See Rankins, The
Rankin, Jimmy
　See Rankins, The
Rankin, John Morris
　See Rankins, The
Rankin, Raylene
　See Rankins, The
Ranking, Roger
　See English Beat, The
Rankins, The **24**
Rapp, Tom
　See Pearls Before Swine

Rodney, Red **14**
Rodriguez, Rico
  See Skatalites, The
  Also see Specials, The
Rodriguez, Sal
  See War
Roe, Marty
  See Diamond Rio
Roeder, Klaus
  See Kraftwerk
Roeser, Donald
  See Blue Oyster Cult
Roeser, Eddie "King"
  See Urge Overkill
Roessler, Kira
  See Black Flag
Rogers, Dan
  See Bluegrass Patriots
Rogers, Kenny **1**
Rogers, Norm
  See Jayhawks, The
Rogers, Roy **24**
  Earlier sketch in CM **9**
Rogers, Willie
  See Soul Stirrers, The
Roland, Dean
  See Collective Soul
Roland, Ed
  See Collective Soul
Rolie, Gregg
  See Journey
Rolling Stones, The **23**
  Earlier sketch in CM **3**
Rollins, Henry **11**
  Also see Black Flag
Rollins, Sonny **7**
Rollins, Winston
  See Jamiroquai
Romano, Ruben
  See Fu Manchu
Romm, Ronald
  See Canadian Brass, The
Ronstadt, Linda **2**
Roomful of Blues **7**
Roper, De De
  See Salt-N-Pepa
Rorschach, Poison Ivy
  See Cramps, The
Rosas, Cesar
  See Los Lobos
Rose, Axl
  See Guns n' Roses
Rose, Johanna Maria
  See Anonymous 4
Rose, Michael
  See Black Uhuru
Rosen, Gary
  See Rosenshontz
Rosen, Peter
  See War
Rosenshontz **9**
Rosenthal, Jurgen
  See Scorpions, The
Rosenthal, Phil
  See Seldom Scene, The
Ross, Diana **1**
  Also see Supremes, The
Ross, Malcolm
  See Aztec Camera
Rossdale, Gavin
  See Bush
Rossi, John
  See Roomful of Blues

Rossington, Gary
  See Lynyrd Skynyrd
Rostill, John
  See Shadows, The
Rostropovich, Mstislav **17**
Rota, Nino **13**
Roth, C. P.
  See Blessid Union of Souls
Roth, David Lee **1**
  Also see Van Halen
Roth, Ulrich
  See Scorpions, The
Rotheray, Dave
  See Beautiful South
Rotsey, Martin
  See Midnight Oil
Rotten, Johnny
  See Lydon, John
  Also see Sex Pistols, The
Rourke, Andy
  See Smiths, The
Rowberry, Dave
  See Animals
Rowe, Dwain
  See Restless Heart
Rowlands, Bruce
  See Fairport Convention
Rowlands, Tom
  See Chemical Brothers
Rowntree, Dave
  See Blur
Roxette **23**
Rubin, Mark
  See Bad Livers, The
Rubin, Rick **9**
Rubinstein, Arthur **11**
Rucker, Darius
  See Hootie and the Blowfish
Rudd, Phillip
  See AC/DC
Rue, Caroline
  See Hole
Ruffin, David **6**
  Also see Temptations, The
Ruffin, Tamir
  See Dru Hill
Ruffy, Dave
  See Aztec Camera
Run DMC **25**
  Earlier sketch in CM **4**
Rundgren, Todd **11**
RuPaul **20**
Rush **8**
Rush, Otis **12**
Rushlow, Tim
  See Little Texas
Russell, Alecia
  See Sounds of Blackness
Russell, Graham
  See Air Supply
Russell, John
  See Steppenwolf
Russell, Mark **6**
Russell, Mike
  See Shudder to Think
Russell, Pee Wee **25**
Rutherford, Mike
  See Genesis
  Also see Mike & the Mechanics
Rutsey, John
  See Rush
Ryan, David
  See Lemonheads, The

Ryan, Mark
  See Quicksilver Messenger Service
Ryan, Mick
  See Dave Clark Five, The
Ryder, Mitch **23**
  Earlier sketch in CM **11**
Ryland, Jack
  See Three Dog Night
Rzeznik, Johnny
  See Goo Goo Dolls, The
Sabo, Dave
  See Bon Jovi
Sade **2**
Sadier, Laetitia
  See Stereolab
Saffery, Anthony
  See Cornershop
Saffron,
  See Republica
Sager, Carole Bayer **5**
Sahm, Doug
  See Texas Tornados, The
Saint-Saëns, Camille **25**
Sainte-Marie, Buffy **11**
Sakamoto, Ryuichi **19**
Salazar, Arion
  See Third Eye Blind,
Salerno-Sonnenberg, Nadja **3**
Saliers, Emily
  See Indigo Girls
Salisbury, Peter
  See Verve, The
  Also see Pizzicato Five
Salmon, Michael
  See Prefab Sprout
Saloman, Nick
  See Bevis Frond
Salonen, Esa-Pekka **16**
Salt-N-Pepa **6**
Saluzzi, Dino **23**
Sam and Dave **8**
Sam, Watters
  See Color Me Badd
Sambora, Richie **24**
  Also see Bon Jovi
Sammy, Piazza
  See Quicksilver Messenger Service
Sampson, Doug
  See Iron Maiden
Samuelson, Gar
  See Megadeth
Samwell-Smith, Paul
  See Yardbirds, The
Sanborn, David **1**
Sanchez, Michel
  See Deep Forest
Sanctuary, Gary
  See Aztec Camera
Sanders, Ric
  See Fairport Convention
Sanders, Steve
  See Oak Ridge Boys, The
Sandman, Mark
  See Morphine
Sandoval, Arturo **15**
Sandoval, Hope
  See Mazzy Star
Sands, Aaron
  See Jars of Clay
Sanford, Gary
  See Aztec Camera
Sangare, Oumou **22**

Sheppard, Rodney
  See Sugar Ray
Sherba, John
  See Kronos Quartet
Sherinian, Derek
  See Dream Theater
Sherman, Jack
  See Red Hot Chili Peppers, The
Shines, Johnny **14**
Shirelles, The **11**
Shirley, Danny
  See Confederate Railroad
Shively, William
  See Big Mountain
Shock G
  See Digital Underground
Shocked, Michelle **4**
Shocklee, Hank **15**
Shogren, Dave
  See Doobie Brothers, The
Shonen Knife **13**
Shontz, Bill
  See Rosenshontz
Shorter, Wayne **5**
  Also see Weather Report
Shovell
  See M People
Shudder to Think **20**
Siberry, Jane **6**
Sice
  See Boo Radleys, The
Sidelnyk, Steve
  See Aztec Camera
Siebenberg, Bob
  See Supertramp,
Siegal, Janis
  See Manhattan Transfer, The
Sikes, C. David
  See Boston
Sills, Beverly **5**
Silva, Kenny Jo
  See Beaver Brown Band, The
Silver Apples **23**
Silverchair **20**
Simien, Terrance **12**
Simins, Russell
  See Jon Spencer Blues Explosion
Simmons, Gene
  See Kiss
Simmons, Joe "Run"
  See Run D.M.C.
Simmons, Patrick
  See Doobie Brothers, The
Simmons, Russell **7**
Simmons, Trinna
  See Spearhead
Simms, Nick
  See Cornershop
Simon and Garfunkel **24**
Simon, Carly **22**
  Earlier sketch in CM **4**
Simon, Paul **16**
  Earlier sketch in CM **1**
  See also Simon and Garfunkel
Simone, Nina **11**
Simonon, Paul
  See Clash, The
Simons, Ed
  See Chemical Brothers
Simple Minds **21**
Simpson, Denis
  See Nylons, The

Simpson, Derrick "Duckie"
  See Black Uhuru
Simpson, Mel
  See US3
Simpson, Ray
  See Village People, The
Simpson, Rose
  See Incredible String Band
Sims, David William
  See Jesus Lizard
Sims, Neil
  See Catherine Wheel
Sin, Will
  See Shamen, The
Sinatra, Frank **23**
  Earlier sketch in CM **1**
Sinclair, David
  See Camel
  See Caravan
Sinclair, Gord
  See Tragically Hip, The
Sinclair, Richard
  See Camel
  See Caravan
Sinfield, Peter
  See King Crimson
Singer, Eric
  See Kiss
Singer, Eric
  See Black Sabbath
Singh, Talvin
  See Massive Attack
Singh, Tjinder
  See Cornershop
Sioux, Siouxsie
  See Siouxsie and the Banshees
Siouxsie and the Banshees **8**
Sir Mix-A-Lot **14**
Sir Rap-A-Lot
  See Geto Boys, The
Sirois, Joe
  See Mighty Mighty Bosstones
Siverton
  See Specials, The
Sixx, Nikki
  See Mötley Crüe
Sixx, Roger
  See Less Than Jake
Skaggs, Ricky **5**
  Also see Country Gentlemen, The
Skatalites, The **18**
Skeoch, Tommy
  See Tesla
Skillings, Muzz
  See Living Colour
Skinny Puppy **17**
Sklamberg, Lorin
  See Klezmatics, The
Skoob
  See Das EFX
Slash
  See Guns n' Roses
Slayer **10**
Sleater-Kinney **20**
Sledd, Dale
  See Osborne Brothers, The
Sledge, Percy **15**
Sledge, Robert
  See Ben Folds Five
Slick, Grace
  See Jefferson Airplane
Slijngaard, Ray
  See 2 Unlimited

Sloan, Eliot
  See Blessid Union of Souls
Slovak, Hillel
  See Red Hot Chili Peppers, The
Sly & the Family Stone **24**
Sly and Robbie **13**
Small, Heather
  See M People
Smalls, Derek
  See Spinal Tap
Smart, Terence
  See Butthole Surfers
Smashing Pumpkins **13**
Smear, Pat
  See Foo Fighters
Smith, Adrian
  See Iron Maiden
Smith, Bessie **3**
Smith, Brad
  See Blind Melon
Smith, Chad
  See Red Hot Chili Peppers, The
Smith, Charles
  See Kool & the Gang
Smith, Curt
  See Tears for Fears
Smith, Debbie
  See Curve
  Also see Echobelly
Smith, Fran
  See Hooters
Smith, Fred
  See MC5, The
Smith, Fred
  See Blondie
Smith, Fred
  See Television
Smith, Garth
  See Buzzcocks, The
Smith, Joe
  See McKinney's Cotton Pickers
Smith, Kevin
  See dc Talk
Smith, Mark E.
  See Fall, The
Smith, Michael W. **11**
Smith, Mike
  See Dave Clark Five, The
Smith, Parrish
  See EPMD
Smith, Patti **17**
  Earlier sketch in CM **1**
Smith, Robert
  See Cure, The
  Also see Siouxsie and the Banshees
Smith, Robert
  See Spinners, The
Smith, Shawn
  See Brad
Smith, Smitty
  See Three Dog Night
Smith, Steve
  See Journey
Smith, Tweed
  See War
Smith, Wendy
  See Prefab Sprout
Smith, Willard
  See DJ Jazzy Jeff and the Fresh Prince
Smithereens, The **14**
Smiths, The **3**
Smyth, Gilli
  See Gong

Stewart, Winston "Metal"
  See Mystic Revealers
Stiff, Chris
  See Jackyl
Stills, Stephen 5
  Also see Buffalo Springfield
  Also see Crosby, Stills, and Nash
Sting 19
  Earlier sketch in CM 2
  Also see Police, The
Stinson, Bob
  See Replacements, The
Stinson, Tommy
  See Replacements, The
Stipe, Michael
  See R.E.M.
Stockman, Shawn
  See Boyz II Men
Stoll
  See Clannad
  See Big Mountain
Stoller, Mike
  See Leiber and Stoller
Stoltz, Brian
  See Neville Brothers, The
Stoltzman, Richard 24
Stonadge, Gary
  See Big Audio Dynamite
Stone, Curtis
  See Highway 101
Stone, Doug 10
Stone Roses, The 16
Stone, Sly 8
Stone Temple Pilots 14
Stookey, Paul
  See Peter, Paul & Mary
Story, Liz 2
Story, The 13
Stradlin, Izzy
  See Guns n' Roses
Strain, Sammy
  See O'Jays, The
Strait, George 5
Stratton, Dennis
  See Iron Maiden
Strauss, Richard 25
Stravinsky, Igor 21
Straw, Syd 18
Stray Cats, The 11
Strayhorn, Billy 13
Street, Richard
  See Temptations, The
Streisand, Barbra 2
Strickland, Keith
  See B-52's, The
Stringer, Gary
  See Reef
Strummer, Joe
  See Clash, The
Stryper 2
Stuart, Mark
  See Audio Adrenaline
Stuart, Marty 9
Stuart, Peter
  See Dog's Eye View
Stubbs, Levi
  See Four Tops, The
Styne, Jule 21
Subdudes, The 18
Sublime 19
Such, Alec Jon
  See Bon Jovi

Suede 20
Sugar Ray 22
Sugarcubes, The 10
Suicidal Tendencies 15
Sulley, Suzanne
  See Human League, The
Sullivan, Jacqui
  See Bananarama
Sullivan, Kirk
  See FourHim
Summer, Donna 12
Summer, Mark
  See Turtle Island String Quartet
Summers, Andy 3
  Also see Police, The
Sumner, Bernard
  See Joy Division
  Also see New Order
Sun Ra 5
Sundays, The 20
Sunnyland Slim 16
Super DJ Dmitry
  See Deee-lite
Superdrag 23
Supertramp 25
Supremes, The 6
Sure!, Al B. 13
Surfaris, The 23
Surfin' Pluto 24
Sutcliffe, Stu
  See Beatles, The
Sutherland, Joan 13
Svenigsson, Magnus
  See Cardigans
Svensson, Peter
  See Cardigans
Svigals, Alicia
  See Klezmatics, The
Swarbrick, Dave
  See Fairport Convention
Sweat, Keith 13
Sweet Honey in the Rock 1
Sweet, Matthew 9
Sweet, Michael
  See Stryper
Sweet, Robert
  See Stryper
Sweethearts of the Rodeo 12
Swing, DeVante
  See Jodeci
SWV 14
Sykes, John
  See Whitesnake
Sykes, Roosevelt 20
Sylvain, Sylvain
  See New York Dolls
T. Rex 11
Tabac, Tony
  See Joy Division
Tabor, Ty
  See King's X
TAFKAP (The Artist Formerly Known as
  Prince)
  See Prince
Taggart, Jeremy
  See Our Lady Peace
Tait, Michael
  See dc Talk
Taj Mahal 6
Tajima, Takao
  See Pizzicato Five
Takac, Robby
  See Goo Goo Dolls, The

Takanami
  See Pizzicato Five
Take 6 6
Takemitsu, Toru 6
Takizawa, Taishi
  See Ghost
Talbot, John Michael 6
Talcum, Joe Jack
  See Dead Milkmen
Talking Heads 1
Tampa Red 25
Tandy, Richard
  See Electric Light Orchestra
Tangerine Dream 12
Taree, Aerle
  See Arrested Development
Tate, Geoff
  See Queensryche
Tatum, Art 17
Taupin, Bernie 22
Taylor, Andy
  See Duran Duran
Taylor, Billy 13
Taylor, Cecil 9
Taylor, Chad
  See Live
Taylor, Courtney
Taylor, Dave
  See Pere Ubu
Taylor, Dick
  See Rolling Stones, The
Taylor, Earl
  See Country Gentlemen, The
Taylor, James 25
  Earlier sketch in CM 2
Taylor, James "J.T."
  See Kool & the Gang
Taylor, John
  See Duran Duran
Taylor, Johnnie
  See Soul Stirrers, The
Taylor, Koko 10
Taylor, Leroy
  See Soul Stirrers, The
Taylor, Melvin
  See Ventures, The
Taylor, Mick
  See Rolling Stones, The
Taylor, Philip "Philthy Animal"
  See Motörhead
Taylor, Roger Meadows
  See Queen
Taylor, Roger
  See Duran Duran
Taylor, Teresa
  See Butthole Surfers
Taylor, Zola
  See Platters, The
Te Kanawa, Kiri 2
Teagarden, Jack 10
Tears for Fears 6
Technotronic 5
Teenage Fanclub 13
Television 17
Teller, Al 15
Tempesta, John
  See White Zombie
Temple, Michelle
  See Pere Ubu
Temptations, The 3
Tennant, Neil
  See Pet Shop Boys

Turner, Sonny
  See Platters, The
Turner, Steve
  See Mudhoney
Turner, Tina **1**
  Also see Ike & Tina Turner
Turpin, Will
  See Collective Soul
Turre, Steve **22**
Turtle Island String Quartet **9**
Tutton, Bill
  See Geraldine Fibbers
Tutuska, George
  See Goo Goo Dolls, The
Tuxedomoon **21**
Twain, Shania **17**
Twist, Nigel
  See Alarm
Twitty, Conway **6**
Tyagi, Paul
  See Del Amitri
Tyler, Steve
  See Aerosmith
Tyner, McCoy **7**
Tyner, Rob
  See MC5, The
Tyson, Ian
  See Ian and Sylvia
Tyson, Ron
  See Temptations, The
U2 **12**
  Earlier sketch in CM **2**
UB40 **4**
Ulmer, James Blood **13**
Ulrich, Lars
  See Metallica
Ulvaeus, Björn
  See Abba
Um Romao, Dom
  See Weather Report
Unruh, N. U.
  See Einstürzende Neubauten
Uosikkinen, David
  See Hooters
Upshaw, Dawn **9**
Urge Overkill **17**
US3 **18**
Usher **23**
Utley, Adrian
  See Portishead
Vaché, Jr., Warren **22**
Vachon, Chris
  See Roomful of Blues
Vai, Steve **5**
  Also see Whitesnake
Valdès, Chucho **25**
Valens, Ritchie **23**
Valenti, Dino
  See Quicksilver Messenger Service
Valentine, Gary
  See Blondie
Valentine, Hilton
  See Animals
Valentine, Kathy
  See Go-Go's, The
Valentine, Rae
  See War
Valenzuela, Jesse
  See Gin Blossoms
Valli, Frankie **10**
  Also see Four Seasons, The
Valory, Ross
  See Journey

van Dijk, Carol
  See Bettie Serveert
Van Gelder, Nick
  See Jamiroquai
Van Halen **25**
  Earlier sketch in CM **8**
Van Halen, Alex
  See Van Halen,
Van Halen, Edward
  See Van Halen
Van Hook, Peter
  See Mike & the Mechanics
Van Rensalier, Darnell
  See Shai
Van Ronk, Dave **12**
Van Shelton, Ricky **5**
Van Vliet, Don
  See Captain Beefheart
Van Zandt, Townes **13**
Van Zant, Johnny
  See Lynyrd Skynyrd
Van Zant, Ronnie
  See Lynyrd Skynyrd
Vandenburg, Adrian
  See Whitesnake
Vander Ark, Brad
  See Verve Pipe, The
Vander Ark, Brian
  See Verve Pipe, The
Vandross, Luther **24**
  Earlier sketch in CM **2**
Vanilla Ice **6**
Vasquez, Junior **16**
Vaughan, Jimmie **24**
  Also see Fabulous Thunderbirds, The
Vaughan, Sarah **2**
Vaughan, Stevie Ray **1**
Vedder, Eddie
  See Pearl Jam
Vega, Bobby
  See Quicksilver Messenger Service
Vega, Suzanne **3**
Velocity Girl **23**
Velvet Underground, The **7**
Ventures, The **19**
Verlaine, Tom
  See Television
Verta-Ray, Matt
  See Madder Rose
Veruca Salt **20**
Verve Pipe, The **20**
Verve, The **18**
Vettese, Peter-John
  See Jethro Tull
Vicious, Sid
  See Sex Pistols, The
  Also see Siouxsie and the Banshees
Vickrey, Dan
  See Counting Crows
Victor, Tommy
  See Prong
Vienna Boys Choir **23**
Vig, Butch **17**
  Also see Garbage
Village People, The **7**
Vincent, Gene **19**
Vincent, Vinnie
  See Kiss
Vinnie
  See Naughty by Nature
Vinton, Bobby **12**
Violent Femmes **12**

Virtue, Michael
  See UB40
Visser, Peter
  See Bettie Serveert
Vito, Rick
  See Fleetwood Mac
Vitous, Mirslav
  See Weather Report
Voelz, Susan
  See Poi Dog Pondering
Volz, Greg
  See Petra
von Karajan, Herbert **1**
Von, Eerie
  See Danzig
Vox, Bono
  See U2
Vudi
  See American Music Club
Waaktaar, Pal
  See A-ha
Wade, Adam
  See Shudder to Think
Wade, Chrissie
  See Alien Sex Fiend
Wade, Nik
  See Alien Sex Fiend
Wadenius, George
  See Blood, Sweat and Tears
Wadephal, Ralf
  See Tangerine Dream
Wagoner, Faidest
  See Soul Stirrers, The
Wagoner, Porter **13**
Wahlberg, Donnie
  See New Kids on the Block
Wailer, Bunny **11**
Wainwright III, Loudon **11**
Waits, Tom **12**
  Earlier sketch in CM **1**
Wakeling, David
  See English Beat, The
Wakeman, Rick
  See Yes
Walden, Narada Michael **14**
Walford, Britt
  See Breeders
Walker, Clay **20**
Walker, Colin
  See Electric Light Orchestra
Walker, Ebo
  See New Grass Revival, The
Walker, Jerry Jeff **13**
Walker, T-Bone **5**
Wallace, Bill
  See Guess Who
Wallace, Ian
  See King Crimson
Wallace, Richard
  See Mighty Clouds of Joy, The
Wallace, Sippie **6**
Waller, Charlie
  See Country Gentlemen, The
Waller, Fats **7**
Wallflowers, The **20**
Wallinger, Karl **11**
Wallis, Larry
  See Motörhead
Walls, Chris
  See Dave Clark Five, The
Walls, Denise "Nee-C"
  See Anointed

Wilborn, Dave
  See McKinney's Cotton Pickers
Wilburn, Ishmael
  See Weather Report
Wilcox, Imani
  See Pharcyde, The
Wilde, Phil
  See 2 Unlimited
Wilder, Alan
  See Depeche Mode
Wilk, Brad
  See Rage Against the Machine
Wilkeson, Leon
  See Lynyrd Skynyrd
Wilkie, Chris
  See Dubstar
Wilkinson, Geoff
  See US3
Wilkinson, Keith
  See Squeeze
Williams, Andy 2
Williams, Boris
  See Cure, The
Williams, Cliff
  See AC/DC
Williams, Dana
  See Diamond Rio
Williams, Deniece 1
Williams, Don 4
Williams, Eric
  See Blackstreet
Williams, Fred
  See C + C Music Factory
Williams, Hank, Jr. 1
Williams, Hank, Sr. 4
Williams, James "Diamond"
  See Ohio Players
Williams, Joe 11
Williams, John 9
Williams, Lamar
  See Allman Brothers, The
Williams, Lucinda 24
  Earlier sketch in CM 10
Williams, Marion 15
Williams, Milan
  See Commodores, The
Williams, Otis
  See Temptations, The
Williams, Paul 5
Williams, Phillard
  See Earth, Wind and Fire
Williams, Robbie 25
Williams, Terry
  See Dire Straits
Williams, Tony
  See Platters, The
Williams, Vanessa 10
Williams, Victoria 17
Williams, Walter
  See O'Jays, The
Williams, Wilbert
  See Mighty Clouds of Joy, The
Williams, William Elliot
  See Artifacts
Williamson, Gloria
  See Martha and the Vandellas
Williamson, Robin
  See Incredible String Band
Williamson, Sonny Boy 9
Willie D.
  See Geto Boys, The
Willis, Clarence "Chet"
  See Ohio Players

Willis, Kelly 12
Willis, Larry
  See Blood, Sweat and Tears
Willis, Pete
  See Def Leppard
Willis, Rick
  See Foreigner
Willis, Victor
  See Village People, The
Willner, Hal 10
Wills, Aaron (P-Nut)
  See 311
Wills, Bob 6
Wills, Rick
  See Bad Company
Willson-Piper, Marty
  See Church, The
Wilmot, Billy "Mystic"
  See Mystic Revealers
Wilson, Anne
  See Heart
Wilson, Brian 24
  Also see Beach Boys, The
Wilson, Carl
  See Beach Boys, The
Wilson, Carnie
  See Wilson Phillips
Wilson, Cassandra 12
Wilson, Chris
  See Love Spit Love
Wilson, Cindy
  See B-52's, The
Wilson, Dennis
  See Beach Boys, The
Wilson, Don
  See Ventures, The
Wilson, Eric
  See Sublime
Wilson, Jackie 3
Wilson, Kim
  See Fabulous Thunderbirds, The
Wilson, Mary
  See Supremes, The
Wilson, Nancy 14
  See Heart
Wilson, Orlandus
  See Golden Gate Quartet
Wilson, Patrick
  See Weezer
Wilson Phillips 5
Wilson, Ransom 5
Wilson, Ricky
  See B-52's, The
Wilson, Robin
  See Gin Blossoms
Wilson, Ron
  See Surfaris, The
Wilson, Shanice
  See Shanice
Wilson, Wendy
  See Wilson Phillips
Wilson-James, Victoria
  See Shamen, The
Wilton, Michael
  See Queensryche
Wimpfheimer, Jimmy
  See Roomful of Blues
Winans, Carvin
  See Winans, The
Winans, Marvin
  See Winans, The
Winans, Michael
  See Winans, The

Winans, Ronald
  See Winans, The
Winans, The 12
Winbush, Angela 15
Winfield, Chuck
  See Blood, Sweat and Tears
Winston, George 9
Winter, Johnny 5
Winter, Kurt
  See Guess Who
Winter, Paul 10
Winthrop, Dave
  See Supertramp
Winwood, Muff
  See Spencer Davis Group
Winwood, Steve 2
  Also see Spencer Davis Group
  Also see Traffic
Wiseman, Bobby
  See Blue Rodeo
WishBone
  See Bone Thugs-N-Harmony
Withers, Pick
  See Dire Straits
Wolf, Peter
  See J. Geils Band
Wolstencraft, Simon
  See Fall, The
Womack, Bobby 5
Wonder, Stevie 17
  Earlier sketch in CM 2
Wood, Chris
  See Traffic
Wood, Danny
  See New Kids on the Block
Wood, Ron
  See Faces, The
  See Rolling Stones, The
Wood, Roy
  See Electric Light Orchestra
Woods, Gay
  See Steeleye Span
Woods, Terry
  See Pogues, The
Woodson, Ollie
  See Temptations, The
Woodward, Keren
  See Bananarama
Woody, Allen
  See Allman Brothers, The
Woolfolk, Andrew
  See Earth, Wind and Fire
Worley, Jeff
  See Jackyl
Worrell, Bernie 11
Wray, Link 17
Wreede, Katrina
  See Turtle Island String Quartet
Wren, Alan
  See Stone Roses, The
Wretzky, D'Arcy
  See Smashing Pumpkins
Wright, Adrian
  See Human League, The
Wright, David "Blockhead"
  See English Beat, The
Wright, Heath
  See Ricochet
Wright, Hugh
  See Boy Howdy
Wright, Jimmy
  See Sounds of Blackness